To Jack W. Jayce
in Memory of our

The D.A.'s Man mutual friend.

Harold "Danny" Danforth
James Rudy
May. 15th 196...

★ Harold R. Danforth

★ James D. Horan

The D.A.'s Man

CROWN PUBLISHERS, INC. ★ NEW YORK

To the memory of Leon Racht, a newspaperman . . .
a fine core in a hard shell.

ACKNOWLEDGMENTS

MANY HELPED us in the preparation of this book, particularly District Attorney Frank S. Hogan and Thomas E. Dewey. I would be remiss if I did not thank also James O'Leary, confidential secretary to District Attorney Hogan, and such friends as Chief Investigator Tom Fay and investigators Tony Scanlon and Eddie Whiteside. Many others, now in private life, also gave me their time and patience: Frank Severance and William Devine, now an investigator with the legislative Watch Dog Committee. Also, I wish to offer my particular thanks to Tom Devine for devoting so many hours to going over his records and for supplying me with the picture collection of his "ten months in a tree-house."

And Dan and I both thank Gertrude, my wife, who painstakingly took down all stories. We always knew they were good when, instead of typing, she listened.

JAMES D. HORAN

Horan's Boondocks
September, 1957

CONTENTS

LIST OF ILLUSTRATIONS

AN INTRODUCTION TO . . .

I MET "Dan" Danforth in 1942 while I was engaged in a newspaper investigation of the Harlem underworld. We worked together on one of the most terrifying assignments I have ever had. Our trails crossed in a number of other cases and we became friends. During this period I learned of some of Dan's amazing exploits. One day as we were discussing his career he remarked, "When I retire, Jim, I'll give you all my records. Perhaps you can do something with them."

"That's a promise," I replied. "Call me when you retire." And one day Dan called.

"I've retired from the D.A.'s office, Jim," he said.

"Say no more, Dan," I said, remembering his offer. "When can you come over?"

"How about tonight?" he asked.

And that's when this book began.

. . . HAROLD R. DANFORTH

THE NAME of Harold R. Danforth is virtually unknown to the newspaper-reading public although he has been called "one of the finest criminal investigators in the country" by Thomas E. Dewey, former Special Prosecutor and later District Attorney of New York County, and also by the present District Attorney, Frank S. Hogan. Dan has worked behind the scenes on almost every major criminal case of our time, yet his name has appeared in the press only four times. So closely knit were Dewey's security precautions that no one outside the District Attorney's Bureau of Investigation staff knew Danforth's real identity.

In personality and appearance Danforth is a vivid contrast to the traditional "private eye" detective. He is soft-spoken, courteous, well-

DISTRICT ATTORNEY
OF THE
COUNTY OF NEW YORK
155 LEONARD STREET
NEW YORK 13, N. Y.
RECTOR 2—7300

FRANK S. HOGAN
DISTRICT ATTORNEY

ADDRESS ANSWER TO THE DISTRICT ATTORNEY,
ATTENTION OF THE SIGNER OF THIS LETTER AND
REFER TO NUMBER_____

November 9, 1951

Dear Dan:

It is a matter of sincere regret to me that you
have decided to leave the staff of the District Attorney.
I accept your decision to make a change with great reluctance, although, of course, I quite understand the personal
considerations which have caused you to accept the splendid
opportunity that has come to you.

For sixteen years you have been an outstanding
member of our Bureau of Investigation. During that time,
you have performed the most difficult assignments with
great courage, ability and loyalty. Your entire service
in this office reflects great credit upon yourself and
constitutes a distinguished contribution to good government.

You take with you the friendship and respect of
all our associates. I know that I speak for every person in
the office when I say that we shall miss you very much.

With every good wish for your continued success
and happiness, and with warmest personal regards.

Sincerely,

Frank Hogan

Frank S. Hogan

Mr. Harold R. Danforth

educated and dresses conservatively. In the twenty years that I have known him I have never heard him raise his voice.

But this is no sign of softness, as a certain husky champion of the fleet can testify. One night in 1942 a young seaman in a Harlem barroom boasted that he could flatten anyone who wanted to take him on. He swaggered over to a nondescript man who sat at one end of the bar, swung the civilian off the stool and started to shake him.

"Why the hell aren't you in uniform?" he demanded.

A short from-the-shoulder blow caught the young bully on the chin. He crumpled to the floor and two of his buddies went to his assistance.

"Hey, Mac, you knocked out the ship's champ!" one called to the civilian walking casually out the door of the tavern. Joined by another man, the civilian walked rapidly down the block, turning into a doorway to watch a radio car pull up in front of the bar.

The young seaman had blundered into a perfect "stake-out" involving two criminal investigators' nightly watch over a key witness whose testimony, months later, led to an important conviction.

"When he started to push me around I had to hit him hard and fast, or else the place might have erupted into a riot and our suspect, who was on the edge of the law, might have quietly disappeared," Dan recalled. His companion that night was Tom Fay, now Chief Investigator of the District Attorney's office. As Fay recalls, he didn't know whether to move in and help his colleague—perhaps ruining a case that had taken months to prepare—or let Dan slug it out alone.

This was not, by far, the closest call Dan has had in his more than twenty years of sleuthing. On several occasions he almost lost his life. He was once struck on the head by a gallon can dropped from a four-story building. He took a murderer at gunpoint, blundered into a desperate gang of jewel thieves, found himself trapped while installing a dictaphone in the office of a tough waterfront mob, and had other narrow escapes.

Someone once suggested to Dan that he should apply to Actors' Equity Association for a membership card because of the varied roles he has played during his career. To gather evidence he has had to infiltrate the ranks of the underworld. To obtain vital information he has played the part of a waterfront thug, a bordello-keeper, a loan-shark, a longshoreman, a gun-for-hire killer, a tramp, a school-teacher, a homosexual, a piano-player (he can fake a good tune), a drunk (in all stages of intoxication) and many more. Each time he was successful in avoiding detection by the real article.

Before he adopted the guise of a longshoreman he hung about the Hudson River docks—eating, drinking and even living with long-shoremen. He got to know their language, gripes, union factions, favorite meeting-places and the nicknames of longshoremen in other cities. His favorite fictitious home port was Boston and he spent many days memorizing its local ship movements, pier numbers and pier bosses.

He admits he had some difficulty posing as a bordello-owner in the Luciano investigation, but found the task not insurmountable. He sought out a known prostitute, flashed some money, "talked big— all prostitutes dream of mink and pearls—told her I wanted to open up. Before long I knew the names of all the important procurers, top bail bondsmen, madams and so on."

Dan can claim a fascinating stable of personal informants—a small-time criminal grateful for a few dollars to tide him over his rent crisis, a thief who wants a parole recommendation, a criminal who seeks to gather a storehouse of favors for the winter's day when he may be forced to ask one in return. These range from a former member of the Five Points gang, which ran the Lower East Side of New York in the nineties, to an eighteen-year-old drug addict for whom Dan arranged admittance to a narcotics' rehabilitation center.

I saw "Bob," a white-faced boy, the perspiration beading his forehead, his body trembling like an aspen as he approached Dan.

"There's three pushers selling horse near P. S. ———," he blurted out.

Dan made a note; the information would be forwarded that afternoon to the District Attorney's office, the Police Department's Narcotics Bureau or the U. S. Treasury Department. He asked the names and addresses of the narcotics peddlers and the boy supplied them.

"Can you let me have some money to get home, Dan?" the boy begged.

Dan counted out twenty-five dollars. Three days later an informer called Dan to tell him "Bob" had got a "fix" with the money. Dan didn't believe it. A week later a postcard arrived from the boy's home town.

"I wish I had given him fifty," Dan said.

He has worked on many notable criminal cases, but he has also had a part in resolving numerous unknown ones. His favorite case never rated a paragraph in the metropolitan press; after six months' work he was able to prove a young Negro boy innocent of a crime he was accused of having committed. The boy, who might have been sentenced to twenty years in Sing Sing, never fails to send a Christmas card "to Dan, the man to whom I owe my life."

Danforth is a dedicated man; his whole life is the law. He reads pamphlets and books of awe-inspiring thickness on criminology, psychology and sociology. Juvenile delinquency is his special interest; he has on several occasions volunteered his services in cases involving young offenders.

He is a tenacious man. Those who violate the law must face the prospect of such men as Danforth relentlessly dogging their footsteps, no matter where they go. In the end they find there are no places left to hide. The elusive, still unsolved cases remain a part of Dan's life. Although he is no longer associated with the District Attorney's office he still checks the Missing Persons' Bureau periodically to learn the status of the case of a young girl who vanished from a Harlem marijuana den, and keeps in touch with her mother, who has never given up hope.

Except for an occasional movie he has no hobbies. Like many men engaged in criminal work he likes to read detective stories, and he is perpetually astounded at the ease with which television and movie sleuths solve their cases. One night we watched such a program. The crime—less the commercials—was solved in 22½ minutes. Dan, at my request, joined me in making up a similar hypothetical crime and sketched a program of how a real investigation agency would go about solving the murder. We made a list of the witnesses who would have to be contacted, both in and out of the city, computed the amount of time that would be required to obtain the medical examiner's report, the toxicologist's analysis, stenographic statements, etc. By our reckoning it would have taken much longer than 22½ minutes merely to get the Police Department photographs taken of the corpse and to remove the body, with the medical examiner's approval, to the Bellevue morgue.

In his more than sixteen years as a D.A.'s man Dan has worked on thousands of actual criminal cases. Obviously, all of these could not be included in this book. The incidents were selected on the basis of their importance and variety. In our re-creation of the gangster era he helped fill in details of the period by producing a scrapbook, notes and copies of reports he had made on famous cases. He is also blessed with an impressive memory.

. . . AND THE D.A.'S OFFICE

THE STORY of the D.A.'s man is inevitably also the story of the D.A.—the District Attorney's office. Actually, the District Attorney's office of New York County is one of the largest law enforcement agencies in the United States. It performs a variety of tasks, not only the legal prosecution of the accused but the detection and investigation of crime, the counseling of those who ask assistance in matters beyond the jurisdiction of the office and the protection of individuals falsely accused of criminal acts. As District Attorney Hogan has described it, "In a collective sense the District Attorney on any given day is part lawyer, part policeman, part defender of the innocent, part youth counselor and part community adviser."

New York County is Manhattan Island which, although it constitutes little more than seven per cent of the total area of the city, has a resident population of 2,000,000 with another million pouring in regularly from commuting areas, besides additional transients from other states and other countries. This great population and its centers of trade, fashion and wealth make up the honey which attracts criminals from all over the world. Nowhere in America is there found the astonishing volume and variety of problems of law enforcement. The grafter, racketeer, swindler and killer are the criminals who make the headlines. Less publicized but more important in the aggregate is the mass of smaller, less sensational crimes of fraud, theft, assault, etc.

In the Criminal Courts of New York County some 40,000 matters are considered each year. The District Attorney's office presents evidence to grand juries in some 4,000 cases. More than 3,000 defendants a year answer felony indictments which are disposed of in the Court of General Sessions, while another 15,000 are prosecuted on misdemeanor charges in the Court of Special Sessions.

Under the supervision of District Attorney Frank Hogan today are 76 assistants, ten certified public accountants, ten investigators, 30 clerks, 42 law stenographers, 25 process-servers and a number of specialized employees such as a psychiatrist, a civil engineer and a photographer. Thus, Hogan commands a small army of 214 men and women. In addition, he has assigned to his office 60 detectives from the New York Police Department, many of whom have served since the "racket-busting" days of the late thirties all under Captain Freddy Hains, veteran police officer. The nonprofessional personnel of the office are civil service employees for the most part. The members of the legal staff are in the exempt class of civil service. Competition for jobs on the legal staff is keen. Most of the appointees are honor students, some editors of their law school review. Each legal assistant is required to devote full time to the office.

For years the office had been more or less of a political tool. When Thomas E. Dewey was elected District Attorney after a brilliant term as Special Prosecutor, he brought to the office many successful techniques he had used to unearth fragments of evidence which, when painstakingly pieced together, formed the basis for many of the state's cases against leading racketeers and politicians.

Before Dewey's era there were no effective facilities to carry forward the battle against organized crime and corruption. To fill that virtual void he established special bureaus in 1938 as integral parts of the office; each of these was a complex unit designed to combat crimes with skill, patience and resourcefulness. They were to become the District Attorney's keen-edged weapons in the battle against organized crime.

The first point of contact which the public has with the District Attorney's office is the Complaint Bureau, where each year many grievances, real or fancied, are heard. In many cases this office does not have jurisdiction and advises the complainants as to the proper legal procedure. If a complaint is found to have real merit an arrest is ordered. In some cases the specialized bureaus of the District Attorney's office make a further investigation of the complaint or the evil complained of. In less serious matters the complainant may be referred to the Police Department or to the Magistrates' Courts to request a summons.

The citizen's complaint is one way in which a case may be started. Arrests, reports of crimes or misdemeanors committed are other ways. In addition, many cases are initiated by the office, which does not sit back and wait to have cases brought to its attention. Rather, it is alert to evils and is quick to probe the possibility of crime when there is reason to believe one has been committed.

Transgressions of the law are divided into misdemeanors (minor) and felonies (major). In a misdemeanor case the defendant is brought directly to trial. In a felony case, an indictment by a grand jury must be obtained before the defendant is brought to trial.

The assistants in the Special Sessions Bureau are responsible for the trial and disposition of all misdemeanor cases in the Court of

Special Sessions. One of the assistants is detailed to Gamblers' Court, a unit of the Magistrates' Courts.

The Indictment Bureau supervises the duties of the grand juries. One member is assigned as the People's attorney in Felony Court. Cases of defendants in Felony Court are channeled to the Indictment Bureau where the assistant sifts the evidence in order to present it to the grand juries, four of which are empaneled each month. There are six so-called "holdover" grand juries engaged in long and extensive investigations. The bureau advises the juries as to the law and drafts the "true bills" when they are voted. A grand jury consists of 23 persons. It hears the evidence presented by the District Attorney and the defendant if he wishes to testify, and decides whether a *prima facie* case has been made out. If so, it indicts the defendant by bringing in a "true bill." Otherwise it brings in no bill of indictment.

When there is a "true bill" the indictment may go to the Court of General Sessions, the oldest court of criminal jurisdiction in North America. Part I of this court is reserved for motions and arraignments, Part II for youthful offenders. Three sections are concerned with bail cases, while two cover trials of prison cases which must be disposed of expeditiously to assure an imprisoned defendant his right to a speedy trial, and two sections hear only homicide cases.

A verdict does not always mean the end of a case. For the District Attorney's office a verdict of guilty may be only the beginning of a long and arduous trail through the higher courts, even perhaps to the United States Supreme Court, before a final decision is made. Attorneys assigned to the Appeals Bureau write the legal briefs, argue the contested points and carry the cases to the last ruling. Five top third-year law students from the New York University School of Law serve without compensation as volunteer law student clerks. They help the assistants in the Appeals Bureau by researching the facts and preparing memoranda.

Other bureaus in the District Attorney's office are the Election Frauds Bureau; the Abandonment Bureau, which tries to locate missing husbands; the Bail Bond Bureau, which examines the collateral furnished by defendants and handles forfeitures. The District Attorney's medical assistant heads the Medico-Legal Bureau; in addition to normal forensic medical services, this bureau's aid is vital in trials in which psychiatric and psychological questions arise. Affiliated with this bureau is the Youth Counsel Bureau, which handles the cases of juvenile offenders.

All the bureaus in the District Attorney's office are indispensable in the work they perform, but the drama and the headlines center chiefly around two important bureaus, the Homicide Bureau and the Rackets Bureau.

The Homicide Bureau investigates all cases of fatal violence in New York County. Twenty-four hours a day, every day of the year, an assistant is on duty, ready to go out immediately on notification of a homicide. Accompanied by a man from the stenographic unit, he speeds to the scene of the murder, questions witnesses or perhaps takes a death-bed statement. On-the-spot questioning often minimizes the possibility of subsequent lapses of memory and serves to perpetuate the evidence.

The Rackets Bureau investigates governmental, commercial and industrial enterprises when there are indications that the underworld has moved into their operations. It cultivates and jealously guards its confidential sources of information. It constantly seeks out those who have been injured by racketeers, then coaxes or compels them to tell the truth as state's witnesses before a grand jury. The bureau is now headed by Chief Assistant District Attorney Alfred Scotti, a fiery, peppery lawman who has helped to shatter many New York rackets and send their political protectors to jail. No well-known racketeer or criminal makes a move that this bureau doesn't know about. Many cases involving rackets and politicians might never have been broken if Scotti and his assistants had not initiated action.

The bureau is constantly on the alert for overt acts of violence. A waterfront union boss on one occasion publicly stated at a meeting that if a union rival appeared in Brooklyn he would run him back to Manhattan. The next morning Scotti sent for him and when he arrived flung a newspaper at him.

"Did you say this?" he demanded.

The tough waterfront boss, now very meek, began to explain in Italian and broken English.

"Don't pull that immigrant English on me," Scotti snapped. "I know you speak English—speak it and fast!"

He left with this warning from Scotti: "If I get one man to tell me you did this I'll throw you in jail. Now get out of here before I lock you up on general principles!"

The Rackets Bureau is charged with a great deal of public responsibility. Since ill-advised action or impulsive investigations could cause irreparable damage, evidence relating to individuals, commercial and banking houses must be as clear and hard as a polished gem before any prosecution is initiated. This unit also acts as a policing

agency in the regulation of the businesses which perch on the fence
of the law and in the matter of violation of city statutes. For example,
the Rackets Bureau accumulated the evidence for a grand jury's
presentment against a city councilman; the charge was that he had
violated the "conflict of interest" clause in the city charter.

A great deal of preliminary work must be done in each case to
assemble sufficient incriminating evidence with which to confront a
potential defendant. This is the job of the Bureau of Investigation,
and the work of its investigators such as Harold R. Danforth is often
essential to the successful prosecution of a case.

The members of this department have played major roles in the
trials and convictions of racketeers and politicians which made the
headlines during the thirties, forties and fifties. They are not "detectives," but "investigators." Their work is long, tedious and often
dangerous. They are mostly middle-aged men; some are bachelors
and others are married with families. Each is selected with care and
his background as thoroughly checked as that of any FBI recruit.
Their names rarely appear in the newspapers and never their pictures,
yet their reputations in the world of law enforcement are so high that
their services are sought by prosecutors of many states. They may
work on criminal cases involving as many as ten states. Yet in such
cases the investigators are not paid extra; their work is done in the
spirit of cooperation so that justice may be served. New York City
is far from their sole stamping ground; they are constantly flying to
the West Coast, to Florida or even to Europe on the trail of criminals.

In this department are kept voluminous dossiers of known gangsters and criminals with information which could quickly lead to
their apprehension if it became known that they were involved in a
criminal case. Each case has an extensive file, including the confidential reports of investigators who worked on the case. Sometimes
in an extensive investigation as many as six men will each handle a
different phase; all six reports are studied, then woven into a master
report. Although it has access to the Police Department's Rogues'
Gallery, the bureau has its own extensive files, or "morgue." Other
state, federal and local law enforcement agencies frequently request
information from this bureau.

Of course this bureau holds a strong attraction for would-be detectives. Almost every day some eager amateur writes or telephones,
anxious to know how he can become a member. "I have just taken a
course in learning how to be a detective. I am sure I can help District Attorney Hogan break up the rackets. Please call me at ————.

. . ." Or "I used to be a deputy in ———— and I am sure you need a man like me in your office. I am afraid of no one. My address is ————." Or there's the one who mentions his district leader's name and asks to be put on at once. "Politician" is a forbidden word in this bureau; it is the one word *not* to mention in asking for a job, although it is one bureau to which the politicians would give anything to have a pipeline.

The structural twin of the Rackets Bureau is the Frauds Bureau. Occasionally their areas of jurisdiction overlap. In the intricate world of New York finance many fraud cases involve a financial maze of contracts, negotiable instruments and complicated documents the meaning of which is disputed by all parties concerned. When it has been established that a crime has been committed, corroborating evidence must be found among a wilderness of dummy corporations and devious bookkeeping devices. To acquire a thorough understanding of a complex case it may be necessary for the Frauds Bureau staff to study the particular customs of the business or trade involved.

Since the cases investigated are largely commercial in nature the complainant who has been the victim of chicanery is often more interested in getting his money back by the threat of prosecution than in obtaining a criminal conviction. Thus the Frauds Bureau must be on the alert to avoid becoming merely a collecting agency and must channel those cases which properly belong in the civil courts to these courts rather than the criminal courts.

An important phase of the District Attorney's office which is little known to the general public is its cooperation with legislative committees and investigation commissions such as the Kefauver Committee and the Senate Rackets Committee. The committees may make the headlines, but it is Hogan's office which provides much of the material for the momentous disclosures Americans see on their television screens and in the newspapers.

"Seeds of lawlessness on a wholesale scale must be rooted out before the evil growths run wild through the community." This is Hogan's conception of the nonpolitical way in which a public prosecutor's office should be run. It has won wide recognition and acceptance. The Kings County District Attorney stated a similar philosophy in almost identical language. In 1951 a candidate campaigned in Philadelphia on the platform that he would set up an office similar to Hogan's in New York.

Prior to 1938 Assistant District Attorneys were appointed from the political clubhouse. In 1942 for the first time in New York County came an unprecedented political event: Frank Hogan was endorsed by all parties and elected as the unopposed candidate. "I interpreted this to mean a mandate from the people of New York to continue the administration of my office on a nonpolitical and nonpartisan basis," Hogan said, "and that's the way it will remain as long as I am here."

Shortly before this book went to press Hogan was again endorsed by all parties for re-election this fall.

This is a brief summary of the progressive development of the office. It is a far cry today from the dusty, creaking D.A.'s office I covered in the Tombs in the early thirties. I was a fresh-faced young reporter then from the hinterlands of New Jersey, but it didn't take me long to realize it was more of a Tammany Hall clubhouse than a public prosecutor's office charged with the solemn responsibility to stand steadfast in its fidelity to the constitutional safeguards to our lives, our liberty and our pursuit of happiness.

JAMES D. HORAN

1. ISLAND OF INFAMY: THE APPRENTICE YEARS

I BEGAN my apprenticeship in this business of law enforce‐ ment on the lowest rung of the ladder: as a guard at the toughest reformatory in the country, the House of Refuge on New York's Randall's Island. I'm glad I began my career this way. The tough young hoodlums under my charge—most of them gang-leaders of the Prohibition and Depression eras—helped to knock many of my illusions galley-west and turned me into a realist.

When I walked out of the big gates of the House for the last time, there was little I didn't know about crime, criminals, perver‐ sion, brutality, official corruption and official ignorance. The place was quite a proving ground for my college ambition—to be a shield for justice and a guide for delinquents seeking the road back to a decent, law-abiding life.

It began on a December morning in 1925, a day in contrast to my exuberant mood. It was cold and foggy, with a bone-chilling wind whipping up whitecaps on the East River. I could scarcely wait until the ferry, *Refuge,* left its dock. I was in my early twenties and armed with the faith of a thousand men.

Springfield College and Boston University—where I had majored in philosophy and sociology—were now behind me, and although my mother had advised me to go on for a master's degree in phi‐ losophy, I was determined to find someplace where I could work with the young—the tougher the better.

I had mentioned this one day to one of my instructors at Boston University.

"You want a real tough place to start, Danforth? Why don't you try the House of Refuge in New York?"

"Thanks, I will, sir," I said, and that night I wrote a long letter to the office of the superintendent.

I waited anxiously and in a week's time the postman rang the bell of our house in Haverhill, Massachusetts. There was a terse letter from the superintendent, Edward C. Barber, asking me to come down for an interview.

1

Somewhere beyond the swirling fog was the House of Refuge.

I paced the deck of the ferry anxiously. The buildings on Randall's Island were grim and fortress-like and for the first time I felt a tug of apprehension. I imagined it was like young Oliver Twist's first sight of the London workhouse.

I was directed to the superintendent's office, and there, standing behind a desk, was a dignified-looking man of about sixty, with cold eyes that took my measure in a matter of seconds, and an impassive face.

His voice, like his eyes, was cold.

"Why did you come here for a job?"

"Frankly, sir, because I heard it was a tough institution. I thought I had better start out learning the hard way."

"Who told you it was tough here?"

"My philosophy professor."

"Where was that?" he asked.

"Boston University," I said with pride.

The thin lips twisted just a bit. "You can't handle these animals with stuff you learn from books, Danforth."

I was shocked at such a brutal description.

He suddenly seemed tired of talking to me. "What do you want?"

"A job."

"Anyone starting here takes a guard's job."

"Fine, sir. I accept."

"You start tonight," he said. "You won't get a uniform for three months . . ."

I had started for the door, but something in his tone made me turn around.

"Three months, sir?"

"I doubt that you will be around here three months. If you last one month it will surprise me. I'll have one of the guards show you to your quarters. You're on the night shift."

The guard who had met me at the door was named Tony and it was he who took me in tow for the rest of the day. He was a tough, illiterate brute, who seemed quite puzzled with me. When I convinced him I wasn't from Albany—the place was usually being investigated by the state—but from Boston, he became friendly. He took me on a tour and I was shocked by the physical conditions in the sprawling building. The place housed roughly five hundred boys, all in their teens. The average age was eighteen. Tony was frank in his description of the rampant sex perversion and the brisk trade in smuggled tobacco, candy, cigarettes and other luxuries in which some guards "made a few bucks."

Once when we were going down a corridor I saw a burly tough of about eighteen or nineteen half-dragging a young boy toward what I thought were steps leading to a boiler room or cellar. He grinned at Tony, who just chuckled and waved. I thought nothing of it until we had passed out of sight, then I casually asked Tony what they were doing.

"That's Rocky, the leader of one of the toughest gangs in here," he said. "He's got a new girl. His 'wife' went home last week."

I didn't get the implication immediately. I would in a few days. . . .

My mattress was unyielding as iron and my room small and not too clean, but even if my quarters had been first-rate I doubt if I could have slept. I was due to report on the night shift at 11:00 P.M. to work until sunup, and I couldn't wait to get started. My assignment was night guard in one of the dormitories. For the first few nights I was to be accompanied by an experienced guard, who would train me in the routine.

My station was a raised platform in the center of the dorm in which a hundred and fifty beds were lined up on both sides of the room. The only light was a small night light above a bookkeeping-type desk.

I relieved the surprised guard at least an hour before his quitting time. After a brief rundown of my duties, which were to maintain watch over the sleeping boys and to keep a sort of rough log, I was left alone. The other guard wasn't due for an hour

I can still see myself, dressed in my best suit, white shirt and black tie, the model of formal municipal neatness, sitting uncomfortably on a high stool, bathed by the naked light of the bulb under a wide green metal shade, anxiously listening to the rhythmic breathing, with an occasional cough and sleepy murmur. Once, to relieve my nervousness, I walked up one side of the room and down the other, staring at the young faces and feeling like the guardian of all mankind. My charges were safe. I returned to my post on the high stool.

In a moment I leaped out of the seat. The most terrified screams I had ever heard in my life were still echoing in the room.

Not a blanket moved, not a boy raised himself on an elbow to see what was happening.

Then I realized that since I had taken my post one hundred and fifty pairs of eyes had been watching my every move! Not a boy was asleep.

I ran toward the sound of the screams. "What is wrong?" I kept calling. "Where are you?"

There wasn't a sound from the beds. I ran frantically up and down, searching for the injured boy. The screams had now dwindled to a few sobs. Finally I traced them under a bed. I pulled out the boy from under the bed, my hands slippery with blood.

Under the light I could only gasp with horror at what I saw. His scalp had been split from ear to ear. I could see the bare bone of his skull in the open slit. One ear had been badly mangled and it looked as if his jaw was broken.

I ran out into the hall with the half-conscious boy—he was about fifteen—the blood running down my suit and along the floor. Luckily I ran into an older guard who was on his way to join me. This man, one of the more humane employees of this hellhole, took in the situation quickly and guided me to the infirmary. There at least seventy-five stitches were needed to close the boy's wounds, his broken jaw had to be wired and part of his ear had to be stitched back.

The boy, a slight Italian boy with large black eyes, just shook his head to my questions.

"You're new here, aren't you?" the nurse asked.

"Yes," I said. "I think we ought to notify Mr. Barber."

The nurse gave me a sick grin. "Get him out of bed for this? Do you want to be fired tonight?"

"Come on, Danforth," Andy, the other guard, said. "Save your breath."

On the way back to the dorm I asked Andy, a bald-headed Irishman, if we should attempt to find the boy's attacker, but he put his hand on my shoulder and said, "Do you know what would happen to a kid in there who would tell you anything, Danforth?"

"Well, they might rough him up," I agreed.

"They'd probably cut his heart out," the guard said. Now I believed it.

The dorm was still as before, but I had the feeling I was being watched. After a few hours of listening to Andy's explanation of the fundamentals of the night watch, I sauntered back to the wounded boy's bed. I felt about the floor in the darkness; in the pool of blood I found something hard. I pulled it out from under the bed and slid it inside my shirt. It felt heavy and cold.

I waited, then told Andy I was going to the washroom. On the way to the door the weight inside my shirt felt tremendous. I wondered if the eyes knew what I had found. Outside in the corridor I took it out. It was a firehose nozzle. I recalled seeing a coil of hose hanging near number-one bed in the front of the dorm.

I walked back and showed the nozzle to Andy. "I'll check the hose," I said. It was without a nozzle. I screwed it back on.

Back at my post I told myself I was quite a guard. While I had sat so prim and official the nozzle had been quietly slipped from bed to bed, then had been wielded with a savage fury.

"Shouldn't we question the boys who sleep next to him?" I asked Andy.

He shrugged. "Waste of time," he said. "I'll tell the colonel about it . . ."

"Who's the colonel?" I asked.

"Barber," he said. "He likes to be called colonel."

For the rest of the night until daylight filtered through the barred windows, Andy told me of what was going on inside the walls of the House of Refuge. When he had ended I told myself that if this were true this institution was a human bomb with a sizzling fuse. . . .

The following day I had concrete evidence that I was the new target. As I was walking down the stairway I heard something clank against the side of the stairway somewhere above me. I jumped aside and a canvas bag crashed at my feet. Had it hit its mark, the bolts and nuts in the bag would have crushed my head like an eggshell.

I stayed on the night shift for three months. It was the same quiet jungle I had met on my first night. There were more assaults. Once a boy's liver was punctured with a homemade shiv—a table knife worn down to razor sharpness. Again it had been passed from bed to bed. The assailant slashed his victim and at the moment of his outcry the weapon was passed back, hand to hand, to its hiding place or skimmed across the floor.

I found the lack of interest and the cynical attitude on the part of the House's officials outrageous. The guards only shrugged. Once when I reported an attack to Barber he said coldly, "We'll look into it, Mr. Danforth."

Perhaps he did look into it, but if he did, the boys who should have been questioned were never summoned.

I found some of the guards brutal, illiterate and almost totally corruptible. They sold everything from food to cigars. One guard—by rumor, I couldn't get the proof—had a still and was selling alcohol to the boys.

The brutality was incredible. I once saw a guard club a young boy, scarcely more than a child, into unconsciousness. He stopped when I told him I'd use the club on him. Some guards used stern, but proper disciplinary measures, but on the whole it was the law of the club and the boot.

The boys themselves were mostly from the tenement areas of New York City, schooled in thievery and assault since infancy, some motherless and fatherless, most of them from broken homes. However, on the other hand, there were boys who came from excellent home surroundings, with a background of religious training and parents of fair education. The reasons for their defections from society lay deep within themselves. They obviously needed treatment, but they never got it on the Island.

They did get an excellent course in vice and crime. When they left there wasn't anything about vice they didn't know. I also got an excellent course in practical criminology, in the drives and twists of the criminal personality.

After three months on the night side I was shifted to the cell division. I took on this new assignment with a great deal of apprehension. My new assignment was the least desirable on the island. I found that when an inmate could not be controlled in the dorms he was placed in the cell division at night. Here were the future gangsters, killers and robbers who within the next few years would supply newspaper headlines. Seven of the boys I watched during those long nights died in the electric chair. At least that many were "ride" victims or were killed in gang fights. A few were mentioned in the forties when the Kings County District Attorney's office was smashing the Murder, Inc., ring, and I came across several others during my criminal investigation work in later years.

Because of the tighter security measures in the cell division, there were fewer assaults but there was the constant strain of knowing that a riot might start at any hour. There were always rumors of a mass break and it was quite uncomfortable pacing up and down outside the cells, wondering which boy had a gun under his pillow, ready to use.

After two months of this duty I was detailed to the storeroom. There I made several enemies by refusing to deal with guards who had been stealing supplies and selling them at exorbitant prices to the inmates. But also I made an important discovery.

I perceived that deep down inside the toughest kid on the island there was some core of decency, some unbreakable code of personal honor. I tried a sort of personal honor system, and in most cases it worked. Some boys completely ignored it, but others obeyed it and even helped to enforce it. Strangely enough, the boys who maintained the code were those with the longest records.

I don't want to give the impression that I was a dreamy-eyed reformer; I was never brutal, but I was firm.

One day a slim young boy named Vincent was assigned to work under me. He was a quiet type with cold blue eyes and thick blond hair. He did his work grudgingly, especially when I gave him a direct order.

"Do you have anything against me, Vincent?" I asked him one day.

"Not you, Mr. Danforth," he replied, "only your uniform. It reminds me of a cop's."

"What have you against cops?" I asked.

"They killed my friend," he said. "A cop shot him in the back."

"What was he doing?" I wanted to know.

"Running away," he said.

"From a holdup?" I inquired.

He nodded. "But they didn't have to shoot him in the back," he argued.

For days I tried to win this boy's confidence. He would listen, shrug and say, "Well, Mr. Danforth, let's say I don't see it your way."

I had the frustrated feeling that I was throwing words to the winds. I was to remember Vincent many times in the years to come when I would read the headlines—when he was known as Vincent "Mad Dog" Coll.

In the winter of 1927 the tension in the place began to mount. The guards felt it and the brutality increased. The guards were now wielding their clubs in a frenzy of fear. I had made a few dents in the hardened personalities of the boys working with me in the storeroom, but even these were becoming surly and arrogant again.

Then one night the pent-up violence exploded. The frenzied clanging of the fire bells shattered the stillness. As I jumped into my clothes I could see through a window that one of the buildings was on fire.

The place was in an uproar, the boys totally uncontrollable. They raced up and down the corridors fighting, screaming, laughing, sometimes in a state of hysteria. They ripped beds apart, smashed tables, flung furniture through windows. They were like creatures possessed by the devil. For one of the few times in my career—and I have been close to death many times—I was physically afraid.

The mobs broke through the doors of the dorms and poured out into the grounds. Those still in the cells kept up a wild clanging, rattling their tinware up and down the bars. I saw two guards swept under the wild rush. They fell, rose, and fell again. Under fists and feet I tried to push through, but was flung aside. A blow in my face made my ears ring. I almost went down when someone tried to kick my legs from under me. Other guards joined the fray, flailing clubs. Some of the boys seized their clubs from them and beat them. The mobs broke up into smaller groups. Rivals began battles with rocks, broken bottles and clubs, all against the lurid glare of the burning buildings.

We finally managed to organize some of the boys in a bucket brigade, but it was hopeless.

"We got the mainland," one guard shouted. "They're sending emergency and fire trucks."

A ferryboat finally brought fire department equipment but the angry mobs tried to overturn the engines, only to be driven off by high-powered hoses. While some of the firemen fought the blazes others invaded the cell blocks where some of the prisoners had overpowered the guards. They rescued the guards and pushed the boys back into their cells.

Although the firemen fought valiantly and got the blazes under control, the island was still at the mercy of a raging mob of boys, gathered together in one part of the buildings, many armed with lead pipes, knives and an assortment of homemade tools.

"This is a job for the cops," one firemen told us.

Colonel Barber, as detached as though this riot were happening in some other place and not in an institution under his supervision, finally summoned the police.

Again a ferryboat ground its way into the dock and the police roared up. After a brief reconnaissance they decided tear gas was to be used. The first burst of gas brought out roars of rage and curses, but it soon took the heart out of all of them. They began staggering out, crying, rubbing their eyes, stumbling around hopelessly.

The riot was over. I was surprised to read a newspaper account the next day describing the riot simply as a "dispute" over a ball game.

Discipline was tightened and guards became more brutal than ever. One boy, about fifteen or sixteen, who worked for me on a few occasions, was the target of a guard notorious for his brutality. Once he came in with a swollen eye and a badly cut lip. I brought him to the doctor and insisted that he be X-rayed and treated. I also told the guard that I would take off my uniform and meet him in the gym for a session in the ring if he hit the boy again. A protest to the superintendent's office was "noted," but nothing happened.

The boy went to work in another department and I didn't see him for several weeks. Then one afternoon he came in and said he was leaving and had just dropped in to say good-by.

I assumed he was going on parole or had served his sentence, and I wished him luck. The next day his body was found in the river. He was a rather frail boy and I said aloud that I couldn't understand why he tried to escape.

Later one of the boys passing me in a corridor told me in a whisper, "He wasn't trying to escape, Mr. Danforth. He couldn't swim. He just walked off the dock. . . ."

The year turned. In 1928 Barber left and a man named Fred Helbring took his post. He had been a former inmate of the island himself and had lost three fingers of one hand in the laundry. For some reason he was called "Kinch" by the boys.

He was as brutal as the most brutal of the guards. He would not hesitate to smash a boy across the face for the most trivial of incidents. One time I saw him knock a boy down and cold-bloodedly kick him in the back and ribs.

The place became a worse hellhole after Helbring took over. Once a boy tried to stab him with a fork. Another boy, just seventeen, attacked a guard, and beat him to death with a hose nozzle. The boy, who was ready to disclose the terrifying conditions on the island, was allowed to plead guilty to a manslaughter charge and was sent to Sing Sing.

I soon was top man on Helbring's list of unwanted persons. He told me quite bluntly and truthfully, "I don't like you or your God-damned honor system, Danforth, and I'm going to get rid of you as fast as I can. From now on you take over the Discipline Squad. Got to harden you up, young man!"

In the Discipline Squad of the Island were gathered the vicious, the uncontrollable, the violent and the feeble-minded inmates. The usual punishment was to require them to stand upright all through the night at attention. Only at certain times was the command "at ease" given so they would not topple over in a faint or collapse with cramped limbs.

It was either take the job or quit, so I took it. It was a miserable chore. The boys hated me or any guard and even though they knew they were being punished for breaking a rule they resented any order. Without being too soft, I tried to do my job. Finally I hit on an idea of letting them discipline themselves. For example, if someone made a noise and wouldn't admit it, the whole company received a penalty. In time they came around to accepting this Navy-type of punishment.

"You are only as good as the man next to you," I told them. "If all of you respect the rules there will be no punishment. But it has got to be all or nothing."

I had this assignment for a month. Then one night Helbring appeared at the door. He went into a tirade and nothing I could do to explain would help. I was then shifted to the prison yard from 4:00 P.M. until supper and then until lights out.

Here I discovered the true inside of the gangs who really controlled the island. In their own "oligarchy" there was the leader, always the toughest or the smartest, then his body of henchmen who enforced his laws, then the "scouts" who found out advance information from guards through bribery or threats. Offenders were judged by a kangaroo court held in the yard in the late afternoon. Fear sealed any boy's lips. They would rather die than squeal. The usual weapon was a razor blade taped on the inside of the leg or arm. The number of boys who left the island with scars is almost incredible.

I will never forget one who aroused the anger of one of the gangs and was slashed down one side of his face, leaving a nasty scar. I don't think he was more than fifteen. I watched the boy when he came out of the hospital but he never made a move to avenge his attack; he became a lone wolf.

One bright spring day in 1928, I saw him among those lined up in the yard who were to be released that afternoon. "Kinch" stood by as the names were read out.

Finally this boy's name was called. His name was the last called out and in the moment of silence before the order to break ranks was given, his actions were so startling and so unexpected that no one made a move. I thought he was making a break for the gate or had suddenly become deranged—not an unusual happening on this terrible island.

He ran halfway down his row and stopped in front of a dark-skinned boy.

"You see this!" He jabbed at his own scarred face. "I got *this* to carry—now you carry this!" He slashed at the other boy's face with a razor held between his fingers. In a second the blood spurted. He screamed and other boys grabbed the boy who had done the slashing. He didn't try to tear away, but just stood looking at the anguished boy.

The yard became a bedlam. The guards began running around, waving their clubs and shouting hysterically at the group milling about the two boys. The inmates seemed only casually curious; this had been expected for a long time. In this primitive world, justice had at last been served.

The incident never saw the light of day in the city's press. The boy who had done the slashing was transferred to another reformatory; later I heard he was released after a few months. The other boy left that island eventually, a vivid scar down both cheeks.

To what lengths the boys would go to escape the House of Refuge was underscored by the case of two boys, one fourteen, the other eighteen, who swam the East River on one of the coldest of winter nights. A cold spell had gripped the East for weeks. It was so cold that the river was virtually frozen from shore to shore. All day we watched the huge ice cakes grinding their way down the river to the Bay.

The ice must have given the boys the idea. After midnight they had scaled the twelve-foot wall in their pajamas when the younger boy confessed to the other that he couldn't swim. The older one, a bull-like Polish boy, helped his companion skip from cake to cake and when they reached open water he put the younger boy on a cake of ice and pushed it to the Manhattan shore line. Both boys were clad only in flannel night clothes. How they made it we never knew. A policeman found them, their pajamas sheets of ice. The older boy was half-carrying his unconscious companion. They were rushed to the hospital with pneumonia and for a time it looked as if both would die, but they survived.

The case of the young Negro boy in the dining hall is another dramatic demonstration of the brutality rampant on the Island. I was walking across the hall when I noticed this small boy slumped in a chair. I went over to reprimand him for being asleep on the job, but when I came closer I could hear him breathing very heavily.

"What's the matter with him?" I asked a boy passing with an armload of trays.

"He's sick," the boy replied. "We told Mr. ———— but he said he wasn't sick and had to do his work."

I touched the boy's forehead; it was burning with fever.

"This boy is sick," I called out to the guard in charge.

He sauntered over. "That black bastard has been trying to get out of cleaning his tables all day," he said.

"The boy needs a doctor," I told him.

"Doctor!" the other guard snorted. "He needs a kick in the ————" He leaned over to yank the boy to his feet by his shirt but I pushed him aside, picked up the boy and carried him to the infirmary. The next morning he was dead. When I left the guard was still on the Island.

Another Negro boy complained of a sore eye. Someone in the infirmary administered iodine instead of argyrol. The boy lost his eye, but no action was taken.

Some boys found that by eating handfuls of ground-up prune pits violent cramps would result and they could plead appendicitis. This worked for a while until the secret leaked out. Then peaches replaced prunes.

For a time there were rumors that liquor was being sold somewhere on the island. I didn't put any stock in it but one day I noticed a boy staggering up the boiler shop stairs. I watched, and soon a second boy followed. Then a third and a fourth. All were in serious stages of intoxication. Finally, when no more appeared, I tiptoed down to the boiler shop. It was easy to follow the strong smell which led to a small still concealed behind one of the closets.

I dismantled the still and advised the superintendent. He was interested only in finding the four boys who had broken *his* rules but he wasn't interested in questioning the guard who patrolled that section of the building. It was obvious that a still with its attendant odor could not operate without the connivance of someone.

It was shortly after the still incident that the food began to deteriorate—if that were possible. There were many complaints, but no improvement. By this time I had been on the Island long enough to develop that certain unexplainable premonition that guards and inmates acquire in all institutions.

One day I sensed that something was brewing. The boys were surly or abnormally quiet, standing about with uneasy looks on their faces. When they laughed it was in sudden, high-pitched voices. I knew something was up.

In the dining-room the boys were lined up at the tables waiting for the whistle, which was their customary signal to sit down. When the whistle shrilled, a roar rose from the crowded room. Tables crashed with a bang of tinware, heavy china cups, knives, forks and pitchers of milk. The inmates, in a wild fury, began hurling plates and pitchers at the guards. Monkey wrenches, bats, screwdrivers appeared. From my post on the balcony it seemed that all the boys had gone mad. They were slashing, kicking, clawing at themselves as well as at the few guards, who were fighting for their lives.

The alarm brought reinforcements of guards on the double. They waded into the clawing mass, clubs swinging. Boys screamed. Some went down under the feet of others. Several boys rushed a guard, lifted him up and hurled him against a wall. The guard never got up. I saw one small boy, his face a bloody mask, feel his way along a wall. A guard spun him around and lifted him almost a foot off the ground with his heavy boot. Screaming in pain, the boy crawled to a corner and lay there like a beaten dog.

Tear gas broke up the mobs into groups. These were chased and tracked until they broke up into quartets, then pairs, then singles. Finally by nightfall the riot was over. I recall that the food was better for a day or two, then lapsed back again.

One day a new boy—let's call him Dom—was brought to the storeroom as one of my helpers. The guard pushed him into the room.

"Here's one for you, Danforth," he said. "Turn your back and he'll have a knife in it."

The boy, about nineteen and a splendid physical specimen with the shoulders of a fullback, eyed him insolently.

"All Irish eat ————," he said coolly.

The guard made a lunge for him, but I stepped in the way.

"Let him go," I said, "I'll take care of him."

"Don't cross my path, kid," he muttered, "or I'll break your skull."

"He means it," I told the boy.

"———— him," he said.

"Mind your tongue," I said. "If you can't talk without cursing, don't talk."

He shrugged. I pointed to some bags. "Help store them over there across the room," I told him.

He walked nonchalantly to where some other boys were piling up bags and grabbed one from a smaller boy. With ease he flung it up on a pile. Then he turned around and grinned.

For the rest of the afternoon he helped to pile boxes and bags. He was extremely powerful and didn't seem to mind the work. Before an hour was up he was telling the other boys what to do. There was little doubt he was a born leader. The other boys didn't seem to mind taking orders from him. I knew from their snickers and giggles he was probably telling dirty jokes out of the corner of his mouth. But the work progressed rapidly.

"So long, Captain," he said solemnly as he and the others filed out for lunch.

"The name is Danforth," I said.

"So long, Captain Danforth," he said with the solemnity of an altar boy.

In a way he was refreshing and I had to fight back a grin.

For the next few days Dom was assigned to the storeroom. He was not nineteen as I had suspected, but sixteen. He was about 175 pounds, superbly conditioned with dark coloring and hair. He was an easy kid to deal with, but when he was crossed he was a holy terror. One morning he came to work with a black eye and a bruised cheek. I knew better than to ask what happened. But one of the smaller boys later told me he had slugged it out with three bullies who messed up his bed, the usual initiation.

Dom was no tenderfoot to juvenile institutions. He had been in three elsewhere but, as he later admitted, the Island was much rougher than any of the others.

When I gained a little of Dom's confidence, I found that he came from a large family of six brothers and four sisters. They lived on Third Avenue in East Harlem in a rotting tenement apartment of five rooms. They had to share an outside toilet and one of the brothers usually had to stand guard for their sisters, to prevent any of the tenants from molesting them.

The hallways were always filthy, redolent of alley cats and urine, with one electric bulb—when someone didn't steal it—the only illumination. It wasn't unusual to find a drunken man sprawled on the stairs. There were two bedrooms, one for the parents and the other for the boys. The girls slept on cots in the living room and kitchen. It was fortunate, Dom said, that some of his brothers were able to get jobs working nights. In that way the beds were usually going twenty-four hours a day.

"One thing, in the winter it was warm," Dom used to say philosophically.

When he was seven, he was a veteran of pocketbook-snatching or stealing fruit and groceries. By ten he was in and out of juvenile courts. He was the leader of his own gang, and rock and knife fights were common.

Dom's hero was his oldest brother, who was a hired gun for the "188th Street Gang," a bunch of small-time thugs who hired themselves out as drivers for bootleg truckers or armed protectors. To follow his brothers' footsteps was all that mattered to him; to own a fancy car, carry an automatic revolver and know the satisfaction of seeing other men step off the sidewalk to let him pass by were his chief ambitions.

One day we accidentally started talking about his brother and it opened a flood-gate. I tried as gently as I could to point out to Dom that this way of life could only lead to misery, violence and perhaps the electric chair. But the boy's response was a laugh, edged with contempt. Who was I, a miserable two-bit guard, to talk to him about his brother, who had all the money he wanted, women, fine clothes—and a brand new gun. . . .

One day I found a crumpled piece of paper on the floor after the boys had gone. Curious, I pressed it open. It was a crude but imaginative drawing of the ferryboat coming into the dock. Something told me Dom had done this. When I asked him he actually seemed angry. "Kid stuff," he growled.

On my next trip back to the city I bought him a cheap book giving the fundamentals of drawing. When I gave it to him he glanced at it, then tossed it aside.

"Bet you a dollar you can't draw a picture of the waterfront," I said. He just grunted.

But when he left the room I noticed he had taken the book with him.

Dom's arrogance earned him enemies both among the boys and

the guards, especially the one who had brought him into the store-room. One day this guard, who had been drinking heavily from the hidden still, came on Dom, who was mopping a hallway.

He cursed him and said he had slopped his shoes. The boy insisted he had not. Shouting abuse, the guard clubbed the boy to his knees, then dragged him to the solitary cells and flung him in. The boy stayed there for three days, the blood clotting on his face and head.

When he came out he had changed. A cold hatred had replaced the old smooth, nonchalance. He worked steadily in the storeroom. One side of his face was puffed up and he had a piece of court plaster on his head. He ignored anything I said to him. The look in his eyes was something terrible to see. When I saw the guard I upbraided him, but he just sneered.

"That's the only way to treat 'em," he said. "Now he'll be a good little boy."

Ironically, it was the hatred of this particular guard which almost led to my death. Later I found out that Dom had carefully plotted to trace every move this guard made throughout the day. He didn't have to seek very far for recruits to help him—in each ward was a ready victim of this guard's brutality, eager to join forces with Dom.

One afternoon I was told by the chief of the guards that I was to take the place of this man, who had been sent with some papers to the mainland. I went to the prison yard and began patrolling his section, which included walking about a building that was more isolated than the rest.

I had just passed under a fire escape when the world exploded in a shower of stars and sparks, followed by utter blackness. Two days later I woke up in the hospital with a fractured skull, the sight in one eye gone and more than fifty stitches in my scalp.

"What happened?" I asked the orderly.

"Some kids dropped a gallon can on your head from the fourth floor," he said.

I was now dimly conscious of a far-off throbbing pain. It kept growing in intensity until I thought my head would burst. When I groaned the orderly gave me some pills and I slipped back into a world of soft blackness.

For more than two weeks I lay in the hospital, alternating between agonizing head pains and the newly developed pains in my right eye. The doctor was frankly pessimistic; if the sight didn't clear up, he said, my eye would have to be removed.

It was not only the pain that bothered me, it was the knowledge that I had failed. Evidently I was hated even more than the other guards. They were despised, but no one had ever hated them enough to fracture their skulls.

Then one day a note was smuggled to me. It was in a childish scrawl. I don't recall the exact language, but it said something to the effect that they were sorry they had "conked" me; they had been after the other guard.

There was a perfunctory investigation of the incident and Helbring frankly told me it was my fault because I had been too soft with the inmates. I tried to warn him that the boys might still try to get the other guard, but he laughed.

"It was you they were after, Danforth," he said, "not ————."

I told him about the note.

"They are a bunch of young liars," he said. "You can't believe any of them."

Within the week the inmates had refuted him. One day about dusk, several of the boys caught this guard when they were working outside the walls. He tried to make a run for it but they cornered him, gagged and tied him with his own belt, spread-eagled him to the wheel of a cart. Then they took turns systematically beating him with heavy coal shovels. When his face was a bloody pulp they fled. As I recall there were seven in all; three of the boys pushed off on a crude raft they had previously built and hidden. In midstream it fell apart and tossed them into the whirling currents of Hell Gate. Their bodies were found later. The others were flushed from hiding places along the shore line.

One of the drowned boys was young Dom. Among his personal possessions sent to his family was the cheap book on the fundamentals of drawing. There was evidence he had dipped into it; one of his sketches was of the Manhattan waterfront. I guess he had been determined to win my dollar.

Another incident, the breaking of a boy's arm by a guard who clubbed the child unconscious, leaked out to Albany. Assemblyman Louis A. Cuvillier, in a biting letter to Mayor James J. Walker, disclosed the terrible beating and demanded a wholesale investigation.

The Island was on the alert. The guard who had injured the boy was dismissed and lofty statements were issued. One thing that the continuous threats of investigations accomplished, was a temporary improvement in the quality of the food—until the thunderheads disappeared from the horizon.

That investigation died but it flared up again in April, 1928, when Governor Al Smith, who detested the House of Refuge and all it represented, asked for a state probe of the use of state funds to maintain the institution. Smith was outraged when he was informed that although New York State contributed $292,000 a year to the House of Refuge, the institution could not be brought under the Department of New York State Charities because the place was governed by a board of nineteen, comprising the Society for the Reformation of Juvenile Delinquents. Shades of Dickens!

The superintendent intoned in his public statement the following day that "We are dealing with human souls . . . we are doing it as clearly and economically as possible . . ."

I looked forward to a public hearing. I remember being approached by someone and asked what I would say if I were questioned.

"The truth," I said.

Looking back over a span of twenty-eight years, I can smile a bit at my remarks. I can also stand a bit in awe of my arrogance and confidence. I felt sure that a flock of sharp-nosed investigators would descend on the Island and put the superintendent and his men under a merciless grilling.

As the years slipped by I would lose some of this starry-eyed confidence in politicians. Although the Island stayed on the alert, I didn't see any sharp-nosed young men. But the fires were smoldering in Albany and the rumors were that something was about to break.

Actually it never did. Six years later, in October, 1934, a severe riot broke out among the boys, with the result that a large police unit was dispatched to the Island to set up machine guns, fire scores of tear-gas bombs and keep up a constant firing over the heads of the boys until they could be corralled and pushed back into their cells. One gang even cut the hawsers of a tug and escaped with it, with a fireboat in pursuit. The inmates set fire to the thick, fall-dry shrubbery and thousands on the Manhattan shoreline watched the columns of smoke rise in the autumn sky. At least two boys were badly wounded by the firing and several were fished out of the Hell Gate whirlpool, half-drowned.

About 1930 there were rumors of a new investigation. This seemed to be stronger than the others and from the press accounts it looked as if the state officials were really ready to move in.

Then one day the superintendent summoned me to his office. He seemed unusually cordial.

"I've watched your work, Mr. Danforth," he said. "It's been excellent."

I murmured thanks, wondering what was in the wind. Only a few weeks ago he was berating me for being too easy with my charges.

"You're making a career out of penal work, I understand," he said.

"I hope to make rehabilitation of the young my work," I told him.

"I think I am able to offer you a fine opportunity," he said. "There's a course opening next week on Institutional Management, Sociology and Psychology at Children's Village in Dobbs Ferry. I have been asked to send a representative of New York State to take the course."

"Under whose auspices?" I asked.

"New York School of Social Work," he said.

I knew this to be an excellent course and a fine opportunity.

"You'll represent New York State," he said.

"Why did you pick me, sir?" I asked.

"Because you're the best qualified," he said.

And the biggest nuisance, I told myself.

"Thank you, I'll take it," I said.

He nodded. That ended our interview. I had no illusions about my qualifications. I knew I was being removed from the Island for obvious reasons.

I attended the six-month course at Children's Village, where the superintendent offered me the job of taking charge of the discipline cottage. I accepted, and turned it into an honor cottage.

Dobbs Ferry was delightful, but my injured eye was giving me a great deal of difficulty. Even in the weakest sunlight I was unable to open the lid. The doctors told me it would be like this for quite a while and suggested I find a night job. I subsequently took a position as night supervisor of the New York Parental School in Flushing, Long Island. This was a school strictly for truants and not for the type of young criminals who were sent to Randall's Island. I felt that I would have more experience in rehabilitation with these children, whose wrongdoings were minor.

When I set out for Long Island I had high hopes that I would find at last an institution that really helped misguided youngsters— although some of my idealism and fervor were now slightly worn about the edges and I was developing a jaundiced eye.

2. THE QUEENS INCIDENT: THE NEW YORK PARENTAL SCHOOL SCANDAL

AT THE New York Parental School I tilted for the first time with professional politicians. I was appalled at their callousness and their ability to shout down those who disagreed with them or who attempted to show all was not well in their own backyards.

I came out of this affair slightly bruised and with my illusions showing. But I also discovered that if you hit the politicians hard enough with undeniable facts, they tend to muffle their roars, silence their guns and take to the hills. That is especially true if you have a newspaper as your ally. Any politician, from the smallest ward-heeler to a Washington nabob, dreads seeing scandalous headlines informing the public that his party or administration houses thieves, not Galahads.

I found the Parental School situated on a pleasant, rolling hillside in Flushing, Queens, surrounded by 107 acres of farm and pastureland. The inmates, who ranged in age from eight to sixteen, had been sent to the school for habitual truancy. There was nothing of the grimness of the House of Refuge on Randall's Island; here there were grasslands, trees and flower gardens. It was a joy to walk along the winding paths. As I passed the clean Spanish-type cottages, I thought of the boys back at Randall's Island and wondered if some of them, like young Dom, would not have had a better chance had they been sent here.

The superintendent was Thomas M. Donohue, a man who proved totally incapable of managing a disciplinary institution of this type. Within a week after I had been at the school, I had first-hand evidence that the fine cottages, winding paths and perfectly-cared-for flower gardens hid a world of undernourishment, mismanagement, vice of every description, horror and savagery as terrible as any I ever saw on Randall's Island.

In all my twenty-five years as an investigator dealing with all types of criminals from murderers to racketeers I have never witnessed such scenes as I did in Flushing. They are as vivid in my mind as if they had taken place only yesterday.

Sadistic guards stationed themselves nightly at the exit of the shower room to catch boys coming out, dripping wet. They made the boys hold on to a pipe while they beat their wet bodies. That made it sting more, one told me. I told him that the day I left the school I would make sure to look him up.

Each cottage was in charge of a "house father," and almost every one was a brute. One, who boasted to me that he had been a guard on a prison chain down South, beat a small boy with his fists until the poor child was bleeding from his nose and mouth and whimpering for his mother.

I saw boys, mere babies, beaten black and blue with hoses, sticks, fists and heavy shoes. Boys, white and black, were forced to fight each other with stones and fists—no holds barred—for the enjoyment of brutal house fathers. Mass punishment was approved; a boy would be turned over to five or six other boys and the house father would sit by, encouraging the boys to "muss him up." Older boys were ordered to string up smaller boys and whip them with hoses until their victims screamed with pain. I heard young boys with both eyes swollen shut, their teeth knocked out, noses smashed, and faces bruised, mumble "I fell" when they were asked how they were injured. Later they admitted a house father gave them a "muchachos," a dread form of beating that was a feature of the school.

This was an example of "the muchachos." A small boy had run away. On his return, one of the guards took the runaway and other boys in his cottage down into the cellar. For more than an hour he beat the boy with his fists and a rubber hose until the boy was a bloody pulp, with both eyes closed, teeth knocked out, bruises and contusions all over his body.

The guard, gasping for breath, then told the other boys, "Now you can have him." They were supposed to pounce on their companion, but fortunately the boys, instead of hurting him, washed his cuts and helped him to bed.

When the superintendent heard of the beating he told the guards, "Don't let that happen again," and sent the guard back to his job!

Following the superintendent's warning, the guard returned to give the same boy a beating every night for two weeks! He stopped only after the brother of the boy and three others grabbed him in the hall.

"If you touch my brother again," the older boy warned, "I'll cut your guts out."

He had a broken butcher knife to show he meant business. Only then did the guard turn his fury on another boy who didn't have an older brother.

I also found that the cottage masters appointed "captains" to help maintain discipline. These older boys told me that if they didn't beat the smaller boys, they in turn would be given a "muchachos."

The New York City Board of Education resisted any investigation, and even after the facts had been bared, refused to admit they had existed, while Queens officialdom acted only after it had been prodded by the newspapers. In the case of the New York Parental School, New York City officials, including those at City Hall, were content to let sleeping dogs lie.

In 1931, after months of witnessing the perversion and brutality existing at the school, I found in all conscience I had either to resign my job or bring some official attention to what was going on. It was during the Depression and jobs were scarce. Also it is not in my make-up to run away; it's the Yankee in me. I'm one of those men who must battle for what he feels is right but which inevitably brings heartache and probably financial disaster.

I stayed on and collected an impressive amount of affidavits. These I forwarded to District Superintendent Lucile Nicol on June 12, 1931. They detailed the vice and brutality at the school. In my letter I wrote:

"Homosexuality is running rampant in many parts of the institution. There are cottages which are little more than houses of vice. In these cottages I can offer proof that every shade of degeneracy which it is possible for boys to practice can be found, with little or no interference from those in charge. The smaller boys are beaten and kicked around and forced to commit all sorts of vicious and degrading acts."

A short time after Miss Nicol had received my report, the superintendent took an enforced leave of absence and retired before returning. William D. Pulvermacher was appointed acting director. It was a change in title which eliminated the necessity of his taking a competitive civil service examination. In order to install him the Board of Education changed its by-laws. A year later the board created the position of director, also exempt from examination, and Pulvermacher was appointed permanently under this title.

Mr. Pulvermacher had a good educational background but he didn't have what the Civil Service would have required, three years' experience in a truant school position.

We hoped that as a "new broom" Pulvermacher was coming in to clean up the place, but after a short time realized that this was not true; he only whitewashed the facts. I had the distinct impression he didn't want cited instances of vice or brutality which I and some of the decent guards and employees brought to his attention. I knew he wasn't ready to clean up the place when we found out he was turning the names of the boys who complained to him over to the cottage masters, who, of course, beat them.

The Board of Education continued to keep its head in the sand. When I protested to Pulvermacher one day he shrugged.

"Look, Danforth," he protested, "the job was wished on me."

I realized that it was hopeless to expect the Board of Education to act, so I decided to gather more affidavits and present them to a higher body. I made this decision after one of the guards mercilessly beat an eight-year-old child with a rubber hose, a thick rubber shoe and a stick. The child limped for days. The infraction: he had followed his older brother into a playground.

Pulvermacher heard about my activities and summoned me to his office.

"Danforth, where are those affidavits?" he asked.

"In a special place," I told him.

"Hand them over; they are city property," he said.

"I collected these affidavits after my regular tour of duty," I said. "They belong to me."

For three hours we engaged in a furious battle of charges and counter-charges. Finally he summoned two policemen from a nearby precinct and ordered them to search my room. Fortunately I had engaged a private room in a Flushing boardinghouse and had hidden most of my clothes and the incriminating material there in a trunk.

I was fired the next day.

Four days later Pulvermacher summoned me to his office. "If you promise me you will destroy those affidavits," he said, "you can return to your old job."

I told him what I thought of him in no uncertain terms and he showed me the door.

Despite my cockiness I was troubled. I told myself from now on

I'd turn my back like the rest. If the taxpayers didn't complain of such horrible conditions, why should I? But I knew deep in my heart I could never do that. Mother had pounded what was right and what was wrong into me from my early childhood and it was rock-hard. I was lonely, too, and on those summer nights in 1934 I sat on the porch of my boardinghouse and talked about the case to a fellow boarder. I talked too much. He had a relative on the New York *Daily News* who broke in that paper a sensational story about the investigation. It was premature, but it did throw the spotlight of public attention on the school.

Then Leon Sevirsky, school editor of the New York *World-Telegram,* published a series of stories on the conditions in the school. He interviewed me and I contributed my own material.

This exposé rocked the city. Mayor La Guardia rushed out of City Hall for an "inspection tour." But the Mayor's plan to visit the school leaked out and by dinnertime, when he arrived, the boys were enjoying roast chicken, strawberries and ice cream—it was quite a feat to whip up that menu in such a short time.

The newspaper series prodded Queens District Attorney Charles S. Colden to bring about a grand jury investigation. In July, Colden announced that the boys at the school had repudiated my affidavits and he called me "a damn publicity seeker."

Colden's remarks made me angrier than I had ever been in my life. The *World-Telegram's* school editor had gathered his own affidavits which paralleled what I had found, but this was ignored. *I* was singled out. Within an hour after this statement I sought out the three boys who Colden claimed had repudiated their statements to me. I found all three terrified; they had been warned they could be sent to a reformatory until they were twenty-one. After I asked them to testify before a grand jury and explain to the jurors why they had repudiated their statements, they agreed they would return and tell the truth.

This was done and in August, 1934, a Queens County grand jury handed up a searing denunciation of the school, its managers and its barbarity. A presentment found that the boys had been beaten, the food was poor and the institution had failed to live up to its aim of rehabilitation. County Judge James C. Kadien, Jr., remarked that he was "deeply shocked at the conditions the investigations showed at this institution, supported by the taxpayers at a loss of $200,000 and I am only sorry that you [the grand jurors] have not been able to hand up any indictments."

Mayor La Guardia at City Hall that afternoon blithely informed reporters that he was "heartily in accord with the findings of the grand jury, and I will get in touch with Dr. Campbell (Superintendent of Schools), and start working on many things that need correcting. We will make it a scientific school for salvaging these boys."

Mayor La Guardia forgot to tell the taxpayers that a similar report, called the Bayne Report, which had also detailed the brutality and neglect in the school, but which he had not made public had been sat on. I also learned later that Commissioner of Accounts Blanshard had made a report which had been given to City Hall five months before the grand jury had handed down their presentment. It also had not been made public.

"Well, Mr. Danforth," the elderly gentleman at the boardinghouse said as I was packing my bag, "you certainly stirred up quite a row in Queens."

"So I see by the papers," I said.

He chuckled. "You raised a row and kicked yourself out of a job."

"As we say in New England, sir, you are as right as rain," I told him.

"Where you going?" he asked.

"Home," I said. "I want some fresh air."

3. ON A SLAB IN THE MORGUE: THE LUCIANO INVESTIGATION

I RETURNED to Haverhill, Massachusetts, weary of windy politicians and cynical public officials, and began to look for another job. I found one in the precise, quiet world of a bank not far from Boston. The man who agreed to employ me was a soft-spoken, middle-aged man. The bank was clean and quiet; a dropped match would have sounded like falling slate. It was a gentle world, it was security in a day when the slow tide of the Depression was creeping across the land.

I returned home on a Wednesday, prepared to start at the bank on Monday. It rained all that day and I can recall staring out the rain-streaked window, wondering about Randall's Island and the New York Parental School. What was happening there?

I thought of the quiet bank and its quiet, reserved people.

I said out loud, "I should be glad I have a job."

My mother, who was passing, turned and asked me, "When are you going back to New York, son?"

I took a long time in replying. Finally, I said, "I'll wait until Monday." My mother is a very wise woman.

That night I wrote a letter full of gratitude to the bank official. I didn't say why I had turned down the job. Frankly, I wasn't sure myself. I had no prospects in New York, but I was determined to find a niche in some city department as an investigator. I knew now more strongly than ever that I wanted to work for the law.

On Monday when I arrived in Manhattan I rented a small room on West 72nd Street and started to look for a job. I recalled that during the Parental School probe Commissioner of Accounts Blanshard had a small staff of investigators so I decided to start with his office.

As luck would have it, Blanshard recalled the work I had done in gathering the affidavits at the school and he hired me.

I stayed with Blanshard for a year during which I helped investi-

26

THE D.A.'S MAN AND THE D.A.S.

The D. A.'s man,
Harold R. Danforth.

Danforth, in the guise of "Dan O'Brien," longshoreman from Boston, when he was working on the waterfront rackets investigation.

To Harold R. Danforth
With Warm Personal Regards
Thomas Dewey

To Harold Danforth   Nov. 9, 1951.
With sincere appreciation for able and
devoted service to the District Attorney's
Office and with warmest regards
                    Frank Hogan

POLICE DEPARTMENT
CITY OF NEW YORK

WANTED FOR GRAND LARCENY

COLONEL HALE HEATHERINGTON HALQUIRE
Aliases ALFRED E. LINDSAY, "LINDSEY," "LINDSLEY"

DESCRIPTION: — Age, 76 years (looks younger); height, 5 feet, 8½ inches; weight, 234 pounds; blue eyes; gray hair; ruddy complexion; bulbous nose; wears eye-glasses; neat dresser; American. Usually carries a cane, and may limp. May apply at some hospital for medical treatment for arthritis. Poses as a Washington, D. C. lobbyist, representative of big business, and an Army Officer. Former resident of Philadelphia, Pa., and Washington, D. C. New York Gallery No. B-55126.

This Department holds an indictment warrant, charging Halquire, with Grand Larceny, 1st Degree, obtaining $15,000 in U. S. Currency, during November of 1940, by false representation, regarding United States Government Contracts.

Kindly search your Prison Records, as this man may be serving a sentence for some minor offense. If located, arrest and hold as a fugitive, and advise Detective Division, by wire.

RIGHT HAND

LEFT HAND

+ is to be delivered to him Either upon his request, or in case of anything happening to me. Such as my death, accident or serious sickness — H.H.Halquire

Police Department "Wanted" circular. See Chapter 10, "The Fabulous Colonel: The Halquire Case."

gate minor affairs in various other departments, and complaints which arrived by phone or mail. It wasn't particularly exciting, but I did at least learn to find my way about the city and grasp a working knowledge of municipal government.

The year 1935 was a stirring one in New York. After the grand jury's spotlight turned on District Attorney Dodge came the appointment of young Thomas E. Dewey, a former U. S. Attorney, as Special Prosecutor of the rackets that held New York in its grip.

Dewey's name was on everyone's lips. Most of the assistants in Blanshard's office scoffed at the idea that Dewey could hope to break the powerful grip the underworld had on New York's waterfront and industries.

One day the office buzzed with the news that one of the young attorneys had been summoned by Dewey as a prospective assistant. I met the attorney out in the hall, and after offering my congratulations suddenly asked him, "Do you think Mr. Dewey would hire me as an investigator?"

The lawyer looked quizzical. "It certainly won't do any harm to find out, Dan," he said.

"Will you?" I pressed.

"I'll ask him within the week," he said.

Weeks passed. Finally one day in the fall of 1935, I received a call requesting me to be at Mr. Dewey's office at 4:00 P.M. that same day. That afternoon, with the wind toying with the dead leaves in the park, I walked across City Hall Park to the Woolworth Building on Park Place, where Dewey had his headquarters, telling myself that there wasn't a chance I would be taken on. I had heard that only top-flight people were being hired.

An elevator whisked me to the 14th floor and the moment I stepped off I was impressed by the security arrangements. I was shifted from guard to guard and finally reached the office of Dewey's secretary. I identified myself and in a few minutes she came out.

"Mr. Dewey will see you now," she said.

The door closed behind me. The man who stood behind the desk was slim and mustached. We shook hands and he got down to facts immediately.

"You have asked for a job as an investigator," he said. "What are your qualifications?"

I told him the work I had done in the New York Parental School and he nodded. Then he asked a series of questions which led me to believe that this man knew what he was doing. Once when I was describing a situation he shook his head.

"That's gossip, Mr. Danforth. Tell me the facts—what you saw or heard."

When I had finished he asked about my previous employment. I told him about the House of Refuge on Randall's Island.

"You can get a recommendation from the superintendent, of course," he said.

I took a deep breath. "No."

He looked surprised. "Why?" he asked.

"Because the last time I saw him I told him I hoped our next meeting would be before a grand jury."

He smiled faintly. "We will call you, Mr. Danforth." We shook hands and I left.

A week passed. I felt sure I had been passed over, when a call came in for me. The cool crisp voice identified the speaker as Mr. Dewey's secretary. Would I come in the next day at 10:00 A.M.? I managed to say I would.

The next morning Mr. Dewey was brisk and businesslike. I did not qualify as an investigator, he said, but because of my work in the New York Parental School probe I could have a job as a process server, if I were interested. I was. Dewey nodded, told me to see the chief investigator and we shook hands. A week later I was a member of a team of dedicated men. There was an *esprit de corps* that would do justice to a crack Marine platoon. The hours were long, but no one complained. It was an honor to be included in this organization. Our work was tedious and frustrating. The gangsters had held New York in their grip too long to make slips that could be easily unearthed. Books had to be examined minutely, wire taps installed, suspects followed.

But the one thing that had to be conquered above all was fear. I could sense it the moment I handed a man a subpoena. He would stare at it, his face paling. He knew what would happen if he talked and he also knew what would happen if he lied. The grapevine into the underworld was humming with the news of "Dewey's technique" to get the top racket leaders. He first obtained evidence which would convict the small fry. When they talked it would lead to another link, then another, until the whole sordid mess was laid bare. They also knew that Dewey was using the full weight of the law as a powerful weapon. If you lied you would be convicted of perjury, and that stern-faced man in the black robes, Justice Mc-Cook, hated perjurers and liars.

In the beginning I was relegated to minor duties, but as the investigations quickened I was given more and more important assignments. The serving of subpoenas, as can be imagined, was at times not an easy job. It would be quite an understatement to say that the subjects of our subpoenas were not eager to testify before a grand jury. But on several occasions I managed to seek out certain members of the racket fraternity and serve them, even though they had employed an alias or had moved their operations to another part of the town and disguised it by the façade of a responsible business house. It wasn't anything brilliant; it was just legwork, which, I was beginning to learn, was a large part of police work. Apparently my accomplishments pleased Dewey and one of his chief assistants, Murray Gurfein.

One day I received a call to see Mr. Gurfein. He was a medium-sized man whose youthful appearance made him look like a prodigy instead of a racket-buster. When I used to see him in the corridor I thought of him as a young student who would be more likely to be carrying an armful of textbooks than a briefcase containing secrets of the underworld.

He praised my work in locating one or two difficult witnesses, then arrived at the heart of the matter.

"I understand you want to be an investigator, Dan?" he said.

"Very much so," I said.

He toyed with a pencil. "Well, Dan," he said, "we have an assignment here—purely a volunteer job—but if you succeed your appointment as an investigator will be assured. We feel you may be able to pull it off because of your success in finding those witnesses."

"I would like to try it," I said.

"Have you heard the name Luciano?" he asked.

"Vaguely," I said. "I have no knowledge of who or what he is."

Gurfein then went on to sketch Dewey's keen interest in Charles "Lucky" Luciano, who, at the time, was undisputed king of most of New York's rackets. Today Lucky is a bespectacled, graying man, living out his years in Italy, repeatedly protesting his innocence every time he is linked to dope smuggling. But in 1935 Luciano bossed with gun and club a small army of "enforcers" who milked millions of dollars into their own greasy pockets.

This investigation had been conducted with great secrecy. Dewey's first targets had been Louis "Lepke" Buchalter and Jack "Gurrah" Shapiro, the garment-center racketeers who kept the multi-million-dollar garment industry in line. The witnesses had been so terrified of possible retribution by killers of Murder, Inc., that the investigation had slowed down. Dewey also had been quietly probing the racket kingdom of Dutch Schultz and the activities of Schultz's chief attorney, Dixie Davis, and on several occasions had struck paydirt. But Luciano and his control of New York's vice rings were to be the prime targets.

Gurfein described to me Luciano's henchmen—Little Davie Betillo, Tommy (the Bull) Pennochio, Jimmy Fredericks, Danny Brooks and others—and gave me their pictures to study. My job was to act as an undercover investigator and to connect, if possible, these men with Luciano.

"Where do you suggest I start?" I asked Mr. Gurfein.

"We believe their hangout is in the back room of a bar on Mott Street near Hester," he said. "Our information is sketchy, but we believe Little Davie usually eats there."

"I'll start in a few days," I said.

"How do you think you'll go?" he asked.

"Probably as a longshoreman," I said. "I think I'll spend some time on the docks just to get the feel of it."

"Take care of yourself," he said, and we shook hands.

That afternoon I walked about the waterfront section of Manhattan near the Staten Island ferry terminal. Finally I found the type of old clothes store I wanted. I bought a pair of dungarees, with the knee section a pale white from many washings, two well worn flannel shirts, slightly worn shoes, thick socks, a turtle-neck sweater and a pea-jacket. I also bought one of those curved, deadly baling hooks that longshoremen hang from their belts. Going into a rendezvous for gangsters with brand-new working attire would have instantly pinpointed me. As it was, these people are suspicious of any strange face in their meeting places.

I also moved into a small seaman's hotel on West Street. For a few drinks I gained the friendship of a couple of longshoremen and spent a few evenings with them discussing the waterfront situation. They were great gossips and before the week was over I could put over a fair acting job. I was now Dan O'Brien of the Hoboken waterfront. One of my new friends was from Hoboken and a ferry ride there helped to familiarize me with that section.

The following Monday night, my heart beating a little faster, I wandered into the bar on Mott Street. It was small, dim and smelled of spaghetti sauce, strong cheese and sour wine. I had a few drinks, then a spaghetti dinner. After I had finished I promptly left. I wanted to establish a routine in the bartender's memory. I did this for about a week, gradually staying later and later and getting in the bartender's good graces. I also got to know the "regulars," and a large bar mirror allowed me to get a glimpse of some of them who walked quickly through to the rear room. I found out what the activity was in the rear room—a card game. It was plain our office had the wrong information.

Before I could report my findings to Gurfein I received word to come in. Gurfein looked haggard that morning and waved away my information on the downtown bar.

"We got it right this time, Dan—it's Jamison's Bar on West 57th Street just off Broadway. You'll find Little Davie and the whole gang there, but Lucky's never seen."

"I'll start tonight," I said.

"This time, Dan, for the protection of the office and your personal protection, don't call or contact this office again until your assignment has been completed. Next Tuesday night be on the 6:00 P.M. Staten Island ferry. Someone will give you your pay and tell you the next meeting-place. Then you can tell him where you're staying. Good luck."

I was now completely on my own. I went home, had a hot tub, a good dinner and then wandered over, dressed in my best, to Jamison's. I had no particular role in mind; I just wanted to see the setup.

It was a typical New York West Side bar and grill, one so ordinary you would pass it by without a second glance. The entrance was several steps down. The heavily-curtained window was filled with the usual cardboard cut-outs distributed by the liquor companies. Inside, several men at the bar were drinking and talking in low tones, a bartender was listening to a small radio and at a table in the rear were two men. One was Jimmy Fredericks, the other Danny Brooks. In those days gangsters wore what seemed to be a universal outfit a chesterfield coat with a velvet collar, white shirt and dark tie or dark blue shirt and light tie, highly polished black shoes and a snap-brim hat. They were playing cards, but when I came in I knew they had given me the once-over in a matter of minutes. I had a drink, frowned over some papers as if I were engrossed in some private business, then left.

Back home, I made my plans. This time I had pinpointed the subjects and their rendezvous, but it certainly didn't call for a longshoreman's role. They were vice racketeers; I had to make them believe I was one of their kind.

I recalled that about a year earlier I had come across a young Italian seaman who seemed to know something of what was going on in the city. I had seen Tony once or twice and we had parted on friendly terms. He knew me only as "Dan O'Brien from Boston." I had hinted that certain police departments were eager to talk to me, but I had ignored any specific questions. I now decided that if I were to act as a procurer or a bordello owner I would have to enlist his help.

Tony, a husky young lad of about twenty, had been a merchant seaman since he was fifteen. He had been raised on the West Side and there was little he didn't know of vice and depravity. I hinted to him that I wanted to do "business" in New York City and intimated that if I were successful he would be "taken care of." He nodded knowingly and agreed to meet me the next night.

The first thing I did on the following morning was to rent a room in a small, shabby, West Side hotel. My only contact with the office would be the man I was to meet on the Staten Island ferryboat on Tuesday evenings to whom I would give my verbal report. If I failed to make it, he would take the ride every night for a week until I showed up. If I didn't show up then . . . I supposed the next thing they would do was to check the morgue.

I also mapped out a plan with Tony. I told him that in Jamison's Bar were certain individuals who I hoped would help me, but that they had to seek us out. Tony agreed.

That first night we sat at the far end of the bar, sipping our drinks, conferring in low, conspiratorial voices. We stayed that first night until 11:00 P.M. and for a week we followed the same routine. Whenever someone came close to us I would stop talking. I also insisted that Tony wear the clothes of a merchant seaman, while I was well dressed. I knew this would arouse the curiosity of the racketeers who frequented the place. Anything out of the ordinary will always attract the attention of the underworld.

I knew that the men in the dark suits and snap-brim hats would soon be asking questions of each other: what were that well-dressed guy at the bar and that seaman talking about? Where did they come from? Why such low, confidential tones? Was it something they should have a piece of . . . ?

We kept up our schedule; we met at 8:15 and stayed until 11:00

P.M., interrupting our "conferences" for an occasional game of pinball. Some of our low and confidential discussions were on the day's baseball scores.

The strategy worked. Gradually, when we stopped to play the pinball machine one or two of the men in dark coats would drift over casually, perhaps to offer a suggestion as to how to get a high score. Once or twice they offered to play for money. We just shrugged and went back to the bar. I did this for a whole month before I made my first move.

This night I went into the bar alone. As I took off my coat one of the men—it was Danny Brooks the "booker"—hurried to my side.

"Here's a hook, Mac," he said. I could see him weighing the coat as he hung it on a hook (an old trick to see if it contained a gun). Two others flanked me and offered to buy me a drink. To the inexperienced their slight brushing movements would have meant nothing; I knew I was being frisked.

I refused a drink and went to the machine. Danny and a tough-looking Irishman, who I learned later was a gun-for-hire killer, followed me.

"How are things, Mac?" Danny asked.

I nodded. "Good."

The Irishman pushed next to me. "Where are you from?" he asked in a hard, gritty voice.

"Boston," I said. I pulled back the lever. "One more and I'll have top score."

The gunman put his hand on the plunger. "How come you hit Jamison's?"

"I like the beer here," I said.

"Who sent you here?" he insisted.

"The doorman at the Flamingo," I said. "I was there one night and he said this was a nice place."

His voice was icy. "That's a nice story, but the Flamingo closed two months ago."

I felt as if a cold hand had suddenly clutched my heart. I bent over the glass of the machine as if to add up my score. He had said this loud enough and I could sense the eyes studying me.

Now I knew the Flamingo had been open a month ago, but I suddenly began to doubt my memory; had I made a mistake in some way? I bent over the glass as if concerned with my score. By the time I straightened up I had made up my mind I was going to brazen it out.

"Pretty sure of that, mister?" I said.

"Pretty sure," he said.

"Money talks," I said.

He looked surprised for a moment and I knew I had him.

"Are you sure for fifty?" he asked.

"No," I said. "A hundred."

"We'll give it to the bartender and take a cab up there," he said.

I was already walking toward the bar, opening my wallet and starting to take out some tens and twenties. I had counted fifty when he laughed.

"Put your money away, kid," he said. "I was only fooling."

"I don't like that kind of fooling," I said, and put the money back in my wallet. Then I ignored him and returned to the machine. I felt almost exuberant. I knew he would follow—and he did.

"Play you for a buck," he said.

I nodded and we began to play. I won a few dollars and we went to the bar. I could see he was curious and I played him on the line. He would throw out casual questions and I would answer them in the same offhand manner. Once he asked me what "line" I was in and I just smiled. For the rest of the evening we fenced, played pinball for money and drank. At 11:00 P.M. I slid into my coat and went out.

I walked back to the small hotel to get the smoke of the place out of my lungs. Almost unconsciously I found myself on the street where the Flamingo was located. I could see the garish neon sign blinking on and I wondered what would have happened if we had taken the cab there and it had been dark . . .

The next day I arranged more play-acting with Tony. He was to have one of his friends call me at the bar. I would leave hurriedly and probably, as soon as I was gone Fredericks and the others would try to pump him.

"What do you want me to say, Dan?" Tony asked.

"About the joints I ran in Boston," I said.

"Jeez—so that's what you did," he said. "How many did you have?"

I gave him that mysterious smile routine and it seemed to impress him.

That night we took over our own station at Jamison's. Fredericks was there and gave me a big hello when I arrived. One of the boys took my coat—again carefully weighing it before he put it on a hook. We went through the same routine again—from the bar to the pinball machine.

At about ten o'clock the telephone rang. I could feel my stomach muscles tense. One of the men at the bar answered it.

"Dan O'Brien?" he called.

"That's me," I said, and went to the phone. In a moment I hung up, whispered hurriedly to Tony, grabbed my coat, nodded to Fredericks and went out. There was nothing to do, so I grabbed a cab and went back to my hotel to await Tony's report.

He came over about midnight quite impressed. "These guys are real big, Dan," he said. "I know one of the guys at the bar and he said they control the town." He cleared his voice. "This guy said the dough is brought there Saturday morning."

"What dough?" I asked.

"You know," he said. "The dough they get from the joints."

"Did they ask you about me?" I wanted to know.

"The guy with the pearl gray hat bought me a drink," he said. "We spoke in Italian. He wanted to know all about you. I told him you ran some joints in Boston. He said the next time we came in he was going to talk to you."

I now felt that at long last I was beginning to get my foot in the door.

"Tony," I said, "when I get set up I'm really going to take care of you."

Tony looked pleased.

That night Tony and I concocted our next move, which, to put it mildly, shocked Mr. Dewey no end. I had now been established in the minds of the vice racketeers hanging out in Jamison's as a fugitive and possibly a big-time bordello operator in Boston. I had to clinch that identification in their minds by concrete evidence rather than stage whispers. I was a big-time procurer—I had to have some girls.

I discussed this with Tony and he agreed. Knowing the members of Dewey's investigation staff, I was sure that there were no female detectives who could play the role of a hardened prostitute. The only thing we could do was to go out and recruit some ourselves. Tony knew of a spot called The Bucket of Blood on Eighth Avenue, a notorious hangout for prostitutes, criminals and petty thieves on the fringes of the underworld.

"Can we hire some girls in this place?" I asked Tony.

He just winked. "Leave it to me, Dan," he said. "I know some of them. They're starving down there."

The moment we opened the door a blast of juke box music, mixed with drunken laughter, singing and jeering, hit us. The smoke hung so low it could be cut into solid chunks. Business at the bar was brisk. Seamen and soldiers moved, body to body with young girls, on a postage-stamp dance floor. In booths on every side, men and women, young and old, pawed each other, oblivious to the pointing and snickers of the drunks at the bar. Most of the girls were in their early teens.

Tony seemed well known. He waved to those who had called out and guided me to a booth at the far end of the room. When the waiter came over he said casually, "Send Joan over."

In a few minutes a pretty, hard-faced young girl joined us. She gave me a quick glance and then hugged Tony.

Tony took her hand and led her to the dance floor. They moved in and out of a revolving blue-white light. I could see Tony speaking earnestly in her ear. Once she turned and squinted through the smoke at me. When they returned Tony winked.

"Joan's in, Dan," he said.

I then went into a long spiel, inventing the stuff as I went along. Two of my girls in Boston were now mistresses of big financial men, I told her. They wore diamonds and dripped mink. They had penthouses, cars, etc. I don't know how she swallowed it, but she did.

"You got customers here in town?" she asked.

I brought out a small book in which I had written down more than fifty fictitious names and fashionable East Side addresses. "I don't usually keep this around," I said. "Look at the addresses."

She seemed impressed when she gave the book back.

"I need four more girls," I said. "They have to have your class."

She smiled, obviously flattered. "I know four right here," she said.

"Bring them over, kid," Tony said with a grand air, "and we'll do our selecting."

It was a strange few hours. Joan kept bringing over girl after girl; Tony meanwhile kept whispering his lies into their ears and before the night was over it was known that a big-time whorehouse owner was in, looking over the stock.

It was a dangerous game and only luck let me get away with it. If one of the pimps in the place had informed a syndicate member I might have been found in the river.

But the whole foolish scheme worked; by the time I was queasy from the smoke, stale beer and stench of cheap perfume we had a stable of five pretty girls. (Two were later picked up by the Missing

Persons' Bureau on my information and returned to their midwestern homes as runaways.)

Tony and I made a date to meet three of the prettiest the next night for dinner and a few drinks afterward at Jamison's. I thought it was a grand plan, but it almost backfired.

After dinner the following evening we piled into a cab for Jamison's. I was feeling quite the accomplished investigator; could anyone else have pulled this off so neatly? I paid the driver with a flourish and with Tony coming up in the rear I escorted the three young whores into Jamison's.

The moment I walked in I felt a ripple pass along the bar. I saw Fredericks and waved. He turned his back. I felt I had missed a step somewhere along the line but I couldn't put my finger on it. We swept to the end of the bar, where we stayed for a while. Then when I felt the chill closing in on me we retired to the back room. When the bartender came in to serve us I knew he was nervous.

We had a role to play and there wasn't anything I could do. The prostitutes took it all very gaily, teasing Tony and asking in undertones when we expected to start in business. I told the usual lies and after a while I suggested we leave for a place that was livelier. Tony said "The Bucket of Blood," and I assented. Anything to get out of Jamison's. I wondered if I had been found out.

On the way out I waved to Fredericks, but he ignored me. Even Tony seemed to sense the change.

"What's up, Dan?" he whispered.

"I don't know," I said truthfully. "I wish I knew."

I got out of accompanying the others by pleading a mysterious appointment. Tony didn't care as long as I slipped him some money. I left with a flurry of gay goodbyes from the girls. I never was so happy to get back to the quiet of my room, dismal as it was. I paced the floor most of the night, wondering if I should contact the office or go through with my act. I decided to go on.

The next night Tony and I went back to Jamison's. The same heads swirled as I entered. I hung up my coat and Tony and I took our regular places. We had arranged another phone call and when it came I answered the call, but this time it was Tony who left after a whispered consultation.

A moment later the bartender came over to me.

"You're wanted at the end of the bar."

I saw that Fredericks was sitting there. Apparently he had come out of the back room.

"Hello there," I said, with a great deal of assumed joviality.

"Don't ever do that again, mister," Fredericks said softly.

"Do what?"

"Bring those whores in here," he said.

"I only wanted to buy the girls a drink," I said.

"Buy it somewhere else," he snapped. "If Tommy was here he'd bust you up."

Tommy Pennochio was Luciano's "treasurer." I was glad he hadn't been there. I felt quite deflated as I realized how foolhardy I'd been.

"I'm sorry," I said. "I didn't mean any harm."

He waved his hand. "Forget it . . ."

"Can I ask why it was so wrong?" I asked.

"A cop comes in, nabs the whores and we lose the license or pay off. We're paying too much now."

We went into the nightly routine: coarse jokes, playing the pinball machine, drinking Scotch and soda, talking women, sex, baseball. Fredericks gradually warmed and we were soon back on friendly terms. As the hours passed I felt that he wanted to talk to me alone. Several times he seemed on the verge of saying something but then changed his mind when one of the other hoods joined us.

I finally gave him an opportunity by starting to play the pinball machine by myself. He joined me. As the metal ball rattled around the game he said in a low voice, "The kid said you came from Boston, Dan."

"That's right."

"You run a joint there?"

"Not one," I said, "three."

He asked, "How many girls do you have?"

"A few," I parried.

"One, three, four, five?" he insisted.

"More or less," I replied, continuing to play.

"What kind of setup?" he asked.

"Good enough to last me a few years," I said, "so I guess it's pretty good."

"Where are your places?" he asked.

"Washington Street and two in Back Bay," I told him.

He looked impressed. "Two for the carriage trade," he said. "Not bad. What's your take?"

"Five G's a week," I said.

He whistled through his teeth. "Good setup. What's the ice?"

I said indignantly, "Too much."

He grinned. "Same here," he said. "Going back?"

I gave him a steady look. "No," I said.

"Trouble?" he said.

"Let's say I like New York," I told him.

"Goin' to set up?" he said.

"Pretty soon," I said. "Just as—"

He held up his hand. "Not so fast, Dan," he said. "This isn't Boston."

"What's wrong?" I asked innocently.

"Things are organized differently here," he said. "Do you know Luciano?"

"Never heard of him," I said.

He leaned over, inserted a nickel and began to play. We both watched the ball hit the ring and the bell clanged furiously.

"He's the boss," he said.

"In other words, I've got to get his okay," I said.

"What Lucky says goes," he said. He looked up. "I help him."

"Who's this guy Lucky?" I wanted to know.

"He's just the guy you need to know," he said. "Let's leave it at that. Let's have a drink."

We joined the others and spent the rest of the evening talking and playing that damned pinball machine and lying about our conquests. I'd always wondered what the bar-hound does night after night in the same smelly place; now I knew. No wonder some of them go home and turn on the gas. Such evenings, to anyone with normal intelligence, can be horribly degrading.

Night after night like this went by. On the windy decks of the Staten Island ferryboat, in the bar in Roseland Dance Hall, on Broadway, in subway stations, in Grand Central, I would meet other investigators from our office and gave them reports of my progress. I was close to linking Luciano with these men—soon the game would be up.

The long nights, the terrible tension, the dread of making a false move or saying a wrong thing were beginning to weigh on my mind. I found myself becoming jittery, irritable and unable to sleep. The hotel room seemed shabbier than ever. There were times when I walked as far north as 50th Street from 14th Street along deserted Eighth Avenue, just to relieve my nerves.

I also began visiting Jamison's at odd hours. I abandoned the routine of leaving at 11:00 P.M. I was curious who came in after I was gone. Fredericks was always there and I was always welcomed. He never questioned my late hours; I guess he assumed I was about my business.

One morning just before closing a man came in, looked around quickly, handed the bartender a small leather bag and went out. He put it under the bar and went on counting his bar receipts. About fifteen minutes later another man, a gorilla if I ever saw one, came in. He was followed by two hard-looking men who kept their hands in their pockets. Fredericks casually nodded to all three, the bartender handed up the bag, the man took it without a word, and then all three left. I heard a car pull away immediately and assumed a fourth man had been idling the car outside. It was plain the transaction involved receipts, what and whose I hadn't the slightest idea. Of course, I avoided looking at the transfer and never asked Fredericks any questions. Later, when the raids were made our office confirmed my suspicion that the bag contained receipts the combination was taking in from Manhattan bordellos.

One night Fredericks came in, calm and well-dressed as always.

After the usual routine talk, he came to the point.

"Ready to open up, Dan?"

"One more week and I'll be okay," I said. "But as you say, I have to meet Lucky."

"That will be arranged at the party," he said.

I was surprised. "Party?"

"Lucky's surprise party," he said. "We're going to throw it in a joint on the West Side. You're going to meet a lot of people you need to know . . ."

"Will I meet Lucky?" I asked.

Fredericks stared down at his drink. Hastily I changed the subject. I tried to appear enthusiastic. "I'm ready to open. What about a bail bondsman and a lawyer?"

He looked pained. "Didn't I tell you we take care of everything?"

I made a show of looking over my shoulder. "In Boston I had a little trouble," I said. "Somebody came up to see me and said he wanted a piece."

He leaned over. I'll never forget those black eyes, flat as a snake's. "Dan," he said. *"Nobody* muscles in on Lucky."

He had his hand on my arm and kept patting it. *"Nobody,* kid. . . ."

We shook hands. "Okay, I'm satisfied," I said, trying to look relieved.

The rest of the evening Fredericks and some of the other mobsters described Lucky's surprise party. If their plans had worked out it would have been one of the bawdiest orgies New York had ever seen. It was a strange scene in Jamison's that night; the two racketeers, whose pockets were lined with money taken from pimps and procurers whose heads they had smashed with lead pipes and iron bars, carefully going over a list of racketeers, murderers, thieves, crooked politicians and show girls, weighing each potential guest's importance to see if they should or should not be invited to Lucky Luciano's surprise birthday party.

One of them would mention a name and Fredericks would look scornful.

"That bum," he would snarl. "That —— bum. He's hot. Do you want the G-men raiding the joint! What'll Lucky say if his party's raided!"

It was as if he had uttered a shattering state secret. The others nodded gravely.

"You're right," he said. "The hell with him."

Thus were Lucky's guests selected. . . .

I passed the information along in my reports and at the next meeting with our investigator I was ordered to come to the office late one evening.

I took a roundabout route by cab and subway to make sure I wasn't being followed. I was ushered immediately into the office. I was surprised to find Murray Gurfein, flanked by Inspector John Lyons of the Police Department assigned to our staff, Wayne Merrick, chief investigator, and Sergeant William Grafenecker, of the grand jury squad of detectives assigned to the investigation.

"Sit down, Dan," Gurfein said. He looked so grave I thought I was about to be sacked for some mistake.

When I sat down Gurfein leaned across the desk.

"I have been going over your reports, Dan," he said. "They are very interesting, but it seems that you're getting too close for comfort."

He picked up one report. "Now, where," he said with emphasis, "did you recruit these women?"

I went into a detailed explanation. They listened as Gurfein questioned me. He shook his head when I described The Bucket of Blood, and from the look on John Lyons' face, I knew that it wouldn't be long before a raiding party would be visiting that saloon.

Gurfein questioned me closely about Tony and I convinced him the boy knew nothing of who I was or what I was doing.

When I had finished, he asked Lyons what he thought. Lyons was a blunt man and so were his words that night.

"Mr. Gurfein," he said, "get this young man off this investigation or the next time you'll see him will be in the Bellevue morgue. He has gone as far as he can with this mob."

Gurfein nodded. "I think so, too, Dan. We're too close now. One false move and the entire investigation will go out the window."

"I'd like one more evening," I said, and then went on to explain about the plans for Luciano's surprise party and the bag that had been delivered to the bar. I wanted to know just a little more.

There was a warm discussion, with John Lyons insisting I should terminate my phase of the investigation. I talked fast and I think my sincerity impressed the boss. Finally it was decided I would have one more night and then drop out of sight. I was to wait at my own home for further orders.

I left the office in the early hours of the morning, my exit cleared by investigators who searched the deserted neighborhood for possible watchers. After another roundabout trip I finally arrived at the West Side hotel, putting on a drunk act as I stumbled upstairs.

Needless to say, it was another sleepless night.

The following evening I arrived at Jamison's at the usual time. As I opened the door I had the curious feeling that all eyes were on me, searching my secret thoughts. In all the time I had spent with these hoodlums I had not known a qualm. Now I was afraid.

Fredericks joined me and afterward, Little Davie Betillo, slim, well-dressed, his choirboy's face hiding his killer's heart.

Fredericks called out, "Hey, Davie, come on over." Betillo walked slowly toward me, his eyes on me every moment.

"This is Dan, the guy I was talking to you about. Dan, meet Davie."

The big man put out his hand; his handshake was limp and sweaty.

"Dan is going to open up soon," Fredericks said. He spoke rapidly, as if he was trying to convince the other man. Davie just stared at me, then turned away.

Fredericks turned to me. "Davie's a nice guy," he said softly, "if he likes you."

I told myself I didn't think Davie liked me. I now realized what Lyons had meant. I couldn't get out of the place fast enough. But strange, this night, my last, when I just wanted to walk out, was the hardest to leave. Fredericks wouldn't think of it; he insisted on my having one last drink. I could feel the fear gripping my guts. Suppose —suppose I had been found out . . . was I being set up for something . . . ?

Suddenly off to one side, a drunk at the bar slapped his companion. There was a brief flurry of fists and curses. The bartender was quick as a cat. He swung a small bat used to poke ice down the cooler; the thud on the man's skull sounded like a club hitting a melon. The man crumpled. As if they had rehearsed the act many times two men grabbed the unconscious man to pull him into the back room.

I was frozen on my stool, waiting, but nothing happened. Fredericks just grunted.

I'd had enough. I felt that if someone had plucked one of my nerves the sound would have reverberated in the room like a taut harp cord.

But Fredericks still wanted company. "Give you a game, Dan," he insisted, and I had to go along. We played five games and he won them all. That seemed to satisfy him. I started to say good night but he ordered a nightcap.

I tried to sip the drink, but it almost gagged me. Then suddenly Fredericks began talking about the party for Lucky. He talked freely, more than he ever had. He told me I would meet Luciano and the setup would be okay. He asked casually if I would take a girl he knew and I told him I would. Then he told me the address of the place where the party would be held and gave me some details of the so-called surprise.

I was saying a final good-by when Davie came out of the back room.

"Good night, Davie," I called, but he just nodded.

Good night, Davie, I said to myself, Good night, Jamison's. Good night, Fredericks—I'll see you all in jail, God willing. . . .

I didn't learn until later that while I was getting advice from the mob on how to set up my "joint," Dewey's staff was carefully building up cases against the principal madams, prostitutes and "bookers." Then, on the evening of February 1, 1936, 150 detectives and patrolmen were assembled at precincts throughout the city. They were sent out in teams—with orders not to open their sealed envelopes until 8:55 P.M. Each envelope contained instructions for a raid. Promptly at 9:00 P.M. the teams went into action. Forty houses of prostitution were raided simultaneously.

The girls were brought down to the Woolworth Building and I

doubt if such a scene will ever be seen again—sleek-haired pimps with their harlots; tough gangsters' molls, dyed blondes, redheads, young, old, sick, bored, weeping, bewildered, many of them diseased, herded down the marble halls to be questioned by the D.A.'s assistants.

After leaving Jamison's for the last time I had gone back to my own apartment for my first real good night's sleep in many weeks. When I awoke I was impatient to know what was happening. For the first and last time in my life as an investigator I disobeyed orders; I went downtown.

It was Sunday morning. The corridors were humming with action; I felt like sinking into the floor when I saw Wayne Merrick.

"Are you crazy," he said, "coming down here? My God, what's the matter with you?" He grabbed me by the arm and hustled me into an empty room.

"They made the raids this morning," he snapped, "and the mob is in. Stay here and don't budge until I send for you."

I sat motionless for a long time. I told myself I would never disobey orders again, and I never have. As time wore on I began pacing the floor. Suddenly the door opened and several men entered. They were in handcuffs. One was small, swarthy and curly haired: Little Davie Betillo.

Jimmy Fredericks, who was handcuffed to Betillo, stopped dead. He jerked his handcuffed hands around and said something to Davie. I opened the nearest door and fell into another predicament. The room was stinking with cheap perfume, smoke and the chatter of many women. It seemed there were bevies of women sitting on chairs, desks and standing about.

The conversation died. A woman who was knitting looked up.

"Hello, honey," she said. "Coming along for the ride?"

The other women began laughing and calling out suggestions that had to do with their profession.

I retreated from Lucky's whores as best as I could. Outside, I met Merrick, who just groaned when he saw me.

"Go home, Dan, and stay there! Stay there until I call you!"

I almost ran to the elevator. And this time I did stay home until I was ordered to come back to the office.

While I ate, slept and took long walks, one of Lucky's bigger bookies, Dave Miller, had talked. This was the first crack in the wall of the underworld. It widened and finally, when Mildred Harris, Nancy Presser, Cokey Flo and the rest of the girls and madams became state's witnesses, Lucky's underworld empire crashed about his ears.

Ironically Danny Brooks, my first contact with the Luciano mob, was not sent to prison by Dewey; shortly after I left Jamison's Brooks was arrested in Westchester County and sent to prison for seven and a half years on a charge of compulsory prostitution. The alert authorities there found a small black book in his car and this was turned over to Dewey's office. It provided some good leads.

Other investigators had picked up bellboys, waiters and hotel maids who would testify to having seen the mobsters in Lucky's suite at the Waldorf. These were the most impressive witnesses of all. There were 68 madams, pimps, bookies and other disreputable persons to take the stand for Dewey. This was a crashing blow to the defense of Luciano, who had denied knowing the mobsters.

My part of the investigation was important because I also had linked Lucky to the gangsters I associated with in Jamison's Bar. I did not have to testify. Fortunately the bookies and the prostitutes had turned state's evidence. No District Attorney wants to put his investigator on the stand. After his first public appearance, an investigator is likely to be useless.

When I was finally called downtown the office was quiet. Luciano, arrested in Hot Springs, Arkansas, had been indicted and the witnesses all wrapped up. I met Murray Gurfein that day and he said in his quiet way, "That was a good job, Dan. There is no more need for you to serve any more subpoenas. From now on you are an investigator for this office. Report to Wayne for your next assignment."

After a sensational trial, Luciano and his gang were found guilty. Lucky received a sentence of 30 to 50 years in Sing Sing; Tommy (the Bull) Pennochio, 25 years; Little Davie Betillo, 20 to 40 years; Jimmy Frederico, or Fredericks, 25 years; Little Abie Wahrman, 15 to 30 years and Ralph Liguori seven and a half years.

4. TRIALS AND TRIBULATIONS OF AN INVESTIGATOR

AFTER THE Luciano case was finished, I underwent intensive training in investigative work. My first chief was Wayne Merrick, a former FBI man and a fine fellow. He was succeeded by John F. O'Connell, also a former FBI man who had been Merrick's assistant. If I can be considered a good investigator today and a fair criminologist, it is a credit to O'Connell's training. O'Connell, who was later, for 12 years, chairman of the New York State Liquor Authority and is now in business, was a fearless and tireless public servant.

After the Luciano case, O'Connell seemed to take an interest in me and immediately put me on a job-training course. He was a stickler for detail and accuracy and despised stupidity and lack of aggressiveness. There were some assignments in which I failed miserably and I can still hear John's biting, cold voice asking me where I had left my brains.

For three years, at first when we were in the Special Prosecutor's office and later when we were in the D.A.'s office, he gave me every kind of investigation under the law; I was in every type of situation and gained an experience few men who are in criminology can boast. During this period I learned the technique of tailing a suspect, wire tapping, the installation and camouflaging of the dictaphone; the interrogation of witnesses and suspects; rules of evidence in the establishment of a prima facie case; undercover work in which one assumes another character than his own for the purpose of obtaining vital information, and so on.

My classroom was New York City; my teachers former FBI men and veteran detectives. This was no textbook course; I learned by doing. When I was learning how to shadow a suspect, I was out on an actual case with an experienced man and I hung onto his coattails until, as the saying goes, we "put the suspect to bed."

The investigator's assignment begins the moment he is summoned into the office by his chief, handed a dossier and told to study it. For example, I might be given the case of John Doe, wanted as a suspect in a racket investigation. The dossier, if he is a criminal, contains his picture, former reports about him from other investigations, his rogues' gallery picture, perhaps snapshots taken from him or his room when he was arrested, his "yellow sheet"—police record of arrests and convictions—a probation or parole report. Many times there is a single report summing up the man's entire criminal record.

I would then make copious notes, list the names of former hangouts, criminal associates, names of women companions and would have the subject's pictures copied.

Checking out all of Doe's former addresses and looking up his associates would be my next step; tough hoodlums are D.A.-wise and they don't scare easily. But I have found they dread jail. Let's say John Doe had a friend named Lefty, who is currently on parole. His yellow sheets show he owes the state ten years. Lefty no doubt will tell me what I want to know; he knows how cooperative the parole board is with law enforcement agencies. That business of honor among thieves is just a worn cliché; Lefty, like most of the hoods, would sell his sister to stay out of jail. To be behind bars means one thing in his caste-strict underworld society: You're in because you're stupid and you don't have any influence.

Once we have located John Doe we stay with him from sunup until his lights go out, usually twelve-hour shifts shared with another investigator. A D.A.'s man is no clock-watcher. If the subject has a telephone a Supreme Court order is obtained and "a wire man," usually a detective expert in installing dictaphones and wire taps, is ordered to the house. The wire is installed and two men "sit on the wire," sometimes for months—in a coal bin, a darkened and damp cellar, or in a woodshed. But the main part of my assignment is to tail my subject. It is a difficult, dangerous task, yet many times a fruitful one.

I have found from sad experience that it is easiest to lose one's subject in the crowded streets of New York. In such busy sections you must stay within six feet of the man you are following and keep your eyes on him at all times. The hour-by-hour events of busy Manhattan can easily catch the eye or the ear of the investigator and in a flash his suspect is gone.

As an example, I had been tailing a man all day. He was a suspect in a rackets case in which Dewey was exceedingly interested. I kept at his heels, in and out of subways, office buildings, restaurants and bars. It was shortly before 5:00 P.M., the time when he was expected to make contact with a racketeering group; for me this would have meant striking paydirt after a tiresome day. At 44th Street and Broadway my suspect was about six feet ahead of me and I was carefully doing everything O'Connell and the boys had told me to do. A few more blocks and I would have successfully fulfilled my assignment. Suddenly there was a crash, the sound of steel twisting and glass splintering. I jerked around and saw that a taxicab had hit another car. I glanced at it only briefly, then swung back to my suspect.

He was gone, seemingly swallowed by the sidewalks. I pushed frantically through the crowds, dashing into stores, running around corners, looking into cabs and cars, but there was no sign of him. I went into the nearest phone booth and slowly dialed the office.

"Mr. O'Connell," I reported, "I lost the tail."

"It's a wonder you didn't lose your head," snapped his reply. "Report back to the office. You are relieved of the assignment."

Back at the office O'Connell gave me a tongue-lashing. "We are not interested in accidents, Danforth," he said. "You had an important job to do and you failed to do it."

I thought I would be sacked but he gave me another assignment, and this time I followed the suspect as close as his own shadow.

When a street is deserted it is best to take a position on the opposite side of the street about half a block away. There are times when one must adopt the casual air of a window shopper. The suspect may use the same technique but you can be sure he's using the glass as a mirror. Getting behind a parked car is the best cover.

It is very difficult to tail a suspect who is suspicious of being followed. Criminals have a thousand and one tricks up their sleeves as I have learned from experience. One of their favorite tricks on the subway is to jump out the door just as it is closing. In my early investigation days one man did this and I plunged after him. The door caught my arm, half-dragging me along the platform. Fortunately, I was able to yank it free before being swept off the platform and perhaps under the train.

I had no trouble catching up with the suspect. He was watching. Later, when he was finally arrested I asked him why he had waited around.

"I wanted to see you break your ——— head," he said.

There are some types of criminals, such as Costello, who make surveillance very difficult. As far as I know all attempts to tail him have failed. Investigators discovered *they* were being tailed by Costello's henchmen. During his peak as gangland's number-one man, he was as closely guarded as a king on a parade route. Thugs would be in doorways, in parked cars, in cruising cars and on street corners. Their job was to see that the boss wasn't tailed and if he was being followed they were to follow the follower. Word would also be passed along in relays to go ahead of Costello and warn him to be careful whom he saw and visited.

In some of the larger hotels Costello's big tips gained him a small army of informants among barbers, bellboys and doormen. We tried several times to get close to him at the Waldorf-Astoria barber shop, but failed. If we wanted to take the chair next to him we would find it occupied by one of his hoods. If we followed him into a bar the grapevine would be humming within seconds, from bartender to waiter, that a stranger had followed him.

When an investigator finds himself entering an almost deserted street he swings to the opposite side of the street. If the person he has under surveillance turns the corner he can cross to the opposite corner and observe whether the suspect enters a building, continues down the street or enters a car.

One of my first solo attempts at shadowing a suspect was slightly ridiculous. I was in our office in the Woolworth Building and some minor witness was leaving. O'Connell told me to hop to it and see if he met anyone.

I recall it was a dreary, rainy November day. The suspect had his umbrella thrust against the rain and seemed oblivious of anything but getting to the subway station. I hurried after him along the same side of the street.

When he turned the corner I hurried up, gave him a few seconds, then swung around.

The suspect was standing against the building. For a moment we eyed each other. Then with a marvelous aplomb, he said, holding the umbrella to cover both of us, "Shall I walk with you back to Dewey's office?"

I never made that mistake again.

One of the most difficult phases of surveillance is shadowing a suspect by car. I have learned by experience that the best way is to be always on the right of the suspect's car so he cannot see you in the mirror, and have one or two cars between yours and the suspect's, with the exception of heavy traffic when you may be tricked by the lights.

When a suspect turns a corner and you believe he has become suspicious, you either put on your dim lights or your fog lights to give your car another appearance. When a suspect stops you never park immediately behind him but ahead of him or around the block so you can slip out and come around on foot.

One case I recall demonstrates the difficulty of tailing an experienced criminal. It involved my trailing a fur thief suspect from his home in Flatbush to Times Square. I had no trouble "making him" and followed him onto a subway train. He seemed absorbed in the newspaper he was reading. When we reached Times Square he got off and walked slowly up the steps, apparently still deeply engrossed. I was about twenty-five feet behind him. As soon as he reached the street he turned left. By the time I reached the top of the subway stairs he had disappeared. I was completely dumfounded. I did not understand how he could have made the entrance to the first building, about thirty feet away. The only store was a cigar store near the corner, which I immediately entered. On the pretext of making a phone call, I gave the interior a quick examination. But my suspect was nowhere to be found.

I did the same thing the next day, cutting down the distance between us. Again he disappeared, although it took me only a few seconds to bound up the subway steps. Again it seemed he had been swallowed up by the earth. I examined the street and it was obvious that for him to enter any other building except the cigar store would have been impossible. I stayed around the neighborhood all morning, but he did not reappear.

The following morning I decided to work it from the other end. This time I took up surveillance directly outside the cigar store at the subway exit. The little man appeared on schedule, still with a newspaper. He walked slowly as he came out of the entrance, then suddenly darted into the cigar store. I was on his heels. He slipped behind the counter, sat on a little stool and continued to read his newspaper. He remained there most of the day. When he came out I trailed him successfully to a fur drop in a loft building on West 39th Street. We later raided the place, recovering thousands of dollars' worth of stolen furs. My elusive subject and his entire mob were arrested and are now serving long sentences in Sing Sing.

Wire-tapping technique was another facet of the investigating business I had to learn. At the time of his Special Rackets probe, Dewey was one of the first big city prosecutors to use wire tapping extensively. The evidence and leads which were obtained helped to break many of the sensational cases.

I did not do the actual wire tapping. That was done by detectives O'Sullivan and Adams, assigned to Dewey's office. Both were fine detectives and electronics experts. My assignment was to sit on the "plant" after it was finished and take down notes which were then transcribed into a report to O'Connell.

Many times the wire tapper must assume the role of a gas-meter reader, water inspector or telephone repair man so he can get into the premises and find "the pairs," the proper wires to tap. Those sitting in on the tap are not necessarily in the building; in the majority of cases they are blocks away. If the "plant" is at a distance, the officers listening in usually hire a furnished room or work from a cellar.

The subject of wire tapping is a controversial one. Many states, like New Jersey, have laws against wire tapping, but in New York County a telephone may be tapped if an order is signed by a Supreme Court or Court of General Sessions justice giving permission to the District Attorney or Police Department to conduct a wire tap. This permission is granted only after the judge has been shown proof that the person whose wire is to be tapped has been associating with known criminals or is engaged in criminal acts.

There have been many unlawful wire tappers, some of whom have been sent to jail. On the other hand, the solution of many an important case involving vicious criminals had as its genesis the report of some legal wire tapper. I don't mean that wire-tap conversations are necessarily valuable evidence, but the leads they produce are of tremendous value to the office of a prosecutor.

Dictaphones were also extremely helpful when properly placed in rooms or hangouts of criminal suspects. The hearing of one's voice uttering an incriminating remark produces a tremendous psychological effect.

It is quite a job to install one. First of all there is always the danger of the suspect unexpectedly appearing, and this necessitates a team of investigators. It is necessary to have a complete and accurate schedule of the suspect's activities to know how to select safely the hour or two hours needed to install the machine properly.

The first thing the investigator does is carefully examine the room to determine the spot which the subject would be least likely to find obvious. Also the habits of the suspect must be known beforehand to guide the installation. For example, if the subject is a heavy reader it is clear that the last place in the room to put the dictaphone is in the bookcase. Dictaphone wires are also another problem, because they must be covered up by running them across the ceiling and painting them, or running them along telephone wires or under a carpet.

One case involving the installation of a dictaphone is worth reporting. The District Attorney's office had received reliable information that a phony doctor living in a midtown hotel had a widespread and lucrative abortion practice.

I was put on the case with Irving Barst, an intelligent young investigator who died in World War II. Barst had an excellent sense of humor and such a scholarly, bookish look that no one ever took him for a criminal investigator.

We were ordered to find out what was going on in the doctor's office from morning to night. This, of course, would involve the installation of a dictaphone in the physician's lavish offices.

Barst and I hired the room next to the doctor's. We took off our coats and sat on the bed wondering how we were going to install the machine. We traded ideas, but each one was more dangerous than the last. Finally we were joined by O'Connell, who was also stumped. I believe it was Irving's idea which saved the day. John okayed it and went back to the office. Before he left he warned us, "This man has no idea he is under investigation. Now, for God's sake, be careful!"

After he left we brought the manager of the building into our confidence. The idea was to pose as maintenance men who were installing ventilators because of a broken pipe. I recall fishing back in my mind for all the terms for all kinds of pipe and fittings; we had to make this look good.

The manager fitted us out with work clothes and tools and also he called the doctor to tell him we were on the way up. In addition he sketched the layout of the room, which fortunately had a hanging ceiling. Our plan was to open the ceiling, toss the dictaphone wire into the direction of our room, then break through our ceiling and hook up the machine.

The doctor was a man of about sixty-five and well built. From the moment we were in his office he kept his eyes on us.

"There's a broken pipe two floors above," I said. "We have to install a ventilator to dry out the plaster."

He looked up at the ceiling. "I don't see any signs of dampness," he said doubtfully.

Irving picked up his bag. "Okay, doc," he said. "If you want your furniture ruined it's all right with us."

That did it. The room was expensively decorated and plainly dear to the doctor's heart.

"Very well," he said, "but don't make any dirt."

I climbed to the ceiling and made a great show of measuring and tapping. Once when he climbed up the ladder to hand me a tool Irving whispered, "I'll go out and get the damn vent. I hope you know how to put it in."

Irving left—later he told me he walked all over Third Avenue and Second Avenue looking for a ventilator and found one in a second-hand shop. He finally returned with the vent.

The doctor kept standing at the bottom of the ladder until I said, "Do you have a pot, Doc?"

"A pot? What for?" he demanded.

"When we open the ceiling the water will spill on you," I said.

That cured his curiosity. He went back to his patients.

We managed to cut a crude square into the ceiling, toss our wire across to our room and then somehow hooked up the vent. I recall we hammered the damn thing in with nails instead of screws and Irving said we would be expelled from the Carpenters' Local that night.

We returned to our room and hooked up the dictaphone. This was in the late afternoon. I don't think we had the wire open for more than a few hours when Irving beckoned to me. I slipped on my head set.

Someone had entered the doctor's private office.

The dialogue went like this:

Doctor: "You have come for the job, Miss?"

Girl: "Yes, Doctor."

Doctor: "I am a very particular man. I must know that you are in perfect health. Please disrobe."

Girl: "My clothes?"

Doctor: (impatiently) "Yes, yes, girl. Hurry, I have patients."

Sounds of girl removing dress. Rattle as if doctor was opening door of his cabinet and taking out a stethoscope.

Doctor: "Throw your head back. Breathe deep."

Girl: (indignantly) "Doctor!"

Doctor: "It's only part of the examination."

Silence.

Doctor: "Remove *all* your clothes. This is a *complete* examination."

Girl: "I don't think so."

Doctor: "You want the job?"

The girl suddenly yelled.

Girl: "Don't touch me."

Doctor: "Come here, honey."

Girl: "Don't come near me. Don't touch me."

The girl began running around the office. A table overturned. She kept yelling, and over the dictaphone we could hear the stumbling gait of the doctor. He kept telling the girl how he would take care of her, and how important physical examinations were.

Irving looked at me. "What are we going to do, Dan? This guy will rape the kid."

"And if we go in," I said, "O'Connell will have our scalps for messing up this investigation."

Meanwhile the chase continued. Once he caught the girl, but she hit him with something and he let go. Apparently he was an old hand at this sort of thing.

Finally, after the girl let out a yell I picked up the tool case.

"I'll go in and say I have to fix the vent," I said.

I ran for the door but Irving yelled at me. "He's run out of gas, Dan."

I slipped on my head set and could hear the old lecher gasping for breath.

"All right, girl," he managed to say, "get dressed."

Then after a bit I thought we'd both howl when he added seriously, "I just wanted to find out if you're a good girl."

The girl never came back for her job but we had the pleasure of arresting the doctor some weeks later when our investigation proved he was a vicious and corrupt physician who had made a fortune out of the misery of women.

Next on the investigator's list is the art of interrogation. The business of using the person most cherished by the suspect to lead him to confess is, I believe, vividly demonstrated by the case of a sixteen-year-old boy from Brooklyn who was the leader of a teen-age band of fur thieves and already a hardened criminal. He had been picked up by the police on suspicion and from the corroborating evidence we knew he was leader of the gang. It was just a question of his admitting it. The case involved an older man, who, like Dickens' Fagin, taught the young to steal for him. We all took turns with the boy. Investigators and Assistant District Attorneys questioned him throughout the day, but all we got from him were curses and threats. Once we had to handcuff him to the chair when he tried to assault one of the members of our staff. It soon developed that the boy hated his father and disliked his mother. At one point we had evidence that the man had had supper at the boy's house. In his mother's presence the boy was asked if this was true. He denied it.

"Why, you know it's true, son," the mother said. "I cooked supper that night."

The boy looked up at his mother and said, "You're a rotten liar."

Because I was usually given juveniles to question I had spent most of the day with the boy, pleading, cajoling, doing anything that the law allowed to get a boy to confess to a crime. We desperately wanted evidence on the older man. I was chagrined to find that I, like the others, was rebuffed in no uncertain terms. Outside in the corridor I said to the mother, "Surely there is someone the boy loves, isn't there?"

"There is only one," his mother said, "and that's his grandmother."

I arranged for the aged grandmother to be brought in a car to the District Attorney's office. I opened the door of the conference room where the boy was and said, "I have a surprise for you. There's someone to see you."

I ushered the old lady into the room. The boy stared at her for a moment in silence. Tears were running down the old woman's cheeks. All that could be heard in the room for those few tense minutes were those muffled sobs.

Suddenly, like a dam bursting, the boy broke down and wept bitterly, throwing himself in his grandmother's arms. Within ten minutes he was dictating a detailed confession which led to the conviction of the man, who was sentenced to a long term in jail. The boy also received a suspended sentence in consideration of his services as a state's witness and was sent to a place of rehabilitation.

Courtesy is an important facet of interrogation. The investigator should never be abrupt even when the complainant seems to have no logical basis for his complaint. With an investigator, patience must be a virtue.

Interviews are often conducted under great stress. I have found from experience that injury, excitement, prejudice, fear and anger must be taken into account when questioning complainants or witnesses. Even superstition may cause them to distort, perhaps unconsciously, the report of what they have seen or heard. Frightened people remember little except the object of their fear and this is usually exaggerated. Enraged persons are usually suspicious of the investigator.

I learned also that seemingly meek and naïve witnesses—I found a few in the racket probes who were dumb as foxes—sometimes attempt to learn from the investigator the gist of the stories told by other witnesses. It is the inexperienced man who answers an inquisitive witness with information obtained from others.

Experience has taught me the value of copious notes. On the other hand, I discovered that a pencil and a notebook can be danger signals. One day I had a witness talking freely about the taxicab racket. Names, dates and payoffs fell from his lips. I eagerly took out a pencil and notebook.

He gulped. When I sat with pencil poised he said, with a blank face, "I just forgot everything, even my name."

It took days for me to groom him back to our side before he would talk. Later he told me, "The minute you took out that book I felt my heart turn over."

To many witnesses a pencil or pen and notebook means permanency, an indication that their remarks are being preserved, perhaps to be used against them. The best procedure, as I found from another sad experience, is first to establish a friendly relationship with the potential witness. It's the old cliché; honey attracts.

The first interview should be informal. Questions are casual, without any intensity. Never produce a pencil or notebook, but memorize the really important answers; then at the first opportunity record pertinent material. A trick I always used was to visit at intervals the men's room, where I would jot down notes while they were still fresh in my mind.

Questions asked in the second, or formal, interview are based on the information obtained in the first interview. O'Connell always told me to make it a habit, when dictating my notes, to include on the top of the statement the place, date and time of the interview, the file number and title of case, name of the person interviewed, his or her telephone number and address. I still do it to this day.

O'Connell always stressed interrogation as one of the investigator's main weapons and the thousands of persons, criminal and innocent, from whom I have taken statements, confirm his opinion. The investigator must learn the psychological weaknesses and strengths of those questioned and take advantage of his own particular ability in questioning the suspect or reluctant witness.

Experience has taught me never to use such words as "guilt," "guilty," "crime," "crook," "robbery," "rape," "murder" or "burglary"—words with sinister connotations. Such words arouse the suspect's instinct of self-protection. It is simpler and more effective to frame questions along the line of: "Just what *did* you do? . . . All I want is the truth . . . All I want to know is this, just what did you do . . . ?"

Timing is important in interrogation. A suspect should be questioned promptly, but if he is not taken into custody until a considerable time has lapsed, a great deal of thought must be given to the questions to be asked. In such a situation, the criminal's complete dossier is carefully studied for details of his background, associates, previous criminal acts, dispositions, personal weaknesses—alcohol, drugs, women. Secondly, before he is placed in custody, a technique must be devised to induce him to reveal his movements—wire tap or surveillance. This sort of preparation is time-consuming, but a successful questioning of a witness or suspect can wrap up a case in short order.

Perhaps this is best illustrated by the episode of the young thug arrested in one of the racket investigations. Before I brought him in I had sat on a wire for days and had shadowed him around the clock. When we sat across from each other in the conference room of the D. A.'s office I knew his most intimate thoughts.

In the beginning he was sleek and arrogant. Before the hour was up he was sweating. We asked questions that stunned him. Finally he threw up his hands. "What the hell? You know more about me than I do. What do you want to know . . . ?"

We told him. When we turned him over to the detectives to be booked at Oak Street we had a detailed signed statement.

5. THE TERRIBLE THIRTIES: THE DUTCH SCHULTZ–JIMMY HINES INVESTIGATIONS

PART I: PORTRAIT OF AN AMERICAN GANGSTER

I WORKED on the Dutch Schultz and Jimmy Hines investigations for more than two years and I consider the work I did on both cases to have been the most important in my career as a D. A.'s man. Violent death stopped us from putting Schultz behind bars, but we did arrest and convict Hines, one of New York's most powerful politicians. I am proud to say that witnesses I uncovered helped put him in jail.

In a way I have always regarded both cases as symbols of their times, the halfway mark of the "terrible thirties." It was the beginning of a national waking up, a shrugging off of the lethargy that had sunk in from the days of bread-lines and apple-peddlers. A sense of public morality was tightening and we were beginning to be aroused about the power wielded by gangsters, racketeers and criminal syndicates who, with the aid of crooked politicians, controlled our larger cities.

It was a time when the new term, "racket-buster," caught the fancy of newspapermen and script-writers. Instead of the "Little Caesar"–type gangster, the young crusader of law and order became the hero of Hollywood's stories. It was a time, as they say in the small English pubs, that "has been and gone." I doubt whether the country will ever see such days again.

One of the two central figures in this drama was Arthur (Dutch Schultz) Flegenheimer. One of the paradoxes of his short but lurid career, is that he should perch as a doubtful footnote to the history of his violent era as the typical American gangster overlord. As I sit here reviewing my yellowing reports and notes I close my eyes and see again the figure of the Dutchman in his ill-fitting gray suit, looking for all the world like an unsuccessful salesman. To me he always appeared slightly haggard, as if pressed with the details of his intricate violence-ridden empire. In his late years he was exceedingly moody and jumpy. If it was true, as he once told George Weinberg, his henchman and his betrayer, that he intended to get out of the rackets, no doubt what preyed on his mind was the terrible truth that he had passed the point of no return. Behind him the path was blocked with the burned and garroted bodies of dead men and ahead were the menacing figures of those who were waiting to kill him. We knew those shadows were moving in on him in his last days.

Schultz was far from the Hollywood-born illusion of the American gangster. He always looked like a small businessman ready to announce his bankruptcy. He was proud of this appearance. In Syracuse, when he was on trial for tax evasion, he was told that a man of his position should wear tailor-made clothes.

"Such display is vulgar," he replied blandly. Then, forgetting his careful front, he added in a growl, "Personally, I think only queers wear silk shirts." When a reporter pressed the silk shirt question, Schultz expanded: "Now, you take silk shirts," he said. "I never bought one in my life. A guy's a sucker to spend fifteen or twenty dollars on a shirt. Hell, you can get a good one for two bucks!"

Schultz looked shabby as compared to his associates, Abe (Bo) Weinberg; Bo's brother, George, who was to become one of our chief witnesses; and Dixie Davis, the now forgotten mouthpiece of the underworld, who is living out his years in peaceful obscurity on the West Coast with his showgirl wife, Hope Dare. When I was guarding Dixie's family during the subsequent trials, I was astounded at his array of tailor-made suits, shirts and shoes. Every suit he wore had to be hand-pressed.

The Dutchman's wealth is legendary. Several of the investigators still working in the District Attorney's office can tell you of the mysterious iron chest which Schultz had made for him in the early thirties. George Weinberg said, not once but many times, that he had seen Schultz put only thousand-dollar bills into it and that once he had had to kneel on the lid to close it. In the chest was a king's ransom in diamonds, the proceeds of a Broadway jewelry-store robbery. Schultz, acting as a fence, bought the loot from two safecrackers. Weinberg said he had heard, but could never prove, that Schultz had both men shot down by a gunman, who then returned his money to him. I doubt that Weinberg made this up. Weaving fancy tales was not part of his nature; he was a realist.

Weinberg and Davis agreed that Schultz loved money more than anything else in life. Dixie said: "You can insult Arthur's girl, even steal her from him, spit in his face, push him around and he'd laugh it off. But don't steal even a dollar that belongs to him. You're dead if you do."

Weinberg and Harry (The Horse) Schoenhaus both described Flegenheimer as a penny-pincher. They once told me how the Dutchman, in order to win over a West Side politician, promised him a hundred turkeys to distribute among the poor in his district at Christmas. Dixie was ready to pay for them, but the Dutchman said scornfully, "What the hell are you doing, Junior? Send a couple of boys down to the market and make 'em cough up."

When Dutch Schultz's guns ambled into the poultry market the owner was only too eager to supply the fowl and forget the bill.

Schultz had a commonplace background. He was born in the Bronx on August 6, 1902, the son of Herman Flegenheimer, a saloon-keeper and livery-stable owner. His mother was Mrs. Emma Neu Flegenheimer, a hard-working housewife who tried to teach her son how to live the good life. In 1906 a daughter, Helen, was born. She and her brother would be almost total strangers in their adult years.

Schultz in his boyhood days was already a delinquent. He was always harassing his teachers and finally left school in the sixth grade. In later years Dutch became quite sensitive about his lack of education. He once insisted that Dixie Davis arrange for him to meet "guys like book writers and singers," and he would never disclose to reporters which elementary school he had attended in the Bronx.

"I don't want you guys to bother the teachers," he would say indignantly. "They're nice people."

Herman Flegenheimer deserted his family when Dutch was fourteen years old. His mother took in washing to support her son and daughter. In later years Schultz would never accuse his father of desertion. Once to a reporter covering his tax trial in Syracuse he said simply, "He just died."

Schultz sold newspapers for almost a year while he was becoming acquainted with the old Bergen Gang, a band of young toughs who terrorized the neighborhood along Third Avenue and 149th Street. He subsequently became an apprentice to a roofer, a clerk in a grocery store and a printer's devil. ("I once worked in your racket," he was apt to tell reporters.) Schultz was not eager for hard work; he slipped in and out of jobs. However, he did maintain his card in the roofers' union primarily to show arresting detectives that he was "gainfully employed," as the statute reads.

At Christmas time in 1917, he was arrested for the burglary of an apartment in the Upper Bronx. Under the alias of Charles Herman he was sent to Blackwell's Island for an indeterminate sentence. He was a difficult prisoner to handle, so the authorities had him transferred to Westhampton Farms. There he slugged a guard and escaped. When he was found he had been free fifteen hours. Two additional months were added to his original sentence; in all, he served fifteen months.

Back in the folds of the Bergen Gang, he gained the nickname "Dutch Schultz." He wasn't Dutch; his parents were German Jews. Dutch Schultz was the name of a young fighter known for his raw courage in the ring. There was a ring of solid toughness in the name and Flegenheimer wore it with a swagger.

Retired detectives tell stories of seeing the husky young thief on Friday nights walking down Third Avenue with a kosher chicken under his arm. His mother was of orthodox religion, but her gangster son lived without God, and he listed himself variously as Jew, Protestant and Catholic on the police arrest records.

Curiously, during his tax trial in Syracuse, he accepted a string of rosary beads in the morning and a Jewish mezuzah in the evening.

"I'll need all the luck I can get," he explained to his attorneys.

One of the major mysteries to all of us who investigated Schultz's background was how Schultz, a coward and essentially a weakling, was able to amass such tremendous power. The only explanation may be in Schultz's excellent sense of organization; he selected the best men. He was as ruthless as a big business baron. The weak were gobbled up, money was spent to amass more money. In the end the killers and the thugs knew the empire they had built could not operate without him, so they accepted him as their leader.

Schultz made his first important moves in the underworld after he was released from Westhampton Farms. He managed to get a job as helper for Otto Glass, a moving-van owner, who had turned to beer-running during Prohibition. Schultz ran beer to speakeasies in New York for three years, then bade goodbye to Otto to go in business with Joe Noe, who owned a speakeasy on Brook Avenue in the Bronx.

One source of supply of beer for the speaks came from a massive old-time brewery in Union City, New Jersey, operated by Frankie Dunn, later to die under a hail of machine-gun bullets. Dutch rented two ancient trucks, hired three big bruisers and contracted with

Frankie to pick up his barrels of beer on the New York side of the Weehawken ferry entrance.

The Brook Avenue speakeasy flourished and Dutch opened another on Third Avenue. The ferry-truck supply was not enough to wet the throats of his dry customers, so Schultz tied in with Frenchy Dillon and Jay Culhane, who operated breweries in Paterson, New Jersey, and Yonkers. Beer flowed and money came in. From the retail side Dutch went into the wholesale end of beer-running; he bought out Dillon and Culhane's Yonkers plant.

Within a year he was paying off politicians and had formed the nucleus of his gangland court; Abe (Bo) Weinberg, who specialized in murder; my former storeroom helper, Vincent Coll, and his brother, Peter; and gaunt Larry Carney.

In my researching of Schultz's life, Carney particularly intrigued me. There are a multitude of legends about his relationship with Schultz, but from what George Weinberg said, at least one legend may have been born of fact. In the late twenties, while Schultz was running his speakeasies, Carney was critically ill of tuberculosis. Schultz loaned him money enough to stay at an upstate sanitarium, where the disease was arrested. From then on, Carney was a devoted follower whose gun was always ready to defend him.

Schultz began to demonstrate his superior organizational abilities. He expanded his mob and his business. By 1931 police estimated he had seventeen beer drops where he stored large supplies of the stuff, which was sold on the spot to other speakeasy owners. One warehouse, near the Mott Haven Railroad yards in the Bronx, had an elevator on which empty trucks were placed and lowered into the basement. When the elevator reappeared, the trucks were loaded with beer kegs. Dutch Schultz's hoods carefully guarded every drop. They were armed to the teeth, ready to cut down any rival who might be tempted to take over control of his rapidly-expanding beer empire.

I have gone through the testimony of the Malone and the Syracuse tax evasion trials of Schultz, which form the framework for the true story of the growth of the American gangster overlords. Government witnesses, including the old-time beer-runners who were in on the racket in the early days of Prohibition, gave a vivid picture of how the illegal sale of beer mounted month after month while the mound of dollars grew higher and higher.

Wealth came with stunning suddenness to Schultz. Government accountants, never given to fancy, put down Schultz's beer fortune as about $7,000,000. His caravans of trucks were everywhere; no longer was he forced to buy from other breweries; besides his Yonkers plant, he had his own on Manhattan's West Side.

But his expanding empire began edging across the borders of such rival lords as Waxey Gordon and Legs Diamond. Schultz, as a good businessman, abhorred gunfire because he knew it would hurt business, but it was inevitable that violence would seek him out. Joe Noe, who gave Schultz his start, died in a midtown shooting fracas.

The legend-makers have the Dutchman witnessing the shooting and killing one of the gunmen, but police later ascertained that Schultz was far from the scene, busy making money on his beer business. When Legs Diamond, the amazing clay pigeon of the underworld, was slaughtered in October, 1931, the underworld grapevine hummed with the rumor that Schultz was in on the killing in retaliation for Noe's death, which he attributed to Diamond's gunmen. He was questioned, but released.

The year turned on violence. In the gaudy Club Abbey, whose four walls could tell the history of that era, Schultz met Charles (Chink) Sherman, in a battle royal over some unknown reason. He was shot in the shoulder, the only time he was ever wounded. Sherman was stabbed and clubbed with a chair. He gave himself up but was released. Though Sherman came out of the hospital vowing revenge he ended up on a county dump heap.

In 1931 the menacing shadow of Vincent Coll, the "Mad Dog," moved across the underworld. Coll, who feared neither death nor dying, had broken with Schultz. He turned in his hired gun and sent word to him that he was taking over the Bronx territory. Schultz was hit in his most beloved possession, his purse, but he dared not cross guns with this young killer.

Coll was arrested on a Sullivan Law charge and "The Mick," as the underworld called him, brazenly sent his brother Peter to Schultz demanding $10,000 for court expenses. The story George Weinberg told us is indicative of the fear this young man could instill in the hearts of other men. That night he said, Schultz, his forehead damp with fear, counted out the money Coll had demanded and gave it to Peter, who calmly put it in his pocket and walked out of the office of the brewery.

Fear paralyzed Schultz, George said; Bo Weinberg had to be constantly at his side. In Schultz's mind "The Mick" with his gun was always around the next corner, or peering from the window of a passing black sedan.

Coll's reign was brief. With Charles (Fats McCarthy) Papke, a gun-crazy thug, his own brother Peter, and a few other hoods, "The Mick" put fear into the hearts of the underworld such as it had never known before. Coll demonstrated his fearlessness the afternoon he led his men into one of Schultz's warehouses on College Avenue in the Bronx, destroying with crowbars all of Schultz's slot machines, to the tune of $100,000.

He raided beer-truck caravans, shot down drivers and stole their loads. He slipped into warehouses to kill Schultz's gunmen where they stood. The invaluable Larry Carney wilted under a blast of bullets while Schultz shivered in his hideout. The authorities thundered that Coll must be captured, but "The Mick" even walked into the homes of Schultz's lieutenants and killed them in their beds. New York was shocked when Coll and his gang, trying for a Schultz gunman, machine-gunned a small child. Newspapers demanded that action be taken, but it was the lawless who beat the law; they killed their own. A phone call lured Coll from his hideout in the Cornish Arms Hotel on West 23rd Street. While he was in the phone booth arranging another gangland kidnapping, a man calmly walked in and machine-gunned the booth. The young Irish killer was dead at twenty-three.

There have been many statements as to who that machine-gunner was. He is walking around New York today. The gangster overlords had decided that Coll—for the good of all of them—had to die. For a large sum, this man arranged the call with a gangland Judas and killed Coll.

After Coll's funeral, Schultz emerged from his hideout to pick up the pieces of his business. Moreover, he decided to move into the lucrative policy (numbers) racket, the criminal empire J. Edgar Hoover has called a sore on the nation's life. A pudgy Negro, Casper Holstein, was the current boss, but Schultz nudged him out. José Miro, another Negro, who liked silk shirts and fancy clothes, was another policy boss. Schultz forced him out also. Big Joe Ison also felt that retreat was the better part of valor and left his banks behind him. Now Schultz, backed by his gunmen, was the boss of a racket which brought in millions.

Now Schultz swaggered about town and was often seen in the company of politicians. Although it was known he was paying a king's fortune for protection, he never talked directly about who was being paid, George Weinberg told me, not even to his most trusted henchmen.

Labor unions and crooked prize fights were the next to catch his eye. His gunmen proceeded to take over control of several unions; when honest men protested they were shot down on the street in daylight. Schultz's dapper Jules Martin moved into legitimate tax-icab companies. Millions poured into Schultz's strong-boxes and vaults. He had the power of the chairman of a large American business empire, and wealth far beyond the dreams of such a chairman, yet he continued to buy his cheap suits, shirts and shoes. He never distributed large gifts or lavish tips. The acquisition of money was as necessary to Schultz as his intake of food.

He became more brutal as his power increased. He was intensely jealous of his leadership and although George Weinberg would not talk about it, the underworld insists that Schultz killed George's brother, Bo, in a West Side hotel room, had the room freshly papered, the body stuffed into a barrel of cement and dropped off East 23rd Street into the East River. Until the body is found the true story can never be known.

George Weinberg, however, did tell me the true story of the murder of Jules Martin in Cohoes, New York. It took place in a room in an old-fashioned hotel. Dixie Davis was with Schultz, who was increasingly moody as it became apparent that the government was moving in on him with a tax evasion suit. Martin, he suspected, had stolen $21,000; Schultz demanded an accounting.

Martin arrived at the hotel about 8:00 P.M. Schultz, snarling and vicious, cursed Martin for hours while the gangster protested he was loyal and honest. Davis, who hated violence, tried to act as a peacemaker, coaxing and cajoling Schultz into listening to Martin's explanations. Finally, at 5:00 A.M. Schultz grunted, "Let's go."

Davis stepped into the living-room of the suite. He was about a foot in advance of the others when a gun crashed. He spun around to see Schultz with a .45-caliber revolver in his hand and Jules Martin's body sprawled at his feet, a pool of blood from Martin's shattered head spreading across the floor.

"Get Bo and the boys," Dutch snarled.

Davis ran downstairs to return with Bo Weinberg and three of the young hoodlums who gloried in hanging around Schultz.

"Get the stiff out of here," said Schultz.

Two of them wrapped some towels around the dead man's head

and dragged him down the back stairs. The corpse was stuffed into a trunk to be dumped later.

Upstairs, Schultz pointed to one of the young hoods. "Hold his arms," he said.

When the others obeyed him Schultz told Bo Weinberg, "Break his nose."

"What do I want to hurt the kid for?" Bo asked.

Literally foaming at the mouth, Schultz shouted his orders again. Bo shrugged, then turned to smash the face of the man who was held. Under his huge fists the young gangster's face was soon a bloody pulp.

"Put him in the chair," Schultz ordered. Then he held the boy's head over the pool of blood from Martin's head which was seeping down through the old floor. Bo was speechless, Dixie Davis, weak with fear, while the others just stood there watching the blood from the battered face of their companion leak over the floor. Finally Schultz ordered the half-conscious youth put on a couch. The hotel doctor was summoned and Dutch casually told him it had been a fight over a card game. They wiped up the blood, paid the doctor and left with a perfect alibi.

Dixie Davis told me: "I had never seen a murder before this one. I couldn't sleep for a week."

I believed him. He was a cowardly little man, vain as a peacock with the morals of a package thief. But he never lied to us.

After the Martin murder there were hints of dissension in the ranks of Schultz's hoods. Cracks appeared in the wall of his empire when the government indicted him for income tax evasion. The gangster leader had a great deal of political influence in New York and Connecticut but he couldn't fix his government. He was indicted finally but then disappeared.

Responsible for the formal charge in the indictment voted by the federal grand jury was a solemn, bespectacled Assistant United States Attorney, Jacob Rosenbloom ("Jack" to all of us). Rosenbloom, with whom I was to be associated under Dewey, worked as many as eighteen hours a day with a battery of bookkeepers and accountants, assembling the figures which resulted in the indictment. Although he knew more about the case than any one, he never got to try Schultz.

The Dutchman surrendered in Albany. After eighteen months as a fugitive, he and his attorneys had mapped out their plans. The trial was scheduled to take place in Syracuse in the northern federal district. An outsider was chosen as federal prosecutor. Rosenbloom was stunned, but like a good soldier obeyed his superior's orders and gave what help he could.

George Weinberg told us that Schultz had contacted one of the best known public relations counsels in the country and paid him $10,000 to "create a good press and feeling among the local citizens."

Advance agents were sent into town with large bank rolls. They followed the trail of the government representatives, who were working on the usual stringent federal budget. Their tips—as friends of "Mr. Flegenheimer"—were several times larger than those left by the federal people. When they went into a bar everyone got a drink on the house; sometimes bottles of whiskey were given away. There was a wave of children's parties; everyone in town—men, women and children—was touched with Schultz's money. These press agents also spoke long and earnestly about Schultz's trouble with the government, "the same trouble that you and I have." The government was made out as the enemy and Schultz a poor, misguided taxpayer. The strategy was simple; from these people would come the jury which would try Schultz.

After a long and interesting trial, the jury disagreed. Schultz was worried. *The New York Times* quoted him as charging the government with persecuting him. "I offered them (Washington) a million bucks as a settlement when there was almost a revolution, but did they take it? No, they wanted blood," the Dutchman said bitterly.

The second trial was held in Malone. Somehow it was impressed on Schultz that the money he had spent in creating good will in Syracuse had not been spent in vain. Before the second trial opened, he redoubled his spending in Malone. The farm people had never seen a similar situation. This man of blood and violence appeared in the small border town seemingly humble and contrite. He was always on the streets, smiling and bowing to the ladies and patting heads of small children. One day a lavish distribution of flowers and candy for the sick children was made throughout the Malone hospital—compliments of Mr. Flegenheimer. He hired the largest dance hall in the town and invited everyone in town to dance and drink beer as long and as much as he wanted—free. He dropped large tips. He never appeared in a bar without turning around, waving his hand and calling out with assumed geniality, ' Everybody's drinking on me tonight, gents! Come and get it!"

The simple people of Malone were soon won over. It is natural they would be. To them Schultz had been born in the headlines. These people, so far from the big city, had assumed that, like a Western desperado, he wore guns, was continually surrounded by bodyguards and would probably shoot down anyone who talked to him. When they saw this man in baggy pants and crushed hat with a smiling face and open pocketbook they found it hard to believe that he was a man of blood and murder.

In the end a jury of these same farm people said that they had found Arthur Flegenheimer not guilty. They and their decision earned one of the bitterest excoriations a federal judge has ever delivered. Schultz celebrated that night, then disappeared. Malone slipped back into its bucolic calm.

It was at this point in his life, George Weinberg told me, that Schultz was determined to quit, but found it impossible. He was now a prisoner of his own creation. For a time he hid out in Connecticut, to enjoy the riding he loved so well. (Here I discovered one of the most important links in the Hines case, one which I am proud to say I developed.)

After a rest in the country, Schultz announced he was returning to New York City. Mayor La Guardia let it be known to Police Commissioner Valentine in no uncertain terms that he wanted "this bum" arrested on sight.

What few people knew at the time was that Schultz had been married to a former cigarette girl and a son had been born to him during the tax trial in Malone. His boy was a source of pride to him and Schultz bragged to his henchmen that he would slip in past the city cops. But then it became known that the government wanted to arrest him and was still amassing evidence for a new tax case against him, so he stayed, fuming, outside the New York limits. But horses and the countryside began to pall. A plan was concocted to have him arrested in Perth Amboy, New Jersey. We always understood from Dixie Davis that the Dutchman nursed a scheme to fix his tax case by means of political influence while he was free on low bail. Schultz hated prison.

Schultz's plan worked flawlessly—for a time. He surrendered in Perth Amboy to be released in $10,000 bail by a police recorder as a fugitive from justice. He then appeared before U. S. Commissioner Morris Spritzer, expecting to be arraigned. Instead he was confronted by Assistant U. S. Attorney J. Howard Carter, who presented a bench warrant signed by Federal Judge William Clark, calling for the arrest of the Dutchman as a tax evader. Turned over to federal officers, Schultz appeared before Clark, who set the very high bail of $75,000, after remarking that he believed an "odd situation" existed in Schultz's surrender to a police recorder.

Carter then told the court that federal authorities had never stopped investigating Schultz since the Malone verdict. Our people at the arraignment reported that Dutch's head jerked up when Carter added, "We know a lot more about this man than we did twelve months ago. There may be some new developments soon."

Schultz read the portents in the sky. Dewey.

In New Jersey Schultz made his headquarters in the rear of the Palace Chop House in Newark. On a fall night in 1935 he was sitting with Lulu Rosencranz, Abe Landau and Otto ("Aba Daba") Berman, going over his policy receipts, when Schultz got up to go to the men's room. As he closed the door a lone gunman entered. Schultz emerged in a rain of bullets. It has been said that Charlie (The Bug) Workman, now in a New Jersey prison, was the gunman, hired by Murder, Inc., who had received orders from Lepke to kill off Schultz, who was making too much trouble.

It was not Workman who killed Schultz. Essex County Prosecutor Wachenfeld's report shows beyond a doubt that Schultz had been killed by a bullet from the revolver belonging to Rosencranz. He had been cut down by the very gun he had hired.

It was a sort of poetic justice.

PART II: DAYS OF THE RACKETS

LONG BEFORE the night the gunman shot Schultz in the Palace Chop House we had been busy with wire taps, trailing suspects, evaluating information whispered by underworld informants and checking thousands of court records in an effort to build up a case against Dutch Schultz and to destroy his racket empire.

As the investigation continued the shadowy figure of a political protector took form: the blurred outline of James J. Hines, one of the leaders of Tammany Hall. We all knew we now had two goals to achieve: the conviction of Schultz, then Hines.

After the government failed to convict Schultz for tax evasion at Malone, Dewey contacted Jack Rosenbloom to offer him an appointment in the Special Rackets probe. Rosenbloom, who has the tenacity of a bloodhound, refused to admit defeat after Schultz's acquittal. During the trial, covered daily by our own staff, Schultz made one mistake; he admitted he had not filed state tax returns.

It was now Dewey's goal to get the Dutchman on three separate counts for three different years he had failed to file. Rosenbloom had a tailor-made case and was eager to come to grips with Schultz. He accepted Dewey's bid and joined our staff. Rosenbloom went on to prepare his state tax evasion case against Schultz while another part of our staff set out to link Hines and his political power with the Schultz underworld.

One of my first jobs in this extensive scheme was to join three other investigators in examining thousands of records in the New York City Magistrates' Courts. We spent months in searching records in West Side, Washington Heights, Yorkville and other courts throughout the city. I recall that when I had finished my phase of this assignment I had uncovered more than fifty cases in which Schultz's henchmen had been acquitted of violating the Sullivan Law, selling numbers or paying off in the policy games, simple assault and such various crimes. When all of the reports had been put together we found that we had established a pattern which showed that only certain judges heard these particular cases. In fact, the cases would be postponed until these judges could hear the cases.

This appeared peculiar but it was far from evidence. Surveillance, raid after raid on policy drops and banks, and convictions of those who ran the places as well as invaluable wire taps brought out the evidence. Dixie Davis was the mouthpiece for this policy setup, run by Schultz and his hired guns; Hines was its political protector.

For a long time we had a wire tap on Dutch's favorite hideout. On a Christmas Eve the two detectives who transcribed the conversations reported back to Dewey that he might as well remove the tap.

"Why?" he asked.

One detective read from his notes: "Davis called at 10:00 P.M. 'Merry Christmas, Arthur,' he said. A voice we identified as Flegenheimer's replied, 'Merry Christmas, Junior. And a Merry Christmas to those ———— from Dewey's office who are listening in.' "

Dewey was confident finally that he had enough evidence to place before a grand jury which could indict Schultz. There was a strong feeling in our office that Schultz might be ready to make a deal and talk. This was not fancy. Schultz was aware that Rosenblum had enough on him to hang him and this, combined with the desire to get out with the money he had, might have persuaded him to talk.

On October 21, 1935, Rosenbloom and the State Tax Commissioner discussed the case against Schultz until 10:00 P.M. in Dewey's office in the Woolworth Building. The following morning he began to present his case to our blue ribbon jury.

Then the gunman walked into the Palace Chop House.

Schultz's murder only intensified Dewey's determination to link Hines to the gangster's policy empire. For almost three years we had been collecting an enormous amount of evidence, linking piece by piece until the whole sordid picture was completed.

One fragment was found in the tally sheets our investigators located in Schultz's apartment in the Robert Treat Hotel after his death. The sheets showed a policy profit of $826,916 over a five-week period. There were also many items such as "flowers" (presumably for dead rivals), "ice" (graft) and "fixing" (for police payoffs), along with the names of hundreds of small-time and big-time gamblers across the country. Among them was the name "Mr. Erick."

The lists, with the names and totals, were turned over to a special bureau of the New York Tax Commission, headed by Spencer E. Bates, Deputy Tax Commissioner. He was aided by Nathan M. Mitchell, of the New York State Tax Department, who brought along the "figure hunters."

Dixie Davis dropped out of sight, but the bureau questioned his accountant, who insisted the gangland lawyer never kept books. Investigators were then put on the trail of Davis' employees and came up with an account at the Manufacturers Trust Company, 11 Essex Street, in the name of Max Fruchtman. The deposits were in cash, some as large as $20,000.

The laborious job of tracing all entries began. One entry of $2,500 caught the eye of the bureau, who gave it their attention. It led into a southern distillery. The distillery's subpoenaed books also showed a $100,000 "loan account" of a "Mr. Erick," who was identified by the distillery's officials as a real estate operator on Manhattan's West Side.

The name clicked immediately; "Mr. Erick" had also been found on Dutch Schultz's tally sheets. Vague as it was, this was a lead. Chief Accountant Al Goodrich threw all his accountants on the audit of the distillery's outgoing checks until several repaid loans to Mr. Erick were found. Retracing every item, the man was finally found.

Operations were now transferred to New York's National City Bank, where the Erick checks had been deposited. Every day for months accountants examined bank deposit checks and check clearances. Finally an "Erick" check appeared payable to Milton Bernard, Dixie Davis' accountant. It was endorsed by Bernard and reindorsed by a New York lawyer.

The lawyer refused to bring his books into the office, so the investigators turned to searching for his bank accounts. One appeared. After an examination the attorney was given a bill by the State of New York for $25,000 estimated due on his income tax. He promptly came down to our office with 500 cancelled checks, insisting that most of the checks were Bernard's, who shared the account.

One check was payable to cash and endorsed by "J. R. Davis," "J. Hines" and "Eddie Holly."

One more link had been forged between Dixie Davis, Schultz's mouthpiece, and Jimmy Hines. There were to be many more before the chain of evidence would be completed.

But Dutch Schultz and Jimmy Hines were not the only targets Dewey had in his sights. The Dutchman's powerful rival, Louis Buchalter, alias Lepke, was also high on our list as the boss of the industrial rackets. Dewey was also concerned with the $2,000,000 restaurant racket, which had been organized by Schultz and financed by his policy racket. All these investigations were going on at the same time. These racket empires were complex organizations with leads from one investigation tying in with another. A Dutch Schultz gangster would suddenly emerge as an organizer in the restaurant racket, while a Lepke man would be discovered in a trucking racket, with links to a union already under investigation.

From 1936 to 1938 the underworld grapevine hummed with the news that Dewey was getting nearer to Lepke. Then one day we found Lepke was among the missing; now he knew that Dewey was trying to get evidence to send him to the chair.

Every detective and investigator was working around the clock. I can recall sitting on a tap on a racketeer's telephone for seventeen straight hours, crouched in a coal bin with sandwiches as my only meals. I ached for days afterward. We were tailing every known member of Lepke's mob from New York to Canada, from Canada to Cuba and the West Indies. I think we would have followed them to hell itself; such was the spirit of Dewey's staff in those days.

Tom Devine's experiences in following the mob and recording their conversations supplied many leads for us to work on back in New York. One spring day in 1938 we received information that some members of the gang were leaving for Havana on a White Star liner. Dewey ordered Tom and Barney Dolan, our expert on wire tapping and dictaphone installation, to get on the boat under any circumstances and install a wire in the gangsters' cabin.

Somehow they got aboard the liner as the gangplank was being hauled aboard. They explained their mission to the captain, who promised his cooperation. After studying plans of the ship Tom and Barney selected their post—for the rest of the voyage they sat in a closed ladies' room below the gangsters' cabin, listening to the tapped conversations. Before they reached Cuba, Tom arranged by radiogram with Police Chief Eddie Melchen of Miami to contact his friends in the Cuban secret police. So when the boat landed Tom and Barney were met by five crack secret agents. Together they trailed the gangsters all over the island. They also canvassed every hotel, bar-room and brothel trying to get a lead to his hideout. For two weeks they fine-combed the island, but no sign of Lepke. The wire-tap conversations proved of little value; evidently the gangsters were on a genuine "Cook's Tour" of the Caribbean.

The day Tom returned he checked into the office and was told a chartered plane was waiting for him at Floyd Bennett Airport; his next assignment was to lead a delegation of detectives and Chief Investigator Wayne Merrick to Montreal, where other segments of the Lepke mob had been located in a hotel. The incidents that followed are now legendary in the D.A.'s office.

They arrived separately at the hotel, then met later with the manager, who promised to cooperate in any way possible. The main task was to install a dictaphone in the gangsters' suite. There were five altogether, among them Harry Harris, a loft thief; Sommerman, a deadly killer; and Benny Levine, one of Lepke's underworld friends. Strict surveillance showed that while three of them were spending money freely in a tour of the night spots, two men were always left behind in the suite, probably waiting for telephone calls. There was no way to get the dictaphone set up, no time when all the mobsters were out.

After a week of waiting Tom became quite anxious. Finally he summoned his men and the manager and announced a plan; he would drive them out by a false alarm of fire, but to make it sound real, a fire had to be staged. The manager was stunned, but Tom and the local Montreal detectives assured him no damage would be incurred.

Tom and Wayne, playing the role of watchmen with time clocks strung about their necks, began checking the corridors about 10:00 P.M., while the other detectives, dressed as bellboys and elevator operators, took up their stations. A fire was started in a huge jardiniere filled with paper napkins and scraps. Tom and the local cops kept smothering the flames until the corridor was filled with smoke. Then Tom and Merrick pounded on the door of the suite. "Fire—everybody out . . ."

People emerged from other rooms on the floor, but the gangsters' suite remained closed.

Tom and Merrick pounded again on the door. "Fire . . . all out . . . fire."

The suite remained silent. The manager kept saying, "Look, I want to cooperate with you fellows, but this is still the finest hotel . . ."

Finally Tom persuaded him to open the door with a pass key. Devine peered inside.

"They're drunk," he said. "They couldn't be awakened with a siren."

While the mobsters snored in drunken sleep, Tom and Merrick entered the room on tiptoe, hung the mike in the heavy drapes, then carefully lifted the window an inch and pushed out the wire. They tiptoed back across the room and gently closed the door.

They hurried to the roof, and in their stocking feet ran across the small roof. Tom scrambled down the fire escape to get the wire. Just as he was jimmying the screen aside to get the wire, the window drapes parted slowly and Sommerman's face appeared. He was staring directly at Tom.

Tom froze. For a long moment Sommerman's dull black eyes stared at him. When nothing happened Tom guessed correctly that because of the heavy rain, the darkness and the well-lighted room, the gangster could not see him crouching on the fire escape. Then the drapes closed and Tom again was in the darkness. Crouching like a coiled spring in the wind, he found that he had gripped the screen with such force that his fingers ached for hours afterward.

Slowly, cautiously, he picked up the wire, replaced the screen and tiptoed to the fire escape.

Merrick, shivering in the cold, whispered, "What happened . . . I couldn't see you . . ."

"The mob's awake," Tom whispered. "Let's get the wire working . . ."

Soaked to the skin, they tiptoed across the roof to their room.

Minutes later they had the wire tap working and were listening to Sommerman complaining about the weather. The investigators had done their job but they did not get the result they hoped for. Lepke was not in Montreal.

From Montreal, Tom was sent to Florida, when leads from the Montreal stake-out showed that Sommerman and the others were headed there simply to spend the winter. In Miami he contacted his old friend Chief Melchen and together they toured the town. The second night they spotted Sommerman and tailed him to a hotel where the mob had taken a suite.

The manager of the hotel readily agreed to cooperate with the provision that no scandal be linked with the hotel. Devine agreed. That night he was given the room adjacent to the mobsters' suite. For seven long months Tom sat there with a dictaphone headset, listening to the gangsters boast of past murders, robberies of all descriptions and details of New York and national rackets. The room seemed to be the magnet for visiting mobsters, who stayed for the night, drinking and smoking opium—"kicking the gong around" as the old-time mobs called it.

When the gang were out sunning themselves on the beach, Devine, using a special, hair-fine drill, bored a peephole in the thick oak door separating his room from the gangsters' suite, then installed a tiny, but powerful mike under the door jamb.

Almost every night the gang would gather to smoke opium. Through the tiny hole Tom watched their ritual preparations. Harris, the safe and loft thief, would spread a white tablecloth on the bed, then someone else would unlock a trunk to get a small tin of opium, while another would get a bottle of Coca-Cola. The fumes were inhaled from a tube in the bottle and passed from gangster to gangster, while they sat tailor-like in a circle; it was "like an Indian peace-parley," Tom said.

As the dope took hold they became talkative. Tom, lying on the floor of his room, took down as many as forty pages of notes per night. Once the gang neglected to cover the windows and tape the door; the fumes gathered in the room, giving the smokers extra pleasure. Tom, on the floor, became aware that the fumes were gradually seeping into his room.

Once he heard Harris ask Sommerman, "What about the joker next door?"

"To hell with him," was the grunted reply.

As the hours passed, Tom became drowsy from the fumes, then

finally passed out. He awoke in the early hours of the morning, his
headset still on, his head splitting.

There were days during that long winter when the gang held meetings in the room which lasted for hours. One night Tom stayed on
the wire for seventeen straight hours without eating or sleeping.
But the taps bore fruit. Whenever Tom's airmail special delivery envelopes came in we held a conference to go through them for leads.
When we spotted one, I, Tom Fay, Tony Scanlon, or anyone available would check it out.

Once Tom was startled to hear Harry Harris discussing the robbery of a famous movie actress which was making headlines.

The robbers were coming to Miami to dispose of the loot through
Harris.

"The bums want $500 for the mink," he told Sommerman.
"They're putting the shake on us . . ."

Sommerman's cold, harsh voice replied, "When we get the stuff
I'll give it to them . . ."

They calmly discussed the murder of the thieves while Tom scribbled furiously. When they were finished he picked up the phone
and whispered to Chief Melchen to meet him on the beach. Melchen
agreed with Tom that they were in a spot; they had to arrest the
thieves but they could not tip their hand. Melchen finally came up
with an idea. He had a good friend, a Pinkerton detective, who
could make the arrest. The thieves arrived and were arrested as
they waited for Harris. That night Tom overheard Harris berating
another mobster whom he blamed for having been a stool pigeon
for the police.

Once, in order to get a picture of the interior of the room and
the opium set-up, Tom did a risky thing: two of the gang had set up
the pipes and drugs, and then stepped across the hall to summon another gangster. They had just closed the door when Tom opened
his and took a quick flash picture. He had just closed his own door
when the gangsters returned. He had his hand on the key but
couldn't lock the door because the click would have given him
away.

Once Sommerman wrote a letter and slipped it down the mail
chute. With Melchen's help Tom retrieved the letter and quickly
X-rayed its contents. It was to a collector for the gang in New
York regarding one of the factories Lepke controlled in Baltimore.
It was an important clue in the complex maze of garment rack-
eteering.

As the weeks passed Tom noticed the mob very carefully locked a large trunk every night after they had taken out their opium-smoking equipment. The mystery of the contents of the trunk plagued him. At last he told Melchen he was going in open it and examine it. Melchen warned him of the dangers. Tom said he had an alibi all prepared. If they caught him he'd fight his way out like any sneak thief. . . .

The room was seldom empty, but one hot afternoon the lone remaining mobster put on his trunks, threw a towel over his shoulder and set out for the beach. He had just closed the door when Tom entered the room. As one of the best known safe and loft detectives in the country, Devine can open any lock. In a moment he had the trunk opened. With Melchen standing guard with a gun he pored through the letters and other documents he found.

His heart leaped when he saw a picture of a cab driver. Lepke! He threw it into his pocket and was locking the trunk when Melchen hissed a warning. Tom dived for the door just as one of the gang who had raced up the stairs bolted into the room. Evidently he had forgotten to make a phone call to his girl. They could hear him trying to catch his breath as he gave the number.

Tom leaned against his own door. Chief Melchen mopped his brow. It had been a close one.

Together they examined the picture. The cab driver was not Lepke, but looked enough like him to be his twin. The picture puzzled both Tom and Melchen until one night one of the mob, examining the trunk, exclaimed: "What happened to the picture?"

Another asked, "What picture?"

"The picture we took of the joker who looked like Lepke. We were going to give it to him. . . ."

They virtually tore the room apart looking for the picture. Now they were suspicious. They went over the list of their gangster guests who had stayed overnight or who had been left alone in the room and hit on one from Detroit; he was the culprit, he had stolen the picture. They ranted and raved and Harris even wrote a letter to someone in Detroit asking him to "look up the man" and get back their picture.

Finally in the spring the gang called New York to tell their friends they were flying back. Tom wearily packed his bag and returned home to his family for a short rest. When he had left them they were putting up the Christmas tree; now, they were cutting roses.

We never did catch up with Lepke, but the long hard days of trailing the mob paid off in leads in other racket investigations, such as the restaurant racket. Louis Beitcher was the collector for the Schultz gang, which controlled this $2,000,000-a-year racket. In February, 1936, Beitcher vanished as the extraordinary grand jury was about to indict him on a total of 48 felonies, including 41 shakedown charges and seven extortions amounting to $250,000 in tribute from frightened restaurant owners.

In Beitcher we had the whole key to the vast racket—if we could find him. He came from a large family and closest to him was his brother Joseph. We grabbed Joe in the hope that he would lead us to Louis. Milton Schilbach, one of Dewey's Special Deputy Assistant District Attorneys, was handling the case with one of Dewey's chief assistants, now Federal Judge William Herlands.

When we picked up Joe, Tom Devine, older and more experienced than any of us, wisely counseled Schilbach to let Joe go on a sort of office parole; we were not to tail him or to bother him. Schilbach thought it over a moment, then said he would take Tom's advice.

In early December, 1936, Joe called Tom, "Come up and see me."

Tom rushed up to Joe's place to be told that Louis was hiding out in a house near Yale University in New Haven. That same afternoon, Tom, Schilbach and several detectives were on their way to New Haven.

"I think I know the house but not the address," Joe told Devine.

They cruised about New Haven for three days without finding the house. Meanwhile, Devine felt instinctively that Joe was withholding something. One bitterly cold night, Tom took Joe aside.

"You love your brother, Joe?"

Joe nodded.

"Well, if you want him to live take us to him. You know this mob; if they find out where he's staying it's curtains for Lou . . ."

Joe was silent for a moment, then said:

"Let's drive over to Baldwin Street . . ."

On Baldwin Street he pointed to a shabby two-story house. Tom and Joe walked down a narrow alley to stop at a lighted window. The shade was raised a few inches; inside a man with reddish brown hair and mustache was reading a paper.

"That's Louis . . ." Joe whispered. They tiptoed out of the

alley. Minutes later Louis Beitcher was staring into the guns of Devine and the other detectives.

"For a moment," he said in a relieved way, "I thought it was the mob coming for me. . . ."

His arrest halted a nation-wide search in which 15,000 "wanted" posters had been distributed by orders of Commissioner Valentine. His bail was set at $100,000. In the end he pleaded guilty and became Dewey's star witness. At Beitcher's arraignment Dewey announced that his office had indicted nine men in the restaurant racketprobe.

The restaurant shakedown had been a long and intense investigation which sent all of us flying across the country checking hundreds of leads. Many of these rackets dovetailed into one another. For example, Jules Martin, when he had bossed the restaurant racket, had been delegated by Schultz to take over the taxicab racket. We found Martin's plant in Elkhart, Indiana, where he had cabs built from parts salvaged from automobile graveyards.

The restaurant racket was probably one of the most important criminal cases investigated and tried in this country; its setup was so near legal that it took sixteen months to build up a case. The enterprise included several departments. Members of the strong-arm, or collection department, collected the cash shakedown after the victims had been intimidated. They also took care of the throwing of stench bombs to "persuade" reluctant restaurant men, selected the victims and decided how much they had to pay to stay in business. Another echelon included the crooked union men, whose job it was to call strikes, threaten to post picket lines and make demands for such large wages that the restaurant owners would have to go out of business if he granted them, or risk being beaten or even killed if he refused. Then a representative of the "association" would come around and offer to take care of the union for a fee. Various prices were fixed; if the owner didn't want a union contract he was charged so much; if he contracted for an increase of fifty cents or a dollar for his labor another price was set.

The Metropolitan Association, the so-called owners' association, was one of the most vicious racket groups Dewey had to fight. The association had as its goal the shakedown of each restaurant in New York City for a $250 "initiation fee." In addition it demanded dues of five dollars a week. This organization gave the gangsters an opportunity to operate legitimate offices in which the union leaders and the association leaders could meet. There were few New York restaurants that weren't touched. Many were forced to join.

I investigated numerous cases in which gangsters had thrown stench bombs into restaurants. It was incredible how the sickening smell seeped into the woodwork, furniture, drapes and plumbing, where it remained. In one case the malodorous stench lay dormant for three months, only to emerge in full strength during a rainy period.

Our investigation was stymied by gunfire many times. Labor bosses whom we had induced to talk to avoid a lengthy jail term, were murdered in daylight on the streets. Naturally, witnesses whom the investigators located were petrified with fear. I remember particularly one owner to whom I showed my proof that he had paid protection. Weeping and holding on to the lapels of my jacket, he begged me not to bring him in. Downtown in our office, he shook like a man with the palsy as he answered questions. Another man I found hated the racketeers because they had driven him out of business. He wanted to testify but he demanded absolute maximum protection; he was so frightened that the day he talked to me, outlining Coulcher's activities, we had to ride around town in a taxicab for three hours (for safety and privacy) while I took down his statement. After every sentence he would turn and peer out the window to be sure we were not being followed.

Each man who gave us a statement knew he was marked for murder. In the courtroom, Herlands, Dewey's assistant, exhibited a chart we had prepared, showing the organizational framework, from the kingpin Dutch Schultz down to the smallest gunman. Of the seventeen names on the chart, four were dead, four were missing and one had committed suicide just before the trial began.

After a lengthy trial before Justice McCook in the winter of 1937, a jury convicted the gang and the restaurant racket was smashed.

Next on our list of racketeers was "Tootsie" Herbert, the mobster who controlled the poultry racket.

Tootsie Herbert—he got his nickname from his mother—was overlord of a racket that cost city consumers $10,000,000 to $16,-000,000 a year. But he made a mistake in a $2.18 item, which caught the eagle eyes of our accountants. This actually broke up his criminal empire.

In this investigation Dewey used our accountants more than he used his investigators. Tootsie Herbert's trick books were as hard to crack as the steel vault of the Chase Manhattan Bank, but these men finally accomplished the apparently impossible.

Herbert had long exerted a strangle hold on the city's poultry industry. Tootsie forced himself into a lifetime job in the Chicken Drivers Chauffeurs' Union, Local 167, as business agent, boosting his salary from $60 to $200 a week. On the side he organized feed companies. Of course, the poultry people had to buy from Herbert or else go out of business. As a result it cost twice as much to unload poultry here as in Philadelphia, and the housewife paid the difference.

When Herbert had been brought up on a federal contempt charge in 1934, his books had mysteriously disappeared. New books were set up which showed that the treasury of the union had only $257.50. What faced Joseph M. Gasarch and other C.P.A.'s was the almost impossible task of rebuilding the lost books. This took an entire year. Checks had to be traced, outside accounts all over the country had to be examined.

The big break had come when our accountants found a notebook with the item: "Ins. pre. ref. $2.18." This was believed to be a notation that Herbert had received an insurance refund. The refund would have been paid by check. Find the check and you trace it to a bank account in which it was deposited.

Together with other investigators, I checked insurance companies and agents. Finally the long and tedious job clicked—we found the insurance company that had paid the check to Herbert. Now the accountants took over again. The cancelled check was found and traced to a bank and a business account—listed under a woman's name. Deposits in this account tallied with the dates of special levies placed on his union members by Herbert. This account showed transfer of funds to other accounts, all under names strange to us. A half-dozen bank accounts finally were uncovered; all contained union funds. Before the search was ended Gasarch and his band of "figure hunters" discovered that Herbert and his racketeers had stolen $38,875 from the union funds. On January 7, 1937, Herbert and his two union officials went on trial.

The evidence produced at the trial was staggering. As the skein of hidden bank accounts unraveled Herbert interrupted the trial to change his plea to guilty along with the two other union officials. At 38, after long defiance of the law, Tootsie, the small-time hoodlum who became boss of one of the city's largest industries and looted his own union members, went to Attica Prison for six years.

After our efforts in the Special Rackets probe were finished a final report was prepared for Governor Lehman. I began to wonder where I would find myself next.

One night I asked John O'Connell if he thought I should stay on. John smiled. "I'd stay if I were you, Dan," he said.

"Why?" I asked.

We were both looking out of the window of our Woolworth Building office, across the park from City Hall.

"Maybe we'll just send our files over there," he said.

He was looking out over the towers of the smaller buildings to the Criminal Courts Building.

This was where the offices of the District Attorney of New York County were located.

I decided to stay. I had always wanted to be a D.A.'s man. And there was still a lot of unfinished business on hand—like putting Jimmy Hines in jail.

PART III: TEN MONTHS IN A TREE-HOUSE

AFTER THE Special Rackets Investigation ended in 1937 Dewey, against his wishes, ran for the office of District Attorney of New York County. During his campaign for that office he publicly described for the first time the whole shocking picture of New York's politically-protected underworld. At the time there were some who thought he was going out on a limb, but we in the office knew how right he was; week after week the evidence was mounting that James J. Hines was the political protector of Dutch Schultz's policy kingdom.

In the beginning it was difficult to believe that this genial white-haired politician, who recently died on Long Island, could be in league with gangsters. It was almost unbelievable that this man, who had helped elect Franklin D. Roosevelt, was accepting tarnished money. Ironically, he would almost send Dewey to the same White House.

With the other investigators I was assigned to compile a dossier on his life. Hines was born in Manhattan on December 18, 1876. In his formative years "politics" was a household word. His grandfather had been one of Boss Tweed's workers, his father a loyal follower of Boss Croker. When Jimmy was eight his family moved to the area known as Manhattanville in the Eleventh Assembly District, where he grew up. At fifteen he left school to shoe—as he would boast—40,000 horses.

The smithy was a favorite rendezvous for the colorful, old-time politicians. From them young Jim learned all the in-fighting tricks of their rowdy political battles. When Jim was twenty, his father died, leaving him as a legacy the captaincy of the district. A year later he and his friends organized the James J. Hines Association, with headquarters at Eighth Avenue and 116th Street. In 1910 young Hines led a torchlight parade winding in and out of the West Side streets. Jimmy lost that year, again in 1911, but in 1912 finally won the district leadership.

Before World War I Jimmy Hines' power increased. He was well liked by the people of the district, especially the poor, who knew they could count on Hines for a Thanksgiving basket or a Christmas handout. In the war Hines served honorably as a lieutenant in the Motor Transportation Corps. On his return Hines found Tammany boss Murphy had set up a rival organization, but in 1920 Jimmy won the election by a large vote. He married, had a family of fine boys and continued battling Boss Murphy. When Murphy died in 1924 Hines maneuvered John F. Curry in as head of Tammany. Jimmy ruled the roost, with his clubhouse as one of Tammany's focal points. His sons went on to Harvard and Yale to make impressive records scholastically and in athletics.

In the Prohibition era a thousand years separated Jimmy Hines, the politician, from Jimmy Hines, the blacksmith. Jimmy got to know the beer barons and was often seen at ringsides with Dutch Schultz and others. Judge Seabury tried unsuccessfully to hook him up with the racketeers. In the 1932 Chicago convention, Hines bolted from Tammany's support of Al Smith to join Roosevelt's supporters. When F.D.R. went to the White House he repaid Hines' loyalty by making Jimmy the federal patronage-dispenser in Manhattan.

But the gossip linking Hines and the gangsters was beginning to leak into print. In 1932 United States Attorney George Medalie startled the city when he announced that friendship with Hines would disqualify prospective jurors trying a policy racketeer. When Dewey, Medalie's protégé, took over the rackets investigation in 1935, he soon found that the tentacles of the Schultz gangster investigations always seemed to embrace Hines.

Dewey was elected District Attorney by a landslide and, as John O'Connell predicted, we moved our precious files from the Woolworth Building to the Old Criminal Courts Building.

These files were the nucleus of our first major investigation—James J. Hines. Dixie Davis was disbarred, then promptly disappeared. In January, 1937, after three months of intensive investigation in Harlem, Dewey planned a major raid on a series of policy banks. Two nights later, with a small army of police who were not aware of their sealed instructions until an agreed hour, we raided 25 banks, collaring 72 prisoners.

Cases had been carefully prepared against each banker; some broke the rule of the underworld and talked. The evidence was growing. Then in February, 1938, Dixie Davis, Hope Dare—his show-girl mistress—and George Weinberg were located in Philadelphia. Two days later they called Harry (The Horse) Schonhaus at his hideout and persuaded him to surrender.

Then Dixie began talking, followed by Hope, George and Schonhaus. On May 25, 1938, Hines was indicted by a New York County grand jury on 13 counts of conspiring to protect Dutch Schultz's policy racket. Among the strongest of the links in the chain of evidence was the sight of that check to "Mr. Erick" that our accountants had found.

Davis also told me that while they were hiding out, Hope paid a visit to Hines at his clubhouse to plead with him for money and legal aid. But Hines refused to see her. Finally she forced her way in, only to be waved away by Hines.

"I'm not interested," he said.

"Hope was very bitter," Dixie said. "She came back and pleaded, 'Let's go to Dewey and make a deal.' "

Then began one of the most fantastic assignments I or any member of the District Attorney's office ever had. Our job was to take care of Davis, Hope, George Weinberg and Schoenhaus until the trial. The members of this important quartet were not steadfast in their determination to testify against Hines; they could be more accurately described as being on the fence.

In my mind's eye I can see Davis pacing the floor and crying, "I can't testify against the old man. I can't—I can't."

It was our job not only to guard these people, but also to try to banish their fears. We were guards, confidantes and father confessors to a murderer, a disbarred lawyer, his show-girl mistress and a phlegmatic gangster who lived only to eat and play cards.

The first two weeks we dodged about New York City, hopping from hotel to hotel. Naturally, Dewey was apprehensive but we were plain jittery. There were all kinds of rumors; the Purple Gang was gunning for Davis, free-lance killers were on the loose, the underworld grapevine was humming with the report that the gang overlords had sent out word: "Kill them before they reach the witness stand."

Finally at a conference it was decided that we should hide our witnesses on Long Island. We hired a house on several acres of ground which was patrolled day and night by our investigators and detectives. Tony Scanlon, Tom Fay, Jimmy Malone, Jimmy Canavan and others kept constantly at the heels of Davis, Harry the Horse, and Weinberg.

We were there exactly twelve days when the landlady, a spinster of about sixty, knocked at the door.

"I'm sorry," she said, "but you people will have to leave. There are just too many men about the place day and night. I'm afraid what the neighbors will say."

It was Tom Devine who came to Dewey's rescue. Tom had a summer place at Rocky Point, seven miles west of Riverhead, then quite sparsely populated. Dewey agreed with Tom that the tenacious newspapermen would have little chance of finding us there.

Tom is really one of the New York Police Department's living legends. His arrest records are still talked about; in the underworld his enemies are legion. They hate him, but respect him.

As the senior member, it was understood Tom was the boss. And when he gave an order it was best to execute it promptly and intelligently or you would find yourself back in the office. We all realized the national importance of the case; the incompetent or lazy were not welcome. Tom made that fact plain.

Before we moved out of our worried landlady's house, Tom had his country place fenced with barbed wire and two searchlights mounted at the entrance. He contacted the Police Department for additional weapons, a machine gun and automatic rifles.

Then, with an armed guard, the caravan of cars set off for Rocky Point. Tom was in the center car with Dixie, Harry the Horse and Weinberg. Two cars filled with investigators and detectives, hands on their guns, preceded and followed Tom's car.

As Tom swung into the grounds Dixie cried, "Stop!"

When Tom jammed on the brakes Dixie pointed to a log house, whose slanted roof rose out of the top of a clump of oak trees.

"What the hell is that, Tom?" he asked.

"That's my tree-house," Tom said.

"You mean a regular house in a tree?" Dixie asked.

Tom nodded. "It's a regular house with a stairway that can be lowered and raised."

"Let's go over and see it," Davis said.

They drove across the yard. Tom escorted the three prisoners and his curious men about the tree-house, then showed them how the stairway was raised and lowered by weights.

"What's that?" Dixie asked, pointing to a name carved on a log by the door.

"Otonogan—that's an Indian name for House-in-the-Tree," Tom said.

Dixie looked at Weinberg. "This is where I'm going to stay."

Weinberg added, "Me, too, Tom."

Schonhaus nodded. "Looks perfect."

"Okay, that's it," Devine told the others. "This is where they'll stay until we leave."

And that was the hideout for ten months for the three witnesses who helped put Tom Dewey on the road to the White House nomination.

That morning Devine split our group into round-the-clock shifts. Some patrolled the grounds, others patrolled up and down underneath the tree-house. Machine guns were set up and every man was ordered to carry his firearms—even when swimming, playing horseshoes or badminton.

As the blue twilight thickened, Devine ordered the searchlights turned on. In the country blackness the strange little treetop dwelling was starkly revealed in the pool of hard, white light.

That first night no one could sleep. George Weinberg tossed and turned while Davis kept getting out of bed. At last Tom said, "Want to sit outside, Dick?"

"Yeah, let's do that, Tom," Davis said.

"I'll go along," Weinberg said.

"Me, too," said Schonhaus.

They sat on the floor of the porch, protected from the glare of the floodlights by the oak leaves. The warm stillness was broken only by the chorus of country night life, the occasional chirp of a sleepy bird, the rise and fall of the cricket orchestra and the continuous rustle of the grass as the guards with machine guns paced back and forth beneath them.

"Jeez, this place gives me the creeps," Weinberg said. "Can't hear a trolley or cars or anything."

They sat in silence for a time, then suddenly Dixie began to talk. They were still talking at dawn.

It began with Dixie's story of the day he returned to their Bridge-port, Connecticut, hideout from Washington where he had attempted to fix Schultz's income tax case. It was about 2:00 A.M. and the hotel was deserted. As he reached the second floor he heard loud voices. He froze when he heard his name. Then, as the voices continued, he tiptoed to the door.

"It was Arthur talking," Dixie said. "He was drunk. He was planning my murder.

" 'Dickie's got to go,' he said. 'He knows too much. I'll give it to him tonight.' "

" 'Let me blast him, Dutch,' another voice said.

"Then there was a crash as though someone had slammed the table with his fist.

" 'Damn you, shut up. *I'm* killing Dickie!'

"There was the clink of glasses, then Schultz said, 'I'm going to kill Bo soon. He's getting too big. The wops [Italian mobs] talk to him, not to me. Who the hell does he think he is?'

"I felt my skin crawl when he began screaming. 'I'm Dutch Schultz. I'm the boss—Bo Weinberg—I'll kill him . . . I'll kill him . . . !'

"I had heard enough. I tiptoed down the corridor and went out. I ran until I dropped. I remember leaning against a stoop, my lungs almost bursting. I kept telling myself, 'I'm going to die. That bum is going to kill me.' For hours I walked aimlessly. I think that was the first time I knew I was trapped. I knew as long as Schultz lived I was his prisoner. I almost cried. Then because there wasn't anything else to do I went back to the hotel. This time I made a lot of noise as I walked down the corridor, whistling and so on.

"I opened the door and almost dropped dead. Schultz and four hoods, all hired torpedoes from Detroit, were standing with .45's in their hands—all aimed at me!

"One walked over and kicked the door shut. Arthur came close to me. He was so drunk he was reeling.

" 'Junior,' he said, 'I have to kill you. Do you want it in the head or the guts?'

"One other bum staggered over. 'Let me do it, Dutch,' but Arthur hit him in the face with the gun barrel and cursed him. The hood fell down and lay there.

"Suddenly—I don't know why I didn't think of it before—I recalled the Bronx brewery. I knew if I hit the Dutchman's wallet he'd soon forget killing me.

" 'If you kill me, Arthur,' I said, 'the brewery will go to my relative. Remember how you insisted you list her as owner for you?'

"The Dutchman just kept swaying in front of me, his eyes like a pig's, red and bloodshot, the big .45 about two inches from my stomach.

"Then it finally got to his drunken brain. He put the gun back inside his belt.

" 'Yeah, yeah . . .' he said. 'Let's all have a drink. I'll kill Bo instead.'

"He kept drinking until dawn. That night I knew Bo was going to be killed. For a long time I had a feeling there was bad blood between them. But now the Dutchman was spilling the hate he'd kept pent up for so long. Finally the amount of whiskey he consumed was too much for him. He became sleepy and dropped off. The other bums stretched out on the bed and on the floor. I'll never forget the picture as I tiptoed out. . . . Schultz, mouth open, snoring and drunk, the butt of his .45 just above his belt, with the other killers, guns in their belts, sprawled out, snoring like a bunch of cattle . . .

"I wondered to myself just how many men all of them killed . . .

"Back in my own room I lay on the bed, my heart pounding like a drum. I felt my black ace had turned up and eventually my body would be found on some dump heap . . . Every time a step sounded in the corridor I jumped like a rabbit and put my ear to the door, listening and waiting . . ."

There was a moment of silence. Then George Weinberg said, "Tell Tom what Schultz said later, Dick."

Davis shook his head. "I thought he had forgotten about the brewery crack I had made. But he didn't. About two weeks after that incident he said casually, 'Let's do something about that brewery contract, Junior. If something ever happened to your relative I'd lose a lot of money.'

"He brought up the subject many times but I was always able to stall him. In a way I figured that contract was my life insurance."

They continued to smoke in silence, the tips of their cigarettes glowing red in the gloom.

"That's why I flipped when I saw Jimmy Canavan today," George said. "He looks like Bo's twin."

"Did Schultz kill Bo?" Tom asked.

"Ask me another," George said softly.

"Did the Dutchman go after you any time, Harry?" Tom asked, switching the questions.

Harry replied, "Six months before he got it he called me down to his office one day.

" 'How much you got in the kitty?' he asked. This was the four vaults we had in the bank. As treasurer, I had to make sure we always had a bundle on hand in case we had to buy off some cops, put in a fix or put up bail. The largest one was the biggest the bank could offer. It was packed so full that whenever I opened it bills fell out on the floor.'

"So I told the Dutchman, 'Three hundred and fifty thousand, Arthur.'

"He just sat there, looking up at me in that mean way of his. Then he said, 'You sure, Harry, did you count every buck?'

"I said, 'I'm sure, down to the last dime.'

" 'Okay,' he said. 'Okay, now get out of here.'

"The next day at nine o'clock he called me again. 'Come right down,' he said. 'I want to see you.'

"I went down and the same act took place. After that at least twice a week he would repeat the routine. I got so nervous I couldn't eat. Finally I saw the light. I was next on his list. So one day when he called me down, I said, 'I've been thinking it over, Arthur. After all, I got a wife and two kids. I think I'll leave the rackets and open a store or a small business.'

"The Dutchman just kept staring up at me. Then he smiled. 'Harry, that's just fine. Just fine. Maybe I can help you . . .'

"The way he said it and the way he smiled I knew that the only help he wanted to give me was getting me out of this world. I forgot all about retiring after that meeting."

"Did you ever tell Bo about that threat, Dick?" Tom asked Dixie.

Dixie nodded. "I thought about it for a long time. Then I decided I had to go to Bo."

"I don't know if you cops know it, but Bo was the big man in the underworld. All the mobs looked up to him. And he was tough as iron. He didn't know the meaning of fear. One day in Chicago he entered a saloon, walked over to some of Capone's mob sitting at a table, leaned over and said to one of their hired guns, 'I understand you're out to get me.'

" 'Go back to Brooklyn or be carried out,' the hood said.

"Bo broke this fellow's jaw, fought the whole saloon, wrecked it completely, then walked out. As he told me later he didn't have to pull a gun; it would have been foolish to waste a bullet on a bunch of punks.

"The Dutchman knew all this and was deathly afraid of Bo. In '34 and '35 Bo was the boy who was keeping the mobs in line. Finally I decided to tell him about that night, so I met him 'way uptown in a bar where we wouldn't be recognized. Bo shook his head after I finished.

" 'It's been a long time coming, Dick. I knew he wanted me,' he said.

" 'What can we do, Bo?' I asked.

"He shrugged. 'Nothing—just wait. If he makes a false move I'll kill him with my bare hands.'

"Then he held up one of his big hands and slowly closed it. I felt chills running down my back.

"Before we left he said, 'I promise you, Dick, if I hear anything I'll let you know in time. If you hear anything, let me know.'

"He held out his hand and we shook on it. We consider that our pledge.

"Three weeks later I got a call from Bo. He wanted me to meet him at 125th Street and Broadway. When I got there he was sitting in a convertible.

" 'Get in, Dickie,' he said.

"I knew in a moment he was boiling. He was not an emotional man but from his face I knew he was on fire.

" 'What's up?' I asked.

" 'Schultz shot his mouth off last night for the last time. Now I'm going to shut it for him.'

"He pointed to the seat. For the first time I noticed a gun between us.

" 'What do you intend to do?' I asked.

" 'I'm going to kill him tonight,' he said. 'I'm going to get that bum and make him get down on his knees. Then I'll give it to him in the face.'

"He said it so calmly I had to look twice at him. But I knew he was serious. Then I did something I'll regret all my life . . ."

Tom asked, "What was that, Dick?"

"I talked him out of it," Davis said. "For three hours I talked like a lawyer summing up for a condemned man. At last he agreed to look at it my way, to wait awhile. So we drove over the bridge and I threw the gun in the Harlem River.

"We had a drink, then shook hands, with Bo reminding me of our

FROM AN INVESTIGATOR'S CASE BOOK

Payoffs in front of the Half Moon Bar & Grill, photographed by a concealed small but powerful camera with a telescopic lens.

Danforth (in light jacket, last row) accompanies the "dynamite" witnesses to the Hines trial.

This is the photograph of Mrs. Doris Coppola (wife of Trigger Mike) and her father that Danforth used to track down these key figures in the Scottorigio case.

Tom Devine on the trial of Lepke Buchalter. *Above left:* using a dictaphone headset to listen in on the gangsters. *Above right:* peering through a peephole to watch the mob "kicking the gong" around. *Below:* the flash photo of the opium setup in the mob's "den."

The Basketball Scandal. At left Danforth with Assistant District Attorney Vincent O'Connor *(center)* and Detective Nicholas Barrett, who accompanied Danforth when he captured Eli Kaye *(below)*.

Virginia Cogswell, Miss America of 1921, who was a key figure in the Fritz Kuhn case.

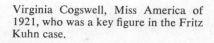

promise. That was the last I ever saw of him. He vanished the next day."

On a hunch Tom asked, "Where were you boys when Schultz got it?"

Dixie said, "We were all home."

Tom said, "Well, that means you knew beforehand about the shooting?"

In the long silence George said softly, "Ask us another, Tom."

"Why was the Dutchman killed, George?" Tom asked.

"When Bo got it the Dutchman signed his death warrant," was the reply.

Now the east was glowing with the first light. Dixie and George said they would take a nap. Harry was already asleep.

And so the first night in the tree-house was over . . .

In the nights to come Dixie, George and Harry the Horse told Tom and Tony Scanlon many strange but true stories of that dark and dreadful cesspool, the American underworld. Dixie gave a hint of Schultz's penuricus nature when, in telling how he burned the Dutchman's books after word reached him of the gangster's death, he said, "When I examined the books I found Schultz was so cheap that he itemized a pack of cigarettes."

Although they gradually got used to the country quiet, the three prisoners never really got over the fears that hired killers were after them.

Each night about eleven Tom would lower the stairway, preparing to retire.

At the first creak George's hoarse voice would ask nervously: "Who's that . . . who's that?"

And Devine would answer, "It's Tom, George, everything's okay."

And Weinberg would say in a relieved way, "Oh . . . Tom . . . goodnight."

In the first week Tom Devine's greatest problem was that a nearby neighbor who knew him might accidentally give away their hide-out. He wondered what explanation he could give for the men and the fence until Tony Scanlon turned up with a beard.

"I'm not going to shave until we leave here," Tony said. "I've always wanted to sport a beard."

Tom suddenly had a bright idea. "Come out into the yard a moment," he said to Tony.

Tony, wondering, followed him. As he suspected, Tom could see his neighbors standing on the porch wondering who the men were

The great Fascist O'Brien
Can never be mine
He may have once had a brain
I thought it seem to me to have been
waisted in vain. drained
He may yet see the light
But it will require a
　　Communist to set him right
　　　　　J. Richard Davis.

O'Brien the ~~Fascist~~ Fascist and
Dick the Communist are both
full of a lot of hot airism
~~isms~~　　　George Wlenberg.

Are you ready. Friske - Points.
Had a helluva swell time with
a helluva bunch of fellows
　　　Sig Harry (the fur buff)
　　Harry Schonbaum

Inscriptions from the tree-house guest logbook.
92

who were prowling about the yard in shorts, or playing badminton, or just sleeping in the sun. And what about the barbed wire that was strung about the Devine place . . . ?

"I'm going over to see my neighbor," Tom said. "When I get there and we turn to look at you, scowl and look real tough. I'll explain when I return."

Leaving Scanlon standing in the yard quite bewildered, Tom walked across the road. After some small talk the lady asked, "I can't help wondering who those people are over at your place, Mr. Devine. I'm sure some of them have guns in their belts."

"Oh," Tom said casually, "they're the guards for the poor boys."

"Poor boys . . . guards?" the lady echoed.

Tom said in a low, conspiratorial voice, "Just between us, ma'am, these poor boys are from a seminary and they suffered breakdowns. The doctors ordered them to go out into the country and have complete rest and plenty of sunshine . . ."

The woman shot a fearful glance toward the fenced yard. "Are any of them dangerous, Mr. Devine?"

Tom waved his hand. "Oh, I wouldn't say exactly dangerous, ma'am, but that big one over there . . ."

He turned to the yard. Huge Tony Scanlon, who will obey an order if he has to jump off a cliff, scowled and looked ugly. In shorts, with his barrel-like chest, dark beard and .38 in his belt, he looked like a man who had just stepped out of an African safari.

"Pardon me, Mr. Devine, but I have something in the oven," she said nervously.

"You won't say anything about the boys, ma'am?" Tom asked gently.

"Oh, no," the lady said. "But you will keep them *behind* that fence, won't you?"

"I certainly will, ma'am," Tom said, then added under his breath, "if I don't Tom Dewey will have my scalp."

When Tony heard about the play-acting he always managed to scowl or bare his teeth when the neighbors stopped to look. He never failed to send them scurrying back into the house.

I think the most graphic memory we all had of those ten long, weary months with these three criminals, was how they were tormented by their consciences. At night their minds and their memories were relentless. Dead men, old plots and schemes, all the evil they had committed, came like Hamlet's ghost to haunt them. When they couldn't sleep they poured out stories—true stories—of the underworld that only a few of the top racketeers knew. Some were hair-raising, some bawdy and hilarious.

As the months passed we all got a good insight into the mentality and the thinking of these three men who represented one of the largest racket dynasties in the history of our country.

Dixie was an egomaniac who adored fine clothes, good food, easy living and serenity. He liked the feel of silk against his well-cared-for body, but he dreaded the violence which bought it. Typical of his sense of values was the pride he took in his ermine-lined slippers. And this was in 1938.

Weinberg, in the beginning, stood in awe of Dixie's knowledge of law and education. He was always shaking his head, "That Dickie boy—he's a real smart guy."

But as the hot days dragged on, he grew less confident. In the end he was scornful of the racket lawyer and said openly he didn't trust him.

Weinberg was the moody one. He adored his wife and their two children and constantly worried about them.

He was closest to Tom Devine and obeyed him implicitly. In one of his dark moods, in which he paced endless miles under the trees, his thoughts known only to himself, Tom joined him. For a long time they walked in silence.

"What's wrong, George?" Devine said softly.

Weinberg shook his head. "When I think and remember I could cry . . ."

From what Davis had told us, we knew that he and Weinberg, before their capture, had hidden two pellets of poison on their person and had sworn they would die rather than go to prison. We saw the pellets.

With this in mind Tom said in an undertone to Weinberg, "I'm worried, George."

George looked at him. "About what?"

"About you . . ." Tom said. "I hope you would never do anything foolish. You know what it would mean to me . . ."

George stopped and put his hand on Devine's shoulder. "Let me say this, Tom," he said, "I would never do anything foolish—while you were on the job . . ."

And George Weinberg kept his word.

Another thing that bothered Weinberg was the knowledge that he had broken the iron code of the underworld of "don't talk." As he once told me, "It's not like fingering some hood to jail, it's squealing on Pop [Hines]. God, how I dread the day I have to take the stand and look into his face . . ."

While Dixie and Weinberg fretted and went sleepless, Harry the Horse slept like a log and thoroughly enjoyed himself. He was the most phlegmatic man any of us had ever seen. He lived only to eat and play cards. A glutton, he virtually pushed the food into his mouth until we wondered when he would explode.

Someone always had to play cards with him. He was a real shark but never could beat Jimmy Malone. This slender, witty Irish detective was the only one who could stir anger in him. When Jimmy laid down a winning hand, Harry would slam down the cards and walk away. As he belched, sucked at his teeth and plopped down the cards with a heavy hand Tom observed that he wasn't exactly the kind of person one would invite to the Colony.

Schoenhaus had been Dutch Schultz's collector. He could have been seen any day waddling down the street, a copy of *The New York Times* under his arm. He would go into a building, emerging within a few minutes, the newspaper still under his arm. He was never without it.

"What the bums didn't know," Harry the Horse would chuckle, "was that I stashed the loot in that paper. Some days I would be carrying more than $100,000 in that paper."

One day I asked him, "Suppose some young hood held you up, Harry?"

He gave me a look of scorn. "He'd be dead before he could spend a dime," he said. "This was the Dutchman you were robbing!"

During the hot, dry summer of 1938 we lived minute for minute with these people. Our lives were never our own. From the day Davis was taken into custody until the end of the second Hines trial I lived day and night with Davis' family, answering the doorbell with one hand on my gun. Davis was always afraid that the underworld would take one of his family as a hostage to make sure his tongue would be silenced. To calm his fears Dewey ordered me to live at the house. When Davis wanted a new suit, which was almost every day, two detectives had to make the 180-mile round trip into Manhattan. I would select his ensemble, hoping it would suit his lordship. Needless to say, the Davis family hated the sight of me before the case was finished. And I was certainly weary of them, their son and his suits.

Fortunately, it was summer and the outdoors saved our people from contracting a severe case of cabin fever. They could swim, there were makeshift handball and softball games, and horseshoes banged constantly on the ground.

Dixie was scornful of athletics, Harry the Horse wanted only to eat, while George Weinberg was a health fan. This man who had carried a .45 revolver stuck in his belt would walk blocks every day to keep in shape. Schultz, whose only act of exercise was opening a window, used to shake his head; George, he always said, was a nut on health. Not a day passed that Weinberg didn't do setting up exercises or swim up and down with a strange intensity. He was an excellent swimmer. One day he came up to the surface 25 or 50 feet out. He started to swim out farther with long, powerful strokes. Tom Fay, who had his pants over his trunks, with a .38 strapped outside, shaded his eyes and called, "Come on back, George."

Weinberg replied over his shoulder, "I'll see you in Bridgeport."

In a flash Fay was out of his pants. He swam up behind Weinberg and tapped him on the shoulder.

"Turn around and head back, George."

Weinberg turned. We never knew whether he was fooling or in earnest. But in those days you had to be not only an investigator but a valet, swimmer and expert horseshoe player.

I remember Big Tony Scanlon teaching Dixie Davis how to swim. Dixie would cautiously approach the water, then hold on to Tony as they entered. When it was over his head Tony would hold Dixie in his arms while Dixie taunted, "Don't drop Dickie boy, Tony, or your Uncle Tom won't have a case . . ."

During that summer the worst times were when we had to take the witnesses into Dewey's office for questioning. The newspaper reporters and photographers were all persistent. To try to fool them we had to keep on hand sets of specially prepared fictitious license plates and even changes of cars. All this maneuvering was vital; if the newspapers ever printed pictures of our hideout and that tree-house, Davis and the others might have refused to testify. Fear had them wavering. If their secret hiding-place had become known, no one knows what the results might have been.

When Hope Dare came to Dewey's office he never knew whether to expect a blonde, redhead or even a silver-haired beauty. In the hotel where she was under guard the investigators had a whole array of wigs. It was up to Hope which she wanted to be.

Davis, a married man, was in love with Hope, and this affair gave us some bad moments, particularly after the time a newspaperman using a telescopic lens got a picture of Dixie and Hope in a midtown apartment.

Dewey, I thought, came in for unwarranted criticism. The public didn't seem to realize that he was not custodian of the morals of these people; he had to keep them happy in order to get them to the witness stand. Without their testimony Hines could not have been convicted.

The long summer dragged on. Other evidence besides the testimony of our star witnesses—testimony from co-conspirators which would come under heavy defense fire—had to be gathered to show links between Hines and Schultz. To obtain such evidence I was taken off from my assignments with the Davis family and ordered to report to O'Connell at once.

Within the hour I was in John's office. He eyed me as I sat down.

"You're going to get one of the most important assignments in the case, Dan," he said. "We have information now that Hines was seen with Schultz in Connecticut. Your job is to confirm that by eyewitness. Needless to say, such evidence will be highly important. Dewey asked that you be given the assignment."

"Where do I start?" I asked. "Connecticut is a big state."

"We have vague information putting them in the Bridgeport area," he said. "Beyond that we can't help you." He stood up and we shook hands.

"Good luck, Dan," he said. "Don't bother to report to the office unless you find something."

Three hours later I was sitting in the smoker of a Connecticut-bound train. In my valise I had a collection of pictures of Schultz, Weinberg, Dixie Davis and Hines, along with a number of rogues' gallery photos which had nothing to do with the case.

In Bridgeport I registered at the Barnum Hotel, three blocks from the Stratfield. That first evening was spent in a leisurely walking tour of the city. I ended at the Stratfield Hotel Bar and for some reason had a hunch that here was the place to start. Before the evening was over I was at least on friendly terms with the bartender, who liked horses and baseball and prizefighting, subjects on which I like to think I am somewhat of an authority. We struck it off. Back in my room at the Barnum, I told myself that at least I had made a start.

I followed this same procedure for the next four days and nights. I wanted to become known. I went out of my way to become acquainted with the master of ceremonies at the club in the Barnum. I also made the acquaintance of the assistant manager and the owner of an after-hours club, who gave me a card. All this was done to try to reach people who might have known Schultz or who could direct me to those who might have known him.

Within two weeks I had made friends with some 15 people. After the first week I casually began to mention Schultz's name. Different persons would nod their heads and say they had heard the gangster did stay in town but that they didn't know too much about him.

I widened my circle of acquaintances, contacting people of varied interests, storekeepers, clerks, businessmen, auto dealers. One was Jimmy McKay, a bright young man who seemed to know everyone in Bridgeport.

My meeting him demonstrated how links are forged in a case. The bartender had introduced me to the master of ceremonies. He in turn had introduced me to McKay. The boy in turn would lead me to an important witness in the Hines-Schultz case.

After I had gained his confidence I told McKay that I was a writer doing some research for an article on Schultz and how he had lived in Bridgeport.

Jimmy seemed impressed. "Jeez, a writer!" he said. "Say maybe I can help you. Do you know Eddie Corbett?"

"No," I said. "Who is he?"

Jimmy said, "He's a former prizefighter who runs a health club in the Stratfield. I heard some of the Schultz gangsters used to go down there for a steam bath and massage."

"What kind of fellow is Corbett?" I asked.

"A nice guy," Jimmy said, "and an honest man."

After a few drinks he left, promising to check with some of his friends who might know something.

Late the next afternoon I went up to see Corbett.

He was a short, thick-set man with a broken nose, who couldn't be anything but an ex-pug.

I told Corbett I wanted a series of treatments for a cold I couldn't shake. I started off with a steam bath cabinet, which was horrible. After I had dropped about five pounds he turned a cold hose on me that shocked the devil out of me. Then he put me on a table and gave me a brisk massage.

I found Corbett a talkative man who was ready to discuss anything and everything. His hobby was health and he went into a long discussion of foods, diets and fads. I left that night promising to return the next day. On the second day he was tied up with another client and I met him later at his office. It was at this time in the relaxed atmosphere of his office that I cautiously mentioned Schultz.

He leaned back in his chair. "Oh, Schultz," he said. "I know him. They have guns and everything."

"Oh, did you see Schultz?" I asked.

Eddie nodded. "Yes. One of the bellhops went into their rooms and said there were guns all over the place."

"Did you know the men who were with Schultz?" I inquired.

His reply was, "Oh, I guess I've seen all of them at some time or other."

"Did you ever hear of a man named Hines?" I asked. "Jimmy Hines."

When Eddie shook his head I took out the series of pictures of the Schultz mob, Hines and the five or six others who had nothing to do with the case.

"What are you, a cop?" he asked suspiciously.

"I'm from New York," I said, "and I'm doing some research for an article in a magazine."

Corbett didn't buy that. "Who are you?" he asked. "FBI?"

I threw the pictures on the desk. "I'm from New York," I said. "I'm doing research."

Corbett wasn't to be thrown off. We fenced for a long time before I finally disclosed I was from the District Attorney's office in New York.

Dewey's name seemed to impress him. "You people are regular racket busters down there," he said admiringly. "What do you want to know?"

I spread out the pictures. He picked out Schultz, Bo Weinberg and several of the mobsters.

Then he stared at the others. I held my breath. He slowly picked up the picture of James J. Hines.

"Who is this?" I asked.

He shrugged. "I don't know. But he was with Schultz. I have seen him here in the hotel with Schultz."

Now I felt I was getting somewhere. I didn't press Corbett for fear he might become uneasy, so I switched the conversation back to health and listened for the next hour on how to keep in shape.

What exuberance I felt vanished the following day when I saw Corbett. Twenty-four hours made a difference. When he saw me he rubbed his chin. Now he wasn't sure; he would have to see Hines in person to be sure. That, of course, was impossible so I reluctantly put

Corbett on the shelf to continue looking for others who had seen Hines and Schultz together.

I saw the banquet manager of the Stratfield, Mr. Pucher, a heavy-set man who knew a great deal about fine foods. I came right to the point. I showed him the group of pictures I had. I told him to look at each one carefully, then to pick out those he knew.

Without a word he took the pictures and spread them out on his desk. One by one he picked out the mobsters. "These people here belonged to the Schultz mob," he said. He then picked up Hines' picture and I held my breath.

"This man is not one of the gangsters but I saw him several times with Dutch Schultz in the dining room," he said. "He is a very dignified man and must be a big businessman or a politician or something like that."

"Are you sure?" I asked.

"Positive," he said. "I noticed him because he looked so out of place with these people."

His positive attitude impressed me. I knew immediately he would make a fine, unshakable witness.

My next contact was with William Hunt, manager of the Hotel Barnum. I was looking for one of his former employees named Hughes, who had been at the hotel for a long time. Hughes had remarked once that he had seen Schultz and his gang together on several occasions.

Hunt telephoned to a former bellboy who told him that Hughes was somewhere in New England. While Hunt waited on the phone and I mentally chewed my nails, this former employee looked through his desk for Hughes' address. At last he came back on the phone and said he not only had his address but also his phone number in Gardner, Massachusetts.

When Hunt relayed me this information I told him, "Ask him to call Hughes and ask him if I can see him."

The former bellboy told Hunt he would and promised to call us back.

Time seemed to stand still. I haunted Hunt's office, my heart leaping each time the phone rang. Finally Hunt nodded at me—it was our call. The conversation was brief. Hunt smiled when he hung up.

"Hughes will be here at 9:30 A.M. tomorrow," he said.

Hughes arrived on time. I found him to be a soft-spoken, highly intelligent boy, who spoke so deliberately I could almost hear the cogs turn in his head. In the coffee shop of the Barnum Hotel I showed him the group of fifteen pictures and asked him to pick out those whom he knew. He picked out the pictures of Schultz and Hines.

"I have seen both of these people together on several occasions."

"Why did you remember these people?" I asked. "After all, you see thousands."

"Everyone knew Schultz was a gangster and anyone who walked with him or talked to him would be noticed," he said. "And this white-haired man looked so different from that hoodlum."

"Are you positive?"

"Yes, this is the man who was with Dutch Schultz."

I now had my second positive witness.

In the weeks that followed I added to these two witnesses four others: Charles Wall, a bellboy; William Matowski, a bellboy; John Hanson, a hotel employee, and a Mr. Bean, another hotel employee. All of these witnesses could testify to the close association of Hines and Schultz.

Schultz was dead, but he was still a power in the underworld as I discovered in the next few weeks. At least seven persons who positively linked Hines and Schultz disappeared overnight. In the case of one witness I was called by his wife.

"My husband has just received a phone call," she told me frantically. "He was told he will be murdered if he goes to New York with you."

"Where is he now?" I asked.

"Where you will never find him," she said, and hung up.

I began to make daily trips to the office with these witnesses, where they were turned over to Frank S. Hogan, then Dewey's chief assistant. Then they received subpoenas as state's witnesses.

I returned to Bridgeport on August 10, 1938, two days before the Hines trial started in New York's Supreme Court.

George Weinberg, who was the second witness to take the stand, proved to be a devastating witness. Dressed in a quiet brown suit, and tanned from months in the sun at the Long Island hideout, George outlined the entire $20,000,000 policy racket which he ran for the Dutchman, then exploded a political bombshell when he calmly described how Hines was the man who had put former District Attorney William Copeland Dodge in office with campaign funds and floating votes supplied by Dutch Schultz.

He quoted Hines as saying he wanted Dodge because he was "stupid, respectable and my man."

During his testimony Hines broke for the first time. When George pointed him out, when he was describing how Hines, his brother Bo and Schultz met with him in the Dutchman's apartment, Hines said in a loud, clear voice, "You lie! You know you lie!"

Weinberg paled, but went on testifying. That night when he returned to the hideout he was downcast and subdued.

But he was a shell of the man the night he returned after a blistering cross-examination by Hines' counsel, Lloyd Paul Stryker, in which he was called every kind of a thief, knave and even a murderer.

Stryker thundered, "Did you kill Dutch Schultz . . . ?"

That night Weinberg couldn't eat. He kept whispering to Tom Devine and Tony Scanlon, "I couldn't go through that again . . . I just couldn't . . ."

Then on September 10, Lyon Boston, former Assistant District Attorney under Dodge, was summoned to the stand. Dewey asked Boston, "Do you remember any testimony about Hines and the poultry racket there by him?"

The storm broke. Chief defense counsel Stryker was on his feet in a split second.

"I move for a mistrial," he shouted. Everyone in the courtroom knew that he regarded the implication of criminal involvement in another matter as highly improper. Dewey insisted the defense had opened the door for the questions but Stryker, shaking and quivering, kept shouting, "I demand a mistrial."

Dewey suggested a conference at the bench but Stryker turned his back on it. After a stormy morning Judge Ferdinand Pecora recessed until Monday morning. It was a long, hot and muggy weekend. Not only New York, but the whole country seemed on edge. The story was blazoned in headlines from New York to California. Radio commentators made it their choice subject, while in his office Dewey prepared his 25-page memorandum to be delivered to Pecora.

Monday morning Pecora came to his chambers early. At 10:00 A.M. he walked to the bench and read his decision granting a mistrial. Dewey, tight-lipped and grim, listened to what seemed at the time the death knell of his most celebrated case and his political future.

When the court clerk intoned, "Do you agree with the court's decision?" he gave a loud, clear answer, "I most certainly do not . . ."

I was in a deep sleep in a Bridgeport hotel room after an all-night-long investigation when the phone rang that Monday morning.

It was John O'Connell. Even in my drowsy state I sensed disaster. "Pecora granted a mistrial, Dan," he said. I lay back on the bed, refusing to believe what I had just heard. Just fourteen words could destroy months and months of dangerous, round-the-clock work; more than $50,000 for the trial alone could go down the drain . . .

If he was heartsick Dewey never showed it. He was grim-faced and said little. To meet the challenge of the mistrial he threw all the forces of the New York County District Attorney's office into the preparation of the second trial. I have always considered Dewey's darkest hour his greatest. If anything, that defeat drew us all together and we bared our teeth at the sneers and sniping from those who will always chortle at a mishap, and the political opportunists who watched to see how the ball bounced. It was not only Dewey's setback, it was ours—right down to the humblest office boy.

But there were many more dark days ahead. After the mistrial we hid our witnesses in the old Chappelle mansion, Mamaroneck Road and Miles Road, in the outskirts of Westchester. The lease was signed in the name of Harvey Miller, one of our detectives. On Harvey's name hangs one of the few humorous incidents of those bitter days.

It began one day when Weinberg looked out the window.

"Let me have that shotgun," he growled at Tony Scanlon. "That guy behind those bushes is watching us all day."

Tony peered out the window. He saw a colored servant from the adjacent estate lying on the ground behind a tall hedge, evidently watching our house.

"He's just curious, George," Tony said. "Think nothing of it."

"In the old days, I'd blast a guy who'd do that to me," Weinberg grumbled.

A few days later a man rang the front doorbell. We had hired one of Weinberg's relatives as a sort of handyman and I believe he answered the bell.

A heavy set man stood on the porch. When our man opened the door, this fellow flashed a badge.

"Chief of Police, White Plains," he said. "This your house?"

"Yes, sir," was the reply.

"What's your name?" the chief asked.

"Harvey Miller," the doorman replied.

"I think I'll just have a look around," the chief said as he walked inside.

We were all sitting around, about fifteen detectives playing cards with Weinberg and Davis. Some of us were in shirtsleeves, lumberjack shirts and jackets. I guess we really looked like a rough bunch.

At first everyone thought the visitor was a tailor or some delivery man. But when he walked into the room all of us were on the alert. He didn't look dangerous, so we just sat there and continued to play cards.

The chief tapped Tom Devine on the shoulder.

"You live here?"

Tom said, "That's right."

"What's your name."

"Harvey Miller," was the reply.

The chief tapped Tony Scanlon next.

"Live here, mister?"

He looked up. "Yes, sir."

"I suppose your name is Miller?" he said.

"Harvey Miller," Tony corrected him.

After questioning three more of the detectives only to have each one identify himself as Harvey Miller, the chief was boiling. He knew something was going on but he wasn't sure what. Finally one of the boys drew him aside and told him we were detectives up in the country for a rest. The chief didn't swallow that, but when they got Chief Investigator John O'Connell on the phone, things were smoothed out. It seems the people on the neighboring estate had complained. They thought we were conducting a gambling house or a still. The Negro servant had been employed to watch our movements.

The chief was a nice fellow after we got to know him. I think his parting crack is a classic.

As he opened the door he turned and said, "Know what my name is?"

Tom looked up, "What is it, chief?"

"Miller," the chief said, and slammed the door.

Finally the day grew near when the new trial would open. Weinberg said constantly he didn't want to testify against "the old man." More than once he said he dreaded the moment when he would have to take the stand.

Weinberg sincerely liked Tony Scanlon and Tom Devine. On several occasions he told both he would never do anything to embarrass them.

Tony Scanlon, over Weinberg's protests, was assigned to another phase of the case. On Sunday, January 29, 1939, Tom Devine had finished his tour of duty. He called out good-by to Weinberg, who waved back cheerfully. The substitute investigator who replaced Devine left the room momentarily. Weinberg listened as Tom's car traveled along the driveway. In the quiet he probably heard the shifting of gears, then gradually the sound of the car fading into the distance. Satisfied that Devine was safely on his way home, Weinberg took the guard's revolver and tiptoed upstairs to the bathroom. He locked the door, lifted the gun to his head and pulled the trigger. The shot echoed for days in the lurid headlines. Weinberg's body crashed down, wedging itself between the side of the tub and the wall in such a fashion that most of the plumbing had to be ripped out to remove his body.

Devine heard the news when he stepped into his house; Tony Scanlon was dining with friends when the radio blasted out the news.

"I almost choked," he recalls.

Weinberg's death was a major blow to Dewey's case, but it wasn't fatal. Dixie was like a stunned man. He just kept shaking his head. "Why did he do it—Why?"

This was the pitiful side of Davis—he never fully realized the enormity of his crimes. Could you tell such a man that dead men have a way of perching on a murderer's shoulders?

My assignment in Connecticut was now more important than ever; Frank Hogan, who was working day and night, summoned me back from Bridgeport.

"Dan," he said, "I have a tip that Schultz liked horseback riding. It is possible he went horseback-riding in or around Bridgeport. Maybe there's a Hines connection there."

I now started one of the most laborious searches in my investigating career. I contacted every stable and riding academy in that part of Connecticut. I hired a car and paid each one a personal visit with my collection of pictures. Two weeks after my search began it paid off.

I drove up one afternoon to the riding academy of Dudley Brothwell, in Fairfield, Connecticut. Mrs. Brothwell met me at the door.

I introduced myself and showed her my group of pictures. She immediately picked out the pictures of Schultz and Hines.

"These two men came here frequently as riding partners," she said. While we were talking Brothwell came in. He was a tall, lanky New Englander, whose integrity was as hard as Yankee granite.

He took the pictures, looked at each one, tossed it aside with a grunt. When he came to Hines and Schultz he brightened up.

"This is Dutch Schultz, the gangster," he said. "I saw this white-haired man in his company."

"Are you positive this is Schultz?" I asked.

"Yes, positive," he said firmly.

"Why are you so positive?" I asked.

He sat down, took a deep breath and told me:

"Well, I had Mr. Flegenheimer's horse here at the stables and boarded it and took care of it. After I read the story in the newspaper that he was shot in New Jersey and died, I got the address of his wife from the *Daily News* and I wrote a letter to find out what I should do with the horse. It was a very valuable animal and frankly I didn't want it on my conscience that I had taken it as my own property."

"Did you get an answer?" I asked.

He nodded. "Yes, I received an answer. Mrs. Flegenheimer said to take good care of the horse. She said that she would see that all bills would be paid."

"Do you have that letter here?" I asked.

A faint smile appeared on his solemn face.

"I thought I'd need it," he said. To his wife he said, "Mother, do you have it handy?"

Mrs. Brothwell nodded. In a moment she was back. In her hand was the letter. I could have hugged this Yankee.

I pointed to Hines' picture. "What about this man?"

"He and Schultz used to ride together," he said.

"Are you positive?" I pressed.

"I swear it is the truth," he said.

I saw Dewey the next morning and told him the news. He is not an emotional man, but when I finished he was beaming.

"Dan," he said, "If you never do another thing in this office you've earned your Oscar."

The second trial began and my job was to corral my witnesses, some of whom were terrified after receiving death threats if they should testify. My job was to bring them down one by one. Back in Bridgeport the next day, after I had delivered Brothwell, I received news that staggered me. I heard that the riding master was once arrested on some sort of a Prohibition charge.

I rushed down to New York and caught Dewey minutes before the Brothwells were to take the witness stand. I recalled I pressed the driver from Grand Central so much we were almost killed in a head-on collision at Union Square.

When I told Dewey about Brothwell's Prohibition violation he slammed his fist in his hand.

"That's wonderful!" he said.

I was on pins and needles all day in the courtroom. But I had no need to be apprehensive. The Brothwells were wonderful witnesses. When Mrs. Brothwell had finished on direct examination, Mr. Dewey said casually, "Have you ever been arrested, Mrs. Brothwell?"

She smiled. "Well, during Prohibition we had a little wine in the house and the police came in and took it."

Dewey walked back a few paces, turned and leaned forward.

"Tell me one more thing, Mrs. Brothwell."

I thought the whole courtroom had sucked in its breath and was waiting.

"Yes?" Mrs. Brothwell asked.

"Was it good wine?" Dewey inquired softly, and the courtroom roared.

This apparently was a blow to Lloyd Paul Stryker, Hines' counsel, who undoubtedly envisioned the earlier arrest as an opportunity to discredit the witness. Dewey had trumped his ace.

The importance of my witnesses was underscored by the vigorous cross-examination they underwent at the expert hand of Stryker. Each one had to retrace his movements with me, recall the exact words of our first interviews and go over and over the moment when they had picked out Hines' pictures from the batch I had shown them. Despite the sharp cross-examination Mr. Stryker couldn't shake their stories.

It amused me to hear myself described as "Mr. William Danforth [sic], the Dewey detective." In his summing up for the defense Mr. Stryker denounced what he called "a Danforth type of investigation." To this day I don't know what he meant and, frankly, I never much cared. What I was most proud of was the conduct of the bellboys and employees of the hotel and Brothwell. Out of respect for our country's laws, they defied all the threats and gossip to come to the big city to testify at an important trial.

The great and impressive-looking lawyer had a battering ram of a voice and steely eyes, but in their quiet simple way my witnesses outdueled him all the way.

Hines was found guilty and was sent to Sing Sing.

6. PHILIP MUSICA AND THE McKESSON & ROBBINS SCANDAL

MY NEXT case was to take me back to Bridgeport and also to Long Island. I will always remember the unraveling of a fabulous fraud and a certain stormy night.

The large living room in the mansion in Westbury, Long Island, was suddenly plunged into darkness. The thunderclap which followed the flash of lightning shook the house; the winter rain, riding the back of a strong gale, flayed the window panes.

The man seated across from me said in a low, sad voice, "It's just as well . . . there's no more to tell."

We sat for a while in the darkness watching the lightning zigzag across the sky and listening to the peals of thunder retreating across the sky.

Finally he said, "I will get a candle and let you out."

As he started to leave the room he suddenly froze at the far-off sound of a siren. We listened in tense silence as it neared, then passed down the road.

"I thought they might be coming for me," he said in a relieved way.

"They won't," I said. "No one knows I'm here."

He returned in a few minutes with a lighted candle to show me to the door. The rain was still coming down. I knew I would be soaked before I reached the depot.

"Good-by," he said.

We shook hands and I dashed down the steps to the road. When I looked back the house was in darkness.

The man who had closed the door was George Dietrich, alias George Musica, brother of Philip Musica, alias F. Donald Coster, who, only a few weeks before, had been revealed as the man who had swindled millions from McKesson and Robbins, one of the nation's oldest, largest and most respected drug firms. He had just finished relating to me the last installment of the amazing story of his brother's life.

Up to this writing I have never revealed any of my findings in this sensational case, except in interviews with Dewey, then District Attorney, in which we and Assistant District Attorney Frank Severance were the only ones present. I have kept the documents on which I base this chapter locked in a vault for eighteen years, bringing them out only now to refresh my memory. Among the notes is my original report of an unpublished suicide note left by Coster; the only other copy is in the files of a federal bureau in Washington. This suicide note was never released. It contained the names of more than ten of the nation's leaders—men who were confidantes of President Roosevelt—men who Coster charged had accepted bribes from him in the form of stocks or hard cash.

In my interviews with George Musica, he told me the detailed story of his brother's fantastic swindles, of the staggering sums his brother paid to extortioners, some of whom were judges and politicians prominent in both the Democratic and Republican parties. My reports included charges made by Musica's brother against one of the important figures in the United States government. On the basis of these reports Dewey went to Washington and personally gave the whole story to Federal Bureau of Investigation Director J. Edgar Hoover. I cannot name these persons because they were never charged with a crime. And I feel it would be an injustice to indict in print those who were not indicted by the law.

Despite the explosive revelations which George Musica made to me, the District Attorney's office could not take action because the federal arm of our law had jurisdiction over this case.

However, before we go into the District Attorney's phase of the Musica case I believe one must have a knowledge of the background of Coster—Philip Musica—and his entire family. I discovered some of this information in the basement of the Criminal Courts Building in reports written by an unknown Assistant District Attorney more than forty-four years ago.

The Musica story really begins on New York's lower East Side, where Antonio Musica owned a small barber shop. He was a shy, rather reserved man, with a full beard and a penurious nature. His young wife, Assunta, had borne him four sons and two daughters. Their first was Philip, who was six when they came to this country in 1883 from their native Italy.

Philip was a wild, headstrong boy, who scoffed at entering the barber's trade. He resisted attending school and when his mother searched for him she usually found him hanging around his friend Fernando Costa, a printer.

There is a blank in his formative years, but we do know that when Philip was twenty-one he talked his father into selling the shop and investing his savings into the business of importing Italian wines, cheese and olive oil. Father and son set up the concern, with Philip guiding its destiny. He was a smart businessman and the firm prospered so much the family moved to a large house in the Bay Ridge section of Brooklyn.

Then the government learned that Philip and his father were escaping heavy duty taxes by bribing government weighers to mark down import invoices. Antonio's name had been signed to some, but, as he said tearfully, he was only doing what his oldest son told him to do. They were both indicted, but Philip insisted on taking full responsibility; the case against the father was dismissed. His son was fined $5,000 and sentenced to Elmira Reformatory, then used as a federal house of detention. Philip served only five months and fifteen days. He managed to get President Taft to pardon him because of "extenuating circumstances."

Shortly after his release Philip got his father to go back into business, this time as the United States Hair Company. In the days when switches and high coiffures were popular the company made money. Philip was a strong believer in distributing the wealth among his family, so he brought his brothers, Arthur, then twenty-one, and George, nineteen, in as minor executives. Louise acted as telephone girl and general clerk; Lucy Grace kept house for Assunta.

Philip, who now wore opera coats with silk linings and shiny top hats, was the boss, not only of the firm but of his family. All of them basked in his reflected glory.

On March 12, 1913, Assunta took the two youngest children to Naples for a visit. Just before they waved good-by Philip had paid a visit to the Bank of the Manhattan Company, to apply for a loan for the full value of 216 cases of human hair, worth $370,000. As security he offered bills of lading, warehouse receipts and bills of exchange. But investigators for the bank found the boxes held hair of poor quality worth only $213.

On March 13, 1913, Philip paid a visit to the District Attorney's office in the Old Tombs Building, regarding the shipping documents. He went into a long explanation and promised to bring some documentary proof the next day.

That night the Musica family fled to New Orleans, where they were arrested. Sums totaling $96,000 were found on various members of the party, including Louise, who hid the bills in her corset.

A New York County grand jury indicted Antonio, Philip, Arthur and George and on March 20 they were extradited. On April 11 they were arraigned on the indictment in New York, and through their counsel, George Gordon Battle, entered a formal "not guilty" plea.

What follows is an excerpt I copied in 1937 from a dusty document I found one day while rummaging in the files of the District Attorney's office. The heading on the faded folder is "Philip Musica vs. The People of New York City." It read:

It was apparent from the first that the eldest son, Philip, had been in full control of the business and was primarily responsible for the frauds which led to the flight and subsequent indictments. He immediately sent word to the District Attorney that he was willing to make a full statement, and on the following day, he was brought to District Attorney Charles Whitman's office and there made a detailed statement of how he had discounted bills of exchange attached to bills of lading purporting to cover valuable merchandise, whereas the cases described in the bills of lading, in many cases, contained worthless hair and waste. According to Musica's story some half-dozen banks in the City of New York were in this way defrauded in the amount of about one-half million dollars.

During the next few days Philip Musica gave to Mr. Stern, of Rushmore, Bisbee & Stern, representing the Manhattan Company, and John Munroe & Company, a detailed statement, which made a record of several hundred pages. This statement afterward proved to be of much value in straightening the bankrupt estate of A. Musica & Son and an allied corporation known as the United States Hair Company.

On the 27th day of May, 1913, Philip Musica pleaded "Guilty" before Judge Swann upon indictment #93,630, in which he was charged with stealing $16,793.33 from the firm of J. & W. Seligman & Company.

Afterward he testified before the Grand Jury which found an indictment against Hans Shapiro, who had been the Paris agent in the Musica frauds. [Shapiro is still a fugitive.]

Afterward Philip Musica testified before the grand jury which found an indictment against one Frederick Holder, a New York

customs broker, who had also participated in the Musica frauds.
Philip Musica says that Holder was his instructor in crime. [The
Holder case is still pending.]

On the 11th day of July, 1913, George Musica pleaded
"guilty" before Judge Swann on indictment #93,624, and after
hearing Probation Officer Conway's report and statements by Mr.
Rice of Whitridge, Butler and Rice, Mr. Stern of Rushmore,
Bisbee and Stern, and Mr. Embree of the District Attorney's
office, sentence was suspended.

On the 14th day of January, 1914, Arthur Musica pleaded
"guilty" before Judge Swann on indictment #93,625 and, after
hearing the report of Mr. Conway and the statements of Mr. Rice,
Mr. Stern and Mr. Embree, sentence was suspended.

At the request of the attorneys for the receivers of A. Musica
& Sons and the United States Hair Company the sentence of
Philip Musica was postponed from time to time in order that he
might appear as a witness before the referee in bankruptcy.

Page after page followed, detailing receiverships in which Philip
Musica was chief witness. One action took fifty sessions. The résumé
of the hearings and the subsequent investigations showed that Musica
was an excellent informer. He even named his closest friends who
had been involved in his human hair fraud. They were either arrested
or became involved in civil actions.

Musica proved such an expert informer that he was hired under
the name William Johnson as a District Attorney's investigator!
When World War I began he transferred to the Attorney General's
office to do counterespionage work for the government.

After the war, Prohibition presented a wide and fertile field for
Musica's operations. Under the name of Frank Costa, his former
printer friend, he formed the Adelphi Pharmaceutical Manufacturing
Corporation, in partnership with Joseph Brandino and Leonard Jenkins.

The firm was granted a legal permit to buy 5,000 gallons of
alcohol a month. The liquor of course, was sold to bootleggers, who
made it into "20-year-old Scotch, just run in."

Apparently Costa feared Brandino, and again played the informer.
To get Brandino he tipped the Treasury Department, who raided the
place and revoked the liquor permit.

Costa vanished for a short time. When he next appeared he was
F. Donald Coster, a wealthy man-about-town, employed in the broker-

age house of Clark & Hubbard. Carol, the sister of Jenkins, Coster's old partner, was married to one of the partners in the financial house, Edward Hubbard. There was a divorce and Carol married Coster.

Coster again returned to his family to invite them into another venture. This time he founded the Girard Company, in a small, neat brick building in Mount Vernon. It was the same setup as the Adelphi—a drug firm which sold alcohol to bootleggers.

Philip also gave his brothers new names: Arthur became "George Bernard"; George, "George Dietrich"; and Robert, "Robert Dietrich." To make the façade more realistic he bought a mansion out in Westbury, Long Island, and installed his mother and sisters in it under the name of P. Horace Girard with a signpost erected prominently at the entrance of the property.

Meanwhile, he and Carol settled in an imposing house in Fairfield, Connecticut.

Here he made up the "W. W. Smith & Company," which was simply brother George in a one-room office in Brooklyn Heights. The Girard Company's alcohol was sent by the Smith Company to various warehouses. Bootleggers would send "George Bernard" the cash and he would transfer it to the Girard firm by check.

Coster expanded as the money flowed in. He increased his circle of legitimate businessmen, notably Julian Thompson, a Wall Street investor who assumed Coster was a brilliant operator.

Thompson unwittingly helped Coster make contacts with the bankers of Bridgeport, who in turn were also charmed by this middle-aged merchandising genius, whose black eyes peered so brightly behind the rimless glasses and whose clothes came from the smartest Fifth Avenue men's shops. When the Girard Company moved to Bridgeport the bankers congratulated him.

Coster's next major move was to take an option to buy, for $1,000,000, McKesson and Robbins, a century-old drug concern of fine reputation. Thompson, with whom he discussed the proposal, thought that with Coster at the controls the old firm would go on to greater achievements.

Now Coster began his greatest swindle—one which makes the manipulator Ponzi's pale in comparison. He made Thompson treasurer of the drug firm, and the entire business, with one exception, quickened legitimately—that exception was the crude drugs department.

Coster let it be known he had a Ph.D. in chemistry, and an M.D. from Heidelberg, and that it was there at the university that he became interested in crude drugs. He talked learnedly about such things as oil of orange, snakeroot, dragon's blood powder, benzoin of Siam, and so on. It was assumed Coster's thorough network of agents bought up large stocks of crude drugs when the price was low or when the market was glutted. The stocks were then stored in warehouses. My investigation disclosed that one time his books showed he bought so much of a certain drug that (according to the United States Public Health Service), he would have captured the entire drug crop for that current year and the three years following.

Coster's closest associate was "George Dietrich," who was treasurer of his department. He had an office next to Philip's. It was generally known that George had been with Philip since the early days at Mount Vernon—"Robert Dietrich" worked with George. In fact, when George was cut, Robert would sit in for him. No one but the Dietrichs and Coster ever handled the records of the crude drug department.

This department was a small empire in the firm dominated by Coster. He bought and sold as he pleased. It was accepted that the drugs were purchased through a chain of wholesale houses in Canada. When Coster wanted to buy a large quantity they quoted a price. It was George who selected which one to buy from. The order would be made in quadruplicate. Three copies would be sent through the firm's billing and accounting departments; the Dietrichs would keep one copy. Invoices from Canada were then filed by George Dietrich.

Later, invoices would arrive from Manning & Company, a private bank in Montreal, indicating they had paid the wholesale house for the drugs, in the name of McKesson and Robbins. These items would be listed in the books of the Fairfield firm, in favor of the Manning bank.

On the reverse side of the business the disposal end of the crude drug department was handled by the Montreal office of W. W. Smith & Company, Ltd., supposedly an old established London firm which had been in business before the start of the Civil War. Their offices were listed in almost every part of the Empire. Smith & Company received .75 per cent of all sales and a monthly fee of $1,500. This income averaged about $150,000 a year.

To summarize, this is the gist of the operation: Manning bought the drugs and placed the lot in a warehouse. Smith sold it at a big profit. Then McKesson and Robbins had Manning buy a larger amount of drugs, with the original investment plus the profit. Smith sold that and the round robin was repeated. Thus, in time a big profit was built up, but the profit was all in drugs in warehouses. Actually there were no drugs, no warehouses. But on the books of McKesson and Robbins there was an asset of more than a million dollars of drug inventory. The only money that actually changed hands was the commission money paid to the Smith firm by Mc-Kesson and Robbins. The payments for the purchase and sale of the drugs were essentially just bookkeeping items. The money paid to Smith and used by Coster was not the major purpose of the swindle. The crucial thing was the earnings increase that McKesson and Robbins showed as a result of the enormous (declared) profits of the drug department. McKesson and Robbins' credit became absolutely gilt-edge, the price of its stock was boosted far beyond its true worth. The total valuation of the company as represented by all its common stock at the price quoted on the New York Stock Exchange contained many million dollars worth of air.

Coster and George Dietrich were together every business day, but nobody could recall when the Costers and the Dietrichs entertained. George had an attractive blonde wife, Claire, and five children. On the side, he and his wife dabbled in real estate. Robert Dietrich was married to a quiet little woman named Anne and had two children. He was quite active in civic affairs and liked baseball.

Coster ruled his company with an iron hand. He was a stickler for anonymity and the reason became obvious to his fellow executives after the scandal broke. He once stated in an office memorandum: "I have experienced no difficulty personally in keeping publishers of trade journals, curiosity seekers and manufacturers from making inquiries. All of these have come to me one time or another—but only once. Then they have kept away from me thereafter."

Thompson was the only person for whom Coster seemed to have a friendly regard. They were an odd pair as they walked down the hall or appeared together on the street; Coster, impassive, cold, unfriendly—his brown eyes suspicious and alert behind his heavy-framed glasses; Thompson, his face thin, gaunt and ascetic-looking.

Thompson was not only a financial expert but also a Broadway playwright. In 1932 his *Warrior's Husband* starred Katharine Hepburn. There were times, George said, when Coster and Thompson lunched together, that the conversation was so desultory that they would eat the entire meal in silence, speaking only after coffee.

"It seemed to me they just didn't have to talk," George said. "It was as though they understood each other so well that words were superfluous. They just seemed to like each other's company."

By 1929 the firm was doing a volume of $14,000,000 legitimate business a year. In the spring of that year a shabbily dressed man who said he was an iceman appeared in General Sessions Court before Judge Francis X. Mancuso, to ask that an ancient perjury case against Philip Musica be dismissed. He identified himself as Musica. There is no record of the disposition of this appeal. In fact, all of the Musica records have mysteriously vanished from the files of the District Attorney's office.

While the country moved slowly toward the Wall Street disaster and the Depression, life with the Coster-Musicas went on smoothly both in Connecticut and on Long Island. Coster and Carol moved into an 18-room Italian style villa on Mill Plain Road in Fairfield, Connecticut. The décor was baroque—heavy walnut furniture, thick draperies, pedestrian oil paintings of pastoral scenes, overstuffed furniture and thick rugs. There were many ferns and plants in the windows which looked out on a large garden. Behind the house was a two-story garage in which Coster kept his Packard and Cadillac. The household staff included three house servants and a chauffeur. Mrs. Coster, who loved chow dogs, kept a kennel with a dozen of the breed, a pet parrot and a St. Bernard.

The Costers usually kept to themselves. The only visitors they had were Mrs. Carrie Jenkins, Mrs. Coster's mother, and her two brothers, Leonard and John Jenkins. When they did invite some neighbors in for the evening Coster kept mostly to himself. He smiled at quips, inquired politely about children, sipped ginger ale while he offered his guests 20-year-old Scotch and generally gave the impression of being a grave, deep-thinking man who was being polite for politeness' sake but who actually didn't give a damn whether or not you were having a good time.

Coster was not a flashy man. The only thing that he seemed really to like and over which he could sound a bit enthusiastic was his 284-ton yacht *Carolita,* named after Carol. He had bought it for $40,000 and had spent another $85,000 replacing the hull and engines and installing a two-way radio. There was a captain and a crew of six. The few times he had executives from his firm up for the weekend he would take them out on the *Carolita* for a day of fishing. Only then did he abandon his role of the grave businessman. He joked, laughed heartily and grew excited when he had a strike. These cruises took him and his friends as far as Nantucket and Marble-head and sometimes to Maine waters.

In Westbury, Long Island, on every Sunday morning you could see "the Girard family" attending services at St. Brigid's. "Old Mrs. Girard" usually had a visitor who drove up in a handsome limousine at least once a week. Gossips in the neighborhood whispered that it was her son from an earlier marriage. F. Donald Coster would have smiled had he known the talk his visits created.

Then there was another member of the clan whom the towns-people called "Robbie," who each Christmas played the fat, jolly Santa who gave out handsome toys at the firehouse children's party. That was brother Robert, of course.

In 1929 Coster, after he was told he was suffering from a heart condition, founded the Bridgeport Heart Clinic. To their neighbors the Costers were a wealthy, quiet-living, middle-aged couple, who seemed devoted to each other.

Away from the quiet of his suburban home, Coster was the energetic, dynamic executive. He flooded his assistants with memos of the most trivial nature, became irritated when they were filed and forgotten and banged on the desk when his orders were not carried out fast enough. Most of the company executives disliked his arrogance, but the crude drugs department showed such a profit they felt he had become indispensable. One thing they grudgingly admired was his refusal to take more than a $40,000 annual salary.

The stock market crash caught him in his own network of swindling. To make up the losses he swindled more than before, increasing by millions the company's inventory of crude drugs. Firm after firm fell into bankruptcy, but with Coster's phony drug supply on the books, the firm sailed serenely through the turbulent Depression years.

In 1937 came a brief business recession. To many firms it was the portent of another depression, so the board of directors directed Coster to convert his $2,000,000 drug stockpile into cash. Coster said he would, but promptly ignored the board's order.

Coster's refusal a second time made Thompson curious, but not suspicious. In the winter of 1937 he sent for a copy of the contract with Smith and Company. He was surprised to find that it was not a Canadian company but a New York City concern. He was relieved, however, when a telephone book informed him it was "W. W. Smith & Co., Ltd." Under the name was the list of several warehouses, some which held McKesson and Robbins drugs.

But he received another shock when a Dun & Bradstreet report showed that the Smith company office was but a "small space put at the disposal of persons traveling from Liverpool." Thompson said later that it was then he began to feel that the addresses were simply mailing drops. A bank check in Liverpool produced the startling news that "they [the Smith company] were unknown in banking circles there."

Although he had sufficient evidence to warrant at least a semi-official probe by the officers of the company, Thompson hesitated. He was still telling himself that this man in whom he had placed so much trust could not be a thief.

As he said later, he continued to "proceed tactfully and unostentatiously." He discovered that John McGloon, the company's comptroller, also had been suspicious of the crude drug department. McGloon said he had taken it up with Coster but the company's president had satisfied him that everything was all right.

Thompson began to dig into the company's records which revealed that the Smith company was being paid from the funds of McKesson and Robbins, not from the profits of the crude drug department. He was stunned to learn that "real cash," as he later called it, was leaving the company. The summer dragged on. After he had found that the Smith bank account was small and inactive, Thompson decided he had enough evidence to move. He went up to Fairfield to see Coster, but got nowhere. Coster kept circling the question of who and what was Smith and Company, Ltd. At lunch the following day Coster smiled when Thompson pressed the question.

"I want to smoke you out," he replied.

"What do you mean by that?" Thompson said.

"There's a conspiracy behind this—a conspiracy in the New York office."

"There's a conspiracy all right and it's right in your office," Thompson said with newborn courage. "In fact, it's in your treasury and I will let you smoke me out."

Coster got angry, accusing Thompson of a lack of faith. Then suddenly he said bluntly, "Don't you believe my crude drug department has any assets?"

"You're too smart not to have assets," Thompson replied, "but I must know."

When Thompson asked him why he had never insured such a

valuable store of crude drugs, Coster waved his hand and said, "Oh, the Smith company takes care of that."

After assuring Thompson he would discuss the "matter in detail" Coster left. On the next day, November 29, Thompson tried unsuccessfully to get in touch with Coster.

Meanwhile, Thompson received another shocking report. At his request Dun & Bradstreet contacted their Canadian office and the report they filed on Smith & Company was at odds with the report in Coster's desk. That one was plainly a forgery.

Thompson returned to Fairfield to find Coster ill with a heavy cold. He was obviously agitated as he paced up and down the room, croaking angry replies. Suddenly he turned and in a hoarse, cracked voice said, "If you're not careful I'll throw the whole company into receivership."

Thompson could only stare at him. "But you would be the biggest sufferer," he cried.

Coster turned his back on him to stare out of the window. Thompson, who felt his world beginning to crumble about him, took his hat and coat and left.

On December 5, Coster was still ailing. That evening Thompson, weary and heartsick, went home early. He had decided on a light supper and early bed. It was shortly after seven o'clock when a reporter from the *Wall Street Journal* called to ask about the receivership granted in Connecticut.

All Thompson could whisper was, "I don't know anything about it." Coster had made good his threat; he had filed a petition to throw the drug firm into receivership.

At about this time the stock list committee of the New York Stock Exchange was about to consider an application by McKesson and Robbins for permission to list three million dollars' worth of debenture bonds. Sidney Weinberg, a prominent Wall Street broker and director of many corporations, was having dinner at the Sherry-Netherland with several other prominent businessmen when he received a call from a partner in the law firm representing McKesson and Robbins. Weinberg was shocked when he hung up. The drug company's total stock and bond issues were valued at about forty million dollars. Its common stock, regarded as excellent in the Street, was selling at $7.50 a share. Weinberg knew that the federal court's action would postpone or cancel the debenture issue, might even suspend all trading in the drug company's securities.

Weinberg hurried to join Julian Thompson and the other Mc-

Kesson and Robbins executives. A feverish meeting followed. Calls to Fairfield went unanswered. Finally late that night Weinberg reached Coster.

"My God, this is a terrible thing, Donald," Weinberg said. "What is it all about?"

Coster protested. "I don't know anything about it. Here I'm living right in Connecticut, Sidney, and no one has told me a thing about it. We'll have to discuss this thing in the morning."

"You'll be in then, Donald?" Weinberg asked.

"Yes, I'll be at the office," Coster replied.

Weinberg, meanwhile, roused William O. Douglas, then head of the Securities and Exchange Commission to ask him to look into the strange happenings of the past afternoon. Douglas drowsily replied that he would, then went back to bed. Weinberg and the others, still bewildered, had a stiff drink, said good night and went home to bed. Few of them slept.

The legal machinery rolled on. The receivers took over, changing the locks on the plant. Coster appeared, still hoarse, but dapper, surprising everyone in the office. He opened a bottle of Scotch and downed a large tumblerful. Then he sat at his desk staring straight ahead, without saying a word. The whole office had a funereal atmosphere. That same day the Board of Governors of the Stock Exchange ordered suspension of trading of McKesson and Robbins securities. William O. Douglas in Washington broke into the act by sending a pair of agents to question Coster.

State, federal and local law enforcement agencies moved in from half a dozen different directions.

Investigators for the Attorney General's offices and Douglas's SEC agents quickly confirmed the suspicion that had lurked in Thompson's mind all that summer: there were no warehouses; they existed only on paper and in Coster's fertile imagination.

The private bank of Manning and Company was located at 1396 St. Catherine Street West in Montreal. It was nothing but a tiny office with one employee, a woman. She told investigators she had been hired in 1930 to simply sit in the office and send on to a Brooklyn address all mail she received. She also established several other mail drops throughout Canada with the help of friends and relatives. These friends and relatives would forward what mail was received to her; she in turn would send it on to Brooklyn. She received $28.00 a week.

Down the street, investigators found the offices of Smith & Company, Ltd. Instead of a huge Victorian-type office busy with its branches in the Empire, the Smith company also turned out to be little more than a mail drop presided over by a bored young stenographer, who just sat in the office for $7.00 a week. A week before they arrived the blonde told federal agents she had received a call from New York with instructions to burn the records.

Upon this disclosure, Chief Investigator O'Connell summoned me into his office.

"Dan, I want you to go out and make a complete and thorough investigation of this company in New York County. Here are copies of reports made up by the Stock Exchange people and the Attorney General's office. No one really knows where it will end . . . I suggest you start with one of the officers of the company . . ."

That afternoon I was on my way to Bridgeport where I had once scored a triumph in the Hines investigation; I wondered what lay before me in the Coster case.

Strangely enough it was a newspaperman, Arthur Kornfield, with whom I had become acquainted during my investigation of Hines, who started me on the right track in this investigation. It was only a few hours after I had arrived in Bridgeport that I called Kornfield.

"Who in town knows F. Donald Coster or any of the people in that scandal?" I asked.

There was a pause over the phone. "Well, Dan, the truth is I'm a close friend of George Dietrich."

"The treasurer of Coster's department?" I asked.

"Yes. Would you like to meet him?" he asked.

"I sure would," I replied and Art said he would call later. He called and said George was willing to see me. After dinner that evening he picked me up and drove me to George's home in Fairfield. It was a palatial place, set in the center of well-kept lawns and shrubs. Dietrich himself let us in. He was seemingly tired and worried.

We retired to his book-lined library, and for the next hour I listened in disbelief to the story he told of corruption and bribery of high government officials. He mentioned names—with amounts of bribes—of men I had thought were of impeccable integrity.

"How could you prove these charges?"

Then he said in that calm way of his, "F. Donald Coster called me over last week and I spent five hours alone with him checking and rechecking every item in his books and private papers."

"You mean he kept an account of all the bribes he paid," I asked.

"Exactly," he said. "Every penny for fixing and bribes and black-mail. He kept a black notebook."

"Where are the papers?" I asked.

"They are hidden in a secret drawer in the file in his study," he said.

"Can we get them tonight?" I asked.

He shook his head and smiled. "Not so fast, Mr. Danforth. First I want a deal with Dewey," he said.

I smiled back. "What kind of a deal, Mr. Dietrich? I can't make any, but I can send him your message."

"I want the indictment against me and the others squashed," he said.

"In return for what?" I asked.

"We will prove to Dewey every charge we made," he said, "by documentary evidence." He shook his head. "We have nothing to worry about from the government—but, frankly, we are afraid of your Mr. Dewey."

"Well, the government and our office have similar cases," I pointed out. "Why worry about one and not the other?"

"The New Deal will never allow this scandal to be dragged into the courts," he said bluntly. "It will involve leaders of the Democratic Party, even men who are close to Roosevelt."

"When do you want the answer?" I asked.

"As soon as possible," he said.

"Why are you in a hurry?" I asked.

"My brother has been carrying a gun in the pocket of his dressing gown for seven days," he said. "He's going to use it on himself if a certain thing happens."

"What is that?"

He said firmly. "That I cannot tell you, Mr. Danforth." He looked at Kornfield, who had sat through the interview in obvious bewilderment. "That's something I can't even tell my dear friend here."

I left in a daze, scarcely believing the shocking story which I had just heard. Outside in his car, Kornfield turned to me.

"How am I going to print it?"

"You can't," I said. "But if he gives us those papers we might be able to prove it."

We rode in silence. At the hotel we stopped for a cup of coffee. I don't think we said two words to each other; each of us was thinking of his own job; he had to print it; I had to prove it.

The next day I went back to New York City and told John

O'Connell the whole story. He just whistled softly and went out of the office. In five minutes he was back.

"The boss wants to see you, Dan—in a hurry," he said.

We hurried. Dewey listened and read my notes. He just kept shaking his head when I reeled off the names with the amounts paid to them in bribes.

"Get right back there, Dan, and get those papers," he said.

"What about his deal?" I asked.

Dewey said, "Tell Dietrich that if he cooperates, tells us everything he knows and proves it with those papers that I will inform the court of his cooperation and he can be assured of consideration. . . ." He turned to John. "What else can I tell him?"

When he asked me my opinion I told him I felt that Dietrich would cooperate. The next morning I was on the train back to Bridgeport. I registered at the Barnum Hotel at about noon. I was putting my things away when my phone rang. It was Kornfield.

"Dan," he said.

"Yes," I replied.

"If you're standing, sit down," he said. "This is a shocker."

I sat down.

"Coster killed himself a few minutes ago," he said. "Two marshals were at the front door."

When I gasped Kornfield said, "And there's more. Coster is really Philip Musica."

"Who the hell is Philip Musica?" I asked.

"A big-time swindler, bootlegger, what not," Kornfield said. "And get this: Dietrich is his brother. He has another one named Robert."

"How did it come out?" I asked.

"In New York," he said. "I believe the Attorney General's office found out."

I groaned. I knew what reception would be waiting for me back in the office. I could just hear John O'Connell's biting sarcasm. Dietrich, my "wonderful" contact, had made a fool out of me.

The rest of the day I tried to find George, but he was behind the closed doors of his brother's house arranging the funeral. That night he sent me word he was too grief-stricken to talk; I was to return the following week.

Back at the office I was given a biting criticism of my work, although I protested that the name of Musica meant nothing to me and I had no possible way of finding it out. Why George had not told me was unexplainable, but undoubtedly he would tell me his reasons when next I saw him.

The week passed slowly. While I waited I searched our files on the U. S. Hair Company case, but I found only an empty envelope from General Sessions Court. I checked at the Police Department headquarters for Musica's prints, where I learned the Attorney General's office had tried to locate his fingerprints but found them missing. Fortunately, a detective had recalled some old files in the Sheriff Street warehouse and spent a day digging into the dusty papers until he found an old print of Musica's. He compared the print with those taken of Coster at the time of his arrest and declared they were similar. That is how Musica was unmasked. I also spent a week reading all the old newspaper accounts of Musica's activities before World War I. By the time I left for Bridgeport I had an excellent background of the whole Musica family.

According to my original notes which I have kept in a vault all these years, I saw George Musica for the second time shortly after I returned to Bridgeport. We sat in his study for five hours, during which he outlined for me the first part of the story of bribery, corruption and thievery by which Musica had built his fabulous empire. This I have recounted above in the story of how Musica became the respected F. Donald Coster.

George's face was deeply lined and his hands shook. When I asked him for an explanation of his failure to tell me the whole story he held up his hands.

"Please, Mr. Danforth—I told you there was something pending which might change everything. And that was our real identity. Philip was so sure he would never be found out."

I pointed out, "But certainly you knew there were records—fingerprints."

He smiled sadly. "My brother paid more than $50,000 to have his records and fingerprints stolen from the Police Department headquarters and the files of the courts."

"Who stole them?" I asked.

He shrugged. "I don't know, but they were sold to him by ———" and he mentioned one of the largest law firms in the United States. Then he said, "I have promised myself to tell you everything, Mr. Danforth. I want Dewey to know because I feel the government will whitewash the case; we are all finished now. All I am living for is to expose the political rats who are responsible for sucking Philip's blood all these years. We are all guilty, Philip more than any of us, but these men who appear to be such good citizens and leaders of their country are as guilty as we. In fact, they are worse because they have taken advantage of their trust."

"That is not for me to say," I told him, "that is for a jury. All I want is proof. Let's start from the beginning. Where is that black book?"

"Gone," he said. "When we are at the funeral the police raided the house and took it." He smiled grimly. "But I have something here that should interest you." Then he gave me the suicide note in which Musica charged that many important New Dealers and Republicans were taking bribes.

The note read:

"George: The slush fund book, wherein by and with the consent of ———, checks for postage and other false expenses were drawn, cashed and turned over to you—I have burned. There was 200 left which I have used to live since they closed and attached my accounts. This money was used to pay off politicians.

"——— is a witness that I paid money to ———* to bribe the Atlanta officials for liquor permit money paid through ———** and rest for defending chain store legislation and all sorts of company dirty political work. No use involving outsiders. This is only to acknowledge you turned over to me books and cash as I ordered you to.

"I have also burned many records. I am sorry as they would prove what the truth really is—remember Simon's treachery and the others that has taken us through Hell.

[signed]   D. F. Coster

"You should also know from memory the larger amounts for political contributions both to Republicans and Democrats.***

"Assure them there are no hidden millions. The stockholders and bondholders got dividends we didn't make. The hole got bigger and the more they will investigate the more they will eat up the stockholders' money."

"Who has seen this?" I asked.

"I believe federal agents have the original," he said. "But I feel nothing will come of it. For example, why didn't they release this note?—they released the other two Philip wrote."

---

* Here Musica named a Republican leader, a Wall Street financier and a leader in the Democratic party.

** Another politician.

*** Here he again named prominent politicians of both parties in several states.

"Let's start from the beginning," I said.

He leaned back and rubbed his eyes. "You can expect to see me for at least a week," he said. "It's impossible to tell you of a lifetime in a few hours."

He first outlined the entire business swindle as I have described it, then described how Coster had them all change their names legally in 1920. This was done by paying $600 to a man in the Attorney General's office, who got a judge to sign the court approval. Then to assure favorable reports on his assets, he had phony Dun & Bradstreet papers made and also purchased special typewriters used by Dun and Bradstreet to type up his own reports, which gave a glowing picture of the nonexistent assets of this nonexistent corporations.

During Prohibition, George said, Philip fixed all of his bootlegging violations and patent infringements through a high government official who in turn introduced Coster to a man who later became an important American ambassador. The future ambassador, in turn, introduced Coster to a close friend and adviser of President Roosevelt. This man later became the key, George said, in the network of political corruption which protected Coster for years.

From George I also found out that Coster was plagued by blackmailers who were usually paid off by Benny Simon, a slight, soft-spoken man who was associated with Coster for years. The blackmail money came from what George called "Philip's slush fund," a small black tin box which Coster kept locked in his office desk. Coster had a unique way of furnishing money for the fund. He instituted a series of fraudulent patent infringements suits against his fake companies. When the suit was "settled" the money paid by McKesson and Robbins would go into the tin box.

I left late that night, my hand cramped from writing. Back in my hotel room, I stayed up most of the night drinking black coffee and nibbling on a ham sandwich as I wrote my first report. At dawn I tumbled into bed, to be awakened by the phone at 9:00 A.M. It was George.

"Come at once," he whispered, and hung up.

I hired a car and raced to his house. He met me at the door.

"Don't bother to come in, Mr. Danforth," he said. "I can't talk to you any more."

I was bewildered. "But why?" I asked.

"I have just received a call from the Attorney General's office in New York City," he said. "They know I was with you last night and they told me that if I told Danforth of Dewey's office any more they would throw the book at me. Good-by."

I was left on the porch staring at the closed door. Back at the hotel I called O'Connell and told him what had happened.

"Stay there, Dan, and make him talk," he said. "The boss wants the whole story."

That afternoon I was in my room lying on the bed, wondering how I could persuade George Musica to talk, when the phone rang. A man's voice told me to come to Musica's house at 11:00 P.M. that night but to be careful not to be seen and to come through the cellar. Then there was a click.

At 10:30 P.M. I hired a cab and had it stop four blocks from George's home. I pretended to walk up to another house until the driver vanished down the block. Then I turned back to George's house. I found the cellar door open and carefully went down the steps. I struck a match and for a moment I stood there, the match a tiny pool of light in the blackness, the pulse roaring in my ears. Suddenly a shaft of light appeared in the blackness as a door opened above me.

"Mr. Danforth?" a voice inquired softly. It was George.

"It's me," I said. I found the stairs and went up. But when I walked into the hallway George switched off the light and led me by the hand along the dark hall to his study. When he switched on a lamp there I could see that the blinds had been carefully drawn.

"I kept thinking about you," he said, "and after you left I decided to take a chance. You can come here every night at this time but for God's sake don't be seen. If you see a light in my study that will tell you I have visitors. Don't come in. Always use the cellar, which I will leave open."

I took out my notebook and he continued his story.

I left as the sun came up. In my notebook were the names of a Senator who had been paid $2,500 to modify sections of a bill Coster thought would hurt his drug business; a high official of the Attorney General's office who took $48,000 to fix Coster's liquor permits for his Maryland branch; several bankers who were aware that in 1931 Coster had kited, first $700,000, then $900,000 worth of checks so he could face the New York State auditors and finally a high federal official who George claimed had received $1,500,000 from Coster in a year and a half.

I also had the name of the go-between in the law firm who sold

Coster piecemeal-style all records which would identify him as Philip Musica.

"First they sold him his fingerprints," George said bitterly. "Then they sold him original indictments from General Sessions. Then again they came up with his bankruptcy petition, arraignment records and so on. Philip would get a call, then tell me: 'Get $10,000 from the slush fund. The thieves want more blood.' I would get the money and put it in a briefcase. Philip would take the train from New Haven even though he hated trains—and would meet this man in the lower level of Grand Central. The man would take the briefcase and leave without a word. Philip told me he never said two words to the man. For a few months he would have peace; then another call would come in. Sometimes he sent Benny Simon down to the station; other times he went himself."

The following day I decided to visit the Bridgeport police chief. I found him in his office in the local police headquarters. He was a stocky man with graying hair. He was anything but cooperative when I told him I was from Dewey's office.

"Why is Dewey interested?" he asked bluntly.

"He wants to find out if any crime has been committed in New York County," I told him.

He did give me some bits of information, but when I asked him in a casual way if he had staged a raid on the Coster home while the family was at the funeral, he stiffened.

"I was at the Coster house, but it wasn't any raid," he said.

As he was talking I happened to glance down at his desk. A pen caught my eye. On one side I could see gold lettering. Then I picked it up and read: "F. Donald Coster."

"Where did you get this?" I asked.

"Mrs. Coster gave it to me," he snapped. "Coster was a friend of mine. And that's all I'm going to tell you. Get out of this office."

He was obviously angry. There wasn't anything I could do but obey his wishes. If he didn't want to cooperate with our office that was his business.

From that day on my troubles began. Federal Bureau of Investigation agents dogged my footsteps. I realized I was being tailed by FBI agents when I visited a lead George had suggested.

When he admitted me he seemed surprised.

"Why, I saw your assistant last night, Mr. Danforth," he said.

"My assistant!" I exclaimed. "I have no assistant."

"He was a young, well dressed man of about twenty-five," he

said. "He said he was from the FBI and because you were working together he asked me to go over the story again. I did so while he took notes."

That put me on the alert. Later that same day I revisited another witness suggested by George. Again I found that FBI agents posing as my "assistants" had taken down the same story as the witness had given me.

This ridiculous situation of law enforcement agents competing with each other in a criminal investigation so infuriated me I took the next train to New York and had a conference with Frank Severance, one of Dewey's young assistants, who had been assigned to the Musica investigation.

Like myself, Frank was indignant and reported at once to Dewey. After listening to his report, Dewey got J. Edgar Hoover on the phone and told him that he had to get his agents to stop interfering with my witnesses. I don't know what Hoover's reply was, but I do know that Special Agent Foxworth, in charge of the New York office of the FBI, appeared at our office the next day to "explain" why their agents were tracking my witnesses.

Evidently Dewey's call had been effective. When I returned to Bridgeport I was no longer tailed, nor were my witnesses interviewed by my "assistants."

On June 12, 1939, I accompanied George to Lake Monatan to interview William Williamson, Philip's butler, who was dismissed after the swindler's suicide.

"Don't identify yourself as being from Dewey's office," George warned me. "He does not want to be connected with any investigation and will not talk if he knows who you are. I'll just say you're an old friend."

Williamson turned out to be a slender, calm man, who looked more like a retired broker than a gentleman's gentleman. When George brought Musica into the conversation, Williamson began talking freely. He told us that Musica had two guns which Mrs. Musica ordered him to hide. He said he placed the guns under a box wedged beneath the last step of the stairway in the garage, which led to the servants' quarters over the garage.

The next morning he said he was startled to see Musica walk to the garage and return with the two guns; he kept one in the pocket of his robe. Several times during the day, Williamson said, he watched while Musica took the gun from his pocket, stared at it for several minutes, then slowly replaced it.

"Once I told him, 'Please, sir, don't do anything rash . . . it's not hopeless.' "

But Musica shook his head. "It's all over," he said. "It's all over and I'm finished . . ."

While the national headlines recorded the progress of the many investigations racing each other for indictments and glory, the servant said Musica paced miles in his large living room.

Although he kept himself impeccable, he never dressed; he only wore a dark red robe, sagging a bit on the right side with the weight of the revolver.

Williamson also was a witness to the burning of vital papers by Musica. One whole day, from dawn to dusk, Musica sat on the floor of his Chinese study, sorting out papers. Those in one pile were put in a fireplace and burned. The others were placed in a worn briefcase.

Someone was in the room with Musica while the papers were being burned, Williamson said.

"I heard him say rather loudly—as if the man was across the room: 'You look over the rest of the papers . . . you know what should be saved as well as I do . . .' "

On the trip back to Bridgeport, George told me more about the politician friend of Roosevelt's who was the key in Musica's network of bribery.

"He was arrested and indicted for rum-running in Rhode Island," George said. "But he used his friends in Washington to square the case. One day a newspaper got hold of the story, but through a crooked editor he managed to fix the story."

"Oh, he had the story killed?" I asked.

George shook his head. "That would be the easy way," he said. "He paid a man to stand in for him and let the photographers take his picture. The newspapers used this man's picture on page one, along with the story of a fictitious man who had been connected with a rum-running outfit. It was a completely phony story and picture."

Another vital part of the investigation was Musica's luxurious yacht, the *Carolita,* because its log and guestbook could corroborate some of the things George had talked about; the visits of high government officials, some of whom had written letters to Musica, thanking him for the excellent time they had cruising and fishing.

The captain of the *Carolita* had completely vanished. I tried for days to find him, until we learned he had gone to Florida. But the yacht itself was still somewhere in the Sound. If the FBI agents hadn't visited it the log and guestbook would still be aboard. At one of our midnight meetings, George sketched the interior of the boat and gave me instructions exactly how to find the books.

I returned to the hotel before sunup and slept most of the day. I had my meals sent up and deliberately kept off the streets. When it grew dark I hired a cab and drove to the waterfront. At a fishing-tackle store I bought some line, worms and the usual gear, then hired a boat to do some night fishing.

It had been years since I had wet a line and had done some serious rowing, but I bent to the oars and pulled out into the night. It was a chilly, star-shot night and craft of all kinds were silhouetted in the pale light. One was the *Carolita*— but which one?

I don't like to recall that frustrating night. I rowed until my hands were rubbed raw. I drowned a small army of worms—I caught three fish without even trying—but I never found the Musica yacht. Twice I thought I had discovered her, but the name on the bow in the light of my flashlight always told me I was mistaken.

I stayed out for more than five hours before I gave up. I think I can say without exaggeration that I was one of the weariest and coldest men in Connecticut when I docked my craft, then headed back to my room.

The next midnight I cautiously opened the cellar door of George's home to step into the now familiar darkness. George was there to meet me and we again tiptoed down the darkened hall to his study.

This night he detailed for me the activities of one of the President's closest friends, who had taken advantage of his position to put through many of Coster's deals.

"Two years ago Philip informed him he was getting too expensive," George said. "He wrote a letter in reply in which he tried to justify his expensive hire. In his letter to us he listed many of the fixes he had put through with Senators and other high officials."

"That letter could hang him," I said.

George smiled. "Sure it would—if you can get it from them."

"Who has it?" I asked.

"I think the federal people," he said. "If they have it I don't think they're going to give this out."

We continued to meet late at night. Each time George laboriously went over his notes. At the end of the morning, although we were both weary, he would insist I review what he had given me for the sake of accuracy.

What was emerging was a fantastic picture of official corruption, unrivaled in my experience. Not a night passed that some man in a high place was not implicated in a shadowy deal or an outright bribe. Legally, this was only one man's word, but the evidence that could corroborate George's charges did exist—in the black book, the memoranda, the checks, the self-incriminating letters that had been confiscated by the government agents.

In the late thirties, George said, Musica sensed the rumblings of war across the sea. He decided it was time to move in for a big profit, so he contacted Benny Simon. His plan was to buy up as much arms as possible in this country, then sell them for a vast profit. In the spring of 1937 he made an offer to sell arms to Mexico. In fact, he even went as far as drawing up a contract for 100,000 .30-caliber rifles made for the United States Army after World War I, to a "non-belligerent consignee." The contract was drawn up between Mc-Kesson and Robbins and a fictitious English company. The consignee was China.

George claimed that mixed up in this deal were a high official close to the President, and a well-known Boston businessman. But the deal fell through.

George was particularly bitter about Bernard Simon. He insisted the little man had extracted blackmail money from his brother on many occasions. Once he persuaded Musica to pay $10,000 demanded by another blackmailer but kept the money himself. That particular scoundrel couldn't collect it; he had been dead a year and a half.

In 1937, George went on, Simon notified Musica that Joseph Brandino, his former partner, was making plans to kidnap him for $100,000 ransom. Simon insisted he could pay off Brandino for $2,500. Philip told George in Italian, "They want more blood," and instructed him to get the money.

The tin box gave up $2,500. George gave the money to Philip, who took a cab to New Haven, then a train to New York City. Meanwhile, another brother, Robert, had hired two rooms at the then Pennsylvania Hotel, under the name of Robert Dietrich. George arrived later and witnessed the payoff.

At one of our midnight meetings, George gave me the name of a prominent Connecticut state physician, the model of propriety, who was involved in Musica's affairs.

The next day I paid a visit to the doctor's fashionable office. I told him frankly what I knew. He sat there, his face growing dark red.

"I understand you have some correspondence from Musica," I said. "May I read it?"

"I have no such letters," he said.

"I have information that you do," I persisted.

"I don't give a damn what your information says," he snapped. "I haven't any such letters."

He was telling the truth. Later I found out from a maid that on the day of Musica's suicide he had been seen burning quite a number of letters which he had hastily removed from a private desk.

After my interview with this uncooperative physician, I followed a tip I had received from one of the firm's officials and talked to Leon A. Danco, head of McKesson & Robbins' cosmetic division.

Danco, a personable and alert executive, had an amazing story to tell. Four years before the scandal broke he had conducted his own investigation into Coster's affairs. When he had obtained evidence pointing to the existence of a swindle of enormous proportions, he turned it over to the U. S. Attorney's office, together with Coster's fingerprints, which he had obtained by a unique trick. But the federal prosecutor never summoned Coster for questioning. Furthermore, so far as is known, no matching fingerprints were found in the federal files, although Coster's prints should have been there under the Musica name.

After questioning Danco myself, I hurried him to our office, where he told his incredible story to Assistant District Attorney Frank Severance. Francis Weisberg, our stenographer, made an official report of the questioning.

Here are excerpts from this hitherto unpublished report:

Q. What papers did you turn over to the U. S. Attorney's office?

A. My attorney wrote two letters outlining the investigation and our belief. After that the U. S. Attorney made a copy of our conversation.

Q. Have you got a copy of that?

A. Yes, I have, and I went to see the head of the narcotics division for New York at the Custom House.

Q. You gave him [U. S. Attorney] the facts but you did not give him any particular documents?

A. No, sir. I couldn't take a document out of the file without an accountant.

Q. Didn't you tell me when you first came in that there was a rumor that he had formerly been a bootlegger?

A. Yes, that's right.

Q. And you thought it was a good idea to get his fingerprints?

A. That was a suggestion; either I got it from my attorney or the U. S. Attorney's office.

Q. The request for fingerprints was made after you had a conference with the U. S. Attorney's office?

A. That's right.

Q. Tell me the details whereby you obtained Coster's fingerprints.

A. I got a piece of untouched cardboard, white cardboard, to which is attached a drawing . . . for his [Coster's] approval and made certain that the bottom part of this piece of cardboard had not been soiled or touched with my own fingers. Taking it by the top I handed it to Coster in his own office in Bridgeport in such a manner that he was forced to take it and put his fingers, at least his thumbs, on the bottom part of this piece of board. We discussed the drawing together and when he handed it back to me I made certain that I took it by the top part which already had my fingerprints on it before, and when I got back to my office I cut with scissors the part that had been touched by Coster, wrapped it in cellophane and mailed it or delivered it personally to my attorney, I don't remember which way. My understanding is that those fingerprints were compared in Washington and that no evidence or any comparison was found with any in the file.

Q. You turned it over to your attorney and he told you he turned it over to whom?

A. The U. S. Attorney's office.

Q. And subsequently he told you that the investigation had not revealed that the prints you had submitted were on record?

A. That's right.

Q. Now, did you or your attorney make any attempt to find out whether or not there was a file in the office of the U. S. Attorney for the Eastern District of New York containing your communications of 1934 and memos of your investigation of 1934?

A. He advised me that there was no file available of any investigation of 1934 in the Eastern District.

Q. Do you have copies of the letters that were sent to the U. S. Attorney?

A. Yes.

Q. By your attorney?

A. Yes, sir.

Q. Do you have a copy of the memorandum taken of your conversation with the U. S. Attorney?

A. Yes, sir.

I repeat: this clear tip, this important lead, fortified by real evidence, could have broken this enormous fraud years before it came to light, had a thorough investigation then been conducted.

George also gave me the name of a state trooper stationed in Connecticut who had a hint of Musica's real identity and apparently had been blackmailing the swindler. He was arrogant and insulting when I interviewed him, and of course denied knowing anything. I hadn't any proof of his criminal acts, but because of his sneers and insults I decided to let him simmer on the griddle for a while.

"Of course you'll be subpoenaed for the grand jury," I told him.

"I'll make you and Dewey look like fools," he snapped.

"Think so?" I said.

He boasted, "I know so."

I paused at his front door. "I wonder how you're going to explain those yearly trips to Europe?" I said. "You, your wife and kids, and even a grandmother, on your salary?"

I slammed the door. I know he didn't sleep many nights. He tried several times to get me on the phone but I hung up on him. He was no longer arrogant; now he was pleading.

Week after week this story of crime and corruption continued. Twice a week I returned to New York to give Dewey my reports. Only Frank Severance and I knew what I was doing or what was in my reports.

I wondered many times as I watched the countryside slip past, what the man next to me would say if I suddenly named five of the country's leaders and told him I had just left a man who swore they had taken bribes . . .

After about our seventh meeting, I returned to New York. At a very private conference I outlined to Dewey all that George had told me. Of course the material was dynamite politically, but legally the only violations came under federal laws not the laws of New

York County. Dewey saw to it that the information in my reports
was funneled to the proper agencies in Washington.

During one of my meetings with George Musica, he told me Benny
Simon had called to make an appointment. "He wants some money,"
he said.

"When is your appointment?" I asked.

"Tomorrow night at eight," he said.

"Fine," I told him. "We'll put him on tape. I'll go down to New
York, pick up a dictaphone and record the conversation."

I hurried back to the office, obtained the wire, microphone and
recording device, and returned to Bridgeport. It was a difficult room
to bug. The microphone was hidden in a lamp. I had to run the wire
all around the molding of the room, down the hall and into the basement, where I set up shop behind a pile of coal.

Early the next day I slipped into the house to take up my post
behind the coal. The house was tomb-quiet. Occasionally I could
hear a footfall above or a car passing outside. The light in the
cellar faded into blackness. I couldn't do much more than just sit
there; a light might have alerted Simon.

A few minutes after eight the doorbell rang. I could hear George
walking down the hall, opening the door, then returning to his study,
followed by another man.

Then the dictaphone came to life.

According to my original notes, this dialogue took place:

Simon: "Windy out tonight."
George: "Yes, it is."
Simon: "I'm sorry it came out [Musica's real name and crim-
inal record]."
George: "Philip is dead—it doesn't matter now."
Simon: "I want to help all I can."
George: "How can you help me?"
Simon: "How about a fix in Dewey's office?"
George: "You can do that?"
Simon: "Maybe I can reach someone in his office. Nothing much
can happen to you with the New Deal boys but it's that
little mustached bastard you have to worry about."
George: "There's no more money, Benny."
Simon: "The rest of you people made money—why not me?"
George: "The payments stop—as of now."
Simon: "Don't be sure."

George: "No more blood money. Brandino bled my brother for years."

Simon: "I got paid for services rendered."

George: "I don't need your help."

Simon: "You will before you're through. My friend can take care of the whole case."

George: "I'm not worried about Dewey's office."

Simon: "Why not?"

George: "Anything that took place took place outside of New York County."

Simon: "Don't be so sure, George. You'll need my help . . ."

George: "No more money, Benny. I'm through paying. My brother is dead. All I want now is to see those crooked politicians and blackmailers who bled my brother all these years behind bars. Now, good night."

There was more small talk, then I could hear the footsteps crossing the room, the opening of the door, the steps going down the hall. The front door opened and closed. The gears of a car could be heard shifting, then driving away. Upstairs in the study I found George, gray-faced, looking tired and worn, seated in the large leather chair he liked, staring down at the floor.

At that moment I felt genuinely sorry for the man. I believe he suffered for his sins, not in the jail to which he would be sentenced, but in those days following his brother's suicide. He who had been closest to his brother now bore the blame for his crimes.

I coiled the wire and we sat for a moment in silence. Then, as if he wore an anvil on his shoulders, George slowly straightened up in the chair.

"You heard it?" he asked in a hollow voice.

"I have it all," I said.

"Vulture," he said bitterly. "Nothing but a vulture."

"The law will eventually take care of Mr. Simon, George," I said.

He stood up. "I'm sorry," he said. "I don't feel up to talking any more tonight. I'll see you out."

"I'll go by the cellar," I said.

"No," he said firmly, "tonight you'll go out the front door."

At the front door he shook hands, then growled in a bitter way "The hell with them—let them know I'm telling Dewey the whole story."

I walked down the path. When I looked back he was standing in the doorway.

He had switched on the lights.

Apparently George's bravado failed or Benny Simon's threats made him uneasy. A message was sent to me to meet George at a hunting lodge about twenty-five miles from Bridgeport. I hired a car, and after a very difficult time, finally located the lodge. It was a fairly large place with an open fireplace, two bedrooms and bath.

"One day Philip said he wanted a hunting lodge," George said wryly. "He bought this place but never set foot in it. He never fired a gun nor had the slightest inclination to go hunting. The nearest he came to athletics was to throw a line over the side of the *Carolita* and fish."

"What didn't bore him?" I asked.

"Making money," was the prompt reply.

I said, "Stealing money, you mean."

"I guess you're right there," he said.

We had three meetings at this lodge, during which George continued to outline and document as much as possible the endless stories of blackmail and official corruption.

The lodge rendezvous was abandoned after I found I was being tailed by a light blue car. I checked the license plates with our office and found the car belonged to a local detective.

When I went to police headquarters to complain they told me to leave.

The meetings were then shifted to Meadowbrook, the rambling, 12-room house three miles from Westbury, which Philip Musica had bought for his mother and sisters. His mother was a silent woman with silvery hair; the sisters appeared to be recluses. They wore old-fashioned dresses and disappeared the moment George issued some orders in Italian. We met twice at Westbury before George had exhausted his story.

Eventually the three Musica brothers, George, Robert, and Arthur —were indicted for conspiracy and fraud, to which they pleaded guilty. George received two and a half years in prison, Arthur, three, Robert, one and a half. Mrs. Coster's brothers, Leonard and John Jenkins, also pleaded guilty to conspiracy charges. John was sentenced to a year and a day, Leonard received a suspended sentence.

Benny Simon also was indicted, and pleaded guilty. He received a three-year term. McGloon, the company's controller, was found guilty after a long trial by a jury who thought he should have been suspicious enough of Coster's juggling of the books to warn the SEC. He was sentenced to a year and a day and was fined $5,000.

As I have pointed out the material I received from George did not come within our jurisdiction. However, after I had completed my investigation and had made my final report, Dewey traveled to Washington where he conferred with J. Edgar Hoover, turning over to him the charges George Musica had made to me against the high government official.

Down through the years, whenever I had the chance, I tried to keep in touch with the Musicas, more out of curiosity than anything else. After their prison terms had been served, George, Robert, and Arthur drifted into various businesses. Arthur and Robert worked in defense plants during World War II, while George engaged in real estate. He died in 1947. Assunta, his mother, died in 1941, while her sons were in prison. One sister died and the other, who still wore old-fashioned attire, sold the Westbury house. She, too, dropped out of sight. Mrs. Coster, or Musica, remarried in 1947. Julian Thompson died a few months after the close of the Attorney General's investigation.

On March 19, 1939, Joseph Brandino, his brother John and sister Mary were indicted for conspiracy, extortion and blackmail by Special Prosecutor John Harlan Amen's extraordinary grand jury. Amen, a former federal racket-buster, had sent such underworld figures as Lepke, Gurrah and Joe "Socks" Lanza to jail, and was appointed by Governor Lehman to clean up Brooklyn's corruption.

However, in the winter of 1942 the indictments which had been transferred to the Kings County District Attorney's office, were dismissed because of insufficient evidence. But the law wasn't finished with Brandino. It wasn't long after the indictment had been dismissed that the federal agents raided his Brooklyn home and found him operating a 750-gallon still. He was sentenced to a year and four months in prison and fined $1,100.

I have always wondered what would have happened, had Philip Musica, that swindling genius, turned his talents to a legitimate enterprise.

7. THE CARDBOARD HITLER AND THE BUND: FRITZ KUHN

IN 1935 Adolf Hitler, the former paper-hanger, was the German Fuehrer, moving closer to his date with an infamous destiny which would plunge the world into the terror of World War II. To most Americans he was a sight made familiar by the newspapers and newsreels, as hands on hips he shouted into the microphone behind the bullet-proof glass shield his fanatical threats to the world, while hundreds of thousands of Germans roared "Heil . . . Sieg Heil . . ." in response to his declaration that their savage world would last a thousand years.

Here in America, the "heils" echoed in the barrooms of Yorkville, the beer stubes of Queens and in northern New Jersey, where the German-American Bund gathered to honor the Fuehrer of the new Germany. Like their Storm Trooper brothers, they swaggered about, cursing Jews and Catholics, swilling beer and stabbing the air with upraised right arms as they "heiled" their leader: Fritz Kuhn.

Kuhn, a burly, belligerent man with cold blue eyes, was the principal exponent in this country of Nazi principles. He was the organizer of the German-American Bund, whose members dressed in blue-gray Storm Trooper uniforms, marched under a swastika banner and gave the Nazi salute.

In New York at carefully staged rallies in Madison Square Garden, Kuhn, surrounded by a ring of tough bodyguards, would stalk down the aisle in isolated splendor under a solitary searchlight, mount the stage and roar out his threats and predictions in a guttural German. These meetings were repeated in many parts of New York and New Jersey.

Details of Kuhn's background were meager. He was born in Munich in 1898 of middle-class parents. He was said to have been a lieutenant in a German machine-gun outfit in World War I. His followers insisted he was among the original members who took part in the Munich "beer hall putsch," which was generally associated with the rise of Hitler and his party. The story was fictional; Hitler always honored the members of his original gang and Kuhn was never on the list.

Kuhn had studied chemistry in Germany and in the twenties went to Mexico to establish some chemical companies, all of which failed. In 1926 he entered the United States, worked for a time in a Ford plant, then became an American citizen. In 1933 he organized the Bund, whose members were made up of American citizens of German extraction interested in showing their support of the Nazi movement in Germany. Kuhn tried to take over the old-line German-American societies but was rebuffed. It has been said but never proven that Kuhn was only a front for such other Bund leaders as Heinz Spanknoeble and Fritz Gissibi.

The reaction against the Bund in the New York area was violent; whenever the Bund had a rally it took a small army of policemen to maintain order. Kuhn and his followers were constantly picketed. Newspapers denounced him editorially and sent reporters to infiltrate the Bund and write exposés of Kuhn's goal, which he boastfully admitted was to be "dictator of the United States."

Kuhn and his family lived in Jackson Heights, Queens; the goose-stepping and "heiling" of his gang made it necessary to maintain a 24-hour guard in front of his house. At the headquarters of the Bund on East 85th Street, Kuhn could be seen almost every day, his feet propped up on the desk, a picture of Hitler glaring down at him, while he bossed a small office force which enrolled new followers and collected dues.

Under the Constitution of the United States, Kuhn could not be silenced until war was formally declared and his status became a matter for the federal agencies. But before the FBI could step in, we grabbed him—not for treason but for common thievery.

One day not long after photographs of thousands of so-called citizens "heiling" and roaring out Nazi songs had appeared in every New York paper, we held our usual conference with Dewey on active investigations. On the way up to his office, John O'Connell threw aside his tabloid which had Kuhn's arrogant face on page one.

"I'd like to get that pig," he said.

"Let's ask the boss if we can look into him," Tom Fay said.

"I'll think about it," John replied.

After the other business had been disposed of, O'Connell took up the matter of the Bund with Dewey.

Dewey nodded. "Let's do some work on Kuhn," he said, "and see what we come up with."

That morning I, with several others, started out for Yorkville, to begin the rounds of German bars and restaurants, just to listen. It didn't take long to find out that a large percentage of Yorkville was pro-Kuhn and Hitler, but there was also a small hard core of Yorkville residents who hated Kuhn and his type. It was through them that we gradually began to infiltrate into the Bund. We attended meetings and picnics in New Jersey, and more than once I had to shout and cheer Kuhn, although it almost turned my stomach.

I found out that he was a glutton, a hard drinker and notorious with women. He spent a great deal of money, so much that we began to get suspicious. Gradually we learned of some of the members of the Bund who didn't like what was going on. After circling around them for some weeks contacting neighbors, tradespeople and so on to learn more about them, we hit them with a proposition that they help us.

It wasn't long before we knew the evidence against Kuhn lay not in his "heiling" and Storm Troopers, but in the books and ledgers of the Bund. After a conference with Dewey and O'Connell, a raid was made on the Bund headquarters.

It was a very quiet raid; no doors were kicked in, no guns drawn. An elderly office manager and a frightened young bookkeeper gladly turned over all their books in answer to our subpoena. Our accountants did a superb job and before long we had evidence that Kuhn had stolen at least $2,000 from the treasury of the Bund.

After we took his books we had him under 24-hour surveillance—there were rumors he was ready to skip to Mexico, then Germany—and within an hour after a grand jury had indicted him on sixteen counts of grand larceny we had him in the office.

His face and bull-neck a brick red, he kept shouting, "I am being politically persecuted," but we ignored him and took him down to the Oak Street precinct, where he was booked.

"Hey, Fritzie, why don't you ask Adolf for some help?" a man called out as we walked up the precinct steps.

"Swine," he grunted.

After Kuhn was released on bail, we continued to look into his activities, especially those concerning the women with whom he had associated. From an informant we received information that Fritzie's favorite girl friend was a Miss Virginia Cogswell, the Miss America of 1921, known as "The Georgia Peach."

What interested us more than anything about Miss Cogswell, was that she was reported to own a diary which gave a day-by-day account of the activities of Kuhn. If this were true, the diary might be an important part of the state's case, perhaps even the key to other crimes. My assignment was to find Miss Cogswell in Atlanta, Georgia, and persuade her to come to New York with her diary.

It was a few days before Memorial Day when I arrived in Atlanta. A telephone book gave me Miss Cogswell's address and I took a cab there. She lived in a beautiful pre-Civil War mansion, complete with white pillars and a garden.

A rather faded brunette, who surely had once been a beautiful girl, answered the doorbell.

"Miss Cogswell?" I asked.

"I am Virginia Cogswell," she said. "Who are you?"

"Harold R. Danforth, from District Attorney Dewey's office in New York City," I said.

She smiled. "I guess you're on the Kuhn case."

"As a matter of fact I am," I said. "May I come in?"

"Please do," she said, and showed me in.

We went into a spacious living room and when she sat down on the sofa she said, "Now, what can I do for you, Mr. Danforth?"

"We are interested in obtaining your cooperation," I said. "We understand you were friendly with Kuhn."

"Oh, Fritzie and I were old friends," she said.

"We also understand you have a diary?" I asked cautiously.

She smiled. "I have."

"Would you bring it to New York?" I asked.

Her big brown eyes opened real wide. "Well, Fritzie is an enemy of our country, isn't he?"

"I'd say he is," I said.

"Well, as for the diary . . ." she hesitated. "Will you let me think it over and give you my answer tomorrow, Mr. Danforth?"

"Dan," I said, turning on the charm.

"Dan," she repeated, and gave me a big smile. "Until tomorrow."

The next morning bright and early I was on the porch ringing the bell. Miss Cogswell opened the door to show me in.

Back in the living-room she said, "I've slept on the idea and I'll come to New York with the diary."

"Fine," I said. "When can we leave?"

She smiled and held up a hand. "Not so fast, Mr. Danforth. Mr. Dewey will have to pay my expenses to New York . . ."

"How much will that be?" I asked.

"One hundred and fifty a week," she said.

I gulped. "I'll have to clear that with the office," I said.

The big brown eyes opened wide. "Why, of course, Danny. Now will you have some tea?"

After tea I rushed back to the hotel to call the office. John O'Connell groaned, but said, "Okay, tell her we'll pay her expenses. But get that diary."

I returned that afternoon and told Virginia—it was now Virginia and Danny—that the office had okayed the expenses. She smiled and brought out a typewritten paper.

"What's this?" I asked.

"Oh, the contract," she said, innocent as a lamb. "Even *you* prosecutors can forget things."

"Well," I said, "I'll have to check with the office."

"Of course, Danny," she said. "Will you have some lunch?"

I had lunch, then raced back to the hotel. Over the phone John O'Connell roared: "A contract! What does she think we are—an actor's agency!"

"Look, John," I said. "That's what she wants. No contract, no diary."

O'Connell said a few ungentlemanly things, then told me to call back. On the next call he said, "Okay, sign that contract but get her to New York fast."

That night I rang her bell again. "How nice, Danny," she said. "Three visits in one day."

"The office said I could sign the contract," I said. "But we have to take off tomorrow."

"I'll be ready," she said. "Won't you step in and have a drink?"

"I'm sorry, Virginia," I said. "I have to make out some reports. I'll pick you up first thing in the morning."

The brown eyes opened wide. "Fine, Danny. I'll see you in the morning."

The next morning I signed the damn "contract," as she called the slip of paper, and we caught the first plane for New York. I noticed the city seemed unusually quiet when we rode in from the airport, but I didn't realize why until after I had signed Miss Cogswell in at the New Yorker Hotel late that afternoon. We were on the eve of a three-day holiday.

For a moment it bothered me until I realized that O'Connell had told me in my last call to set up a 24-hour guard for her when we arrived. Actually the idea of her being harmed wasn't too far-fetched. A number of Hitler fanatics still roamed about Yorkville and some of our witnesses against Kuhn had received threats they would be killed if they testified. In fact, one of our witnesses was Mayor La Guardia, who had received a death threat. They all might have been from crackpots, but no prosecutor takes chances on the safety of his witnesses.

"I'll have some policewomen over here in a jiffy," I told her.

Ten phone calls later I realized that due to the holiday there just weren't any matrons or policewomen to be had; those on duty were in jails or detention pens or special assignments. I shuddered to think what Virginia would say if I suggested she spend the hot, three-day holiday in jail . . .

There was only one thing to do; check in the hotel and guard her myself.

When I told her of my plans she giggled. "To tell you the truth, Danny," she said, "I'd rather have you guard me than some old policewoman . . ."

It would be an understatement to say I was becoming somewhat apprehensive about this assignment.

I checked in, managing to get a room just two doors from her room. After dinner I escorted her to her room. Back in my room I was just taking off my shoes when the phone rang.

"Danny?" a soft voice asked.

"This is Danforth, Virginia," I said. "Everything all right?"

"I feel better, now that you're around," she said.

"That's fine—sleep tight," I said.

The phone rang many times that night; Virginia, it seemed, just couldn't sleep. It got so I sat by the window watching the lights of Manhattan, and picking up the phone to assure her she was well guarded, that no Nazis would be breaking down her door.

I was rather hollow-eyed when we had breakfast; she was as chipper as a spring swallow.

"Tonight we'll go to a night club," she said briskly.

"Night club!" I said. "We can't do that. You'll be recognized!"

"We're going to a night club," she said firmly.

We argued over breakfast but she was adamant. Finally I gave in and settled for a small Greenwich Village spot. The rest of the day I had to escort her on a tour of the closed shops, window shopping. By night I was half dead, but Virginia was full of life.

I soon found she was no stranger to Scotch and she loved to

dance. We closed the night club and when we arrived back at the hotel she was still raring to go. Now I put my foot down; not even for Tom Dewey would I take her to an after-hour club for more drinks and more dancing. I had had it. She was put out, but went upstairs.

I was asleep before I reached the pillow. Once the phone rang, and half asleep I answered it.

"Danny . . . ?"

I could have strangled her, but she *was* a potential witness.

"Yes, Virginia . . ."

"I just wanted to make sure you were guarding me," she said. "Good night."

"Good night," I said, and fell into a sleep so deep that even the damn phone couldn't rouse me. Virginia, at breakfast, was a bit peeved. She couldn't get me during the night, but I finally smoothed her ruffled feathers. Again we went on a tour of shops and again she danced my feet off that night. I was not only tired but somewhat jittery when we were in the club. I almost fell over when two waiters began speaking in German behind my chair; I couldn't get her out of there fast enough.

Monday was the last day of the long weekend, one of the longest of my life. On Tuesday morning, weary but triumphant, I brought her down to a conference with the assistants working on the case. I thought I was finished, but at noon, after the long conference, O'Connell ordered me to take her on a tour of apartment hunting. We canvassed several places from Greenwich Village to the Central Park West area, with the rental price going higher and higher with each visit. Finally she settled for a suite in the Park Central, complete with sunken living room.

Late that afternoon we returned to the D.A.'s office, where she insisted upon a police guard. O'Connell assigned her six detectives and three policewomen on a 24-hour basis. When she left she had more guards than the President.

"Good-by, Danny," she said.

"Good-by, Virginia," I replied.

After she left O'Connell gave me a look. "Danny, eh?"

I ignored him but I noticed that during the afternoon whenever a call came for me, he would say innocently, "Just a minute and I'll get Danny . . . Danny, it's for you . . ."

The others took it up with winks and sly looks. But I made believe I just didn't hear them.

Two days later O'Connell called me in. He was scowling.

"Take a cab up to the Park Central and see Cogswell. She's unhappy."

I began, "I just received a call from an informant on the waterfront . . ."

John held up his hand. "Go up to the Park Central and see . . ."

Well, it was a good try, I told myself, as I ran for a cab. When I arrived she was in tears. Now there were too many cops around her.

"But *you* asked for protection," I pointed out.

She said stubbornly, "There are too many cops . . . they make me nervous . . ."

Miss Cogswell wasn't the only one with complaints. On the way out two of the policewomen politely asked to be relieved of their assignments. When I asked why they rolled their eyes upward.

The following day Dewey sent word he wanted her to come down with the diary. From what I could gather from the assistants, she had been feeding them information piecemeal.

I was in the room when Virginia swept into Dewey's office. After some small talk the subject of the diary came up.

"I'll bring it in tomorrow," she said.

"That's fine, Miss Cogswell," Dewey began, but Virginia broke in, "I have a complaint, Mr. Dewey."

"Yes, ma'am," Dewey said politely.

"I don't mind having policemen during the day," she said, "but I don't want them at night."

"You must be guarded at night, ma'am," Dewey said. "In fact, *you* asked for it."

She said, "I don't mind them in the daytime, Mr. Dewey, but at night can't I have Danny?"

In the deep silence Dewey slowly turned to where I was sitting. He slid his heavy-rimmed glasses down on the bridge of his nose to stare over them at me. Then he swung about to Virginia.

I wondered how I could get the floor to open up and swallow me. "No," he said softly. "I don't think that can be arranged."

Virginia was disappointed but finally calmed down.

"I have another complaint," she said.

Dewey looked tired. "Yes, ma'am."

"A year ago I left some baggage in the Pennsylvania for an unpaid bill. Could you get it for me?"

Dewey made a note. "We'll do what we can," he said. Then to O'Connell: "Why don't you send *Danny* up there, John?"

I was sure every damn one of them was just busting and I knew my face was flaming.

On the way out Johnny said slyly, "You be sure and check that hotel, Danny . . ."

Actually it was this assignment that gave us a clue into Virginia's rather lurid past. In the dusty packages I found her scrapbooks with accounts of nine marriages; Virginia, it appeared, was one of the most married women in America. I could just see her under a biting cross-examination. Obviously her credibility as a state's witness wasn't too good.

I returned to the office with the information, which we checked out. All of it was true. Then we got another shock in the form of a bill from a woman doctor who had been called in every night. The "injections" turned out to be drugs.

In an interview the following day she confirmed our suspicions, then admitted she had had *three* diaries; one she had sold to a government agency, the other to Congressman Dickstein, then hot on the trail of American Nazi groups.

"How much did you sell it for to Dickstein?" I asked.

She opened her purse to take out a cancelled check. "He gave me a $2,000 check," she said sadly, "but it bounced."

The existence of three diaries completely destroyed the credibility of Virginia as a state's witness. When she was informed she wasn't going to be used, she stormed down to Dewey's office, waving the "contract" I had signed calling for $150 in expenses. This, she said, included dresses, hats, shoes and so on. Dewey was mad as a hornet, but I pointed out to him I was only acting under orders from the office.

To smooth things over, I went back to the Park Central to retrieve my contract from Virginia. I persuaded her to return it after I had made her realize the seriousness of the case. I confess I had to do a little flag-waving that afternoon.

On November 29, 1939, Kuhn was found guilty of forgery and grand larceny for stealing money from the Bund. General Sessions Judge James G. Wallace sentenced him to two and a half to five years in state prison. Sent to Sing Sing, Kuhn was transferred to the toughest of New York State's prisons, Clinton Prison at Dannemora. He was later released, but his citizenship was taken from him on the grounds that he had obtained it through fraud. In 1945 he was deported to Germany, escaped from Dachau in 1948 and died unwept and unknown in 1951. He was fifty-five years old. His name was so obscure to the postwar generation that his passing was not mentioned in the German press.

But it was a long, long time before John O'Connell and the boys in the office stopped calling me "Danny" or "Danny boy."

8. TALK AND YOU'RE DEAD: THE WATERFRONT

IN 1940 racketeering on the waterfront had increased so much that Dewey ordered the office to begin an all-out war against the loan-sharks, the crooked bosses who collected kickbacks, narcotics peddlers and the gun-for-hire thugs.

Fortunately, before we could begin, a longshoreman who had been victimized so badly by a moneylender that he would be paying off his debt for years came in to the office and gave us a complete picture of the conditions existing along New York's waterfront. O'Connell turned the informer over to me and for a whole day I listened and made notes. These notes I transcribed into a report which O'Connell, then Dewey, read. The following day O'Connell called me into his office.

"Good-by, Dan," he said.

"Where now?" I asked.

"The waterfront," he said. "Don't contact the office except in case of emergency. I'd suggest Tuesday or Thursday in the waiting room of the Staten Island ferryhouse to turn over your reports and collect your pay."

We shook hands. John said there would be no limit to the investigation; Dewey wanted the waterfront cleaned up.

I went home and reverted back to the character of Dan O'Brien, the thug from Boston. But now instead of being a bordello owner as I had been in the Luciano investigation, I had to become a longshoreman. I knew some of the records of brutality and violence of some of the hoodlums bossing the waterfront, and I did not intend to make any mistake. My background had to be flawless.

I went home for a few days' rest, saw Mother and the new roses, then went to Boston and its waterfront. I hung around the area for a few weeks, soaking up the atmosphere, names of the bosses and their nicknames, possible police records, union factions at war, the local loan-sharks and the bosses of the shape-up, that notorious traditional arrangement which causes a man's livelihood to depend on how much he can pay off and the whim of the boss of the pier.

151

It's simply this: You stand around with the other men, while the hiring boss looks you all over. He picks the men he wants and the rest of the men must wait for the next shape-up. If the boss doesn't like you, you'll never get hired.

When I returned to New York I had a good working knowledge of how a Boston longshoreman works, eats, sleeps and who he likes and doesn't like. I even had a card admitting me to a waterfront bawdy-house. The information wasn't hard to get, nor the card; a free hand at the bar, a willingness to listen are a considerable help.

Not only mentally but physically I had to play the part of Dan O'Brien. I could not carry even a hint of my real identification. Back on South Street, below the Fulton Fish Market, I found the old second-hand clothes store and once again bought a used pair of washed-out dungarees, heavy shoes, pea coat, flannel shirt. I still had my old baling hook. The only part of the disguise I didn't like was smoking cigarettes. I am a habitual cigar smoker. I like the long panatelas. But they belong with brandy and after-dinner talk and certainly would stand out among the waterfront gangs.

I took a room at a small, smelly hotel over a bar, and started the old grind of idly toying with a stale beer, listening, and talking only when spoken to; of sitting at the marble-topped tables of waterfront restaurants, drinking black coffee as the interminable arguments went on.

Before long I discovered the principal bars and restaurants where the racket bosses hung out, and these I made my headquarters. Within a week I was on speaking terms with the regular longshoremen who spent most of their free time in these bars and restaurants. And in that time I found that a man named Frankie Salvio was the local loan-shark with a good band of strong-arm men as his "collectors."

In the beginning it was just a name one man had whispered to me when I suggested I needed a few dollars. But bit by bit I gathered information on Salvio's activities. It was obvious he was operating a wide-spread and lucrative loan business. I also learned that those who didn't pay didn't work. Word would be passed along to the hiring boss and the man in debt would be faced with the choice of finding the money in some fashion or letting his family starve.

From the bars and restaurants I went into the daily shape-up. Actually this was a dangerous move on my part. Longshoring is not just a human pack horse's job; there are skills and tricks that come only from long experience. If, ironically, I was selected to work, any boss in the hold would know within an hour that I was faking, that I was an alien among them. The waterfront is always suspicious. If they suspected I might be an undercover agent or a police officer I might have earned a broken head or other broken bones. A case or box tips over an open hold, or breaks loose from a swing—it has happened many times, maybe by accident.

I shaped every day, and as luck would have it, I never caught the eye of the hiring boss. But I did acquire a nodding acquaintance with some of the union delegates. One was Bull Piccarelli, a union agent for the International Longshoremen's Association, whom rumor connected with the loan-shark racket.

Piccarelli made his headquarters in the Half Moon Bar and Grill on South Street. I decided to seek him out indirectly. I took a station at a section of the bar that was not filled. I had to stand out to catch his attention.

He came in, waved to some friends and ordered a drink. While waiting he surveyed the bar. Out of the corner of my eye I saw him stop, frown, turn away and come back to me. I could also almost see the cogs in his mind working . . . where have I seen that guy?

After two drinks he sauntered over to where I was standing.

"Where are you from, Mac?" he asked.

"Boston," I said.

"What's your name?" he demanded.

"O'Brien," I answered. "I'm looking for work."

"Why did you leave Boston? Plenty of jobs there."

I smiled. "Let's say I had reasons for leaving."

He nodded in a knowing fashion. "Got a [union] book?" he asked.

"I intend to join up," I said.

"Did you belong to the union in Boston?" he asked.

I gave him the name of a hiring boss on a Boston pier and told him we had an "arrangement" so that he gave me work when I needed it but I didn't have to belong to the union.

"It'll cost you $110 to get a book here," he said. "Got that much?"

"I have a C-note," I said, "but not much more."

"No book," he said, "no work."

I shrugged. "What am I supposed to do?" I asked, "Stick up a bank?"

"Come along and have a drink," he said. "Let's talk it over."

We moved to a table in one corner of the room and he started to buy drinks and pump me slyly about Boston. He was so crude he was boring. I rattled off pier numbers, nicknames of bosses, landmarks on the waterfront, loan-sharks, and then tossed him the whore-house card.

"May's the madam," I told him, "an old friend. Go down and get some of the stuff for free. Tell May Dan sent you."

He seemed impressed. "See me tomorrow at my office, Dan, and maybe I can help you."

I felt I had taken the first real important step. The next morning promptly at ten o'clock I entered Piccarelli's office on South Street, a short distance from the Half Moon. It was one flight up, a dingy two-room office with bare walls, grimy windows and naked light bulbs. The Bull was sitting behind his battered desk when I entered.

"Close the door," he said. "Let's make this private. Take a seat." He waved me to a rickety chair and I sat down.

Then he leaned across the desk and gave me a wide, oily smile.

"I'm going to do you a favor, Dan," he said. "I'm going to do you this favor because I like you. I know how it is being a stranger in town and hard up for dough. I'm going to give you a union book and your button for only $25.00." Then he stabbed the air with a fat forefinger. "And furthermore you don't have to pay me the 25 bucks right away. You can wait a couple of weeks until you get paid." He leaned back in the chair and chuckled. "I'm going to make sure you get work because I'm going to introduce you to the man who's going to give you work. Meet me tonight in the Half Moon and I'll introduce you to Thompson."

This was a new name. "Who's Thompson?" I asked.

He replied vaguely, "Oh, one of the fellows. He'll give you work, Dan. Don't worry about it."

My exuberance was tempered with caution. If Thompson hired me he would notify Piccarelli before the night was over that I was a phony who didn't have the slightest knowledge of longshoring. My only hope was that the few weeks I had on the docks had given me a superficial knowledge that could allow me to put up a reasonable bluff.

At the Half Moon, Bull introduced me to a big burly Irishman fairly bursting out of his lumber jacket with ruddy, good health. Then Bull took Thompson aside. When they returned Thompson sized me up.

"Looking for work?"

I nodded. "I'd like a job."

Thompson said shortly, "You got one. At the shape-up tonight

I'll pick you as one of my gang. We unload that ship across the street at midnight."

I almost groaned at the thought of starting that back-breaking job at midnight. I had been up since dawn, but it was a job that had to be done. I joined them at the bar and stuck with Thompson for the rest of the evening. It was just at the time when Thompson was finishing his last beer after shouting "Let's shape," that I had an amazing turn of luck.

A man came running into the saloon shouting, "She's sinking."

As one man, all of us poured out of the tavern and dashed across South Street. The ship—the one I was supposed to help unload—was listing. It seems that sometime during the day she had sprung a plate and water had been pouring steadily into her hold. As a consequence her cargo had shifted.

We stood on the pier's edge watching the other gang frantically trying to unload the cargo, but it wasn't any use. While we watched she went under.

"No shape tonight, boys," Thompson called out. To me he added, "Sorry, kid. Come around in a few days and I'll take care of you. He leaned toward me and said softly, "If Bull says it's okay it's gotta be okay . . ."

I was saved by the bell.

In the next few days I avoided Thompson, which wasn't too difficult because, as I had learned, he was a North River boss who came to the East Side piers only to unload certain ships.

Piccarelli was consoling. "No matter, Dan," he said, "I'll get you another gang real soon."

While I avoided Thompson and work I found that loan-sharking was at its peak on Friday, when the men were paid off. I contacted our office and a meeting at Union Square with our original informant was arranged. The possibility of being seen—you'll be surprised how small New York can be sometimes—with your informant must be explained beforehand. In this case I had already made an alibi I could easily explain: that I had met him on the East Side docks.

The informant told me the men did not receive their pay envelopes at the pier but that Salvio and his hoods would collect the envelopes, take them down to their office on Front Street to exact their pay-offs and then dole out the wages to the longshoremen. Each man had to pay (1) his loan-shark debts; (2) a certain kickback to the racketeers according to the hours they worked.

"How can I get into the office?" I asked.

"Longshoremen go in and out there all day long," he said. "Guys hang out there when they're not working and you can just drift in."

I asked, "Can I get a loan?"

"Sure," he said, "if you get an okay."

"Can you okay me?" I asked.

He nodded. "First we have to be seen together for a while at the Half Moon."

I then outlined a plan in which we would appear to meet in friendly fashion at the Half Moon and from then on seem to strike it off. This we did. It was a casual meeting with a great deal of easy laughter.

I made sure that Frank Salvio and his brother, Carl, were always on hand to see us together. After a while it became accepted that we had hit it off and were friends.

After a week of this play-acting I moved in. My informant contacted one of Salvio's hoods to arrange for me to get a $20.00 loan. I was to return $24.00 the following Friday.

The thug was a short tough with the battered face of a clubhouse fighter. He kept nodding while I talked.

"Okay," he said, laboriously counting out four five-dollar bills, "here's your dough." Then he jabbed a blunt finger at my informant. "If he doesn't have the twenty bucks you pay the interest." He stared at me. "That we don't let go, Mac."

When he walked away my informer said grimly, "He means that if the D.A.'s office doesn't get up four bucks by next Friday, I'll have my brains kicked in."

I counted out ten to ease his mind. But I wondered what happened to the poor unfortunate who didn't have it to pay or who paid and begged the corner grocery store for more credit.

The next few days I visited the Front Street office. It was a large and barren place, but it had a big old-fashioned belly stove around which we sat, trading lies and coarse obscenities. But I was also getting an inside peek into Salvio's operations. He had been operating so long with seeming immunity he didn't bother to hide what he was doing.

On a Friday afternoon I took a station in a doorway about a half-block from the pier entrance. In the afternoon Carl and his hoods drove up, then left shortly with a small valise. I followed in a cab and watched them stop at the Front Street office. I left the cab around the block and joined the line of longshoremen moving up

the stairway. It was amazing—there they were waiting calmly to get
the leavings of their own pay envelopes which had been taken,
opened and depleted by the loan-shark racketeers.

Upstairs, Salvio and his gang were seated behind a large table. I
watched as they tore open the envelopes, took out their kickback
and handed each man his partially emptied envelope. But although
I had seen with my own eyes how the racket worked I still had to
gather more substantial evidence to support a grand jury indictment.

I collected the names of a number of these victims and of some
who had been severely beaten. A few told me their stories—speaking, as they imagined, to a fellow longshoreman and not to a D.A.'s
man. But I was still short of what I wanted. So I hit on this plan.
I stayed away from the docks for a week, I dropped my longshoreman's clothes, obtained a small but powerful camera and started in
gathering pictorial evidence. With a telescopic lens I shot hundreds
of feet of film from a cab window—I had a driver who was absolutely trustworthy. I photographed the Salvio brothers actually lend-
ing out money on the piers and also collecting.

But I needed also a pictorial record of the kickback racket, prin-
cipally of the men who were victimized and who might be potential
witnesses. I arranged with our office to hire the loft in a building
directly across from the Front Street office of Salvio and on a Friday
I went to the loft before dawn and took up a station at a window
with my camera.

It was a long wait, but finally in the afternoon the droves of
men began to appear. I took a picture of every man who entered and
left Salvio's office that day.

My job was almost completed. Besides the moving pictures of the
longshoremen I felt that a wire tap installed in Salvio's office might
yield a great deal of incriminating evidence and leads on the petty
racketeers who frequented the place. Dewey agreed and Detective
Bill O'Sullivan, a good-looking, jovial fellow, one of the finest experts on electronics, was assigned to help me install a dictaphone
in Salvio's office.

I explained the setup to Bill and we agreed the best time to install the apparatus was in the early hours of the morning when, my
investigation had confirmed, the office was always dark.

Bill and I gained a pass key from the building owners and entered
the cold barren office. About midnight we turned on a small light in
the back room and went to work. Bill decided the best place to put

the dictaphone was behind the large picture of Abraham Lincoln, on the wall. The mike was hung from the ceiling with what is known as invisible wires. From the mike wires were strung along the molding and dropped outside to be connected with the machine in the next building where we would set up a listening post. We didn't have to paint the wire because the molding hid it.

We had just installed the microphone and dropped the wire out the window when the door swung open and all the lights were switched on. Three tough-looking hoods stood in the doorway. One, who seemed to be the spokesman, said, "What the hell are you doing?"

I would like to say that it was my quick thinking that saved the day but actually it was Bill O'Sullivan's agile mind. In a voice full of indignation he said angrily, "Don't you people have any consideration?"

The trio seemed to have been taken off balance for a moment. One of the gorillas said, "What do you mean, Mac? This happens to be our joint."

Bill dramatically pointed to the electric clock on the wall. "Do you see that Western Union clock?"

One of the fellows said, "So what?"

"That clock of yours was out of order," Bill said, "and because you people didn't have the consideration to call us, every clock on the West Side is out of order."

The three tough-looking gentlemen actually looked surprised. Bill went on to describe very graphically how all over the city from Fourteenth Street to the Staten Island Ferry hundreds of clocks were stopped and had to be reset.

"Do you know it has taken us an hour and a half to fix this one clock?" he demanded.

"Hell, Mac," the spokesman said, "I'm sorry. We didn't know the clock was broken."

"Well, make it a habit to look at it once in a while," Bill said. "Let's gather up the tools," he said to me. I threw everything in our bag.

As we went out Bill turned and said, "Will you boys lock up?"

The three hoods, just staring at the clock, nodded dumbly.

We jumped into our car and left in a hurry. We thought sure they would discover the wire. The next night, more out of curiosity, Bill and I paid a visit to the alley. In the darkness Bill felt along the wall while I stood guard.

"The wire is still here, Dan," he whispered. "They didn't find it."

We picked up where we had left off and had the entire apparatus working before morning. For three days we listened in on their racket secrets. A large amount of information on other allied rackets on other docks was channeled daily to other investigators and assistants working on other cases involving fugitives and loan-shark activities on the West Side.

Then one day we heard the door slam and several voices raised in greeting. We both recognized the name of a young labor racketeer who had just entered. A card game was in session and he took a hand. The conversation was desultory until one of the racketeers said:

"That clock right?"

"Sure—I check it every day now," another voice said.

"What's this clock bit?" the young labor gangster asked idly.

"It went out the other night and threw all the clocks out along the West Side," a voice said. "Two guys had to come down and fix it."

"You know, boss," a voice said hesitantly, "I was meanin' to ask you. How did those guys get into the office?"

We could hear a moment of silence. It was broken by the young racketeer.

"What office?"

"This office. Joe saw a light on and tipped us off. We thought someone was robbin' us."

The younger man asked excitedly, "What were they doing?"

The other answered: "They were fixin' the clock."

Chairs scraped. "You crazy bastards," he shouted, "they bugged the joint. There's a dictaphone in here. Let's find it."

We could hear the noise of chairs, curses and men running about.

"Who would want to bug us?" someone asked.

"The D.A.," someone replied. "Get that bug!"

Bill cut the wire while I swept our stuff into a bag. In minutes we were running downstairs to the car.

I returned to the District Attorney's office and a conference was held with Dewey. It was agreed that I had obtained enough to allow the office to move in. We hired ten city buses and loaded them with a small army of selected detectives from precincts as far away as Queens. At a late conference in our office Dewey and Gurfein plotted a layout so that the busloads were placed at strategic points to block off the entire waterfront along the lower East Side. It was my job to go from pier to pier and pick out Salvio and his hoods; all longshore-men on the piers were to be picked up for questioning.

It was a bright winter's day. At an arranged signal we moved in. I went from pier to pier pointing out the racket boys who were un-ceremoniously pushed into the buses. They were then taken to the District Attorney's office. It was a madhouse. Every assistant, on Dewey's orders, was taking part in the questioning. It was a long and frustrating day. The answers were shrugs and blank looks. Not one of the 200 longshoremen would admit he had been victimized by these thugs.

Finally it was decided to try a psychological approach and let them see the movies. It can be quite a shock to a man to realize that his illegal actions are on film. To see your face leap out of the screen in a darkened room can create panic in many a man's heart.

The longshoremen were assembled in the largest room in the Criminal Courts Building. They sat down, muttering among them-selves and staring at the covered movie equipment at the rear of the room. At a signal the lights were switched off. The rhythmic sound of the film clicking into the projector from the roll filled the room. Faces appeared and disappeared; men walked in and out of Salvio's office, stared at the hidden camera, lit a cigarette and walked away, some fingering their torn pay envelopes.

Finally it was all over. Nothing was said. The lights went on. The longshoremen stared straight ahead, or eyed each other suspiciously, then filed out. Again the tedious, fruitless questioning went on. In the early hours of the morning we started to let them go. The rule of fear had won out—at least this time. Although we had gathered some information that was helpful, not one of the victimized long-shoremen would point an accusing finger at the loan-sharks and job-racketeers who had stolen their wages, beaten them, hounded them, robbed their families and on whose whim their livelihood depended.

In a way I couldn't blame them. There are few men who are willing to risk their jobs and their lives in the vague defense of civic duty. It was so easy to miss your footing on a high deck, or for a sling to break loose and hurtle down on an innocent victim tons of crates or boxes. . . .

I can recall one young fellow who just shook his head. "Who the hell wants to be a dead hero, mister?"

But all our efforts were not in vain. Despite the refusal of the longshoremen to talk we did catch Salvio and his gang on other charges, such as violation of the Sullivan Law. Piccarelli was picked up and held on one thousand-dollar bail as a material witness.

The most difficult task was to face our original informant, who had risked so much. But surprisingly, he wasn't bitter.

"I knew they wouldn't talk," he said. "The word was passed along before we even got into the buses."

"What was it?" I asked.

"Talk and you're dead," he replied.

9. SEARCH FOR A HIRED GUN: LEPKE'S TRIGGER-MAN

ON A RAINY April evening in 1933, the Needle Workers' Union meeting at 131 West 28th Street erupted into a riot carefully staged by the mobsters of Louis (Lepke) Buchalter. Men shouted, cursed, fought or threw chairs as the hall was thrown into bedlam. Under the cover of the noise, a tall man in a topcoat fired several shots at two men, Manny Burdy and Harry Gottlieb, two workers who had been threatening Lepke's domination of the garment district. Both men were critically wounded. Union men produced arms and in the exchange of gunfire six men were wounded. In those racket-ridden days the shootings received the usual one-day headlines, then vanished from the metropolitan press. To readers satiated with stories of men found burned to death on dump heaps, garroted, stabbed or trussed like poultry, this was just some more gangland violence.

From reluctant witnesses the gunman was identified as Sam Turtletaub, alias Sam Green, alias Big Greenie, Lepke's trigger-man, a cold-blooded hired gun who had terrorized the garment district for years. Greenie was picked up and charged with felonious assault, violation of the Sullivan Law, and inciting a riot. As always, he was calm and impassive. Curiously, he was allowed bail of $10,000, which was produced within an hour. By the following morning, in which time both men had died, Greenie had vanished. He was named in five indictments.

In 1935, when Dewey began his investigation of Lepke's racket empire, the name of Big Greenie constantly swirled to the surface of this dark pool. Yet a quiet but intensive hunt failed to turn up Greenie. The search was carried over into the District Attorney's office when Dewey was elected but the underworld took care of its own—especially, in those days, when the fugitive was one of Lepke's men.

Lepke had always been one of Dewey's main targets and by 1940, after years of the most frustrating work, we managed to corral enough evidence for an indictment, charging him with running a racket in the flour-trucking industry. The name of Big Greenie was heard again and again, but to the investigating corps he was fast becoming a shadowy figure who seemingly no longer existed—until the day when our office received a whispered phone call from an underworld informant.

I had just returned from Detroit, where I had found a fugitive in another racket case, when Chief Investigator O'Connell summoned me to his office.

"Dan," he said, "I have a job that's right up your alley. We found Big Greenie's girl friend."

Now it has always irritated me that since the Fritz Kuhn case I had been dubbed a sort of ladies' man who could charm secrets out of the opposite sex, when actually, as a bachelor, I've always been rather shy with the ladies. But all my explanations and rejection of this unearned reputation had been met either with knowing grins or soft whistles. All I could do was ignore them. Weakly I accepted my assignment.

"Where is she?" I asked.

"Her name is Edith and she occupies a room on the second floor of this flat," he said, tossing me an address on a slip of paper. "We understand it's a railroad flat rented by one woman who has four boarders. All we want you to do is give her some of that Danforth charm and get her to tell us where Greenie is hiding."

"Is that all?" I asked sardonically.

"You might persuade her to get Greenie to surrender," John said with the innocence of a choirboy.

I left amid much whistling and comments.

I found the brownstone house on West 93rd Street just off Broadway. A sign read, "Rooms to Rent." The rooms were on the second floor, as Tom had said, and the white-haired landlady showed me one for $12.00 per week, not including breakfast and dinner. She told me there were three other boarders, one a lady.

I moved in that afternoon as Dan O'Brien of Boston, and set up shop. In the early evening I managed to be out in the corridor to catch sight of the other male boarders, one a young man about thirty-five and the other two both elderly men. Then Edith walked in.

She was tall, with a striking figure. One look at her hard, carefully made-up face and I knew she had been around. I purposely ignored her as she walked by. I was sure as I lighted a cigar before closing my door that she had paused on her own threshold to study my back. I closed my door and in a moment heard her door shut.

The next week I kept to myself but made it obvious to the others I did not go to work. When I paid my rent I pulled out a roll of bills and peeled off a note of a large denomination. I knew I would be talked about. Later I found I was the topic of much speculation. During this time I went out of my way to ignore Edith. It was simple psychology. What attractive woman in an all-male household will allow herself to be ignored . . . ?

When I discovered she was friendly with the younger boarder I set my sights on him. After going through the routine of smiling and passing the time of day, I managed to leave at the same time as he did one morning and suggested he share my cab. I dropped him off, saw a movie and returned home, hoping I looked like the proverbial cat who had swallowed the canary.

The next night, a Saturday, I was invited to the weekly poker game. When I saw Edith at the table I readily accepted. I slipped in the chair directly opposite her and during the evening ignored her. I'm no particular card shark, but luck was with me that evening. Edith looked impressed. I felt she was about to make a move. When the game ended I went to my room. A moment later there was a soft knock.

"Come in," I called out.

"Feel like some company?" she asked.

I grinned. "The landlady said it was against the rules."

She smiled in return. "Rules are made to be broken."

"I like that," I said.

She pouted. "You haven't even said good morning."

I said, "We haven't been introduced."

She held out her hand. "I'm Edith."

I took her hand. "I'm Dan O'Brien."

We sat and talked in this fashion for about an hour. When she left I said, "I'll drop by tomorrow."

She looked surprised. "What for?"

"We're going out to dinner," I said.

"I'd love to," she replied.

When she closed the door I knew we had taken a step on the right road to Big Greenie's hideout.

For three weeks we went twice a week to the movies, had dinner several times and took walks together. I never mentioned Big

Greenie, of course, but I did know from her background that she had been in Chicago and knew several racketeers who lived there.

One night I said casually I might have to fly to Chicago for a few days.

"You working?" she asked suddenly.

This was a familiar underworld salutation. If a safe-cracker met a burglar and asked this question it was simply a what-job-are-you-on-now salute.

"Not now," I said, "but there are times when I work."

"Steady?" she insisted.

I gave her the mysterious smile routine. "Why steady, Edith? I'm getting along the way I am . . ."

Then she dropped the bomb. "Know Big Greenie, Dan?"

"I heard he's a torpedo," I said, "but I don't know him." Then I shrugged off the question. "I don't deal with hoods."

Then she mentioned the names of three members of Chicago's hierarchy of crime and I made a show of brightening up and nodding.

"They're more my speed," I said.

"I know them," she said proudly.

We went on like this for another week or two and to my dismay she was now constantly at my elbow. I was watching her mail which was placed on a table in the hall, but she received nothing of importance. One night she was bragging about her friendship with notorious gangsters and again mentioned Big Greenie's name.

I pretended to frown. "Wasn't he in the papers a couple of years ago?"

She nodded. "The law's after him for a killing on 34th Street." She gave me a sly look. "Do you know he used to be my boyfriend, Danny?"

"Maybe I'd better pull out," I said. "They say Greenie's real tough."

She waved her hand. "He's in Cincinnati," she said. "He'll never come back."

"How do you know he's there?" I asked. "Maybe he's in town looking for you right now?"

She shook her head. "I heard from him only last month. He's carrying a gun for ———" and she named a notorious midwest gambler.

Suddenly she came over and sat on the arm of my chair.

"Want to know something, Danny?" she said softly.

"What's that?" I asked.

"I think I've found the guy I want to go with to Chicago," she said.

"Who's that?" I asked.

She leaned over. "You," she said.

I recalled the report we had on this woman's activities as mistress of a half-dozen thugs and murderers, most of them crawling with disease, and I was so repelled I could scarcely control myself.

"You like me, don't you, Danny?" she kept insisting.

I made a serious attempt of trying to impress her but it was hard going. I felt a great impatience to get on the phone, tell Fay the news, to get out. But this night was the toughest; I just couldn't get rid of her. I believe it was about 2:00 A.M. when I finally managed to get her back in her own room. I didn't dare try to leave because I could see her light was still burning in her room. A foolish impatience now might ruin the case. Minutes after she left in the morning I was on the phone with Fay.

"Good work, Dan," he said. "I'll get someone on the way to Ohio. You'd better stick around for a while."

"I can't," I protested. "This woman is getting serious."

I could just see him grin over the phone. "The orders are just a few more days, Dan," he said. "Then we'll get you out."

I grudgingly realized that it would be too suspicious for me to drop out of sight. I had to stay.

It was the worst week I ever spent. She constantly dogged my footsteps, asking me when we were going to "blow New York," as she put it. Finally I set a date and got on the phone with Fay. This time I meant it; I wanted out.

"Okay, Dan," he said, "but we'll have to stage a raid. What time do you want it?"

I arranged the time for the phony raid and returned to the rooming-house to resume the hounds-and-hare game with Edith. The raid was set for that Saturday, at 11:00 A.M. At 10:30 A.M. I ambled into Edith's room. To make sure she stayed I began picturing the wonderful time we would have in Chicago.

Promptly at 11:00 A.M. Fay and two detectives who had obtained the key from the frightened landlady tried the lock.

I jumped to my feet. "The cops," I whispered. "Where can I hide?"

She pointed to a closet. I jumped in behind her dresses as Fay and our detectives entered the room.

"Edith ———," Fay asked.

She nodded.

"The District Attorney would like to talk to you," he said.

"You have nothing on me, copper," she replied. Then she cursed the boys with such savagery that they just stood there. Edith certainly had been around.

"Search the apartment," Fay ordered.

In the stifling darkness of the closet I could hear them going through the place with a fine-tooth comb. Then suddenly the door opened. A big hand pushed the clothes aside to yank me out.

"Who's this bum?" Fay growled.

The detective shook me like a terrier shedding water. "Just another punk," he grunted.

"Leave Danny alone," Edith cried.

Fay stuck his face close to mine. "Danny, heh! What's your last name? You got a record?"

"I want to see my lawyer," I said in my best underworld fashion.

Fay swung at me and I rolled with the punch. Edith began yelling that they were not to hurt me and while I struggled with Fay and the detectives I managed to whisper, "Take it easy, fellows," but they just grinned. When she asked Fay why I was wanted he answered, "He's Dan O'Brien, lady. Wanted by Uncle Sam and seven states. . . ."

Downtown, we were separated and they began grilling Edith. Surprisingly, she did give some odds and ends of information which were helpful to us later on.

The next morning as she was released, she asked, "What did you do with Danny, Mr. Fay?"

As Tom said, "I told her you were repaying Uncle Sam for some time. But you certainly had a narrow escape, Dan."

"How's that?" I asked.

"She told us she was planning on getting married to you in Chicago. She said she thought it would be nice to settle down with such a nice young feller."

But that wasn't the last of Edith in my life.

By the time our office had staged the raid to bring me in, Investigator Joe Kaitz and Detective Bill Devine were on their way to Cincinnati to follow up the information Edith had given me.

They contacted the local police, who supplied a detective who knew the underworld as he did the back of his own hand. But Cincinnati produced nothing. The stool pigeons, the gamblers, and the fancy bordellos which a man of Big Greenie's type would frequent, had never seen him. As both Kaitz and Devine were aware, it was a dangerous game. Greenie was a tough, unprincipled killer who would not hesitate to start shooting if he were boxed in. Facing him was a life sentence, and his philosophy was quite simple; he'd rather die in trying to break out than spend the rest of his life behind bars.

After they had scoured Cincinnati, the local detective asked them if they would like to visit Keyport, Kentucky, across the river.

"Keyport?" Bill asked. "What's over there?"

The other law officer just grinned. "It's quite an interesting place and there's a good chance you'll pick up a lead."

Both of our people were amazed at what they found. Keyport was as wild and unruly as any western frontier town. Every second house was a gambling den or a brothel. It was a town dominated by crime.

"I'll show you the local gambling setup," the Cincinnati police officer said, and guided them to the Beverly Hills, one of the largest gambling houses. It was a luxurious place, with an adjacent restaurant which supplied elaborate steak dinners.

Following the detective, they walked through a door into a small, dimly lighted alcove. As Devine's eyes got accustomed to the gloom, he suddenly nudged Kaitz. Kaitz looked up. Two giant Negroes, both armed with machine guns, which they cradled in their arms, were sitting on a small balcony. The gunmen stared down impassively. Then another door opened. They walked into a large smoky room, filled with every known gambling device. Croupiers in evening dress were constantly gathering in large piles of greenbacks. Dice rolled, bird cages flipped and stickmen called out the points for the crap-shooters.

"Every hood on the lam eventually gets here," the local detective said in a whisper.

"Suppose he's here?" Joe said.

"What do you boys think you'll do if he is?" the Cincinnati cop said with a grin.

"Can we take him here?" Bill asked.

The detective jerked his head. Bill followed his glance. Two more big Negroes with machine guns, half-hidden by phony palm trees, sat on a small balcony above the gambling room.

"What did you say you boys would do?" the detective whispered.

Bill said, "Not a damn thing."

They walked leisurely about the crowded room, watching fantastic amounts of money change hands on the roll of a pair of dice.

They carefully noted each player or watcher; Big Greenie was not among those present.

It was decided to return to the restaurant for a discussion of the next move.

Over the coffee the local police officer said very bluntly, "If he's not here—he's not in this state, gentlemen."

"I guess you're right," Bill said.

Just before they said good night, Bill and Joe went to the men's room. The large, gaudy room was deserted. Bill recalls looking at his watch; it was just 2:30 A.M. He was combing his hair when the club's doorman came in. He was a huge, genial Irishman, whose name, even now, must remain a secret. It was obvious to both Kaitz and Devine he had been drinking.

"Well, gents," he bellowed, "having a good time?"

"Very good," Bill said.

"Good crowd tonight," the doorman said. "I saw. . . ."

He reeled off a roster of the underworld with what seemed a touch of pride. "Know every one of them, too. Good tippers. Well, good night, gents."

When he left Bill and Joe stared at each other. Each knew what the other had in his mind. What had they to lose if they showed the half-drunken doorman Big Greenie's picture . . . ?

They joined the doorman outside and after commenting on the town and its setup Bill said they were looking for someone.

The doorman froze. "Local?"

Joe said quickly, "Not local, strictly out of the state, and if he hangs around here he might cause your boss some trouble. He's a killer."

"Cops?" the doorman asked.

"New York District Attorney's office," Joe said.

The doorman asked again, "Not a local boy?"

"Strictly New York," they told him.

"Got a picture?" he asked.

They showed him the picture of Big Greenie. The doorman held it up to the small single light under the canopy. Then he whirled around, his face flushed with anger.

"What you guys doing to me?"

Joe said, "What's the matter?"

"What kind of games you guys playing?" the doorman asked, "Calling this bum Greenie or whatever the hell you said his name was!"

Bill put in, "But that's his name."

"You ask my help, then phony up on me," the doorman said belligerently.

"Believe us, that's his name, Big Greenie," Bill said quickly.

The doorman was now plainly incensed over something in connection with the picture.

"Do you know him?" Joe insisted.

The doorman waved the picture away. "Know him? Of course I do. Greenie! Hah!"

"What's his name?"

The doorman shook his head. "Why should I help a couple of New York phonies? You gave me a bum rap. You could get me in trouble."

"Look," both Joe and Bill pleaded. "We only want his name."

They stood aside while he helped some guests out of a cab and escorted them into the club. Both Bill and Joe waited on tenterhooks. When the doorman came out both detectives grabbed him.

"What's his name?"

The doorman shrugged.

"You must know every hood that comes in here," Joe said soothingly.

"What a memory," Bill said softly.

The doorman softened. "Never give me a steer like that again."

"Do you know him?"

"Sure—that bum's name is Baker."

"Where did you see Baker last?" Joe asked.

The doorman pointed to the ground. "Right here. Why, that bum thought he was a big shot. He came up driving with a couple of hoods and walked right in. 'I'm taking a piece of this joint,' he says. The boss didn't say anything, just wined and dined him and patted him on the back, as if he was afraid. After dinner he took Baker and his hoods into the gambling setup and showed him our staff. Meanwhile those guards—you saw those boys with the hardware, didn't you?—well, they just slipped out and sat in the back of this bum's car. When he and his pals came out I waved them into the car.

"Then the boss leaned over and said, as his boys put the guns to these crumbs' heads: 'Now you're going for a little ride—this time we'll take you home. The next time I see your kisser around here it's going to be full of little holes. Now, get the hell out of here.'"

"Did they come back?"

The doorman grinned. "Would *you* come back to have those fiddle-players practice on you?"

"Where's Baker now?" Joe asked.

"You'll find your New York bum in Cincinnati," the doorman answered.

"But where?" Bill asked. "We've been all over Cincinnati."

"He's got a new Dodge, that's all I know," was the reply.

Joe asked hopefully, "Got a license number?"

The doorman shook his head.

They gave him ten dollars to keep his eyes open and then rushed back into the restaurant for the local detective. A police-car escort took them to the airport for Columbus, Ohio, headquarters of the state's automobile registration bureau.

They had one chance—had Big Greenie registered a car under the name of Baker . . . ?

They arrived at the Motor Vehicle Bureau at 7:00 A.M. After a hasty breakfast they contacted the superintendent of the office, and he opened the office. Bill and Joe then started on the monumental job of checking the automobile registration file.

At 10:00 A.M. Joe Kaitz jumped up, waving a registration blank.

"I got it!" It was a Dodge registered in the name of Joseph Baker and gave a Cincinnati hotel as his address.

Both investigators flew back to Cincinnati, picked up their local police officer friend, and rushed out to the hotel.

Bill and the local detective covered the front, and Bill told Joe "You watch the window and the first head that comes out, blow it apart. Greenie probably will make a run for it."

Bill and the Cincinnati man kicked in the door and rushed in, guns ready. The room was torn apart. Bureau drawers were open and clothing strewn on the floor; there had evidently been a tip-off. Greenie had fled. Bill ran to the open window.

"Joe," he called.

Joe Kaitz, with his gun pointed at the window, replied wryly, "Well, your head is the first I've seen, Bill. What'll I do now?"

The day the gangster had fled was January 10. The District Attorney's office in New York had sent out a flyer and a photo of Greenie on January 10. It was a strange coincidence.

Bill and Joe kept on Greenie's trail all across the Southwest until it petered out. They returned to the East as Tom Devine, Bill's brother, was leaving New York. He was on another case, but District Attorney Dewey ordered Tom to drop flyers all along the way to the Coast—just in case. The flyers did it. Tom had just reached Los Angeles to begin work on his own investigation when word was flashed from the Tucson police: "Big Greenie, listed in your flyer No. 23645 as wanted for suspicion in murder arrested this city. Please advise."

Within the hour Assistant District Attorney Jack Rosenbloom was leaving New York for Arizona to take Greenie into custody, while Tom Devine was moving back from Los Angeles to meet Jack in Tucson. That night we received word that Greenie was captured.

Subsequently Big Greenie was returned to New York, the only metropolitan gangster dressed as a cowboy. He swaggered into Grand Central in the heat lightning of the photographers' flashbulbs, resplendent in a colorful cowboy shirt, high-heeled puncher's boots and a ten-gallon hat.

But Greenie was still a city boy at heart. "What a joint out there," he complained to the investigators who returned him to our office for questioning. "Nothin' but sand and lizards."

Big Greenie was sentenced to spend the rest of his life behind bars, but I hadn't heard the last of the case. Several months later I was tailing a suspect in the subway. We both got off at 50th Street and Broadway. Suddenly someone grabbed my arm.

"Well, Dan O'Brien," a woman's voice, dripping with sarcasm, said, "how are things in the District Attorney's office?"

I felt like jumping back into the car. I knew only too well who that was.

"Fine, Edith," I said. "Look I'm very sorry—"

"Let's step over here," she said. "I've been looking for you for a long time."

We stepped over to one side and for the next half hour I took the tongue-lashing of my life. Every time I started to move away she stepped in front of me. The gist of her complaint was not that Big Greenie had been arrested but the way I had trifled with her affections.

Then she started to weep. Here I was on an uptown subway platform, with a gangster's mistress weeping on my shoulder and everyone eyeing us. I guess words finally failed her because she wiped her eyes.

"You're a no good ——," she said loudly and walked off. With a great deal of relief I watched her board a subway train.

What had someone said about a woman scorned?

10. THE FABULOUS COLONEL: THE HALQUIRE CASE

THE YEAR 1942 saw Thomas E. Dewey elected Governor of New York State and Frank S. Hogan made District Attorney. The people of New York County never regretted their selection as prosecutor. I doubt that his record of convictions as a law enforcement officer has been duplicated by any other prosecutor in the country.

To most New Yorkers Frank Hogan is a quiet, pipe-smoking man who looks like somebody's uncle. Actually he is a tough, realistic prosecutor whom Tammany Hall would like to see retire. It is known in the underworld that the New York County District Attorney's office is absolutely uncorruptible. Fixes are a thing of the past and political influence means nothing to Hogan.

He is absolutely dedicated to law enforcement and rules his office with a firm hand. We had a strict set of rules to follow; any deviation meant dismissal. His assistants can't work outside the office, as do assistants in other District Attorneys' offices outside New York County. They can't visit night clubs or race tracks unless they have permission, and they can't make a speech without clearance from Hogan or his chief assistant. An assistant can be immediately dismissed if he is photographed with a defendant. Courtesy is a by-law in our office. "When I was in private practice I was kicked around in too many public offices," Frank once told me.

Few New Yorkers realized the tremendous spot he was in when, shortly after he took office, a batch of wire taps from our department was placed on his desk. The taps established that gambler Frank Costello was a power in Tammany Hall circles and that Supreme Court Justice Thomas Aurelio had thanked Costello for his help in obtaining the judgeship. Hogan, who is a registered Democrat, was bitterly criticized by his party for releasing the wire taps to the public. "I figured the public had the right to know what was going on," was Hogan's answer.

Actually, few New Yorkers know the real Frank Hogan story.

He was not born to wealth or position. In a sense, his story could be a lesson to those who complain that you can't get anywhere unless you have money or pull. Hogan had neither, but he did have integrity and determination.

His story begins in Waterbury, Connecticut, where he was born, the son of a County Clare immigrant who was a buffer and polisher in a New England watch company. While he attended grammar school, he ran errands in a grocery store. At thirteen he was a high-school freshman, and during the summer he worked in a factory, dipping watch backs in an acid vat. Up to his junior year he was successively a timekeeper, apprentice carpenter and a clothing-firm collector. The last job was the most lucrative—$23 a week.

After graduation he worked as a foreman in a brass rod factory. In 1920, at the age of eighteen, he entered Columbia. His mother, who had carefully saved all her son's money, staked him with $1,400. That first year he played a good game of varsity football and waited on tables.

His first summer was spent selling "The People's Home Library" to upstate farm people (three books in one for $10.50.) In September he had sold 150 sets to earn $750. People liked the earnest young man and inevitably invited him to stay for supper, then suggested he spend the night—thus he saved on bed and board.

In his sophomore vacation he worked for the Pullman Company and in the summer of his junior year as a waiter on the old *Leviathan*. He augmented his income by house-managing the Cosmopolitan Club, a Sunday night dining club—later the International House—and managed to win a $250 scholarship. In his senior year he was elected president of his class and of his fraternity, Beta Theta Pi.

After graduation he worked for a time with a Russian baron, Eugene Fersen, a physicist, who gave lectures across the country. The baron's big theme was that the civilized man had lost the ability to contact universal life energy, or something of that sort. Hogan stayed for three months to help the baron prepare his pamphlets, pass the hat and sell his book, *Science of Being*. Guatemala and a job with a gold-dredging company followed. Then in 1925 he shook the dust from his feet to return to Columbia Law School. He formed a law partnership in 1930, then in 1935, about the time I was taken on, he joined Dewey as an assistant.

Hogan is a strict taskmaster, but he has achieved a fine team spirit in the D.A.'s office. Without this kind of coordination the complex cases involving Fay, Moran and many others could not have been handled successfully.

One of the first assignments I received from Hogan, the newly elected District Attorney, was the case of Colonel Halquire, one of the most evil yet fascinating criminals I have ever hunted.

His file—it weighs 25 pounds and is more than a foot high— is the largest in the New York County District Attorney's office. Police of 11 states and the Federal Bureau of Investigation have files of similar bulk on his activities, some dating as far back as the turn of the century.

In almost a half-century of crime, he has stolen hundreds of thousands of dollars without resorting to bloodshed or physical violence. He was arrested only once, to serve five years in Sing Sing. Uneducated but highly intelligent, he has fooled the most level-headed of businessmen, countless women, politicians, bankers and investment men. He has always been versatile and inventive, mastering the intricacies of many industries. Stealing money and playing false roles have been his life's work, but the only time he lost his composure was when a woman accused him of being a fraud.

My associates in the District Attorney's office and I have covered several thousand miles searching for him. We have gone as far as Holland and have traced his family tree back to the beginning of the seventeenth century when an ancestor emigrated to America with a small group of people escaping from religious persecution.

Twenty years ago, when we began our investigation of Halquire, we had only his two favorite aliases and a vague physical description; we now can boast of a huge file, which includes a description of his most intimate habits. As a matter of fact, I probably know as much about Halquire as he does himself.

He is a short, rotund man with a smiling, genial manner. Sharp eyes glint behind rimless glasses as his wizard's brain works continuously. His I.Q. is extraordinary, although he never went beyond the fourth grade in a Manhattan grade school. He is an authentic expert on the tobacco and shoe industries and can converse intelligently on almost any subject, especially the classics and great themes in music.

He has the appetite of a Henry VIII, the manners of a Chesterfield, the morals of a tomcat and the cold impersonal cruelty of a knife blade. Although physically he resembles a beer keg with legs, he has an incredible fascination for women. In more than ten cases he swindled them out of their life's savings, their bank accounts, jewels and even their homes. Perhaps the reason for their gullibility is best summed up by one of his middle-aged victims, who told me, "He robbed me, but I will never forget his thoughtfulness and generosity." His generosity is part of his *modus operandi;* $50 may yield $50,000.

The man's cruelty is almost beyond belief. He has indirectly caused the deaths of two businessmen who collapsed when they learned he had stolen not only their own savings, but those of their friends and business associates. Two women, one dying of tuberculosis, are today wards of the State of Colorado: the colonel had stolen their life's savings. The poignant last line of my report on their cases reads: "They are now penniless."

Although Halquire is king of the confidence men and one of the most wanted criminals in the United States, there can be no end written to his story, simply because no one is sure whether he is alive or dead. A week before this was written, two investigators rushed to a midtown hotel in New York City to track down a tip that he had been seen in the lobby. It turned out to be false. He was last seen alive about 1946, when I missed him on Christmas Eve.

Although I have no evidence except my own deductions, I believe he came to a dramatic end, which you will see is woven through with much poetic justice.

We traced the colonel's family back to Tyne and Adrian Post who arrived in New Amsterdam in 1637 from Holland via London. The colonel's real name is Alfred Banker Post and he was born on February 26, 1874, in New York City at 271 West 21st Street, then a fine neighborhood. His father, Alfred McCarem Post, a descendant of one of the oldest Dutch families in America, was a well-to-do prominent businessman. He was born in this city on February 21, 1853, and died in 1922, the year his favorite son committed his first major crime.

The elder Post married an attractive, well-educated woman of good breeding, Aramneta Mansfield Banker, who was a few years younger than her husband. Four sons were born, Alfred (the colonel) was the only one to survive.

Alfred was a strong-minded boy who resisted schooling—although he was to seek education eagerly throughout his criminal career. On July 18, 1893, he married a neighborhood chum, Amelia Beyer. Four sons were born; two died at birth, one shortly afterward, one survived.

●

He holds an important banking position today and is a highly respected member of his community. He hasn't seen or heard from his father since his infancy.

Shortly after the third son was born, the family moved from 336 West 15th Street to Jersey City. There the colonel, weary of the restraints of domesticity, deserted his family. His wife bravely carried on, found a position and raised and educated her son, who believed his father dead. In 1933 on her deathbed in Rutherford, New Jersey, she gave her son a sealed envelope.

"This is your father's story," she whispered. After her funeral the contents were opened and for the first time the young man discovered that the man who had deserted them was a criminal.

"I met your father only twice after he deserted us," his mother had written. "Once in 1917 when he begged me for money. I gave him all I had, and again a few years later when he took what jewelry I had, promised to pawn it and rejoin us to start life anew. I never heard from him again. In 1922 I read of his arrest and for the first time knew he had become a criminal."

I first encountered the colonel through a criminal complaint made in 1941 and began to piece together the story of his life to the time of his latest fraud. Through old court records, newspaper files and prison records, we located his former criminal associates and those he had victimized. From the combined information we fitted together the jigsaw pattern of his life.

His early pictures show he was an impressive-looking man, handsomely dressed and with an air of confidence. He looked successful. Even before his marriage he was the weaver of grand schemes, some of which had the air of respectability.

In 1908 he gained an audience with J. P. Morgan to unfold before the giant of American finance a plan to set up a protection agency which would guard American banking institutions. Morgan was impressed with the plan, but he left for England and the colonel never reappeared. We next found him dabbling in stocks and mines. Then in 1917, shortly after he robbed his wife of her jewels, he set up an office in Washington, posing as an intelligence officer investigating German spy activities. He was then Colonel Alfred Lindsay.

The colonel claimed his main assignment was to check the backgrounds of young women applying for government work and in this capacity he interviewed scores of women. Some he used to gain contacts with government officials. One girl reported the colonel to the Department of Justice and Halquire was arrested on a white slavery violation. Evidently by threats or bribery he persuaded the girl to withdraw her complaint; the case was dropped when she failed to appear.

The following year he was arrested for impersonating a federal officer, but again the charge was dropped. The colonel next returned to the world of finance, forming a corporation which dealt in mining stocks. The New York State Attorney General's office raided his luxurious Park Avenue office and charged his two partners with fraud. The colonel escaped a prison sentence by cooperating with the state and testifying against his two partners.

A hint of his magnetic charm is detected in the testimony of a prominent Park Avenue surgeon who was one of the chief victims of the colonel; he simply refused to believe the state's charges and offered to make good the losses of the other victims!

In 1922 the colonel was again arrested for fraud; this time his immunity failed. He was found guilty and sentenced to Sing Sing for five years.

There Halquire met Henry Boerum, a mild-mannered former postal clerk from Brooklyn, who was also serving time for fraud. It was apparent from several letters from Boerum, which we found in a raid on the colonel's hotel room—the colonel had skipped a few hours before I kicked in the door—that he also was engaged in some mysterious fraud. On District Attorney Hogan's orders I began building up a separate dossier on Boerum, who we thought at first was the colonel's partner.

Again the hunt for information was a long and tedious task of searching old police and jail records; of seeking out and interrogating reluctant criminals and victims of fraud.

Boerum, we found, left Sing Sing before the colonel and they corresponded regularly. One letter revealed that Boerum was anxiously waiting for the colonel to finish his term so they could set up in business.

The colonel emerged on parole and promptly vanished. It was very difficult to find any trace of his and Boerum's activities from 1925 through the thirties, but by plodding police work and the use of official records we traced them to a South Nyack, New York, mansion, the home of a very wealthy woman.

The estate was also the headquarters for Doctor Hugh Carruthers, a mystic from Tibet, who walked about in a flowing blue gown. Carruthers, of course, was Henry Boerum, the postal clerk. But the real boss of this fraudulent setup was a short, roly-poly man with a steel-trap brain and a winning personality—Colonel Alfred Lindsay, Halquire, of course. He had absolute control over the society woman and her fortune. From a local garage man I found he had three Cadillacs—we tracked down their licenses—and a yacht. At his insistence a private dock was built.

Although he had this rich woman under his domination the colonel surrounded himself with young girls, to whom he gave rich gifts.

The Wall Street crash wiped out the woman's fortune—what was left after Halquire had finished with it—and the jailbird friends calmly washed their hands of her. The double disaster—the loss of all her money and the revelation that the man she had loved so devotedly was nothing but a common thief who had robbed her—brought about the woman's mental collapse. She died a few years ago in a mental institution, a ward of the state. Her total estate at one time was more than $2,000,000.

There must always be a falling out among thieves, despite the old cliché about their loyalty to one another, and it came to pass that Halquire and Carruthers quarreled and parted.

Boerum had now established himself as Doctor Hugh Carruthers and there was no reason why he should have abandoned such a lucrative racket so we started to hunt for a phony mystic from Tibet.

New York's vital statistics files supplied facts about his early background such as his father's history—he was a fireman—his former addresses, birth certificate, marriage license, school records and so on. About a year after we started to search for him we located him, in his Chicago Loop office, where he was still Doctor Carruthers, now the head of the Neological Foundation, which peddled phony Eastern wisdom, hair tonic and laxatives.

He was known to his followers as the "High Priest of Kum Bum Lamasery of the Mystic Blue Lakes of Tibet," also the "Daily Visitor" and "The Human Engineer." In addition he posed as a former student of Changu Nrain, Katmandu, Nepal, on the shore of the mystical blue lake. We found he still preyed on the gullibility of middle-aged women, reaping more than $290,000 on the sale of his hair tonic and laxatives. He had 11,000 members, who paid him a yearly fee of two dollars. These same members bought the ludicrous pamphlets he wrote, titled "How to Influence the Opposite Sex" and "How to Hold a Husband, Wife or Lover." One woman we talked to gave us an idea of how gullible she was when she quoted Carruthers' instructions: "The left nostril is negative and the right one is positive. Therefore you should inhale with the left nostril and exhale with the right."

The woman told me, "I understood clearly what Doctor Carruthers meant, but it was difficult to do."

I also found his "haven of retreat," which Carruthers advised his members to visit. It was supposed to be a luxurious estate of many acres with glittering lakes and air brisk with the smell of pine. All I found was a run-down ten-room farm on a rocky patch of land.

Carruthers now sported an impressive beard. He appeared indignant when we questioned him, but that dignity faded when we produced a complete dossier on his life and activities.

Once he returned to earth Carruthers supplied us with some vital information on the colonel. I was positive he would return someday to see Carruthers and so I gave his secretary one of our flyers, which she pasted in a desk drawer. She promised us she would call the local police the moment she saw him.

Carruthers' activities did not come within our jurisdiction, but we channeled the proper information to the federal authorities.

We now had complete dossiers on both Carruthers and Colonel Hale Heatherington Halquire, as the swindler was now known to us in the New York County's District Attorney's office, to the FBI and to the police and prosecuting attorneys of several states.

In 1940 I received authentic information from a businessman that Halquire was living in Queen Lane, Germantown, Philadelphia, as Colonel Lindsay. I rushed down there but somehow—and to this day I don't know whether he had been tipped off or whether his marvelous intuition had warned him—the colonel got wind of my visit. I opened the door of his apartment with a pass key only to find that he had fled. I traced him to the Philadelphian Hotel but missed him by a day.

Although he had escaped us I stayed on in Philadelphia, retracing the colonel's life in that city, and locating and interviewing those he had swindled.

I began by checking all the exclusive clubs. As I suspected he belonged to all five. He was also highly regarded, and an elderly businessman I interviewed spoke warmly of his vast knowledge. It was apparent to me, examining some of the correspondence he had left behind, that he was in between frauds, so to speak, but still maintaining a lively correspondence with several government agencies, trying to arrange contracts. He wasn't neglecting the ladies either;

three were writing him endearing letters. All, of course, were wealthy.

I found that the colonel had moved with ease among the blue-bloods. At one club he had arranged to have the *maitre d'* transferred to a more exclusive boat club of which he was a member; in gratitude the man named Halquire as the executor of his estate, which represented his life's savings. Halquire attended the man's funeral, extolled his virtues, then squandered the estate and left $500 in debts when he skipped.

Enroute to Washington, he met a Philadelphia engineer, and after the colonel had discovered he was fairly well-to-do he defrauded him of $5,000, which was supposed to be invested in a revolutionary development, perfected by the colonel, in medical photography. And the colonel really knew what he was talking about. We found he had spent endless hours in a medical library.

That same year two more women fell to the colonel's charm and parted with $12,000. We were also amazed to find that a well-known band leader, the most sophisticated of men, had given the colonel $1,000 to invest in a "revolving nut" scheme.

"He just made it sound so damn good," he told me. "I really believed him."

In the winter of 1940 he became acquainted with a well-to-do matron and after a magnificent sales talk she gave him her Chester estate to sell. When he asked for $125 for "expenses" she gave it to him gladly. Months later she demanded the money back because "I have lost faith in you." The colonel returned it by messenger that same afternoon.

His promptness dispelled her doubts as to his honesty and they resumed their friendship. It is not surprising when he offered his personal note for $5,000 she did not hesitate to give him the money—which she never saw again.

War came and the colonel made the most of it. He embezzled hundreds of thousands of dollars from gullible businessmen. There was scarcely a month in which one of us wasn't winging across the Middle West or flying to Washington or Chicago to track down a tip that the colonel had been seen.

In 1942 word came into the office from the Du Pont family that Halquire, who usually told his victims he was on his way to "Pierre's" for a business conference, might possibly be trying to sell a smokeless powder project to some citizen in a small community in northern Pennsylvania.

Tony Scanlon had just finished a case nearby and was told to stop off at the place enroute to New York.

It was 2:30 A.M. when Tony's train pulled into the village. Tony stepped out into a snow-covered wilderness of unbroken white, unmarked by a single footprint. The only sign of civilization was a mail rack; the only light that picked up the dazzling snow came from the car windows.

"Where's the town?" Tony asked hurriedly of the conductor.

He scratched his head. "I braked out of here forty years ago," the man said.

"That's fine, but where's the town?" Tony insisted.

He swung up on the car steps and waved the lantern. "Somewhere down in that direction," he said vaguely and pointed to the left.

Tony watched the train lights grow smaller and smaller. Finally they winked out. The only light was the starlight that here and there caught a snow crystal and made it shine like a diamond in the cold and frosty night.

Tony started off. The only sound was the crunching of the snow that sounded like crumbling match boxes. It seemed he had walked for hours when he saw a tiny light to his right. He approached cautiously, not knowing if he was walking on a lake or in a canyon. There wasn't a sign of a road. Finally he came on the light; it was coming from the frosted window of a house. Tony looked in and saw that the front of the house had been fashioned into a tiny restaurant. Several men who wore peaked railroaders' hat were sipping coffee and eating towering stacks of pancakes. At it turned out, he had struck the house, patronized by railroaders, as if he had been heading in a straight line. Had he missed it he would have walked all night before he reached the outskirts of the village.

All heads turned when he came in. It was 5:00 A.M. and this was the early shift. He had been walking for two and a half hours.

"Just come in on the No. 8, mister?" a man called out. Tony nodded. He eyed the pancakes, but he was so exhausted and cold he could only mumble that he wanted coffee. After he thawed out someone gave him a lift to the nearest town. There he found a room in an old-fashioned small hotel, whose owner eyed him when Tony asked for the elevator.

He pointed to the stairs. "Right there," he said. After a few hours' sleep Tony made a tour of the tiny community, then decided to hit the barber shop, in most small towns the gathering place for local gossips.

Happily the barber was a garrulous man. "Just come in?"

"This morning," Tony said. "Nice town."

"A salesman?" the barber probed.

"Real estate," Tony said, using the same line of business as the man who was the object of his search.

"Buying?"

"Looking, maybe buying."

The barber's razor slipped over his face. "Hate to tell you, mister, but you just missed a big deal. Only ten of us in it."

"What's the deal?" Tony said.

The barber needed some coaxing, but he was fairly bursting with pride and he let it out. It seems a stranger had appeared and had made it known he was in real estate. He was seen examining a piece of property and the gossipers soon had him coming in on a deal of some magnitude. Finally he admitted he was interested in a site for a big smokeless powder plant which the Du Ponts were financing. Ten of the village's most prosperous citizens flocked to him with their money, but strangely enough he had refused to take any. Tony frowned; this certainly didn't sound like the colonel.

"Yep," said the barber, "we walked down to the pond and even took samples of the water."

"Samples?" asked Tony. "What for?"

The barbor looked at him with scorn. "Anybody knows if you have a powder factory you can't use water with iron in it. Blow the whole place sky high."

Tony closed his eyes. As Barnum had said. . . .

The barber went on to say that the real estate man had even scooped up a bag of dirt to have it analyzed for minerals and then had dropped pebbles into the water to check the "rippling content."

Tony learned that the man owned a Cadillac and lived in a cabin high on a nearby hill.

That afternoon he contacted our office. Glynn, then Chief Investigator, in turn called the state troopers and the District Attorney of the nearest city. They joined Tony and after a tedious journey up the hill made the arrest. One glance and Tony knew this slight, pale-faced man was not Colonel Halquire.

It developed that the man had been born in the community and then moved away when still a small child. He had contracted tuberculosis, and remembering that his mother always said the air of the hills was excellent for sick people, he returned to his home town.

No one knew him and he was under persistent questioning in the barber shop.

"They kept up their prying until I told them I was in the real estate business," he told Tony. "When they insisted I was here for some secret deal I finally made up this story and went through the motions of testing the land and water. Then a committee tried to make me take almost $10,000 to cut them in on the deal. It was all I could do to refuse. Every day they kept asking me when I wanted the money. It got so that some of them were getting mad and accusing me of trying to do them out of the money they would get from my investment. I only told them this yarn so I wouldn't have to confess I had TB and was sick, in case I had to try to get a job. . . ."

Tony caught a ride back to the nearest city after they let the man go.

Our office continued to press hard on the colonel's trail. In 1942–43 we traveled to Ohio, Pennsylvania, Illinois, Delaware, Maryland, the District of Columbia, North Carolina, Michigan and Connecticut, checking on the stories of Halquire's latest frauds and swindles.

On April 21, 1942, District Attorney Hogan ordered 20,000 flyers bearing the colonel's name and description sent out across the country. He also arranged with the National Association of Better Business Bureaus, an organization very valuable to law enforcement agencies in this country, to circularize the colonel's face and description. They were asked to call us collect or to notify any local law enforcement agency if he were seen.

In addition we arranged with the American Hotel Bulletin to distribute 5,800 flyers to that many hotels and several thousand more to the American Bankers' Association. We also contacted the Motor Vehicle Bureau of every state in the union, requesting them to consult their records to see if within the last few years they had a registration under Halquire or one of his many aliases.

Finally, because we had received reports that Halquire was in bad health, our bureau sent a personal letter giving the aliases and descriptions of the colonel to the Bureau of Vital Statistics in every state, asking each to consult its records to see if he had died. Today notices are still posted in these offices across the nation and clerks check periodically.

This was in addition to running down the many tips and complaints which came from the West Coast, the Middle West, New England

and the South. Each complaint was checked out. If the preliminary check showed that the suspect vaguely resembled Halquire we sent an investigator personally to supervise the investigation. Once or twice the information was good and the suspect was Halquire, but each time he had vanished. As always the victim, lulled into a false sense of security by Halquire's glib ways, had waited weeks, sometimes months before contacting the authorities.

But each time we learned a little more about him. In Chicago we talked at length with a wealthy widow who reluctantly agreed at last to file a complaint. The colonel had talked her out of $5,200.

"But he was such a nice man," she cried. "I would have given it to him if he asked for it."

From this woman we obtained two shirts and a few collars. These were rushed back to New York and delivered to the technical Bureau of the Police Department. There the ultra-violet ray brought out hidden laundry marks. These, with the visible laundry and trade markings, were valuable. Now here was a whole new avenue of approach which might lead to Halquire's apprehension. As you may or may not know, the laundry industry in this country has a bureau which has helped solve many a crime. This bureau has a file of every laundry mark made by every laundry in the United States. The mark on your shirt is as valid in court as your fingerprint.

We found a laundryman in Chicago and even a shirtmaker in Washington and Philadelphia, who had made custom-made shirts for the colonel. We knew he had a bull-size neck, was fastidious, had fine tastes and bought only the best material, an item which could well stick in the mind of a clerk. Flyers slipped across the land again to thousands of shirt-makers, and the Laundry Institute of America in Chicago devoted a page to the colonel's picture and an account of his crimes.

In the spring of 1942 Halquire pulled off one of his most lucrative and vicious coups, in which he demonstrated his *modus operandi* in the minutest detail.

The story opened on a blustery winter day when Kathryn, an attractive, rather shy woman of about twenty-five, was standing on a street corner waiting for a bus to take her to her Lincoln Park home where she lived with her well-to-do widowed mother in a two-story stucco home. The only blight on their lives was the threat of tuberculosis which shadowed the young woman.

Kathryn, who was devoted to the arts and literature, worked when her health permitted as private secretary to an official of the Chicago

Red Cross. She and her mother lived sheltered lives; in the evening Kathryn would read aloud or play Chopin. They were regular parishioners of the local Catholic church.

During the first week of January they decided that they would rent the large hall bedroom to an elderly man or woman with unquestionable references. There is evidence that the world of loneliness in which they had been living for so long had begun to press closer and closer on them. And with the periods during which Kathryn needed bed rest becoming more frequent, her mother felt it would be safer if someone else were in the house in case of emergency.

It was about six o'clock and the street lamps were on. Kathryn, bundled up against the cold, was peering down the street when a soft voice made her jump.

"Kathryn?"

She spun around. Standing in the gloom was a short, squat man in a fine tweed overcoat. He wore a Homburg. Warm dark eyes twinkled behind his glasses. He was leaning on a cane and she thought he looked the part of a diplomat.

"Kathryn ———?"

Kathryn naturally was startled. "Yes," she said. "That is my name but who are you, sir?"

He stepped forward. "Colonel Hale Heatherington Halquire," he replied. "I was your father's friend in Springfield. In fact I left shortly after you visited the funeral parlor the night your poor father passed away. That's how I remembered you."

"You knew Daddy in Springfield?" she asked.

"Quite well," Halquire said. "Didn't he ever write to you about me? We went to the theater several times together."

Kathryn had loved her father dearly and cherished his memory. It had been a stunning blow when he had died in Springfield, where he had gone to attend to some banking matter. She was instantly drawn to this soft-spoken stranger who seemed to know so much about her dear father.

They talked at length about him and it wasn't until later that she recalled how carefully chosen his questions had been.

Unknowingly she revealed a great deal—most of which he was to report to her mother as his own version of her late husband. Kathryn, in her loneliness and naïveté, supplied the colonel with all the props he needed.

The meeting had been carefully planned. Halquire always made a

A GALLERY OF ROGUES

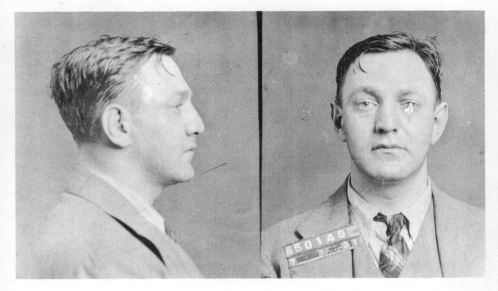

An early rogues' gallery photo of Dutch Schultz.

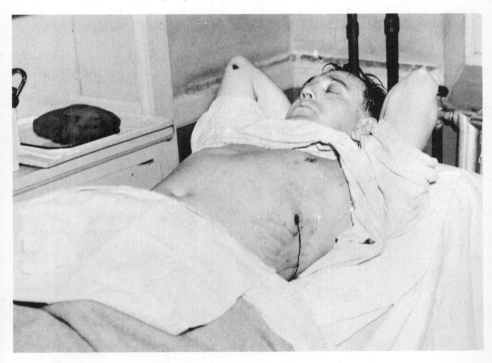

Dutch Schultz, photographed as he lay dying.

Bernard ("Lulu") Rosencranz, a Schultz henchman. The bullets that were fatal to Schultz came from Lulu's gun.

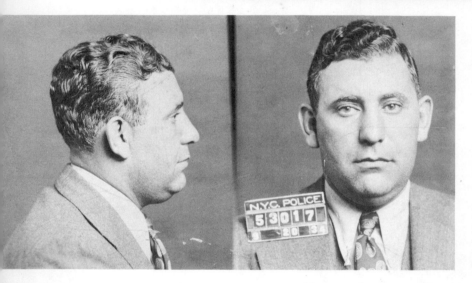

Abe ("Bo") Weinberg (*above*). Abe Landau (*below*).

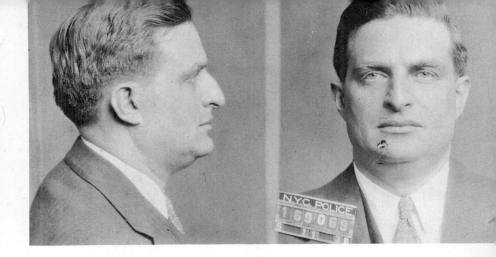

Harry "The Horse" Schonhaus *(above)*. George Weinberg *(below)*.

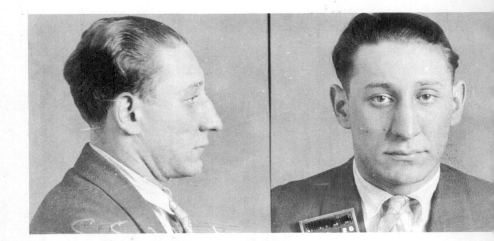

Lawrence Carney.

Ross Colarco, the former clubhouse fighter captured by Danforth at gunpoint.

Louis "Lepke" Buchalter (from a New York Police Department circular).

Anderson T. Herd (the Florida Land Office case).

practice of checking notices offering rooms to rent, but only if the house was situated in a good section. If the prospects looked good he investigated the late owner's background in the libraries of newspaper offices, by studiously reading hundreds of back issues of newspapers to saturate himself with the background of the late husband, son or brother. Sometimes he established himself in the immediate neighborhood and, by shrewd questioning of tradespeople, built up a fund of information about the potential victim. This was what he had done with Kathryn; her father's death was the opening wedge.

"Where are you living now, Colonel?" Kathryn asked.

"On the North Side," he said with a shake of his head, "in a dreadful hotel. It is always cold and there's never enough hot water. The food is atrocious."

Almost without thinking the girl burst out, "Why, we have a room Mother's trying to rent, Colonel. Why don't you join me and look at it? Mother'll be glad to see a friend of Daddy's . . ."

The colonel demurred, but the more he resisted the more the girl insisted. In fact it was only after she pleaded with him that Halquire gallantly acquiesced to her wishes.

"I really should be on my way back to the hotel," he said, "but I would like to see your mother."

Of course this old fraud was welcomed with open arms by the lonely old lady. Before the night was over they had begged the colonel to rent the room—in fact, she cut in half the rent she had been planning to ask. She gave the colonel the room for eight dollars a week and three meals a day!

He moved in the next day. For the next few months he gave a magnificent performance as a kindly retired Army officer whose family had helped to settle the West. He thrilled them with stories of the opening of Oklahoma, the vanishing of the frontier and the great Run of '89 when he and his father had lived under a wagon and he had ridden bareback to claim the section that was the basis of the great fortune he and his father had collected.

He never let on what the great fortune was based on, but he made many telephone calls from the hall, knowing that Kathryn and her mother could not help but overhear his conversations. For example, he would call a New York number or a Chicago broker, "Colonel Halquire speaking," he would say, then ask for the last quotation on a whole list of stocks. It was evident to the ladies he was a man of wealth. He also made calls to Washington—some undoubtedly with his finger pressed down on the receiver hook—to the White House and to the Office of the General Staff. On the telephone it appeared as if he were running the war. And when the headlines appeared of reversals in the field he would growl angrily and ask what those dumbheads were doing in the Pentagon with the last suggestions he had sent them. There were always plenty of toll charges on the telephone bills for calls actually made by the colonel so that the colonel's deceptions were not detected.

It was all quite thrilling to these lonely women. They were completely taken in, which is not surprising when one realizes that two of the shrewdest of New York's garment center merchants also had succumbed to his charms.

Christmas holidays that year were the happiest the two ladies had known for some time. The colonel completely dominated their lives. He was a gourmet and cooked them many a fancy and exotic meal. He bought them presents, many and costly—the colonel's philosophy was that if you invested a little you would make a lot. To their joy, he made his personality felt in their church affairs.

For example, he had strolled into the parish hall, surveyed the decorations and then announced he was throwing a monster Christmas party for the children. He organized the decorations, hired the orchestra, told them what selections to use, played a magnificent Santa and donated the presents. The children and the parents loved him; the two ladies glowed in his reflected glory.

The colonel meanwhile knew what he was doing; he had learned just before Christmas that the two women had more than $30,000 between them. That was Halquire's goal.

The colonel, always the advocate of the fluid front, had branched out. During the time he was charming Kathryn and her mother, he had read that a Gay Nineties Club was being formed and he was present at the opening meeting. It is not surprising he was elected treasurer and wrote the bylaws.

In the next few meetings Halquire selected a few of the likeliest victims, all widows or spinsters, from the club's list. He quickly charmed each one. One woman told me, "Unfortunately, the colonel discovered I had to work for a living as a secretary."

"Why was that unfortunate?" I asked her.

"He dropped me like a hot coal," the woman said wistfully.

The colonel encountered opposition, however, in at least one case. He had assiduously courted an attractive woman who also had a physician as an admirer. Once the colonel escorted her to the doctor's office and the doctor, after a blistering tongue-lashing, ordered him out of his office.

In his gravest voice the colonel turned to the woman and said, "Madam, you have your choice of hearts."

Naturally the woman took his and lost $5,200 as a result.

In the meantime Halquire never neglected Kathryn and her mother. The evenings he was away—he was usually in bed by 10:00 P.M. —he explained that he had spent in the library or playing chess with old Army friends.

Halquire was beginning to suffer greatly from swollen legs and intense headaches. He inquired from one of the ladies in the club the name of a good physician and, concerned over his health, she made an appointment for him with one of the best in Chicago.

The physician told us he found Halquire suffering from phlebitis and high blood pressure, and prescribed some medicine which the colonel took twice, then threw away. The doctor discovered he was a glutton and then gave him medicine to curb his appetite, with a firm warning to cut down on food.

"I warned him he could suffer a fatal stroke if he did not take care of himself," the doctor told us later.

Yet the doctor was so won over by the colonel that in two weeks he was taking Halquire on the rounds of his calls and for drives in the country.

One day the colonel told him, "The trouble with you, doc, is that you are a fine medical man but a poor businessman. I bet half your patients have owed you money for years."

"As a matter of fact many of them do," the doctor said. "I've always thought of hiring an accountant to take over my books."

The colonel was thoughtful for a moment, then said, "Doctor, have all your books ready for me tomorrow."

"Tomorrow? Why?" the doctor asked.

The colonel waved his hand. "I'll let you know."

More out of curiosity the physician had his books together on the following day. The colonel brought them home and came back within a week. He dropped the books and a sheaf of papers on the doctor's desk.

"Here is a complete bookkeeping system," he said. "Follow it faithfully and you'll find that in the next year you will double your income. Your patients will have more respect for you—they've been cheating you for years but you're too soft-hearted to dun them."

The doctor told us he followed the colonel's system and it worked.

When we interviewed him, he refused to believe that Halquire was a cruel thief. It took most of an afternoon of talking to convince the man, so strong were his convictions that Halquire was a wonderful friend. Even seven months after the colonel had disappeared the doctor hoped it would turn out that the colonel had *not* stolen the funds of the victims in his community.

The colonel's plan was ripe; he was ready to take the money Kathryn and her mother had and flee. He had his getaway all arranged. He would only have to transfer his belongings from his hall bedroom to the cozy apartment of his next victim, a widow who was eagerly waiting to make him comfortable and share her life's savings.

Halquire moved slowly but surely. He told Kathryn and her mother his Oklahoma venture had prospered. Wells and derricks were criss-crossing the western sky; black gold was pouring into his pockets the day round. The women whispered together, then Kathryn shyly asked the colonel at dinner one evening if he would invest some of their money for them.

The colonel appeared startled. "Do business with women? My dear ladies, I never do business with the opposite sex."

It was the usual swindler's trick: tell a woman what she couldn't do. Refuse her and she'd be on your heels until you surrendered. They badgered the colonel, begged and cajoled him until he reluctantly accepted $10,000. Ten days later the mother drew out her savings of $20,000 and forced him to take it.

The colonel wasn't in a hurry to leave—he kept up the phony long-distance calls and each time emerged, rubbing his hands and bringing in more wells than there were in all Oklahoma. Then gradually he began to appear worried. He seemed to be distracted, to be staring constantly at some far-off point. He grudgingly confessed that he "couldn't trust those people out there—they never did anything right."

The ladies sympathized with him; it was a shame, they agreed between themselves, that the colonel couldn't get someone to carry out his specific orders.

Then one Sunday morning the colonel received a telegram which he had arranged to be sent to himself, urging him to visit the oil fields at once.

He packed a bag, careful to leave some clothes behind. "If you want something done," he fumed, "you'll have to do it yourself.

Ladies, adieu. I will see you when I have straightened out affairs in my fields."

They saw him to the taxicab and waved good-by. The house seemed strangely silent and all night they talked of Halquire's "goodness and generosity."

The colonel, of course, did not go to the airport to board an Oklahoma-bound plane; he was settled down in his widow's place, sipping a Scotch and puffing on a corona.

Incredible as it appears, Kathryn and her mother did not report the loss of their money for several months. When the colonel did not return in a reasonable time, it was not their money—their whole life's savings—they worried about but the state of health of their thieving guest! They wondered if they should check some Oklahoma hospitals only to realize that they didn't know the exact town or even the part of the state in which the colonel had invested their money. They hadn't even requested a receipt.

It seemed that Kathryn and her mother had a sharp-eyed friend who had never liked the colonel and his expansive ways. She had been their treasured friend, only to be replaced by a stranger.

It took some digging on her part to learn the story. When she suggested she go immediately to the police they were horrified and ordered her not to. Fortunately, she had a great deal more horse sense and reported the fraud to the police. His description matched that in our flyer and we flew to Chicago to cooperate with the local police in the investigation.

Kathryn and her mother collapsed when they heard the news. Halquire had made them penniless, wards of society. We traced all the members of the Gay Nineties Club. For a time it appeared Halquire's doctor might be his confederate, but an investigation proved him to be an innocent victim. So shocked was he at the disclosures which followed that he undertook to treat Kathryn, now desperately ill of tuberculosis, without charge. He drove her and her mother to Colorado, where he arranged for Kathryn to be placed in a state institution and her mother to be cared for in a home.

Our investigation took us all over Illinois. Many persons were naturally reluctant to expose their own stupidity. We learned that the colonel had patronized the finest of restaurants: Henrici's, St. Hubert's Grill and Jacques'. He ordered two of everything; two steak dinners, two orders of mutton chops, even three banana splits, topped off by a candy bar and a plate of vanilla ice cream.

After his trip to one restaurant he lumbered to his feet and had the waiter escort him on a tour of the kitchen. When he engaged the French chef in a lively debate on the importance of certain sauces, the chef bowed him out and told the waiter that this was indeed a real gourmet! The waiter, who later recalled he had been astounded by the man's capacity, received a five-dollar tip.

At Marshall Field's we picked up a pair of custom-made shoes with special arches the colonel had ordered. This, the doctor said, indicated that Halquire's legs were bothering him. This was confirmed when we heard from one witness that the colonel wore elastic stockings. This set us off on a tour of the city's drugstores. Finally, after much legwork, we found a clerk who identified the colonel as the man who had bought an expensive type of medical stocking.

In New York, Chief Investigator Glynn sent on a letter to the manufacturers requesting full information about the stocking we had as a sample and in what states it was sold. The information we received indicated that the garter size was variable, depending on Halquire's health, and that the stocking was sold in fifteen large cities.

While we were busy in Chicago the office canvassed each city from jobbers down to the drugstores. Somewhere, we felt, the colonel had to buy another pair of these stockings because of the inevitable changes in his health which would be reflected in the swelling of his legs.

In Chicago we slowly continued to pick up the colonel's trail; sometimes the things we found could not be explained. Why, for example, did Halquire go into the Tribune Towers Building, purchase expensive tobacco and cigars and hint he was on his way to a conference with "Charlie," a mythical official, only to go out another door? Was he sizing up someone who patronized the shop?

And why had the colonel been so enraged the day Kathryn accepted a registered letter for him while he lay in bed nursing a swollen leg . . . ? "I am the only one who accepts Halquire's letters," he thundered, and so Kathryn had wept. Later that night he begged her forgiveness; the pain in his leg had made him forget his manners. Who had sent the letter—another woman?

We also found that the Gay Nineties Club had been suspended for a while, but upon its reorganization the colonel was the first one to be invited by the ladies.

He had been at his peak that night. Sitting quietly in a large chair, his soft, magnetic voice had drawn them together, welding them into one little group whose happiness would defeat the loneliness they all felt. It was so wonderful one lady cried. But Halquire refused to accept the presidency; he preferred to be the power behind the scenes. He knew someone might send to a newspaper an innocent news item listing his name and some sharp-eyed cop would have him in custody before he could skip.

One day the colonel had arranged an old-fashioned picnic.

The members sat under the trees, ate sandwiches and drank soda, sang old songs, listened to the marvelous lies only the colonel could spin. It had been a glorious day, they all agreed, because of the colonel. . . .

We also discovered that the colonel could become impulsive. One day in a Chicago grill a young man was explaining to his friends that he was entering the new field of insurance and if anyone wanted to take out a policy. . . .

The young men all laughed at the new agent but stopped to look up in wonder at the distinguished gentleman who stood behind them.

"Here is my card, young man," the colonel said. "I couldn't help but overhear you. I want to insure my personal belongings for $2,500. Please make out the policy. Good day."

They were so impressed they all stood up.

The policy was issued, but the colonel never paid the seven-dollar premium.

We found that in Chicago he had lived high off the hog; he had bought 15 tailor-made suits, 12 pairs of special shoes, dozens of custom shirts, scores of handkerchiefs and an assortment of his favorite Homburgs.

But the colonel had definitely flown.

False leads now began popping up across the country like exploding firecrackers. From Chicago I flew to East Grand Forks, Michigan, to track down a tip we had received in a letter from an ex-convict. The man he had identified as the colonel looked something like him but that was all. I returned to New York and wrote another report for the big file.

A few months later a businessman who had read of the colonel's activities in a trade journal called our office from the Waldorf-Astoria to report that a man who looked like Halquire had made a reservation for the afternoon train to Albany and had requested a wheel-chair. The man was short, stout and had swollen legs!

The clerk at the Waldorf-Astoria insisted to me that the customer was a fine old man whom he had known for years. That could be; the colonel had been around for a long time and more than one clerk had been won over by his charm.

I checked the train in Albany and found the man in the wheel-

chair was on the way to Saratoga. Our office contacted the state
police headquarters and an officer went out to get the details on the
old man and his background. That evening a long report came from
the young trooper who had interviewed many witnesses who positively identified the gentleman as a retired and ill judge from Georgia.
We obtained his picture and the resemblance was astonishing.

A year passed while we checked many false leads and gossip. We
all thought surely it was only a matter of days before the vast network of state and local police, the trade journal notices and the
thousands of flyers District Attorney Hogan had ordered distributed
around the country would enmesh him. But luck was on Halquire's
side; he was never caught.

In the spring of 1943 his money was apparently running out for
he boldly returned to Chicago to see his old friend and cellmate,
Doctor Carruthers, the phony mystic, in his Loop office.

He was expensively dressed and smoking his favorite cigar. He
looked serene and prosperous. He gave his name to the secretary
and was admitted. Inside, he came to the point.

"I want in," he said. "I'll be back in a few days after you think it
over."

As the colonel bickered with her boss, Carruthers' secretary slid
open her desk drawer, studied our flyer and picked up the phone.
She told our investigators that she informed the patrolman on the
phone that Halquire, wanted by the District Attorney's office of New
York County, was in her employer's office. The patrolman, to be
charitable, may have had plenty of local trouble to worry about,
without having to be troubled by the frantic call of a woman who was
telling him a man wanted in New York was in a downtown office.
But whatever the reason, the police did not arrive. When she called
a second time she was advised to go out and get the policeman on
the nearest beat.

The woman was on the fifteenth floor, the only one in the office,
and naturally she concluded that if the police weren't interested, why
should she worry? She hung up moments before Halquire emerged.

When Halquire started to put on airs she pulled him down a peg.

"Don't 'colonel' me, you old phony," she snapped. "You're nothing but a con man on the make . . ."

Then, in the only scene we have from an eyewitness in which the
colonel dropped his play-acting and turned violent, he spun around
and tried to strike her with his fist. It was as if he had dropped a
mask, she told us, which, for a few fleeting seconds, revealed the

true criminal. His face was livid as he cursed her savagely. When he called the next day, his manners and voice as smooth as oil, she hung up on him—on Carruthers' orders.

This was the nearest any law enforcement agency in the country came to nabbing the fabulous colonel.

In 1943–44, the colonel apparently made his headquarters in Wilmington, assuming a role as a man of wealth, a lobbyist, a speculator and a "friend of Pierre Du Pont."

Halquire sized up his victims on the train rides to Washington, in the parlor cars of course. His impressive bearing and courtly manners won him friends among the porters and waiters. He was always "Colonel Halquire" or "Colonel George Lindsay Smith," manufacturer of explosives, shoes, machinery, dealer and promoter in oil, lobbyist, former government official who knew men in high places and could establish a liaison with the Army, Navy, and the whole vast machinery of the United States government. Never was Halquire questioned or asked to provide identification or references. I guess it wouldn't have made much difference; he would probably have forged them himself.

One of his classic swindles began in a smoky parlor car in 1944. The colonel, with his sharpened instinct, had picked out a Baltimore manufacturer as a possible victim. The Baltimorean struck up a conversation. Halquire was a skillful interrogator and soon the bored manufacturer was speaking quite frankly of his business, family and friends.

At one point Halquire learned the man had a friend in the shoe industry who was ready to expand. Halquire knew one question was inevitable; what line was *he* in . . . ?

"The shoe industry," he said promptly when it was asked. "In fact, I'm going to Washington now to conclude a million-dollar shoe contract with the Army."

"Gosh," the other said, "my friend would certainly like to know you. Maybe you've heard of him."

Halquire shook his head. "I don't deal much with small stocks," he explained. "I usually sell and buy factories. In fact, just before the war I sold an entire community which was built around my business."

By the time they arrived in Washington where Halquire said he was enroute to the "Hill," the Baltimore man was begging the swindler to come to Baltimore to speak to his friend in the shoe line.

After putting on a show of reluctance Halquire agreed and a date was made for the following week.

Halquire spent that week in several libraries. He had a photographic memory and a love of research. He read from morning until night, until by the time he arrived in Baltimore he had a comprehensive knowledge of the shoe industry.

His new victim had lined up ten men, including his friend who had spent thirty-five years in the shoe industry, waiting to meet the colonel. They enjoyed a fine luncheon, and Halquire appeared really angry when someone tried to pick up the check. Then they returned to a small meeting-room at a hotel to try to persuade Halquire to come in with their shoe expansion program; they had the land and the factory sites, Halquire had the ability and the money. Between them they could raise about $100,000.

Halquire demurred; surely they could not believe that he, a man who dealt in millions, would join their small proposition. They begged him but Halquire kept putting them off, insisting rather upon discussing shoes with the veteran of thirty-five years in the industry. At one point he held up a piece of fine leather and some shoemaker's thread and gave them a vivid demonstration of the mistakes made currently by shoe men in the threading of soles.

The shoe man later recalled, "He was superb. Never in my life have I met a man, and that includes leaders in my field, who knew so much about shoes. He talked for hours and never repeated himself."

Another fine meal followed and Halquire left—with $30,000.

The blow came slowly. When they didn't hear from Halquire they met again; all were reluctant to believe they had been swindled. Finally they went to the police and we entered the investigation. All we could do was chalk up another victory for the colonel and wonder about the universal gullibility of men.

As in many cases, there was a tragic twist to the colonel's crime. The man who had met the swindler on the train and induced his friends to put up their money suffered a heart attack. When our investigator interviewed him he could speak only a few minutes at a time, so severe had been the attack. It took the investigator seven hours to get the entire story.

The colonel next appeared in New Haven, Connecticut, where he fleeced a hard-headed businessman out of $5,200 with the aid of a fine act and a "prop" telephone. I was assigned to this phase and interviewed the colonel's victim and his colleagues, who had been ready to make a big investment. For some reason the colonel folded his tent rather abruptly. Perhaps his instinct told him he had stayed too long in one place, and he left before making a larger haul.

From the victimized businessman I gathered the entire story.

The colonel had established an office in New Haven, including his trick telephone, and had so impressed the businessmen of the city with his brisk and friendly way of addressing the country's great— over the unconnected phone—that this particular businessman invited the colonel to inspect his plant.

It was a grand tour. The businessman showed the colonel every nook and cranny and cited past performances of efficient production with a great deal of pride. The colonel had casually mentioned that he, of course, had ways to obtain war contracts.

But back in the main office the colonel carefully lowered his big bulk into a leather-covered chair and shook his head.

"My dear fellow," he said, "your plant is much too small. The contract I had in mind calls for a million dollars. If you got it you would have to expand your plant buildings and operations or lease a much larger building."

The businessman asked the colonel to give him a little time. A few weeks later he found a large plant, which he leased.

The colonel was still reluctant. He said that he doubted that the two plants were large enough to carry off the big production deal he had in mind, but after a great deal of discussion and pleading on the part of the businessman, the colonel reluctantly agreed to obtain the contract.

That afternoon in his office, with the businessman eagerly listening, the colonel pulled off a grand performance. With his trick telephone he called everyone from the President's secretary down to some Senators. All of them happened to be out to lunch, but he left messages for them to call him back. Of course they did, because all the colonel did was reach over with his toe and tap the button under his desk to ring the telephone. His booming voice filled the room:

"Colonel Halquire speaking. Oh, Senator, how nice of you to call back. About that business I was speaking to you about at lunch at the Willard last week, I think I have the gentleman with the exact equipment you were so anxious to find. Yes, he's right here and he's willing to start at once. No, I can't be there Tuesday—but just a moment now." Then the colonel would lean over, wink at the businessman and flip through a calendar engagement book. "But I can be there on Wednesday. Lunch? That's fine. I'll meet you at the bar at the Willard."

Then his voice would lower to a conspiratorial whisper.

"Incidentally, Senator, will the other people concerned be there also? Fine. I trust you will contact them. Good-by, Senator. Nice talking to you."

The colonel hung up his telephone, swung around in his chair, and said to the businessman, "Well, you've as good as got the contract. Of course, you know in a deal of this kind you will have to be prepared to spend some money. I think $5,000 will take care of the entertainment and a few gifts we will have to give to the proper people."

The businessman, visualizing a lush million-dollar contract, hastily agreed. He was no longer a logical reasoning man; he was now a man consumed by greed.

I spent some time in town checking on the habits of the colonel in an attempt to find a new angle in his mode of life. It was the usual story of gluttony, high living and big tips.

While I was working in Connecticut, Halquire had moved back to Washington, where he made his stand in one of the exclusive tobacco shops. There is no doubt from our investigations that Halquire is a legitimate student of the tobacco industry. There is little he doesn't know about the business of growing, mixing and selling tobacco. He is also quite fluent in describing the history of tobacco.

The colonel made several visits to the store during which he bought many expensive pipes and jars of tobacco, which he said were for his friends on the "Hill." Each time he let slip something that made the tobacconist look up in surprise. After one visit the man said, "Lord, you certainly know your tobacco, Colonel!"

The colonel only smiled.

Gradually the colonel became an accepted visitor at the shop. In fact, we found that a special chair was placed to one side of the counter to assure his comfort.

One day a tall and distinguished-looking man walked into the store and stared at a large case of pipes. The colonel sized him up as a possible victim. He was just about to strike up a conversation with the man when the customer walked to where he was seated.

"Pardon me, sir, can you wait on me?"

The colonel rose to his feet. "Certainly, sir, right this way."

The colonel was so superb he sold the man three pipes at ten dollars each, a large jar of his own Erin Moore mixture, along with a lecture on how to break in the pipes. The man reached into his pocket, then looked into his wallet.

"I'm terribly embarrassed," he started to say and I can imagine the colonel's eyes begin to narrow—was this a fellow con man?—when the customer took out a card.

"I'm Congressman ————," he said. "If you send the purchases to my office my secretary will pay for them."

The clouds of suspicion vanished from the colonel's brow. "I will see that they arrive there tomorrow, sir. And thank you, sir. Please feel free to call upon us for any advice; we are most happy to please you."

The tobacconist was delighted but dismayed that his friend and favorite customer had been mistaken for a clerk, but the colonel chuckled and seemed quite pleased. He had begun to stalk Congressional game.

The next morning the colonel himself delivered the pipes. The embarrassed Congressman fell all over himself apologizing when he found the "clerk" was the distinguished Colonel Halquire. They had lunch, then dinner and the Congressman was quickly won over. In fact, we discovered that on the day the colonel disappeared, the Congressman had been reading a protest against socialized medicine written by the colonel, which he hoped to get into the *Congressional Record*.

I was puzzled by this until I learned that the colonel was attempting to shake down some medical society by showing them that his power on the "Hill" could be used to defeat socialized medicine.

"Don't really introduce it as a bill, just read it aloud so it will appear in the *Congressional Record*," the colonel said. "It's only to please some doctor friends."

The colonel was never a man to let a dollar go by.

He was often seen in the Congressman's office and in fact gave him some small souvenir elephants as gifts for his office. As usual, he began using the phone to call his brokers and the talk was in the hundreds of thousands. He was again in oil fields and bloc stock-buying.

One day while he was waiting for the Congressman, his secretary told the colonel, "Please, Colonel, don't tell the Congressman, but I would like you to take some money I have and invest it."

"Madam, I never do business with women," the colonel said. "It is my policy."

The woman insisted on other visits until finally the colonel agreed to accept $10,000. She was in the process of getting ten other women together to put up the same amount when she confessed to her employer what she had done.

When Halquire walked in the following day the Congressman was plainly annoyed.

"Look here, Colonel," he said, "the money you took from my secretary represents all she has in the world. She's on in years and after she leaves here she'll need it . . ."

The colonel listened in silence, his face impassive. Then he rose with the dignity of a peer.

"My dear sir," he said, "the woman asked me to help her and I reluctantly agreed to take her money. However, if you doubt my word or ability I will gladly return it to her."

Then, while the Congressman watched, he laboriously raised his swollen leg to the top of the desk, pulled up his pants leg and his long underwear, then reached down into the elastic stocking to take out a roll of bills.

He flipped them before the amazed eyes of the Congressman.

"One hundred and ten thousand dollars," he said calmly. "Do you wish to count it?"

The Congressman was now sure he had made a mistake.

"Now, don't be angry, Colonel," he said. "I was only looking out for her interest. Suppose you give her back half her money and keep the other half . . ."

"Suppose I give her back *all* her money," the colonel said. "Will that assure you, sir?"

The Congressman held up his hand. "No, no, just half."

Halquire slowly counted $5,000 and, picking up an envelope, put the bills inside and handed it to the Congressman.

"Please inform your secretary that in 90 days her money will be doubled. Good day, sir," he said and walked out.

The colonel felt he was treading on thin ice, and after all half was better than none. He still had 90 days to make another strike.

His next victim was an official of an A. F. of L. union with headquarters in Washington. This man of the world, himself a lobbyist, was taken for $2,000 by Halquire. A very pretty redhead now appeared in the picture. She had introduced Halquire to the union man, and for a time we thought the colonel had acquired a partner.

If the woman were indeed the colonel's partner, we expected she would eventually lead us to him. So Tony was sent to Washington, and with the assistance of the Washington police arranged for a phony long distance call to be made to the woman.

Tony was near by when the phone rang in her apartment.

"This is long distance," the operator said. "I have a call for Miss ——— from the colonel."

She excitedly replied: "Please put him on at once. Colonel, is that you, Colonel . . . ?"

There was only silence and sputtering of the wires, then the operator came back on.

"I am sorry but your party hung up."

"Well, call him back at the number," the woman insisted.

"I am sorry, it is a booth," the operator said. "Whoever answered the phone said your party walked out."

The whole operation, of course, was completed by one operator working with the police. The woman then made several frantic calls, and within an hour the victimized union official appeared in the apartment. It was plain that the woman could not be working with Halquire, so Tony approached her and made a great play of being frustrated when she told him the colonel had called only an hour before. She promised complete cooperation and did give us some leads and tips.

The colonel was still free, but now his former cellmate and partner was on his way to jail. Doctor Carruthers was indicted by the government for fraudulent use of the mails in connection with the sale of his junk and he was convicted. The self-styled mystic was given five years in federal prison to meditate. The background information we had unearthed was effectively employed in the trial.

In the summer of 1944, I was on the colonel's trail in Chester, Pennsylvania, where I found Halquire had sold several homes in a series of fast deals which netted him anywhere from $320 to $9,200.

Philadelphia . . . Chicago . . . St. Louis . . . Detroit . . . Saratoga . . . Albany . . . New York. . . .

From the meager reports we were able to get, the colonel's health was going downhill. We knew this from doctors and from the different sizes in the elastic stockings he was buying. Suddenly the complaints and tips winked out. There was a strange silence from the colonel. Now he had become an obsession with me, as he was with all of the men in the office, and our office kept in touch with law enforcement agencies all over the country, waiting for the colonel to reappear.

One Christmas Eve about 1946, I received an urgent assignment to fly to the Middle West on a fugitive case. When I returned I found a note from a woman in New Jersey that the colonel had been seen in that state, but had vanished.

From the information I have been able to pick up from conversations remembered by those who had caught the colonel in a mellow mood, I have written an unofficial ending to his story.

That Christmas Eve he was on his way to visit a home for the aged run by Catholic nuns. The colonel, it seemed, had been one of their best contributors for the reason that he was again playing for big stakes—he was planning to get the pastor to invest the building funds in one of his schemes—a postwar development. On a visit to the home he died of a heart attack and was buried in the small church yard or perhaps in a potter's field. However, we checked the death certificates in every state in the union and have found no record of a death under his many aliases.

The small, waddling man with the twinkling eyes, steel-trap brain, and merciless heart may be sitting this very night in some soft-hearted lady's estate, telling her in his quiet, confident manner that his heart is hers or, over brandy and cigars, dazzling a prospective businessman with a "sure-fire" proposition. If he is, be sure that a District Attorney's man will someday close in on him.

11. THE WAR YEARS ON "THE AVENUE": TEEN-AGE RUNAWAYS AND DELINQUENTS

DURING THE years of World War II, Times Square—ugly, garish, tinseled—beckoned like a flashing beacon to thousands of teen-age boys and girls. Here, they thought, they would find romance, excitement, glamour; instead they found sordidness, ugliness and cruelty.

After the attack on Pearl Harbor our office was besieged with inquiries from parents all over the country, begging us to find their children who had run away to come to New York. It is not our job and legally it does not come within our jurisdiction to seek out runaways, except when they are implicated in a felony, such as rape, robbery, compulsory prostitution or other serious crimes.

After a conference with District Attorney Hogan I was given a roving assignment to see what was going on in the Times Square and Harlem areas.

From the Luciano investigation and others I was familiar with the rotten bars and dives on "The Avenue," as Eighth Avenue, in the 40's, was called, so I adopted my usual "Dan O'Brien of Boston" role—the mysterious fellow who has been around—and began prowling on "The Avenue."

The Bucket of Blood, the most infamous, was the natural beginning. I was known—as Dan O'Brien—to some of the bartenders and hangers-on, who assumed I was in the rackets. They welcomed me like a prodigal son to these gin mills with the smoke thick as a fog, the din a mixture of blaring jukeboxes, shouting servicemen, bellowing drunks and barber-shop quartets.

The place was jammed with servicemen, few of them over twenty. The whole atmosphere was "Live-today-for-tomorrow-we-die." The boys were trying to consume as much liquor as possible; the young girls' idea was to give them as much comfort as possible.

The girls, whether they were runaways from a Missouri farm or a cosmopolitan city, dressed alike; saddle shoes, ankle-high sweat socks, tight sweaters and skirts. They wore their hair long and piled high in front. They talked in loud, shrill voices, laughed at anything, drank, chain-smoked, danced like dervishes and seemed to be on the verge of hysteria. In a way they were a symbol of the times; frightened of the uncertain future, insecure, desperate for some happiness before it was too late.

The first night I just drifted from bar to bar, letting it be known that I was looking around for some fun—young fun. In no time the panderers, both male and female, as well as some of the bartenders who acted as pimps as a side-line, were aware of what I wanted.

One night a bartender leaned over and whispered as he poured a drink, "Little Petey has something for you."

I slipped him a five-dollar bill. Little Petey was a notorious young thug and panderer.

"Tell Pete I'm free tonight," I said softly.

He nodded. A half hour later he was back. Pete was on his way over to say hello.

Pete soon appeared. He was a stocky man of about 25 with a face that looked like dough kneaded out of shape—a souvenir of his days as a stumblebum fighter. He twirled a key ring.

He slid next to me after pushing a young drunken soldier off his seat.

"I'm Pete. I understand you want some young stuff," he said out of the corner of his mouth.

I nodded.

"Who are you?" he asked.

I turned and gave him a long stare. "The name's Dan," I said softly. "Suit you?"

He seemed taken back. "I was just askin', Dan."

"Well, don't ask," I said. "How much is she?"

"Ten bucks and she's yours for an hour," he said. He grinned. "She's fresh. I broke her in myself." After handing me a card on which he made a small circle, he gave me a number of a room in a dingy West Side Hotel, then held out his hand. I gave him ten dollars.

As I stood up he said, "I'll come by and tell you when your time's up." I had all I could do to keep from hurling him across the bar.

When I reached the hotel room I tapped softly. A frightened voice answered, "Yes—who is it?"

"Pete sent me over," I said and slipped the card under the door. In a moment the door was opened by a pretty young girl with one blackened eye. She was clad only in a man's worn dressing robe.

"Hello," I said, closing the door. "My name is Dan. Pete said you wanted company."

She said, "Pete said I had to get money before I do anything." It was obvious she was frightened to death. Tears were welling. Then she bowed her head, weeping bitterly.

"Please don't make me do it," she kept saying. "Please don't tell Pete . . ."

"Don't worry about Pete," I said. "I'll take care of him." Then I identified myself.

"Did you run away from home?" I asked.

She nodded dumbly.

"From where?"

The sordid story poured out. She was the only daughter of a well-to-do Pennsylvania surgeon. At college some classmates returned from a weekend trip to New York. They had sat up most of the night describing for Rose, as we will call her, the excitement of a date they had with two servicemen who had taken them night-clubbing and dancing. Rose was intrigued. When she pleaded they agreed to take her the next time. The following week the three girls came to New York. Unfortunately, the two servicemen couldn't get a third date for Rose but promised they would the following night, a Sunday. After her friends had left Rose decided to see the fabulous Times Square she had heard so much about.

She said she was standing on the corner of 42nd Street and Seventh Avenue for only five minutes when she was conscious of a man standing next to her.

"Stranger in New York?" he asked pleasantly.

She nodded. "It's fascinating," she said.

He started to point out prominent buildings to her and before she knew it they were walking down Broadway. She hesitated when he suggested a show but a name band on the marquee made her say yes. After the show he took her on a tour of wild bars which enthralled her. Not used to liquor, she was an easy conquest. He got her drunk and brought her to his shabby hotel room. When he started to undress her she screamed and he hit her, blackening her eye. As she said, she was half-conscious when he raped her.

When it was over he showed her a knife. "From now on you do as I say," he said. "We're going to check into a hotel and when I send up a man with a card you do what he wants. For everyone you take care of it means two dollars for you."

He also threatened her with arrest if she talked. He raped her twice during the night, once knocking her unconscious. Late that night he brought her to a fourth-rate hotel where he had a friend as a clerk. He insisted on having intercourse with the girl before he checked them in. The girl was forced to submit. Then she was stripped and given the filthy bathrobe. Fortunately, I was the first customer.

I told her to try to calm herself. I'll never forget the slow passage of that hour while the unfortunate young girl kept choking dry sobs despite anything I could say in a vain effort to comfort her.

It was less than an hour when the knock came. I slipped off my coat and motioned to her to open the door. When she slid back the lock Pete swaggered in.

"Did you fix up my friend?" he demanded.

The girl just stared at him. With a curse he started toward her, his fist raised.

"Just a minute," I said.

At that moment he knew he had been trapped. He made one leap for the door and my fist caught him on the side of the jaw. He flew over a chair and slid half under the bed.

I dragged him out and threw a basin of water over him. Eventually he was booked on a rape charge. I brought the girl to the Children's Shelter at 105th Street and Fifth Avenue. Later I had the distressing task of informing a heart-broken father what had happened to his daughter and advising him to come to New York and bring her home.

I arrested the hotel clerk the next day. After he had been booked I returned to the hotel, purely on a hunch. A drunken old Irish woman who acted as a maid told me what I wanted to know. She gave me a passkey to a room where I stretched out on a bed to wait.

I was half-dozing when the door opened. Two 12-year-old girls, both drunk, followed by four servicemen, in various stages of intoxication, staggered into the room.

The soldiers started to bolt when they saw me, but I reached the door first. They were too frightened to lie. They told me the story in a very short time. The girls were runaways from a West Virginia mining town, who had been attracted to the lights of Times Square by some movie they had seen. Two days after their arrival their money had run out; the rooming-house operator suggested they could pay their rent by having intercourse with him. From this they graduated into prostitution for meals or a few dollars for food; their only clients were servicemen.

"We wanted to be patriotic," one child said.

I sent the girls to the Children's Shelter where a subsequent medical examination revealed one had contracted a venereal disease. The rooming-house proprietor was also booked on a charge of rape. He, Pete and the clerk received long terms in Sing Sing.

An anonymous letter led me to the next crime against a child. The letter, which arrived at our office, read:

District Attorney's Office,
Centre St., New York City.
Dear Sir:

I am reporting a case which I am quite sure you will take action upon. The case is one wherein a married man who has three children by his first wife and one by his second (common law) took advantage of a little 15-year-old girl during the month of December: results, she will soon give birth to a child . . . There is not only a case of rape involved but also one of bigamy, for as he never did obtain a divorce from his first wife, he is therefore guilty of unlawfully marrying another person . . . The parents of the girl in question, and especially the father seems to take the matter as a joke, but I cannot see where this joke comes in unless the father thinks a term in Sing Sing is a joke. The father of this child is guilty as an accessorer not only after the facts in the bigamy complaint, but also in the rape case, for he never lifted his hands to see that American womanhood was protected and reported to the authorities . . . This same party is constantly running after little girls. On last Wednesday he attempted to entice a little girl who he spoke to on West 42nd Street . . . I looked around for a policeman but none was in sight, hence, he went on his way.

In the name of decency and for the good of the community, I appeal to you to apprehend not only the principle but the father of the child for they are both guilty of a felony . . . the time to act is now and not tomorrow, for tomorrow may be too late . . . The girl in question is Fanny ———, residing at ——— 10th Avenue.

This letter is to be treated as confidential.

Anoum.

I learned more about this case after talking to the girl's father.
After José, the seducer, had endeared himself to the family he be-

gan taking Fanny to the movies. For the first few times he was meticulous in his behavior, always returning her home before 10:00 P.M. But one night he took her to his apartment and raped her. After that he made the child submit to him twice a week.

"What about your wife?" I asked the girl's father. "Where is she?"

The man hobbled to the next room. I followed. It was gloomy, lighted only by a candle in front of a tiny statue of the Virgin. He pointed to a corner where a woman sat, staring into space. I had to bend over to convince myself she was breathing. Saliva rolled out of her mouth down her chin. Her lips moved but the whispers were incoherent. Back in the kitchen, the father told me a harrowing story of hardship, poverty and desperation. His wife had been helpless for five years after the birth of their last child; he had to feed, dress and undress her.

I asked the father, "Why didn't you go to the police when this man molested your daughter?"

He shrugged, hobbled across the room to a chest of drawers, took out a paper and handed it to me.

I read it with disbelief; it was a marriage certificate. Later we learned that José and the child had been married in an obscure church. The clergyman who had performed the ceremony had left the city when we went to interview him; I still cannot understand how any man could have accepted that tiny girl as a lawful bride. Legally, this marriage certificate protected José. If the state was to punish this man we had to build up another case against him.

I interviewed the father for four hours, probing, digging, trying to find some clue to other criminal acts José might have committed.

During the interview the father told me that José had given the little girl a bicycle for her wedding present! Later he had given her a ring and bracelet. The girl had the cheap jewelry set for a month. Then one day, the father recalled, a man came and took them back. José had never paid more than the initial down payment of a dollar . . .

I was doubly shocked when I asked the father if he had ever given his daughter any understanding of sex. The father nodded, "That's why I can't understand how Fanny got herself into this mess. I always told her to use a contraceptive when she went with a man . . ."

I could only stare at him. Later in reviewing the conversation in my report I could understand and pity this poor family.

The father, a cripple and a foreigner in a strange city, had never gone to school. The mother was mentally incompetent and belonged in an institution. Fanny had never gone to school. They had always lived in dire poverty. In this dim, shabbily furnished railroad flat, a stone's throw from Times Square where the price of a theater ticket could have provided a feast for these poor people, their daily supper was either a can of beans or a can of sardines on stale bread. This was the little known, bitter side of Manhattan. I wondered, as I finished typing my report, how many other Fannys there were in the city who had been raped and seduced and bought off with a cheap trinket or a toy . . .

I just couldn't let go of the case. The face of her one-legged father haunted me. I returned to the neighborhood where José lived and began a house-to-house questioning of neighbors and tradespeople. From one of the more talkative neighbors—and there is always one in every investigation—I learned that José had been seen with another child about Fanny's age, whom he described as his daughter. The neighbor thought they lived in the Bronx.

The marriage license bureau proved that José was already married. The Department of Health records showed he had two children.

I paid a visit to his wife, who told me they had been married 16 years. His daughter, a nice-looking dark-eyed child of 15, said quite candidly: "We don't see much of Daddy any more; he's got a girl downtown."

"Is her name Fanny?" I asked.

The girl shook her head. "Oh, no, her name is Mary. She lives on 23rd Street."

Downtown, I found the other girl in José's life. She was also his "wife" and the mother of a baby girl.

I took statements from his two wives. Their marriages made the child-marriage null and void, which meant I now had José on a rape charge as well as on a bigamy count.

After a conference at the D.A.'s office, I returned to Fanny's house with Jack Lawler, one of our veteran grand jury detectives. When Jack saw the pregnant child his eyes narrowed. I felt sorry for José if he tried to use the knife which Fanny's father had warned us he carried in his belt.

"It will be good if you can find his letter," the father said suddenly.

I was surprised. "What letter?"

He sighed. "I did not want to tell you before. José said he would kill me with his knife if I told." He shifted uneasily in his chair. "When he did that to my daughter he wrote me a letter telling me what he had done. He said Fanny would have a baby and I should not stand in his way."

"Where is the letter?" I asked.

"After he sent it to me he took it back," the father said. "He said he would keep it always, and if I went to the police he would show it to everyone and disgrace me with my friends . . ."

"Does he come here every day?" I asked the father.

"Only when he wants her body," was the bitter answer.

"If I send one of the children with a story Fanny is ill and wants him, will he come?" I asked.

The father nodded. "I think he will come."

I gave the oldest boy a half-dollar to tell José Fanny needed him. The child returned with the news José was out but that he had left the message. While we waited the father prepared coffee and a sandwich of stale bread and dried ham. It wasn't particularly appetizing, but we both made a fuss over the humble meal. The children were washing the dishes when the bell rang. The oldest boy went out, then returned.

"José," he hissed.

Lawler shifted his chair near the door and I swung to the other side. When the door opened and a flashily dressed man walked in I kicked the door shut and stood against it. He just stood there; it was clear he knew what was up.

"Raining out, José?" I asked.

Lawler spun him around for me to frisk him. He was clean but defiant. We shook him up for a few minutes to make him realize it was useless to resist, then marched him downstairs. At his flat we searched for the letter the father said had described the rape. I found a knife, the one he had used to intimidate the father, and some letters and pictures. But I couldn't locate the one important letter. Lawler and I went over the place piecemeal, but no luck. After a two-hour search we were ready to give up. As I stood in the middle of his living-room a mirror garnished with roses along its border caught my eye. As I moved toward it José excitedly began to berate us for disturbing his property.

Of course we found the letter and more pictures pasted on the back of the mirror.

By 6:00 P.M. José was booked on a charge of rape at the West 37th Street precinct. He later received ten years in state prison.

A month later I received a telegram from Fanny, who was in a New York hospital; she wanted to see me.

"She had a baby girl yesterday," a nun from the hospital told me on the phone.

Fanny, who was a slight child, was almost lost in the big hospital bed. She gave me a big smile when I came in and her eyes lighted up when she saw the flowers and candy I had brought. She told me this was the first time anyone had ever given her a present.

It was difficult for me to talk to this child, now a mother, but I tried to make some small talk about her brothers and her father.

Fanny didn't say much. Finally she reached out to hold my hand. Big tears rolled down her cheeks.

"Please, Mr. Danforth, tell me . . . should I give up my baby . . . ?"

It was a stunning question. What could I tell this poor child? Should she bring a baby to that dingy tenement and try to care for it amidst such poverty? Should she give up the baby, which, it was plain, she now loved with a great intensity?

Now the words kept pouring out. She talked of the baby and how much she wanted it; she said she would get work, even washing dishes if necessary. . . .

Fortunately, I recalled she was a Catholic and sought out the hospital chaplain. I explained the entire story, which shocked him, but he promised to see and advise the child.

Three days later the chaplain called; Fanny had given up the baby for adoption.

"She leaves the hospital tomorrow, Mr. Danforth, and she asked to see you," he said.

The next day I came up with some more flowers, which again brightened her big black eyes.

The nuns had dressed her in a new white dress, shoes and stockings. Her hair was neatly combed and braided. She looked all of ten years old. I promised I would do anything I could to help her father get a job, which I later did, and when I turned to go something made me stop.

"Fanny," I said, "as I came up here I saw a big doll. Would you like it?"

She nodded. I waved good-by and went out. I took a cab to Macy's and bought the biggest doll I could find, then returned to the hospital.

Fanny silently took the doll and hugged it. I turned at the door. She was cradling it the way a mother does her newborn baby.

As the months passed it became quite clear that Times Square was fast becoming a center of juvenile delinquency and crime. "The Avenue" offered me insights into shocking and savage situations.

One morning I received a call from the office. A lawyer had reported that the 12-year-old son of a friend had been missing for a week. He described the child as an unusually shy boy, home-loving and very obedient.

Chief Investigator Glynn ordered me to look into the case so I called the lawyer. He was insistent that the boy was not a runaway.

"I know Bob," he said. "I'm sure he wouldn't cause his mother any grief. I think he's being held by someone."

Later that night I visited the family in a fairly good section of the East Side. The couple were grief-stricken and bewildered by the disappearance of their only child. They gave me a picture of the boy, which showed him to be a slight, good-looking child. We went over everyone who could have possibly been in contact with their son. I interviewed their friends and relatives, but not one could offer a solution. The next day, just on a hunch, I went back to the family. Again we went over the list of relatives and friends. Just as I was about to leave the father hesitated.

"Anyone else?" I asked.

"Well," he said, "there's a fellow named Pepe who works in a restaurant not far from here who used to give Bob half a dollar for walking his dog." Then he shook his head. "But he hasn't been around for months. The last I heard he was in California."

"Where did he work?" I asked.

The father wasn't sure of the address but did have a general location. Something made me impatient to find that restaurant. I visited every restaurant in the neighborhood until I found the one where Pepe had been working as a chef. None of the help knew where he had gone, but one waiter recalled that he had been friendly with an assistant chef. I located this man in Queens. The moment I saw him I knew he was a homosexual.

"Where's Pepe?" I asked, after showing him my shield.

Like most homosexuals he was happy to inform on others as long as his own personal life wasn't being investigated. Twenty minutes later I left with Pepe's home address and the name of the restaurant where he worked. I decided to hit the apartment first. Using the procedure we always followed, I checked in with my bureau, then picked up a detective from the local precinct. The apartment was on the second floor of an old brownstone building in the east fifties. I rang the front bell, then knocked on the apartment door several times.

"I think there's someone in there," I whispered to the detective. He pressed his ear against the door and nodded.

"Let's kick it in," he said.

He was a burly man and the door flew open as he slammed against it.

What we saw then was one of the most pitiful sights I have ever seen. The boy, both eyes closed, his lips swollen and his body a mass of bruises and cuts, huddled nude on a daybed, one leg chained to the leg of the bed. He whimpered when we came in.

"Don't hit me, mister . . . don't hit me. . . ."

We wrapped the boy in a blanket and rushed him to the hospital. There doctors said he had been beaten savagely by a sadist and had been sexually assaulted. Later, when he had calmed down and was in his mother's arms, he told us how he had met this man on the street and had gone to his apartment to earn another quarter for taking care of the dog. After attacking him, the man warned the boy he would tell the police and his parents of what he had done if he tried to get away. The threats silenced the child. Each night this degenerate would dress the boy in woman's clothes, drink heavily, then attack the boy.

We had all we could do to prevent the father from returning home for a gun and killing the chef.

That night we arrested the degenerate in the kitchen of the restaurant. Later he pleaded guilty in General Sessions Court, where he was sentenced to five years in state prison.

The following week I was back on "The Avenue." By the end of the year I had stumbled across a loan-shark racketeer, a drug peddler and a purveyor of pornographic films. All were arrested and found guilty.

By early 1942 conditions became even worse. I remember particularly the case of a young girl named Mary, one of eight children, a deeply religious girl who went daily to Mass. Mary lived with her poor family in the seventies. She was a junior in high school and to help out she worked as a baby sitter. At a small luncheonette near the school she met an attractive blonde woman who several times gave her jobs minding children. One day she asked Mary if she would like some steady work in the afternoon and a few evenings a week.

Mary was delighted. "I'll meet you this afternoon right after school and take you to see Martin," the woman said.

"Who's Martin?" Mary asked.

"Oh, he's my boss," she said with a smile.

The "steady work" was prostitution; her "boss" was a vicious pimp named Martin Gatoff, a brutal criminal. This is one man I tried to put behind bars for as long as the law would allow.

Late that afternoon the blonde picked up Mary and brought her to an apartment on West 78th Street. Mary didn't observe that the woman carefully locked the door. Although it was spring, all the windows were tightly locked. Gatoff, about 30, was all smiles when Mary sat down. When she refused a drink Gatoff came to the point.

"You can earn as much as ten dollars a night," he said.

"That's wonderful," Mary said. "I can help with typing and I know some bookkeeping."

Gatoff laughed. Then he went to a drawer and took out a small book. He gave it to Mary who riffled the pages bewilderedly.

"What's this, Mr. Gatoff?" she asked.

"These are your ten-dollar-a-night boys," he said. "Are you a virgin, kid?"

Now Mary knew what he meant. When she started for the door Gatoff pulled a gun and the woman dragged her back. Gatoff grabbed her long hair, then slapped her, splitting her lower lip. Then while the woman held her he stripped her nude and dragged her into the bedroom.

"This is just what I've been looking for," he told the woman, "a nice young girl to break in. I can get fifty bucks a throw for her."

Though Mary tried to fight him off she couldn't stop him. But he had only begun. After raping her twice he forced her to commit unnatural acts. Then he dragged the bloody, almost hysterical girl into the bathroom to hold her under a shower. After the woman helped her to dress Gatoff pushed her out of the apartment with this warning: "Come back tomorrow ready to work or I'll tip off the cops you're a whore and tell your priest and family."

The girl wandered at midnight through Central Park until she was found by a man walking his dog; he notified the police. Incoherent from shock and internal injuries, she was treated at a hospital then transferred to the Children's Shelter. The next day the case was referred to our office. Because it came within my scope of investigation involving juveniles it was turned over to me.

I questioned the girl for some time, then summoned two policemen who arrested Gatoff. That afternoon I received a call from Mary, who had been transferred to Welfare Island.

"Please, Mr. Danforth, come and see me," she whispered into the phone.

"What's wrong, Mary?" I asked, but she had hung up.

I hurried to the Island, only to hear another shocking account. She was in a ward with a group of young prostitutes, some of them lesbians. They had threatened to "work her over" that night if she refused to join their orgies.

It must be recalled that this child was not a criminal, but a witness for the state against a particularly vicious sadist. . . .

When I interviewed an official, he indignantly denied Mary's charges. He as much as told me I was a liar. I didn't have any proof to support the girl's story, so I had to remain quiet. But that night I returned to the Island and slipped into the ward. What I saw confirmed everything Mary had told me.

I immediately called the Chief Investigator, who exploded over the phone when I told him what was going on. He got in touch with District Attorney Hogan, who blistered the Department of Hospitals. The next day the doctor was transferred and a general shake-up of personnel followed.

Gatoff was finally found guilty and sentenced to three years. But we shall return to Mary and the ending of her story. It's not very pretty.

I continued with my investigation, living the role of Dan O'Brien, unearthing cases which sickened even my case-hardened soul. The more setbacks we had in Europe or in the Pacific, the wilder the Times Square area became. The runaways continued to flock there from all over the country. I found girls in squalid hotels sleeping with soldiers, sailors or marines, usually only in their teens themselves; some were pregnant, some infected with a venereal disease. In 1942 pimps from Harlem began to move down into the Times Square area; before long we found that a loosely organized band of procurers was picking up runaway girls in bus stations, hotel lobbies, Grand Central or Penn Station, bringing them up to a jitterbug dance hall, filling them with whiskey or marijuana, then "breaking them in"—raping them. The rest was easy. Either by threats or because they wanted excitement these children were made prostitutes—some at the age of thirteen—or subjects for pornographic movies or sex exhibitions in the rear of Harlem bar rooms and private flats, where spectators paid from $10.00 to $25.00 a ticket.

On any street corner—if you knew the pushers—you could buy heroin. Teen-agers bought marijuana openly, mostly in the wash-rooms of restaurants.

The Police Department, the M.P.'s and Shore Patrol and the S.P.C.C. agents did what they could, but the situation, because of the times, worsened.

In April, 1942, a worried mother from Maywood, New Jersey, paid a visit to our office. She brought a picture of her pretty 17-year-old daughter, May, who had been missing for two weeks. When I heard her story I knew it wasn't just a runaway: this girl was either murdered or had disappeared in some vice setup in Harlem.

May had been a happy, dance-loving high school girl, who brought home excellent marks and seemed like an average American teen-ager. One day at a dance she met a girl whose sister, unknown to the neighbors, had once been committed to the New Jersey Reformatory for Women at Bordentown.

May seemed attracted to the sister, who was about 19. Once she took both girls to a Harlem dance hall. The first night they had a wild time, coming out second in a jitterbug contest. They arrived home shortly after midnight and made plans to return the following week. In the interval the female ex-convict alerted two colored pimps, who danced several times with May and her girl friend. Later they went to a private party where the two girls passed out.

It was the old story; they awoke in the morning raped. Both pimps threatened them with physical harm, the usual tips to local police, their family and so on if they talked. The girls returned home, explaining their absence by lying about a visit they had made to a girl friend in another part of New Jersey.

There is a blank in the girl's life for the next three months. I later traced her to the dance hall where she was becoming known. Obviously she had been used by the pimp. A month later she fell ill and ran a high fever. The father called in a physician, who, after an examination, said the girl required an emergency operation and was seriously ill from a venereal disease. The shocked father and mother rushed her to a hospital. The girl was bed-ridden for three months; she emerged from her illness silent, bitter. The parents tried to talk to her but she refused to disclose what had happened.

One day in the spring of 1942 she kissed her mother. "I'll be back in an hour," she said.

Her worried mother watched her walk down the street. A flashy
green car with New York license plates, which evidently had been
waiting nearby, drove up. A Negro leaned out and spoke to the
girl. As the mother started to run out of the house her daughter got
into the car, which sped away. The police were notified, but the
car and the girl seemed to have vanished.

Two weeks later there was a long-distance call from Boston.
Speaking in a whisper the girl said, "Please help me, Mother . . .
Tell the police I am . . ."

The mother heard her daughter scream and then the phone
clicked. The girl has never been seen or heard from since that night.

I made a preliminary investigation of the case and checked out
all of the facts. I interviewed her friends and found a shocking situation in which other young high-school girls, fascinated by the excitement of jitterbugging, flocked to the Harlem ballroom, where
they were recruited by Negro pimps. After I had gathered several
statements of young girls I wrote out my report. District Attorney
Hogan immediately ordered a sweeping investigation of the Times
Square and Harlem vice rings. My assignment was to infiltrate the
Harlem underworld to gather all the evidence I could, particularly
against men and women using children as prostitutes.

The Harlem underworld is unlike the white man's jungle; it is harder
to penetrate, simply because of the problem of color. The Negro
lawless are tougher and more unpredictable and are engaged in
more primitive kinds of crime. For example, few colored gangsters
have penetrated into the ranks of legitimate business, as Lepke once
throttled the garment center. They are involved mostly in vice, narcotics, "numbers" gambling, etc.

I believe that Harlem is one of the most dangerous sections in
New York City because of conditions spawned by poverty, official
corruption, and miserable housing conditions. Where in America do
you have the same beds used by two or three people during a 24-
hour day, or several families using one hall toilet . . . where rats
scurry over the bodies of sleeping men, women and children . . .
where fire hazards are so widespread that they are almost impossible
to cope with . . . ?

Drugs are sold openly on the street corners. Policy (playing the
numbers), which constitutes an established part of community's life,
is protected by crooked cops. Only recently Treasury agents raiding
bookmaking spots in Harlem refused to take along city cops be-

cause they could not be trusted. Few politicians like to attack the problem because of the major vote factor; they don't like to be accused of being anti-Negro. So Harlem remains, despite its decent people who vigorously fight these conditions, a cancer on the face of the city of New York.

In Harlem I began to move about the bars and grills. But it was difficult to mix; men moved away at the bar and gave me sullen, suspicious glances. Fortunately, I had among my stable of private informers a young colored ex-thief, who was genuinely trying to go straight. He agreed to help me make original contacts, but then would drop out of sight.

"I don't want those boys to be usin' my throat for a honin' strap," he used to say.

The first night we met in a Lenox Avenue bar, which Alex, my informer, said was a narcotics drop. More importantly, he said it was also the headquarters for William Chappelle, known as Chappy, the vice leader in Harlem. Alex warned me to be careful of Chappy, who was armed, and had reportedly killed a man in a dice game.

The first few nights we just sat about, drinking, laughing, and watching a young drug addict named "Blackjack" do a soft-shoe dance. Blackjack, a happy-go-lucky boy of 19 had been a main liner (one who injects heroin directly into his veins) since he was 15.

"Man, I'm high," he used to chant as he danced, "hangin' on a kite headed for the golden gate."

Blackjack's song was curiously prophetic; he was dead within a year, helplessly insane from drugs.

After a week I began my first cautious moves. Alex had hinted to the others I was a "John" up in Harlem for kicks—especially young girls. When Alex left for a while, I began to drop a phrase here and there about "young stuff" to Blackjack. He caught on.

"Gotta see Chappy about that, Dan," he said. "That young stuff's his department."

"Can I meet him?" I asked Blackjack.

The young Negro said he would try to get in touch with him. Later that night a tall, good-looking Negro, with a pencil-line scar on one cheek, came in with a shorter, powerfully built man known as "Frankie D" who once had been a sparring partner for Joe Louis. Later I learned he was Chappelle's lieutenant.

Alex waved them over. After a round of introductions I invited them to have a drink.

"Chappy, meet Dan O'Brien of Boston," Blackjack said. "He's a good Joe."

Chappelle quickly took my measure. Apparently he decided I didn't look suspicious, because he held out his hand.

"Glad to know you, Dan. The boys been taking care of you?"

"Man, are we goin' to take care of Dan!" Blackjack said as he danced about . . . "goin' to take care of Dan that big steel man . . ."

Blackjack's antics really broke the ice. Chappelle seemed to thaw. He was impressed when I told him cautiously I was in the steel business and was in New York to set up a new office.

"Work all day, play all night, Dan?" he said with a laugh.

He seemed satisfied when I gave him the impression that was the life I was leading. The type of white man I was playing was not unusual in Harlem in the war years. I have the names of white Hollywood stars, musicians, and big businessmen who ignored the risks and came to Harlem to buy sex and thrills. It's a miracle they weren't knifed or mugged. If they had been, the fault would have been theirs alone.

To wave a well-filled wallet, jewels or furs before an embittered boy was to toss a lighted match in a plastic factory. White men were stabbed, beaten and robbed, while I was in Harlem, but I always heard the other side of the story from Blackjack. He knew from the ever-humming grapevine the identity of the muggers and how much they got.

"That white man wanted somethin' he couldn't get downtown," Blackjack would say, "and he got it . . ."

I found Blackjack invaluable in my dealings with Chappelle. This pitiful drug addict was the court jester for the pimps, procurers, madams and thugs who hung around Chappy. When they laughed at Blackjack's antics they weren't suspicious—that was important.

After that first evening with Chappelle I proceeded cautiously. He was friendly, but still somewhat reserved. After the third or fourth meeting he suggested I join him at a bar and grill on West 115th Street. Here he was the undisputed boss. He was constantly answering the phone; men and women, white and black, conferred with him in the back room.

"Looks like you own this place, Chappy," I observed casually.

He laughed. "I do, Dan. This is my joint, free and clear."

The next day the records of the ABC Board confirmed he was the owner. That afternoon we had his phone tapped. But a report from my office a few days later made me uncomfortable. The FBI report on Chappelle showed he was a vicious criminal. He had already spent time in federal jails for violation of the Mann Act—transportation of women across state lines for purposes of prostitution. He was deadly when cornered; the scar on his cheek was a memento of a knife battle in which he reportedly had killed another man in Detroit.

On the surface he was quiet and surprisingly well informed. He was contemptuous of women, who he insisted were good for only one thing. He wasn't a heavy drinker but a serious gambler. When I promised to bring him to a downtown gambling house he was impressed. From then on his reserve thawed.

One night, about the second week of just sitting and drinking, he asked casually, "How about some tea, Dan?"

Tea is marijuana. It meant I could get a look inside one of the dens, so I nodded.

It was about 1:00 A.M. when we set out in Chappelle's bright red Cadillac. We pulled up at a rickety tenement on West 110th Street. I followed Chappelle and Blackjack down into a cellar, the foulest I had ever been in. The stench was almost overpowering. By this time I felt a small, hard lump forming in my stomach. Unarmed, I was in the company of a drug addict, and a killer. I could only hope Chappelle's excellent spy system had not found me out.

I held on to Chappelle's arm as a guide across the cellar to a fire door with a bare light above it. After he banged on the door we could hear chains on the opposite side. The heavy door swung back to reveal a small black man in overalls.

Chappelle grunted something, then moved into what appeared to be the cellar of the adjacent building. This led us to an alley, down another cellar, to a basement apartment. The door opened to Chappelle's knocks. The brackish smell of marijuana hit me. The door closed. The only light was from a blue bulb in a jukebox. Pinpoints of light circled about the room.

"Sit down, Dan," Chappelle said.

I joined him on a couch. As my eyes got accustomed to the gloom I could make out men and women, white and black, on chairs and sofas, or sprawled on pillows on the floor. All were smoking. There would be sudden bursts of laughter, then giggles. A young girl clad in a bright red dress that showed every curve, came up with a sort of silver bread tray. On it were piles of marijuana cigarettes.

"You smoke tea before, Dan?" Chappelle asked.

"A few times," I said.

"We'll get you real gauged tonight," he said. This was the term to describe a form of intoxication resulting from smoking the cigarettes and breathing in the stagnant smoke that was so thick it burned my eyes.

To simulate smoking I blew into the thin cylinder at intervals so that its tip would glow, then exhaled lustily.

"There's snow [cocaine] in the back," Blackjack said.

"This house's got anything you want," Chappelle said.

Suddenly one of the men, laughing uproariously, leaned over and tore the front of the dress of a girl who was starting to weave back and forth before him. In a moment she was nude; everyone laughed.

Then Chappelle shouted, "Let's get that young stuff and have a circus, Marge."

Marge—one of Chappelle's procuresses who was later arrested—went into a back room. She returned with two white girls about fourteen, a colored child no more than twelve and a light-skinned teenage boy, who was staggering from whiskey. Everyone began shouting and laughing as Marge turned on a floor lamp.

"Let's go," Chappy shouted. The children, solemn-faced as if they were on a school stage, took off their clothes. Any description of what followed would be unprintable.

"Anything you like there, Dan?" Chappelle asked.

I tried to make some excuse which was plausible but I don't think it even registered with him. The whiskey he was drinking, combined with the marijuana, gave him a glassy-eyed look.

All during the early hours of the morning customers entered and left. There were four girls, one named Ruth, who gave me her address for a "date" before I left.

It was 7:00 A.M. when we emerged from the cellar. My eyes felt like two holes burned in a blanket, my throat was parched, all I could think of was a tall glass of ice water. Chappelle was bleary-eyed and half drunk. Blackjack was left back in the den. Chappy refused to take any excuses, insisting that he wanted to drive me to my hotel. He was half-drunk, but still shrewd. Chappy wanted to know where I was living. I told him the Warwick which seemed to impress him. He dropped me off, then with a grin asked if I would be back "uptown."

"I'll see you tonight about ten o'clock," I told him.

I hurried inside and registered. Upstairs, I took a shower and lay on the bed waiting. It didn't take long for the phone to ring. It was Chappelle calling . . . he just wanted to make sure I was coming up. . . .

I associated with Chappelle for six weeks, seeing a side of Harlem that few white men are ever permitted to witness. I saw many other dope "tea pads" (marijuana dens), after-hour clubs, brothels which could be equaled only in Singapore or Hong Kong, and many children, boys and girls from the age of 12 to 17, being traded by pimps and procurers.

As the weeks passed it became clear to me that the vice network led from Times Square to Harlem; in the background was a shadowy mob which Chappelle hinted was the "Hamilton Mob." At this point I had no idea of who these vice procurers were or how they operated. The leader was said to be a man named "Frank the Sheik."

After a few weeks I returned to the office to outline in reports all that I had witnessed, along with my recommendations. After District Attorney Hogan had read the reports it was decided that we should move into Harlem and Times Square, and also try to seek out the mysterious "Hamilton Mob." Army and Navy Intelligence and the National Defense setup in the Police Department were notified of our moves. Our liaison was Alexander Dreiband, who was in charge of all vice matters in our office.

I returned to Harlem, well armed. I had a special holster strapped inside my shirt for emergencies. At the bar Chappelle welcomed me like an old friend. I was lavish with the District Attorney's expense account that night, hinting I was doing well with a war contract. Before the evening was over I had gathered quite a collection of pimps, thieves and musclemen who were used by Chappelle as his enforcers.

There were the usual, dreadful tours. Each morning I carefully added addresses of apartment houses and bars to my growing list of brothels, narcotic centers, after-hour clubs and side-street hotels.

There were some close calls, like the early morning I was walking down Lenox Avenue accompanied by Blackjack. I was on my way home after another terrible visit to one of Chappelle's brothels, where the inmates were two 15-year-old girls, one a runaway from Brooklyn. Chappelle had boasted they had been picked up in the Dixie Bus Terminal, raped by a pimp in a West Side hotel, then transferred to Harlem. From there Chappelle said he was going to send the prettiest child to Schenectady. It was the first time he had revealed to me he was transporting girls to another part of the state.

I recall I was chewing on the stump of a dead cigar, going over in my mind the various addresses I had memorized, when suddenly two men slid out of a hallway to block our path.

Blackjack just grunted "Muggers."

The pair didn't say anything, but I heard a click. One of them had a switchblade knife; the blade looked as long as a saber. Blackjack stepped up to them, but one pushed him aside with, "Get out of here, nigger."

As soon as I saw them I started to slip my hand inside my shirt but the man with the knife started for me. I think it was Blake who said something like "Beware of a frightened rabbit." I was both frightened and indignant: frightened because I knew the percentage of muggers and robberies in this area—indignant that these two bums were holding me up.

I drop-kicked him in the groin, then as his hands dropped, instinctively I hit him one of the hardest blows I had ever swung. I rushed at the other one who started to run. I grabbed his topcoat to yank him up short. He swung at me but I ducked. Behind him was an areaway with a three-step drop. I gave him a hard push. He toppled back, then vanished into the hole.

Blackjack, who now had the knife, was kicking and pummeling the prostrate mugger. I had more trouble getting the weapon away from him than I had from our attackers. It was important not to be found by a prowl car, so I literally dragged Blackjack down the street to the next avenue where I hailed a cab.

The last I saw of the pair was the man I had kicked. He was sitting on the bottom step of a stoop holding his stomach. I guess the other fellow was in the areaway. I felt quite satisfied.

On another occasion I was in a "tea pad" when it was actually raided by some holdup men. No shots were fired but the two strong-arm men who guarded the place fought a fierce hand-to-hand battle with the bandits in the outside hall. One man returned with a badly slashed hand.

Such incidents were not unusual. As Chappelle said later that night, "The cops never hear about them. We have our own ways of catching up with those ———."

As my investigation continued, I was introduced to Harlem's most famous after-hour club, called "Papa Joe's," on West 115th Street. There I heard the pimps talk about a girl named Kitty, about 15. It seemed she was particularly desirable because none of them could touch her. From what I could understand she was a runaway from a small Massachusetts town.

"I can't even get next to the little —— myself," one pimp named "Carnation" said.

This was the nightly topic, their stock in trade. They discussed young girls who had been put into West Side hotels to be groomed for the upstate trade. It wasn't unusual for one of the pimps to bring Chappelle a small snapshot which had been taken in one of the Times Square mechanical portrait machines. I made a pretense of getting a perverse thrill at having young girls' pictures, so in this way I managed to get three pictures of child victims of rape which helped to bring about convictions. I also had a working arrangement with an official of the Children's Society to notify me if any young girls arrested by the police were turned over to the Shelter.

One morning about 9:00 A.M. when I was about to tumble into bed after a night spent with Chappelle, my phone rang. It was the Children's Society man.

"I've been calling you since last night," he said. "Come up right away, I got a young kid who should talk to you."

I was at the Shelter within a half-hour. The girl was a slender, pretty blonde in her early teens. Her eyes were red from crying. She had a bad bruise on her cheek. Here is my official report which I submitted to Assistant District Attorney Dreiband the next day:

INVESTIGATIVE REPORT

March 2, 1942

TO: Mr. M. Glynn, Chief Investigator
FROM: Harold R. Danforth
RE: Vice Investigation

NATURE OF INVESTIGATION:

Continuation of the investigation started in December, 1941, concerning vice conditions in Harlem and Times Square involving conspiracies by certain procurers to force into prostitution young teen-age girls who have run away from home and who have been picked up in the Times Square area.

RESULTS OF THE INVESTIGATION:

Previous reports submitted by this investigator have described conditions in certain areas in both sections. At least 15 individuals are now under surveillance by other investigators. (See prior report on Chappelle's vice setup.) The following is a statement made to me at the Children's Shelter, 105th Street and Fifth Avenue in the presence of the Supervisor, by a child, Kitty ——, 314 East —— Street, New York City, who has been classified as a Missing Person, reported to the Missing Persons Bureau, December 15, 1941.

I am 14 years old. I ran away from my home because I wanted some excitement. I thought Times Square was fun so I went there. I was in the Dixie Bus Terminal sitting on a bench when a nice fellow came in and sat down beside me. He introduced himself as Shorty.

After we talked he asked if I was hungry. I said I was so he took me to Bickford's on 42nd Street between 7th and 8th Avenues. There I met a woman named Ann. Shorty said she would take care of me. Ann took me to her room in a hotel on Eighth Avenue and told me if I was nice to Shorty I would be wearing furs. When I said how would this come about she just smiled and said I would see.

I stayed with Ann for a week. Twice when I saw Shorty he asked Ann if everything was okay. She said it would take time. I didn't know what she meant until one night she told me I should go and live with Shorty. She said he would break me in. I knew then what she meant and I said I was a virgin and I would never do anything like that.

When she told this to Shorty he got mad and said I would have to come across. I became frightened and didn't go back to that apartment. I sat all night in the bus terminal but Shorty came in and found me. He said he would take care of me. I told him I didn't want to go with him but he said all he wanted to do was buy me a meal. I went with him to a cider mill somewhere near 50th Street on Eighth Avenue. He ordered me some food, then left saying he would return shortly.

About 20 minutes later a man walked in and showed me a badge. He said he was a detective and was arresting me. I went outside with him into a taxicab. He showed me a gun and said he would kill me if I didn't obey him.

We then went to an apartment on West 81st Street—I don't know the address but I can pick out the house. There he ordered me to disrobe. When I refused he hit me with his fist. Then he threw me on a couch, ripped off my clothes and raped me.

When I screamed he struck me again and showed me the gun. I cried for a long time but he said now that I was broken in Shorty could send me to Harlem to earn a lot of money. He also told me Shorty had contact with a man named Chappy who could use a young girl like me. He said by this time next year I would be working upstate and would have enough money to buy anything I wanted. Then he began drinking.

I asked him if I could go into the bathroom. When he said yes I went in and stayed there a long time. When I opened the door he was on the bed snoring. My clothes were ripped and I couldn't put them on. I took the shower curtain and used that to cover me; then I ran out. A cab driver took me to the police who sent me up here.

By ten o'clock that same morning Kitty had been treated by a physician, who administered a sedative. The next afternoon I took her on a tour of the west eighties. She picked out the apartment of the man who raped her. This information was turned over to the police and the occupant was arrested.

He confessed to the rape and told us he had been paid to do it by Shorty, whom we also arrested. Both had records of arrests for procuring. Kitty proved to be an invaluable witness. Conversations she had overheard gave us clues to other procurers working in the area. From Kitty we also learned of an after-hour club on West 50th Street which catered to servicemen. A quiet raid picked up three 15-year-old girls, two of whom were diseased. They confessed to having had relations with numerous servicemen.

Kitty also supplied us with the names of other young girls who were staying in the cheap rooming-houses and shoddy West Side hotels. Their stories were a dreary, tragic recital of children in these hectic war years seeking excitement, only to find degradation and remorse. One particular story which still haunts me concerns a 13-year-old girl named Mona, who had run away from Massachusetts on December 6, 1941, a few hours before the Pearl Harbor attack.

With another girl she came to New York with $20.00 between them. A cab driver took them to a cheap hotel on the West Side, where they shared a $6.00-a-week room. The day following their arrival they met another young runaway named Mickey. This girl, it later developed after her arrest, was employed by the Times Square pimps to solicit runaways.

Part of my report on Mona deals with that first afternoon:

Mona states that Mickey took her to see the sights, as she called it. They went to a Times Square movie, then toured such places as Diamond Jim's, Grant's Bar, the Marine Bar and Grill. Mickey introduced her to several men, all known pimps, who urged her to let them get her and her girl-friend jobs as waitresses.

One of the men, known to this writer as Cowboy Danny, a notorious procurer, who is now a fugitive from a warrant obtained by our office, took the girl to his apartment, beat and raped her, then transported her to Schenectady where he placed her in a house of prostitution. Because of her inexperience in sexual matters she became pregnant. The pimp was notified and brought the girl to an abortionist in New York. The operation was bungled and the girl became desperately ill. In her weak state she contracted pneumonia. The procurer, Danny, left her alone for one full day. In the evening he called the superintendent to go up and "have a look at the kid."

The superintendent whom I interviewed and from whom I took a statement, found the child delirious. He notified the police, who sent an ambulance from Columbus Hospital. The child died two days later.

This procurer was arrested months later and sent to prison on charges arising from another case. Unfortunately, the evidence of the abortion death was too weak or he would have been indicted for manslaughter.

It was my sad task to notify the girl's parents and bring them to the morgue where they identified the body of their daughter.

With evidence now linking the Harlem vice setup to Times Square procurers, I rejoined Chappelle. My "raid list," as we called it in the office, named restaurants and after-hour clubs where teen-age girls were used for purposes of prostitution. Added to this were the names of more than 60 pimps, madams and dope peddlers.

Among them was a fabulous and truly amazing woman. She was Evelyn Fox, alias the Duchess. Then about 45, she was a tall, poised, obviously well-educated woman, but evil to the core. As

Chappelle's lieutenant, she ran his string of brothels with a firm and shrewd hand.

She got her nickname legitimately. In the District Attorney's office she produced evidence which convinced Alex Dreiband that she was a White Russian of the nobility. How she ended in Harlem is still a mystery—one she refused to discuss.

At my suggestion the Duchess was put under surveillance, earmarked as a potential witness for the People after I heard her complain about Chappelle's withholding some of the profits.

By now I also had uncovered a shocking amount of official corruption. In my report of March 5, 1942, I wrote:

> There is no doubt the places [brothels] are police-protected. As one owner of a Harlem brothel told this writer: "They say the cops are raising hell on this vice business but they will never bother us people in Harlem because they don't want to kill the goose that lays the golden egg."
>
> This man went on to explain to the writer that all you had to do to run a "joint," as he called it, was to have the right connections and know the right people. He went on to say that as long as the owner kept on the right side of the cops and gave them their cut, he would have nothing to worry about. This opinion is general in Harlem. As a result of information this writer has received from a former vice operator and from recent association with many of Harlem's underworld leaders, the writer's opinion is that there is no one syndicate controlling vice in Harlem but that Harlem is controlled by several different groups or rings which operate separately and yet cooperate with each other. It appears that the various leaders of these groups constantly keep in touch with one another in their various hangouts.
>
> There is little doubt in this writer's mind that police in certain precincts know of the activities of these pimps but have been paid off not to interfere. Chappelle, one of the major vice leaders in Harlem, told this writer quite casually the other night that he was on his way downtown to "take care of two cops" who had arrested one of his lieutenants. . . .

My reports were later sent to Police Commissioner Valentine, but I was never notified exactly what happened to those police officials whom I listed as receiving "protection money."

In February, March, April and early May, 1942, I was constantly shuttling between Harlem and Times Square. The latter section was now completely covered by our people, with other investigators shadowing 15 or more pimps and procurers who were living off the proceeds of young runaway girls. Wire taps on many bars and grills yielded excellent information on dope peddling and transporting of women for purposes of prostitution. One gave us the location of an apartment where any kind of vice was sold.

Following up a phone conversation clue, I mentioned to Chappelle that I had heard of "Harry the Book," alias Harry Jacobson, a notorious procurer, who had some unusual forms of entertainment to offer.

"Harry? I know him well," Chappelle said. "Let's go up there tonight."

We visited the apartment on West 118th Street. From the exterior I assumed it would be a dingy, ill-lighted flat, but I was surprised to find this brothel to be expensively furnished with a bar and an assortment of children from 11 to 18, four of them runaways, who were prepared to engage in any form of vice or perversion the customer wanted. Jacobson also told me he supplied male and female homosexuals.

"I get a big trade from downtown," he said proudly. "My house will supply anything for money."

During the evening I managed to get near the phone to memorize the unlisted number. The next day we were sitting on a wire. Within a week we had all we wanted to convict Jacobson.

On May 3, 1942, a final conference was held with District Attorney Hogan. It was decided to turn over to the police all available information so that they could make the raids; we would prosecute the guilty.

Our target date was 8:00 P.M., May 12, 1942. Three days before that Chief Investigator Glynn, myself, and all the other investigators who worked on the case gathered in the office of Alex Dreiband to synchronize the staging of the raids. A Deputy Police Commissioner and chief inspectors were ordered by Police Commissioner Valentine to supply us with teams of police and the best the detective bureaus could offer, to accompany us on the raids.

We planned the raids with maps. The squad room of the West 128th Street precinct was to be our field headquarters. All Assistants were put on a 24-four-hour duty by District Attorney Hogan, the Department of Correction was alerted and the warden of the Tombs was advised to have enough empty cells prepared. The Children's

Shelter was prepared to house a small army of runaway children who had to be taken into custody, while additional matrons were summoned, along with doctors and nurses.

Because of the official corruption I had uncovered it was decided that sealed envelopes containing the addresses of the places to be raided, along with the names of those to be arrested, be given the police teams. These envelopes were to be opened only when they left, accompanied by a D.A.'s man. This irked the honest cops no end, but it made for a more successful operation.

That day the office was tense. Over a tapped telephone I called Chappelle, discussed some "young stuff" which he had promised to have on hand; then, to set him up for arrest outside his racket hangout I made a date to meet him on Columbus Circle. I told him I had finally made arrangements to take him on the oft-promised visit to the downtown gambling house.

During the morning we learned that the police were moving pieces of emergency squad equipment from midtown to Harlem. By noon all of the top police brass had gathered at Police Headquarters. Reporters who covered headquarters naturally assumed something big was brewing.

At 12:30 P.M. the then City News Association, a local news-gathering wire service which has since been absorbed by the Associated Press, sent out a bulletin. It read:

BULLETIN   BULLETIN

SEVERAL HIGH RANKING POLICE OFFICIALS WERE SUMMONED TO POLICE HEADQUARTERS TODAY (THURSDAY) BY POLICE COMMISSIONER VALENTINE TO DISCUSS WHAT ONE CALLED "A BIG DEAL RAID." COMMISSIONER VALENTINE REFUSED ALL COMMENT.
    (MORE LATER)

All that morning stories and bulletins came across the city desks of large metropolitan newspapers, but so tight was our security that none of the veterans at Police Headquarters learned what was up.

At 6:00 P.M., after a last briefing by Alex Dreiband, the police set out. All over town, both in the Times Square area and throughout Harlem, raids were soon in progress. It was one of the largest and most concentrated series of raids in the history of the Police Department, comparable to Dewey's loan-shark and racket-busting raids in the early thirties.

When Blackjack and Frank, Chappelle's lieutenant, were arrested, detectives rushed them down to the D.A.'s office. They steadfastly denied they knew Chappy or had been in any of the places we had raided.

"Get Dan in here," Dreiband said.

When I walked in, Blackjack just said, "Oh, man . . ."

Frank threw up his hands. "What's the use?" he said. He stared at me. "Boy, you really took us."

Within an hour they had signed statements to be the witnesses for the People against Chappelle.

When Chappy was brought down to the office he sullenly denied everything.

Again Dreiband summoned me. When I walked in Chappy started to rise from the chair, but a detective pushed him back. I have never seen such hatred in a man's eyes.

"Dan is a D.A.'s man, Chappy," Alex said. "Do you want to talk now . . . ?"

"I don't know him . . . I never saw him in my life," Chappy said. He kept repeating these words even after Dreiband read him the statements of Frank and Blackjack.

In the early hours of the morning the Duchess was brought into Dreiband's office. She fainted when she saw me. After she had been revived she signed a statement. She was another important witness against Chappelle.

While the questioning of the important witnesses went on through the night in the D.A.'s office, police continued their raids until dawn. By 6:00 A.M. we had more than 200 prisoners, some of the most vicious of the Harlem underworld.

By 10:00 A.M., 28 teen-age girls from the ages of 11 to 17 were in our custody. They were the most pitiful of this sordid mess. Some wept, the more hardened smoked and chatted excitedly.

Within three days our assistants had shaken down the prisoners and lined up the cases against them for compulsory prostitution, sodomy, rape and assault. A grand total of 205 men and women were arrested. Many were released by magistrates on the payment of fines, but at least 15 went to prison for long terms. All of the children, after medical attention, were returned to their homes. Chappelle pleaded guilty and was sentenced to an indeterminate sentence on a charge of compulsory prostitution. This could mean up to three years in Riker's Island.

Through Frank, Chappelle warned me: "When I get out—watch out."

But Chappelle never got out. He died of paresis in Blackwell's Island Hospital.

The Duchess, who cooperated with the state, was sentenced to 30 days for medical care.

But the assignment was not concluded. The mysterious "Hamilton Mob" of procurers was uncovered through information supplied by defendants caught in our raids. The mob turned out to be 11 men operating a nationwide vice syndicate from the Hamilton Hotel on upper Broadway. They maintained combinations of brothels from upper New York to Los Angeles, transferring young girls and hardened prostitutes from state to state. Our wiretaps showed that in one night they sent 25 girls to as many as seven different states.

In June, 1942, District Attorney Hogan ordered a raid on the "Hamilton Mob" led by "Frank the Sheik." On a late Friday night we moved in, cornering the whole mob as they were sitting down to divide the profits of that week. Along with thousands of dollars in cash boxes, we found scores of small tickets, similar to the type used in cafeterias, which had various numbers punched. Each ticket had a woman's name on the back, and thus gave irrefutable evidence of her night's work. These 11 men were arrested and charged with compulsory prostitution. All were sent to jail for from one to five years.

The fight to combat juvenile vice in both areas continued until the war was over. I spent four years on "The Avenue" gathering information against combinations of pimps which seemed to multiply overnight despite the arrests. The Police Department's National Defense group also pitched in to clean up the area.

Then in 1944 we received information from an informer that foreign ship captains were using an expensive brothel on the upper West Side operated by a woman suspected of Nazi affiliations. We quickly confirmed the information through wire taps and by questioning ship captains who were picked up as they left the apartment.

The raid caught the women, mother and daughter. There is little humor in this sordid business but what happened during the questioning of the young woman is now a bit of bawdy folklore in the D.A.'s office.

Accompanying Alex Dreiband was a high police official later slated to be Police Commissioner. The girl, a striking redhead, was clad only in a bathrobe. Dreiband, an intense and serious prosecutor, was firing questions at her when her robe began to slip. Inch by inch it gave way until it was entirely open.

"Close that damn robe," Dreiband roared.

In the silence the weary police official sounded almost wistful. "Why, Alex . . . ?"

All during the war years the case of the young New Jersey girl, who vanished after that last terrifying phone call to her mother, continued to haunt me. Once or twice a year I would contact the family or Police Chief Herzog of Maywood to keep in touch with the case.

On February 2, 1943, I received a call from Herzog that the girl who had been May's closest friend had returned home. That same night in Herzog's office I interviewed the girl with her tearful parents. The year and a half she had been away had wrought shocking changes in her. Now a hardened prostitute, she was adamant in refusing to discuss her activities, but she did give me all the information she had on May. She said that shortly after May had disappeared she had seen her on the Seventh Avenue subway platform at 50th Street with two men. Unfortunately, she was on the opposite side and could not attract May's attention.

According to my original notes this interrogation followed:

Q. Where do you think I should look for May in Harlem?
A. The Fat Man's place on 155th Street. I bet they took her there.
Q. Were any young girls seen there?
A. There are always four or five who hang out in this place.
Q. Are they runaways?
A. Yes, I believe they are.
Q. How do you know about this place?
A. The State Police [New Jersey] picked me up there.
Q. How old were you then?
A. Fifteen.
Q. Where do you think these men took May?
A. Probably to a house. Either in Harlem or upstate.

I went back into Harlem but the Fat Man, a former pimp and procurer, was now a fugitive. His place had been closed by the Alcoholic Beverage Control Board after an investigation based on my reports. Ironically, I had helped close the one source of information which might have helped find May.

She was never found. As the years went by I kept in touch with her parents, who never gave up hope that someday May would walk back into their lives. . . .

The vice investigations lasted for four years. By 1945 Alex Dreiband reported to District Attorney Hogan that numerous procurers and panderers had been sentenced to terms totaling 125 years, while a small army of teen-age girls and boys had been returned to their homes. The break-up of Chappelle's ring and the Hamilton mob of pimps ended syndicated prostitution in New York City, at least up to that year.

There was to be one final chapter for me. On a fall afternoon in 1955 I was about to enter a store near 72nd Street when I bumped into an attractive young woman. She wore a great deal of jewelry, furs and a heavy scent. I mentally catalogued her as a high-class call girl.

I was pulled up short when she smiled. "Hello, Mr. Danforth. Remember me?"

I studied her hard, young face. "No, I'm sorry, I don't," I said.

She said softly, "Remember Mary—in the Gatoff case?"

"Why, of course," I said. "How are you, Mary?"

Her smile was bitter. She held up the rings and pointed to the furs. "Being in the custody of the state taught me a lot."

12. THE RELUCTANT WITNESSES: THE POWELL CASE

IN 1942 conditions on the waterfront had become so bad that District Attorney Hogan assigned me to a roving assignment on the docks to uncover what crime and criminals I might find.

Of course I assumed my usual role of Dan O'Brien of Boston. By this time I was so familiar with the act I could play it with a natural ease. I began drifting casually along the West Side docks, hanging out in cheap bars and restaurants, listening and carefully making friends.

One day in a bar a longshoreman with whom I had struck up an acquaintance called over to us a stocky, tight-faced man with a cast in one eye.

"This is Dan O'Brien from Boston," my friend said.

The man with the cast stared at me. "Yeah," he said out of the corner of his mouth and that was all.

When he left the longshoreman said, "That was Cockeyed Johnny Dunn. He's the real pistol for the pistol local."

I began hanging out in the same place and before long I had a nodding acquaintance with Dunn and his gunmen. Within a few weeks I had the framework of my coercion case; Dunn and his gang were extorting money from ship owners.

Gradually I managed to get inside their union hangout where they sat around playing cards. After a time I was accepted as a dock drifter who made his money in mysterious ways. Dunn was not, as one would suspect, secret in his crimes. He had enjoyed so much immunity through the terror he wielded on the waterfront that he was brazen in his discussion of criminal enterprises in which he was engaged. When I had enough I passed the information to Chief Investigator Fay. One day I was quite happy to see Fay and several of our detectives quietly enter the union office and take all concerned into custody. After questioning I was let go with some of the others.

Dunn was arrested, charged with extortion and was convicted. He was sent to Sing Sing for five years, only to emerge and murder another dock worker. He died in the electric chair a few years ago, boasting that he killed men "like buying a cup of coffee."

With Dunn gone I returned to the waterfront. One day in April, 1944, I was standing at a bar near the West Side Highway, drinking beer with a huge Negro longshoreman. Since I had discovered that there was a great deal of segregation on the docks I sought out Negro dock workers who gossips said had been beaten, stabbed and physically driven from their jobs.

I had spent a week's time with this man and had seen at first hand how he was ignored at the shape-up. Now as we stood at the smelly bar the door opened and a husky, curly-haired man of about 30 walked in.

"There's a bastard who gets away with murder," he grunted.

"Who is he?" I asked.

"Powell," he said. "One of the most miserable ———— on the docks."

That night I went downtown to look up what we had on Powell. I found that he was the son of former Sanitation Commissioner William Powell and a man of violent temper who had brought much grief to his respected father. I learned that Powell had once been arrested for the murder of a longshoreman but had been acquitted.

"Powell's a bad egg, Dan," Fay said. "See what you can get on him."

The following day I joined my friend, the colored longshoreman. After a while I casually brought up Powell's name. The Negro greeted it with a bitter curse.

"That ———— almost killed three men with a hatchet," he said.

"Was he arrested?" I asked.

The Negro looked at me, eyes wide. "Who's goin' to arrest him!"

Later another Negro joined us and the first, still fuming, brought up the hatchet assault.

"You tell him what happened, man," the first said.

The other shook his head. "Not me—not me."

As much as he tried my friend could not get the other man to tell me. But a second man joined later and he reluctantly described the events. It seemed that Powell had used a hatchet in a savage fury, inflicting serious wounds on three men.

"How do you know all this?" I asked.

"The man that got his head busted is a friend of mine," the Negro said.

"Were any complaints made?" I asked.

The Negro laughed. "Man, we're black," he said.

When this was reported to Hogan he said angrily, "Get all you can on this assault, Dan. I want it."

Without their realizing it, I managed to have my two Negro friends bring in others who had witnessed the assault. This was not too difficult; the first longshoreman was eager to get others to confirm his story and each time he saw someone who he knew was a witness to the assault, he would call him over to repeat his story for my benefit.

Finally I managed to meet one of the men who had actually been assaulted. One night we found him sitting in a corner of a bar.

"Tell him what Powell gave you," my friend said.

"That's done with," the man said hastily. "Forget it."

"He's a regular guy," the first longshoreman said. "Go ahead."

The other just shook his head.

For almost a week I trailed this man, trying to make it appear that our paths were crossing accidentally. Each time, still casual, I would bring up the assault. Gradually he relaxed and told me bits of the story. Before long I had the entire version. Through him I found the other two men who had been assaulted.

At last I knew they were becoming suspicious, so I put them in a cab one night and we went across town to an East Side automat, far from the waterfront. There I told them I was a D.A.'s man gathering evidence for a grand jury; they must come downtown with me at once.

For hours these three terrified men refused, but one of them was so bitter he joined me in persuading the other two to come down. In the early hours of the morning we left Criminal Courts Building. All three had given statements and had supplied the names of other witnesses.

But one said bitterly, "So what? He'll be back and we'll get another hatchet in the head or pushed off a dock."

"Then we'll sign another statement," the most courageous of the three said.

I finally gathered together nine witnesses. Powell was indicted for felonious assault but as the days slipped by my nine witnesses began to disappear. It was like trying to control drops of mercury. A man would disappear and after I had spent three or four frantic days prowling around Harlem to find him, I would return downtown only to learn another had vanished.

By now the case had become a personal challenge. I think I averaged only three or four hours of sleep a night, going from house to house, assuring my witnesses and their wives that they would be protected.

One morning I received a telephone call from the wife of one of the witnesses.

"Mr. Danforth," she said, "please come at once."

"I'll be there in ten minutes," I told her.

It wasn't much longer than that when I was listening to her story. The night before a city detective had paid her a visit.

"I don't want your husband to testify against Powell," he said.

"Why not?" asked the frightened woman.

"Because there's 200 bucks waiting for him down on my desk at the precinct," the detective said. Then he took out a scrap of paper and wrote his number and name.

"Give this to your husband and tell him to come down and collect the dough," he said.

I checked the precinct number and found it to be correct. Then I hurried downtown and gave Fay the story; he in turn informed Hogan. Within minutes he was on the telephone with Captain Hammill, one of the most efficient officers in the New York Police Department. Later, after a trial the detective was fired from the force.

Despite the phoned threats and the reluctance of the witnesses, I had three when Powell's trial opened. And these three, with a great deal of courage, told of his vicious attack with a hatchet. This time Powell did not beat the charge; he was convicted and sentenced to five years in Sing Sing.

13. MURDER: THE CLASSIC CRIME

As PHIL CURTIN said in his *Noted Murder Mysteries,* the interest in murder is as old as the race—the interest of humanity in its own drama. The files of the District Attorney's office supply just that. The voluminous confidential reports cloak the trappings of drama. Here are two vagrants roused from a drunken slumber by a patrolman who peeked into a soggy cardboard box one was cradling, to find a battered revolver with only the framework of a grip; two hours later we fitted tiny pieces of plastic glued together into the stock to start the pair on the road to prison for life. . . . Here is the story of a relative who happened to examine a locked window, an act which would send her brother-in-law to prison for life.

And what a terrible coincidence it is that Carlos Rodriguez, seeking a year to find Carlos Ramos and kill him, should hail a cab one day and find that its driver was none other than his prey.

As I have pointed out before, murder *per se* is not the District Attorney's task. It is up to the police to solve the murder cases. The D.A. prosecutes.

However the Bureau of Investigation has on many occasions been assigned to murder cases to augment the evidence collected by the police. I have selected several for variety and human interest. Among the clues you will find a toy elephant, bits of plastic, three spent bullets and a curious woman.

The first is the Wayne Lonergan case; here are all the ingredients of a sensational big city murder—beautiful women, wealth, position in society, sex perversion and a development so weird it seems fictional.

The case began about 6:30 A.M. on a crisp day in October, 1943, when Mario Gabellini, 40, an interior decorator who vaguely resembled Rudolph Valentino, escorted a beautiful raven-haired woman to her front door at 313 East 51st Street, said good morning and jumped back into the waiting cab.

The woman who let herself in the front door was Patricia Burton

Lonergan, heiress to a $7,000,000 estate, which came to her from a great-grandfather, Max Bernstein, a New York brewer.

Patricia entered her bedroom, threw her dress, underwear and stockings on a chair and, nude, slipped under the covers. In a minute she was asleep.

During the day the lavish duplex apartment was quiet, even more quiet than the usual Sunday. Elizabeth Black, nurse for Patricia's 18-month-old son, Wayne, Jr., fed, bathed and played with the child until noon. Then when her mistress did not emerge from her room, she began to worry.

At first she knocked gently on the bedroom door, then harder. When there was no response she called Mrs. Lonergan's name several times and tried the door. It was locked.

At 8:00 P.M. she notified Patricia's mother, Mrs. Lucille Burton, who lived at the Hotel Elysée, 60 East 54th Street. Mrs. Burton came over with Pat's friend, Captain Peter Elser, USMC.

Captain Elser knocked several times, then turned to Mrs. Burton.

"I think I had better break it down," he said.

"Please—do anything," the elderly woman said.

Elser, a former Harvard football player, threw his shoulder against the door several times, but the thick and heavy wood resisted his efforts. Finally the officer found a screw driver and hammer to remove the hinges. He stepped inside, took one look and barred the doorway so the two women could not enter.

"Call the police quickly," he told Mrs. Black. The hysterical woman rushed to the phone. Within minutes radio cars and detectives from Homicide East swarmed through the front door, up to the second-floor bedroom.

The room was a shambles. Pat's nude body lay sprawled across her large Georgian bed. Her head had been battered to a pulp; both hands were crossed in front of her face as if to ward off the fatal blows.

The group of detectives from the Homicide Bureau were under the leadership of Captain Dan Mahoney. While the police photographers took a picture of the corpse, Dan and his men questioned Elser and the two women, then began a careful foot-by-foot search of the house.

Two bent brass candlesticks, obviously the murder weapons, were found, along with a smudged bloody print in the bathroom. The window was slightly open, the door locked. The murderer must have gained access to the room from the fire escape.

On the hall table Dan's men found a mechanical elephant in a carton wrapped in paper from F. A. O. Schwarz's famous Fifth Avenue toy store. If Patricia had bought it Mrs. Black said she had not known of it. Of course anybody—the child's grandparents—could have left it when Pat was still sleeping or out.

Within an hour after the discovery of the body the detectives began their usual grueling legwork—a door-to-door canvass of the neighborhood. Their efforts paid off when they found a tenant on the floor above who had heard Pat scream: "Don't . . . what are you doing to me . . . ?"

That was early in the morning.

When the usual address book of names was found more than 50 detectives began checking on each one. They finally gathered that Pat had been out with Gabellini, along with Joan Goodman, a pretty model; Thomas Farrel, editor and reconteur; John Harjes, scion of Morgan, Harjes & Co., a Paris banking firm; Sylvia French, and Jeanne Murphy Jaburg, an attractive young divorcée.

All of the women were pretty, sophisticated and had had their photographs in the society pages many times.

By Monday the relentless investigation with its questioning was in full blast as the case made lurid headlines. As is usual, the Bureau of Investigation kept in close touch with the Assistant District Attorney in the Homicide Bureau, who was immediately assigned to the case the moment the Medical Examiner announced the victim was "DOA" (Dead On Arrival).

The autopsy report showed she had been strangled to death, with accompanying lacerations of the scalp, skull fracture and concussion of the brain. There was no doubt in our minds that the murder was premeditated. Our man on the scene noted at once that it took the murderer 18 steps to reach the dresser to pick up the candlesticks, then another 18 steps to return for the second after the first had fallen apart under his savage blows. The law does not specify that premeditation be any special length of time; a decision to kill can be made in seconds.

In the time the murderer walked to the dresser to pick up his weapon, he had committed, in the eyes of the District Attorney, who presents the People's case, an act of first-degree murder. Punishment in the electric chair is mandatory if the jury does not recommend life imprisonment.

By Monday it was known from questioning the friends and relatives of Pat that her husband, Wayne, had been in town on a pass from Montreal, where he had enlisted in the RCAF and was taking courses at the University of Toronto.

Lonergan, it was learned, had cashed a check for $25 at the Plaza and had spent the night at Harjes' at 140 East 79th Street, where he had been seen Saturday in uniform, Sunday morning in a dressing gown, and later in civilian clothes. A valet so informed Harjes, who arrived home later that afternoon. Later they learned that Lonergan had stopped off at Sylvia French's apartment to pick up two bottles of brandy and a toy he had bought for his son—the mechanical elephant that the detectives found in the hall. This placed Lonergan in the house on Sunday morning.

Mahoney and his men knew that if Lonergan had a bloody uniform or scratches on his face they probably had their man. . . . So detectives William Prendergast and Nicholas Looram were sent to Canada to interview Lonergan.

But the man who was probably more concerned with the case than anyone else was Mario Gabellini. Witnesses had placed him with Pat up to the hour of her death. No cab driver could be found who could support his alibi that he had just taken her to the door, then hurried back to the waiting cab to be driven home. Newspapers appealed to cab companies to examine their tripsheets in an attempt to find the driver. But as the days dragged on and none made his appearance Mario sweated.

While the police doggedly continued their house-to-house search, our office was also occupied with the murder. All of us in the Bureau of Investigation, working with our homicide chief, Assistant District Attorney Jacob Grumet, who would eventually prosecute the case, were building up a dossier on Lonergan and his friends. Like the police, we climbed stairs and rang doorbells. Lonergan belonged to the purplish fringe of New York's café society who practiced and boasted of their sex perversion. He had been turned down by his draft board because he was bisexual. I was given the assignment to find several of his effeminate friends. One in particular proved the hardest to find but he became an important witness in the case.

Then requestioning of Harjes' valet produced a startling find: after Lonergan had left the apartment the valet had found two soft-boiled eggs wrapped up in a napkin and hidden under some shirts in a drawer. The servants also found a Max Factor make-up kit, which Harjes said he had never seen before.

Here was a disturbed or sick man who could not eat and hid his

food and who had bought a make-up kit . . . to hide scratches . . . ?
We all waited eagerly for a call from Canada . . .

Then on Wednesday a cab driver notified his company that he had
driven Gabellini and Pat home; he verified the interior decorator's
story. When he left our office, Mario was wiping a very pale, but
relieved-looking face.

In Canada, Lonergan calmly insisted he had been to New York
City on Saturday and Sunday, saw Harjes, Sylvia French and Jeanne
Jaburg, and had left the toy outside his wife's apartment when he
did not get any answer to his repeated knocking. He told detectives
he had joined the air force after constant quarrels with Pat and
went to Canada "just to get away from her."

Lonergan's alibi for the hours in which the crime was committed
was this: he had picked up a soldier named Maurice Worcester and
had taken him to Harjes' apartment, where they had indulged in a
sex orgy. Later he woke and found that Worcester had stolen his
money and uniform. That was why he left in one of Harjes' suits. It
seemed like a logical alibi when Lonergan's sordid background was
considered.

Under the relentless questioning of the police Lonergan refused to
change his story. Then in late October, a slender, bespectacled man
walked through the revolving door into the lobby of the Criminal
Courts Building. Under his arm were copies of New York and
Bridgeport newspapers.

"Where can I find District Attorney Hogan?" he asked the elevator starter.

"What do you want to see him about?" asked the starter, who has
gently guided thousands of crackpots to the ever-suffering Complaint Bureau.

The man slapped the newspapers. "I'm mentioned in this case and
I don't know the first thing about it . . ."

The starter took one look at the headline: "Lonergan Brought to
New York for Questioning," then pushed the man into the elevator.

"Seventh floor," he said tersely.

The door slammed shut in the face of some indignant lawyers, but
in a few minutes our receptionist was ushering the man into the
Bureau of Investigation, where I talked to him.

It was plain he was very angry. "It says here that Lonergan was
with me on Sunday," he began, "but I never met the man, never
saw him and don't know what the devil he's talking about . . ."

He didn't get any further. "What's your name?" I asked.

Then came his stunning answer: "Maurice Worcester. . . ."

I took down his statement, then rushed him into Grumet's office. Worcester, who had become a defense plant operator after his honorable discharge from the army, had been many miles from New York the Sunday of the murder. A few phone calls established that his story was authentic. By a weird coincidence Lonergan had manufactured the name of a man who really existed. . . .

We decided to play a long shot. Worcester was given some preliminary instructions in acting as one of our investigators, then we brought him into the interrogation room where Lonergan was sticking doggedly to his story that he had been with a soldier named Maurice Worcester when his wife was murdered.

As we entered the room Lonergan turned to study us. We all held our breath, but he turned away without a sign of recognition. We stood around while the questioning went on; time after time he stared at us dully.

Finally a detective brought Worcester up to Lonergan.

"Don't you recognize this man?"

Lonergan shook his head.

"Well, this is your old friend."

Lonergan snapped, "I never saw this man before this minute."

"We know that, Wayne," the detective said softly. "This is Maurice Worcester. . . ."

If Lonergan had not been caught unawares, he would have said calmly "That's not the Maurice Worcester I met, whatever his name is. That's not the man." But he was caught off balance and reacted without thinking.

I could see the blood rush from his face. He wet his lips and said only, "Oh, no."

From that minute on his reserve began to crumble. He slipped into half-truths, lies and inconsistencies. Within minutes he was dictating his confession. He said he had gone to his wife's apartment about 9:00 A.M. Sunday and had knocked on her bedroom door.

She had opened it, completely nude, and had gone back to bed. He stalked about the apartment angrily reprimanding her for spending so many nights in "gin mills."

"I hear you're the belle of El Morocco," he said.

"You're talking like a drunken sailor," she replied, "and it's none of your business what I do."

Finally after some bitter words she screamed, "Get the hell out of here and don't ever come back. You'll never see the baby again."

Lonergan said he then went berserk, picked up a brass candle holder and smashed her over the head. When the candlestick broke he ran back to the table to get the second one, which he also used to batter her about the head. She tried to ward off the blows, screaming, "What are you doing to me . . . ?"

He said when she tried to struggle to her feet he dropped the battered candlestick, grabbed her about the throat and strangled her.

Almost in a monotone he said: "I held her throat tight for a long time—I don't know how long—maybe two or three minutes and then I stood there and realized she wasn't moving. I stepped back and she fell back on the bed. I was horrified at the blood all over the bed and the walls. I went into the bathroom and tried to wipe the blood off my uniform, gloves and my face where she had scratched me. . . ."

Later he said he went to Harjes' apartment, stuffed his uniform into a duffle-bag, weighed it down with a bar bell and threw the bag into the East River from the pier at the foot of 79th Street. After this he bought a Max Factor make-up kit to hide the scratches on his face. He said he had left the toy elephant on the table outside his wife's door.

"I wanted to make sure my son got it," he said.

While Lonergan was confessing, the weary legwork of the police at last paid off. Even before they heard that Lonergan had confessed to discarding his uniform into the river, Mahoney's men had found a young woman florist who was making a delivery that Sunday morning when she saw Lonergan emerge from Harjes' apartment with a blue bag over his shoulder. He seemed nervous and upset, she said, looking up and down the street as he hurried down the steps of the brownstone house. Then at a rapid pace he started down the street toward the East River.

"He was wearing a blue civilian suit," she said.

The florist was rushed to the D.A.'s office. A line-up of twelve detectives and investigators, all over six feet—like the defendant— was formed. Lonergan was the twelfth man. The young woman walked down the line to pick out Lonergan unhesitatingly as the man she saw hurrying toward the river, a bag over his shoulder.

But our job wasn't finished. Before the trial began we learned that the defense, headed by Edward Broderick, had located a mystery man named John Lovell March, who would be a smashing defense witness. It was necessary that we know March's background, so Assistant District Attorney Jacob Grumet gave me the order:

"Find out who this character is, get all you can on him."

"Where does he live?" I asked.

Grumet grinned. "Westchester."

I first checked the telephone books but found nothing. The next day I began to hunt for March in White Plains, the county seat, checking all municipal bureaus which might have vital statistics. The post office was next. By three that afternoon I knew March lived on Grant Avenue in Pelham Manor with an uncle and aunt. They couldn't—wouldn't—tell me anything about their nephew, so I began canvassing their neighborhood.

There's always someone who will talk. I found a friendly old lady who evidently had spent a major part of her life peering through her blinds to see what her neighbors were doing. She invited me in and over the teacups she gave me a good rundown on March.

A tall, good-looking young man of about twenty-two, he was a professional tennis player. For the next three days I covered most of the tennis courts in Westchester County. I ended that weary tour with a more rounded picture of March. He was lithe, good-looking, hung on the fringes of Manhattan's café society, gave tennis lessons and sold racquets.

The records of the local draft board told me more. On January 25, 1941, he had changed his name from John Massena to John Lovell March. On December 15, 1941, he tried to ship to Bermuda to work for a contractor, but was refused. In February he was classified as 2B. In February 1942, he went to Hoffman's Island to train for the merchant marine.

Police records and Chief Paul A. Werech of Mamaroneck gave me another side of his make-up. On July 27, 1941, he and another man were arrested for second-degree rape of a 17-year-old girl. The grand jury, however, refused to return an indictment against the pair.

Although his family was of moderate circumstances, he hung about with young and wealthy playboys.

I paid a visit to Hoffman's Island to discover he wasn't in the merchant marine but in the chorus of *Follow the Girls,* then rehearsing at the Adelphi Theater.

When I returned to the office I had five pages of notes on March, much of it far from complimentary. At the next preliminary hearing Broderick made a speech to the court about the value of the testimony of a newly discovered witness, John Lovell March.

When he had finished, Jack Grumet said nonchalantly, "Oh, yes, we know all about March. The District Attorney has smoked him out. . . ."

This disclosure obviously startled Broderick and his staff. We never knew what they had, but the importance of March vanished completely that morning after Jack had made his announcement.

Lonergan was convicted of second-degree murder before a General Sessions judge and jury on March 31, 1944, after the first case ended in a mistrial. The second was a long and bitter fight between Assistant District Attorney Grumet and Edward Broderick. He was sentenced to serve from 35 years to life in Sing Sing, where he is still confined.

A few years ago he applied unsuccessfully through his attorney in Surrogate's Court to qualify for a share in his wife's $4,000,000 estate.

A strange aftermath of the case involved Mario Gabellini, Patricia Lonergan's escort that fatal morning. In May, 1951, a pretty redheaded showgirl, Patricia Stousland, 25, died in Bellevue Hospital from an overdose of sleeping pills which she had taken in Mario's apartment. He told police he had been away and discovered the girl in convulsions on his return. He said he was completely mystified by her act. The reason for her death was never learned.

Passion, jealousy, revenge and a curious quirk of fate were involved in another murder case, which is unusual in the files of our office because it rested almost entirely on circumstantial evidence.

It began in April, 1941, when Eva Bilbao met Carlos Rodriguez and went to live with him. Rodriguez, using violence and threats, placed her in a house of prostitution while he spent her earnings playing pool and betting on the horses. In September, 1942, after she had met a hard-working cab driver, Carlos Ramos, she tried to abandon her former way of life but Rodriguez slashed her severely.

After a long stay in the hospital she signed a complaint. Rodriguez was arrested and convicted of compulsory prostitution on the testimony of Eva and Ramos. He was sent to state prison. As he was led away, Rodriguez muttered that some day he would "get" Ramos. Eva and Ramos were married and dropped out of sight.

In 1945 Rodriguez was released from prison. One day he met a friend of Ramos and gave him this message:

"*Voy a limpiarlo. . . .*" A death threat.

Rodriguez, as he later admitted, walked the streets of New York City day and night seeking Ramos. On the early morning of September 3, 1946, the killer found his victim by a strange twist of fate.

Rodriguez and a friend, Alfonso Roman, were standing on a street corner, Rodriguez talking violently of the subject which by now had completely taken hold of him—Carlos Ramos.

"Someday," he vowed, "I will kill him with this," and he made a menacing move with the gun in his pocket.

Roman, who was weary of his friend's constant vows of murder, whistled at a passing cab. When it screeched to a stop both men entered. Roman noticed that Rodriguez suddenly lapsed into a frozen silence. It began raining, and as they passed a corner Roman noticed three men he knew trying to signal a cab. He ordered the cab driver to stop and they picked up the trio. All were chatting and laughing as they drove uptown in the rain—except Rodriguez, who stared straight ahead without speaking.

Finally they arrived at their destination and the men piled out. "I will pay," Rodriguez said.

"Very good," Roman said, and got out of the cab. He had taken only about three steps when he heard a shot. When he whirled about he saw Rodriguez running down the street. Roman took to his heels also. He did not know who fired the shots nor what became of the other men.

The cab driver, of course, was Ramos. Among the 14,500 cab drivers in New York City, fate had selected Ramos to pick up the man who had sworn to murder him. Whether it was because of the rain or the darkness, he apparently did not recognize the killer.

Another driver found Ramos dying in a pool of blood beside his cab. Near him was a bullet and two discharged shells. The murder weapon was never found.

Ramos died without talking. One of the fatal bullets was found in the socket of his right hip. From the holes and tracks left in his body by the bullets it was evident that Ramos had been shot while he was in a sitting position. Ballistics experts established that the bullets and the two discharged shells had come from a 9-millimeter automatic pistol of European make.

It was the assistant in the District Attorney's office who had sent Rodriguez to prison who recalled that the prisoner had muttered a death threat against Ramos. On a hunch he ordered us to bring him in. Rodriguez had a tailored alibi and when he gave his statement, the Bureau of Investigation had to check each item.

We found he never saw the movie he claimed to have seen; the girl he was supposed to be with said she had not seen him for days, and so on. When we came back to the office and fitted together what we had established it was evident that Rodriguez' alibi was shattered and that he was lying.

"Do you want to tell us about it?" the assistant asked when he showed Rodriguez his web of lies.

"He chased me," the prisoner blurted out. "Then I drew a pistol and shot him. It was either him or me."

But the ballistic examinations and the medical reports which showed that Ramos was killed in a sitting position shattered this defense. The jury believed the charts and tiny pieces of the spent slugs. Rodriguez was sentenced to state prison for 30 years to life. In 1948 the Court of Appeals affirmed his conviction.

The dogged type of investigation, rather than flashy sleuthing, solved the next case of murder "as a favor."

The killing took place on January 13, 1948, when Benjamin (Chippy) Weiner, a small-time East Side gangster, was found dying on the kitchen floor of his First Street apartment. A policeman who lived in the building and who had heard the shots was at his side within three minutes.

"Who shot you, Weiner?" he asked.

Chippy shook his head. He died a short time later, still obeying the underworld rule of refusing to talk to the law. Dozens of residents in the neighborhood who had heard the shots were questioned, but if they knew who the killer was, they weren't telling the police.

A month after the murder, Edward Fennessey, arrested for a stick-up in Brocklyn, made an admission to the Kings County District Attorney's office, linking a small-time gunman, Santo Bretagna, and Willie Rosenberg with the murder. The police arrested Rosenberg, but Bretagna vanished.

The Bureau of Investigation of the D.A.'s office now took over. We visited Connecticut, Chicago and parts of New England, mostly on tips from informers which all dwindled into nothing. At a conference it was decided that our next step was to question every known criminal associate of Weiner's. From our dossier on Weiner we began picking up the men with whom we knew he had been engaged in criminal activities. It was day-after-day business of picking up the small-time hoods in East Side bars and restaurants, bringing them downtown and questioning them hour after hour. None of these was the ordinary citizen having his first brush with the law; these were sneering, tough young hoodlums, who knew their way around a D.A.'s office or a police precinct.

We picked up one young tough who seemed uneasy. Instinctively we knew we had our man. He was on parole and was aware that we could send him back. Few like to return to prison, so in a few hours he revealed he was sending money to Bretagna. At 10:00 P.M. that same night we moved in on Bretagna as he entered a bar in Boston's Scollay Square. This was March 13, 1948, two months after Chippy Weiner shook his head in answer to the patrolman's questions.

Bretagna confessed in our office that he had gone to Weiner's apartment with Rosenberg. The latter wanted to collect his share of a hijacking job in which Weiner was holding the profits from the fence. On the way up to the apartment Rosenberg gave Bretagna his gun.

"Knock this guy off as a favor to me," he said casually.

"Okay, I'll give it to him," Bretagna replied. Thus was murder planned.

Weiner greeted them at the door. He waved them to a couch while he went into the kitchen to prepare some drinks.

Rosenberg jerked his head in the direction of the kitchen. Bretagna rose, tiptoed to the kitchen and killed Weiner as he poured whiskey from a bottle. Rosenberg, confronted with the confession, readily confessed his part in the murder. By noon of the 14th we had wrapped up the case. Both men died in the electric chair for the cold-blooded slaying.

Two jagged pieces of plastic, which we kept in a separate file, solved the slaying of an aged grocer in East Harlem. The body of the man was found beside his cash register. The murder props were conventional; the opened till, the man's head battered to a pulp by a revolver butt, the lack of witnesses to the crime. No one had been seen entering or leaving the premises.

All the police found were tiny bits of plastic from the grip of a revolver. They were brought in to our office to be glued together, while the detectives worked day and night to break a case without a clue. Finally, the investigation reached an impasse; there just wasn't anything more the weary detectives could do.

Months later two police officers found a pair of vagrants, Joseph Greenwood and Vincent Gavin, sleeping in a hallway near Canal Street. They were arrested for vagrancy. But one of the patrolmen discovered that one of the men was trying to hide a soggy cardboard box. When he tore it open he found a gun with a taped handle. At the precinct the tape was removed, revealing that the weapon lacked a grip. The information was channeled through the ordinary police routine. Homicide Squad detectives leaped on the item; the gun was brought to our office and the bits of plastic so laboriously glued together slipped into place.

When they were faced with the evidence, Greenwood and Gavin confessed the murder. They said they had wandered into an apartment house intent on holding up a tenant when they encountered a woman, Josephine Pergola. After a conversation they revealed their plans.

"I've got a better idea," the woman said. "Let's stick up the grocery."

They agreed. When the store was empty they held up and then beat to death the aged owner. Their loot was $10.

We picked up the woman later in the day. All three pleaded guilty to second-degree murder and were sentenced to long terms in prison.

The D.A.'s Bureau of Investigation and the detectives of the homicide squad combined forces to break the next murder case, which might have gone unsolved except for a woman's alertness.

The story begins with the usual Signal 30—crime of violence— being sent out by the police dispatcher. Radio cars sped to an upper West Side apartment house. In the courtyard a crowd was gathered about the battered body of Mrs. Herman Jones. In their apartment her husband sobbed out a story that two men had invaded their place through the kitchen window which faced a fire escape. They stabbed him in the arm when he resisted, then threw him out of the apartment. He ran downstairs screaming for help. The superintendent, who was talking with Jones's sister-in-law, heard him, and together they rushed back to the fifth-floor apartment. It was strangely silent. When both men looked out they saw the body of Mrs. Jones in the courtyard.

Jones identified one of the murderers as a former neighbor. He was picked up and identified by Jones. The man strongly protested his innocence but could not account for his movements when the murder was committed. There was nothing to do but hold him.

All of the witnesses were brought down to the D.A.'s office and questioned. The sister-in-law was asked to describe exactly what she did when she entered the apartment.

"When I went into the apartment I went to the kitchen window," she said.

"Why?" she was asked.

"I wanted to see if it was locked," she said.

"Was it locked?" she was asked.

She nodded. "Yes."

(Jones had said his attackers had climbed into the kitchen by the window.)

"What else did you do?" the investigator asked.

"I went into the bedroom. The window was open . . ." she said.

The case was now beginning to fall into form.

A woman neighbor was brought in who told how she had seen Jones leave the apartment and return with his sister-in-law and the superintendent.

"Did anyone leave or enter the apartment?" she was asked.

"No," she said.

"Are you positive?"

"I am," she said. "I was standing in the hall all the time."

The evidence was too strong for Jones. Under requestioning he admitted he had quarreled with his wife, she had stabbed him in the arm with a kitchen knife and he, in return, had knocked her unconscious. Then he pushed her through the bedroom window.

His confession freed the innocent neighbor. Jones pleaded guilty to second-degree murder and was sentenced to a term in Sing Sing.

14. THE WRONG KEY: THE COLARCO CASE

THE INVESTIGATING STAFF of the District Attorney's office is often used by law enforcement officials of other counties and other states in the apprehension of fugitives from justice who have tried to bury themselves in the melting pot of New York, only to discover that the big city can be a small town when it comes to gossip and curious neighbors.

On the other hand, the District Attorney of New York County may send investigators to as many as 15 other states yearly on the trail of criminals; they can count on receiving the cooperation of local police, state troopers and sheriffs. The following case, I believe, underscores the reciprocity which exists between law enforcement agencies in our country.

The first involves a former clubhouse fighter named Ross Colarco, who was wanted for a large fur robbery in upstate New York. In 1944, two deputy sheriffs from that county arrived at District Attorney Hogan's office with his picture and a request for assistance.

As usual, Hogan ordered us to give them complete cooperation. I made copies of the picture and interviewed both sheriffs. They had no specific information, but from close friends of Colarco they had learned that once when he was in the ring he had lived on the lower East Side near Hester Street.

I first went to Stillman's Gym, a gathering-place for fighters in New York, to look up some pugs I knew. They told me they had heard of Colarco, but had not seen him for more than a year. From Stillman's I went on a tour of bars in the vicinity of Hester Street, casually dropping Colarco's name to bartenders and waiters. My role was that of a rather shady character who hinted he had some "hot" furs to unload.

One bartender took the bait; Colarco had been in the neighborhood within the last six months and was hanging out with an ex-convict named Frenchy. The name clicked with me. Back at the District Attorney's office, I went through my files and found that this

253

ex-convict had been involved in a case I had investigated a year before and had cooperated.

I found the ex-convict, who gladly gave me Colarco's address, more in relief to know I wasn't after him than in a spirit of civic cooperation.

"Watch out for him," he warned, "he's got a loaded gun and swears no cop is going to take him."

"Is he alone?" I asked.

He shook his head. "He's got a dame you had better watch, too."

Colarco's hideout was a furnished rooming-house in the forties just off Ninth Avenue. I contacted the deputies and, accompanied by a detective from the West 54th Street precinct, we paid the place a visit. We identified ourselves to the landlady, who gave us a pass key. The room was as quiet as a tomb. The deputy slid the key in while we stood by, guns drawn. The lock turned and we rushed in; the room was empty. We began a search of the apartment and I found a loaded .32 wrapped in a towel in the bureau drawer. I removed the gun and substituted a sock. Ross would be unpleasantly surprised. The landlady insisted we return the key and the deputy did so.

For the rest of the afternoon the deputies helped us set up a stake-out at each end of the block; they arranged to signal us when Colarco came back. At about 3:30 P.M. the detective nudged me. Down the block we saw the deputy take off his hat, the agreed signal. A moment later Colarco, a girl on his arm, strolled into view. To our dismay, at the same time a crowd of school-children, swinging books, began to flood the block.

It was obvious we couldn't take him now; we had one gun of his, but suppose he had another on him?

The detective and I walked away, I on one side of the street and he on the other, to join the deputies. We agreed to give the fighter about ten minutes, then take him in the flat.

The deputies got the key again from the landlady and insisted on going in. I was assigned to the rear window. It was their prisoner and their glory, so I told them it was their pleasure. The local detective took a position in the hallway.

In the junk-cluttered back yard I slipped up to the window, took off my hat and peeked in. I was looking into the kitchen. Colarco, his back to me, was near the door, talking to the girl. Suddenly he put his hand over her mouth as he pointed to the door.

Then he tiptoed to the bureau to get his gun. He grabbed the towel. A look of bewilderment spread over his face when he found the gun was gone. He tossed the sock to the wall and bolted to the kitchen. He flung up the window and as he straddled the sill I leaned over, put my gun to his head and told him he was to get back in the kitchen. For a moment I thought he was going to rush me.

"Try it and I'll kill you," I said.

Few men can look into the muzzle of a gun and still be full of fight. Colarco wasn't one of them. He withdrew and I crawled in after him. I covered both while there was the damnedest racket at the door. Finally they crashed in; both deputies looking as mad as wounded bears.

"What took you so long?" I asked the detective.

"The old lady was so frightened she gave us the wrong key," he said.

Colarco was taken down to the Tombs, then transferred to an upstate jail to stand trial for the robbery. He was convicted and sentenced to a long term in Sing Sing.

15. THE CROOKED LABOR CZAR: THE JOE FAY STORY

ON A bright spring day in 1932, a chartered boat pulled out of a Jersey City pier and proceeded down the bay to meet an incoming ship. Aboard were city and state officials, union delegates and the Jersey City Police Band. When the luxury liner hove into sight, the band struck up "For He's A Jolly Good Fellow," while the officials and guests cheered lustily.

On the liner's deck a broad-shouldered, nattily dressed man raised his hands above his head in the traditional gesture of a champion. Below, on the chartered boat, the crowd roared its approval. Mayor "Boss" Frank Hague, an aging dandy, was at the pier to greet the smiling gentleman as he walked down the gangplank. All in all, it was a royal welcome for Joe Fay, one of the most powerful union leaders in the country and one of the most crooked.

Fay, a big man, handy with his fists, had been one of the top powers in the misty back-room world where certain elements of politics, labor and business connive or collide. Before 1930 he was little known to the public though the New York–New Jersey construction industry was his own peculiar preserve.

He was well fixed before his name burst spectacularly into the headlines, first in connection with murder. He was back in the headlines in 1943 when District Attorney Hogan convicted him of extortion in one of the most difficult cases our office ever handled. His conviction, affirmed by the United States Supreme Court, was one of the most important in the history of American labor. Yet even while in jail, Fay's name reverberated in the headlines, shaking loose one prominent politician from his Senate seat.

Before I go into the investigation and prosecution of Fay, it is best to examine his violent career in chronological order.

Fay started his union career in 1920 by moving in on the AFL Union of Operating Engineers, the union he always claimed as his own. He was soon elected delegate of Local 825 in New Jersey and quickly rose to become its business agent, a position which gave him tremendous power over the men who operate derricks, steam-shovels and other construction equipment.

Then Fay branched out to set up his own construction companies. Needless to say, he soon had an enormous volume of business.

By about 1925 he had become politically ambitious. He ran for Democratic State Chairman of Essex County but was defeated. That ended his interest in elective offices. The following year he turned down an invitation to run for the Newark City Commission.

Behind the scenes, Fay was solidifying his political strength. By 1930 he was the strongest of the "top four" of organized labor in the country.

About this time a prominent Senator told a political gathering in Newark, "I am interested in men like Joe Fay. They represent one of the real forces in American life."

An interesting statement in view of things to come . . .

During Prohibition he conducted the Joseph Fay Association, with clubrooms in Newark, and the Fay Travel Association. The latter scorned hired buses; trains were chartered to Canada where the liquor flowed freely and the stakes in card and dice games ran into the thousands.

Fay, we learned in our later investigations, was one of the wealthiest labor leaders in the United States. He lived in a spacious ten-room brick house in the sedate Forest Hills section of Newark, and maintained a palatial home at Avon, on the North Jersey shore.

In 1937 Fay became a household name on both sides of the Hudson River following the murder of Norman Redwood, a rival construction union leader in Tenafly, New Jersey. John J. Breslin, Bergen County Prosecutor, said flatly that Fay and the late Sam Rosoff, New York subway builder, had plotted the slaying. But neither was indicted and the case remains unsolved to this day. Fists swinging, Fay returned to his stronghold behind the labor scenes. In 1940 he got into a fistfight with David Dubinsky, president of the International Ladies' Garment Workers' Union at an AFL convention in New Orleans, after Dubinsky offered an anti labor-racketeering resolution to the delegates.

Two years later Fay was accused at a state convention in Syracuse of slugging a Rochester business agent of his own union. The complainant disappeared temporarily, however, and the charge was dropped. Later the man got his job back.

It was in 1942 that our office got our first inkling that Fay, then international vice-president of the operating engineers' union and president of the Newark local, and James Bove, another international vice-president, were engaged in extorting money from contractors on the $300,000,000 Delaware Aqueduct Water Supply project for New York City. Fay and Bove were threatening the contractors with strike.

At the time this was merely whispered gossip, innuendo and rumor. It was our job to establish it as legal proof.

At a staff conference District Attorney Hogan ordered every available man put on the case. Assistant District Attorney Tom Moore was assigned to it, but Frank Hogan personally handled every report, guided the investigation and then, in an unprecedented move, prosecuted the case in court.

"If he's acquitted I'll get the blame and no one else," he said.

We started from scratch. The first thing Tom Moore called for was a copy of every contract on the project. Then, because wire tapping is illegal in New Jersey, we reconnoitered Fay's business and private residence. For days I did nothing but amble about the streets, taking down license plates of cars that stopped in front of his office and union hall. I also paid a visit to the hall in rough clothes, seeking a job. I didn't get one, but I did get a good look at the setup.

The barrooms near the union headquarters were not particularly fruitful. Whenever I entered the customers at the bar scrutinized me closely and the conversation broke off. On other investigations, I have found bartenders to be good sources of casual information and leads. But on this case they just grunted when I started up a conversation, even about things as innocent as ball game scores. This was one investigation in which Dan O'Brien of Boston, who hinted he was not averse to making crooked dollars, didn't get anywhere.

However, some of the license plates gave us clues to Fay's associates. Each one was tailed for months by an investigator, who made daily reports about how he spent his time, with whom he did business and how often he contacted Fay.

But the major job was noting all his toll calls. We had a chart made in the office which listed more than 10,000 calls over a span of years. We traced each call, investigated the person who made the call, then built a dossier on the ones we suspected of having criminal dealings with Fay.

From the telephone calls, the license plates and his visitors, a pattern began to form; Fay was intimate with contractors, racketeers, politicians and hoodlums.

Now Assistant District Attorney Joseph M. Gasarch, our chief accountant, and his band of figure hunters, joined us. We served all the contractors with subpoenas calling for a surrender of their books. Each item on the books was examined. Obviously it was a tremendous task. But gradually the items began forming another pattern; bribes to Fay had been listed in many strange ways: promotion, labor expenses, etc.

When the item was clearly not what it was supposed to be Gasarch would send it on to Hogan, who personally handled the questioning of the contractors. When they saw it was useless to try to explain the items away they told the truth to become potential witnesses for the People's case.

Two witnesses were William J. Brewster of Hackensack, New Jersey, president of George M. Brewster & Co., and Miles I. Kilmer, vice-president and general manager of Mason & Hanger. One courageous contractor was Thomas J. Walsh, who gave the District Attorney's office fine cooperation.

Under questioning by Hogan they admitted Fay and Bove demanded $60,000 for the smooth running of their $15,000,000 contract on the $300,000,000 water-supply project. They said Fay had made the demands in August, 1940, in a suite in the Hotel Commodore while a group of labor leaders met in an adjacent room.

The payments were made in installments. When the time to pay arrived Fay would call them with this message: "The time for the annual meeting is now at hand . . ."

The name of Harry McLean, the millionaire, who is famous for his $1,000 tips to bellboys and passers-by, came into our investigation when we questioned Louis R. Perini, head of his own company and also an official of the Seaboard Construction Company, owned by McLean.

Perini admitted to Hogan that he paid Fay $25,000 to avoid labor union trouble. Seaboard had a $10,000,000 contract. Perini said he received a call from McLean in Ontario to meet Fay in a New York City hotel room, where Fay demanded $125,000 to avoid labor trouble.

McLean now emerged as a major witness for the People, so Gasarch was assigned to examine his books in Toronto.

McLean stalled at first, but when Gasarch insisted he see the books the millionaire reluctantly brought the accountant into one of the rooms of his suite and brought in some books.

Gasarch went to work. An hour went by. Then suddenly out of nowhere McLean was at his side, swinging. Gasarch tried to duck but the blow caught him on the side of his head. When he got up from the floor, McLean was gone.

Joe called the office and Hogan was furious. "Go to the Toronto police," he said, "and get assistance. I want this man locked up."

Accompanied by two detectives, Joe returned to the Seaboard offices but a secretary informed them "Mr. McLean has been called out of town." Joe and the detectives searched for a week but never caught up with McLean.

Assistant District Attorney Tom Moore was then detailed to interview McLean. He decided to try McLean's house, a beautiful mansion near Merrickville, Ontario, where the millionaire builder lived in feudal style.

McLean received him in bathrobe, pajamas and slippers.

"Why the hell don't you people leave me alone? I'm a busy man. Tell Hogan to stop hounding me. . . ."

Tom tried to calm him by pointing out it was his duty as a public-spirited citizen to answer at least some of our questions and permit us to examine his books in relation to Fay.

McLean exploded. Tom, who knew of Gasarch's experience, stepped back.

"I'm warning you, Mr. McLean," he said, "not to throw one at me or I'll have to defend myself."

McLean took a look at Tom's six-foot height and decided he didn't want any trouble. But he did the next best thing. He flung open the door with a shout: "Okay, you wise guy—now walk back to the station."

It was seven miles to Merrickville and the day was cold and windy.

Tom began hoofing it back to the depot. He had walked only a short distance when two burly men stepped into the road and barred his path.

After a moment of silence, one said, "He looks like a nice guy. . . ."

Tom just stood there and wondered how he was going to take them both on at once.

"We're supposed to kidnap you," the bigger man said, "but what the hell—you look like a pretty nice guy, so we'll let you go. . . ."

They both stepped aside and Tom kept walking, now a bit faster. . . .

To catch up with McLean now became a major operation. Under Chief Investigator Fay's direction we contacted the Border Patrol, United States and Canadian Immigration personnel and all official offices at Ogdensburg, New York, St. Albans, Vermont, and Detroit, Michigan. At our request these offices promised to contact us if McLean crossed the border.

It was now a game of hare-and-hounds with McLean; we on one side of the border, he on the other. Once on a tip our man, Tom Fay, was sent to Syracuse with a body attachment warrant. We heard that McLean was coming in to turn over a huge amount of cash to one of Joe Fay's men. Tom, playing the part of a quiet vacationer, surveyed the town and quietly looked into the background of the local hotel managers. He selected one who appeared to be a solid citizen.

"McLean?" the manager said. "Brother, I would love to help you. That character came in last time, wrecked the hotel room and caused me no end of trouble. The moment he comes in I'll call you."

Tom also covered the airport, where an employee promised to call him if McLean's private plane was scheduled to come in.

Despite the arrangements and a day-and-night watch by Tom Fay the mission failed. Perhaps the Canadian millionaire never arrived.

While we waited for McLean to appear I was sent upstate to Troy, New York, when we learned in researching Joe Fay's early background that he had been involved in an assault there.

I arrived in Troy on November 6, 1942. Reluctantly I started with the police, hoping I would find an official record of the assault. Police Chief John B. Conroy, a genial, white-haired gentleman, was very courteous but not very helpful.

He looked vague when I mentioned Fay but he did promise to question some of the "old-timers," as he put it, and see what he could come up with. When I returned the next day he just shook his head.

"The records were all burned up in the fire at old headquarters some years ago," he said. "None of the old-timers recalls the case."

I noticed the officer who had just entered looked surprised at his remark.

There was nothing I could do but accept the chief's explanation. My next trip was to the library, where I spent the day going through the files as far back as 20 years. I did find an account of a burning of a police station, but I had a hunch the records had not been destroyed.

I decided to wait in the vicinity of headquarters about the time the shifts changed to try to find one of the members of the force who might stop off at a neighboring saloon.

At 4:00 P.M. when the uniformed men came out, I spotted the officer who had entered the office when I was talking to the chief. Purely on instinct I selected him. When he entered the saloon I followed. He had downed his first drink when I leaned over and introduced myself. He was politely formal until I had bought him a number of Scotches. By 8:00 P.M. he was belligerently drunk and advising me that the chief—whom he disliked intensely—was holding back the records.

Then he gave me an owlish look. "But I like the way Hogan's been operating down there and I'm going to do something for you."

"What's that?" I asked hopefully.

"I'm going to get that record for you," he said.

"How about now?" I asked. "I'll wait here."

He gave me a comic salute and went out.

He returned in a half hour, planked a book in my lap, wheeled about and left.

What I had was the police blotter of the Troy, New York, Police Department.

I wrapped a newspaper around it and hurried back to my hotel. I didn't dare wait overnight, but took the milk train back to New York. At 10:00 A.M. District Attorney Hogan was examining the arrest record of Joe Fay.

My notes taken from the record read:

Monday, March 13, 1916: At 6:00 A.M. Edward Maloney, age 38, white, born in the U. S., a bartender, was arrested on the charge of assault. On his person was a revolver, 60 cents, wallet, purse, keys, a razor and brush. The arresting officer was Jayra. The case was dismissed in two hours.

Monday, 6:00 A.M. Sgt. Ruff called for an ambulance to Broadway and Sixth Street to carry Joe Fay to the Troy Hospital. He had been shot at Broadway and Sixth Street. Fay lives in Port Washington and boards at 129 [illegible] Street, Troy.

Monday, 6:00 A.M. Sgt. Ruff called Doctor Hambolt to the station house to attend Maloney for an assault at Biscates Cafe, Broadway and 6th Street.

It was a curious hodgepodge of facts. Apparently the police had tried to conceal that Maloney was a patrolman. As Hogan wryly observed, "It looks like Joe had influence even then."

I returned to Troy on Hogan's orders to begin piecing the parts together. Finally I confirmed that Maloney was a policeman who had engaged Fay in a gunfight. I obtained this information from an elderly gentleman, Tom Stray, who had been Maloney's partner during their stay on the force.

My next assignment was to reconstruct Fay's early life in Troy, to find out about his associates, his business ties, his political and union influence. This time I became a brush salesman. I brought a small suitcase, a dozen brushes, researched my sales talk on brushes, and set out. My first stop was a neighborhood where Stray said Fay's sweetheart had lived 20 years ago. It was a middle-class neighborhood of two-story houses. I began at one end of the street, ringing doorbells, having doors slammed in my face, but still managing to get a few people to talk, especially a lonely old Irishman with a thick brogue and a yen to talk about anything and everything.

When he was looking over my brushes I casually mentioned that I had lived in the neighborhood many years before.

"What ever happened to Joe Fay?" I asked.

The old man shook his head. "He was buckoo, that one . . ."

He began reminiscing without my prompting and in a half hour gave me some names, particularly the name and address of Fay's old sweetheart and a boarding-house where Fay had lived for many years.

He finally talked himself out. Then, while I was hurriedly packing the brushes which he had minutely examined, he asked me where I had lived in the neighborhood. I told him I had boarded with the O'Briens.

His face lighted up. "Sure, they were a fine family," he said. Apparently my fictitious family had a counterpart in real life so I had to stay and listen to his memoirs about the O'Briens.

At Fay's old address the landlady told me that Fay had moved to Newark where he was "in the union business." She even bought a brush and said she remembered me from years back. . . .

I dropped the brush salesman's role when I looked up the address of Fay's girl. Knowing the caliber of a girl who would hang out with this man, I thought I had better appear as a flashy, horse-playing type. I bought a racing form, which I stuck in my coat pocket and set out.

The woman who answered the bell was sharp-eyed and had been around. She was a peroxide blonde of about forty. She gave me a quick once-over when I asked for Fay's girl, then invited me in. We got along famously. After a few drinks I confessed I was a bookmaker from Boston and an old friend of Fay's and the girl's. After a few more drinks we went out to dinner and it didn't take too long to learn the whole story of the relationship between Fay and the girl, how Fay got into the local unions and who his friends on the police force were.

The most important thing she gave me was the current address of Fay's girl. I was startled to find it to be in Newark.

"When Joe left she followed him," she said. "She's married now and has a couple of kids . . ."

I had one bad moment when she insisted on calling the girl in New Jersey, then putting me on the wire. I got out of it by telling her it would spoil a wonderful surprise and by buying her another drink.

In the early hours of the morning I gladly put her in a cab, said good night, after promising to see her the next day, and went back to my hotel. The following morning I was on my way to Newark.

Fay's former girl-friend lived in a rather good section of Essex County, in a fashionable garden apartment. On my first call she was out and I talked to the next-door neighbor, fortunately a talkative housewife, who told me that she didn't think much of her neighbor—the woman I was interested in—because she was close-mouthed and didn't mingle with the others in the house. From her I got an inkling it wasn't going to be easy to get her to talk. Evidently she knew how to handle police or D.A.'s men. That same day I called again and found her at home.

She opened the door just a few inches. I didn't waste any time but flashed my badge.

"I am from the District Attorney's office in New York. I would like to ask you a few questions," I said.

"About what?" she asked.

"Joe Fay," I said.

She slammed the door in my face.

"Maybe I'll wait until 5:00 P.M.," I said loudly, "and we'll both talk to your husband. About the time . . ."

She opened the door slowly.

"Come in," she said sullenly.

I left an hour later, my notebook filled with certain details of Fay's background, with names of contractors, union rivals, and so on. Not all of the information was pertinent to the investigation, but some was very important.

I was next sent to Chicago on the trail of a millionaire contractor, Steve Healey, who Hogan considered an important witness in the investigation. He had begged Healey to come to New York City to be questioned, but the contractor dodged each query.

My job was to tail Healey day and night and grab him the second he crossed the border into Michigan. Illinois does not have a reciprocal witness arrangement with New York State, but Michigan does.

I first stopped off in Michigan to make arrangements with the State Police to accompany me in the arrest, then went on to Chicago, where I registered at the La Salle Hotel.

The next morning I started at Healey's office. I paid it a visit on the pretext of seeking a job. I didn't get the job, but I did obtain a good look at Healey without his seeing me.

It was a cold, windy day and I stood for seven hours outside the building waiting for him to go home. Finally he ran out and dived into his car. Luckily I was able to flag a cab to follow him to his home just outside of the city. From his action it was evident that Healey was on the alert for a tail.

After I tailed him for three days I got to know his routine fairly well. I also discovered that there was more than one entrance and exit to the building. All I could do while waiting was to move from exit to exit.

I soon concluded that to maintain an effective security detail I needed help, so I paid a visit to all airports, made a contact in each with someone who could and would scan the passenger lists daily, then did the same with the railroads and two private airfields.

Through the cooperation of the telephone company I made up a chart of toll calls made from Healey's home and office. These numbers were rushed to my office to provide invaluable leads.

I also made arrangements by which I saw all copies of communications going in or out of his office. Because this is a secret arrangement presently used I cannot disclose its workings. But it was very fruitful. I learned Healey was flying to New York in a chartered plane. Fortunately the pilot's name was used.

I went to the airport, posing as a New York contractor interested in hiring a plane for weekly trips to New York. Soon I found Healey's pilot and we sat down to outline a tentative contract.

"Do many businessmen use your planes?" I asked.

"Why, on Thursday I'm flying a millionaire by the name of Healey to New York," he said proudly. "He always uses my plane. I have his number here. Give him a call and ask him how we take care of him . . ."

"Maybe I'll come out on Thursday," I said.

"Fine," the pilot said. "Be here by 8:00 A.M."

I was there at 7:00 A.M. but Healey never showed. Finally the pilot called his home to find he had cancelled the flight. The pilot was disappointed and I could sense the let-down over the phone when I notified the office to call off the detectives who were staking out the airport.

I trailed Healey for two long months. I never let him out of sight from the time he entered his office until the lights went off in his house. Several times I sat next to him at night clubs; most of the time I could have touched his coat tails.

I had one embarrassing moment while trying to keep him in sight. He had gone to a hotel where he frequently stayed, but after several hours passed and he hadn't appeared I was afraid I had lost him.

I took out my wallet to get Healey's room number, which I had scribbled on a card when Healey suddenly passed the booth. As he started into the crowded lobby I jumped up to follow him. It wasn't until I was downtown in a cab trailing Healey to his house that I suddenly recalled I had left the wallet in the telephone booth.

And on the wallet was my D.A.'s badge.

I went cold all over. It was an inexcusable blunder. As soon as I saw Healey enter his home I hurried back to the hotel. The wallet, of course, was gone. I checked with the hotel's missing articles department, but it had not turned up.

I recall how I sat in my hotel room, just sweating. After I had checked with the lost and found department several more times without hearing anything about the wallet I reluctantly called the Chicago police, as required by law. There wasn't anything else to do.

The detective's voice sounded bored until I identified myself as an investigator from District Attorney Hogan's office.

"I'll send a man over," he said.

I don't think it was ten minutes later when not one, but four detectives walked into my room. They were friendly and courteous, but very, very curious.

Who was I after . . . what did Hogan want in Chicago . . . ?

I had a story all ready. I showed them a picture of a notorious confidence man and told them we were searching for him in Chicago.

One detective took a long look at the rogues' gallery picture.

"I know that bird," he said. "I saw him on the West Side only last week."

The others nodded.

I had a great deal of difficulty in keeping my face straight. The convict whose picture I had shown them had been dead for ten years. . . .

For four days I had to go through with the act, meeting them at night for a tour of Chicago's night clubs and restaurants seeking my dead swindler.

I finally told them he had probably skipped; they reluctantly agreed. Their reluctance was natural. I had been picking up all the tabs.

They were so solicitous they saw me to the station. I waved good-by, walked in one entrance, then came out another. I registered in another hotel under another name and picked up Healey again that afternoon. I never did find that wallet or the badge.

One night in the third month of my surveillance I thought I had him. He motored out to a night club near the Michigan border. I alerted the Michigan State Police, who posted radio cars on the main highway.

The night club was a pleasant place and Healey looked content to stay all night. Twice he started out and twice his friends urged him to stay. Finally in the early hours of the morning he left and started for the Michigan border, but then, apparently realizing what he was doing, he ordered his chauffeur to swing around. Wearily I called the Michigan police and told them to pull off their cars; Healey was home in Chicago in bed.

At the end of the third month I notified the office it was useless for me to remain; Healey was not leaving the safety of Illinois. A few days later I was recalled. Eventually Healey did come into New York County to be questioned after arrangements had been made through his attorney. Hogan said his story was fanciful.

After I left Chicago Tony Scanlon was sent to Battle Creek, Michigan, where he located McLean in the Post Sanitarium.

In McLean's entourage was an old gentleman who did nothing

but magic tricks to amuse his boss, and an elderly housekeeper. Through surveillance Tony found the amateur magician spent his mornings in the park across the road, sunning himself.

One morning when he appeared, he was surprised to find Tony seated on his favorite bench. Naturally they fell into conversation about the usual topics of strangers, the weather, progress of the war and the world in general.

When the magician suddenly plucked a coin from his ear, Tony put on a good show of looking startled. Then as trick followed trick, he enthusiastically applauded.

"Gosh, mister," he said, "you belong on the stage!"

An amateur loves applause and Tony gave him plenty. Every morning for a week Tony proved an eager and responsive audience. Finally when he felt he had the old man's friendship, he cautiously identified himself.

"Maybe you can get me in to see Mr. McLean," he said. "I only want to ask him to come to New York . . ."

"You got a subpoena?" the old man asked.

Tony raised his right hand. "So help me, I haven't got one . . ."

The old man left, promising to talk to McLean. That night Tony received a call.

It was the magician.

"Mr. McLean wants you to come right over," he said. He added, "I'll give you a tip. He likes his guests to enjoy themselves, so when I do the tricks laugh like hell."

"I'll split a gut," Tony promised.

That night he visited McLean in his suite. He found a big, handsome man, ruddy-faced and sharp-eyed.

"Sit down," he boomed. "Now what the devil does Hogan want from me?"

After Tony had told him, McLean waved his hands.

"I'll think about it," he said. Then he winked at the magician, who started his tricks. Tony put on a show of being vastly amused at the purely amateur parlor tricks. This seemed to please McLean, who invited Tony to come back the next night.

Day after day Tony sat in the millionaire's suite, listening to his fund of endless stories of how he had built dams, bridges and railroads all over the world. The only thing he found wrong with Tony was that he was a non-drinker.

Meanwhile, Tom Moore was enroute to Michigan with a subpoena. It was served on McLean who, although he was furious, did admit he had paid a $125,000 bribe on the Delaware water-supply project.

But that night McLean slipped out of the sanitarium to flee back to Canada.

Despite these setbacks District Attorney Hogan ordered the investigation to continue at high speed. I can't recall the number of times I flew to Michigan, Chicago, Florida and other places following leads. We were all working day and night, from the District Attorney down to the last investigator. Gasarch and his figure-hunters were constantly digging up new veins of evidence. Many contractors were brought in for questioning. They all denied paying bribes until the hard cold facts were bared. It was only then they could be persuaded to tell the truth.

One told how he had paid Fay $125,000 wrapped in paper in a shoebox. Another said he had been ordered by McLean to pay Fay and Bove $50,000. Both labor racketeers had been smart not to come out with threats. As one contractor told me, "They would come into the office, smile and look around. 'Well, things seem to be going along on an even keel . . .' they would say. In other words if we wanted to maintain the even keel we had to pay and pay promptly or face a walkout and picketing. To protect my investment of millions I had to pay. There just wasn't anything else I could do. . . ."

After fourteen months of intensive investigation the evidence we obtained was placed before the grand jury. Both Fay and Bove were indicted in May, 1943, on charges of conspiracy to extort $703,000 from contractors, including the extortion of $420,000 from companies building the $300,000,000 water system in New York, Westchester, Putnam, Dutchess, Ulster and Orange Counties.

The first count was attempting to extort $703,000 and the other six were of extortion totaling $420,000, upon threats of the withdrawal of skilled labor and of sabotage to the machinery on the job.

We had discovered that the extortions went as far back as 1936, the year the tunnel-digging on the water project began. The country's major construction companies formed syndicates on the job and the city fixed a prevailing scale of wages for the various types of labor. From the evidence we had obtained, Fay and Bove went to the companies before they signed contracts and demanded that they be paid or they would see that higher rates of pay would be required, labor troubles would plague them and skilled labor would be withheld.

The companies that paid were the Seaboard Construction Company, $125,000 demanded and approximately that much paid; Associated Constructors, Inc., $250,000 demanded and $150,000 paid; John F. Shea Company, Inc., and Henry J. Kaiser Company, $109,000 demanded and paid; Utah Construction Company, $129,-000 demanded and paid; Walsh Construction Company of Davenport, Iowa, $120,000 demanded and $62,000 paid; B. Perine & Sons, Inc., of Framingham, Massachusetts, $50,000 demanded and $35,000 paid; Mason and Hanger Co., Inc., of Lexington, Kentucky, $60,000 demanded and $36,000 paid; and New York Traprock Corporation, $12,000 demanded and paid. This last company had no contract on the project but furnished material.

Almost immediately after we had taken Fay and Bove to the Oak Street precinct to be booked and fingerprinted, our witnesses began to be intimidated.

I received a call from one contractor, who had confessed to paying bribes only after we had proved it by items obtained through examining his books. Needless to say, his tongue also had been loosened when it was pointed out to him that paying a bribe also constitutes a crime.

I went up to see him at his office. He was pale and nervous.

"I got a call today," he said. "The man on the other end just said, 'Say nothing and tell nothing, if you know what's good for you.' Now I'm not only afraid for my personal safety but I have millions of dollars invested in this project. What can I do . . . ?"

This same thing happened again and again. We were constantly soothing and guarding our witnesses. Even up to the very day the case opened—before a Supreme Court justice instead of a General Sessions justice, in itself an unprecedented move—we were uncertain as to how some of the witnesses would testify. In no other case that I have worked on in my career in the D.A.'s office here have I ever seen such pressure put on the People's witnesses to recant or to disappear.

Without a doubt the issue at stake was not only Joseph Fay and James Bove, two powerful labor leaders, against the District Attorney of New York County, but it was the forces of crooked labor and racketeers against the People.

District Attorney Hogan built up his case carefully against the two thugs and, after long deliberation, the jury convicted them. But the case was far from finished. Fay and Bove's attorneys fought the conviction to the United States Supreme Court, where the decision of the jury was upheld Only then did the prison gates close on Fay and Bove.

The incredible strength of these labor racketeers was vividly underscored a few years later when the New York *Journal-American* disclosed that a long line of politicians, labor leaders and millionaire construction builders were visiting Fay in his cell.

Leading the list was Arthur H. Wicks, Lieutenant-Governor and State Senate Majority Leader.

The public was shocked. Wicks blandly explained that he had visited the convicted extortionist to settle labor troubles in upstate New York. Everybody knew, said Wicks, that Joe Fay was still the boss of the construction industry.

16. INNOCENT UNTIL PROVEN GUILTY: CORRECTING MISCARRIAGES OF JUSTICE

PARADOXICALLY, the brightest hour of the District Attorney's office is when it proves itself wrong, and reverses a decision its own law enforcement machinery has brought about, to release an innocent man from jail. It is a moment supreme in law enforcement. I have been fortunate enough to take part in investigations which cleared eight young men accused of crimes ranging from rape to robbery. In each case District Attorney Hogan ordered the full force of our office to be employed to establish beyond doubt the innocence or to confirm the declared guilt of the boys.

It is interesting to note that of the eight persons cleared, not one had influence, money or high-priced attorneys. One investigation was started by a scrawled, barely legible letter received by Hogan, who personally ordered me "to ascertain its truthfulness beyond the shadow of a doubt." In the other cases our people worked long hours on their own time to establish the true facts. In another a police officer attached to our staff was forced to prove that his own colleagues had made a mistake in collecting evidence that almost sent two men to prison for long terms if not to the electric chair.

The most striking case involved Thomas Oliver, an 18-year-old Negro of West 59th Street, Brooklyn. On October 23, 1945, he and another boy, Eddie Lee Wilbur, 20, of West 53rd Street, had been arrested and convicted for the brutal assault of Mrs. Sophie Wright, a 70-year-old widow who lived in a tenement on West 53rd Street.

The facts in the case were brief. On the night of October 22, 1945, two unidentified men attacked and brutally assaulted the aged woman in her apartment.

Both boys were sentenced in General Sessions to from 10 to 20 years after Mrs. Wright remained steadfast in her identification of them as her assailants. In December, 1946, Hogan received a letter scrawled in pencil from Oliver stating that he was innocent of the crime. The letter was referred to our office with the notation: "Check all the facts in this case and report to me." It was signed by Hogan.

Eddie Whiteside was sent up to Sing Sing to interview Oliver, who told a straightforward story. In a subsequent interview Wilbur broke down and admitted he had lied. He said he had implicated Oliver for fear of his real partner. The name of his confederate in the robbery was "Jay." Beyond the first name he knew nothing of him. He did, however, recall the addresses of several bars frequented by this man.

When Whiteside's report was given to Hogan he ordered the Bureau of Investigation to proceed immediately to obtain proof bolstering Wilbur's confession, which in itself was not strong enough to warrant a move for a reversal of Oliver's conviction.

Assigned to the case by Chief Investigator Fay, I began recreating the crime by reading the police reports and trial testimony. The heart of the whole case rested on the testimony of the victim, Mrs. Wright, who had suffered such grievous injuries. It was a brutal robbery-assault and I personally had doubts that Oliver was innocent. Wilbur, I thought, despite his story, might be trying out of friendship to free his partner.

I paid several visits to the old lady in her neat West Side apartment. Over tea we went over the events of the night, step by step. After the first two visits I began to realize that a terrible injustice might have been done to the boy.

Mrs. Wright told me it was very late at night and she had been sleeping for some time when she was awakened by a crash of someone breaking down her kitchen door. She got out of bed and as she switched on the light she was struck on the side of the face with an iron bar with such force that her eye was torn from its socket.

According to my notes the interrogation went as follows:

Q. Did you have a chance to see your assailants, Mrs. Wright?
A. I had just turned on the light when they knocked me out.
Q. But you didn't see them?

At this point in the questioning Mrs. Wright put on a pair of glasses with extremely thick lenses.

Q. Do you wear them to bed?
A. [Laughing] Lord, no.
Q. Did you have the glasses on when you were struck?
A. No—I only had time to turn on the light when they hit me.

The questioning was done in a casual, almost leisurely fashion. In between the interrogation we sipped tea, talked of the old days and current events. I went back to the office, made some notes from her trial testimony and returned to her place the next day.

After the usual cup of tea I asked her:

Q. According to your testimony, Mrs. Wright, in the trial, you described the color of the boys' jackets, shirts and trousers. Is that true?

A. Yes, I did.

Q. But you didn't have your glasses on when they struck you and you said you didn't have time to get a good look at them when they hit you.

A. That's right.

Q. Well, then, how were you able to describe their clothes?

A. Well, I had seen them in the neighborhood—they're neighborhood boys.

After Mrs. Wright amplified her story I knew what had happened. Both Oliver and Wilbur were neighborhood cronies. Mrs. Wright had seen them often and had given their description as she recalled it from seeing the boys on previous occasions.

At the police station she was shown their pictures and identified them. When they were picked up they had on the clothes with which she was so familiar.

I will never forget the look of distress which spread over her face when I asked her, "In fact, Mrs. Wright, if you were struck as you turned on the light and you were not wearing your glasses, it would not have been possible for you to have seen their clothes in such detail as you so testified. Isn't that a reasonable conclusion?"

She stared down at her hands for a long time. Then she looked up and said slowly, "Mr. Danforth—have I done wrong?"

I assured her it was a mistake, but one which must be corrected at once. She agreed to do anything to right the mistake.

When I investigated the case in more detail I found that when Wilbur had been confronted by the woman at her bedside in the hospital he confessed that he had struck her. She had seen Oliver and Wilbur together and felt sure they were both involved in the attack. She told this to the police who picked up Oliver. In the precinct squad-room she identified both boys as her assailants.

While I was interviewing the old lady, detectives were keeping all the bars mentioned by Wilbur under surveillance. One night they saw a man answering "Jay's" description enter one of the places and they closed in. Hours later, after identifying himself as James W. Campbell, 24, of Manhattan Avenue, he confessed that he had been Wilbur's accomplice.

To right the wrong the District Attorney's office moved as fast, if not faster, than it had in bringing both boys to trial. Hogan appeared in court to set aside the verdict, which was done. Campbell was sent to prison and Oliver returned home. Eventually Governor Dewey signed a bill permitting Oliver to start suit against the state for false imprisonment.

The case, however, did not have a happy ending. Before the suit was resolved, Oliver was implicated in another felony. He was found guilty but in view of the time spent unjustly in Sing Sing, he was given a suspended sentence. Oliver's suit was then dropped.

It wasn't long after this case that I was assigned to investigate a second case in which some boys charged with felonies claimed innocence. The youths were charged with beating and robbing a one-legged war veteran. From the basic facts handed out by the police they all appeared to be brutal young sadists.

The oldest in the quartet was 21. They came from middle-class families and certainly weren't angels. In fact, had they been taken more often to the woodshed for a lick of the strap, they would have been, in my opinion, better adults. They were wild and arrogant, with a taste for beer and dance halls. To the cops they were all young ruffians.

The night of the crime they had left a Broadway dance hall after hours of drinking and dancing. Near 47th Street and Broadway one of the younger boys felt sick. He rushed to the curb and vomited. As he did so a cab swerved to the curb and the fender and hood were dirtied. A passenger in the car stuck his foot out the door and kicked the boy in the face. After an exchange of curses and punches the four youths walked down Broadway. Four blocks from the scene a detective's car squealed to a stop; two officers rushed out and arrested them.

At first I thought this was surely a manufactured tale. Fortunately, one of the boys, a juvenile, had been separated from his companions and lodged in the Youth House.

I questioned him extensively for two hours but the boy repeated the same story the others had told. When I reported to Chief Investigator Fay and Frank Hogan they both told me to continue until the true facts were ascertained.

The police report showed that the driver charged the boys with robbing him of his wrist watch and $90.00. I summoned one of the two arresting detectives, who repeated the same story that appeared on the police blotter but seemed startled when I asked where the money was.

"I think it was lost," he said.

"All the boys had on them was $30.00, according to this report," I pointed out. "Where's the money they supposedly took from the cab driver?"

He fumbled around with some answers but I was far from satisfied. The money was evidence, I told him, and should be in the property clerk's office.

A few days later both detectives returned. This time they had a Knights of Columbus card belonging to the man who charged he had been robbed.

"We found this yesterday at the scene," one said.

I was dumfounded. "Do you mean to say you just happened to be walking past the scene and you just happened to see this card?" I asked.

"It was lying in the gutter," he insisted.

I examined the card. It was spotless. I told the detectives I would talk to them later. When they left I made a list of the dates of the days from the time of the assault to the day the card allegedly had been found in the gutter by the two detectives. Then I went down to the United States Weather Bureau to check their daily reports.

I found that in between the assault and the finding of the card it had rained three times, once all night. Yet the card was not soiled, warped or grimy. . . .

While I was pursuing my investigation the family of one of the boys had sold their furniture to retain an attorney. He came down to the District Attorney's office and was referred to me. He was a brisk, businesslike little man and wanted to come to the heart of his visit at once.

"In the case of ———— I would like to know if it would be possible for them to plead guilty to a lesser charge."

I was shocked. "Have you investigated the case, Counselor?" I asked.

"No," he said, "but on the face of the facts it seems they might have robbed this man."

"And you think they're guilty?" I asked.

"I'm willing to plead a lesser charge," he said.

"These boys are no more guilty of assaulting this man or robbing him than you are," I told him. "I would advise you as an officer of the court to look into your client's case, or return the fee to the family who retained you. I intend to turn my report in to Mr. Hogan today."

A few days later the boys walked out, free. The attorney, I heard, returned his fee. I always wondered if his conscience hurt him when the mother and father thanked him so profusely. . . .

In another case three young men were accused of rape and robbery. Like the others, they were wild and hard drinkers who should have had some sense of values pounded into them by their fathers' strong right arms. But it was after the war and they were living high and handsome on the 52-20 club, with a check always handy on weekends to spend on whiskey and beer in their neighborhood bars.

Living in the neighborhood was an attractive young woman who was loose with her favors. On this particular night the three, hungry for sex after a night of drinking, paid the woman a visit. She liked two of the boys and willingly submitted to intercourse; the third she refused. He insisted and finally she submitted. On the way out, one of the boys picked up a piece of imitation jewelry from her dresser. The woman reported she had been raped by the three boys and robbed.

On the face of it technically she had been robbed of the piece of jewelry, but as the boys told it, there was no rape. I began a quiet investigation of the woman's past and found she was a barroom tramp and, on occasion, a prostitute. When I saw the headlines I was horrified; it seemed the boys had ganged up on a lily-white maiden, a respectable woman who had fought fiercely to protect her womanhood. I reported my findings to the assistant in charge of the case and the rape charge was dropped. The technical robbery charge was, however, valid. At the time there was a wave all over town of assaults and robberies on women. The boys decided to plead guilty; the judge, mindful of current conditions, could not find it within himself to decide on mercy. He sent each of them to Sing Sing for three years.

It was a bitter sight to see the disbelief on the faces of their parents as they watched their sons led away in handcuffs. None of them had any previous record of ever being in trouble.

One boy, then only 19, sobbed to me in the detention pen, "Three years for a five-buck piece of junk and three minutes with a whore."

Justice was stern that day, too stern, I thought, but the stiff sentence—they were all released on parole after a year—proved to be a checkmate for all of them. When they came out of prison they put the beer, whiskey and cheap women behind them to settle down to regular jobs. Today all are married with growing families, respected by the community they once viewed with such contempt.

Another example involves the strange case of two men accused of robbing and almost killing the manager of a loan company. It is a classic reminder that innocent men and women can be and occasionally are imprisoned for crimes they did not commit. On the other side of the coin is the remarkable tenacity of a police officer, working to destroy a case built by his own colleagues, in an attempt to clear the innocent. The officer in the case was Detective William Devine, who worked with me on many cases when he was attached to our office.

The story began when Bill was summoned to confer with Assistant District Attorney Charles Breitel, now an Associate Justice of the Appellate Division, First Department, New York State Supreme Court. At this conference was a slim, dark-haired young man, whose face was soon to be familiar to the citizens of New York as Mayor Vincent Impelliteri. Seated alongside Impelliteri, then an attorney, was his client, a blonde Breitel introduced as Mrs. Lawrence Corrado.

Breitel came to the point of the conference at once; Mrs. Corrado's husband was in the Tombs as one of the men accused of robbing and shooting Frank Burgert, owner of the Metropolitan Finance Company in upper Manhattan. The robbery and shooting had been witnessed by several girl employees. It had been a particularly vicious shooting; the robbers had fired point blank at the owner, wounding him five times in the face and neck. The man was in critical condition and there was a grave possibility that the felonious assault and robbery charges would be replaced by a murder indictment.

Detectives had made the arrest of Corrado and a companion, both of whom had police records, in this fashion:

Following the shooting two men had run downstairs to get into a getaway car, driven by a third man. About an hour later the car squealed to a stop ten blocks from the scene of the crime and three men jumped out and ran away. Meanwhile police had done some fine work canvassing the neighborhood where the getaway car had idled and luckily had found a man who had been attracted by its sudden departure and had jotted down the license number.

It was a simple task of tracing the license plate to the owner, who was brought in with his friend, Corrado. Both suspects were placed in a line-up. Four out of five girls employed by the finance company had seen the bandits during the robbery and scuffle, and had picked out Corrado and his companion as the robbers.

Detectives brought the men over to the hospital to be confronted by the critically wounded man, but he refused to make a positive identification.

When the District Attorney's office took over the case, another line-up was conducted and the girls again identified the prisoners and made statements to that effect. Our office had no alternative but to place the case before a grand jury.

Mrs. Corrado made daily visits to the Tombs to see her husband. Every day she noticed a man come into the visiting room and speak in low tones to the owner of the car, who had been arrested with her husband.

Although they did not know each other—she had never seen the owner of the car before the arrest—Mrs. Corrado and the man struck up a conversation as they left the Tombs. Mrs. Corrado learned that he was the brother of the man arrested with her husband. Drawn together by tragedy, the two became quite friendly. Soon after they left the prisoners they would visit a restaurant and discuss the case over cups of coffee.

"I know my husband is innocent," Mrs. Corrado would sob. "He was with me all that afternoon when the robbery took place. The police say they are guilty and if that man dies . . . what will the words of a wife mean?"

The question always hung in the air. The man sat staring silently into his coffee.

One afternoon when they were leaving the restaurant the man suddenly whispered into Mrs. Corrado's ear, "You have nothing to worry about."

The woman turned around. "Nothing to worry about!"

The man said casually. "He is innocent. They are not going to be convicted."

With bewilderment plain in her face, Mrs. Corrado asked, "Why do you say this?"

He smiled and walked away.

All that night the smile and confident air of this man haunted Mrs. Corrado. She paced the floor, scarcely able to keep herself from going out and searching the city for this man and demanding to know what he had meant.

On the next visit she pulled him aside.

"What did you mean, last time, when you said they could not be convicted? How can you be so sure."

The answer was a shocking one. "I was in on the holdup. And your husband and my brother were not with me."

Mrs. Corrado grabbed his arm. "You—you took part in the holdup? How?"

His answer was casual. "I drove the car."

Mrs. Corrado was almost afraid to ask the next question.

"Did my husband have any part or any knowledge of this crime?"

He shook his head. "I never saw him before I saw him in jail."

It took all Mrs. Corrado's reserve to keep from screaming. She managed to make some excuse to dawdle in the restaurant, and the stickup man, who seemed proud of the effect his knowledge was having on the woman, said he would take her home.

When they were alone he told the story; he had been the driver and he knew the two other men who had been the actual robbers.

"My God!" Mrs. Corrado said. "You have this knowledge and you let two innocent men be accused of a crime and perhaps go to the electric chair—and one your own brother!"

He waved his hand. "In this country no innocent man can be convicted of a crime."

"But they have four witnesses!" Mrs. Corrado said.

He shrugged and doggedly insisted, "No innocent man can be sent to jail for a crime he didn't do."

All through the reports which I have read on this case is the thread of this man's weird reasoning; the innocent can never be convicted of a crime he didn't commit . . .

Mrs. Corrado haunted the man. She argued constantly, calling him on the phone, seeing him after the visits to the Tombs, pleading and cajoling—but wisely never threatening. She knew she had a chance while he stayed in the city but if he decided to flee it would be only her word that such a story was true.

As Breitel told the story, Devine must have looked skeptical. Mrs. Corrado, tears running down her cheeks, said, "I know he doesn't believe me."

Breitel said soothingly, "It's not a question of believing you, Mrs. Corrado. It's a problem of proving that what you say is true. And that is our job now. . . ."

Impelliteri told Breitel, "I am convinced that this woman's story is true."

"It sounds authentic," Breitel said, "but we have to disprove the state's witnesses and that's Bill's job."

Devine was given the assignment and from then on it was a ticklish, 24-hour-a-day job of trailing Mrs. Corrado while she kept her dates with the guilty man.

Finally after a meeting with the District Attorney it was agreed that a tape recorder should be installed in the woman's apartment and she should try to get the man to admit his guilt so that a record of his admission could be made.

Mrs. Corrado arranged the meeting. For two hours Devine and another detective listened in on the conversation. Mrs. Corrado was a superb interrogator.

She kept insisting to the man so many times that Devine grew restless. "But you are sure now that my husband had nothing to do with this holdup and shooting?"

And the man always replied, "No, Mrs. Corrado. I tell you he was not there. I was the driver of the car. Your husband and my brother had nothing to do with it."

Then she started on the track of learning the identity of the two other men. The conversation shows the woman's native shrewdness.

"What are the names of the two other men?"

"What's the difference?"

"I must know."

"Why do you insist on knowing, Mrs. Corrado?"

"I think you are lying to me—there are no other men."

"No, no. Your husband wasn't in on the job."

"If he wasn't, who were the other men?"

She kept attacking his vanity. He knew all and when this sense of power was attacked it offended his ego.

Finally he weakened.

"One guy's named Irish."

"Irish what?"

"Stephen Farrell—we call him Irish."

"Who was the other man? Please tell me."

"He's a Swede. Name's Bjorn Reed."

"Where do they work?"

"What do you want to know that for? You got their names."

"You're making it up."

"Okay. They work at the Westchester Auto Wrecking Company."

In the cellar below Devine said to his partner, "Okay, you take over. I'm going to that wrecking place."

Devine picked up another detective and they drove to the wrecking company. After looking the place over they walked inside, playing the role of a couple of men trying to find certain parts for their cars. The three men in the office looked neither Irish or Swedish. Devine had just decided to leave and set up a stake-out when two men walked in, one a blond who looked to be a Swede and the other an Irishman.

"Irish?" Devine said.

"Yeah," the Irishman said.

"You Reed?" he asked the Swede.

"Yeah," the other man replied.

After Devine identified himself, he and his partner took both men into custody. Devine then rode back to Mrs. Corrado's apartment and picked up the third man—the confessed driver of the getaway car—as he left.

By now the case was becoming a major part of Bill's life. He felt it was up to him to prove Corrado innocent. He had the two men identified in the tape recording as the robbers, but this was far from sufficient proof. One thing that disturbed him was that the men taken into custody were totally different in appearance from Corrado and the other man in the Tombs.

At first he had thought he was working on a case of mistaken identity which had resulted because of a similarity in appearance of the prisoners, but obviously this couldn't be the case.

Devine and his partner took the pair to night headquarters, then under the supervision of Inspector Tom Hammill, the night chief, who was helpful.

Hammill arranged a line-up of detectives, clerks and other workers in the building and the girl witnesses were sent for. It was then early in the morning. Devine, I know, was ill at ease at the thought of what this might possibly do to the original detectives who had collected the statements of the girls which led to the imprisonment of the two men.

He was so upset he called Breitel and asked for his advice. Should he contact the original arresting detectives and ask their help in correcting what seemed to be a grievous mistake? Breitel decided he

THE TREE-HOUSE

The hideout of the Hines case witnesses.

Another view of the tree-house.

Tony Scanlon, with the butt of his .45 sticking out of his shorts.

A mixed group at the tree-house. Standing (left to right) Harry Schonhaus, Investigator Tony Scanlon, Detective Jack Lawlor. Seated: George Weinberg.

Tony Scanlon batting, Dixie
Davis catching.

Dixie Davis puts one over.

Detective James Dwyer, George
Weinberg, Investigator Tony
Scanlon, Detective George Sa-
layka, Dixie Davis.

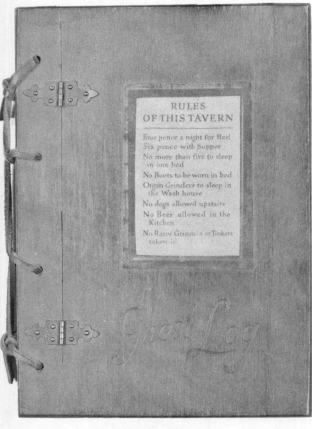

Detectives, investigators and witnesses all dressed up ready to go to New York for the Hines trial. Standing *(left to right):* Weinberg, Schonhaus, Detective James Dwyer, Davis, Detective James Malone, Investigator Tony Scanlon. Seated: Detectives George Salayka, John O'Brien, Max Rumack, Jack Lawlor.

The logbook of the tree-house.

had to go it alone—the District Attorney's office had to start from scratch.

The girls arrived at headquarters one by one. The first walked into the line-up room. Without hesitation she picked out the Irishman and the Swede.

"Those are the two men who held up our office," she said.

Devine tried hard to conceal his exuberance. "Please go closer and make sure," he asked the girl.

She shook her head. "There's no need," she replied. "These are the men."

All four girls were brought in. Without hesitation all identified the men. Two became hysterical and kept crying over and over:

"What have we done to those other two men . . . what can we do to help them . . . ?"

Devine told them it was a sincere mistake and there was nothing they could do except tell the truth. Later the wounded victim of the robbery faced the two suspects and unhesitatingly identified them. The poor victim's neck was permanently crooked and he had lost his voice. Weak as he was, he tried to claw his way past the detectives to get at the two thugs.

There was a great deal of mystery in the courtroom on the day of the trial. Everyone was trying to guess what was under the leather covers on the state's table. Finally the word was whispered about that a recording machine was under the cover. For the first time in the history of General Sessions, recorded testimony was about to be heard. Judge Donnellan presided.

The state's first witness was the man who had installed our tape recorder in the basement of Mrs. Corrado's apartment house. After he left the stand Assistant District Attorney Breitel started the recordings. The words, loud and clear, filled the quiet courtroom, "Are you sure my husband had nothing to do with the robbery and the shooting of that man?"

"No. No. I drove the car. I never saw him before I saw him in the Tombs with my brother." And "Why worry, lady? In this country you can't convict a man of a crime he didn't commit."

The man whose voice filled the courtroom quickly consulted with his attorney, who offered to plead his client guilty.

The other two men elected to stand trial and were subsequently found guilty and received long prison terms.

There's an ironical ending to the what-should-have-been a very happy story.

A young policewoman who had been assigned to a facet of the case lost the suspect she was shadowing and Devine found her outside the apartment house weeping bitterly. It was her first investigation and she had failed. Devine consoled her by explaining that surveillance is very difficult and he himself had lost many "tails."

Devine, a kindly man, tried to cheer her up and in his report placed the blame for losing the witness on himself. After the case ended he was hailed to Police Headquarters. The late Chief Inspector John J. Ryan, a splendid police official but a stickler for discipline, interviewed Bill in his office. In a biting interview he took Bill to task for muffing the tail. Somehow a reporter got his facts twisted and the story came out: "Rookie Girl Cop Teaches Veteran Cop." There was another interview with Ryan which had Bill's ears burning for days.

The young policewoman pleaded tearfully with Bill to allow her to go in to Ryan and explain, but as Bill told her, it would only make it worse; Ryan could accuse him of falsifying the police report and would really blister him then!

So the young policewoman got the credit and glory for the investigation and all Bill won was a tongue-lashing. But all that was superficial. Down deep in his heart Bill Devine was satisfied. He had done his job. He had faithfully served the law and John Ryan's biting brogue could not take it away from him.

17. A LAND-OFFICE BUSINESS: THE FARMLAND SWINDLER

"MY CLIENT has been swindled out of $80,000," said an irate attorney to Francis X. Clark, then head of the Complaint Bureau. "And I want some action from you people."

The attorney's client, it seemed, was an elderly lady—72 to be exact—and very wealthy. Unknown to the attorney she had been the target of several so-called charities, who had persuaded her to give them donations amounting to thousands of dollars. The attorney was sure a fraud had been perpetrated.

"Actually, she lost $70,000 to those phonies," the lawyer explained when he was calmed down. "And $9,100 went for that so-called grazing land. . . ."

Clark's head jerked up. "What land was that?" he asked.

The attorney waved his hand. "Oh, that stuff she bought in some jerkwater place in Florida. I don't think it's worth a dollar an acre. . . ."

"Who sold her the land?" Clark asked.

The lawyer thought for a moment. "Some old fellow named Anderson T. Herd."

Bells clanged in Clark's memory. He carefully took down all the information the attorney had. Then after he had left, he opened his file of old complaints. He skipped through the folders; then it appeared . . .

"Alexander T. Herd . . . fraud complaint. . . ."

He had received it about a year before from a woman who had been swindled by Herd, but the evidence had been too flimsy to bring before a grand jury. However, Clark had looked into Herd's background and was intrigued by what he had found. Herd was born in Kentucky of a genuine old Southern family, which had been one of the wealthiest in the South before the Civil War. He also discovered that Herd was well known in Washington's official circles. In fact, his career paralleled in some aspects that of Colonel Halquire.

285

Herd had been arrested six times on various swindling charges—twice by the FBI—but each time he had been acquitted or the evidence had been insufficient and he had escaped prosecution.

One of the most interesting reports Clark had received from Washington concerned a $20,000,000 suit Herd had pending against the government, an outgrowth of a business deal in which he had participated before the outbreak of World War I. Herd and a syndicate of wealthy businessmen had purchased six ships from Austria shortly before the United States entered the war. When war was declared the government bought the ships from the combine, giving them each about $150,000 profit. One clause in the contract was that the combination would operate the ships and reap something like a 5 per cent profit. Once the ships were in actual operation, the government refused to consider that clause and operated the ships itself.

After the war Herd petitioned Congress to pass an act allowing him to sue the government. He opened headquarters at the Washington Hotel, where he could wine and dine influential persons in an attempt to corral enough votes in the House to pass the act. Just before we entered the case he had lost by just two votes but the suit was gaining sympathizers and was actually being revived.

As Clark reviewed this earlier case he became more convinced that this time the swindler had stepped into a trap of his own making. He asked to interview the attorney's elderly client.

"Are you going into it, Frank?" the attorney asked.

"Of course," Clark said. "I think we'll get Herd this time. Isn't that what you wanted?"

There was a short pause. "Well, there's one thing I didn't tell you, Frank," the lawyer said. "The lady is very old and has a faulty memory."

Frank said heartily, "Oh, she'll probably recall the basic facts. Make a date and I'll hop up there."

The next day Clark paid a visit to her old-fashioned apartment. She was a white-haired, flustered old woman, still living in the world of the Gay Nineties, when she had been the toast of the town. Now she was senile, scarcely able to recall anything that happened from hour to hour.

Frank had to stifle a groan as the old lady rambled on about everything but the case. He knew he couldn't possibly bring her before a grand jury. Finally he got permission from the attorney to go through the old lady's papers in an effort to find some incriminating evidence. It was a bothersome task, interrupted frequently by invitations to stop his work and join her for tea. Finally Frank found what he was looking for; cancelled checks she had given to Herd. The old girl might have had a bad memory but she had been shrewd enough to list in detail on each check what the payment was for; for example, Frank found checks for "taxes on the land," or for "produce and crop taxes" raised on the so-called fine fields.

He found that on April 10, 1943, she had purchased 40 acres for $3,200. On June 26, the same year, she had given Herd an additional $4,000 for farming her land which she had noted "was full of rich crops." On November 17, also in that same year, she gave Herd $300 for "taxes." On December 1 Herd obtained another $1,600 check for another "tax bill."

"Well, ma'am, I think we have enough on this man Herd to stop him from bothering you any more," Frank said cheerfully as he stood up to leave.

The poor old soul gave Frank a blank look. "Who is Mr. Herd?" Frank gently shook hands and let himself out.

Back in the Complaint Bureau, Frank carefully put together what papers he had found. He quickly came to a conclusion that he had far from a watertight case. Someone would have to go down to Melbourne, Florida, to try to obtain statements from disinterested persons who could plug the holes in the case, check the condition of the land and so on.

This was a job for a smooth-talking, shrewd investigator; Tom Fay, now our Chief Investigator, was selected. Tom took a plane for Florida. Among his assignments was to find the old lady's land in Brevard County, determine whether it was actually farmed and cultivated, check the amount of crops it produced, find and consult records of all trucking or freighting corporations in the district, learn the tax rate, the amount of money it cost to drain similar acreage, locate the number of head of cattle (Herd claimed 6,000), study the records of all the banks in the district for Herd's income and output, complete a title search, locate the headquarters and check all records of a ranching organization in which Herd claimed to own two-thirds of the stock. It was a difficult assignment for the area was dominated by Herd, who owned 22,470 acres and was well known in this cattle country.

Fay saw most of the town in a brief tour. Melbourne was a quiet little town with one main street, two banks, the usual needle-spired churches and sun-bleached houses. He had to start somewhere, so he selected the local billiard parlor. After a half hour he gave it up;

there were only high school kids, yipping, hooting and drinking cokes.

His next stop was the local bowling alley. Tom, who is an excellent bowler, stood by one alley to watch a quartet of bowlers. As the balls spun down the polished alley he shook his head; these were far from the teams against which he had competed every Thursday night in New York. Some of the men who noticed his apparent interest smiled and nodded as they wiped their hands and took their positions.

Later Tom joined a man who was buying a beer.

"How's chances of getting in on a frame?" he asked.

The man, big and ruddy, replied, "Sure, mister. Suppose you and I team up against the other two? My partner's got to go home."

"Okay," Tom said. He removed his coat, rolled up his sleeves and went over to be introduced to the others.

"Let's make it interesting," Tom said. "I'll put up a dollar."

His partner nodded. "Okay with me; I'll put one up too."

The other team was glad to make the wager and the match began. Tom sent the pins spinning with strike after strike. However, he was careful not to put on too big a show and make his teammate uneasy. He scored 190 and it was plain the others were impressed.

When he said goodnight, his partner drove him to his hotel and made him promise to return to the alley the next evening. Tom, who posed as a man enjoying a few days' rest, agreed.

For the next three nights he bowled game after game. There was a monthly prize of $20.00 offered and the owner of the alley insisted on writing Tommy's score in chalk along with the other scores.

On Friday night, when the contest ended, Tom had high score. He refused to take the money and gave it to his partner.

"I'm only here for a few days," he said. "You worked for this money all month."

After that Tom was marked as a fine fellow.

The news of Fay's bowling prowess spread as he knew it would. Finally it got to the town's prize bowler, who appeared one night with a challenge for the stranger from the North.

They bowled several games which Tom won, then they teamed up to beat the best the alley could boast. As the evening passed Tom's new partner said, "If you need any money, Tommy, just say the word."

This puzzled Fay until he found an opportunity to ask one of the men, "What's this fellow's business?"

"Oh, he's at the bank, Tommy," the bowler told him.

"Big man in town, eh?" Tom asked casually.

"He has a hand in everything," the man said.

Fay now knew he had the one man who might help him. He was a banker and a public figure to whose civic pride he could appeal for cooperation with a law enforcement agency.

The next morning Tom appeared at the bank promptly at 8:45 A.M. Ten minutes later the banker appeared and greeted Fay with a cordial "Good morning." Tom, who thought the man was probably a cashier, was surprised to find his bowling partner ushering him into a small office marked PRESIDENT.

"Why didn't you let me know you needed money, Tommy?" the banker said. "I'm sure we can arrange a loan."

"I don't need money," Fay replied. "But I do need your help."

"Oh, what's that?" the bank president asked.

Tom showed him his D.A.'s shield and sketched out the case against Herd.

After Fay had finished the banker slapped his hand on the desk.

"Tom, you've come to the right man," he said.

"Why?" Tom asked.

"I've been dead set against the way that tract is being run and I've said so many times," the banker said. "Now let's call on Deputy Drawdy."

Drawdy proved to be a smiling, slender lawman who could have walked out of the pages of the old West. He was an expert woodsman, a crack shot and he knew every acre of the backwoods like the back of his own hand.

The first thing Fay had to do was locate the 80 acres Herd had sold the woman. This was "Section 27, Township 29, South Range 36 E, S ½ of the SE¼ of Section 27, of Township 29, South of Range 36 E."

They obtained a map in order to pinpoint the section. Next day Drawdy and Tom, who was equipped with a movie camera, set out for the tract. After riding as far as they could they began hiking through the thick underbush. They had struggled for some time when Drawdy suddenly stopped in his tracks.

"Damn!" he said.

"What's up, Luther?" Fay asked.

"You got on low shoes," the deputy said, pointing to Fay's muddy shoes.

"So what?" Tom asked.

"Nothing," Drawdy drawled, "except this place is infested with water moccasins. You better let me go first."

After a few steps he turned. "Another thing we got to watch out for are wild steers. They can get real mean. . . ."

Tom looked down at Drawdy's knee-high, tightly-laced boots, then down at his Florsheims. . . .

They started on through the thick undergrowth, sometimes wading across swamps and through high grass. As Tom said later, he had heard bullets whistle many times in his life, but this time he was really frightened. The thought of being bitten, then the long hike back to the car and the journey to town sent chills up his back. The odds on the venom's not killing him before they reached a doctor were definitely in favor of the snakes. Then there were those wild steers. . . .

Finally they reached the section which Drawdy, after consulting the official map, said belonged to the old lady. It was wild without a trace of cultivation; this was the tract that Herd had pictured to the old lady as covered with ripe peppers, corn and tomatoes. All Tom could see was high grass, tangled weeds and swamps. They made a survey of the tract, with Tom taking a complete pictorial record of every part of the acreage.

Back in Melbourne, Tom set up a secret office in the bank and began gathering his evidence. He checked all the freight companies and learned Herd had never sent out any produce from this tract. Tax records disclosed that Herd had not paid $1,000 for taxes on the land as he had told the old lady. Truck companies records gave him more evidence of Herd's swindle. He also discovered that Herd's cattle was 150 head, not the 6,000 he had claimed. The title search revealed that although the woman had bought the land, Herd had never filed the title transfer.

The swindler, the records showed, had originally purchased the land for $2.00 an acre—he had sold it to the old lady for $80.00 an acre.

Tom then began collecting statements. Gathering information from people who might be friendly to Herd, indebted to him or dependent upon him for a livelihood was an extremely difficult task. But Tom is a persuasive fellow. He traveled to Palm Beach, West Palm Beach, Grant, Jacksonville and in and around Brevard County until he obtained seven signed statements.

After completing his investigation in Florida, Fay returned to New York. But the case was far from finished. In the meantime Clark had come upon another aspect of Herd's swindling. And Tom, with the dust of the backwoods country still on his shoes, paid a visit to the cashier's office of the swank Plaza Hotel, where he made some startling discoveries.

Herd, it seemed, had a girl-friend who was a partner in his swindles. Herd had his bank in Melbourne, Florida; his girl-friend's bank was on the West Coast. Their practice was to exchange checks. Then Herd, who always traveled to New York by limousine with a liveried chauffeur, would drive up to the Plaza, usually without a nickel in his pocket, and check in. He would give the clerk his partner's $800 check.

Late in the day, after ascertaining that the clerk who had accepted his check was no longer on duty, Herd would visit the cashier's office.

"I left $800 with the clerk this morning. I would like $400 now, if you please," he would say.

Herd, who had the bearing of a dignified Southern colonel, would be given the cash without hesitation.

Herd usually pulled this act on the weekend. He knew that it took about a week for the check to go through the clearing house and arrive at the Melbourne bank or that of his girl-friend. Thus they had a week in which to make the check good.

Usually the old lady, who never could remember Mr. Herd's name, supplied the money.

Once the old lady was out and they couldn't raise the money. The check bounced and the cashier brought it to Herd.

The swindler put on quite a show. "I'll sue those people," he said indignantly. "Imagine, implying my checks are no good!"

The old lady was persuaded to give Herd $300 for "taxes on the crops." On December 1, 1943, Herd paid the old lady a call. Her land, he said, was just blooming with crops of peppers, corn, tomatoes and beans. All he needed was $4,000 for taxes, cartage and other expenses. The old lady got her checkbook, but as always itemized the purpose for which the check had been issued. Herd's check-to-check existence finally caught up with him when Tom found some of his rubber checks.

The Florida end of the case still required some legal cleaning-up. We had statements, but now Tom had to obtain depositions. The Judge of General Sessions appoints a local commission which takes the deposition. Notice must be filed so that the defendant's lawyer can cross-examine. In short, it is a form of a regular trial. Tom had canvassed the local lawyers in Brevard County and the commission was named upon his recommendations.

It wasn't Tommy the bowler who returned to the Southern town, but Thomas Fay of the District Attorney's office. With him was Assistant District Attorney Newcomb of the Frauds Bureau. The depositions were duly obtained and Newcomb and Fay returned to New York.

The evidence was placed before a grand jury, which indicted Herd on 16 counts of grand larceny. He was brought back to New York where he pleaded guilty. For almost three years he fought to delay his sentence. He pleaded heart trouble and Tom was again put on his trail.

"Let's find out exactly what he's doing," District Attorney Frank Hogan told Clark.

Fay went down to Washington and checked into the Washington Hotel. He first questioned the bellboys and found out that Herd was going about his business in Washington without any apparent sign of being an invalid. He sat at a nearby table in the hotel dining room to watch Herd consume some rather substantial meals. In fact, in Herd's dossier today is a menu Tom brought back to bolster our argument that for a man almost on his deathbed from a cardiac condition, Herd had the appetite of a high school athlete.

Fay also questioned the hotel operator for a list of Herd's requests to be called in the morning.

It read: "May 7. Mr. Herd asked to be called 7:15 A.M. May 8."

The operator told Tom: "I remember that May 7th request very well."

"Why?" Tom asked.

"He had asked me to call him at 7:15 A.M.," the girl said. "But at 5:15 he called and said he wanted to remind me to call him at 7:15."

Tom returned with a full report of Herd's activities. General Sessions Judge Mullen, the terror of all law-breakers, told Herd's counsel, "Get your client in by tomorrow morning or I'll issue a warrant for his arrest."

The next day Herd was sentenced to a year in the penitentiary at Riker's Island. On July 2, 1946, he stepped into the Correction Department van, as dignified as a diplomat beginning his term.

A few days later Clark asked the lawyer who had brought in the original complaint to bring his elderly client to his office so he could return her papers. After briefly reviewing the case and what had happened to Herd, Clark handed the package of papers to the old lady.

"Now Herd is in jail and everything is all right, ma'am," he said.

The old lady gave him a wistful smile. "How nice," she said. "Now can I have the land?"

Another example of the way in which complaints are followed up, is underscored by our bureau's investigations of a loan-shark trio.

It began on September 2, 1950, when a male voice called the District Attorney's office.

"Check Jack Schiff and Freddy," he said. "They're in the loan-shark racket and making good."

The phone clicked. Two days later the same voice called: "Check Schiff and Freddy, they're getting bigger."

After the fourth call, Tom Fay got mad. He called in Frank Mc-Aree, a young investigator and gave him his orders: "Find out all you can on Jack Schiff and this man named Freddy."

Of course, it was very simple: find two men (who may be using aliases) in a city of 7,000,000 people.

Frank took the usual basic steps, checking telephone listings, maildrops and so on. In a short time he had found a SNP (special non-published number) under the name of a J. Schiff. Fay ordered him to set up a stake-out at the address. For a week Frank tailed the man he learned was Jack Schiff. The loan shark's license plates produced more vital information; his garage still more. By questioning employees and neighbors he found that Schiff associated with a man named Fred Bertel.

Frank then shifted his attention to Bertel. He tailed him to his house and set up a watch. Imagine standing on your feet from 9:00 A.M. to 2:00 A.M. in a driving rain, a doorway your only protection from the weather, and you will have an idea of Frank's job. Freddy Bertel drove up in a car and his automobile registration soon provided some vital statistics. We took some pictures of Fred and the rogues' gallery told us he was Freddy Bertolotti, a notorious loan shark and hoodlum.

Frank stuck with Schiff and Freddy day and night. Unknown to the loan sharks, he was at their elbow whenever they moved. One day they turned into a midtown bar. Frank sat down on a stool just in time to see the bartender hand Schiff an envelope. Outside, the pair opened the envelope and took out a roll of bills. The bartender had just made a payment on his loan.

One day McAree tailed the pair to the Abrams Express Company, 308 West 44th Street. This puzzled Fay, so he decided to find out more about Abrams. In addition to tailing Abrams, Frank began checking all license plates of cars which visited the express office.

Frank now became a commuter. Abrams lived up at Lake Mahopac, so McAree regularly caught the 5:20 from Grand Central to Golden's Bridge. There in a cab he trailed Abrams to his house which had a small sign, "Abrams Delivery Company" with the New York City address.

Through our surveillance it developed that Schiff and Freddy were conducting a lucrative loan-shark racket and storing their records at Abrams' country home. When Frank had brought in enough evidence to warrant raids, the stage was carefully set.

Raids as portrayed in the movies show two or three husky cops, guns in hand, kicking in a door. The raids conducted by the District Attorney's office go far beyond this. First, a meeting is held with Chief Investigator Fay, the men who did the undercover work, the assistant District Attorney assigned to prosecute the case and the detectives assigned to our office. The movements of the potential defendants are carefully posted in a timetable. Each detective is given a detailed briefing. The hour of the raid is synchronized so that if more than one place is to be raided, the actions will be simultaneous. Thus the element of surprise is on our side; no telephone calls of warning can be made from one raided place to associates at another nor can vital records be destroyed.

Also subpoenas must be issued by a grand jury to conform with the law. There is one final meeting before the detectives leave. Then a long period of waiting follows; you smoke chain-fashion, drink endless cups of coffee and stare at the clock. The hour strikes, then passes on. The telephone rings in the quiet room and the first detective to call reports that his raid was successful; he has his prisoner and the records. Then the telephone rings again and again. . . . "Fowler speaking. I have the prisoner and the records."

"Bring them in . . ."

"Yes, sir . . ."

The case begins to take shape. But it is only the beginning. There is no overtime pay and few coffee breaks. Fay and his assistants must take advantage of the element of surprise. The questioning goes on. Identifications are made and the accountants pore over the subpoenaed books and ledgers for hour after hour.

This is exactly what happened in the Schiff case. The raids went off smoothly, the prisoners and the books were brought in. After we spent 32 hours without a break in interrogation and checking the findings obtained from the books, one of the prisoners broke and confessed. It was afternoon of the next day when the case was completed to the satisfaction of the assistant who would have to prosecute it in court.

In the face of overwhelming evidence these loan sharks pleaded guilty. Schiff drew an 18-month jail sentence, along with a $2,500 fine. Bertolotti, the ex-convict, received a sentence of two years and a fine of $2,000; Abrams, the expressman, a fine of $1,000; and another defendant, Sydney Borstein, six months and $1,500 in fines.

18. MURDER FOR BALLOTS: THE SCOTTORIGGIO SCANDAL

THE MURDER of Joseph R. Scottoriggio, Republican party worker, on Election Day, 1946, was a crime that shocked the city and the nation. The savage boot-and-fist beating that tore the life out of this slim, bespectacled man, was a "vicious attack on the freedom of elections," thundered the editorial writers. To many indignant citizens in New York and elsewhere, it was a sign that some politicians still employed thugs and hoodlums to coerce voters—just as Tammany Hall had done almost a century ago.

The investigation into this murder still continues. Because it is still an "active" case I must withhold certain information which I possess. More than 800 witnesses have been questioned, the police have questioned twice that many, three grand juries have listened to thousands of pages of testimony and I and other members of the Bureau of Investigation have visited and lived in other states to track down countless clues and leads.

For six weeks I shadowed one of the top gangsters in the country and managed to get him before a grand jury in New York even though he warned me, "If you tell anyone that or show that picture I will kill you."

Frank (Butsy) Morelli, the powerful Rhode Island racketeer, friend of Frank Costello, Joe Adonis and other gangsters high in the hierarchy of the American underworld, was not saying this lightly or with any braggadocio. I had just informed him I had learned two secrets in his life which to this day are shared by only his wife, one other person and myself. I told Morelli I would reveal this story to the press if he did not come to New York and testify before a grand jury on the Scottoriggio murder case.

Over the telephone Morelli's voice was cold and deadly. "I'll come when I'm ready—tell Hogan that." The phone clicked.

This was July 22, 1947. Two days later he appeared before a New York County grand jury to lay the foundation for the perjury indictment of two important witnesses.

These two secrets in Morelli's life can never be revealed by me, because, first, I must protect my source, and, secondly, such a disclosure would only smear an innocent person. What made Morelli testify is not important; the fact is that he did.

My part in the case really started in the fall of 1946, when I was in a restaurant with an old friend of mine, a lifelong Democrat. Politics is not my forte, but the action of the Democratic and American Labor Party in endorsing Congressman Vito Marcantonio for re-election was, for me at least, incredible.

"What's wrong with Marcantonio?" my friend wanted to know.

"He's a Communist," I said, "and I think the Democrats are just plain stupid for endorsing a man with his left-wing tendencies." Then I reeled off his votes in the House, which showed exactly where he stood.

I noticed a man at the next table was listening. When I turned to stare at him he rose and left.

I didn't think anything of the incident until three nights later when this same man tapped me on the shoulder.

"The other night you made a remark I didn't like," he said, "and the man you made the remark about wants to see you."

When I asked who it was he shook his head. "He happens to be right here, in the back room," he said.

My curiosity was aroused, so I followed him. Marcantonio gave me a scowl when I entered.

"You're Danforth of the D.A.'s office, aren't you?" he snapped.

"That's right," I said.

"What the hell is the idea of a man from Hogan's office going around and accusing me of being a Communist?" he said.

The suddenness of his approach drew me up short for a moment, but I told him that under our form of government even employees in a public prosecutor's office have freedom of speech.

"Furthermore," I said, "I don't like your attitude and I still think you're a Commie."

"Why don't you come around and see what I do for the people in my district," he asked, "instead of calling me names?"

"Fine," I said. "Let's begin tonight."

He summoned his secretary and informed him I was going to accompany him for the next few weeks. The following day I reported to Chief Investigator Michael Glynn to request permission to go ahead.

"Why not?" he said. "Who knows what you'll come up with?"

For the next few weeks I sat with Marcantonio, observing at close hand how he ran his district. He was a dyed-in-the-wool Communist but a superb politician. Democrats and Republicans should have borrowed his technique.

Men and women, old and young, some with babies in their arms, were granted private audiences. Marcantonio was never brisk, never appeared rushed. They told their stories, often pitiful ones, generally in broken English. Marcantonio made notes, then told them whether or not he could do anything for them.

The one night I wasn't allowed into his office was election eve. His door was closed—"a conference," his manager said—and I did not get to see him. I left late and went home.

Several hours later, just before a murky dawn, Joseph Scottoriggio, a slender, 37-year-old Republican district captain, kissed his wife, Cecilia, then left his apartment at 400 East 105th Street. Scottoriggio, a meek accountant in a federal bureau, was ready to wade into one of the bitterest elections in the turbulent history of East Harlem.

In the 18th Congressional District, Marcantonio was fighting for his political life against Frederick V. P. Bryan. Marcantonio, as I have said, had the endorsement of the Democratic Party and the American Labor Party and Bryan, the Republican Party. Plans had been made to swing to the support of Marcantonio the Republican votes that could be controlled. This was not uncommon in the political maneuvering that had been going on for years in this district of slums, poverty, thugs and criminals. Scottoriggio was an important factor in the district because he controlled 600 votes.

His wife idly watched him walk across the street, a moving shadow in the morning gloom. For a moment he paused under a street light on First Avenue and 104th Street. It was just 6:00 A.M. Suddenly four men rushed out of the darkness. His wife screamed as she saw her husband sink under a barrage of blows; then the attackers began stomping and kicking him. As many as 30 men and women on both sides of the street watched the attackers, but such is the fear that dominates the area that not one interfered.

After Scottoriggio had been beaten into unconsciousness the four men walked away nonchalantly. They did not attempt to cover up; more than one person had a good look at their faces in the early light.

Mrs. Scottoriggio ran from her apartment to where her husband lay. Others slowly gathered about the unconscious bleeding man.

"Please . . . please . . . call an ambulance . . . my husband is badly hurt . . ." she cried.

The onlookers stared back at her stolidly. But someone on the fringe of the crowd hurried to a nearby confectionery and made a telephone call. Minutes later, Scottoriggio was placed in an ambulance from New York Hospital.

Under the law this was an assault case, still in police hands, but because of the very nature of the case, District Attorney Hogan kept in close touch with developments and ordered our Bureau to seek out additional facts.

In anticipation of possible crimes committed in this bitterly contested election, Hogan had ordered that Edward Whiteside, one of the best investigators in the District Attorney's office, should split the day with me so a D.A.'s man would be on hand at all times.

When I checked into the office at noon Eddie filled me in on the assault. In the office was a young man named Joseph Ferraiolo, who had told police he had been an eyewitness to the beating. Chief Investigator Michael Glynn ordered me to stay with him until given orders to leave.

Joseph, thin and dark, was highly nervous. His hands shook as he smoked one cigarette after another. He described Scottoriggio's main assailant as a short, husky man with black curly hair, apparently an Italian-American. But when we questioned him as to details or whether he had ever seen the men before he just shook his head.

Joe kept saying he was afraid to leave the office to go home. "You don't know how tough the guys in my neighborhood are," he kept saying. "They will kill you as quick as look at you."

I stayed with Joe then as Glynn ordered me to escort him home.

"I want to vote," he said.

"Do you think it's safe?" I said.

"I want to vote," he insisted.

He wasn't a prisoner so reluctantly I had to agree, but I suggested that he walk a few paces in front of me so it wouldn't be evident he was under guard. The purpose of this arrangement was to find out who spoke to him. Obviously no one would contact him if I were present.

He entered the polling booth while I waited outside. Minutes, then an hour ticked by. Finally I entered the place and a woman whispered to me: "He's over there sitting in a chair and frightened to death. He says he's afraid to go out."

I entered to find Joe glued to a chair. I had a devil of a time persuading him he would be safe under guard before he agreed to walk home. Again I trailed a few paces behind as we walked along the crowded streets. Then suddenly he broke into a run and crossed the street to enter a Republican club.

It was the same story; only by a great deal of talking was I able to get him home. Once inside his flat he barricaded the door with a table and chairs, then placed an ugly-looking kitchen knife on the table. This is the way we sat for most of the night; he in one chair next to the knife and I across the room. He kept repeating over and over that he was afraid the "boys" had learned he was in the D.A.'s custody. Nothing I said or promised could calm him.

At about 11:00 P.M. when I checked the office, Glynn told me to go home. The reports from the hospital were good; it appeared Scottoriggio was severely, but not critically, injured. The following day Scottoriggio took a turn for the worse. Governor Thomas E. Dewey visited him, but the half-conscious man probably never recognized him. As Dewey left the hospital he characterized the assault as "a savage beating by left-wingers."

I also interviewed Scottoriggio's brother on his way to his bedside. Frankly, I didn't think he was too happy to see me.

As he waved a cab to the curb he said, "I don't want to discuss my brother's assault."

"I'm sorry," I told him, "I must insist that you do."

He shook his head. "I don't know who attacked my brother—that's all I can tell you."

As he stepped into the cab I joined him, which didn't make him any happier. Naturally he was nervous and upset but at one point during the ride he said bitterly, "If my brother dies I'll give you plenty of information. If he doesn't, I'll settle this my own way."

I included this conversation in my report but when he was questioned later he denied he had said this to me.

Six days after the attack Scottoriggio died. Now the crime was murder. Hogan assigned every available man in the Bureau to the case while Mayor O'Dwyer, in his florid manner, thundered from City Hall that he had ordered the murder solved "if it takes 1,000 men."

His second statement was absolutely amazing. "The second thing," he said, "is to find out what's going on in that area."

That the mayor, himself a former District Attorney, should make such a statement was inexcusable. All he had to do was call up any veteran detective in the area and ask him; it was an open secret that "Trigger Mike" Coppola and Joey Rao, two notorious hoodlums, were bosses of the area. Treasury agents and our office had them constantly under investigation, trying to get evidence for prosecution in either the narcotics racket or other criminal activities. But Coppola and Rao were seasoned hoodlums, wise to the ways of wire tapping and surveillance. Crooked police were known to be paid off by the East Harlem mobs. The hoods operated under the very noses of the cops, though police pressure could have been brought against these two hoods to make it impossible for them to engage in criminal activities. After the Scottoriggio murder the Police Commissioner ordered one of the most drastic shake-ups in the history of the department. It didn't do Joseph Scottoriggio much good; he was already buried.

When news of Scottoriggio's death was flashed to our office, Joe Ferraiolo was immediately taken into custody. I met him in the conference room where he was interviewed. Now his mind had suddenly gone blank. He couldn't remember any details of the assault.

"I just don't know anything," he said. "Not a damn thing."

"You did three days ago," I said.

"Suppose I *did* tell Hogan something," he said, "what guarantee would I have that I wouldn't be killed?"

"You would be guarded day and night," I told him.

"For the rest of my life, Danforth?" he asked.

I tried to tell him how the D.A.'s office had successfully protected Dixie Davis and other witnesses, but that didn't help.

In the conference room there is a trick mirror which is used to view suspects. When several were paraded into the room Joseph took one look through the mirror, then said, "If you think I'm going to send anybody to the electric chair you're crazy."

After he had viewed the suspects his mother walked in. She cried, "Joe," then slowly drew her finger across her throat, the ancient Mafia symbol of silence—talk and you're dead.

He absolutely refused to cooperate from then on and was subsequently released.

I have no way of knowing whether he really knew who Scottoriggio's killers were and had been frightened off by the underworld or whether he was one of those mentally unstable persons we often encounter in criminal investigation who bask in the reflection of their importance as a witness.

After I had dictated my report I continued my investigation in East Harlem. David Levy, elderly, almost blind, the badly frightened Republican leader of the 10th Assembly District North, which is in the 18th Congressional District, was subsequently picked up.

Now the pieces began to fall into place; now we knew what had taken place at that meeting in Trigger Mike's apartment.

Levy said he was in his clubhouse on election eve when two young hoods walked in.

"We're going for a walk," one said. Flanked by both men, Levy walked down the stairs to the street level. His brother, coming up the stairs, gave him a curious look, then said, "Hiya, Dave."

Levy nodded. On the street the hoods pushed him into a car, and drove to Trigger Mike's house. Also present were Mike's wife, Doris, and her father, David Lehman. There was a heated discussion about the various captains, with Levy warning them that Scottoriggio intended to work for Bryant the next day.

Marcantonio was sent for and in the discussion which followed it was decided that someone would "take care of him." It was assumed that the thugs were hired that night. Murder was not intended; they were to administer a severe beating.

Levy was now an important witness and we put him under a 24-hour guard. When he said he couldn't describe the two hoods I believed him; he could barely see a newspaper held up to his face.

It was now decided to put a wire tap on Coppola's phone, so a Supreme Court order was obtained. But we found to our amazement that Trigger Mike didn't have a telephone. It took several days to find out how the gangster operated. Like all mobsters Coppola was wise to wire taps. He had taken the telephone of a woman neighbor three doors down the street, running wires from that connection into his apartment. Each time her phone rang Mike answered the call. For this she was paid a handsome sum each month. Despite this subterfuge Mike was cautious; the tap yielded little.

It was now up to the D.A. to try to get one of those present at the election eve meeting to testify as to the exact language used and to identify those who had participated in the alleged conspiracy to commit a felonious assault. Rao and Coppola were arrested and held in $250,000 bail as material witnesses. In Supreme Court, where they sought the reduction of the bail, their attorneys charged their clients' civil liberties were being invaded. Assistant District Attorney Louis Pagnucco, representing the People, informed the court that both men had been part of the conspiracy and could identify the murderers.

The high bail was reduced to $25,000, despite Hogan's angry protests. The Supreme Court Justice who heard the argument was Aaron J. Levy, who six years later would be the subject of an investigation by the State Crime Commission. After Levy's death it was learned a suitcase containing $600,000 in securities was cached in his hotel suite.

It was useless to try to get Rao and Coppola, both seasoned gangsters, to talk. Marcantonio, as was expected, denied everything. The last two witnesses, Mrs. Coppola and her aged father, were our best bets, but when we tried to serve them with grand jury subpoenas we discovered they had vanished.

Nearly every member of the Bureau of Investigation was assigned to the case. It was obvious that Coppola would entrust his wife and father-in-law only to someone in the underworld whom he respected and trusted. Our dossier on him produced one name; Frank (Butsy) Morelli, the gangster overlord of Rhode Island, an ex-hood with a 20-year police record, who lived in Providence in a home so beautiful it is commonly referred to as "The Mansion."

It was decided that I should go to Rhode Island. So in June, 1947, I checked into the Sheraton-Biltmore Hotel in Providence, to begin the weary, laborious task of locating and questioning everyone who might have had anything to do with the Morelli family. Later I was joined by several Assistant District Attorneys from the office who worked with me night and day—Carl Rubino, Augustus Marchette, John McAvinue, Bill Serignano, Al Melia—a number of investigators and men from the Homicide Bureau. We sought out the milkman, letter carriers, garbage collectors, tradespeople, tax collectors, Railway Express-men, local doctors, even the municipal dog-licensing department. In addition we questioned every resident who lived in and around the Morelli estate.

I would ask, "Have you seen this lady in or near the Morelli house?" and show a picture we had secretly obtained of Mrs. Coppola and her father.

Within three days I had established that Mrs. Coppola, accompanied by Mr. Lehmann, had been in the Morelli home.

I have always made it a practice on an out-of-town assignment not to contact the local police until it was absolutely necessary. On this investigation I had to call at the local police headquarters to get some background on Morelli. I soon found out who the honest and dishonest cops on the Providence police force were.

The night after I had been to headquarters I received a call at my hotel.

"Is this Danforth?" a husky voice asked.

"This is he," I replied. "Who is this?"

"Never mind," the voice said, "just get out of town before you're hurt."

Then the receiver slammed. Soon I was receiving an average of three calls a night. Some would threaten me outright, others would say simply, "Don't you think you've been in town too long, Danforth? Why don't you go back to that —— Hogan?"

The calls were more amusing than frightening, although I was careful to carry a gun at all times and at night tipped a chair against the door to arouse me if anyone tried to enter with a pass key.

Despite the telephone calls and the obstacles placed in my way by certain members of the Providence Police Department, I determined that Mrs. Coppola had been hidden by Morelli at the home of his friend, Anthony Del Guidice, a former New York City patrolman who had been discharged from the force for creating a "one-man riot" at the West 68th Street precinct in 1928.

Apparently Del Guidice had been tipped off that I was on his trail. One day, after interviewing a woman tenant in his house, I started downstairs. Del Guidice, a 200-pounder, was waiting at the bottom.

"Hello, Danforth," he said. "Why don't you stop in? You've hit everyone else but me."

"Fine," I said, "I think I'll do just that."

For the next hour we sat in his well-furnished recreation room. Of course he stoutly denied he had ever seen Mrs. Coppola. I didn't tell him he was a liar; in my pocket I had the statements of four people who had seen Trigger Mike's pretty wife in his apartment.

It wasn't too hard to learn that Mr. Lehmann had been hidden by Morelli in his mansion. It seemed that the old man had injured himself in a fall. I found the nurse who had cared for him. When she learned who I was she dropped out of sight.

My most formidable witnesses were five teen-agers in the neighborhood. Each one had identified the picture and described for me in detail, even to the color of her dress, how they had seen Mrs. Coppola in Morelli's house.

But if the children, four girls and a boy, 11 to 17, talked freely, their parents did not. When I informed them it was necessary that their children testify before the New York County grand jury, they protested strongly. Finally we were forced to bring them to court where the judge ordered them to obey the subpoenas I had served.

"The only condition, Mr. Danforth, is that there be no publicity. We must protect their good names," Justice Robert Quinn warned me. I promised there wouldn't be. I overlooked the ingenuity of the local reporters.

Statements were taken from Morelli, Del Guidice, the children, neighbors and so on. Then I brought the children, their attorneys and their parents back to New York.

I had promised the judge there would be no publicity, but I was shocked to learn that some enterprising Providence reporter had broken the story, which included our arrival time. It seemed every reporter and photographer in New York was on hand when the New Haven's streamlined Yankee Clipper pulled into Grand Central Station.

The bulbs flashed and reporters buttonholed me with endless questions. The children hid their faces with comic books and handkerchiefs as they fled up the ramp with me, their attorneys and their parents on their heels.

"If this is what you call no publicity," a short, fat attorney gasped as we piled into cabs, "I'd hate like hell to be on hand when you really notified the press."

Our witnesses were quartered at the Hotel Barclay. In the dining room, our tables were placed together, with eight waiters rushing about to add to the confusion. The children just ate it all up; one kid went out into the lobby and came back wearing dark glasses. In ten minutes every boy and girl had dark glasses.

The children testified before the grand jury the following day. After the flood of gangsters, liars and crooked politicians, they were to the jurors as refreshing as a sea breeze.

Next Butsy Morelli arrived from Providence to testify. He was a sullen, tight-lipped man, nattily dressed in a gray suit, black-and-white sports shoes and a red-and-blue tie. He was one of the few witnesses who was able to duck the photographers successfully.

I saw him for a few minutes before he entered the grand jury room.

"Don't worry, Morelli," I told him, "those secrets will remain with me."

"They'd better," he said and walked away.

Anthony Del Guidice, the ex-cop, was our next visitor. He was visibly nervous and kept mopping his face.

"What the hell did you do to me, Danforth?" he asked during a recess.

"Why don't you tell the truth?" I told him.

"Why don't you drop dead?" was his reply.

He balked before the grand jury, but District Attorney Hogan, now fighting mad, brought him before General Sessions Judge Sullivan to threaten him with contempt. Del Guidice changed his mind and told all he knew. He was held as a material witness in $7,500 bail.

A new sensation rocked the city when Mrs. Coppola surrendered to our office to testify before the grand jury. She was a reluctant witness, who told little. She admitted being in Del Guidice's house, but her memory slipped when she was asked who had supplied the funds for her trips, who had brought her there, whom she had seen there and why she had left so abruptly. On the basis of her testimony the grand jurors indicted her and her father for perjury.

District Attorney Hogan's strategy was quite clear. Mrs. Coppola and her father now faced ten years in prison, but if she told the truth about the midnight meeting at which Scottoriggio's fate was decided. . . .

Mrs. Coppola and her father, who were already held in $15,000 bail as material witnesses, were arraigned and held in an additional $2,500 bail.

The perjury indictment was based on the pair's testimony that they were not acquainted with Frank Morelli. The People's true bill—the indictment—charged that they had fled the jurisdiction of the District Attorney's office and had given false answers to questions pertaining to the identity of persons with whom she had associated when a fugitive. These persons, the People charged, could supply the identification of the persons who were in on that election eve conference.

As our investigation continued, with investigators flying to Chicago, Florida and many other states, the pattern of the way in which the underworld takes care of its own became more clear. Shortly after Trigger Mike had been picked up on November 16, his wife had fled the city with her two-year-old son, Michael David, and her father. First they had hidden out in a relative's home in Queens. Then, in December, they had gone to Florida, where they stayed on Palm Island, the swank winter resort on which was Al Capone's former winter estate. They remained there until spring, then had traveled north to Morelli's mansion and Del Guidice's house.

Morelli's testimony before the grand jury was fanciful. As it was later brought out in court his story was that a stranger had a heart attack outside his grounds and, good samaritan that he was, he took this total stranger into his house and nursed him back to health. It wasn't until days afterward that he learned this man was David Lehmann, father-in-law of his old racketeering friend, Trigger Mike Coppola!

Another weak link in the underworld's iron shield about this case was Trigger Mike's deep love for his pretty wife. My informers in the district told me he was stunned when the news of his wife's indictment was announced.

The condition of his wife was also another factor that worried him; she was expecting a second child. It is a peculiar facet of the American gangster: he is cruel, vicious, deadly as a wounded rattlesnake, but when it comes to his wife or children, tears well and his gravelly voice becomes soft and caressing.

One night one of my informers called me to describe Mike as "almost out of his head with worry." That afternoon he was heard to say he "wasn't going to jail for that bastard. . . ."

We hoped against hope that this hardened gangster might break the underworld code of never talking to the law, when death, sudden and tragic, defeated all of us. Doris Coppola died in childbirth at St. Vincent's Hospital.

The big break we all hoped for had died with Doris.

Then not long afterward the case took another weird twist when the body of Anthony Lagana, a Republican captain, whom we had held as a material witness for a short time, was found in the East River.

Murder was first suspected but the autopsy showed he had committed suicide.

Because of Lehmann's age and feeble physical condition, it was decided not to prosecute him. But the indictment still stands, pending the state of his health.

Although the case had now reached an impasse District Attorney Hogan was so outraged at the conditions disclosed by the investigation he asked Congress to take action.

Hogan and the November, 1946, grand jury which had been held over for three years to hear evidence in the case, appealed to Representative Joseph W. Martin, Speaker of the House, to have the 80th Congress reopen its investigation of the election of Marcantonio.

In two telephone calls directly to Martin, Hogan asked for action in the form of open hearings. Later Assistant District Attorney Jacob Grumet, in charge of the Homicide Bureau, conferred in the capital with Martin, Representative Charles Halleck of Indiana, majority leader of the House, and three other Congressmen, outlining the evidence in the case.

The Congressmen, who appeared shocked at the revelations, promised Grumet he would hear from them "in a few days." When no word came from Washington, Hogan sent another letter asking that action be taken. The letter was signed by the foreman of the grand jury. When this letter was not answered, Grumet telephoned Congressman Ralph A. Gamble of New York, chairman of the subcommittee investigating election irregularities, but nothing definite came of the conversation.

And there it died, not too much to my surprise. There is often an enormous gap between knowing what happened and proving it, especially where powerful groups or their bosses can terrorize all possible witnesses and informers. We do our best to counteract such fear, but we can't always win.

19. MURDER IN THE TWILIGHT WORLD: THE SADISTIC CRIMES OF RALPH BARROWS

WHEN A HOMICIDE is committed in the County of New York the District Attorney's office's only function is to prosecute the case which the police have prepared against the defendant. Thus, essentially, murder in its early stages belongs in the police category. However, if information is brought to the District Attorney's office regarding the homicide or phases of it, investigators are assigned to establish the authenticity of the facts, which may or may not augment the state's case.

I have been assigned to many such cases but the one which I recall most vividly has to do with a vicious young hoodlum who brutally murdered a Canadian industrialist in the Waldorf-Astoria in the spring of 1949. I got some idea of his make-up when I found that at the age of 14 he had operated a bordello in a studio apartment, had beaten two of the young girls into unconsciousness and spent the money they earned for him on clothes and cars.

Barrows' world was the strange twilight world of the homosexuals. He was a good-looking, powerfully built young man and the "queers" flocked about him whenever he appeared.

Barrows was a male "hustler" who sold himself and who savagely beat and robbed the homosexuals who picked him up. Once or twice a week he would go on a tour of the bars frequented by these people on the East and West Sides of midtown Manhattan, then drift up to the seventies to the "studios" where "cocktail parties" were held by the homosexuals who came in flowing cocktail gowns with their faces made up as expertly as any woman's. Here these half-men, half-women gossiped, exchanged partners, drank and danced by candle-light.

On the night of February 12, 1949, Barrows, who was broke, had made his customary tour but hadn't picked up anyone. In a West 45th Street café he fell into conversation with a soft-spoken, distinguished-looking man who introduced himself as Cameron Mc-

Keller, of Toronto. McKeller, a wealthy Canadian importer, was in New York on business, and more out of loneliness than anything else, walked into the bar after seeing a movie. He was obviously under the influence of liquor when Barrows came in.

At 11:30 P.M. he said goodnight to Barrows, but the hoodlum insisted he would help him to the Waldorf-Astoria where McKeller was staying. They went up to McKeller's room, where they had another drink. Then an altercation took place, with Barrows knocking the elderly man unconscious, then viciously stamping him to death. He ripped off the man's wrist watch, stuffed the bills from his wallet into his coat pocket, then walked to the elevator and casually out of the hotel.

His arrest was the result of a detective's alertness. On the table in the dead man's room was a book of matches with the name "45th Street Café" on the cover. The detectives, during their investigation, visited the café and found a barmaid who recalled serving two men one of whom answered McKeller's description. She described the other, later identified as Barrows.

"How can you be so sure?" a detective asked.

"They drank only Canadian Club all night and the elderly man left me a fat tip," she replied. "That's enough to make any waitress remember them."

A detective wrote down his number. "If the young man ever comes back, call me at once."

The waitress took the slip of paper and promised she would.

The next day Barrows walked into the bar. The barmaid gave him a smile, then slipped casually into the phone booth. Fortunately the detective was in.

"That man came in just now," the girl whispered.

"We'll be there in a few minutes," the detective said. Ten minutes later two of them grabbed Barrows.

Although the police later announced he had "confessed" to the murder, Barrows was far from confessing. He insisted to detectives that McKeller had made an indecent proposal and he had hit the man on the chin, knocking him out. He denied robbing him.

The autopsy, however, had shown that McKeller's intestines had been literally smashed, bursting the blood vessels and arteries, under the feet of someone who had jumped up and down on the stomach of the unconscious man. The autopsy also showed that he had been hit so violently that he had been flung across the room, receiving a fractured skull. But it was the stamping which had killed him.

Assistant District Attorney Harold Birns was assigned to the case. Analyzing it with the cold eye of the law, it was evident to him that Barrows could not be tried for first-degree murder because no premeditation or robbery had been established. What society had against Ralph Edward Barrows was a manslaughter case, perhaps one which a smart lawyer could beat.

After reviewing the facts in the case and Barrows' brutal background, District Attorney Hogan ordered us to make a complete investigation of his activities with the idea of obtaining further indictments for other crimes to make sure he would be sent to jail and removed from society if he were acquitted of the manslaughter charge.

It was about this time that Harold Birns called me into his office. "What do you think of this, Dan?" he asked, showing me a letter scrawled in pencil. I read through it swiftly. It was from a Herbert Diether, Jr., who had written:

"I talked with Ralph Barrows in a bar and grill the night Cameron McKeller was killed at the Waldorf. He told me that he intended to pick up a queer and go to his room and rob him."

"That's the clincher, Dan," he said, "for a first-degree indictment. If we get this Diether we can prove Barrows guilty of premediation."

"That's fine," I said, "but where is his address?"

Birns grinned. "He forgot to sign it."

"That's my job?" I asked.

"A better man couldn't do it, Dan," he said.

"Blarney Birns should be your name," I said.

"Give me a ring when you find our man, Dan," he said.

I reported to Chief Investigator Tom Fay and together we went over our informants who might possibly help us.

"Personally, I think this is a phony name," I said.

Tom said, "I think so, too, Dan, but suppose you just float around the West Side for a few nights and see what you come up with."

Before I went out on the town that night I made up a list of bars and cafés in the city which I knew from previous investigations to be hangouts for perverts and homosexuals. There were about seven in all, all adhering to the rigid caste system of the twilight world of the homosexual. For example, the bars along Sixth Avenue were frequented by the shabbier, more furtive men with the hesitant smiles, but the more elaborate, more expensive places were the rendezvous for those homosexuals who were artistic or who had excellent professional jobs. Here they were more open, more flagrant in their behavior.

The first few nights I merely sat and listened, sometimes allowing myself to be spoken to by an obviously effeminate man. They pranced, strutted, fluttered their hands and even complained that their girdles were too tight. Their voices were shrill and they giggled like schoolgirls. I found the Sixth Avenue bars to be frequented mostly by servicemen, who were constantly being picked up by these creatures. But some, like the sandy-haired seaman first class who was standing next to me one night, would have none of them.

"Scram, Mary," he told one, "before I clip you."

When "Mary" was gone he finished his beer. "I don't mind a joint where the whores are all over you but queers disgust me," he said, and he left.

It was about the third or fourth night that I drifted into a small bar of the intimate type on Lexington Avenue in the fifties. It was about midnight and I was ready to call it a day when I was suddenly conscious of a rather strong perfume. I turned to look into the face of a man about 20, with rouged cheeks and curly blond hair. He smiled, ordered a drink and started to read his *Daily News*. The bartender, who seemed to know him, served him and asked, "What's new, Herb?"

I almost gagged on my drink.

The man lisped, "Nothing, George. I'm just reading about that Barrows boy. Imagine *killing* that man."

The bartender said, "He's a bad egg."

The man lisped again. "I know him, George." He leaned over and said in a whisper, "He robbed a friend of mine and beat him up terribly. It was dreadful."

Another customer came in and George went on to serve him.

"Hello there," I said.

The man smiled, "Hello."

"I knew Barrows," I said. "He was always beating people up."

The man gave me one of those are-you-one-of-us? looks.

"He's dreadful," he said. "Can I buy you a drink."

"Sure," I said. "Herbert, isn't it?"

"Yes," he said. "And yours?"

"Dan O'Brien," I said, "from Boston."

He bought me a drink and we got quite cozy. I strung along with him and we stayed there about an hour. I had found he was a commercial artist and not our Herbert Diether, Jr., but he seemed to know quite a lot about Barrows. His perfume was overpowering. Finally he whispered that he would be very happy if I would join him at his apartment; from the address I knew it was a wealthy section.

I played the game until we were outside. Then I showed him my badge.

"I'm from the D.A.'s office, Herb. Let's go where we can talk."

I thought the man would faint. Then the tears came in a regular Niagara. He wept and pleaded with me not to arrest him.

"I'm not interested in what you do," I told him. "I'm interested in finding out all you know about Ralph Barrows."

Still weeping, he went with me to his apartment, a beautiful place lined with books and costly paintings. I questioned him for more than an hour and gradually I got to know the whole story.

Barrows, it seemed, used to frequent the Ross Bar and Grill on Eighth Avenue, between 42nd and 43rd Streets, and many of his friends still used it as a hangout. Among them was a handsome young Spanish homosexual named Manuel, who had told him a few weeks ago that Barrows had assaulted and robbed a musician friend of his in 1946.

"Where can I find Manuel?" I asked Herb.

Now that he knew I wasn't on the vice squad and wasn't after him, Herb was eager to help and evidently beginning to enjoy his detective role.

"I'll help you," he said. "I'll go along with you."

I certainly didn't relish the idea of traveling with this perfumed, rouged man, but it was an opportunity I couldn't miss. With this character I would be accepted and my job would be made easier.

The next night we went over to the bar, typical of its kind along "The Avenue." Five minutes after we came in I spotted several effeminate men who waved gaily and minced over to Herbert, who introduced me with some knowing winks. For ten nights I played the same role, meeting more than 20 homosexuals of all ages. Once they accepted me they talked freely; a great number of them knew Barrows. In their circle he had quite a reputation. But none of them knew anything about the musician he had robbed and assaulted.

Then one night—I recall it was on the tenth night—Herbert whispered excitedly, "Here's Manuel."

In the mirror behind the bar he appeared to be a dark-faced conservatively dressed man of about 25. He was less obvious than the others who called out to him.

"Manuel," Herbert called. "Come on over."

The Spaniard came over. He spoke with a slight accent.

"I have not seen you for a long time, Herbert. You do not come here much?"

Herbert said primly, "I'm strictly an East Sider, Manuel." He turned to me. "I want you to meet Dan, Manuel. He's very nice."

Manuel gave me a broad smile. "I am happy to meet you, Dan," he said.

"Let's get a booth," I suggested.

Manuel nodded. "Tonight I do not play with the band—I have all night for a good time."

Herbert selected a booth at the end of the bar. After the waiter left he said very seriously, while patting Manuel's hand, "Now, Manuel, I don't want you to be angry with me. But we are citizens and we must help the law."

I saw Manuel give me a fast look.

He shrugged. "I do not know about the law, Herb—this is for the police. I have not done anything wrong. . . ."

Herbert patted his hand. "Of course not, you silly! It's that dreadful Ralph Barrows Dan wants to know about."

Manuel turned to me. "You are the police, Señor Dan?"

As we say, I showed him the tin. "District Attorney's office," I said.

It never fails to impress them, but it also frightens them. It certainly frightened Manuel. He finished his drink so fast he spilled most of it. But I will give Herbert credit; he talked fast and between us we finally convinced Manuel, who told me the story of the assault.

It had taken place in the summer of 1946 when Manuel's friend, Lester, also a musician, met Barrows in an Eighth Avenue bar.

"I was there that night," Manuel said, "when Barrows came in. Right away he talked to my friend. I knew he was trying to make him. We had a few drinks, then Lester said we would all go up to his apartment. I said I did not want to because I was afraid of this man, Barrows. But Lester said he would be angry if I didn't go, so I said I would.

"Lester lived on the first floor. He got out his key and opened the door. He hadn't taken off his coat when Barrows hit him on the chin with such force that his bridgework was driven through his upper lip. When he fell down Barrows jumped up and down on him. When I tried to help my friend, Barrows slapped me. When I fell I watched him take my friend's watch and his wallet, which contained five dollars. Then he kicked my friend and went out."

"Did he say anything, Manuel?" I asked.

Manuel looked hurt. "He called us queers and said he hated us."

"Was your friend hurt bad?" I asked.

Manuel nodded. "I had to take him to Roosevelt Hospital. He stayed there for more than a week."

"Did he file a complaint with the precinct?" I asked.

Manuel smiled sadly. "*We* never file a complaint. It is to be expected."

"Where is Lester now?" I asked.

Manuel shrugged. "Maybe he is home now."

"Let's find out," I said.

It took a lot of persuasion again, but finally we got Manuel to take us to Lester's house. I told him not to reveal my identity—just a friend of Herbert's.

Lester, a piano-player in a well-known orchestra, was home. He was genuinely sincere in his welcome of both Manuel and Herbert and gave me a long look. He was the most effeminate of the three. He wore a long silk dressing gown and his eyes and face had been made up.

His attractive apartment was reeking with perfume and soft music was coming from an expensive phonograph in the corner. The place was utterly feminine in decor; it was hard to believe a man lived here.

He made a drink for us and the three of them chattered like so many women, going into gales of laughter whenever a certain man's name was mentioned. Once or twice Lester would come over, smile down at me, and pat my shoulder.

I almost died when he exclaimed, "Herbert! He's such a big one!"

I had enough of this reeking room and these limp-wristed men, so I managed to indicate to Herbert to swing the conversation around to Barrows.

"Oh, Lester, tell Dan what that dreadful Barrows did to you," Herbert said.

"That beast!" Lester said. "He hit me. Didn't he, Manuel?"

Manuel nodded. "Tell them what happened, Lester."

Then Lester rose and not only described minutely what had happened to him but also acted out the whole performance. He began by going out into the hall, opening the door and entering his apartment.

"I came in with Manuel and Barrows. We weren't in the apartment three minutes when he struck me." He bent over and showed me a scar across his upper lip. "He hit me so hard there was blood on the walls. My blood."

"Did he kick you?" I asked.

He began jumping up and down. "Like this," he said, "but I got against the wall and then he robbed me of my watch and wallet."

"There's no doubt that it was Barrows?" I asked.

He threw his head back. "It was him. I saw his pictures in the papers."

"And you're sure it was he, Lester?" I persisted.

"Of course I'm sure," he said. "What are you, a cop?"

I pulled out my badge. "Not exactly," I said. "I'm from the D.A.'s office. I'll have to ask you all to come down."

Lester was sure he was going away to prison on a morals charge and that Barrows' friends would kill him. I assured him that we would give him all the protection he wanted and his only job would be to testify before a grand jury.

That night I poured a weeping Lester, a glum Manuel and an excited Herbert into a cab and brought them downtown. They were interviewed by Birns and given grand jury subpoenas. The next day they testified. Two days later an indictment was brought against Barrows, charging him with robbery and assault. If convicted he could be given ten to 20 years in Sing Sing. As Birns said, it was a good, airtight case.

A few days later I received a tearful telephone call from Lester.

"A man named Torrio came here last night and said he would kill me if I didn't move away and not testify," he said in a whisper.

"Where does this Torrio hang out?" I asked.

He gave me the address of an Eighth Avenue bar and I told him I was going to have a talk with this hoodlum. I found him in the bar. He was a husky young man of about 20, who knew all the answers. I brought him downtown and Birns and I questioned him extensively. He denied knowing anything about the murder and after we had checked on his movements we let him go. I walked him to the street and pointed to a closed green van just pulling out of the huge gates of the Tombs.

"Know what that is?" I asked him.

He shrugged. "No—what is it—Cinderella's coach?"

He certainly knew all the answers.

"That's a Department of Correction van. They're taking prisoners to the Island. Do you know what, Torrio?" I asked him.

"You tell me," he said.

"You're going to be in that van headed for the Island for a year in the laundry washing a lot of dirty shirts if I find that you're bothering Lester. Is that straight?"

He sneered. "You can't do anything to me."

I grabbed his arm, spun him around and began walking him back into the Criminal Courts Building.

"Hey, where are we going?" he said.

"I'm going to take you back and charge you with intimidating a grand jury witness," I told him. "If the judge hits you with the book you'll get a year and a day, and with your record you'll probably get more. . . ."

It was a shot in the dark, but it worked. "Wait a minute," he said. "I was only fooling. I won't even talk to the queer. Honest I won't."

"Get going," I said. "And don't let me hear of any more threats."

When Lester called the next time he was very thankful; one night he walked into the bar and saw Torrio, who gave him one look and walked out.

There is little use in reviewing the next three months of my investigation into the whereabouts of Herbert Diether, Jr. It was a sordid business of touring dreary bars and cocktail lounges. According to my notes, by June 30, 1949—the investigation had begun on May 1—I had questioned or taken statements from 65 witnesses who had known Barrows or his close friends. All of them contributed some bit of information about Barrows' background or activities.

By this time Barrows was brought to trial. Although Diether was never found, enough evidence had been accumulated and Barrows was found guilty of manslaughter. All of the sordid research I had done was incorporated into the probation report which the judge read before sentencing him to 20 to 30 years in Sing Sing.

This was a case I was glad to see finished. The memories of what I had seen of this strange twilight world of Manhattan stayed with me for a long time like pathetic specters.

20. THE GENTLE BANKER AND HIS BIG FIX: THE NUMBERS RACKET

FROM CELEBRATED murder cases our office swung into the case of a huge gambling racket which I believe has no peer when it comes to the fantastic, Hollywood-type investigation we used to break it.

I believe in this case, more than in any other, District Attorney Frank Hogan proved that wire taps, legally used, are necessary to break up any criminal combination. Without our taps this syndicate, which reaped more millions that Dutch Schultz ever dreamed of, might never have been found out.

The investigation began in a quiet way. Our office was interested in gambler Tony Bender, later to be described by Hogan as "one of the top underworld figures in the East." We discovered that Bender and several ex-convicts, gathered almost nightly at a check-cashing center on West 35th Street.

"Put a wire in," District Attorney Hogan ordered. "Let's find out what they are up to."

A Supreme Court order was obtained and a tap was put on the telephone.

I was sitting on the wire with other investigators, and I can still remember how bewildered we all were when we went over our notes at the end of the day. The dialogue seemed to have come right out of the Mad Hatter's tea party.

For example:

Man's voice: "Thanks for the 35 bucks but you still owe me seven."
Out: "Okay."
In: "I've decided to give my wife a divorce on the 25th and give her custody of the two kids."
Out: "Okay."
In: "This is a 12-horse race and I'm betting position three."

318

Out: "Lay 300."
In: "I'll meet you at 25th Street and 7th Avenue for lunch."
Out: "I'll be there."
In: "It's a funeral—43 cars but no coffin."
Out: "No body, heh?"
In: "I broke my leg in two places, lucky it wasn't nine pieces."
Out: "Got it."

Although the calls appeared to be gibberish, a pattern began to emerge; the calls were made at exactly the same time and the figures each day were in groups of three digits. It was evident that they pertained to some sort of a lottery, but these figures did not jibe with those played at the pari-mutuels. Day after day the messages were funneled through Tom Fay to the Chief of the Rackets Bureau, Al Scotti, to be studied. Scotti reported the latest findings to Hogan.

The Bureau of Investigation put the check-cashing office under round-the-clock surveillance. Finally we came up with one concrete piece of evidence; the outgoing calls were being made to a Tony Bender in Hackensack, New Jersey.

After a conference with Scotti, Assistant District Attorney Andrew Seidler, Chief Investigator Fay and Chief of the Accounting Bureau Joseph M. Gasarch, it was agreed that some form of the numbers racket was the core of this operation—just how it worked and just what it was remained to be determined. Gasarch and his assistants, Alex Finkelstein and Sam Lachter, began scanning newspapers each day, looking for three numbers which would fit in with those in the coded messages. Finally, after reading and rereading hundreds of daily newspapers, it was established that the first two digits were taken from the daily noon bond sales. The source of the third digit was still a mystery until one of Gasarch's boys found it in the daily figures released by the Cincinnati clearinghouse.

On the wire the coded calls kept coming in almost at an exact second. Now we sat glued to the tap, carefully noting each word that came over; now the conversations were beginning to make some sense.

From the wire tap we found that calls were being made from a man named Irving Bittz, a Prohibition hood and a former member of the Lepke-Gurrah gang, who also played a minor role in the Lindbergh kidnaping investigation, and a man named Abe Goldberg; both were employed in the circulation department of a New York newspaper. At a certain hour one or the other would call and give the cryptic message.

The pieces of the puzzle now began to fall into place; these two men were part of the scheme and their part was to pass, by coded messages, the figures about to be printed. They were then passed in code to Nat Levinson, another member of the ring, who had offices in New Jersey.

Numbers, of course, are the heart of the policy racket—it is traditional that three digits are used—in which the player bets on a sequence of figures appearing daily in newspaper statistics. They may be Stock Exchange figures, bond sales, pari-mutuel totals—or they may be a combination of these numbers. There are no ground rules in the numbers game; each mob makes its own. The players, of course, assume that the numbers which they are playing are beyond the control of the persons operating the game.

For a numbers mob they had a perfect setup; they apparently knew the winning number long before the clearinghouse figures were released. We have just seen how they got the first two digits. But how did they get the third? While we were working on that, the calls from the newspapermen were abandoned. Calls began to come in from a Broadway bowling alley. The messages were still cryptic:

To the alley: "You have a date for me at 2:00 P.M."
From the alley: "Got it."

Then, we learned, Kane put in a toll call to a number in Cincinnati.

The calls to Cincinnati were of the same pattern.

Outgoing: "I'll meet you at two—can you make it?"
Incoming: "Two it is. I'll be there."

The following day after this conversation Gasarch and his accountant-sleuths walked in with a newspaper.

"There's your answer," he told Scotti. The number 2 was the last digit of the financial statement issued by the Cincinnati clearinghouse.

We found that by taking the second and third digits of the daily bond sales up until noon as the first two digits of the key number, and the second digit in the Cincinnati clearinghouse figures as the third digit of the key number, they would match the figures heard on the wire tap. For example, if the noonday bond sales amounted to $1,580,000 the second and third digits were 5 and 8, and if the clearinghouse figures for the day were $38,000,000, then the second digit would be 8, making the number 588.

What was crystal clear and yet rather unbelievable was that the gang had some high official of the clearinghouse on its payroll. This man, who obviously had the authority to release the daily number to the press, could rig the last digit to fit the purposes of the mob.

It is important at this point to pause a moment to examine the so-called "innocent nickel-and-dime numbers game" and the average player who has made it a multi-million-dollar racket. Down through the years we have collected evidence that this supposedly innocent game has financed underworld infiltration into unions, supported loan-shark syndicates and organized crime of every description. The dossier of almost every big-time racketeer shows some affiliation with the policy, or numbers, game. It is their financial stepping-stone to more vicious activities.

Who is the typical policy player? He or she—women are heavy bettors—is usually about 40 or older. Mostly, they are embittered, frustrated, shiftless and superstitious. The nickel, quarter or dollar they bet daily represents a dream; a crock of gold spilling into their laps. With one swoop they can retire to luxury and a life of ease. It never occurs to a bettor that he has less than a 1000 to 1 chance of winning. The odds never count, it's the dream, the escape from the humdrum, monotonous, abrasive daily life that must be lived day after day. Sometimes he comes close—if only he had bet 432 instead of 423! The near miss spurs him on. Finally the daily bet is a habit which is never broken. During the Depression we found case histories of men and women who played their relief checks on the numbers. Some spent the money usually set aside to pay a weekly insurance policy premium.

Our office now had the gang's *modus operandi,* but it wasn't sufficient legal evidence to lay before a grand jury. What we needed was proof that the game was being played and a conspiracy was operating to rig that game of chance. Many more hours of surveillance and more wire taps followed; conference after conference was held in Scotti's office.

The biggest problem was to find the mob's office—not the check-cashing drop that was only a message center—but the heart of the policy game—the banks. This is the most difficult part of the whole policy setup to locate. Police congratulate themselves if they find three or four a year. Few operators know their locations, which are visited only by the mob's top bosses. This is not only to protect them from the law, but also from rival mobs, gun-crazy juveniles and stickup men who know the haul may prove as high as $75,000. Of course, no complaints ever reach the police.

What made it doubly difficult was that the numbers rackets in New York are based on local pari-mutuels and as far as any of us knew, there were no policy drops operating on the Cincinnati clearinghouse figures. I contacted some of my informants, who said there were a few spots in the city where you could play policy based on the Midwest figures, but even my underworld informants looked blank when I asked where they could be located.

"Who wants to play the numbers on the Cincinnati combine when you have pari-mutuels in the city?" they asked.

We found the western figures were used by New Jersey policy drops, but that wasn't New York County.

Anthony Perone was assigned to find out where in New York this particular policy ring had its drops. It was a question even the underworld had difficulty in answering.

Tony disappeared for weeks. Because we had a record of a few Staten Island telephone numbers, he decided to strike out there first. He adopted a whole new life; he took a room, walked around with a scratch sheet in his pocket and looked mysterious. He paid visits to bars, grills and restaurants. Tony has a quiet, easy-going nature and it wasn't hard for him to strike up conversations. If he thought he had a likely prospect he would draw him out slowly, then casually wonder where he could play a number.

"Four seven two," he would murmur almost to himself. "I saw the combination on a truck. I just got a hunch I can hit if I can find a spot to lay a buck . . ."

Then one night a milkman with whom he was drinking slapped him on the shoulder.

"Hell, Tony," he said, "that's easy! I got a guy on my route that takes numbers. Let's see . . ." He took out his wallet and finally a scrawled address fell out. "Sure, here it is . . ."

Tony placed his first number that day. He got to be known as a steady player and before long was an accepted customer. From this spot he found others scattered across the island.

Then one night Scotti received a call from Tony, "I have it wrapped up, boss," he said quietly. "We can start knocking off some places tomorrow."

The following morning Tony drew up a list of policy drops to be raided. From these small fry we hoped to get the bigger ones.

In cooperation with the police—the police who were to stage the raids were not told of the purpose or location of the raids until a few minutes before they started out—we staged a series of raids across the island.

When news of the raid appeared in the papers I could hear the puzzled voices of the mob's bosses. . . .

Incoming: "Hear the news?"
Outgoing: "Yeah—so what? Usual stuff."

They were puzzled for a few days, then apparently their fears died down and business went on as usual.

While Gasarch and his accountants studied the records we had seized in the raids, Tony was assigned to shadow a new figure who had appeared in the case; William Tiplitz. Tony found him in the customers' room of a Newark brokerage house at the dot of 11:30 A.M. At 12:05 P.M. the total bond sales appeared on the screen. Tiplitz hurried to a hall phone booth. Tony slipped into the adjacent booth and heard him call a number which we traced to the headquarters of a policy bank operated by Dan Zwillman, a relative of the well-known racketeer, Longy Zwillman. Tiplitz gave the person who answered the phone the noonday bond figures. Apparently the mob had discontinued the arrangement with the newspapermen and now obtained the bond sales figures through Tiplitz.

The way the racket worked was now clear. All policy bets had to be in by 11:30 A.M. At 12:10, after Tiplitz's call, the mob knew the first two digits. Then clerks studied the day's tickets recording the bets to find out which third digit had the lowest play for the day. For example, if the bond sales amounted to $1,580,000, they knew at 12:10 P.M. that the first two numbers would be 5 and 8. They would then hunt for the third number that, combined with 5 and 8, had received the smallest play.

Tony found that Tiplitz would call the policy bank back and receive the third number. Let's say that 583 received no play or very little play, then Tiplitz would be informed by code that 3 was the number the mob wanted.

Tiplitz then returned to the brokerage office and at 12:45 would receive a call from Kane's Broadway bowling alley. Kane's position in the ring now became clear; it was his job to receive from Tiplitz the number the mob thought would receive the lowest play.

The muffled conversation went something like this:

Tiplitz: "There's nothing here [the code that the mob wanted 0]."

Kane: "Okay."

or

Tiplitz: "You got a date at six [the number the ring wanted rigged]."

Kane: "I got you."

I was sitting on Kane's wire and could hear him put in a call to Cincinnati seconds after that.

Kane: "Bill there?"

Bill: "Bill speaking."

Kane: "Charlie wants to see you at six."

Bill: "I'll be there. Good-by."

When Tony made his report we checked the clearinghouse figures and the figure six was the rigged total.

More conferences were held in Scotti's office. It was decided to set our sights for the mysterious Bill. Tony was selected to go to Cincinnati and run down Bill, and if possible, be with him when he called or answered the New York call—clearly a very difficult assignment.

We first checked the Cincinnati number Kane had called and our suspicions were confirmed; it was the official number of the Cincinnati clearinghouse. In Cincinnati Tony carefully made a study of the entire building at different hours. Around noon each day he saw a tall, distinguished, white-haired man enter what seemed to be an empty Board of Directors' meeting room.

Just about the time the call from Kane was due Tony slipped into the building and followed the man into the empty room. The man turned as Tony entered. "What can I do for you, young man?" he asked.

Tony said very earnestly, "Well, sir, I'm looking for a job."

The man smiled in return. "I'm afraid you have the wrong office. You want the Personnel Department."

Tony stalled. He wanted to make sure this was Bill, and if it was he wanted to be near when the New York call came in.

Tony said, "I have some brokerage experience and thought I would fit in nicely here."

The white-haired man nodded. "I'm sure you will, son. Now if you just go down the hall . . ."

Tony interrupted, "Could you tell me, sir, what the starting salary is?"

Although he seemed impatient the man courteously answered all questions. Six minutes passed. Then Tony, who feared he was becoming conspicuous, left to go to "Personnel."

Outside, he carefully lighted a cigarette and waited a moment. The phone rang and Tony re-entered the room to hear the man say, "This is Bill. At six? I'll be there."

Tony hid his exuberance by apologizing and explaining he wanted to make sure on what floor the Personnel Department was located. "Bill" carefully explained.

"Are you the president, sir?" Tony asked with wide-eyed innocence.

The man smiled. "No, son, I'm Dennison Duble, the secretary."

Tony was stunned but masked his feelings and left. For the next few days he cautiously investigated Duble's background. He found the man had been for 20 years an honored resident of the community. He was a popular brokerage-house partner before succeeding his father in the office of secretary of the clearinghouse. When Tony arrived he was being considered as a candidate for mayor of Mariemont, a suburb. He was the father of two children and had an impeccable background. As the cliché goes, "everyone spoke well of him."

Through surveillance Tony found that Duble walked into the empty room at the exact minute every day to take the New York call. It was his job to alter for the mob the clearinghouse figure in his daily report which he released to the press, to fit the desired number which had the lowest play. For example, if the actual total cleared through banks for the day was $38,000,000 and the mob wanted the number six to appear he would release $36,000,000. For this service, we later learned, he received $1,000 a month from the mob.

We now had the members of the gang, their *modus operandi* and proof of a conspiracy to rig a lottery. Back in New York, Tony gave his report and Scotti, under Hogan's direction, organized a huge dragnet which would take in suspects in New Jersey and New York, besides Duble in Cincinnati.

Excellent cooperation was given by Essex County Prosecutor Duane E. Minard, Jr., and the schedule of raids was worked out by Tom Fay, Scotti and Captain William Grafnecker, with all of us assigned to teams.

On July 26, 1949, after a year and a half of intensive undercover and wire tap investigation, our office moved in on the gang. One team picked up Tiplitz, another raided Zwillman's policy bank just as he was hanging up on Kane in New York. That very moment Detective James Canavan walked in on Kane, who, for some unknown reason, had decided to use the phone service in the lobby of the building that day instead of his business phone.

In the lobby a telephone operator took the number you wrote on a slip of paper, then assigned you to a booth to make your call. Canavan, who stood behind Kane, wrote his home number down under the one Kane had written, an invaluable bit of evidence for the grand jury. As the Cincinnati call was coming in Canavan arrested Kane.

While Kane was being pulled out of the booth in New York, detectives in Cincinnati walked in on Duble, who surrendered peacefully. He waived extradition to face arraignment in New York. So perfectly were the raids synchronized that the entire three-state operation took only 13 minutes.

Duble's arrest shocked Cincinnati. The city's leaders refused to believe this pillar of respectability could be on the payroll of Eastern gangsters. The shocked Police Chief of Mariemont said, "I just can't believe it. He is the last man in the world I would think would do anything like that."

Duble removed all doubt of his guilt. Two hours after his arrest he confessed and resigned from his office. He immediately became a state's witness.

Nine men were arrested in the roundup and indicted on charges of conspiracy to contrive a lottery. In January, 1950, eight of the nine were fined and sent to jail for from six months to two years.

Duble, because of his cooperation, received six months and $1,000 fine. Only Tony Bender escaped punishment. He put up $35,000 bail and refused to leave New Jersey without an extradition fight.

The investigation showed the mob could have made millions without cheating their players but they were too greedy; they wanted everything. On some days, because of the rigged numbers, they didn't have to part with a penny.

21. THE CORRUPTION OF SPORTS: THE COLLEGE BASKETBALL TRAGEDY

IN THIS personal story I have given accounts of investigations into major crimes and conspiracies involving murder, rape, prostitution, organized criminal syndicates, the narcotics trade and such evils. The story I am about to tell does not involve such felonies but because it concerns the corruption of our young people and is, therefore, of great concern to law-abiding American citizens, I am setting it down here in full detail. I believe this is the first time this national scandal has been pieced together from the first tip-off to the final legislation.

This investigation and the results we obtained will always be more to me than just one more case. I regard it as a symbol of the way moral standards crumbled after World War II, and greed took the place of conscience. However, I believe that the young men who were corrupted and who lost their honor were not wholly to blame; the tensions of American home life, our hurry-up-and-make-a-dollar philosophy, and our glory-hungry American college alumni must share the blame.

This investigation took four years—1946 to 1950—and as District Attorney Hogan remarked to me after it was over, it was one case he would not like to go through again. Even the most cynical of men would have been moved to see the young athletes who were arrested break down. It is not generally known, but one player tried to leap from the seventh-floor window of the D.A.'s office.

I do not intend to name these young men. They were foolish, but they were not criminals. I feel that they have paid in full for their wrongdoing and today are respectable members of their communities. It would serve no purpose to list their names again.

The scoundrels in this case were the gamblers and bookmakers. In the beginning they were small-time crooks, but about the time we started our investigation we discovered that big-time mobsters were about to take over this lucrative racket. And that would have meant violence or even murder.

Before we had finished our work, with one of our investigators playing the part of a basketball scout, we had trailed suspects across the country as far west as Minnesota and as far south as Miami. The honor of many a young man was tarnished, and in the end, the rules affecting two major American sports were changed.

The investigation of rigged sports began in December, 1946, when, acting on a tip, police wire-tapped the telephone of a wealthy bookmaker. On the eve of a big football game word was flashed to Mayor O'Dwyer, informing him that the taps had finally yielded information that a crooked gambling syndicate was trying to rig a championship football play-off between the New York Giants and the Chicago Bears at the Polo Grounds on December 15, 1946. After an all-night session at Gracie Mansion our office was called in.

Hogan immediately ordered a roundup of the men involved. Before midnight the whole sordid story was incorporated in signed confessions.

The main cog in this crooked machinery was Alvin P. Paris, the brash young stepson of a notorious bookmaker; the combine financed him as their front. Posing as a wealthy man-about-town interested in football, he managed to ingratiate himself with members of the Giants. Champagne parties, the best tables at night clubs and beautiful women put him in solid with some of the players. As an added incentive he offered lucrative post-season jobs as salesmen for novelties which he pretended he was planning to sell, backed by national magazine and newspaper advertising.

Once he had established himself, Paris began pressing gifts of money on some of the players. He insisted that Merle Hapes, an end player, and Frank Filchok, a back and the team's star passer, take $500. He explained that he had bet heavily on a recent game and wanted them to have the money. Both men refused the money.

A week before the big game Paris offered both players $3,500 each if they would throw the game. Paris reported to the combine he had both players in his pocket. On this information the gamblers started placing bets through the bookmakers in New Jersey. Within four hours our wire taps showed they had bet $25,000.

Two days after the offer Filchok advised Paris he wanted no part of the offer. The gamblers went into conference, their phones buzzing constantly. Paris was ordered by the combine to raise the bribe offer to $5,000. Filchok refused him. Then the gamblers began hedging their bets.

The plot leaked out and the police heard about the plan. When newspaper reports indicated an investigation was being conducted, Mayor O'Dwyer summoned both players to his office on the night before the game. Hapes, who acknowledged that he had been approached, was ruled out of the game. Filchok was allowed to play.

That night we moved in. Paris was taken into custody and confessed. The next day he was indicted. Three weeks later he was convicted of bribery.

But from the wire taps and the surveillance of suspects, it was becoming plain to us that this was not the end of the case.

Harvey Stemmer, who was already serving time on Riker's Island for trying to bribe a Brooklyn College basketball player the year before, was our next target. We found that he had been made a trusty in the prison ward at Bellevue Hospital, where he was conducting a large-scale gambling racket from a pay-station telephone. Wire taps proved that. I had him under surveillance for several nights and learned he was slipping out to night clubs or to meet members of his combination. When the District Attorney released this information, Mayor O'Dwyer ordered a wholesale shake-up of the Department of Correction.

But like a cancer, the racket had spread. David Krakower, ex-convict and one-time chauffeur for Louis (Lepke) Buchalter, along with his partner, Zarowitz, manager of a New Jersey bookmaking drop, were pinpointed as ring-leaders. Paris, facing a ten-year term, agreed to become the People's witness. His testimony provided the full details of the widespread plot. All were convicted, with Stemmer and Krakower receiving from five to ten years in Sing Sing. Zarowitz, found guilty of taking part in a conspiracy, was sent to the Riker's Island Penitentiary. Because of his aid to the People's case, Paris was sentenced to one year on Riker's Island.

The District Attorney's job in this case was far from finished. The convicted gamblers brought the case to the higher courts. Although the convictions were affirmed by the Court of Appeals, Stemmer and Krakower carried their appeals to the United States Supreme Court, to test the validity of the use of wire taps as evidence. This was the first such higher-court test of the provision of the New York State Constitution, adopted in 1939, which authorized telephone interceptions by law enforcement agencies, under court order, solely for the discovery of crime. On May 2, 1949, by an equal division of the Justices, the decision of the Court of Appeals was affirmed.

It was a major victory for the assistants in the Appeals Bureau.

The prosecution of this case inspired the introduction into Congress, and in many states, of legislation modeled on the New York statute making bribery or attempted bribery of athletes a crime. The National Professional Football League revised its regulations, as did many other athletic organizations, to require athletes to notify their superiors of bribe attempts. Hapes and Filchok were suspended from professional football indefinitely.

Still the investigation of rigged sports continued. Now we centered on the activities of James Plumeri, alias Jimmy Doyle, a one-time member of the Lepke-Gurrah mob, who had been convicted of extortion in connection with Dewey's garment center racketeering investigation, but who was now out on parole.

We had received rumors that Doyle, as he is better known, was some sort of undercover fight manager. For a front he was using two licensed managers, Sammy Aaronson and Tommy Dio. Wire taps showed that Doyle was trying to get a Canadian fighter to "go along" with one of the fighters in his stable. But the fighter refused to "take a dive" (pretend he was knocked out) and told Doyle so in no uncertain manner.

From Doyle the trail led to another fight manager, Frank Carbo. Here the accountants in our office took over. They finally pinned down Carbo's $300,000 bank account in a New York bank. From the record of his deposits he had apparently accumulated this sum in nine months. It also appeared that he, too, was managing a string of fighters, cloaking his operations behind licensed fronts.

Hogan ordered all New York managers and many fighters to our office, where we questioned them. As a fight fan I was disgusted at what I heard. The sport was now a racket. Managers were victims of Carbo and Doyle, who also did business with promoters such as Mike Jacobs, head of the Twentieth Century Sporting Club, and Nat Roberts, the club's match-maker.

One fighter told me, "He told me I could obtain a match at Madison Square Garden."

"Did you take it?"

"No, I didn't."

"What was the reason?"

"They told me I had to do business."

"What sort of business would that be?"

"Take a dive. This I couldn't take. The stumblebum they wanted to match me with couldn't fight himself out of a paper bag."

Another fighter, no longer young and plainly punch-drunk from the punishment he had absorbed down through the years, painstakingly confessed to me that he had taken a dive.

As he nervously twisted his broken hands, he said in a thick voice: "I needed the bucks. I had to do it."

"Do what?"

"Take a dive."

"Could you have gotten the match without taking a dive?"

"If I didn't take the dive they said they wouldn't give the match to me. I hadda do it. I needed the bucks. . . ."

As the questioning went on it soon developed that unprincipled managers were looting the purses of their fighters by padding their so-called expense accounts.

Another abuse was the deliberate matching of fighters so that favored fighters would establish a string of victories. Such a phony build-up made them contenders for championship matches and favorable headlines.

We also discovered that managers had a fine spy system established in various gyms throughout the city which reported daily on certain fighters. If a fighter kept himself in top-notch condition he was stalled in his attempts to get a match until he let himself get out of condition. Then when the spotter reported he had lapsed in his training he was offered a match. The outcome of the bout was predetermined. The weaker out-of-condition fighter was pummeled unmercifully. A serious aspect of this side of the racket was the manager's total disregard of the possible brain or eye injuries which might have resulted from such mismatching.

At District Attorney Hogan's orders all of the evidence was placed before a grand jury by the Rackets Bureau. In February, 1947, the jury reported that underworld characters, prohibited from holding licenses by their criminal records, were operating behind licensed fronts. Even legitimate ones recognized the power of these men when they tried to arrange matches for their fighters. The jury also found that these managers were violating the State Athletic Commission's rules that purses must be paid directly to the fighter, not the managers, who were taking more than their authorized one-third share.

The jury recommended that the State Legislature make it a misdemeanor for unlicensed persons to act as fight managers. It proposed legislation requiring the fingerprinting of all persons to whom licenses were issued by the State Athletic Commission, including managers and trainers. Another recommendation was that every promoter and manager be required by law to give a sworn accounting for all money received and paid out by him in connection with any fight.

The Legislature adopted the first two recommendations. It also authorized the appointment of a medical board to set up standards and regulations for the examination of fighters and wrestlers, and to act in an advisory capacity to the Commission.

In June, 1947, a grand jury returned a second and more vigorous presentment in which it urged that these abuses warranted prompt action by the Commission. The grand jury minutes were turned over to the Commission on June 24, 1947.

In the office our secret hope was that the Commission would hold open hearings on the basis of the minutes. With the sworn grand jury testimony, the Carbos or Doyles could not deviate from their testimony without risking perjury indictments. Such a public airing of the scandal, we felt, would do much to purge the sport of these racketeers and their evil influence.

The Commission, however, did not hold the hearings, but instead imposed a $2,500 fine on the Twentieth Century Sporting Club for dealing with unlicensed individuals with criminal backgrounds, and refused to renew the licenses of others. The names of the criminals with whom the club dealt were not revealed, nor their dealings.

Instead of a hammer blow, a slap on the wrist had been administered.

From this investigation grew a companion scandal which involved Rocco Barbella, better known as Rocky Graziano.

In December, 1946, we received information that a bold plan had been made to fix the fight between Graziano and Reuben (Cowboy) Shank. On December 24, Rocky had called off the fight, scheduled for December 27, because of a "sore back."

Immediately after the cancellation Rocky left for Miami. But when he came back his first visitor was a D.A.'s man who took him in for questioning. He admitted that a man he had seen previously, but whose name he did not know, had offered him a $100,000 bribe in his dressing-room at Stillman's Gym.

"I'll see you," Rocky said he told the man. Three days later this man and two others returned.

"Is the fix on?" he asked.

Rocky claimed he said again, "I'll see you."

Graziano admitted to us he had faked the sore back as an excuse for cancelling the bout. He claimed that his real reason for doing so had been that the man who had offered him the bribe might believe the deal was on, and he was afraid that, if he fought and won, they would consider that he had double-crossed them.

Graziano repeated his story to Colonel Edward P. E. Egan, then chairman of the State Athletic Commission, and Irving Cohen, his manager. He also revealed that this same man had offered him another bribe a year before when he had fought Al (Bummy) Davis.

"Let me see it," he told us he said.

He quoted the man as saying, "I'll see you Thursday."

The man never reappeared, Rocky said. He knocked out Davis in the fourth round.

Graziano said he could not disclose the names of the persons who had offered him a bribe. He insisted that he did not even know their names although he admitted he knew them from the gym or "The Avenue."

For having failed to report the bribe offer Graziano had his license revoked. It was restored in the spring of 1949.

In the fall of 1948 we thought we had cleaned up the crooked sports, but a new sports racket suddenly erupted in full flower when a tall, serious young man named David Shapiro telephoned the District Attorney's office.

"I would like to see the District Attorney," he said, "I have information about some bribery."

Such calls are immediately transferred to the Bureau of Investigation. I was in the office when Tom Fay, Chief Investigator, picked up the phone. He listened for a moment, then said: "Come down right now. Seventh floor, and ask for Tom Fay."

When he hung up Fay said, "It's a kid who says he's co-captain of Washington's team. He claims some jasper tried to bribe him at summer camp."

David Shapiro turned out to be a fine young man. A law student at George Washington University, he was co-captain of his team, a superlative athlete and a courageous citizen. What he did under such trying circumstances should be an inspiration to all honest men to come forward when they have evidence of a crime.

Shapiro told us a strange story which I report here from the notes I took that day. He said that in August, while at a summer camp in upstate New York, he had received an unusual letter. A total stranger, Joseph Aronowitz, urged him to contact him for "mutual benefit."

In the first week of September David returned to his home. A few days later, when he was packing to return to school, Aronowitz telephoned to explain that it would be profitable if they could get together to discuss some basketball games.

"What do you think he meant, Dave?" Tom asked.

"He indicated he wanted them rigged in some way," Shapiro replied.

"Well, the only way we can get this fellow is for you to cooperate with this office," Fay explained.

"I believe it's my duty to do so," the young man said.

A conference was held that morning with Al Scotti of the Rackets Bureau in order to plan our strategy. It was agreed that Dave should go through with the act.

Under our direction he called Aronowitz from a tapped telephone. The first conversation was brief; he simply said he would meet him at a Broadway midtown restaurant.

Fay, Jim White, Detective Nick Barrett and I staked out the meeting place. We watched as Dave was joined by a flashy man; they spoke together long and earnestly.

"The kid's acting natural, Dan," Fay said. "I hope he doesn't get nervous."

"He looks as calm as an oyster," was the only observation I could make.

When Aronowitz left he was trailed by our people. From that night we kept him under unremitting surveillance, and got reports of all persons who entered or left the house and the license numbers of their cars. Each one was checked and investigated.

When we met Dave Shapiro later he told us that Aronowitz's scheme was simply this: he was to play so that his team, if favored, would win by fewer points than predicted in the betting odds, or if not favored to win, would lose by more points than had been forecast. In this way Aronowitz could make his betting a sure thing.

At the next meeting Aronowitz had another man with him, Philip Klein, whom we quickly spotted as an ex-convict. He was Aronowitz's partner. At this session they told David the whole plan was financed by a "wealthy manufacturer."

Before the next meeting we groomed David with the probable questions he would be asked and the answers the gamblers would want. He had to be nimble, stalling them while leaving the impression he was interested in their proposition.

The conspirators kept after David, trying to pin him down to a decision in the North Carolina and Virginia games. We could move in now, but District Attorney Hogan decided to wait; we had to have the "wealthy manufacturer" to wrap up the case.

Aronowitz and Klein persisted in their efforts to make David accept their offer. When he learned that their big interest was in the George Washington University-Manhattan College game scheduled for the night of January 4, 1949, at Madison Square Garden, he reported it to us.

The gamblers skillfully planned the young player's seduction. They insisted the bargain be sealed at a New Year's Eve party to be held at the Hotel Statler. An attractive young woman was to be there as a feminine lure. David accepted on the condition he meet the manufacturer. We had a stake-out at Pennsylvania Station, but after a few minutes we saw Shapiro walk away. We were puzzled at his action but he later explained, "They reneged on bringing the manufacturer, so I told them I had a previous date." After that we had no doubts about young Shapiro's ability to think fast.

The gamblers were now anxious. Shapiro kept insisting he wanted to meet the backer of the plot, so the gamblers finally agreed to bring him to meet David on the day of the game.

At 10:00 A.M. Aronowitz and Klein and a third man met David. The wealthy manufacturer was immediately identified as Jack Levy, a Florida gambler. Shapiro now made a great show of being willing to accept the $1,000 bribe which was to be paid to his "uncle" that night. For this he was to insure his team's defeat by more than the predicted ten points.

A stumbling block in previous negotiations had been Shapiro's insistence—our plan—on receiving the money before the game. The gamblers were cautious on this point, but when Shapiro told them it had to be this way, they reluctantly agreed to pay his "uncle" that night.

For five hours we shadowed Levy and another man, William Rivlin, who entered the basketball racket picture that day, through the Bronx and Manhattan, while they placed their bets on Washington to lose by more than ten points. They were finally arrested by us as they bought plane tickets for another city.

At 7:15 P.M. Shapiro and his "uncle"—one of our detectives— met Klein and Aronowitz near the Garden. When the money was passed we moved in. The final chapter took place on the Garden floor where Shapiro and his teammates, playing as they never played before, decisively defeated Manhattan in a stunning upset.

A few days later the quartet was indicted for conspiracy and for offering a bribe. They pleaded guilty and were sentenced to long prison terms.

Now the scandal widened. We found the tentacles of corruption had spread across the country into many other colleges. By December, 1950, we had unearthed a major scandal in collegiate sports that dwarfed the notorious "Black Sox" baseball sellout of 1919. Involved now were not only professional athletes engaged in the sport as a business, but young men, ostensibly amateurs, who were corrupted on the very threshold of their careers. The proof showed that they had dishonored themselves, their schools, their teammates, their families, for the easy money from "sure-thing" gamblers. The trail of corruption, which extended across the nation, went undetected for at least four seasons of intercollegiate competition.

These facts sum up briefly the scope of our two-and-a-half-year investigation of the fixed-score operation:

Thirty-three players in six major colleges were shown to have been involved in crooked dealings with fixers. Among them were some of the greatest players in the history of college basketball. Several had been All-American selections, and two had played with the United States Olympic team.

During the four playing seasons from 1947–1948 to 1950–1951, the outcomes of 90 intercollegiate contests were discussed beforehand by players and gamblers, and 49 resulted in deals.

The fixed games were played not only in New York City but in 22 other cities in 17 states.

Twenty-one of the college basketball players were indicted for crimes committed in New York County and all pleaded guilty. Of those implicated who were not subject to prosecution, all but one admitted wrongdoing.

But under these stark facts was a disturbing trend of the postwar days, the knowledge that a sense of ethics had been abandoned for blatant commercialism. What had once been a decent American sport had degenerated into big-time business. Alumni, local boosters and, in some instances, college authorities themselves had also committed the crime of over-emphasis. If the players involved had been scouted and recruited under official or semi-official auspices, subsidies had been provided and scholastic standards relaxed for the players' benefit. In an atmosphere where only money counted, it is not surprising that these youths succumbed to the gamblers' bait.

This major investigation began at the outset of the 1950–1951 basketball season. It was triggered by the arrest of a group of Broadway gamblers who, we learned, had been wagering huge sums on basketball games. Informants told us that the games were fixed. We had rumor and little fact until early in January, 1951, Max Kase, sports editor of the New York *Journal-American* (who was to receive a Pulitzer citation for his work) and Louis Burton, one of his writers, paid a visit to Hogan.

Kase and Burton left after giving our office one all-important lead. It was that Eddie Gard, a former star player for Long Island University, should be watched. This was the spark which would ignite the bonfire of scandal in the sports world.

Hogan immediately held a conference with Al Scotti and the Bureau of Investigation. I put Gard under twenty-four-hour surveillance. A few days' work confirmed Kase's suspicions. Gard was meeting members of the Long Island University and City College teams in the company of a New York University player.

But the big break came for us when we found Gard meeting with Salvatore (Tarto) Sollazzo, an ex-convict engaged in the manufacture of wedding rings, which later turned out to be a front for an illegal gold racket.

Wire taps were put on Sollazzo's and Gard's telephones. It was soon apparent that Sollazzo was the money man, bribing players for his "sure-thing" bets. Gard was the intermediary.

In January there came an unexpected development when Junius Kellogg, center for Manhattan University, reported to his coach that he had been offered a $1,000 bribe to throw the game. The Bronx D.A.'s office nabbed three gamblers and two former players but almost put a stop to our investigation, which was unrelated to the Bronx arrests.

Our wire taps showed that Sollazzo advised Gard and the other players to "lay off . . . the heat's on. . . ."

However, the arrest also prompted the other suspects to make remarks over their tapped phones so revealing that District Attorney Hogan ordered us to move in on the racket. Surveillance produced nothing in the way of actual fixes and there was little prospect of detecting the conspirators in the actual perpetration of a crime. At 3:00 P.M., February 17, 1951, we arrested Sollazzo and Gard. A suspected New York University player was brought in later that same day.

Detectives from our office who were keeping an eye on three

of the City College athletes, had followed the team to Philadelphia, where that evening they saw C.C.N.Y. trounce Temple by a record score. On the trip back to New York the detectives boarded the same train as the players. During the journey they called the coach aside to inform him three of his players were wanted for questioning by the District Attorney's office. All had been members of the fabulous "Cinderella team" which had won two national championships the preceding season. Each player was informed by the coach he was wanted for questioning and advised: "If you have anything on your conscience—tell the truth."

In the office I was assigned to talk to Gard. From the beginning I took the sympathetic approach. I did not accuse him of being a criminal or having committed a terrible crime. I let him talk and, by my remarks, indicated that I realized how much temptation had been placed in his way. For hours we discussed the entire situation of college sports.

While I was comforting Gard, investigators and detectives tried to break Sollazzo. But as an ex-convict he knew all the tricks. He just shook his head to all questions.

Gradually, Gard began to weaken. The telling blow was the record of his own conversations. I will never forget the look on his face when later he heard his own voice on the recording machine.

Then we began to read reports of our surveillance of his daily activities.

"It's no use, Eddie," I told him.

"I guess the jig's up, Mr. Danforth," he said.

"Want to tell us all about it?" I asked.

He nodded dumbly. Then he began to talk, admitting his corrupt dealings with City College players and with a New York University player.

He described how Sollazzo had ingratiated himself with the college players, entertaining them at his home, at night clubs and at Catskill mountain hotels, where athletes from all over the country worked at summer jobs and played in an unofficial, informal league.

Sollazzo's lure was the philosophy that he was not asking them actually to throw a game, only to control the point spread.

"Look," he always argued, "it's not like you're throwing your college."

They agreed . . . a few points didn't mean *too* much. . . .

This warped moral code was encountered again and again. Athletes who refused actually to dump a game, who balked at "fixing" traditional games, had no compunction about rigging scores to accommodate gamblers and taking money to do so.

The three players all denied to us they had taken bribes. Again the recording device was wheeled in. Again appeared the shocked, unbelieving looks when they heard their own voices accuse themselves.

The clincher was when I brought in Gard. He confronted them, told all he knew. It was a bitter scene in the room littered with coffee containers, cigarettes, papers and heavy with stale smoke.

"Did you give this boy money, Eddie?"

"Yes, I did . . ."

"How much, Eddie?"

"Fifteen hundred . . ."

Finally they could do nothing but confess. In tight, strained voices, tears rolling down their cheeks, their words the only sounds in the still room, they told us the sordid details. They admitted accepting bribes up to $1,500 apiece for each of three fixed games at the Garden. At the behest of Sollazzo they had held the team's margin of victory below the point spread by which their school was favored to win.

Thus in the first of these games, played on December 9, 1950, City College was favored to win over the University of Missouri by at least eight points in the published bookmaking odds. On that assumption bets were made. The bribed players agreed to hold their points down to not more than six points—to "go under" in sports world parlance, the "advertised" eight points. Sollazzo, well-warned in advance, could lay huge bets that C.C.N.Y. would not win by eight points. In this case the bribed players more than fulfilled their crooked contract; City College lost the game by 54 to 37. The only winners that night were the gamblers.

Sollazzo, Gard and the players who admitted the bribe-taking were placed under arrest. After 72 straight hours without sleep and hasty meals, we were all sent home.

After a night's sleep, investigators, detectives and assistants returned to the round-the-clock schedule. Another 72 hours of legwork followed leads we had received from Gard. Although Gard insisted he had told all, Hogan felt he was keeping something back.

"Dan," he said, "I want you to stay with Gard, stay with him all night, but get him to tell everything."

All day and far into the night I stayed with Gard, first in our office then in a room in the Hotel Statler. We talked about sports, life, careers and morals. I felt sincerely sorry for this young man. About 11:00 P.M. the entire story came out.

The next day, before Hogan, he repeated the story, which now involved additional players for Long Island University. All were rounded up to be brought to our office.

It was another dramatic and pitiful scene. At first the boys refused to admit anything. Finally one broke, then another. But one held out. At last we had to bring in Gard. Ashen pale, he faced the boys who had been his friends, to repeat his charges. I don't think I will ever forget the grief-stricken faces of these young men as they stared at the husky boy in the rumpled suit.

With the evidence piling up against him, the holdout broke. All admitted accepting $18,000 from Sollazzo and Gard to fix seven games, four in the current season and three the previous winter.

As the days passed the scandal continued to balloon in the smoky conferences of the Bureau of Investigation. As I was the only investigator assigned to Gard, sharing him with members of our detective squad, I had his complete confidence. He continued to enlarge on his story until the full details of the corruption of the City College team were told.

A total of more than $26,000 of the bribe money was recovered at the homes of some of the City College and Long Island University players. It had been cached in such hiding places as a shoebox in a cellar, the lining of a coat hung in an attic, the toe of an old shoe in a closet, a flower pot and an envelope taped to the back of a dresser.

As the investigation proceeded, it was discovered that the bribery of college basketball players had become a well-established practice in earlier years. Sollazzo, it was disclosed, had been approaching Long Island University players during the preceding season, that of 1949–1950. Gard, then one of the team's stars, had been his intermediary. Gard, with his teammates, had each received about $3,500 for "working" three games at Madison Square Garden during that winter.

In the two preceding seasons other fixers had done business with Long Island University players. Gard described how he, as a member of the 1947–1948 team, and a fellow player had taken money to fix games from Jack Goldsmith, who himself had once been a basketball star at the university.

In the following season, that of 1948–1949, Goldsmith had promised bribes totaling $3,500 to four of the Long Island players for holding down the score in one of their games. The corrupted athletes fulfilled their assignment, but Goldsmith reneged on the pay-off, saying he would bet the money for them on a "sure thing." After pestering Goldsmith for nearly a year, they finally collected $1,000 of the promised bribe, which they split among themselves.

Associated with Goldsmith in these earlier fixing activities was William Rivlin, a small-time bookmaker. This was the same Rivlin who had been convicted by the office in 1949 and imprisoned for a year for his complicity in an attempt to bribe David Shapiro.

Goldsmith had also dealt with a New York University star. He and Joseph Serota, a racetrack tout, promised the New York University player $4,000 for himself and a teammate, whom the star falsely claimed he could "deliver," to rig a game at Madison Square Garden on New Year's Day, 1951. Goldsmith and Serota were financed in this crooked scheme by Daniel Lamont, a wealthy gambler and shoe manufacturer of Altoona, Pennsylvania, who because of his reputation had been barred from running his horses at New York racetracks.

After the game in question, Lamont gave Goldsmith and Serota $3,000 to be split between the star and his supposed confederate, telling them that because it was an afternoon contest he was unable to get substantial bets down. Goldsmith and Serota, in turn, held out on the star, giving him only $2,000 and the same hard-luck story. Prior to their own arrests, incidentally, Goldsmith and Serota had been shaking down Lamont, obtaining over $18,000 in hush money from their wealthy backer under threats to embroil him in the burgeoning basketball scandal.

Among City College players, too, contamination had set in at an earlier date. Five players acknowledged that they had accepted bribes from still another fixer, Eli Klukofsky, a bookmaker better known as Eli Kaye.

Their first deal with Klukofsky involved an offer of $4,500 to "shave" points in a game with Southern Methodist University at Madison Square Garden on December 8, 1949. The bribe was never paid because the fixer lost heavily on his bets. The visiting team had performed so badly that the corrupted City College players were unable to live up to their bargain without actually lying down on the floor.

After we received this information, I was assigned, with Detective Nick Barrett, to find Klukofsky (Eli Kaye).

We quickly found out that he had disappeared when Gard's arrest was made public. When a quiet police alarm failed to bring any results, Assistant District Attorney Vincent O'Connor told us to find Kaye if we had to visit every state in the union.

On the assumption that Kaye, an inveterate gambler, would hide out in such places as Las Vegas or Miami, where he had gambling friends, we decided to start in Miami, then move West.

The only clue we had was his bright red convertible. The players told us he loved the car as other men love women or money. He was constantly polishing it or adorning it with gadgets. When we reached Miami, Nick and I started to look for the car instead of the man.

We toured Miami and the Beach, street by street. But there was no sign of a flashy red car. Then one morning, as we passed a garage, I noticed a sign: "Cars—sprayed—$100. Pick your color."

"Stop here, Nick," I said.

When Nick slammed on the brakes I pointed to the sign. We pulled into the curb to begin a tour of every spraying concern in Miami or Miami Beach. Two days later we found what we wanted; the sprayer who told us he had sprayed a bright red convertible with Florida license plates a nice sea green.

The files of the Motor Vehicle Bureau in Miami produced Kaye's new license, his plate numbers and his address.

We staked out his house that afternoon, each taking a 12-hour tour of duty just watching for Kaye. After three days we were both puzzled; Kaye apparently never came home, nor did he drive up in his newly painted car. While Nick canvassed the neighborhood I examined the house. A rear door led to a small fenced-in yard. Anyone who was interested could use the alley from the adjacent street, climb over the fence and enter the house by the kitchen door.

Before we set up a stake-out behind the house, Nick and I decided to make one more grand tour of Miami that night to try to find the car. Instead of canvassing the streets we searched the parking spots of all the night clubs. About 10:00 P.M., with a dozen clubs behind us, we found ourselves staring at the gambler's newly painted car.

Inside the club we found Kaye at a table with some friends. The moment we walked up to him he knew who we were. He just shrugged and mopped his face.

"I knew you'd catch up with me sometime," he said, "but you're not going to get me back to New York."

Kaye really meant what he said. He put up a strong legal fight against extradition. O'Connor rushed down to appear in court as the People's representative. The court agreed with O'Connor's arguments and ordered Kaye returned to New York County to face charges of bribery and conspiracy.

Early in March, 1951, a number of indictments were returned, based on the findings in the investigation. In the principal indictment the arch-fixer Sollazzo and his henchman, Gard, were accused of conspiracy and faced 29 counts of bribery. The charges covered the payment of $26,500 to corrupt college athletes during the 1950–1951 basketball season.

Klukofsky was named as a defendant in a 13-count bribery indictment. Goldsmith, who had also gone into hiding at the outset of the inquiry, but was located after a search of many weeks, was accused of conspiracy and indicted on four counts of bribery. Named as a co-defendant was Rivlin, who was still a fugitive at the time. In a second indictment Goldsmith was charged with conspiracy and bribery, with Lamont and Serota named as co-defendants.

The fourteen players who had admitted their corrupt dealings with the fixers were indicted for conspiracy and for sharing in bribe payments totaling over $40,000. Gard also was indicted separately for accepting bribes during his playing days.

All the players, after making a clean breast of their involvement in the crimes, had cooperated fully in the investigation. They had appeared before a grand jury and were prepared to testify against the fixers. Indeed, without their testimony, the prosecution of the bribers would have been legally impossible. In the light of these facts, the District Attorney's office recommended to the court that they be permitted to plead guilty to the charge of conspiracy, a misdemeanor.

On the date set for their sentencing in November, 1951, the District Attorney urged clemency in view of the severity of the punishment they had already suffered. While not absolving them of culpability, since they "were not boys and their acts were not impulsive, but motivated by the itch for an easy dollar," he noted that in assessing the wrongdoing some consideration must be given to the "moral climate provided by colleges."

He cited the "atmosphere of big business so incongruous to amateur sports, the sham admission requirements for athletes, the snap courses and the lowering of educational standards for the stars who advertise the college and increase its gate receipts, the summer sports professionalism disguised as resort jobs, the unwholesome atmosphere of the professional sports arena, in general the over-emphasis and the commercialization which should be so foreign to sane and healthy intercollegiate sports competition." It was understandable, he declared, that the thinking of the defendants could be perverted and their will to resist temptation weakened.

"Most of these defendants," he continued, "would never have been accepted as college students. With only a few exceptions, their high-school grades were below average. They had neither the aptitude nor the desire for a liberal arts education.

"But all of the defendants were star basketball players. That fact changed the course of their lives. College representatives shamelessly bargained for their services. Inducements were offered. To describe such bidding as scholarship aid is only to add to the hypocrisy practiced. It would be more honest to admit that fees and expenses were promised in exchange for special athletic services to be rendered. The professional advantage of playing under the direction of a famous coach was stressed. The prospect of competing in Madison Square Garden, as a prelude to a lucrative professional career, was emphasized.

"This was the introduction of these defendants to higher education. This was the conception given them of the nature and purpose of a college. Is it any wonder that, at the threshold of life they, in turn, shopped for the best offer? Is it strange that they found the idealism and the search for truth in the classroom inconsistent with their commercial arrangements?"

General Sessions Judge Saul S. Streit, before whom all of the basketball cases were presented, had independently made an exhaustive survey of the subject. He denounced the conduct of college sports in all sections of the country as reeking with professionalism and commercialization and called for a thorough housecleaning.

Sentences were suspended for most of the players, but three of them were required to serve penitentiary terms. The Court noted that these players had not only been corrupted themselves but had been willing agents of the fixers in corrupting others.

The office recommended that a plea of guilty to the conspiracy charge be accepted from Gard, who had cooperated fully in exposing the framework. He was sent to the penitentiary for an indeterminate term.

Goldsmith, on his plea of guilty to bribery, was sentenced to serve two-and-one-half to five years in state prison. His associates pleaded guilty to conspiracy, Rivlin, who finally surrendered in 1953 after hiding out for two years, was imprisoned for a year, while Lamont and Serota received six-month penitentiary sentences.

The severest punishment was meted out to Sollazzo. In the face of overwhelming proof of his guilt, he capitulated on the very eve of trial in July, 1951, pleading guilty to conspiracy and to 27 felony counts. He was sentenced to serve eight to 16 years in state prison.

As by-products of the basketball inquiry, other troubles had accumulated for the master fixer. A Secret Service investigation of his illegal dealings in gold was materially aided by evidence uncovered in Sollazzo's business records which had been seized by the office under court order. Sollazzo, in fact, was the key figure in a ring engaged in the smuggling and black-market sale annually of some $5,000,000 in gold. He was convicted in federal court of illegal dealings in gold and of income tax evasion and in March, 1953, a two-year sentence and a $12,000 fine were imposed. In addition, a deportation warrant was served on him by Immigration authorities while he was in the Tombs awaiting trial in the basketball case.

The indictment of Klukofsky was still pending for disposition at the time of his death in August, 1952.

But, in the meantime, a thorough investigation of his fixing activities had opened up several new lines of inquiry and led to still more startling revelations.

The first news of the scandal involving players of New York schools caused hands to be raised in pious horror at other seats of learning in the nation. Players of the Bradley University team, at Peoria, Illinois, righteously spurned invitations to take part in tournament play at Madison Square Garden and voted to conduct their own championship matches in their home community. Coach Adolph Rupp of the University of Kentucky sanctimoniously observed that the gamblers who corrupted the New York City players couldn't touch his boys with a ten-foot pole.

But, in August, 1952, our broadening inquiry established that moral weakness was not confined to college athletes in the metropolitan area. Members of the Bradley varsity team had also yielded to the blandishments of gamblers, it was found. So had players for the University of Toledo. Three months later, the investigation disclosed that Coach Rupp's University of Kentucky stars had likewise been corrupted.

These discoveries came about as a result of a concentrated investigation of Klukofsky's affairs when he was still a fugitive. Records of long-distance calls made from his New York apartment were obtained. Noticeable at once was the frequency of calls to Peoria and Toledo during the winter of 1950–1951. The only clues to their nature were the numbers and, in person-to-person calls, the names which appeared on the toll slips.

Thus, the telephone company records showed that Klukofsky had called a number in Peoria on six occasions in December, 1950, and January, 1951. For the same period there were charged to Klukofsky four collect calls made from public telephones in the midwestern city. The toll slips indicated that these calls had been placed by a person or persons giving the names "Tim Powers," "Tim Paxton" and "Tim Johnson."

Investigator Jim White, assigned to the inquiry because of his background as a college player and amateur basketball coach, was sent to Peoria. He ascertained that the man called from Klukofsky's apartment was a member of the Bradley University team. He found that the public telephones from which the collect calls to New York had been made were in drug stores in the vicinity of this man's home or en route between his home and the Bradley campus.

Jim examined the local newspapers carrying accounts of Bradley basketball games and discovered that the dates on the team's playing schedule were found to correspond with those on which the telephone calls had been made.

Similarly, inquiry by White in Toledo established that the "Walker" listed on long-distance toll slips charged to Klukofsky's New York number was a member of the Toledo University basketball squad. A study of the Toledo schedule followed to locate contests questionable in outcome or marked by sudden shifts in the pre-game betting odds.

Development of these clues led to the exposure of score-rigging by Bradley and Toledo players and ultimately to the involvement of Kentucky athletes in the scandal. New rings of fixers were turned up in the process. Chronologically, however, the tangled trail of corruption in which players of the three schools were enmeshed had its beginning on the Kentucky campus as early as 1948.

It was a strange tale of a pioneering group of amateur fixers who were taken over by professional gamblers. After that the stage was set for sinister underworld figures to move in for a slice of the easy profits.

It began in the fall of 1946 when Nicholas Englisis, a one-time Brooklyn high-school athlete, played football for the University of

Kentucky, on an athletic scholarship. The following season, when a new coach took over, Englisis lost his "job" and left school.

He returned to the Kentucky campus in 1948 to sound out the possibilities of rigging basketball games. With several of his Brooklyn cronies, he had concocted a scheme to exploit his connections with varsity athletes wearing the colors of his alma mater.

Englisis approached two stars of the Kentucky five, and proposed that they "do business" with him to their mutual financial advantage. They found the proposition quite agreeable.

Back in Brooklyn, Englisis reported the success of his mission to his confederates. These were his brother, Anthony (Tony) Englisis; two former high-school pals, Saul Feinberg, then a Harvard Law School student, and Marvin Mansberg, a truck driver; and Nathaniel (Lovey) Brown, a pool-hall regular. Their combined resources totaled $350. Brown was despatched to Lexington with $300 for the two players lined up by Englisis and their teammate, who had been brought into the crooked combination. Thereafter, Brown traveled with the Kentucky team throughout the season, negotiating deals in behalf of the Brooklyn ring and paying off the players after the rigged games.

Initially, the arrangements called for the players to "go over," that is, to exceed the point spread anticipated in the pre-game betting. Going "all out" to beat the bookmaking odds did not place too great a strain on school loyalty. But from this stage the descent was easy to the practice of "shaving" points, of deliberately holding down the team's margin of victory, often at the risk of losing the game.

The season was a prosperous one for the Englisis syndicate. The original bankroll yielded net returns of more than $8,000. With Kentucky entered in the National Invitation Tournament at Madison Square Garden in March, 1949, the prospects for a real killing were excellent.

The three players received a total of $2,000 to go under the point spread by which they were favored in their opening game. They more than fulfilled their bargain, for they actually lost the game and were eliminated from the tournament. This outcome, however, was quite satisfactory to their gambler confederates, who collected substantial winnings on their wagers.

With Kentucky out of the picture, the fixers began to shop around for other prospects. Saul Feinberg, posing as a commercial traveler, had rented a suite at a midtown hotel where some of the visiting teams were quartered during the tournament. There the gang made its headquarters. Nick Englisis accosted one of the Bradley players in the hotel lobby and brazenly proposed a score-rigging deal. In very short order he had three interested players in Feinberg's room.

Their greed was aroused, but their nerve required some stiffening. By way of reassurance Englisis told them that even Kentucky's All-American heroes had sold out. He offered to provide an object lesson. If the Bradley players wished, he would conceal them in a closet where they could listen in while he staged an incriminating conversation with the Kentucky stars for their enlightenment. This offer was good enough for the Bradley trio. They agreed to rig the score in a scheduled tournament game with Bowling Green for a price of $500 each.

During the game all proceeded according to plan until the closing seconds of play when a Bradley substitute, who was unaware of the plot, sank a field goal which upset the calculations of the conspirators and ruined the anticipated betting coup. The Englisis mob was virtually wiped out financially and there was no payoff. With an eye to the future, however, the fixers gave each of the three corrupted Bradley players about $25.00.

The problem of money confronted the Englisis brothers and Feinberg when these principal members of the ring proposed to resume their crooked operations in the following season, that of 1949–1950. At this juncture, Klukofsky offered his services as a financial "angel." Englisis and his confederates had been placing their bets with this bookmaker. Klukofsky had been astute enough to deduce from their consistent winnings on Kentucky scores that they enjoyed inside information. He further surmised that their substantial though costly wagers on the Bradley-Bowling Green game indicated a corrupt contact with members of the team from Peoria.

With Klukofsky's backing, Englisis began once again to deal with members of the Kentucky squad. Two of the original trio were no longer students, but the remaining one was still susceptible to bribes and two new players were willing to sell out for gamblers' money.

Similarly, when the Bradley team came to New York in January, 1950, Englisis re-established contact with one of the players and lined up a new recruit. He introduced them both to Klukofsky. The bookmaker offered bribes to them and such other players as they could bring into the scheme to rig scores for the remaining games on their schedule. This pair, together with two other corrupted players, split a total of $5,500 in bribe money for fixing two games that winter.

A third rigging attempt with the Bradley team was a fiasco and dramatically terminated the partnership of Klukofsky with the Brooklyn combination. This contretemps came about as a result of the duplicity of the brothers Englisis.

Another big-time gambler, Jack (Zip) West, a bookmaker with a police record, had got wind of what was going on. He approached Tony Englisis and offered to pay the brothers $1,000 a game for information of the fix deals negotiated by Klukofsky. Ever ready to make a dishonest dollar, the brothers agreed.

The first opportunity to capitalize on this arrangement came in connection with the Bradley–St. Joseph's game played in Philadelphia in January, 1950. Klukofsky and Nick Englisis concluded a deal with the conniving players whereby the Bradley score was to be held below the number of points by which the team was favored to win. The players involved each received a $100 good-will payment in advance. Englisis telephoned details of the fix to his brother in New York, who in turn advised West.

Within hours the gambling books were flooded with money wagered against the previously favored Bradley five. Klukofsky, greatly agitated and suspecting the worst, announced he would teach "these wise guys" a lesson. Shortly before game time he reversed his orders to the players, directing them to go over rather than under the point spread. He switched his own bets accordingly. Nick promptly notified his brother of the change of plan and instructed him to pass the information to the West interests.

West was infuriated. He had already plunged heavily and was in no position to hedge his substantial investment on the game. Two strong-arm men seized Tony Englisis and brought him to the bookmaker's Brooklyn apartment, where he was held as a hostage pending the outcome of the contest. In desperation Tony called Philadelphia, had his brother paged among the 15,000 spectators at the Convention Hall and informed him of his plight.

Returning to his seat, Nick caught the eye of one of the players as the Bradley team engaged in pre-game practice and flashed him a "thumbs down" signal. The player took this to mean that the plans had once again been reversed and the orders were now for the players to go under the points. This they did and Klukofsky lost heavily. Nick stoutly denied his partner's accusations of a double-cross, but Klukofsky had nothing further to do thereafter with the brothers Englisis.

But this was not the end of the road. Some time earlier, Saul Feinberg had also been casting about for financial backing. He had approached his half-brother, Sam Feinberg, a Cincinnati sports promoter and ex-convict. The latter, incidentally, was placed under bond as a material witness in the course of the investigation. It was revealed, too, that he had unsuccessfully attempted to bribe two members of the University of Cincinnati basketball team. He was not subject to prosecution in Ohio for these attempts because there was no law in that state similar to the New York statute defining such acts as crimes.

The Feinberg brothers made one independent venture together, flying to the Pacific Coast in an unsuccessful attempt to fix a Kentucky game played in Seattle. Thereafter, the promoter referred the younger Feinberg to none other than Jack West, who now supplanted Klukofsky in bankrolling the Englisis outfit.

This new arrangement meant that the youthful entrepreneurs and the players they had contaminated were to become pawns of the criminal underworld. For West was but the front man for Joseph Benintende, alias Joe Granza, an ex-convict and gangster. This unsavory individual had served time for the armed robbery of a bank and was an intimate of mobsters in New York, Chicago and Kansas City, where he maintained a lavish duplex apartment. He and West had been brought together by Jack Rubenstein, a one-time cellmate of Benintende.

Once this mob had established direct contact with the players, the little group of Brooklyn fixers had outlived its usefulness. Nick Englisis sat in with Benintende at a conference in the gangster's Cadillac when an all-out effort was made to induce a player to accept $10,000 outright to throw a National Collegiate Athletic Association championship match at Madison Square Garden in March, 1950. The player stubbornly demurred at this ultimate act of disloyalty, although he had been willing to take dirty money for rigging a score. As it happened, the Bradley team lost the game anyway.

Later in the year, Englisis accompanied West to Chicago for a parley with the Bradley star on fixes to take place during the approaching 1950–1951 season. Virtually every game on the Bradley schedule that winter subsequently became the subject of fix negotiations although only one contract was actually consummated. For that deal the players received a total of $4,000 in bribe money.

With respect to Kentucky during the 1950–1951 season, West was conducting bribe negotiations directly with an assistant to Coach Rupp.

Thus, not many months had elapsed before Feinberg returned to his law books, Tony Englisis found work as a bartender and Nick went back to driving a truck.

Klukofsky reappeared on the scene in the fall of 1950 in the role of a poacher. He visited Peoria and approached a member of the Bradley squad in the university field-house, offering him money to line up other players for fix deals. However, some of the other members of the combination preferred to continue doing business with West and Benintende. The gambler then made a private deal with one player. He agreed to pay him for tips on the fix arrangements made with the rival outfit to guide him in his own betting. Thereafter Klukofsky was in constant communication with this player by long-distance. (The toll-slip record of these peripheral calls opened up all the later phases of the investigation.)

Meanwhile, Klukofsky had staked out a private preserve for himself, lining up three Toledo University players to control scores for him. The bookmaker, again brazenly invading a university field-house, had accosted one of these players and broached the proposition. He tentatively agreed and found that two of his teammates were ready to go along. For some weeks they were hesitant about concluding a deal, telling Klukofsky that they intended to extend themselves in the games under discussion and win by high scores. The gambler bet accordingly and after one victory forwarded $200 in good-will money to the key player in order to soften him further.

When finally 'a contract was negotiated, in December, 1950, the players barely succeeded in living up to their point-shaving bargain. Thereafter they brought into the combination another teammate, whose stellar playing in the game had almost foiled the plot. Klukofsky, who had won handsomely on his bets, sent the key man a $250 bonus and $500 for each of the three players, twice as much as he had promised. The key man gave his confederates $250 each and pocketed the balance.

The Benintende-West ring was not long in discovering that money could be made with the Toledo five. When Klukofsky next called his contact, in January, 1951, to set up a fix, the latter protested that Bowling Green, the opposing team, was a traditional rival and that the Toledo players intended to do their best. Playing on their home court, he added, they should win handily. On the strength of this enthusiastic prediction, Klukofsky bet heavily and lost, unaware that he had been double-crossed. The players had made a deal with Benintende and his henchman, Rubinstein, to go under the point spread and actually lost the game. They received $2,000 in largesse from these fixers. Another deal with the same bribers soon followed, the players again sharing $2,000.

When Klukofsky was apprehended in April, 1951, he would not talk. With respect to the possible bribery of athletes at Bradley and Toledo Universities, the office had little more to go on than the record of the toll calls to and from Peoria and the Ohio city. But these generated more than a healthy suspicion that Klukofsky had been tampering with basketball players of both schools.

It was determined to resolve the problem by a head-on attack. Simultaneously, on July 24, 1951, Assistant District Attorneys descended on the two midwestern cities and, with the aid of local authorities, located and began questioning the suspected players. The assistants established liaison with each other and with the office in New York in order to coordinate all moves on the several fronts.

One of the players, when shown the record of his long-distance calls to and from New York and a photograph of Klukofsky, admitted his involvement. Another also recognized the photograph of "George," as the gambler was known to the players, and resolved to make a clean breast of it. Gradually the whole story of the corruption of the Bradley team was pieced together.

At the same time, in Toledo, the contact player was admitting his corrupt dealings with fixers. He named the teammates who had connived with him and all confessed their wrongdoing.

The disclosures by these players provided the first leads to the Englisis ring and the West-Benintende syndicate. Word was flashed to New York and the Englisis brothers and their confederates were rounded up. The identities of West and Benintende were still to be determined. The players knew them only as "Ed Turner" and "Pete."

The four Toledo players who were involved in fix negotiations were not subject to prosecution in New York because their corrupt acts had been committed outside the state. Nor were they liable to arrest in Ohio since there was no sports-bribery statute there. They came to New York voluntarily, however, and testified fully before a grand jury.

The situation was otherwise with respect to three of the Bradley players who had entered into the original deal with Englisis in a Manhattan hotel in March, 1949, and, thus, had committed a crime within the jurisdiction of New York County. They waived extradition and with two of their teammates, who came to the city voluntarily, testified about the fixing activities before a grand jury.

The three confederates in the corrupt bargain with Englisis were indicted. They pleaded guilty to conspiracy. The Court, in suspending execution of sentence, again took occasion to assail the corrupting and demoralizing influence of an educational system which set athletic prowess above scholastic accomplishment.

The midwestern developments had a salutary effect on Klukofsky. Already under indictment for the City College fixes, he now saw a formidable case developing against him as well as a prospect of many years behind bars. He abandoned his attitude of hostility and began to cooperate with the office, supplying much information of value to the investigation.

The Englisis brothers, also, were anxious to unburden themselves. They admitted their crooked dealings with the Bradley players and described their relations with Benintende and West. They gave no hint, however, of their bribe payments to players of the University of Kentucky, Nick's alma mater. But the Bradley teammates had revealed the incident in the New York hotel, involving the invitation to eavesdrop while the Kentucky stars exposed their own corruption. This account clearly indicated that the Englisis brothers were holding out. Several days of persistent questioning were required before they gave up the full truth.

Their admissions alone, of course, were insufficient for prosecution. To provide the necessary evidence against the Englisis ring, and to shed whatever light was possible on the subsequent fixing activities of Klukofsky and the West-Benintende outfit, the testimony of the Kentucky players was essential.

Two of the three players with whom Englisis had dealt were now playing professional basketball. They were with the Indianapolis Olympians, one of the outstanding teams in the National Basketball Association, and were part-owners of the club. The third player had become a high-school basketball coach in Louisville, Kentucky. To prevent a premature tip-off to any of the suspects, it was decided to question the three players simultaneously.

The office learned that the first two were to attend an all-star charity game at the Chicago stadium on the evening of October 19. In Illinois, proceedings against them would be possible under the reciprocal witness act. Accordingly, an Assistant District Attorney and detectives journeyed to Chicago. There, the Cook County Prosecutor's office, which had been of substantial assistance in the

Bradley investigation, again cooperated fully. At the conclusion of the all-star game the two players were taken into custody.

Word was telephoned to an assistant and detectives who had gone to Louisville where, with the aid of local authorities, they located and questioned the third man.

Throughout the long night of questioning each group of investigators kept in touch with the other. At the very outset a serious stumbling-block was encountered. When the three former Kentucky players learned of Bradley's involvement in the basketball scandal and the arrest of Englisis, they had entered into a covenant, pledging each other to say nothing if any of them should ever be questioned about their own corrupt dealings.

In the face of the accumulated evidence and in response to an appeal to clear their consciences and aid in cleaning up the sport, the first two at length admitted their part in the fixes. The third still stubbornly refused to cooperate. His resistance was finally broken when his former teammates agreed to speak to him by telephone from Chicago. They assured him that they had told the full story of their wrongdoing and thus relieved him of his pledge to admit nothing.

The three came to New York voluntarily and testified before the grand jury. They were indicted, pleaded guilty to conspiracy, and execution of their sentences was suspended. Once again the court severely castigated the commercialization of college athletics, tracing the plight of the defendants to the "inordinate desire of the trustees and alumni of Kentucky for prestige and profit in sports."

The chief difficulty encountered in the closing stages of the investigation was the clarification of the Kentucky picture during the seasons of 1949–1950 and 1950–1951. In the first place, it was essential to pursue the leads already uncovered in order to obtain vitally needed evidence to secure the conviction of the major fixes. Beyond that, Governor Lawrence W. Wetherby of Kentucky, and Dr. Herman L. Donovan, president of the University, were determined that there be no shadow over the team as it entered upon the 1951–1952 season and that the cloud of suspicion be removed from innocent athletes.

The third player mentioned above had become a cooperative witness. In addition to his admissions regarding the 1948–1949 season, he had told of sharing bribes with other players during the winter of 1949–1950. The grand jury was anxious to question both of these players as well as a certain other star performer of the 1950–1951 season.

An assistant traveled to Oklahoma to question one of the involved players, now in private business, at his home but found he had left for Oregon with his company's basketball team. With the cooperation of his employers, a meeting was arranged with him at Denver, Colorado. When questioned, he would not admit his involvement in basketball fixes and temporized about coming to New York to testify before a grand jury.

Another assistant spent a week in Kentucky vainly attempting to talk with the 1950 star and another player. Counseled by a Lexington attorney, who chose to make local capital out of the "Yankee invasion," they would not consent to be questioned or to come to New York, in spite of all the cooperative efforts of the governor and the president and trustees of the university.

Kentucky at the time had not enacted the Uniform Act to Secure the Attendance of Witnesses in Criminal Cases. Hence there was no legal procedure under which they could be compelled to appear before a New York grand jury. Both were assured through their attorney that they could not be prosecuted in New York—unless they lied before a grand jury—since the acts about which they might be able to testify had taken place outside the grand jury's jurisdiction. Nor would they be liable to prosecution in Kentucky where there was no anti-bribery law. Incidentally, as by-products of the investigation, a reciprocal witness act and a sports-bribery statute were subsequently enacted in Kentucky.

Because of his recalcitrance, one of the players against whom there was concrete evidence of complicity in fixes, was not permitted by the University to continue his studies. He returned to his home in Dayton, Ohio. The star was declared ineligible to participate in athletic activities until he should clear himself of suspicion.

After an interval of two months, the star yielded to University pressure and consented to come to New York. The office promptly moved to bring in the other two, who were now located in states where proceedings under the reciprocal witness act were possible. A court in Eureka, Kansas, where one was then stationed, ordered his appearance before the New York County grand jury while similar proceedings in a Dayton, Ohio, court compelled the other to appear in court. Thereafter, both became cooperative witnesses.

The grand jury found a sharp conflict in the testimony of these two men on the one hand and the story told by the star on the other.

He was notified that the grand jury would permit him to reappear and testify further, but he chose not to avail himself of the opportunity. Thereafter he was indicted for perjury. The indictment asserted that before practically every Kentucky game in December, 1950, and January, 1951, the defendant had discussed with the other two players the possibilities of rigging scores and that he had received $1,000 as a result of such arrangements.

The star's perjury trial in January, 1953, ended in a jury disagreement. There were four witnesses who had knowledge of fix activities allegedly involving the defendant. One of these, Klukofsky, was dead. Another, West, contemptuously refused to testify unless he could make a "deal." There remained only his two former Kentucky teammates, and their testimony was tainted by their admitted complicity. Accordingly, in April, 1953, the office moved for a dimissal of the indictment.

The eight fixers responsible for the bribe payments to players of the out-of-town educational institutions were charged with conspiracy, bribery and attempted bribery in a series of indictments .

West had fled town without bag or baggage on the very day news of the involvement of the Bradley and Toledo teams became public. He surrendered after being sought for six weeks. A month later, Benintende, who had been the object of a nationwide man hunt, was captured at gunpoint as he alighted from a plane at La Guardia Field to keep a rendezvous with a girl-friend. Detectives had been shadowing the woman for days, anticipating such a meeting.

The members of the original Englisis group, all of whom had cooperated in the investigation to a greater or lesser degree, entered pleas of guilty. Anthony Englisis and Brown were sentenced to six-month terms in the penitentiary and Mansberg to a term of nine months. Nicholas Englisis and Feinberg were required to serve indeterminate penitentiary sentences.

West and Benintende chose to stand trial but they capitulated before the first People's witness had concluded his testimony. Their accomplice, Rubinstein, thereupon decided to hold out no longer and entered his plea of guilty. The three were sent to state prison, Rubinstein for a term of two and one-half to five years, West for two to three years, and Benintende for a four- to seven-year term.

The death of Klukofsky in August, 1952, had made further progress impossible along several promising new avenues of inquiry.

The February, 1951, grand jury, after 27 months of fruitful public service, was discharged on April 29, 1953.

An offshoot of the investigation was the discovery that Sol Levy, a professional basketball referee, had entered into corrupt dealings with Sollazzo and Gard and had received $3,000 in bribes to influence the outcome of three National Basketball Association games in 1950.

It was impossible to indict him for a felony under the sports bribery law because the statute was silent as to misconduct of officials at athletic events other than horse racing. Accordingly, he was charged with violations of the commercial bribery law which are misdemeanors. It was the theory of the office that his acceptance of gratuities to influence his actions as a referee constituted acts of disloyalty to his employer, the National Basketball Association.

Levy was convicted after trial in the Court of Special Sessions in February, 1953, and was sentenced to an indeterminate penitentiary term. The conviction was reversed on appeal, however, but not as to the facts. The Appellate Division held with respect to the law that the defendant "may have acted corruptly," but that the commercial bribery section did not embrace the actions of a referee in a basketball game. The State Legislature has since amended the sports bribery law to make the corruption of officials as well as participants in an athletic contest a felony.

Forgetful that the present high reputation of professional baseball is due in large part to the fact that the Black Sox page has been kept black and that players who brought dishonor to the game were permanently banished from organized baseball, some persons were inclined to condone the conduct of the college athletes who sold out.

Coach Rupp of Kentucky had voiced the attitude that saving points for money was less reprehensible than outright dumping. When questioned in his chambers by Judge Streit prior to the sentencing of the Kentucky players, he indicated that he had abandoned his previous liberal attitude about the immorality of point-shaving after his own boys had been implicated in the basketball scandal.

A city official of Wilkes-Barre, Pennsylvania, wrote to the District Attorney inquiring somewhat testily how soon the case of one of the players would be closed as he wanted to put him to work on a professional team he managed.

The two former Kentucky players were required by the National Basketball Association to sell their stock interest in the Indianapolis Olympians and were barred from further participation in the professional league. Member teams were prohibited from signing any other college athlete who had been involved in fixing deals.

In contrast to this attitude on the part of the National Basketball Association, which, incidentally, cooperated fully with the office, was the indifference to the good name of the sport displayed by some elements in the younger American Basketball League. However, the hiring of three involved players by the Jersey City club, and the signing of another by Elmira kicked up a row and resulted in the early disruption of this new association. Judge Streit, who had suspended the sentences of the two former Kentucky players, summoned them before him and sternly reminded them that they were on probation and were to stay out of sports.

The Board of Higher Education of the City of New York prohibited municipal colleges from engaging in sports events at Madison Square Garden and other commercially operated sports arenas and directed other reforms designed to restore public respect and confidence. At City College there was a complete overhauling of the athletic setup. Disciplinary action was taken against members of the coaching staff and an office assistant was dismissed when it was discovered that there had been tampering with the scholastic records of high-school athletes in order to establish eligibility for admission to the college.

Information suggesting improper practices in the purchase of equipment by the college athletic association was turned over by the office to the New York City Department of Investigation. It found that the faculty athletic manager had been purchasing equipment from favored sporting goods merchants at excessive prices and without competitive bidding. In addition, it was shown that an instructor and athletic coach at the college was himself a dealer in sports equipment and in many cases signed requisitions in which he recommended his own company as the vendor.

There were other signs of a moral awakening in academic circles. The American Council on Education approved a program drafted by 11 college presidents to impose stricter control on intercollegiate athletics. Among the reforms proposed were the abolition of recruiting and subsidization of athletes, the vesting of exclusive control of athletic funds in the universities, the limitation of sports to their proper seasons, and the requirement that athletes conform to stated admission conditions and make regular progress toward a degree.

These reform measures were described by the District Attorney as "minimum safeguards that any institution proud of its reputation ought to be willing to subscribe to."

The National Collegiate Athletic Association approved similar housecleaning measures. It placed Kentucky and Bradley Universities on one year's probation and authorized its national council to take disciplinary action against offending institutions between annual conventions. Citing the doctoring of admission records, the N.C.A.A., in October, 1954, placed the City College basketball team on probation for a year, barring it from participation in the 1955 Kansas City tournament.

One immediate concrete result of the basketball investigation was the enactment by the State Legislature of an amendment to the bribery law doubling the maximum penalty to be imposed on a convicted fixer. Under the amended law, the payment or offer of a bribe to a participant in an athletic contest is punishable by imprisonment up to ten years and a fine of $10,000. The recipient of such a corrupt payment may be imprisoned for five years and is also subject to a $10,000 fine.

22. GOOD-BY

FOLLOWING THE basketball scandal I was assigned to a painting industry racket in which I had to pose as a paint salesman. I got most of my knowledge from the public library—"Paints: the origin of," and a few stops at paint stores. A variety of cases followed . . . rent gouging, business swindles, confidence men, more waterfront investigations . . . surveillance . . . wire tapping . . . dictaphones . . .

I was a plumber, a brush salesman, a waterfront drifter, the Boston thug, Dan O'Brien. Then one day I received a call from Tom Moore, a former Assistant District Attorney, who was the first Deputy Commissioner of the New York State Labor Department.

"Let's have lunch, Dan," he said.

"What's up?" I asked.

"I want to offer you a job," he said.

At lunch I found Tom offering me the job of Chief Investigator in the State Labor Department. There was a difficult situation to be cleaned up and Tom was offering me the opportunity. The salary was almost twice what I was getting and the investigation promised to be exciting.

It was a difficult decision to make. One doesn't sever a relationship of 16 years in one office quickly, and primarily I was a D.A.'s man, in one of the most important law enforcement agencies in the nation. Still, I couldn't ignore the better income or the title.

I had a week to make up my mind. On the last day I decided to leave the D.A.'s office. I would tell Frank Hogan of my decision the next day.

The boss, just returned from a vacation, was busy most of the morning and I didn't get to see him until late.

I found him tanned and fit. As always we got immediately to the heart of the matter. He kept nodding as I explained and when I ended he said that he was reluctant to let me go but he realized the opportunity and the economic factors. It seemed a thousand years ago since the day in 1935 when we had met in Dewey's office.

360

I hate good-bys. I have always felt there is too much finality in the formalities. Emptying a desk for the last time to me is distasteful; I dumped the contents of the drawers into my briefcase. I'm afraid my good-bys were almost terse . . . Tony Scanlon . . . Tom Fay . . . Eddie Whiteside . . . Herb Israel . . . Jim Mahoney . . . Frank McAree . . . Emil Johanson . . . Jim White . . . Harry McCabe . . . Gasarch and his figure hunters . . . the assistants.

I reached the street in a drizzly twilight. I looked back only once. Behind the glass doors of the Criminal Courts Building 16 dramatic years waved good-by and I saluted them.

THE
LONG
THIRST

Also by *Thomas M. Coffey*

AGONY AT EASTER

IMPERIAL TRAGEDY

LION BY THE TAIL

THE
LONG
THIRST

Prohibition in
America: 1920-1933

Thomas M. Coffey

W·W·NORTON & COMPANY·INC·
NEW YORK

973.91

27288

Copyright © 1975 by Thomas M. Coffey

Library of Congress Cataloging in Publication Data

Coffey, Thomas M
  The long thirst.

  Bibliography: p.
  1. Prohibition—United States—History.
I. Title.
HV5089.C66   363.4'1   75–17816
ISBN 0–393–05557–4

Published simultaneously in Canada
by George J. McLeod Limited, Toronto

PRINTED IN THE UNITED STATES OF AMERICA

1 2 3 4 5 6 7 8 9 0

Contents

Foreword

At the end of dinner one night, when I was a middle-sized boy, my father stood up from the table, went to the closet, and brought down his hat with the apparent intention of going out. He wasn't necessarily going far. My father wore a hat even when he went for the mail. On this night he turned to me and said, "Come along."

I was astonished because he was not in the habit of taking me anyplace with him, night or day. There was no comradeship between us. As I tagged along beside him, I couldn't imagine where we were going. After a three- or four-block walk in silence, we approached an establishment we neighborhood kids had often pointed out to each other, secretively, as a speakeasy. Today it was no longer a speakeasy. This was the day prohibition ended officially in our state and beer became legal. Though I may not have noted the date at the time, I now know it was April 7, 1933.

We entered the side door of the dimly lit tavern and found about a dozen men standing in clusters with mugs in hand. My father marched me up to the bar and said to the man behind it, "Two beers, please."

Ignoring the fact that I was outrageously under age, the man slid two full glasses to us and my father handed me one as he took the other. "I want you always to remember this day," he said, and I shall.

Even as a boy I thought prohibition a strange phenomenon. It seemed normal enough for adults to forbid children to do certain things, especially since these things were almost always explained as "bad." But it was baffling to see adults forbid each other to do something which, in my family at least, was not considered the least bit "bad." I knew little then about the influences that led to the prohibition of alcohol—the puritan ethic of the people who founded the country and of their descendants; the unswerving belief of such people in the virtues of hard work, piety, and sobriety; their religious fundamentalism and uneasiness about intellectual freedom; their fear of the immigrants huddled in the cities and the religions (Catholicism and Judaism) these "foreigners" had brought with them; the conviction, especially among employers, that alcohol diminished the productivity of the workers; the growing certainty on the farms and in small towns that city life encouraged alcoholic (and therefore sexual) excess—a certainty fostered by the sordidness of the old-time saloons and brothels and by the well-advertised drinking habits of the urban poor.

When I began studying prohibition seriously, and these influences, most of which grew out of the nineteenth century, became apparent to me, I was quickly struck by the realization that many of them still persist in American society. A close look at the Americans of fifty years ago proves that they were very similar to Americans today, that much of the talk about deep, fundamental changes has been exaggerated.

Anyone who doubts this should consider for a moment the last campaign of former President Richard M. Nixon. The "Middle Americans" who so staunchly supported him (until he was found to lack the old-fashioned virtues they cherished) have much in common, often including direct ancestry, with the middle Americans who imposed prohibition on the nation from 1920 to 1933. Nixon in 1972 repeatedly called for a restoration of the work ethic which he said many people had abandoned, and he promised to curb the permissive element which he said was rampant in the nation. His religious mentor, at least in public, was the fundamentalist Billy Graham, a direct throwback to the Bible-shouting prohibitionist, Billy Sunday, of fifty years ago. While Nixon did not appeal to the religious bigotry so popular during prohibition, he did give support to the racial prejudice which has largely replaced it. He also made clear his distrust of intellectuals and threatened, usually through his spokesmen, to curb the "unfair" press as well as the pornographers. The issue of the immigrants in the cities was long since dead, but Nixon warned the nation about other urban evils—the radical young, the street criminals, the narcotics pushers. Like many other astute politicians, Nixon made capital of the nation's narcotics problem. He knew very well how his constituents felt about this issue. Here was the new prohibition. He was as forceful in his promise to stamp out the dope traffic as Harding, Coolidge, and Hoover had been in their promises to stamp out the liquor traffic.

The American people listened to Nixon and returned him to the White House with more than 60 per cent of the votes. While the problems of his opponent may have helped his cause, it is apparent that Nixon would easily have defeated any opponent in 1972. The American people understood his message and they liked it.

The parallels between our current narcotics prohibition and the alcohol prohibition of the 1920s are too striking to ignore. No one can deny the need for some kind of program to counteract the personal and social tragedies which arise out of alcohol and drug abuse. It is appallingly ironic, however, that the same methods which totally failed to suppress alcohol, which on the contrary stimulated its greater use, should now be employed against narcotics. No one ought to be surprised that this latter-day prohibition is as ineffectual, and indeed as aggravating to the problem, as the older one. All the means of circumvention and subversion developed during alcohol prohibition are in widespread practice today. The smuggling, hijacking, bribery, corruption, political maneuvering, gang warfare, and disrespect for law which became institutions in America during the '20s operate again in the '70s.

The contraband commodity has changed from booze to drugs and the volume of business may be smaller, but the profit per customer is greater. Some of our most prosperous gangster dope dealers, especially in the Mafia, are the grandsons of men who were gangster liquor dealers during the '20s, while some of the policemen and public officials who protect them may be the grandsons of men who did likewise fifty years ago. So many policemen, politicians and government agents have been caught doing business with drug racketeers that it is reasonable to ask whether the agencies responsible for stopping the drug traffic are actually being used to perpetuate it. The men in these agencies, like the liquor enforcement officers in the '20s, have big stakes in the continuation of the narcotics prohibition. The honest officers have only their jobs to protect. The others would also lose great chunks of clandestine income if the system were changed. This may be why so many narcotics officials keep insisting that strict law enforcement is the only solution to the narcotics problem. They're using the same arguments the old prohibitionists used. Eventually the public grew tired of listening to the old prohibitionists, but there is little indication that the public is growing tired of the new ones. America's puritan ethic is still strong.

These observations should not lead the reader to expect that this book is a dissertation about the American narcotics problem and how to solve it. It is no dissertation at all. It is a book which tells the story of prohibition in human terms, through the lives of a number of real people, some famous, some obscure, some funny, some tragic, some honest, some crooked. All were either involved in or seriously affected by prohibition. These people include a crooked mayor, a frustrated governor, a slippery bishop, a blustering bigot, a rotund sleuth, a stylish hoodlum, an honest rumrunner, a deceived bootlegger, a militant socialite, a formidable lobbyist, a woman prosecutor, and four Presidents. The book does not suggest parallels between any of these people and specific people active today. But in describing the liquor prohibition of the '20s, the book may also call the reader's attention to some equally strange things happening today.

The gathering of information required research from coast to coast. Among the people most helpful were Associate Editor James Bassett and Lois Markewith of the Los Angeles *Times,* Mary E. Collins, M.D., Los Angeles; June Dieckmann, Wisconsin State Journal, Madison; Frances Forman, Reference Librarian, Cincinnati Historical Society; James Hart, Director, and William Roberts, Librarian, Bancroft Library, University of California, Berkeley; Joseph Kupetz, Strand Book Store, New York City; Elizabeth Mason, Butler Library, Columbia University, Oral History Project; Frederick Morgener, Chief Librarian, Cincinnati Public Library; George Reedy, Director, Marquette University School of Journalism, Milwaukee; John D. Riordan, Operating Director, Chicago Crime Commission; Paul R. Rugen, Chief, and John D. Stinson, New York Public Library, Manuscript Division; Carol Houck Smith, W. W. Norton & Company, Inc., New York; Jess Shaffer, Managing Editor, Cincinnati *Enquirer;* Rev. and Mrs. Hendrick Van Dyke, Alameda, California; Lloyd Wendt, Editor, *Chicago Today;* Walter Zervas, Catherine Lundell, John Baker, and other staff members of the New York Public Library, which offered the special facilities of the Frederick Lewis Allen Room for extended use.

THOMAS M. COFFEY

January, 1975

THE
LONG
THIRST

Chapter 1

Throughout the country it was a surprisingly sober night. The national binge which was widely expected did not take place. Even New York, a city prohibitionists considered the modern-day Gomorrah, was relatively sedate during the last hours of legal liquor on January 16, 1920. The weather there was so bitter that all but the serious debauchers chose to remain at home. The temperature had fallen below twenty degrees by nightfall and a high wind, which had intensified the cold, blew flurries of dry snow along the pavement.

Fortunately for the thirsty, most of them didn't have to go out. During the last several days (and especially since yesterday when federal judge John C. Knox ruled that all privately owned liquor in warehouses or safety deposit boxes would be subject to confiscation) New Yorkers had been stocking their cabinets and closets at home. Here, as in most other cities, the streets had been filled with cars, trucks, taxis, wagons, and even baby buggies, all carrying heavy loads of bottled goods. Pedestrians had burdened themselves with as much as they could lift. Liquor store shelves were picked so clean that few dealers had to worry about being caught at the midnight deadline with seizable goods.

As the midnight hour approached, the snowy streets of Manhattan were almost deserted and the one hundred enforcement officers under the command of New York's Revenue Service Agent, Col. Daniel Porter, were virtually idle. Their boss, oddly enough, had expected this. Colonel Porter was convinced he had the easiest job in town. "There will not be any violations to speak of," he had predicted. The penalties were so harsh (possible $1,000 fines and six-month jail sentences for first offenders) that he could not conceive of anyone risking arrest for the pleasure of a few drinks. It was beginning to look as if he might be right.

In the neighborhood saloons, scatterings of regular customers stood numbly in front of their beers, as if unable to comprehend that this was the last night they could rest their feet on the brass rails, cadge free sandwiches, or spit tobacco juice at the cuspidors. One well-known hostelry in lower Manhattan, Little Hungary, where Teddy Roosevelt used to drink, was much better attended than most saloons. A city alderman named Louis Zeltner presided over a series of toasts to many famous men who had drunk there and some who hadn't. At Healy's Restaurant in upper Manhattan, the proprietors conducted a wake and gave each customer a small casket as a memento of better days.

The bar of mid-Manhattan's Park Avenue Hotel offered a more elaborate funeral for John Barleycorn, which featured black-costumed, weeping girls and maudlin speeches before an audience at black-covered tables. When the theater crowd began drifting into the Broadway area hotels at about 11 P.M., many of the men were carrying their own bottles and flasks. They had already heard the sad news that the big hotels were out of liquor. At the Waldorf Astoria, the Claridge, and the McAlpin, only soft drinks were available.[1]

Across the nation, reaction to the new dry law was equally mild, perhaps because so many people had not yet absorbed the fact that they were forbidden ever to drink again. The president of New Jersey's Liquor Dealers' Protective League, Albert Illinger, told his local chapters on the sixteenth that he expected many states to nullify by special legislation the drastic provisions of federal prohibition. "Just as soon as Governor-elect Edward I. Edwards [of New Jersey] is inaugurated next Tuesday," Illinger wrote to his members, "a bill will be introduced to legalize the manufacture of beers, wines and liquors in the state." Partly on the strength of this assurance, members of the

Newark Retail Liquor Dealers Association voted to keep their establishments open and sell near beer (containing less than one-half of one per cent alcohol) until such a state law was passed.

Many Baltimore saloon keepers, unable to believe they were out of business, stayed open after the deadline but were not molested by enforcement authorities. An estimated four and a half million gallons of liquor were stored and sealed in Maryland warehouses as prohibition began. This volume might have been even greater were it not for the fact that three steamers had sailed out of Baltimore harbor in the last few days, heavily laden with whisky bound for Nassau in the Bahamas. The third ship, the *Lake Ellersie*, departed just a few hours before the midnight deadline, thus saving from impoundment a whisky cargo valued at $5½ million.

In Boston, drinking was heavy as usual but was not allowed to continue after midnight. Police visited hundreds of saloons and hotels at the closing hour to confiscate any liquor found on the tables. In Peoria, Illinois, which had called itself the "greatest distilling center in the world," the "liquor interests" were so reconciled to defeat that several large distilleries were already being converted into food processing plants. In St. Louis, thirteen breweries had closed, throwing three thousand workers out of jobs.

In hard-drinking San Francisco, prohibition enforcement officer Frank Silva tried to intimidate saloonkeepers by threatening to padlock for a whole year any establishment which sold liquor after midnight. Even before the deadline, he confiscated more than one thousand gallons of wine from retail stores. California vintners, however, did not intend to let him get away with this. Theodore Bell, an attorney representing wine interests, announced that several of his clients would invite prosecution to test the constitutional validity of prohibition.

In Los Angeles, where those who drank usually did so at home rather than in saloons, the streets were quiet on the last night before prohibition and there were only a few incidents. At a restaurant called Jim's Chowder House, an officer arrested a tourist couple he found drinking from a "near-beer" bottle after midnight. When the offenders were transported with the evidence to the nearest police station, a sergeant, assuming the officer had failed to see the word "near" on the bottle, dismissed them. Later, when the officer called in, the sergeant said to him, "It wasn't beer in that bottle."

"Of course it wasn't," the officer said. "It was whisky."[2]

In Chicago, most saloons, consistent with one of the city's honored traditions, remained open for some time after legal hours, even on January 16. Their last-night celebrations were quite tame, however, and only a few were planning to open their doors the next morning. It looked as if the saloonkeepers were bowing to fate. Chicago's mayor, William Hale Thompson, sometimes called "Big Bill," sometimes "Kaiser Bill" because of his pro-German, anti-British sympathies during the recent World War, was a dedicated wet, but at the moment he was diverted by a greater menace than prohibition. By coincidence, the League of Nations, President Woodrow Wilson's offspring, was holding its first meeting in Paris on January 16, and while no American delegate attended, there was still a possibility that the United States might join. Thompson was certain that League membership would be catastrophic to America. A staunch Republican, he had nevertheless broken with Republican Governor Frank Lowden of Illinois simply because Lowden, hoping for the party's 1920 presidential nomination, remained cagey about his opinion of the League.

"We all want to know," Thompson said when asked if he would support Lowden at the upcoming G.O.P. convention, "whether he is for America first, or whether like so many other statesmen, he is willing to subordinate the interests of his own country to the interests of three or four countries across the water. We want to know whether he will abide by the policy laid down by George Washington . . . which provides for friendly relations with all foreign powers and entangling alliances with none."

Faced by such a critical internationalist threat, Chicago's mayor had little time to worry about prohibition. Anyway, it was not the kind of issue a true Chicagoan would take seriously. The wartime prohibition law had inconvenienced very few Chicago drinkers, and even when Thompson himself, shortly after taking office in 1915, had ordered all saloons to close their doors on Sundays, no thirst went unslaked. Thompson's measure had been designed to please the churches rather than deprive the drinkers. When he ordered the saloonkeepers to close, they were aware that he meant only their front, not their back doors.

Chicago's police had more to do than arrest Sunday drinkers. The city's crime rate had increased 25 percent during 1919—a year in which there were six thousand burglaries, five thousand robberies, and nine thousand larcenies. If the police were so ineffective in suppressing serious crime, how could anyone ask them to stop people from drinking? And if they were unable, in their thousands, to keep the saloons closed one day a week, how could the federal government hope to keep them closed forever? It would be especially difficult since the prohibition bureau had assigned only 134 agents to stamp out liquor, not just in Chicago but in all of Illinois and Iowa plus part of Wisconsin. However diligent the federal government and the prohibitionists might be, Chicago was unlikely ever to go dry.

Less than an hour after the midnight prohibition deadline, there was evidence to support this assumption. At about 1 A.M. on the seventeenth, six masked men drove a truck into a south side freight yard, tied up the yardmaster and a watchman, herded six trainmen into a shanty, and made off with about $100,000 worth of whisky from two boxcars. It was a slick, professional robbery. Obviously some of Chicago's hoodlums viewed the onset of prohibition as a business opportunity.

The nation's smaller towns observed the end of legal liquor with more celebration in the churches than in the saloons. Thousands of Protestant churches held thanksgiving prayer meetings. To many of the people who attended, prohibition represented the triumph of America's towns and rural districts over the sinful cities. The biggest of these celebrations took place in the nation's biggest "small town," Washington, D.C., where the First Congregational Church was jammed with God-fearing, respectable, and prominent people, many of whom had been born in smaller communities. Under ordinary circumstances these people would have considered the hour of their meeting—midnight—almost indecent, especially since the meeting had been advertised as a "party." They were not the kind of people who indulged in midnight parties. But this was no ordinary occasion. Tonight at the stroke of twelve their most fervent prayers were to be answered, their most cherished ideal fulfilled. They were about to celebrate victory in a struggle which many of their grandparents and great-grandparents had first embraced in the early or middle nineteenth century, a struggle which their parents had intensified and they themselves had finally won. On this night, John Barleycorn was condemned to die. Demon Rum, already reeling back to the nether reaches from whence he came, was on strict notice never to return.

The United States of America, God's country, had finally seen God's light and banished all alcoholic liquor from its shores.

Most renowned of the celebrants on the dais at Washington's First Congregational Church was William Jennings Bryan, three times Democratic Presidential candidate, a devout, fundamentalist upholder of the Bible, and a fierce defender of America's rural or small-town values against the dangers of city license and sophistication. Bryan, the Great Commoner from Nebraska, the "silver-tongued" orator, would of course give the principal address, but there were others who would talk. Navy Secretary Josephus Daniels was ready to say a few words, as were Congressman Andrew Volstead of Minnesota, who had introduced and lent his name to the prohibition enforcement act; Anna Gordon, president of the Women's Christian Temperance Union, which had been fighting for prohibition since 1874; and Dr. Howard Russell, founder of the Anti-Saloon League, which, since 1895, had been more effective than any other group in combatting the "liquor interests."

Also on the platform was a tiny, insignificant-looking man with thinning hair and a thin, stubbly mustache. His name was Wayne B. Wheeler. He was not scheduled to speak, but he was already the most powerful man in the prohibition movement. As general counsel and national legislative superintendent of the Anti-Saloon League, Wheeler, more than any other man, was responsible for the strategy which inserted the liquor-banning Eighteenth Amendment into the U. S. Constitution and propelled the Volstead Act through Congress.

Though many in the crowd may have failed to recognize Wheeler, everyone on the platform knew him well. The League's now elderly founder, the Rev. Dr. Russell, had known him since 1893 when he hired him as an assistant in the war against "the devil's broth." Wheeler, who had been raised on a farm in Brookfield, Ohio, was then a student at Oberlin College. Russell, having just organized at Oberlin the first statewide temperance alliance, asked several professors to recommend a young man who might help him. When he told them the kind of person he wanted, they all suggested Wheeler, who was working his way through school as a part-time janitor. It was in the janitors' quarters at Oberlin that Russell located him. After that day in May, 1893, Wayne Wheeler had devoted his life to the cause of prohibition.

Congressman Volstead had reason to be grateful to Wheeler for the national prominence which had resulted when the prohibition enforcement law became known as the Volstead Act. Though Volstead had introduced the measure in Congress, Wheeler had been its principal author. After ratification of the eighteenth Amendment, January 16, 1919, the Anti-Saloon League had quickly undertaken to prepare an "adequate enforcement law" by combining the best features of the enforcement laws in the thirty-three states which already had some form of prohibition. As the League's general counsel, Wheeler had assumed the task of codifying these state laws into a consensus national law. "When the time came for introducing the proposed enforcement law in Congress," Wheeler later recalled, "Mr. Volstead, the Chairman of the House Judiciary Committee, was the logical man to sponsor the measure. He had been a member of the House for about sixteen years, had been prosecuting attorney of his county in Minnesota, which had voted dry, and had had practical experience in prosecuting bootleggers." Perhaps the audience tonight thought Volstead was the author of the law bearing his name, but Wayne Wheeler could have told them otherwise.[3]

One after another, the people on the platform rose and spoke, most of them keeping their remarks brief so that the loquacious Mr. Bryan could reach the rostrum to welcome prohibition the moment it was official. Shortly before midnight, a wave of excitement swept the hall as the considerable bulk of Mr. Bryan moved toward the podium. His belly was prominent; his grey hair, long in back, was sparse on top. But as he looked down at his audience, it was his eyes that held them. Bryan's zeal for whatever cause he espoused was so intense as to be almost hypnotic.

The clock struck twelve. He waited for the cheering to subside, then in his silver tones cried out, "They are dead that sought the child's life. They are dead! They are dead!"

No one was surprised at his quotation from scripture. Bryan knew the Bible almost word for word and constantly used it in his speeches. Earlier that day at the Presbyterian Church he had informed his listeners that "King Alcohol has slain more children than Herod ever did." He didn't cite figures. Tonight he enlightened his audience with precise statistics.

"Two and one half billion dollars are spent annually in this country on whisky and liquors," he said. "This is three times as much as is spent for education and five times as much as is spent for religion."

But, fortunately, all of this was now changing. As a result of prohibition, churches were receiving more generous collections and colleges were overflowing. Factories were running on a more efficient basis and industry was on a "competent plane."

For the better part of an hour he enlarged upon this theme. Bryan speeches were seldom short. But neither were they dull. Together with his beautiful voice he had an unfailing sense of drama and a command of colorful language. Despite the lateness of the hour, his listeners were still alert when he finally reached his conclusion. After asserting that Europe would be forced to recognize prohibition, since nations across the water would be unable to compete with a sober America, Bryan enlarged his horizons even beyond Europe.

"We must now carry to the world the new doctrine that has found such favor here," he demanded. "The revolution which rocked the foundation of this republic will be felt all over the earth. As we grow better and stronger through the good influences of prohibition, we will be in a position to give greater aid to the world."

Wayne Wheeler, a close friend of Bryan, could hardly disagree with these visionary words, but his current goals were more limited. Wheeler believed there was still much work to be done in America before the prohibitionists could safely turn their attention to Europe and the rest of the world. The Democratic Party, for instance, while solidly dry in the South and the rural West, was deplorably wet in the big cities of the North and East. There was danger in the cities, those bastions of cocktail-sipping intellectuals and guzzling foreigners—the Irish and their whisky, the Germans and their beer, the Italians, Jews, Greeks, French, and Spanish with their wines. Worst of all was New York, a seething mass of wet Democrats. Just two weeks earlier Wheeler had denounced New York in a statement quoting a poem by "an ex-Federal official." The poem succinctly summarized Wheeler's view of the nation's largest city: "Vulgar of manner, overfed, overdressed and underbred, heartless, Godless, Hell's delight, rude by day and lewd by night . . . ruled by boss and prostitute . . . raving, rotten, money-mad; a squirming herd of Mammon's men, a wilderness of human flesh crazed with avarice, lust and vice . . ."

Though not a very politic description, this was Wheeler's honest vision of New York and other large American cities, especially those in the Northeast. The immigrant minorities in these cities were mostly Catholics and Jews, few of whom were blessed with the reforming zeal of the country's Protestants. Prohibition had been from the start an essentially Protestant movement, inspired to some degree by the excessive drinking of the immigrant working classes.

Because there was little support for the "dry" cause among these minorities, and because most of the minority peoples were Democrats, Wheeler felt that despite the passage of the eighteenth Amendment, the Democratic Party still needed his full attention, especially in this presidential election year of 1920. As he congratulated Bryan after his speech, he was keenly aware of the Great Commoner's potential usefulness in this regard. Though Bryan, having failed three times in presidential bids, was not likely to be nominated a fourth time, he was likely to be the strongest single voice at the San Francisco Democratic convention in late June. Wheeler, despite his own unswerving Republicanism, had cultivated Bryan's friendship so diligently that there now existed between the two men what one of Wheeler's assistants called "a working partnership." When prohibition needed a persuasive spokesman at the highest Democratic levels, Wheeler turned to Bryan. It was through Bryan that Wheeler had convinced President Wilson, an undeclared wet, that it would be politically unwise for him to oppose openly the ratification of the Eighteenth Amendment. And it was through Bryan that Wheeler intended to work when the Democrats convened in June. He was confident he could count on Bryan, not only because the Peerless Leader was a dedicated prohibitionist, but also because he was secretly in the employ of the Anti-Saloon League. Wheeler's organization had filtered $11,000 to Bryan during the previous year, 1919.[4]

Wayne Wheeler was not alone in viewing New York City as the primary threat to the nation's permanent acceptance of prohibition. Millions of business and professional people, farmers and white-collar workers throughout the country (the prudent, diligent, mostly white Protestant folks whose descendants became the core of what is now called "Middle America"), looked with puritan distrust upon that eastern citadel of sin and sophistication. New York was a center of low life and high living, a mass of drunken immigrant poor, licentious rich, and radical atheist intellectuals. Even people who had never been there knew this to be so; their certainty was frequently confirmed by their pastors, local newspapers, traveling evangelists, and especially by such groups as the W.C.T.U., the Prohibition Party, and the Anti-Saloon League, which waged a continuing campaign to remind the people where the danger lay, where the battle was yet to be won.

The day before Wheeler quoted the poem disparaging New York City, the governor of New York state, Alfred E. Smith (a Roman Catholic from the city's Lower East Side slums) proposed in his New Year's message to the Legislature that the prohibition issue be submitted to a national referendum. Though Al Smith had never publicly admitted he was a wet (dry sentiment in upper New York state plus his own apparent aspirations toward the presidency would make such a declaration politically unwise), his oblique attacks on prohibition had removed all doubt about his feelings. He seemed unable to grasp the fact that the American people wanted prohibition. The Eighteenth Amendment had now been ratified by forty-six of the forty-eight states, including his own New York, thanks to the dry support outside the City. Only Rhode Island (a bastion of Catholicism) and Connecticut (a virtual adjunct of New York City) had refused to ratify it.

Because of New York's reluctance to surrender to the will of the American people, the Anti-Saloon League had installed its toughest, most aggressive field organizer as state superintendent there. He was a large, gruff, and abrasive Midwesterner named William H. Anderson. Born to Methodist parents in the small town of Carlinville, Illinois, near Springfield, in 1874, Anderson had earned a Bachelor of Science degree at Blackburn College, a local Presbyterian school, before studying law at the University of Michigan. His father was a lawyer, and Anderson had decided on a law career "because I had an idea it might be hard to be a lawyer and still be a consistent Christian, and I rather liked the idea of hard things." He never explained why, as the son of a Christian lawyer, he had developed such a cynical view of the legal profession. After winning his degree at Ann Arbor in 1896, he practiced law in his father's office for more than three years but declined a partnership to accept instead a post as attorney for the Illinois Anti-Saloon League. He decided that in doing so he was embracing the moral principles of a clergyman who was one of his teachers at Blackburn. "I never felt I was called into the ministry," he said later, "but I did feel a sense of call to this work utilizing my profession."[5]

After serving as the League's state superintendent in Illinois and Maryland, Anderson had come to New York in 1914 to accept what he regarded as the ultimate challenge to himself and to the League. He had established offices in the heart of Manhattan at 370 Seventh Avenue, then bought a home for his family in Yonkers. From the day of his arrival, League activity in New York rapidly expanded. Anderson soon became a powerful force in state politics and began to see himself as a permanent New Yorker despite his distaste for certain aspects of life there.

Anderson agreed with Wayne Wheeler that New York was the League's most important target and that Al Smith was prohibition's most dangerous enemy. Smith represented to him a combination of insidious sociopolitical forces—the Catholic Church and Tammany Hall. When Anderson took over the League's state leadership, he had "started out with the assumption . . . that Tammany was wholly and hopelessly pro-liquor, because the saloon was a large part of its political strength." Ignoring Tammany and its New York City stronghold, he had concentrated his initial efforts upstate, which largely explained why, in January 1919, New York had become the forty-fourth state to ratify the Eighteenth Amendment. In Anderson's subsequent report to the Anti-Saloon League, he had declared without undue modesty: "Ratification by New York was the hardest blow struck the liquor traffic. It destroyed forever the plea that it was not fair for small states to put national prohibition over the large states. . . . It was won by outguessing and outgeneraling the foe, by organization, by hard hitting and merciless fighting. . . . To win, it was necessary to build the greatest permanent Anti-Saloon League organization ever built in any state."

Anderson had not mentioned in the report all of the hard-hitting and merciless methods he had used. During the fall election campaign of 1914, for instance, he had become personally disenchanted with Speaker Thaddeus Sweet of the New York Assembly even though Sweet was a Republican and a prohibitionist. In an effort to defeat Sweet, he had hired a private detective to circulate in the Speaker's district (Oswego County) a letter designed to make voters think he had the support of the liquor interests. After investigating the letter, Sweet confronted Anderson at a public meeting and forced him to admit the whole scheme was a hoax. Though Anderson steadfastly denied he had anything to do with it personally, six persons filed affidavits to the contrary.[6] This incident, however, did nothing to impede Anderson's progress in developing "the greatest permanent

Anti-Saloon League organization ever built in any state."

His first battle with Al Smith had come in 1918 when Smith, in his initial campaign for the governorship, allowed a declaration against prohibition to appear in the state Democratic Party platform. That platform plank, Anderson later asserted, "made it possible to compel the Republicans in the Senate (where the margin was close) to caucus and make it a party issue." Thereafter, Anderson and Smith had clashed frequently, the most recent occasion occurring just after the Governor's New Year's proposal for a national prohibition referendum. Anderson had attacked the proposal so vigorously that Smith, on January 8, mischievously suggested the Republicans should run him for governor. "Anderson is the biggest man in the Republican Party in point of influence on prohibition," Smith declared, in an attempt to foment embarrassment for his opponents. He knew, of course, that Anderson, a man who exuded enormous energy but very little warmth, lacked popularity even among those Republicans over whom he wielded so much influence. Anderson, however, had not risen to the bait. With national prohibition approaching, he had ignored the governor's purposeful flattery to focus his efforts on another New York City target—a surprising one, the clergy.

On January 16, instead of traveling to Washington to celebrate victory with Wayne Wheeler and other colleagues, Anderson remained in Manhattan to issue from his office a broadside signed by one thousand pastors representing twenty-five denominations in every one of the state's fifty-seven counties outside New York City. It was, he assured the assembled reporters, "the most remarkable document ever addressed to the clergy of a great city."

According to the document, which Anderson had prepared and the out-of-town clergymen had signed, New York City was the "center of nullification and seditious activity designed to prevent the enforcement of the prohibition amendment."

Who was to blame for this? The Catholic and Jewish immigrant masses, no doubt, but they weren't Anderson's target today. On the eve of prohibition's ultimate victory, he ignored the enemy and goaded instead those slackers in his own ranks, New York City's sophisticated Protestant clergymen. His broadside noted significantly that the pulpits of the city's leading churches, even those which ostensibly opposed the liquor traffic, had seldom been opened to Anti-Saloon League speakers.

"We are compelled to believe," his statement concluded, "that the main reason why so many high-grade members of New York churches of prohibition denominations have not been in sympathy with the prohibition movement is because they have not, through their churches, been brought face to face with the facts and their responsibility."[7]

William Anderson, like Wayne Wheeler, was not deluded by victory. Situated as he was in the very "center of nullification and seditious activity," he saw his enemies all around him, even among his friends. He envisioned the enormity of the struggle ahead, and he was ready for it.

Isadore Einstein, a postal clerk living at 117 Ridge Street in Manhattan's Lower East Side with a wife, four children, and an aging father, awoke to the possibilities offered by the new prohibition law when he learned that enforcement agents were needed and that the job paid forty dollars per week. It seemed to him "a good chance for a fellow with ambition."

Stimulated by the prospect of so much money, Einstein hastened down to the U.S. Custom House across the street from Battery Park at Bowling Green, where the Southern New York division of the Federal Prohibition Bureau had opened offices. After filling out all the necessary forms and awaiting his turn in line, he was duly ushered into the presence of the new Chief Agent, James Shevlin, a man with several years experience in law enforcement.

Einstein soon became uncomfortably aware that Shevlin was looking him "up and down and in the middle"—the latter being his most prominent region. Izzy was five feet tall and at 225 pounds sported a perfect barrel of a belly, which looked as if it would hold even more than the beer barrels the job would require him to seek out and confiscate.

Finally, Shevlin shook his head in rejection. "You're not the type," he said.

"Why not?" Izzy Einstein wanted to know.

"Because you don't look like a detective."

That was exactly why he should be hired, Einstein insisted. "There might be some advantage in not looking like a detective. I could fool people better."[8]

Shevlin obviously didn't want to be impolite but he was a busy man and getting busier each day. His office, still badly understaffed with fewer than two hundred agents, needed help, not laughs. This round little man might be amusing but what could one do with him? "What do you know about detective work?" Shevlin asked. "Have you had any training in that line? Any experience?"

"I'm a postal clerk," Einstein said. "But I used to be a salesman, behind a counter and out on the road. I've never been a detective but I do know something about people, their ways and habits, how to mix with them and gain their confidence."

Though limited in education, Izzy Einstein proved quickly that he was far from stupid. He talked fast and convincingly, pressing home his arguments without giving Shevlin time to reject them. Prohibition had created a new situation which would demand a new kind of detective, he insisted. Finding liquor law violators would be a different game from tracking down thieves and murderers. "Maybe a type like me that would never be spotted as a sleuth," he suggested, "could get results that the regular plainclothesmen couldn't."

Before he finished talking he proved he knew something about people and how to gain their confidence. He had gained so much of Shevlin's confidence that he was hired on the spot. But some of the pleasure he took in his adventurous, new-found job was dissipated when he told his family about it. "Is that any business for the father of four children?" his wife asked. And his father, already disappointed that his son was a postal clerk, became "more disappointed than ever that I wasn't a rabbi."

After this dampening of his spirits, Izzy Einstein approached his first assignment with more fear than enthusiasm. The establishment to which he was sent was a Brooklyn workingmen's saloon which the prohibition authorities believed was selling liquor even though several agents had failed in attempts to buy drinks there. Einstein, instead of walking right into the place, sized it up from across the street. The neighborhood was rundown, so was the old saloon, and so were the men going in and out. Realizing it would be useless to walk in wearing his business suit, overcoat, and gray felt hat, he went home and put on the shabbiest outfit he owned, omitting collar and tie. When he returned to Brooklyn, another man, in working clothes, was entering the saloon. Izzy walked in behind him, wiping his face with a soiled handkerchief. Approaching the bar, he asked for a near beer.

The bartender grinned. "Would you like a lollipop on the side?" The other customers, many with drinks in front of them, began to laugh. Izzy joined in the laughter.

"I'm a stranger," he said, "and I don't know the ropes nowadays in strange places. But just to prove I'm no near-beer piker, I'll buy a pint of whisky—if it's not too expensive."

The bartender produced the pint. Izzy Einstein produced his badge, and a few moments later he had made his first arrest as a prohibition agent.

William S. McCoy, once a mate on Caribbean steamers, now his brother's partner in a Jacksonville, Florida boatyard, gazed idly at their docks as he worried about recent business reverses. Tall, lean, muscular, and physically powerful after twenty years at sea, he was a commanding figure, well known and highly respected along the Florida coast. Like the boats he and his brother built, he was noted for his dependability.

McCoy heard a car engine behind him and turned to watch the approach of "a shiny roadster only a little smaller than a locomotive." He did not immediately recognize the man who stepped down from the running board. Only a few months earlier, the fellow had been "a scrawny brown fisherman in faded dungarees." Now he wore a checked suit, yellow bow tie, and a diamond stickpin in his shirt. Though only casual acquaintances, the two men were on familiar terms.

"Hey, Bill," the prosperous-looking motorist said, "want to make some money?"

McCoy, after admiring the expensive car, admitted that he did indeed want to make some money. "It's one of my chief aims in life," he said.[9]

The McCoy boatyard had done well until the previous season. Bill and his brother, Ben, had built large yachts for such wealthy clients as steelmaker Andrew Carnegie, store-owner John Wanamaker, the beautiful actress Maxine Elliot, who was rumored to be J. P. Morgan's mistress, and several members of the Vanderbilt family. Carnegie had often fished from the end of the pier with the McCoys' father, a retired Philadelphia bricklayer. The two bewhiskered old men dangling their feet together, similar as twins, looked like a pair of retired Scottish sea captains, which indeed the elder McCoy might well have been if he had been educated for it. During the Civil War he had served in the Union navy, sailing on several of the ships used to blockade Southern ports. Always in love with the sea, he had imparted this love to both of his sons. One of them, Bill, had taken two years of cadet training on the Pennsylvania state school ship, *Saratoga,* graduating first in his class to begin his long career in the merchant marine. The other, Ben, had founded the boatyard after the family moved from Philadelphia to Florida in 1900. When Bill gave up the sea, the two became partners, then launched motorboat services on inland waterways from Jacksonville to Palm Beach and from Palm Beach through the Everglades to Fort Myers. They invested heavily and their company prospered. Then someone else launched motor bus services along the same routes. The buses were faster and cheaper than boats. The McCoy brothers were soon out of the transportation business, and though they still owned the boatyard, they were in such financial difficulties that Bill was eager to listen when his visitor mentioned money.

"How would a hundred dollars a day sound to you?" the man asked.

McCoy was incredulous. "You ought to lay off the liquor," he said.

The man laughed. "Liquor," he said, "is just what I want to talk to you about."

Since there were other people standing around the docks, the flashy ex-fisherman took McCoy by the arm and walked him far enough to make sure they would not be overheard. Though America was now dry, the Bahamas in the British West Indies were still wet, he pointed out, and the warehouses of Nassau, only 190 miles from Miami, were bulging with salable liquor. As it happened, he had a contract to carry a load of rye whisky from Nassau to Atlantic City, and he also had a schooner available. All he needed was a skipper, an honest skipper. There weren't many trained schooner captains in Florida, and there were even fewer dependable ones. He knew McCoy could handle a schooner, and he also knew McCoy was a man he could trust. Everyone who had ever dealt with Bill McCoy agreed on that.

"One hundred dollars a day, Bill," the man repeated.

It was a powerfully attractive fee. Bill McCoy wondered where the catch might be. "Let's see your ship," he said.

They drove in the big, shiny roadster to a dock where a seventy-foot schooner, the *Dorothy W.,* was berthed. Bill McCoy gazed at the vessel in silence. A veteran and expert builder as well as sailor, he looked at boats the way he looked at women. To him, as to many sailors, a ship was a person, a "she" with an independent personality. And as in the case of women, there were some ships McCoy liked, others he might "learn to trust," and others he would "suspect on sight."

The *Dorothy W.* was one of the latter. He found her drab and shabby. Even her best days could not have been glorious and she was far beyond them. Convinced that he and she would "never get along together," he turned her down, declined the chance to become her skipper.

He did not put from his mind, however, the opportunity a better vessel might offer. Back at the boatyard, he talked earnestly to his brother, Ben. They were not yet broke. They still owned several small boats. If Bill were to sell them, he might have enough money to invest in a large one. The next day he began looking for buyers. And when he had sold every boat he owned, he would begin looking for sellers. As soon as he could find what he wanted, Bill McCoy was going back to sea as the captain of his own ship.

Throughout the day of February 5, 1920, snow piled up along the eastern seaboard and New York City floundered under the worst winter storm since 1905. Trains and buses stopped as the icy streets filled higher and higher with cold, fine, drifting snow. There were few cars and trucks to be seen; even the horse-drawn wagons had trouble making their deliveries. At the executive mansion in Albany, where the snow was also falling, Governor Alfred E. Smith announced he was not feeling well. Nothing serious, just a slight indisposition. It didn't make him feel any better to know he was expected in Manhattan that night at a fundraising dinner to honor Democratic National Committee chairman Homer S. Cummings. Though Cummings was a good friend, it was no fit day for the 150-mile train ride down to the city, especially since the train might not make it. The snow was getting deeper by the hour. This would be a good night to stay inside where it was warm, perhaps enjoy a toddy or a bit of Scotch before dinner with the family.

Al Smith didn't hesitate to take a drink when he felt like it. Even with prohibition in force, he saw no reason to give up his customary cocktails with friends or family.[10] He was simply unable to reconcile himself to prohibition. It seemed to him a flagrant curtailment of the personal liberty which had made the United States so attractive to the poor and oppressed of other countries, the same liberty which had prompted his own Irish grandparents to endure sixty harsh days on the north Atlantic to reach New York in 1841. Politically it might be prudent for him to soften his continuing opposition to the Eighteenth Amendment, especially since he already had national ambitions. If he were to expose himself openly as the leader of the wet forces, his presidential chances could be damaged badly in the dry sections of the country. But on this issue his feelings were so strong that they threatened to nullify his political instincts.

Abandoning his intention to appear at the banquet in Manhattan, the Governor prepared a message to be read to the diners in his name. Because prohibition was very much on his mind, it became the principal subject of the message. "Do not forget," he wrote, "the time-honored Democratic doctrine that the government is most effective which governs the least. This precept of Democratic faith in the recent past has been grievously and wilfully sinned against, when in the name of Democracy there was imposed upon a hundred million free people, without asking their direct consent, a restriction to their personal liberty which Russia in her palmiest days never dreamt of."

Despite the snow, more than a thousand New York Democrats showed up at the Hotel Commodore that night to honor Homer Cummings, their suburban neighbor from Connecticut, and to hear Governor Smith's message. They also heard a speech by the new Democratic governor of New Jersey, Edward Edwards, who attacked prohibition on the altogether different grounds that it violated the sovereign rights of individual states.

"If the federal government may subvert the doctrine of state rights and without a mandate from the people enter into our homes," he said, "the theory of constitutional government and all the rights incident to home rule and local state government are destroyed."

His audience may have been surprised to hear a northern Democrat so passionately invoke state rights, a concept much more dear to Southern Democrats, whose states had lost some of their rights after the Civil War. Governor Edwards apparently hoped to foment dampness in the predominantly dry South by convincing southerners that prohibition threatened to erode further their state sovereignty, which most of them cherished even more than the dry movement.

Wayne Wheeler, reading his morning paper in Washington the next day, was instantly aroused by the account of the Democratic banquet in Manhattan. When the urban governors of New York and New Jersey openly attacked the Eighteenth Amendment at a dinner for one of suburban Connecticut's favorite sons (who was also chairman of the Democratic National Committee), they could not be ignored. Especially Al Smith. He was the real enemy and had to be answered immediately. Before noon, Wayne Wheeler had a statement in the hands of the press.

The remarks of Governors Smith and Edwards, he said, were evidence that "the work of Americanization and the appeal to patriotism must extend beyond the ranks of aliens within our borders." These were strangely obscure words from a man who usually spoke bluntly and specifically. He apparently meant to say that when even such well established people as state governors could unpatriotically attack the Eighteenth Amendment, it proved that the "aliens within our borders" were not the only people who needed Americanization. Perhaps out of a sense of delicacy, Wheeler refrained from saying who these "aliens within our borders" might be. In the remainder of his statement against the errant governors, he expressed himself with his usual clarity:

> Personal liberty never was guaranteed to the citizens of any civilized government. Civil liberty is guaranteed. . . . The state rights doctrine was settled once for all during the Civil War. To invoke it now to nullify the 18th Amendment is inexcusable. Those who are responsible for it will be characterized in the future as Andrew Jackson described those who attempted to nullify the federal laws in his day, in these words: "These will only be remembered to be held up to scorn by everyone who loves our glorious Constitution and a Government of laws."

Wheeler was making it absolutely clear to Al Smith that if the governor of New York was spoiling for a fight, the Anti-Saloon League was ready for him.

A poor but ambitious cab driver named Larry Fay was cruising the streets of Manhattan in quest of fares when he was flagged by a man who wanted to be driven to Montreal, a distance of about 385 miles. Fay was interested. Since he owned his cab he didn't have to get permission to travel that far. And the tip should be big. The man was flashing a roll of bills. Fay was a dreamer, always yearning for the lucky strike that would someday make him rich, but he was also a hustler, on the lookout for any extra buck that might come his way today.

As a kid growing up in the tough slums of Hell's Kitchen on the West Side, he had learned the value of money from its scarcity, and he had done some things to get hold of it that he wouldn't want to discuss with the police. The only kind of respectable job he had been able to find—wrapping bundles—had been hardly profitable enough, so he had abandoned it to become a fringe member of a West Side gang, and had turned to less gentle pursuits. While he had never been accused of any serious violence, having no stomach for murder, he had come to believe in the efficacy of physical persuasion. It was due to his shrewdness and prudence that, despite his gang activities, most of his forty-four arrests had been for minor traffic violations; only one, in 1915, had been for assault (he was cleared), and only four for disorderly conduct, a term sometimes used as a legal euphemism for gang fights. These offenses had cost him three small fines. He had never served a jail sentence.[11]

Fay was six feet, three inches tall, quick on his feet and quick with his tongue. He still got into his share of scrapes, yet he had much more imagination than one would expect from a common thug. Unburdened by scruples, he kept looking for some big opportunity to make a fortune. The luckiest strike of his life so far had been a bet on a horse at Belmont Park two years before—a 100-to-1 shot named Scotch Verdict that made him "rich" enough to buy his own taxicab. Now, at the age of thirty-one, owning his own cab, he was still making only twenty-five dollars per week. On just this one trip to Montreal he might make that much. After hesitating long enough to assess his passenger's roll of bills, Larry Fay sped north on the first of what would turn out to be many trips to Canada.

In Montreal, having collected his fare and dropped his passenger, he got out of his cab long enough to do some window shopping. Whisky, he noticed, was selling for ten dollars a case. And it was good whisky. With prohibition now in force, how much could he hope to get for a case of whisky in New York? Much more than ten dollars.

He was certain of that. He was not a heavy drinker and he was hardly affluent enough ever in his life to have owned a whole case of whisky. He had never been very interested in it, but at ten dollars a case he now developed an interest. Taking out of his pocket twenty dollars he had received from his long-distance passenger, he invested it in two cases—twenty-four bottles which he sequestered in the trunk and under the seats of his cab.

At the U. S. border on his return trip he had no trouble. Prohibition was so recent that neither the Canadian nor the American officials were worried about people using Canada as a source of liquor. Larry Fay was soon back in Manhattan with his two cases of good Canadian whisky. As a cab driver, he was acquainted with several establishments that might be interested in buying it from him. But how much could he hope to get for it? He quickly found out. Eighty dollars per case.[12] As soon as he could turn himself around, Fay was on his way back to Canada. He was no longer just a cab driver. He was becoming a businessman.

New York state Anti-Saloon League superintendent William H. Anderson, after more than a week in bed with the flu, answered a phone call from the New York *Times* on March 4 to find himself in a potentially embarrassing situation. A Presbyterian minister in the tiny town of Carlisle, about thirty-five miles west of Albany, had told a *Times* reporter an elaborately detailed story about the inner workings of the state A.S.L.[13] The clergyman, Rev. William H. Freeman, had taken a job as a fundraiser for the League three months earlier, but said he had left it after ten days "because everyone connected with the League seemed to be money-mad and far more worried about their personal financial returns than about the success of their movement." Reverend Freeman told of a meeting he had attended in Anderson's New York City office about Christmastime. Rumors were circulating among the staff of fifty or sixty men that the triumph of prohibition would diminish the need for fundraising and thereby put some of them out of jobs.

"They were desperately worried," he said, "until William H. Anderson came in and pacified them. He told them there would be more work for them than ever before. He said that law enforcement would require more money and effort for years to come than the campaign which led to the adoption of the amendment had done."

League fundraisers, Reverend Freeman disclosed, were given small weekly salaries (thirty dollars in his case) but made most of their money on commissions from what they collected. He told in detail how they were instructed to organize their speeches, building steadily toward the climactic moment of consecration when the audience would be asked to contribute. Among the fundraisers, Freeman said, this consecration was called "coin-secration," and sometimes "coin-secretion."

At the meeting in Anderson's office, he said, someone asked the superintendent to explain what was described as his "meat-axe" method of getting results "by violent personal abuse and by attempting to bring scorn and contempt on recalcitrant legislators and ministers."

As Reverend Freeman remembered it, Anderson's reply was that he used the "meat-axe" method because it was effective. But he warned his followers against trying to imitate him. He urged them to be suave and sweet in their deportment, and leave the "meat-axing" to him.

Anderson, still feeling weak from influenza, realized as he heard Reverend Freeman's story that he could not ignore it. That was his usual way of handling criticism of the League or himself, but it wouldn't work if this man had actually been associated with the League. While Anderson could not remember him, it was apparent that Freeman must at one time have been on the staff. Whoever he was, he had caught onto the "meat-axe" method all too well.

Anderson knew various ways of dealing with troublemakers like Reverend Freeman. He could say he had never met the man. He could argue that no one who had worked for the League only ten days could have more than a superficial understanding of its operations. Or he could refute the man's story point by point. But to do the latter would be to invite a public debate with Freeman, a debate Freeman couldn't lose because he would only have to keep enlarging his charges, while Anderson couldn't win because he would be continually on the defensive. He could also, of course, launch a campaign discrediting Freeman, but that would be meaningless. Nobody knew Freeman or cared about him.

The way to deal with such a man, as Anderson knew, was to shrug him off briefly in the most general terms, point out that you were too busy with other important matters to be bothered with him, then mount an offensive against a more significant target, an offensive so dramatic as to make people forget Reverend Freeman. Since the *Times* was pressing Anderson to answer Freeman, he prepared a statement, wording it carefully:

> I have no recollection of this man. We employ many people and if they don't make good, we drop them. I don't know that the Rev. Mr. Freeman is one of those that we have dropped. From the general tenor of his remarks I should say that he takes himself too seriously. According to his own statements he was with the League a very short time and he is hardly an expert witness. . . .
>
> It is true that we are continuing the fight and our expenses are somewhat greater today than they were before the prohibition amendment was adopted. That is because the fight is still on in this state. . . .

He went on to acknowledge that the League did solicit contributions house to house but said it still worked basically through the churches. As for the kind of people who contributed, he knew of no offerings from soft-drink manufacturers or others "who might have a pecuniary interest" in prohibition:

> We have more than 100,000 contributors [in New York state]. We spent in the fiscal year ended last April about $250,000. The total for the present year will probably be about $300,000. Our financial statements have been given to the press every year and widely printed. Everything we have done has been perfectly open and honest.
>
> As for the theory that we may try to run the country [Freeman had also speculated that the League envisioned a "dictatorship" over the whole nation], the man is drawing on his imagination. We are interested in the fight against alcohol only. When our victory is complete in this country, we expect to give some attention to the fight abroad. That is necessary for self-protection. But if alcohol was once completely out of the way, we would be done.

Having thus dispensed with the obscure Reverend Freeman, Anderson was able to concentrate on a much larger, more conspicuous enemy. As it happened, he had written, on March 3, a private letter, not intended for publication, to the Protestant pastors of New York state. The letter said in part:

The time has come to be very frank: The Anti-Saloon League has never been anti-Catholic and it does not intend to begin. But that fact is no reason why we should keep silent when wet Catholics muss into the prohibition situation. . . . We believe most of the officiary of the Roman Catholic Church in this state are indignant over what they consider a Protestant victory for prohibition, and more because of the unenviable light in which the Catholic Church hereabouts is left without having had a larger part in this greatest reform of the country although they had a chance to get into it here the same as elsewhere, and are in sympathy with the Tammany efforts to destroy that victory and bring back the saloons for purposes respecting which your guess is just as good as mine.

The New York newspapers, having learned of this letter, published lengthy excerpts from it in their Sunday, March 6 editions, yet both Sunday and Monday passed and no responsible Catholic offered a reply. By Tuesday noon, at which time Anderson was scheduled to address the Methodist Ministers' Association of New York at their building on lower Fifth Avenue, it was beginning to look as if the Catholics were exercising a disciplined conspiracy to ignore him. Either emboldened or frustrated by their silence, Anderson was prepared to test their discipline.

He began speaking without notes to the five hundred Methodist clergymen, but as soon as he finished his preliminary remarks, he took up a prepared text, copies of which were handed out to reporters. After asserting the function of the Anti-Saloon League in guarding prohibition against those who might attack it, he said:

There is a certain element in the Catholic Church which everyone knows is in politics up to its neck, but which most people have been afraid to say anything about because they are expert in muddying the water by claiming that the Church itself has been attacked. . . . I never have and never shall make any statement that any unprejudiced person can fairly call anti-Catholic. But I will not keep quiet about Catholics who ought to be shown up just for fear I will be falsely accused of an attack upon the Church.

Anderson then undertook to "show up" one of the country's most prominent Catholic bishops, James Cardinal Gibbons of Baltimore, who had been quoted as saying in New Orleans four days earlier that the dry law was a menace and that Congress should legalize the sale of light wines and beer.[14]

The suggestion of the Cardinal to do this and yet maintain the spirit of the prohibition amendment does not obscure the fact that his proposal is nullification because beer is an intoxicating liquor, nor obscure the fact that this is the program of the brewers and would result in bringing back the saloon. . . . In the light of the specific declaration of Cardinal Gibbons for beer and wine it is no wonder that the Catholic Archbishop of New York [Patrick J. Hayes] declined to deny the statement that the Catholic Church in New York is in sympathy with Tammany in its program of repeal and its brazenly announced purpose of nullification pending repeal.

As Anderson spoke, he was repeatedly interrupted by applause. When he finished, the Methodist Ministers unanimously passed a resolution endorsing him and the Anti-Saloon League.

Within a few hours, shortly after the evening newspapers reported his latest remarks, Anderson finally heard from the Catholics. Archbishop Hayes, from his residence on Madison Avenue behind St. Patrick's Cathedral, issued a short statement which said:

While yielding to many pressing demands for a statement on the slanderous attack of the leader of the Anti-Saloon League on the Catholic Church, I feel that, in taking notice of it, I should apologize, first of all, for not leaving the matter to the decent sentiment of New York, which long since has passed judgment on this zealot, his tongue and his methods. . . .

My sole anxiety is that a single person, in or out of the Catholic Church, may be possibly deceived by this sinister figure in American politics, a sower of strife, who sinks so low as to play the un-American role of a brewer of bigotry. . . .

I repeat my public statement of a former occasion that the Catholic Church preaches and practices conscientious obedience to every law, and does not discriminate in favor of one more than another. The Church further demands that law be obeyed, whether we like it or not. Not so Mr. Anderson, who possesses and stresses the Eighteenth Amendment because he wants it observed and is paid for so doing. He seems but little concerned about other fundamental laws guaranteeing personal liberty, protection against unlawful search and seizure, religious freedom, free speech, free press and free legislature.

If Archbishop Hayes was hoping William Anderson would be chagrined or restrained by this harsh personal criticism, the prelate was deceiving himself. Anderson liked attention so well he didn't ask that it be favorable. Many years later he recalled, "I probably made more explosive statements . . . than any hundred others of the Anti-Saloon League fellows. It was kind of left to me to do that sort of thing because it didn't seem to bother me much."[15]

Chapter 2

In his second floor office at 167 North Clark Street in Chicago's Loop, attorney George Remus, one of the city's more prominent and successful criminal lawyers, studied the Volstead Act sentence by sentence and phrase by phrase. He had almost memorized it now. It was a law which had fascinated him since its inception.

Though Remus had earned fame as a trial lawyer (during his first year of practice, 1901, he had represented defendants in eighteen murder cases), he had begun in recent years to feel more strain than excitement in handling criminal matters, especially those which involved capital offenses. It was difficult to keep facing one trial after another in which the stakes for one's client were life or death. Despite a high average of acquittals, Remus had seen enough of his clients hanged to become a crusader against the scaffold at Joliet State Prison. He was an active member of the Anti-Capital Punishment Society.

A son of German parents who had immigrated in 1881 when he was five years old, Remus had grown up in Chicago, where his father had found a job as a lumber scorer. At the age of 14, young George, though a good student, had to quit school and help support the family because his father was incapacitated by rheumatism. He went to work for an uncle who owned a drugstore at Milwaukee and Chicago Avenues on the northwest side, and when his uncle decided to sell the business five years later, George contrived to buy it, procuring a pharmacist's license for himself by passing the required examination and lying about his age. He was then nineteen. During the next five years, he bought a second drugstore a mile and a half from the first one, studied optometry, and earned a certificate which qualified him for limited practice. He also had an affair with a customer in one of his stores, married her, and fathered a baby daughter, decided to become a lawyer, finished a three-year law course in eighteen months of night school, and was admitted to the Illinois bar in late 1900. His legal practice had developed so steadily that by 1920 he was earning about $50,000 a year. But his marriage had failed three years earlier as a result of a relationship he had developed with a young divorcee working in his office, and he was no longer content with his success as a Chicago criminal lawyer. He was ready to try something new.[1]

Remus' sensitivity about his clients was not the only factor in his decision to abandon his law practice. His rapid rise from poverty and obscurity had given him such a taste for money and success that he wanted more. As compared to the great fortunes other men had amassed in the Land of Opportunity, his $50,000 a year looked puny. He was too ambitious, restless, and adventurous to be content with the security he had earned. Had he been born fifty or seventy-five years earlier, he might have gone west to pursue, in the gold fields or on the cattle ranges, the great American dream of sudden wealth. By 1920, however, with the frontier eliminated and the country developed from coast to coast, a man who still envisioned quick riches had to watch for an opportunity others might miss, then pursue that opportunity quickly, ingeniously, relentlessly.

To Remus, prohibition offered just such an opportunity. He had become interested in it because several of his clients who were now bottleggers seemed to be getting the better of the new law. Some of them had already made astonishing sums of money even though they were small operators compared to such famous hoodlums as Big Jim Colosimo and Johnny Torrio on the South Side. Yet Remus did not regard any of his bootlegger clients as intelligent individuals. If men of such limited capacity could pile up small fortunes after only three or four months in the illegal liquor business, then prohibition must surely offer much greater opportunities for an intelligent man. There might even be a way to beat the law without disobeying it. Pursuing this possibility, Remus had begun his first close reading of the Volstead Act.

In Title II, Section 3, there was a provision which immediately caught his eye: ". . . nothing in this act shall prohibit the purchase and sale of warehouse receipts covering distilled spirits on deposit in government bonded warehouses, and no special tax liability shall attach to the business of purchasing and selling such warehouse receipts."

This insertion had been designed to deal with the vast reserves of liquor already manufactured and on hand when the law went into effect. Since there was no provision for the destruction of such liquor, the law had to acknowledge its existence as property. If properly registered, it could not be confiscated. It had to be impounded in government warehouses, where it remained the possession of its owner. Would he then have the right to sell it, even though he could not move it? All property law indicated he would retain that right, and few prohibitionists were in favor of tampering with property laws. To avoid even the suggestion of doing so, they had included this provision in the law making warehouse receipts negotiable.

When Remus read section three, it quickly became apparent to him that despite prohibition, he could buy unlimited amounts of bonded liquor. He would then need only to find a legal way of getting this liquor out of the government warehouses and into circulation. In Title II, Section 6, he discovered what appeared to be an ideal way. This section provided first that no one could manufacture, sell, purchase, transport, or prescribe any liquor without obtaining a permit from the Commissioner of Internal Revenue, but secondly, that any person could buy and use liquor "for medicinal purposes" when prescribed by a physician.

Though these provisions were intended to discourage the medicinal use of alcoholic beverages by requiring a permit for the seller and a prescription for the buyer, Remus saw in them a singular opportunity. Since doctors were allowed to prescribe liquor, their patients had to have places to buy it. Where else but in drugstores, now that the saloons were gone? Wholesale withdrawal permits, then, were likely to be limited to wholesale drug companies, which meant that if a man wanted a safe, legal way to go into the liquor business on a large scale, he should go into the drug business. If he wished to operate on an even larger scale, he should also go into the distillery business, since much of the liquor stored in government warehouses was owned by now-inoperative distilleries. If one owned both distilleries and drug companies, one could become both buyer and seller, a circumstance which would offer excellent discretionary opportunities in bookkeeping, distribution, and other business methods.

Thanks to the prosperity of his law practice, Remus still had about $100,000 in the bank, even after settling $50,000 on his ex-wife and $30,000 on their daughter. In addition, he still had working for him the young divorcee for whom he had dissolved his marriage, thirty-one-year-old Mrs. Imogene Holmes. As intelligent as she was attractive, Mrs. Holmes took more than an ordinary employee's interest in Remus' business affairs. She was his confidante and adviser as well as his lover. He had often discussed with her the possibilities offered by loopholes in the Volstead Act.

He asked her seriously now if she was ready to uproot herself from Chicago (she lived in suburban Evanston) and move with him to Cincinnati. She was aware of his reason for considering Cincinnati. He had calculated that 80 percent of the bonded whisky in the United States was stored in government-controlled warehouses within three hundred miles of this southern Ohio city.

She assured him she would gladly go with him to Cincinnati. Their relationship had now endured for three years and he could hardly doubt that she loved him. In her mind, however, were certain unavoidable considerations. Like Remus, she too had a daughter, Ruth, who was now thirteen years old. As long as they were living in Evanston, the child could be kept reasonably remote from her mother's relationship with Remus in Chicago. But if Imogene were to accompany Remus to Cincinnati, Ruth would have to go with them. And that would be awkward unless, of course, their relationship were to be regularized. If Remus wanted the help and comfort of Imogene Holmes in his new venture, he might have to marry her.

Big Jim Colosimo, his impressive bulk half hidden by expensive tailoring, emerged with his bride of a month from the mansion he had bought her across the street from the Lake Meadows at 3156 Vernon

Avenue, and after giving her a goodbye kiss, got into the back seat of his limousine. He had already explained to her that he had to take care of a business matter.[2]

Would he send the car back, his wife asked, so that she and her mother could go shopping?

He said he would. He was willing to do almost anything for this ex-choir girl, half his age and less than half his size. He had hired her to sing in his restaurant seven years earlier and shortly thereafter had made her his mistress, but she had wanted more, and this spring he had finally divorced his wife of eighteen years to marry her. Upon their recent return from an Indiana honeymoon, he had even invited her mother to live with them.

Colosimo was now the unrivaled first lord of the Levee, Chicago's celebrated saloon and brothel district in the South Side's first ward. When he met his first wife, in 1902, he was a young, virile, but impoverished thug; she was a dumpy, middle-aged brothel-keeper. Within a short time, he was manager of her brothel, owner of another one, and monthly collector from several colleagues for the first ward's most distinguished statesmen, Aldermen Bathhouse John Coughlin and Michael Hinky Dink Kenna.

In 1909, by which time Colosimo owned a modest chain of brothels, he had made a move that appeared now to be the most astute of his entire life. He had imported from Brooklyn a new business manager, thirty-one-year-old Johnny Torrio who, in addition to being his nephew, was one of the most intelligent young men in the New York underworld. Torrio had vastly expanded Colosimo's operations and managed them so wisely that Big Jim was soon a multimillionaire and a more powerful figure in the Levee than even Bathhouse John and Hinky Dink. Since 1915, when Big Bill Thompson became mayor, Big Jim had ruled the first ward, not only because he could deliver both the Italian vote and the saloon-brothel vote, but because he had been quick to reach an understanding with Republican Thompson while retaining his friendship with Democrats Coughlin and Kenna. Both he and his nephew, Torrio, were life members of the William Hale Thompson Republican Club and substantial contributors whenever Thompson called for donations, which he frequently did, to feed his personal as well as his political treasure chest.

With the profits from his brothels, Colosimo had opened in 1910 the cafe at 2126 South Wabash Avenue which bore his name and which had vastly increased his fame. It was here he had met Dale Winter, the girl who was now his bride. When she came to audition for him, he had found this blue-eyed brunette choir singer so beautiful he was ready to hire her before even hearing her sing. She soon became the darling of his patrons, among whom were the most famous people in Chicago as well as the most infamous, plus many of the stage, screen, opera, and sports celebrities who visited the city. In 1917 Colosimo left his wife and began living openly with his protegée. Torrio, who was himself a strict and faithful Roman Catholic husband as well as a ruthless brothel manager, had argued against Colosimo's abandonment of his wife. "Well, it's your funeral," he had finally said to his lovesick uncle.

Colosimo's sin, however, did not seem to stand between the two men. Even now, after Big Jim had divorced his wife and married Dale Winter, Torrio continued to manage his expanding interests. Prohibition had brought complications but it had also brought vast opportunities in bootlegging, a business they had been quick to enter. It was a bootlegging matter that today pulled Colosimo away from his bride. Torrio had called to tell him that two truckloads of whisky would arrive at the café at exactly 4 P.M. this afternoon. Could he be there to receive it?

Big Jim could hardly refuse his nephew's request. Torrio had been doing almost all of the work lately. Colosimo owed it to him to show some interest in their operations. If one of them had to be at the café to check in the whisky, he would go.

His chauffeur dropped him at the north entrance to the café, then headed back to pick up Dale and her mother. When Colosimo entered the building, it looked deserted, like any other restaurant in midafternoon. He walked past the huge mahogany bar, through the green-velvet-walled, crystal-chandeliered main dining room and an equally opulent overflow room, and entered his office at the rear where his chef and secretary were discussing the menu. He asked them if there had been any calls and seemed surprised, even disturbed, when they had none to report. After calling his lawyer but failing to reach him, he talked for a while to his two employees, then left the office.

He walked through the overflow dining room adjacent to the office and into the restaurant's vestibule, toward a phone booth across from the cloakroom. He was facing the door of the phone booth when a gunman emerged from the cloakroom and fired two shots at him. One bullet missed, imbedding itself in the opposite wall, but the other entered Colosimo's head behind his right ear and came out the other side. He died before any of his employees could reach him.

Among the thirty or more suspects questioned by the police were his nephew, Johnny Torrio, and a young man Torrio had recently imported from Brooklyn to act as his assistant and bodyguard—Al Brown, as he was sometimes known, or Al Capone. Both Torrio and Capone were able to prove they were elsewhere when Colosimo was shot. As it happened, one of Torrio's close Brooklyn friends, a skillful gunman named Frankie Yale, had arrived in Chicago shortly before the murder and was discovered by the police the morning after it as he boarded a train for New York. Though Chicago detectives were convinced Yale had eliminated Colosimo at the behest of Torrio, they couldn't prove it. Torrio wept openly at the news of his uncle's death. "Big Jim and me," he said, "were like brothers."

As soon as he was released from questioning, Torrio undertook to make sure his "brother's" share of Big Jim's estate should not be diminished by the new wife's claims. The brothels, the speakeasies, and the rapidly expanding bootleg liquor business were henceforth his. The estimated half-million dollars in cash which Colosimo reputedly kept on hand was never found. The authorities fixed his estate at $76,000 plus fifteen barrels of whisky. Of this amount, Dale Winter Colosimo received from his family $6,000. They gave $12,000 to his first wife, Victoria Moresco Colosimo.

Archbishop George Mundelein of the Chicago diocese forbade Colosimo's burial in a Catholic cemetery, not because he was a thief, a white slaver, and probably a murderer (Chicago police estimated he had killed a dozen men), but because he had broken a Church commandment by divorcing and remarrying.

Despite the archbishop's stricture, six thousand people marched in Colosimo's funeral parade. The fifty-three honorary pallbearers included, as well as hoodlums and whoremasters, three judges, two Congressmen, a state senator, an assistant state's attorney, and nine Chicago aldermen, most prominent of whom were Bathhouse John Coughlin and Hinky Dink Kenna. After a Presbyterian clergyman performed a ceremony, Bathhouse John recited "Hail Marys" beside the coffin.

Mayor Thompson did not appear. As a Republican, and therefore mindful of the support of the better elements in the city, he tried to be discreet about his arrangements with hoodlums.

The nominating speeches at the Democratic convention of 1920 would soon begin. San Francisco's Civic Auditorium was jammed with delegates, spectators, and demonstrators for the various candidates. Most of the buttons, banners, and straw hats boosted "McAdoo," "Palmer," or "Cox," though there was a fair showing for "Smith," especially among the Eastern delegates.

Wayne Wheeler, a Republican himself but so politically powerful as to have the freedom of the Democratic convention, surveyed the scene with apprehension. Secretary of the Treasury William Gibbs McAdoo, a fairly dependable dry even though he was President Wilson's son-in-law, would be the least objectionable of the candidates. A. Mitchell Palmer, the Red-hunting Attorney General, might be tolerable. But Governors James Cox of Ohio and Al Smith of New York would be quite unacceptable to Wheeler. Dry forces throughout the vast auditorium were working actively against them. Wheeler was worried about Cox, whom he had already opposed with all his strength in his own home state of Ohio, because Cox was cagey on the prohibition issue, wet among the wets and dry among the drys. Wheeler, knowing him to be more wet than dry, had arranged for a summary of his wet record in Ohio to be distributed among the delegates.[3]

Wheeler's immediate concern today, however, was the Democratic platform rather than the possible candidates. He was looking for his friend and long-time ally, William Jennings Bryan; he found Bryan at the rear of the hall, lying on "an improvised cot, made of an old door laid across two wooden supports." Bryan was obviously not well. He seemed "dead tired," and his facial expression "indicated that he was suffering greatly." Wheeler, with tender solicitation, put a coat under the Peerless Leader's head for a pillow.

Bryan was at all times an emotional man. Tears welled up in his eyes and he took hold of Wheeler's hand. He was ready to die, he said, if he could only make the Democratic Party take the right course and adopt his resolution in full support of prohibition.

"We don't want you to die," Wheeler said. "We want you to live and continue the fight. We'll do everything in our power to help you."[4]

Actually, Wheeler was willing to do much less than everything in his power to foster Bryan's rigid resolution. The Anti-Saloon League directors had agreed in the spring that since prohibition was now a fact, they need not ask either party for platform planks supporting it.

Instead they would seek strong resolutions demanding its strict enforcement. The Republicans, at their convention in Chicago three weeks earlier, had already given them the kind of enforcement resolution they wanted and, in that already famous "smoke-filled room" at the Blackstone Hotel, had offered up a candidate quite satisfactory to the drys. He was Sen. Warren G. Harding, another Ohioan, a proven friend of Wheeler and of the prohibition cause. Harding, under Wheeler's guidance, had floor-managed the eighteenth Amendment ratification bill through the Senate in 1918.

Since Wheeler's own party, at his behest, had adopted only a prohibition enforcement clause in its platform, he would be somewhat embarrassed now if the Democrats were to adopt a stronger stand. He had tried, therefore, to temper Bryan's zeal. About a month before the Democrats were to convene in San Francisco, Wheeler had written to Bryan, "I have talked with our friends in and out of Congress, and they seem to think that our strongest position is to ask for a clean-cut law-and-order plank in the platform."

Bryan, a stubborn man who did not believe in trimming his strategies, had replied by return mail: "I am in receipt of your letter. I think we ought to try to secure a declaration in each platform in favor of prohibition as the permanent policy of this country, and in favor of the enforcement of the Volstead Law in letter and in spirit. . . . While I agree with you that we ought to make a strong plank on enforcement, I think it would be a mistake to speak of enforcement alone because no person will favor enforcement who does not accept prohibition as the policy of the country. If he looks forward to the ultimate repeal of the amendment, he will endorse the New York position which favors nullification in the meantime."

(By the time Bryan wrote this letter, no one could any longer doubt that the Democratic Party in New York favored nullification. A few days earlier, on May 24, Governor Smith had approved a state legislature measure allowing light wines and 2.75 per cent beer. Though the measure was effectively canceled by a June 7 ruling of the U.S. Supreme Court which affirmed the validity of the Volstead Act, it nevertheless left the position of Al Smith and Tammany Hall unequivocally clear.)

Wheeler, alarmed at Bryan's apparent intention of fighting an unnecessary battle, had written him again suggesting that his priorities were misplaced. He should worry more about the candidates than the platform. "The wets and medium wets are making a terrific drive for Governor Cox," he reminded Bryan in another letter. "They will sacrifice part of the platform if need be to get Cox nominated so he can appeal to wets all over the country. A platform utterance would mean nothing in this case. He must be defeated if there is any way possible to do it. . . . Also, Governor Smith of New York is now getting honorable mention in the press. . . . May the Lord give you strength and wisdom to lead the forces successfully in getting a good plank in the platform and a candidate who is personally in harmony with us."[5]

Bryan, despite his cozy financial arrangement with the League, had refused to heed these Wheeler guidelines. With his usual self-confidence, he had presented his "prohibition as the permanent policy of the country" plank to the Democratic resolutions committee, but to his consternation, it had been rejected. Even the drys on the committee, most of whom were in tune with Wheeler's wishes, had opposed it. Bryan seemed not to notice, however, that it was Wheeler who had pulled the resolution out from under him. Still determined to get it into the platform, he now informed Wheeler that he intended to take it to the floor and submit it to a vote of the entire convention.

Wheeler tried once more to reason with him but Bryan held firm. Finally Wheeler asked him, "What delegations do you think will support your resolution?"

"I don't know," Bryan replied. "I will give them the reasons why they should support it and that will carry the convention."

If the Great Commoner was now so out of touch with reality that he could believe such a thing, it was pointless to keep talking to him. Wheeler wished him well and moved on toward his seat in the gallery.

The day's opening ceremonies were finished and the nominations, with their "man who" speeches and rowdy demonstrations, were beginning. Al Smith's name was about to be presented to the convention, and if Wheeler had been close to the New York delegation he would have observed that the celebration of this event had already begun. The New Yorkers had traveled to California in a special train which carried almost as much whisky as it did coal. They obviously hadn't been able to drink it all on the trip, but they seemed determined to get the job done before their return home. They cheered madly when former Congressman Bourke Cockran, now aging but still regarded as Tammany Hall's most eloquent orator, appeared on the platform and smiled down at the 1,094 delegates to the convention.

"I came here," he said, "to nominate a candidate who in his own life and career constitutes the most perfect platform for a political party." In a lilting Irish voice he proceeded to portray Smith as an amalgam of Washington, Lincoln, and the shoeshine boy on the corner, then concluded, "We offer him reluctantly to the nation. The rest is up to the convention. If you do not take him, New York will claim the privilege of taking back this favorite son of hers, and by making him candidate for Governor assure the success of the Democratic Party in our state."

Smith himself had stood nervously in the back of the hall, listening to this embarrassing eulogy. Fortunately, the crowd was extremely good-natured about it. Though no one believed he would be nominated, or perhaps because no one believed he would be nominated, almost everyone burst into applause as the band, unable to think of the official New York state song if indeed there was one, launched into "The Sidewalks of New York." It was the first time Al Smith had ever been associated with this song which was destined to become his symbol. As the music began, Tammany representatives in the New York delegation grabbed the banners of several states in addition to their own, and within two or three minutes it seemed that all the delegates in the hall were dancing up and down the aisles. The singing marchers were soon joined even by delegates from the dry states. Many of the dry delegates were not so dry, of course, when they got away from home to attend a convention. As Wayne Wheeler knew, there was enough liquor in this building at this moment to stock a dozen saloons.

As he watched the wild demonstration, Wheeler could scarcely avoid feeling that the Democratic Party was a hopeless case. Though a majority of the delegates were supposedly dry, here they were cheering an unregenerate wet. Wheeler could take small comfort in the fact that Smith was not a serious candidate this year. It was beginning to look as if he would be a definite threat in 1924. Meanwhile, at this convention, he and Tammany were most likely to throw their support behind Cox. A lot of dry delegates were also likely to vote for the Ohio governor simply because he was so clever in concealing his true wetness. On top of all this, Bryan, because he was so deluded about the power of his celebrated voice, would probably destroy whatever chance there was of inserting a good prohibition enforcement clause into the Democratic platform. Fortunately for Wheeler, the Republicans, at least, had not let him down. Senator Harding would be worthy of Anti-Saloon League support. Except in one respect. He was an incorrigible drinker.

To Bill McCoy, Gloucester, Massachusetts, with its narrow streets, seventeenth- and eighteenth-century houses, and sharp, rocky hills, looked like a town in a far country after the years he had spent in Jacksonville, with its flat land, wide streets, tropical flowers, and pastel houses. And the cool breeze of August in New England was a diametric change from the Florida heat. Yet Jacksonville and Gloucester had one thing in common—the sea. Both were harbor towns, and it was Gloucester's harbor that had brought McCoy here.

Gloucester, a sizable fishing center, was the home port of some of America's most beautiful schooners. It was therefore a logical place for McCoy to visit when he decided to go into the rum-running business, and his trip here had been productive. He had not been able to buy the most beautiful schooner Gloucester could offer. After selling all the motor boats he and his brother owned in Jacksonville, and putting together all the funds he could lay hands upon, he had come here with slightly more than $20,000, hoping for the best.

The best vessel he could find for the money he had to offer was a ninety-foot fishing schooner called the *Henry L. Marshall*. He had bought it for $16,000, and to refit it properly, he was now spending the $4,000 he had left.

Though McCoy cherished no romantic illusions about the *Henry L. Marshall*, he gazed with a degree of pleasure upon it as it stood rocking gently against its pier. Made of Massachusetts white oak, the boat had two pole masts and a semi-knockabout rig. It also boasted twin engines that would give it at least some chance of escape if it were ever pursued, which it might be occasionally on the voyages he envisioned for it. As to its load capacity, that was no longer to be measured in fish. McCoy had decided the *Henry L. Marshall* would be able to carry 1,500 cases of liquor in standard wooden boxes. But wooden boxes wasted too much space. The most compact way to carry such goods, he believed, would be in burlap packages containing three bottles each. Such packages could be pyramided against each other so snugly that no space would be lost. He calculated the boat's capacity in burlap to be 3,000 cases. Bill McCoy had done a lot of careful calculating, about all kinds of matters, since his decision the previous spring to become a rumrunner.

He had also done some necessary rationalizing. He was an honest, law-abiding man from a law-abiding family, and he felt a nagging uneasiness when he contemplated his intended career outside the law. His primary motive was money. He made no attempt to deceive himself about that. Yet there were some things a man might do for money and other things he would refuse to do if he wished to retain his self-respect. McCoy had always held a fairly high opinion of himself. He was almost excessively proud of his reputation for honesty and fair dealing. How would he look upon himself when he became a bootlegger, a criminal in the eyes of the law?

He would be a criminal, he decided, only in the eyes of one law, the prohibition law. Even though he did not drink, he considered it a stupid law, needlessly restrictive of human freedom. Since the dawn of man, it had never been a crime to sell wine or liquor. Why should it now be a crime simply because a lot of narrow, puritanical people had been able to lobby a bad amendment into the Constitution? According to the history books he had studied, Americans had always "kicked holes in the laws they resented." The Stamp Act was a law during pre-Revolutionary times, but the men who broke it, right here in Massachusetts, were now considered American patriots. And that tea party in Boston, just twenty-five miles down the coast from Gloucester, wasn't "an exactly legal expedition." Before the Civil War, the Fugitive Slave Act was "as much the law of the land" as the Volstead Act today, yet many of the country's best people violated it by organizing the "underground railway" which smuggled runaway slaves into Canada.[6]

McCoy was especially fascinated by one Massachusetts citizen who he thought "might stand as the patron saint of rumrunners." This man had owned a fleet of ships smuggling liquor, silk, and other commodities into the colonies from the West Indies. He was John Hancock, who eventually became the first signer of the Declaration of Independence. If rum-running was respectable enough for John Hancock, it would be respectable enough for Bill McCoy.

At any rate, he had now made his decision and this ninety-foot schooner creaking against the pier was his. Finally he had a ship of his own, and whatever the world might think of him, he would soon be a captain, sailing the seas like any other captain, and, he hoped, getting rich like John Hancock. It wasn't much of a ship, but with a good crew it would do the job. And if he did get rich, he could then buy another ship.

Sunset was approaching and he was standing on the pierhead gazing out across Gloucester bay toward the open water when he suddenly saw, gliding smoothly into the harbor mouth under full sail, the very ship it would have to be.

"Her name was *Arethusa* . . . and she was an aristocrat," he later recalled, "a thoroughbred from her keel to her trucks. The late sun turned her spread of canvas golden, and my throat was tight and stiff as she came walking up the harbor like a great lady entering a room. The lines of her long, low, black hull told the mariner of speed and grace. The *Arethusa,* fishing schooner of the East Coast Fisheries Company, sailed in through the harbor of Gloucester that night and straight into my heart. I couldn't buy her then. I'd spent almost my last dollar on the *Marshall.* She was a fine schooner, but after I'd seen the *Arethusa* I almost hated her."

Captain Bill McCoy, a true man of the sea, had one thing, at least, in common with most other boat owners. Though he had bought a big, handsome schooner just a few days before, he already longed for a bigger, more handsome one.

By mid-August of 1920, most New Yorkers were reaching the conclusion that prohibition was unlikely to threaten anybody's drinking habits. In the theatrical district around Broadway, the city's most conspicuous area, one could enter an endless number of saloons where crowds of men stood at the bars, drinking whisky and calling openly for more. The same was true to a greater or lesser degree all over town, and newsmen, a group who ought to know, were reporting that the liquor on sale now was of a higher quality than what had been available during the last months before prohibition.

Saloons had reopened by the hundreds, perhaps even thousands. Their proprietors were aware that Chief Prohibition Agent James Shevlin, with only a few hundred agents, could not possibly police all of southern New York state. Shevlin was not likely to get much help from the New York City Police Department, which was much too Irish to sympathize with his task. His burden was further complicated by the fact that no civil service examinations were required for prohibition agents, and many of the men who came to him for jobs were sent by Congressmen or other politicians whose recommendations he could not ignore. The forty dollars per week these men received had begun to look like small wages to them when they noticed how much money bootleggers were making, and it was already evident that many of the agents had decided to augment their government salaries with regular stipends from the very people they were supposed to arrest. Under these circumstances, many saloon-keepers were losing their discretion.

This situation presented an open opportunity to agent Isadore Einstein, who liked his work so well that no bootlegger or bar owner had been able to reach him with a bribe. He seemed to enjoy the excitement of a raid more than the possibility of a fur coat for his wife or a better house for his four children. It was beginning to look as if Izzy Einstein might be one of those rare beings, an incorruptible man. After six months of increasing activity marked by astonishing ingenuity, he was now enjoying the added pleasure of seeing his name and forays extolled in the newspapers. He had found a partner, Moe Smith by name, who matched him at least in bulk and energy if not in wit and imagination. Moe was just as round in the middle as Izzy; if he weighed fifty pounds more it was because he was five or six inches taller. The two of them worked so well together they were becoming famous as a team, a fact which they accepted but which complicated their operations. Because so many bootleggers were now on the lookout for them, and because their rotundity was so conspicuous, they had to develop an ever-changing variety of ruses to outwit their intended victims.

On the fourteenth of August, 1920, a hot, dry Saturday, Izzy thought of a new deception. To distract attention from themselves as a pair, he and Moe took along on this project a third agent, a man named Harry Wittenberg, one of the few colleagues they felt they could trust. In a battered old Model T Ford, they drove up and parked in front of an establishment at Columbus Avenue and Eighty-ninth Street on the upper West Side. They entered the place in shirtsleeves, sweating profusely and talking heatedly. Though Izzy had an open checkbook in his hand as if he were about to complete some kind of transaction with the other two, his arguments indicated the deal was not quite settled.[7]

Sixty-five dollars, he insisted, was a high price to pay for such an old car with front tires in that condition.

Those front tires, the other two assured him, would last another thousand miles.

As they moved to the bar, Izzy raised more questions about the car, which his companions answered, one after another. The two proprietors, Joseph Matens and Martin Lane, both of whom happened to be behind the bar, listened with some amusement as the haggling continued. Finally, Einstein, capitulating on the terms of the deal, asked one of them for a fountain pen with which to write a check.

After the check changed hands and the pen was returned, it was only natural that the three men should have a drink to seal the bargain. Matens and Lane, seeing no objection to that, served them without questioning their identity.

Izzy Einstein then promptly announced that they were under a summons for violation of the Volstead Act. Without even raising his glass to his lips, he brought forth a small bottle into which he poured his drink, to be used in court as evidence. Ordinarily, when he bought a drink in a place like this, he poured it into a tiny funnel which he kept in his vest pocket, and which was connected by a tube to a small flask hidden in the lining. Today, however, since he was in shirtsleeves, he had to forego the pleasure of watching his victim's reaction whenever he poured a glassful of liquor into his vest pocket.

Bidding goodbye to the two furious men behind the bar, the three agents hurried out to their Tin Lizzie Ford and sped away. There was a saloon called Sheridan's just a few blocks distant at 601 Amsterdam Ave. Perhaps if they hurried, they could pull their new trick on Mr. Sheridan before the inevitable warnings about them began to spread from bar to bar.

George Remus, having married his mistress and former employee Imogene Holmes shortly after their June arrival in Cincinnati, was now living with her and her thirteen-year-old daughter in a large suite at the Sinton Hotel, where he had also opened an office. These first few months in Cincinnati had been among the busiest of Remus' always-busy life. He had already made himself known in the city by purchasing the first of several distilleries which he hoped would one day be his. It was a small operation—the down payment had taken only $10,000 of the $100,000 he had brought from Chicago. Since his remaining $90,000 would hardly begin to finance his enterprising dream of circumventing the Volstead Act, he had deposited a sizable portion of this money in Cincinnati's Lincoln National Bank, thereby impressing his solvency and respectability upon the officials of that institution, especially the manager of the savings department, a friendly man named Oscar Fender.

Remus' reputation as a lawyer in Chicago, the references he had brought from there, his personal persuasiveness, and his bold but carefully conceived ideas had also intrigued Fender and his colleagues. As a result, Remus had already solved many problems of finance about which he had been uncertain when he arrived in town. After four months, he was in the liquor business on such a sizable scale that he felt cramped both in his living quarters and his office quarters at the Sinton. His wife was looking at a ten-acre estate in Cincinnati's Price Hill district which might be suitable, after major renovations, as a new home for them. And he was looking at an office building on the northwest corner of Race and Pearl Streets in downtown Cincinnati.

By this time he had entered the drug business, in a manner of speaking, through the formation of several corporations which were the nominal recipients of liquors he was able to release from his own distillery and other sources by procuring government permits. Though these permits were legal, Remus' methods of obtaining them would hardly bear close scrutiny by any fastidious local or federal authority. To facilitate the flow of permits and enable him to keep pace with the ever-growing market for good bonded whisky, Remus had cultivated the friendship of every prohibition official he could meet at any level. He had quickly found that by being generous, he could meet as many of them as he pleased. When the news of his generosity spread through their circles, astonishing numbers of them proved eager to visit him openly at his office.

On one day in October, 1920, forty-four men dropped in to see Remus. Some were associates who came to discuss such problems as the transportation of released liquor from its warehouses to the bootleggers who were buying it. Remus was gathering, as quickly as possible, a fleet of trucks and fast automobiles for this purpose. Most of his forty-four callers, however, were politicians, public officials, or prohibition agents, including even some federal marshals. To these men, all of them useful in obtaining either liquor permits or protection from arrest, he happily showed his generosity in cash. He contributed that day an average of about a thousand dollars to the welfare of each.

Though Remus did not yet realize it, he had now become a big enough operator to attract the attention of the Federal Prohibition Bureau. A special agent from New York named William Mellin had installed a bugging device in his office and was able to hear everything he said on this particular day.

With his evidence in hand, agent Mellin went immediately to his supervisor in the Cincinnati office of the Internal Revenue Service and pronounced himself ready to arrest Remus.

Mellin's superior was surprisingly unenthusiastic. "Son, there's times when a man has to be practical in this business," the older man advised him. "It's only a few weeks to election and the information you've dug up is political dynamite. The men you spied on, the agents and marshals, are political appointees. Go back to New York and forget it."[8]

Agent Mellin found out that day what Remus already knew—it is not easy to arrest Santa Claus.

BOSTON, Nov. 1, 1920.—Customs officials searching the *Cretic* of the White Star Line here today for liquor were set upon by members of the crew. Longshoremen came to the defense of the officials and a heavy battle raged on the ship until harbor police, sailors from the Destroyer *Susquehanna* and Boston police arrived to put an end to the hostilities.

The trouble started when the customs officials returned to the vessel today to search for more liquor after having seized a considerable quantity in a raid Saturday. They had unearthed an additional 200 bottles when one of the crew grabbed a crow-bar and attacked an inspector.

The longshoremen then got into it. They are largely Irish and have never forgiven the *Cretic's* crew, largely Italian, for the part they played in breaking a "sympathy" strike of the longshoremen by helping to load and unload cargoes when the longshoremen refused to do it.

Saturday's seizure aboard the *Cretic* was declared to be one of the biggest on record. The customs men confiscated 600 bottles of choice wines and whisky valued at $7,000.[9]

Chapter 3

Al Smith had been depressed even before election day. His campaign crowds had been big and friendly. People had laughed as hard as ever at his jokes. He had been a popular governor. He had fought against rate raises by the public utilities companies. He had increased the efficiency of the state government by reorganization and had passed important social welfare legislation. He had even done his best to bring back beer and wines—a measure which in New York should gain him some votes. Yet as he sat in his headquarters at the Biltmore Hotel election night, he was so certain of defeat in his campaign for a second term that he cast aside the premature congratulations he was receiving from the people around him.

Smith expected to lose primarily because he saw 1920 as a Republican year, in New York and in the entire country. Now that the war in Europe was over, people were blaming the Democrats for getting the United States into it. Distrust of Europe was so deep that President Wilson's proposal to keep peace by forming a League of Nations, a proposal Smith had publicly supported, was now the most unpopular presidential initiative of the century. Even the big city minorities seemed to be turning against the Democrats, the Irish because Wilson had failed to secure the emancipation of Ireland from England, the Germans because Wilson had been associated with the hard terms of the Versailles Treaty, and the Italians because Wilson had not forced France and England to share with Italy the colonial spoils of the war. For all these reasons, Smith was absolutely certain that Harding would beat Cox and he was only a little less certain that he himself would lose the New York governorship. The Republicans had put up a good man against him—Judge Nathan L. Miller, a very able, conservative jurist who, as an attorney, had represented several huge corporations, including United States Steel Company. One of Smith's problems in campaigning against Miller was that he couldn't get angry at him. The man was too decent. The battle, therefore, had been dull, tedious, and unfocused.

The night before the election, Smith had warned his wife, Katie, "Tomorrow night will be no night for getting out the brooms."

In the Second Assembly District, his own lower Manhattan home ground, people used to wave brooms from their windows on election night to proclaim a clean sweep. He expected to see no brooms this year.

"The brooms will be there as usual," Katie assured him.[1]

As the returns began coming in, he could see she was wrong. Everyplace but in the eleven states of the solid Democratic South, Senator Harding, though he had conducted most of his campaign indolently from the front porch of his home in Marion, Ohio, was pulling ahead of Ohio's Governor Cox by a margin of almost two to one. In New York state, Harding's lead over Cox was closer to five to two. It seemed inevitable that if Harding's coattails were that long, Judge Miller would be able to ride in on them. But as the New York gubernatorial results began to pile up, the outlook became less clear. While Miller was ahead of Smith, the race was close and for several hours it remained in doubt. It was not until the early morning hours of Wednesday, November 3, that Al Smith and his Tammany organization knew for certain he had been beaten. Even then he was only about 60,000 votes behind Miller while Cox in New York was more than a million votes behind Harding.

The fact that he had come close was small consolation to Al Smith. He wanted to win. He wanted to stay in politics and perhaps one day even run for the presidency. But all his ambitions seemed hopeless now. Instead of returning to Albany for a second term as governor, he would have to take his family back to the modest place they owned on Oliver Street, in the shadow of the Brooklyn Bridge. Since he had no money, he had better forget politics and find a job to support his children.

Depressing as this election had been to Al Smith, however, it had not discouraged the Tammany organization which supported him. Tammany Hall had been around a long time and had suffered other defeats, but had never been knocked out. Belle Moskowitz, one of Smith's hardest workers and most respected advisers, looked at the almost final tally with a smile instead of a frown. Smith hadn't been beaten, she said. It was Cox who was beaten. Smith had gone down with Cox only because of his loyalty to the party, and because he had refused to let go of the sinking presidential candidate. In another two years, when Smith would be able to run without the weight of Cox upon him, he would go back to Albany. And two or perhaps six years after that, he would be ready for the longer trip to Washington.

Republican headquarters in Chicago on election night, 1920, was City Hall, the fifth floor, where Mayor William Hale Thompson held forth in the corridor just outside his office. Enough returns had come in now to eliminate all doubt about the outcome in Illinois or in the nation. Though Thompson himself was not up for reelection this year, his people were winning as easily in Illinois as other Republicans were winning throughout the country. Thompson didn't agree with his fellow Republicans about everything; few of them shared his colossal tolerance for alcohol. Nevertheless, he was happy to drink to their overwhelming victory.

"We ate 'em alive!" he bellowed at the hundreds of supporters trying to get near him. "We ate 'em alive with their clothes on!" And to an orchestra which had made its way through the boozing, shouting crowd, he cried, "Let the jazz band play! Let's show 'em we're all live ones."

Thompson and his political mentor, former Congressman Fred Lundin, had good reason to celebrate. They were now at the height of their power, having elected today both their hand-picked candidate for state's attorney, Robert Crowe, and their hand-picked candidate for governor, an elderly Kankakee farmer named Len Small, who had often proclaimed Big Bill Thompson "the greatest man in America." Small had defeated his Democratic opponent, state senator J. Hamilton Lewis, by a half-million votes. For a man who was supposed to have more brawn than brain, Big Bill Thompson had done well in the five years since his first election as mayor, establishing effective political control over the state of Illinois as well as the city of Chicago.

Because Thompson's bombastic statements, especially against the war and against the British, had been so widely reported, his success in Chicago had been a source of amusement throughout the country. Here was further proof that the toddlin' town had not yet grown up. If Chicago could tolerate such an ignorant roughneck as its mayor, it must still be the bad boy of American cities. Respectable Chicagoans were horrified at the antics of Big Bill, yet it was they who had produced him. Despite his blustery manners and uncouth habits of speech, Thompson had not sprung from a rowdy environment, and if he lacked education it was by his own choice. He had been born on Boston's Beacon Street into a wealthy New England family. His great-great-great-grandfather had arrived in America from England in 1700 and had acquired large land-holdings in New Hampshire. His great-great-grandfather had fought the British in the Revolution and had been one of George Washington's electors. His grandfather was a naval officer in the War of 1812, and his father was a naval officer in the Civil War.

His mother had come from a wealthy pioneer Chicago family, her father having been one of the signers of the town's incorporation papers in 1833. It was the responsibility of managing her inherited property that had brought Thompson's parents to Chicago from Boston in 1868, when little William was one year old. By the time William was a teenager, his father had added vastly to the family wealth through investments in downtown property. He had also made arrangements for his son to enroll at Phillips Exeter Academy en route to Yale, but William had other plans. He wanted to be a cowboy. It was an ambition to which many American boys succumbed in adolescence, but Bill Thompson's adolescence endured longer than most. Despite his father's wishes he went West, actually became a cowboy, then the manager of a ranch his father bought in Nebraska, remaining there until 1891 when his father died, necessitating his return to Chicago.

Though he had come home to supervise the family real estate

business, he now spent most of his time playing football, water polo, and other games for Chicago Athletic Club teams. He also found time to sail his boat on Lake Michigan, gamble, drink, and visit the brothels on the Levee, as he was once forced to admit in a lawsuit. During a card game at the athletic club one of his friends goaded him into running for the Chicago City Council. He ran and won as a reform candidate supported by the Municipal Voters' League, an organization of wealthy, respectable Republicans dedicated to the overthrow of the "boodlers," mostly Democrats, who were running Chicago as if it were a grab-bag. Thompson had thus begun his political career in 1900 as a crusader against corruption. By 1920, he had traveled a long distance from his starting point.

As the booze flowed and his friends crowded around to congratulate him on the great election victory he had engineered, Thompson's position looked so secure in Chicago that he could now get down to the business of running the state and perhaps even dream, as some of his friends had begun to do, that he would one day run the nation. There were, however, a few problems which would first have to be met. The Chicago police force, of which he often boasted, had gotten in trouble again because of prohibition. The trouble was that in Chicago, thanks partly to Thompson's tolerance, there wasn't any prohibition. The bars and cabarets were wide open ten months after the Eighteenth Amendment went into effect. But the police weren't exactly leaving them alone. They were making regular collections from the proprietors in exchange for protection, and the situation had become so well publicized that a federal grand jury was now poking into it. The police were so busy protecting bootleggers and bar owners they didn't seem to have time for more orthodox business. One banker whose establishment had been robbed of $272,000 in securities was complaining publicly that only by hiring private detectives had he been able to catch the thieves.

The *Tribune* and the *Daily News* were both making so much fuss about Thompson's wide-open-town policies that he had already been forced to make a well-publicized move in the hope of quieting these persistently unfriendly journals. He had ordered the police to revoke the licenses of two of the city's most famous night palaces—Colosimo's restaurant and Ike Bloom's Midnight Frolics, a dance hall which was also one of the biggest bordellos in the Levee. The fact that these two Levee landmarks were closely associated with Democratic Aldermen Bathhouse John Coughlin and Hinky Dink Kenna may have been one of the reasons the mayor had singled them out for closure just a week before election, but their prominence was a much more important consideration. Thompson had no reason to be angry, for instance, at the people who had been in control of Colosimo's since the murder of its proprietor. Johnny Torrio and Al Capone might be friends of Bathhouse John and Hinky Dink, but they were also life-time members of the William Hale Thompson Republican Club. And they were the kind of people who understood the necessity of closing a few well known joints just before elections. Anyway, they needn't remain closed very long. The federal grand jury would soon shut down. The bad publicity would quickly abate and everyone would get back to business. There was no doubt, after all, as to the wishes of most Chicagoans about prohibition. In a 1919 local option referendum, they had voted three to one against closing the saloons.

During the first days after the great Republican election landslide of 1920, rumors of the federal grand jury's discoveries about the Chicago police department became increasingly worrisome, but not alarming enough to distract Mayor Thompson from a vacation he had been planning at one of his favorite getaway resorts, in West Baden, near the southern tip of Indiana. As the daily reports reached him, however, he became more concerned. The word circulated that as many as fifty police officers would be indicted because of their connections with bootleggers. Then there was a demand for the records of Police Chief John J. Garrity's publicized investigation of alliances between his men and prohibition violators. The time had come, Mayor Thompson decided, to silence his critics.

At 1:30 on the afternoon of November 10 he called Chief Garrity and told him he had decided "to make a few changes."

"It's all right with me," Garrity said, anticipating his dismissal. He had already offered to resign whenever he became "embarrassing to the administration."

Thompson then announced his choice for Chicago's new Chief of Police—his own personal secretary, Charles C. Fitzmorris.

Though the mayor did not choose to explain this move to a hostile press corps, he did agree later in the afternoon to talk to a reporter from the one newspaper on whose support he could depend—William Randolph Hearst's *Herald & Examiner*.[2]

"Chief Garrity has done his best," Thompson insisted to the *Herald*

& *Examiner* reporter. "I am satisfied, but I think Mr. Fitzmorris is able to bring about an improvement. The crooks have got to get out of Chicago. We will not quit until they do. Fitzmorris has been in close touch with police matters for sixteen years and I believe him well qualified."

"What is his policy toward enforcement of the prohibition law?" the reporter asked.

"That is a federal law," the mayor reminded him, "and it ought to be straightened out where one begins and where the other leaves off."

Big Bill Thompson may have been less than brilliant, as many of his critics insisted, and his use of the English language might be difficult to follow, but he was not so stupid as to promise that he would enforce the Volstead Act in Chicago.

The long drive to and from Canada was tiresome, but Larry Fay had done it so often now he was accustomed to it. As usual, he was returning with his taxicab full of something more profitable than passengers—Canadian whisky. In the last nine months, Fay had become a remarkably successful entrepreneur. Beginning in the spring with one cab, he had made so many trips north and had brought back so much liquor that he was soon able to buy another cab, then another and another. He now owned several cabs and a few trucks, all of which were speeding back and forth between New York and Montreal or other Canadian cities. Even though he had not yet encountered any trouble with the authorities, Fay believed in varying his routes and his sources.

Today he had come from Trois Rivières, seventy-five miles northeast of Montreal, down through Vermont and New Hampshire toward Massachusetts. New York was his principal market but he might find it just as easy, since this was the day before Thanksgiving, to sell his merchandise in Boston. While some proper Bostonians might look askance at his enterprise, the city in general held as low an opinion of prohibition as did New York. Among Boston's Irish alone there was a constant market for more liquor than all of the area's bootleggers could supply. If he couldn't find buyers any other way, he would be at least half safe in asking a cop to direct him to the nearest pub. One of the advantages of using taxis for these trips was that policemen were usually sympathetic to cabbies, and in cities like Boston or New York, which were full of Irish policemen, they might be especially sympathetic to an Irish cabbie. On the other hand, there was a certain danger in using taxis because they were so conspicuous.

There was danger, of course, in the whole bootlegging business. During the first weeks and months of prohibition, enforcement had been so haphazard and everyone was so unaccustomed to the idea of arresting a man for selling liquor that bootlegging had seemed like an easy route to guaranteed riches. But after ten months, enforcement was better organized and there was an increasing possibility of arrest.

For this reason and several others, Larry Fay didn't exactly like what he was doing, but he found the profits irresistible. He had an overweening desire to become wealthy so he could be looked upon with respect and associate with people of quality. Coming as he did from an immigrant Irish background, he cherished the immigrant dream of acceptance. It was the same dream that New York's Governor Al Smith had nurtured when he envisioned his chances of becoming president of the United States. If Fay's dream was less grandiose than Smith's, perhaps it was because he was more realistic.

Both were lower Manhattan Catholics. Fay was more keenly aware of the limits such an identity imposed. Smith had acquired enough sophistication to make all things seem possible to him. Fay, with little education or culture, and a background of minor arrests, had concluded that nothing was possible for him except through crime. If he wanted the capital necessary to become a businessman, he couldn't borrow it. No banker would let him inside the guard rail. Crime was the only source of capital he could envision, and bootlegging was the most suitable avenue to success he had yet found. He would pursue it, therefore, as long as necessary, but only as a means to an end.

Fay's taxicab had just crossed the Merrimack River from New Hampshire into Massachusetts and entered the textile mill city of Lawrence when he was suddenly led to wonder if he should have chosen some other means. A Lawrence policeman, perhaps surprised to see a New York taxi rolling through town, signaled him to stop. There was no way Fay could conceal what he was carrying. His only hope was that the policeman might be sympathetic, or that a few bottles might make him so. Liquor law violations were now bringing six-month-to-one-year sentences, especially in smaller communities, and Fay did not relish the notion of spending six months in the

Lawrence, Massachusetts jail. But unfortunately for him, the police-man was not sympathetic. Fay soon found himself charged with violation of the Volstead Act: specifically, illegal transportation of liquor.³

He had suffered the bad luck of being stopped by the wrong cop. But in a town this close to Boston, there must be a lot of "right" cops. At the station where he was booked Fay began talking fast in the hope of finding one, and he soon did. A short time later he was on his way out of town with his wallet and his whisky load lightened but with his freedom intact. Though the charge against him still stood, the authorities in Lawrence needn't expect him ever to return and answer it. There were plenty of other routes in and out of Canada.

This arrest confirmed Fay's dislike of the bootlegging business, but he was too near success to turn back. In another year, thanks to his rum-running, he would have a whole fleet of cabs and a lavish office with pretty secretaries. It would be time enough then to go respect-able. However, perhaps the time had already come to leave the driving to others.

CARNEGIE, PA., Jan. 20, 1921.—Bootleggers scored in the first round of their battle with Carnegie ministers last Sunday when they cut the electric wires of the Baptist, Presbyterian, United Pres-byterian, Methodist Episcopal, and Primitive Methodist Churches during simultaneous sermons on "Prohibition in Carnegie." The wires in all five churches were cut at the same time.

The pastors of each of the churches had just launched their sermons when the lights went out. Quick investigations disclosed that the main switch in every church had been thrown and the power lines outside had been cut.

Despite the darkness, the ministers, after communicating with each other by telephone, all decided to finish their sermons. But this plan proved less than successful because most of their parishioners had gone home.⁴

The twin-masted, ninety-foot schooner *Henry L. Marshall*, on its maiden voyage under its new owner and captain, Bill McCoy, sailed proudly around Hog Island, passed the white lighthouse at the en-trance to Nassau harbor, and eased its way toward the row of piers near the center of town. McCoy, gazing across "the blazing pool of emerald, amethyst, and turquoise that is Nassau harbor," observed that his *Marshall* was the only seagoing craft in sight.

He was not alone in noticing this. An American named Billy Hain, who had already found what McCoy was seeking in Nassau, and who had seen the *Marshall* approaching from the north, sped out to meet the arriving schooner in a motorboat. When Hain came aboard, both he and McCoy were surprised to see each other. They were old friends. But Hain wasted little time on greetings. He had bought 1,500 cases of liquor which were urgently awaited in Savannah, Georgia. Would McCoy carry them for him at ten dollars per case?

Before the *Marshall* was tied at a pier the deal was settled, and before McCoy even had time to step ashore, a caravan of donkey-pulled wagons clattered onto the dock, each burdened with twenty-five cases of whisky which Hain had procured from a local wholesaler. A year earlier, when the United States adopted prohibition, proper citizens of the beautiful but lethargic British Bahamas had scorned the notion of making their capital a relay station for liquor en route from European distilleries to American bootleggers. But during the intervening year, it had become clear that the Nassau exchequer would be enriched at the rate of six dollars per case for all the liquor that flowed through its port. Some of the best people in town were now becoming wholesalers themselves.

As soon as the *Marshall* was loaded, Hain came aboard and said, "Let's get out of here. I'm in a hurry."

He had clearance papers to Halifax and he didn't even want McCoy to wait long enough for the seven-man crew to enjoy a few hours of shore leave. When McCoy insisted on this, Hain himself took the men ashore to a remarkably efficient brothel which fulfilled all their desires and got them fairly intoxicated besides within less than an hour. As soon as he returned the crew to the *Marshall* and shepherded them, reeling, onto the deck, Hain announced to McCoy that he would take a seaplane to Savannah and meet them at the mouth of St. Catherine's Sound with lighters onto which their cargo would be transferred. Before nightfall, Captain Bill McCoy with his seven drunken crewmen set sail on his first rum-running voyage, just six months after his decision to enter the illicit trade.

The *Marshall* had not yet reached the Georgia coast when the treacherous February winds in the Atlantic threatened to put her captain out of business. A gale from the northwest heightened the waves, blackened the skies, and increased the ship's speed. As the starless night deepened, McCoy could see that his schooner was going someplace in a hurry, but he wasn't quite sure where. Finally toward morning, as he stepped out onto the wave-swept deck in the hope of getting his bearings, he became alarmingly aware that there was sand beneath his feet. If the breakers were throwing up sand, the ship must be perilously close to running aground. Turning the bow to sea, McCoy started the twin-screw engines and reversed his course just in time. When the sun rose, the Georgia coast was so close astern he could see he had come within a few minutes of being dashed against it.

Despite this near disaster, McCoy was not far off course. When the *Marshall* reached the mouth of St. Catherine's Sound, Hain came out to meet her in a motorboat.

"Can't unload her out here," he shouted. "Too rough. We'll have to go in."

McCoy, whose entire fortune was invested in the *Marshall*, feared that a prohibition patrol boat, perhaps a Coast Guard cutter, might bear down on him at any moment, but after Hain promised him it would be safe, he sailed across the bar into the sound. Hain's lighters appeared and the whisky transfer progressed throughout the day. When night fell and the *Marshall* was only half unloaded, McCoy saw the red light of a patrol boat approaching and pointed it out to Hain.

"Better pipe down," Hain said calmly. "I got them fixed but there's no use rubbing it in."

McCoy could now see a green light as well as the red one on the approaching craft. The drone of the engines became louder and louder. Finally, the boat appeared abeam. It was a cutter, and as Hain had guessed, it was indeed the patrol boat. It bore down so close that its helmsman could not have failed to see the *Marshall*, yet it glided past as if nobody aboard had seen anything. Everyone on the *Marshall* relaxed and the unloading continued without disturbance.[5]

Bill McCoy was amazed at the simplicity of the system. A week later he was back in Nassau with $15,000 in his pocket. Two months later he had acquired an impressive bank account in Nassau and some persuasive acquaintances in New York—a group of Italian gangsters who, in April of 1921, were enlarging an already profitable bootlegging operation. McCoy happened to be rushing through the lobby of

New York's Pennsylvania Hotel one day when a member of this group stopped him. The rum trade as McCoy knew it, the man said, was in its infancy, but was about to grow up fast. His group planned to operate big and there would be a million dollars in it for McCoy if he agreed to haul for them. He would, however, need a larger ship. One which would hold at least 5,000 cases.

"Five thousand cases a load means $50,000 each voyage," the man pointed out. "How does that sound?"

It sounded so good to McCoy that he caught the first train to Gloucester, Massachusetts, with visions in his mind of the schooner *Arethusa,* which he had seen there a few days after he bought the Marshall. In Gloucester, he learned that the East Coast Fisheries Company, which owned the *Arethusa,* was bankrupt, and that a New York firm, George W. Goethals & Son, was acting as receiver. The schooner herself was at Rockland, Maine.

Before returning to New York, McCoy went there to have another, closer look at her. When he saw her the second time, he decided he had to have her. "She was," he later recalled, "the most beautiful thing of her kind in the world. . . . There wasn't an ugly line or a dishonest treenail in her. The lovely turn of her oak hull, the grace of her lofty, tapering spars made my throat swell."

Back in New York, he found that the *Arethusa* was appraised at $42,000, but that due to the East Coast Company's bankruptcy, he could have her for $21,000. Nervously he counted out the cash in one-thousand and five-hundred-dollar bills. The *Arethusa* was his, and after spending another $11,000 to put the schooner in perfect condition, he was ready to enlarge his operations.[6]

When he sailed the *Arethusa* into Nassau harbor in July, McCoy took a hard look at the *Marshall* and decided that, useful as she had been, he ought to sell her. How could he give her the attention she needed when he was so deeply in love with the beauty of beauties he had just acquired? But before he had time to sell the *Marshall,* a man of his acquaintance offered to hire her with crew for a one-trip fee of $15,000 to carry a load of rye whisky to Atlantic City. Though McCoy had reason to doubt the sobriety of the *Marshall*'s captain and crew, and though he didn't especially like the man who wanted to hire her, he liked the money well enough to accept the deal. A few days later, both of his schooners sailed out of Nassau, heavily laden, the *Marshall* bound for the south Jersey shore while the *Arethusa,* now under British registry and renamed the *Tomoka*, headed farther north to the waters outside New York harbor.

There was little reason why either craft should encounter trouble. U.S. authorities were just beginning to show concern about liquor smuggling from the sea. There were only a few revenue cutters on patrol, and as McCoy had learned, some of them could be bought off if they couldn't be outrun. The Coast Guard, which was also supposed to be on the lookout for rumrunners, had other important things to do. There was talk in American newspapers of turning the Navy loose against the growing fleet of liquor boats, and McCoy knew that if this ever happened, he was out of business. But since it hadn't happened, he had reason to feel confident that both of his schooners would soon be safely back at Nassau. As an added precaution, however, he had instructed the *Marshall*'s captain never to sail her closer than twenty-five miles from the Jersey shore.

When the *Tomoka* (which McCoy himself still called the *Arethusa*) approached Montauk Point at the extreme eastern end of Long Island on or about July 25, 1921, representatives of the New York mob and several other bootleggers had already arrived with their motor launches—some at Montauk, some at Fort Pond Bay, some on Block Island—to greet McCoy and do business with him. In addition to the mobsters' consignment of two thousand cases he had about three thousand cases for sale to any purchaser who would come out beyond the three-mile limit. By thus converting his schooner into a floating warehouse where all wholesale buyers were welcome, McCoy was establishing a new pattern. Eventually, Coast Guard authorities were to acknowledge him as the originator of Rum Row, the shadowy conglomeration of vessels which was to hover off U.S. coastlines for several years, supplying any bootlegger who thought his speedboat was fast enough to elude a government cutter.

For three nights the *Tomoka* stood off Montauk, selling and unloading liquor as fast as customers could pull up beside her. Then McCoy, not wanting to stretch his luck, sent her out to sea for a few days while he went ashore to drum up more trade. On the night of August 3, he guided a big customer with four boats out to rendezvous with her and reopened for business very profitably, despite a momentary scare when several naval ships passed by on maneuvers. He had now unloaded all but about five hundred cases, and the following day, after going ashore at Block Island, he found a customer for these. He could congratulate himself for having completed the most lucrative rum-running voyage in history. He would clear more than $50,000 on this first trip of the *Tomoka.* But before he left Block Island on the afternoon of the fourth, he received some bad news.

As he walked with his customer past the island telegraph office, a crowd had gathered to read news bulletins pinned to the door. One of the items quickly caught McCoy's eye:

NEW YORK: HENRY L. MARSHALL, McCOY MYSTERY SHIP, SEIZED OFF ATLANTIC CITY WITH 1,500 CASES OF WHISKY. GOVERNMENT SEARCHING FOR ARETHUSA, RUM RUNNER, SEEN OFF MONTAUK.

That night, after his last five hundred cases had been loaded onto his customer's launches, McCoy sent the now-empty *Tomoka* out to sea. Then, with a full wallet but a heavy heart, he crossed to Montauk and took the 120-mile train ride the entire length of Long Island into New York City. By the time he arrived in Manhattan on the morning of August 5, the Coast Guard cutter *Seneca,* which captured the *Marshall,* had towed her into New York harbor, where the government had impounded her with the intention of confiscating her. McCoy himself, his brother Ben, and the man who had hired the schooner were all under indictment. The captain and first mate were in the Atlantic City jail on a drunk charge, and the rest of the crew had been locked up in New York City's Tombs jail as material witnesses. After talking to them and to his brother, McCoy was able to piece together the infuriating story of the *Marshall*'s capture.

The man who hired the boat had agreed to sell its 1,500-case cargo to a group of New Jersey politicians for forty dollars per case, but he reneged on this agreement when another buyer offered him sixty dollars per case. The New Jersey politicians, understandably annoyed, reported him to prohibition officials as a rumrunner. The Coast Guard, alerted to the presence of the liquor-laden schooner off the Jersey shore, sent the cutter *Seneca* to harass it. Despite all this, the *Marshall* would have been safe from interference if her captain had obeyed McCoy's order to keep her at least twenty-five miles from land, but the captain and his mate had gone ashore at Atlantic City, where they were arrested on the Boardwalk for making a drunken disturbance. With the captain absent, the crew began drinking the cargo and the *Marshall* drifted without restraint toward shore. The

Seneca had only to await its arrival in U.S. territorial water.

Bill McCoy, under indictment but not yet arrested, had to decide quickly whether to stay in New York and perhaps go to prison or escape to Nassau and continue amassing his fortune. It was not a difficult decision for him. Leaving his tangled affairs in the hands of a lawyer, he hastened to rendezvous by motorboat with the *Tomoka*, which was waiting for him offshore, and set sail for the Bahamas.

If it were practical to do so, William Anderson would gladly have spent 100 percent of his time and energy fighting the liquor interests and their principal allies, who were, in his opinion, the Catholic Church, Tammany Hall, and Governor Al Smith. But it took money to fight the war against booze, which explained at least partially why so much of his time and energy were spent on fundraising for the Anti-Saloon League. It also took money to live decently and raise a family, especially at New York prices. This, too, helped explain the energy Anderson put into fundraising and the large staff he maintained for the purpose. If he didn't bring in enough money, he wouldn't be paid even his modest salary of $10,000, which was hardly enough to meet his living costs and the upkeep on his house in Yonkers. His salary was so inadequate, in fact, that he had been obliged to work out an unusual arrangement for augmenting it. And now, in March 1921, this arrangement threatened to cause a small complication.

Four years earlier, in May 1917, he had hired a man named C. Bertall Phillips to solicit business for a job printing plant owned by the League. When Phillips suggested he would rather be a fundraiser, Anderson was sufficiently impressed by his qualifications to employ him in that capacity. The two agreed upon a contract whereby Phillips would be paid 20 percent of the first $25,000 he obtained annually for the League, and an additional 10 percent of all money above that figure.

Within a relatively short time, it was evident that Anderson had shrewdly judged Phillips' skills. One of the money sources Phillips contacted, for instance, was the Rockefeller family. John D. Rockefeller, Sr., had been giving $5,000 a year to the League for several years, but that was the extent of the Rockefeller contribution. As a result of Phillips' solicitation, other members of the family began giving and the total Rockefeller contributions increased rapidly. It seemed likely that even in his first year Phillips would earn more than $10,000, and that would be more than Anderson himself was earning.

One day when Anderson and Phillips happened to meet in the corridor of the Anti-Saloon League office, they stopped to talk about Phillips' gratifying success and about the money he would be earning. After these pleasantries, Anderson casually mentioned a condition of employment which had not been included in Phillips' contract.

"There's one thing you'll have to understand," he said, "and that is that after you've collected ten thousand dollars in commissions, you must split fifty-fifty with me. I will have no one in the League making more than I do."[7]

This, at least, was what Phillips thought he heard Anderson say. As Anderson later recalled it, Phillips himself had made the generous offer as a gesture of gratitude for the help and advice his boss had given him. In any case, from that day forward, Anderson had been receiving, each year, one-half of all commissions Phillips earned over $10,000.

Since Phillips was now bringing in $75,000 a year from the Rockefellers alone, the sums involved were significant. In 1920 he had raised for the League a total of $165,000, thereby earning $18,893 in commissions. Anderson, feeling he was entitled to half of the $8,893 in excess of $10,000, had appropriated for himself a first installment of $2,500 on July 7, 1920. He had arranged this by the simple method of instructing office bookkeeper William M. Potter to make out a check payable to Anderson and charge it to Phillips' commission account. When Potter expressed some curiosity about the transaction, Anderson explained that Phillips had borrowed the money from him, and that the check was in payment of the loan.

On the second of March, 1921, Anderson had arranged similarly for the transfer of $1,375 from Phillips to himself. On the back of the March 2 check was the notation: "For Deposit, William H. Anderson. This check is in settlement of the Anti-Saloon League account with William H. Anderson; charge O. B. Phillips's salary account." Actually Phillips did not receive a salary but his recompense was now listed as such because in June 1917 the Rockefeller family had announced that they would never donate to any cause that paid commissions on their gifts.

This interoffice financial arrangement seemed quite satisfactory to

Anderson, but now, in mid-March, 1921, Phillips complained about it. He was making out his income tax for 1920, he said, and since the League records indicated he had been paid $18,893, he would have to pay tax on almost $4,000 which he had not received. He felt this would be unfair.

When Potter spoke to Anderson about Phillips' complaint, the superintendent was sympathetic. It would indeed be unfair. But it wasn't necessary. Taking pen in hand, Anderson wrote a note to bookkeeper Potter which said:

Mr. Potter: Transfer from salary account of O. B. Phillips $4,400 to his expense account. W. H. Anderson.

The superintendent had been more than generous. Phillips had asked him for relief from only $3,875 in tax liability. By a stroke of his pen Anderson had granted Phillips another $525 in deductions. As it happened, Anderson at the moment had reason to feel even friendlier than usual toward Phillips. Anderson had devised a scheme called "The Yonkers Plan" which he believed could drive all the bootleggers out of any given area. It was based on a carefully designed saturation enforcement campaign. He wanted to try it out in Westchester County, but he needed money to do so. Thanks partly to the efforts of Phillips, John D. Rockefeller, Jr., was about to contribute a supplementary $5,000 to this project. Anderson, therefore, could be grateful to Phillips for helping to get the Yonkers Plan launched. And of course he must have felt some gratitude toward the fundraiser for the personal income he would receive out of the extra Rockefeller gift. He would, of course, be getting half of Phillips' $500 commission on it.

NEW YORK CITY, May 12, 1921.—An alleged dry law violator was freed yesterday because the bottle of whisky in his possession failed to survive the exhaustive experiments which five arresting policemen made to determine whether the whisky was whisky.

The prisoner was William Manning who has a saloon at 1662 Third Avenue. The raiders, Lieutenant John Steinkamp and four patrolmen, found the bottle behind his bar. All five had observed when the bottle was seized that it contained a reddish liquid with a whisky smell. But the police have been repeatedly directed by

Magistrates to disregard the rumors which the inaccurate organs of sense and smell convey to the brain and to depend only on the trustworthy palate.

Consequently, Lieutenant Steinkamp, after the confiscation, ordered every man to do his duty. It was reasoned that if one or two witnesses make a good case, five make a better one. When the case against Manning was apparently iron-clad and copper-riveted, they arrested him and his bartender, John Reilly.

"But where is the corpus delicti?" Magistrate Edgar V. Frothingham demanded in Harlem Court after hearing the testimony.

Lieutenant Steinkamp said, "There's the bottle."

"But there's nothing in it. What's become of the contents?"

The lieutenant looked puzzled and scratched his head. "Well, we all tasted it," he said finally.

"What for?"

"So that we would have a good case."

"We can't hold defendants on evidence that has been verified into a state of nothingness," the Magistrate ruled. "Defendants dismissed."[8]

George Remus' mood was expansive. After less than a year in the liquor business, he was so firmly established that his distillery holdings extended beyond Ohio into Kentucky and Indiana, while his markets had stretched from Chicago in the west to New York City in the east. He had to make frequent trips to New York because many of his best customers were operating there and because some of the drug concerns he owned were supposedly located there. The Central Drug Company, for instance, and the Alps Drug Company had New York addresses, and while they were not exactly in the business of selling drugs, they were such important sources of liquor permits that he closely supervised their paperwork. But now he was on his way to New York for an even more important purpose.

Successful as Remus had been so far, he still had one major problem. The demand for good bonded whisky was so great that he couldn't get enough government withdrawal permits to release as much of it as his customers wanted. He was traveling east this time because he had been promised a New York introduction to a man so well connected he could eliminate this or perhaps any other problem. If the meeting turned out as Remus hoped, he might soon be the nation's biggest liquor dealer. In his Cincinnati base of operations, he had the machinery ready to take advantage of such an eventuality.

He had now purchased the building which had caught his eye at the corner of Race and Pearl Streets and, after renaming it the Remus Building, had set up his administrative offices there. His employees numbered in the hundreds, including a large corps of drivers and armed escort men for the fleet of trucks and fast cars which transported his whisky. He didn't trust the railroads because sometimes as many as twenty-five cases of liquor could disappear from a single train shipment. He owned and operated, on a lonely road near Cheviot, northwest of Cincinnati, a place called Death Valley Farm, where he had installed a complete bottling works and large storage facilities. Here, a full-time crew of men processed liquor which had been released from government warehouses, presumably en route to the drug firms in whose names it had been withdrawn. To this depot, which looked from the outside like an abandoned farm, came also a certain undeterminable volume of whisky manufactured in Remus-owned distilleries and released mysteriously without benefit of government permits. From just one of his holdings, the Squibb Distillery in Lawrenceburg, Indiana, he had already been able to secure the release of several thousand gallons of whisky. Even Remus was not certain how much of this had been covered by legal certificates and how much had been surreptitiously filtered out. He kept no precise accounts, preferring not to commit such matters to paper.

Though Remus was a lawyer, his conscience was quite serene about the open illegality of procuring liquor without permits. It was, after all, his own liquor that he was removing from his own distilleries. He would be willing to pay the tax on it if he could procure enough permits to cover it. He could scarcely be blamed for the fact that the federal government had passed such a stupid measure as the Volstead Act. In his opinion, the dispensation for "medicinal purposes" in the liquor-banning law was "the greatest comedy, the greatest perversion of justice" he had ever known, but if the government wanted to pass such a law, with such a convenient loophole in it, he was willing to make use of it.

When Remus arrived at New York's Grand Central Station, he went straight to the Hotel Commodore. After settling into his suite, he placed a call to a Manhattan attorney named Elijah Zoline, who specialized in federal jurisprudence and had often prepared expert briefs for Remus in connection with federal cases the latter handled while practicing law in Chicago. Remus had maintained his contact with Zoline even after leaving Chicago and this contact seemed about to bear fruit. Zoline was acquainted with a man named Jesse Smith, whose influence in Washington appeared now to be almost limitless, especially in matters concerning prohibition enforcement.

Jesse Smith was a poker-playing pal of President Harding, but, more important, so far as Remus was concerned, he was the confidant of Harry M. Daugherty, Harding's long-time political mentor and now the new Attorney General. Smith and Daugherty had both grown up in the town of Washington Court House, Ohio, and, as the years passed, had become inseparable partners in Ohio politics. In Washington, Smith, once married but now divorced, shared a house with Daugherty and his wife, and rumors had begun to spread that anyone who wanted favors from the Attorney General had better see Jesse. It was not that easy to see Jesse, however, except for men of some importance. The fact that Zoline had been able to get Remus an appointment with him was a measure of Remus' growing fame among Washington insiders who knew what was happening in the liquor business.

When Zoline brought the two men together at the Commodore,[9] the contrast between them was striking. Remus, the stocky, muscular immigrant, showed his ambition and dynamism in the very aggressiveness of his stance. His quick, forceful speech, though at all times clear and easy to follow, was full of elaborate legal circumlocutions, the speech of a man who had not quite digested his education. In his accent there were still gutteral traces of his German ancestry. Smith by contrast was tall, slender, not attractive but comfortably secure in appearance. He wore a droopy mustache on his round, double-chinned face. His smile was friendly and his manner apparently guileless. Only in their clothing were the two men similar, both being expensively overdressed in their efforts to be elegant.

As soon as Zoline excused himself and the two began their conversation, it became clear that they had one other thing in common—both were businesslike. Smith quickly indicated his awareness that Remus was "a reasonably large operator" in the whisky industry, and Remus explained his need for a much greater flow of withdrawal permits (which the government called 1410 permits) to accommodate his expanding enterprise.

Smith, a very direct man, wasted little time on subtle probings and veiled suggestions. For a consideration, he said, he would make sure Remus got as many permits as he needed. The consideration would have to be a certain sum of money per case of liquor released.

Remus had long since reconciled himself to the hidden expenses of the liquor business. He calculated that his "overage" costs—what he had to pay warehousemen, public officials, the police, and so forth—already came to more than $15 per case, but securing the support of people as important as Jesse Smith and the man he represented would be worth at least another two dollars per case. Remus proposed a sliding scale of payments for the permits—between $1.50 and $2.50 per case, depending on the size of each consignment.

Smith found this an agreeable figure, but he made it clear that so far they were talking only about the issuance of permits, which had nothing to do with immunity from arrest. That was another matter.

Remus, realizing this, had come prepared to bargain separately for the kind of protection he would need to safeguard so large an enterprise. Producing a sheaf of one-thousand-dollar notes, he counted off fifty of them.

Smith accepted the money and pronounced himself satisfied with the arrangement. Neither Remus nor any of his people would ever go to the penitentiary, he promised. Even if they were arrested, even if there were a prosecution, there would be no ultimate conviction.

On this they shook hands. George Remus had good reason to feel secure as the two men parted. It was his understanding, though never openly stated, that he had just bought the Attorney General of the United States.

Chapter 4

If there was anyone in the Anti-Saloon League who might be strong enough to challenge the primacy of Wayne Wheeler, it was Bishop James Cannon, Jr., chairman of the League's National Legislative Committee. Cannon was also chairman of the Temperance and Social Service Commission of his denomination, the Methodist Episcopal Church, South. In the field of politics, he was one of the most influential Democrats below the Mason and Dixon Line. A spellbinder in the pulpit, Cannon had also been a college president, an editor, and, though few people knew it, a shrewd businessman. His differences with Wayne Wheeler stemmed from a rivalry which might be considered natural between two ambitious men in the same organization, and also from opposing views as to how the Anti-Saloon League should operate.

Bishop Cannon, perhaps in part because he was a Democrat, entertained a low opinion of President Harding. "He did not impress me," Cannon once said, "as having the mental caliber of the average President."[1] Cannon knew how easy it would be for a Republican as clever and powerful as Wheeler to manipulate the new President, and he looked with misgivings upon such a possibility. If Harding were drawn too deeply into the League's orbit, the general public might begin to think of prohibition as a purely Republican measure. Such an eventuality might damage the prohibition movement among southern Democrats, most of whom now favored it, and might prevent its growth among northern Democrats, most of whom now opposed it.

Cannon also disapproved of Wheeler's apparent intention to use his Washington lobbyist's post as a means of gathering and dispensing political patronage. Cannon knew how much strength Wheeler could accumulate for himself if he were allowed to choose the government's key prohibition officials. But if Cannon hoped to stop Wheeler, he would have to operate with some subtlety and without open opposition, since they were allies in the same cause. The bishop's method was to remonstrate with Wheeler behind the scenes (always, he insisted, "without heat") about the latter's use of Anti-Saloon League prestige to gain patronage and influence. When this method of restraint did not avail, Cannon several times complained about Wheeler to the League's Legislative Committee, which usually supported Cannon's position. Wheeler's method of handling this committee was to agree with its members, even when they reproved him, then continue his policies unchanged, sometimes even calling upon Cannon to abet these policies.

In early January 1921, Wheeler was so concerned about the inadequacy of the prohibition enforcement budget for the coming year that he asked Cannon to help him get it quadrupled. For the year 1920, a Congress which was as optimistic as it was parsimonious had set aside only $2 million. The chairman of the Senate Appropriations Committee, Francis Warren of Wyoming, had estimated at the time that any serious attempt to enforce prohibition might cost as much as $50 million a year. Wheeler, ironically, on April 3, 1920, had argued that $5 million a year would be adequate—perhaps even too much—since he believed that, in the long run, the American public would want to obey the law. Nine months later, in January 1921, Wheeler was somewhat less optimistic about the public. He now wanted Congress to appropriate about $8 million, and he urged Bishop Cannon to write Senator Warren a sharp letter demanding at least that much.

On January 25, Cannon did write to Warren, quoting a resolution recently passed by the Federal Council of Churches, of which the bishop was Business Committee chairman: "In order that the will of the people in the adoption of the Eighteenth Amendment may be carried into effect, we urge that an appropriation be made by Congress of whatever amount may be necessary for the effective enforcement of National Prohibition."

Cannon himself then went on to say: "The Federal Prohibition Department has asked for an appropriation of $7,500,000 for the coming year. This amount does not provide for any increase in the present force, which in the view of the Federal Council should be augmented to whatever extent is necessary to secure genuine nation-wide enforcement."

Cannon considered this a forthright plea in support of Wheeler's demands, but when Wheeler received his copy of the letter, he was so dissatisfied with it that he sent Cannon a note of rebuke. The bishop quickly responded in kind.

"Why do you not admit it when you are wrong?" Cannon's reply to Wheeler began. "My letter to Senator Warren was perfectly plain. The only trouble was that you did not read my letter, but glanced over it, and because it was not drawn up in the style in which you usually write, you did not think it was as effective as it should have been. You are a lawyer and I am a minister. You are expected to present your views in a certain way, and I am not expected to present mine in the same way that you present yours. I may entirely agree with the method you use in presenting your views, but I would very probably think that method not to be suitable for the presentation of my views. . . ."

These two most dynamic men in the Anti-Saloon League hierarchy did not seem destined to work together harmoniously. Two months later, when Wheeler asked Bishop Cannon to write another letter, this time supporting the candidacy of Ohioan Roy Haynes as Federal Prohibition Commissioner, Cannon openly refused. Such knowledge as he had of Haynes, he explained, did not convince him that Haynes had the qualities necessary for an able and efficient administrator. Haynes, a former army officer, school teacher, and editor, had been for several years a devoted protegé of Wheeler in temperance work. His selection would assure Wheeler of almost complete control over the Prohibition Bureau. Bishop Cannon didn't want his colleague and ally to have that much more influence.

Wheeler, however, was a man accustomed to getting what he

wanted. He badly wanted President Harding to appoint Haynes, and he was determined to make it happen. Persistence was one of Wheeler's outstanding qualities. As a Brookfield, Ohio farmboy, he had persisted in his determination to go to college even against his family's firm opposition. "You're a bright boy," his father had said to him. "You don't need an education." Nevertheless, Wheeler took an elementary school teaching job as soon as he finished high school and finally saved enough money to enter Oberlin, where he earned bachelor and masters degrees by working as a janitor, table-waiter, part-time chaplain, book agent, rug seller, and financial manager of the school paper. After a similar performance at Western Reserve University, he won his law degree in 1898. Meanwhile, having embraced the cause of the Anti-Saloon League, he had decided to become the foremost man in this organization, an ambition he eventually fulfilled after becoming its General Counsel and National Legislative Superintendent. As the League's official lobbyist, he had then set out to become the most powerful man in Washington, and by the summer of 1921 he had come close to accomplishing this aim.

During his first six years in Washington, 1911–17, he prosecuted two thousand legal cases against saloons and in 1915 successfully defended the questionable constitutionality of the dry-sponsored Webb-Kenyon Law before the Supreme Court. (The Webb-Kenyon Law impeded commerce in liquor by allowing dry states to turn back at their borders shipments intended for through-passage to wet states.) By virtue of his control over League contributions to national politicians, and his practice of threatening unfriendly candidates with League opposition, Wheeler had built up so much influence over Congressmen and Senators of both parties that the New York *Evening World* called him "the biggest legislative bully the country has produced." The *World* had also expressed the opinion that "The Senate . . . sits up and begs when Dr. Wayne B. Wheeler snaps the whip."

One of the Senators over whom he had developed an exceptional influence was Warren G. Harding from Wheeler's home state of Ohio. In addition to guiding the Volstead Act through the Senate under Wheeler's direction, Harding had for many years both in Ohio and in Washington, accepted Wheeler's advice or dictates on a variety of policies concerning prohibition. Now that Harding was in the White House, some people considered Wheeler omnipotent, an appraisal which was not quite true, as Wheeler himself learned when he tried to prevent Andrew Mellon (the Pittsburgh financier, reputedly wealthier than any man in the world except John D. Rockefeller) from becoming Secretary of the Treasury in Harding's cabinet.

In February, when it became apparent that the President-elect was planning to appoint Mellon, Wheeler had bombarded Harding with a series of protesting letters. Mellon, he pointed out, was a substantial investor in distilleries. Inasmuch as prohibition enforcement was under the jurisdiction of the Treasury Department, appointing him as secretary would be like asking a bandit to enforce the laws against robbery. Wheeler's protests had been so vigorous, and he had inspired such a flood of mail from League members throughout the country, that Harding had felt obliged on February 20 to send him a soothing letter.[2]

"My dear Wheeler," he wrote from St. Augustine, Florida, where he was vacationing, "Mr. Mellon told me quite frankly that he had been interested indirectly in a number of distilling industries through the process of bank liquidations and one process or another and made no effort to disguise it. Moreover he told me just as frankly that since prohibition became effective he was seeking to lawfully dispose of the property. I am unable to find anything wrong about it myself. I know there will be some prejudice, but it is not possible for me to conceive that a man who is willing to sacrifice his own personal affairs to take up a work for the government is going to turn his talents to taking advantage of a situation relating to prohibition."

Though Harding was perhaps the only man in the world who believed in Andrew Mellon's altruism, his estimate was reasonable in the matter of prohibition. Liquor was a minor item in the broad spectrum of Mellon's financial and economic interests. He was so forceful that even Wheeler had to yield to him, but he might be able to use the loss of this battle to help him win another. If Harding planned to ignore Wheeler's plea against Mellon, would he also dare ignore Wheeler's plea in behalf of Haynes? Harding realized that even within the Anti-Saloon League the choice of Haynes was not popular. No one but Wheeler argued that Haynes was a big enough man for the job. Bishop Cannon's opposition to Haynes was so well publicized in Washington that the fate of Haynes' nomination became a test of strength between Cannon and Wheeler.

In early June, President Harding made it clear which of the League leaders he followed. By appointing Roy Haynes as Prohibition Commissioner, he granted Wayne Wheeler veto power over virtually all prohibition appointments.

Wheeler now felt so strong that in his June 13 thank-you letter to Harding he included a scarcely veiled warning about the President's personal habits:

> ... Permit me to thank you for your cooperation in securing the appointment of Major Haynes. I am sure it will inspire confidence in the friends of law enforcement throughout the country to know that a man of his convictions and energy has been appointed to this place. . . .
>
> Do you know anything about the so-called Auto Piano Weekly that is published by the Auto Piano Company On-the-Hudson at 51st Street, New York City? In their weekly report of June 6 I find this paragraph:

> > The continued rush of applicants for federal jobs to the White House is giving wide-spread circulation in the Capitol to a story that is causing the Anti-Saloon League and other "drys" grave concern. At the time the Hardings moved into the executive mansion aspirants for soft government berths had noticed that the incoming President had been the guest frequently of Edward B. McLean (playboy newspaper publisher), who is reputed to have the most extensively stocked cellar in Washington. The first applicants set an example by sending a case of pre-war stuff to the White House offices, it is said, along with their application or petition, and the practice has been continued, so the story goes, until all possibility of a dry spell at the White House has been eliminated.

> After the signature of the Auto Piano Company is a note which says, "This confidential information is secured from special editorial correspondents at Washington and from other sources which we believe to be reliable." I am sending this to you in order that you may know what kind of information is going out from some of the correspondents. . . .[3]

It was not by inadvertence that Wheeler labeled the story "information" rather than rumor. He was so well acquainted with Harding's drinking habits that on one of his first visits to the White House he had remonstrated with the new President for ignoring the prohibition laws. After informing Harding that many people believed he was serving liquor in the White House, Wheeler had said to him, "Mr. President, I am embarrassed. I have been your friend, as you know, but some of our crowd do not believe in you because they say that you, as President of the dry United States, are drinking. Now, what can

I tell them? I don't want to misrepresent things to them; I simply want to know the truth and I will tell them the truth. Will you be good enough to tell me the facts?"

The embarrassed President, instead of chastising Wheeler for his impertinence, authorized him to "tell anyone who really wanted the facts" that he "never served liquor at the White House," but that he did keep legally in his private apartments "a small quantity of whisky," and that he took a drink from that stock when he wanted to do so. This was hardly a satisfactory answer, but it was the best Wheeler could secure in his first efforts to reform President Harding.

Wheeler was discouraged but not reconciled. He would pursue the matter whenever the opportunity arose, and he would eventually wean his friend Harding off whisky, but meanwhile there were other problems demanding his attention. One was the growing campaign by big brewing companies to permit the sale of beer for medicinal purposes. As long as the Volstead Act permitted the whisky distillers to use this subterfuge, why shouldn't the brewers be granted the same privilege? The Anheuser-Busch Company in St. Louis was complaining that it had spent $18 million converting its $40 million plant to the manufacture of legal near-beer, only to learn that it could not compete with bootleggers who were selling real beer. The wets, taking advantage of this logic, had petitioned the Treasury Department to issue regulations which would allow doctors to prescribe beer. Wheeler, seeing this as "the thin edge of the entering wedge of nullification" of the Volstead Act, had opposedany such regulation and had instigated in Congress an "anti-beer" bill sponsored by Sen. Frank Willis of Ohio and Rep. Philip Campbell of Kansas which would effectively prevent any relaxation of the law.

Those who doubted the influence of Wayne Wheeler could have treated themselves to a demonstration of it by attending the House of Representatives debate on the anti-beer bill one afternoon in early July. Wheeler himself was sitting in the north visitors' gallery, quietly and inconspicuously listening to the debate, when wet Congressman John Philip Hill of Baltimore, Maryland, looked up and pointed a finger at him.[4]

"Mr. Speaker and gentlemen of the House," he said, "the discussion this afternoon has been a very interesting discussion and it must have been an interesting discussion to the author of this bill who sits in the gallery beyond us, Mr. Wheeler."

If Representative Hill was hoping to shame the majority of his colleagues who followed the wishes of Wayne Wheeler, he had underestimated their complaisance. Standing up in a body, they turned toward the Anti-Saloon League lobbyist in the gallery and broke into a round of applause.

Wheeler smiled down benignly, delighted almost as much by the wet attack as he was by the dry support. He loved all kinds of attention, and especially the kind which might be publicized in the newspapers, thus demonstrating, not only to the public but to other powerful figures in his own organization, that he had become a virtually irresistible force.

When the applause of the dry Congressmen ended another wet, Rep. Frederick Britten of Chicago, stood and asked a leading question: "Is that the Mr. Wheeler, the $50,000 attorney that has been referred to on several occasions?"

Hill, who was still on his feet, said, "I understand he is the $25,000 attorney for the Anti-Saloon League."

"And he is a good one," shouted Rep. Thomas Blanton, a dry southern Democrat from Abilene, Texas.

Wheeler continued to smile as he savored this valuable publicity.

Rep. John Kindred, a New York City wet, stood up and asked, "Is he paid by Rockefeller money?" John D. Rockefeller, through his son, John D., Jr., was a known contributor to dry causes. He believed, as did many of the most powerful men in business, industry, and finance, that the nation's workers—which is to say, their employees—would be more productive if beer and liquor could be withheld from them.

In answer to Kindred, Hill asserted his understanding that Wheeler was, indeed, paid by Rockefeller money. Though this was not a very accurate understanding, the drys ignored it, perhaps because they saw nothing unseemly in being paid by Rockefeller money.

Rep. Israel M. Foster of Athens, Ohio, quickly arose to supply a more substantial defense of Wheeler. "I had no idea of taking the time of the House," he said, "and would not except for the cowardly way that my friend has attacked the gentleman in the gallery, Mr. Wheeler. I want to say that I have opposed Mr. Wheeler in lawsuits and in politics and have known him intimately, and if my friend from Maryland ever achieves the reputation for honesty, ability, and integrity that Wayne B. Wheeler has he will deserve it."

At this point, Foster was interrupted by a second ovation for Wheeler even more vociferous than the first. When it subsided, he continued: "I happen to know that Mr. Wheeler did not prepare this bill, and that he does not receive one-third of the salary that my wild friend from Maryland imagines he does."

The House of Representatives broke into applause and laughter, mixed with rebel yells from southerners, as the dry majority clapped and shouted its approval of the smiling man in the gallery. Before the outburst subsided, Representative Hill and the other wets who had provoked it were beginning to wish they had not called attention to the presence of Wayne B. Wheeler. The House promptly passed the Willis-Campbell Act on June 27, and after a protracted wrangle, the Senate, on November 18, did likewise. The U.S. government would recognize no medicinal properties in beer as long as Wayne Wheeler was on the job.

The summer of 1921 had been a period of anxious waiting for a 32-year-old Los Angeles lawyer named Mabel Walker Willebrandt. Major Frank Doherty, a prominent Los Angeles attorney, had suggested in June to Hiram Johnson, California's senior U.S. senator, that Mrs. Willebrandt, despite her youth, would be an excellent choice to fill one of the most important posts in President Harding's new administration—Assistant Attorney General in charge of prohibition enforcement, tax prosecutions, and federal prisons. The position was likely to go to a woman because President Wilson had established a politically compelling precedent during his administration by appointing Mrs. Annette Abbot Adams of San Francisco as the first female assistant attorney general in history. Harding was much too fond of women to offend them by ignoring Wilson's example. Whether the job would go to a woman as young as Mrs. Willebrandt was questionable, however, inasmuch as a more mature lawyer from California named Clara Foltz also wanted it, and California's other senator, Samuel W. Shortridge, was working in her behalf.

One advantage Mrs. Willebrandt had was the fact that the formidable Senator Johnson did not want her rival to get the job. On June 24, after Doherty had submitted Mrs. Willebrandt's name, Johnson had sent him the following telegram:[5]

WASHINGTON TIMES PUBLISHED CLARA FOLTZ LIKELY ASSISTANT ATTORNEY GENERAL. SUCH APPOINTMENT WOULD BE UNFORTU-

NATE AND EMBARRASSING. IF YOU ARE INTERESTED IN WILLE-
BRANDT SUGGEST YOU FORWARD ENDORSEMENTS [TO] ATTORNEY
GENERAL, OF JUDGES, MEN LIKE FLINT [FRANK P. FLINT, A CALI-
FORNIA STATE SENATOR], AND OF REPUBLICAN ORGANIZATIONS
AND WOMEN'S CLUBS.

It was not difficult for Doherty to procure such endorsements
because Mrs. Willebrandt was a remarkable woman. Born in a sod
shanty near Woodsdale, Kansas, where her parents were trying without much success to establish a homestead in 1889, she didn't attend
school until she was thirteen years old. Nevertheless, she graduated
from high school at sixteen and went on to Park College (Presbyterian) in Parkville, Missouri, where she was expelled by the president because she refused to accept his Calvinist belief in predestina-
tion. She couldn't imagine that she was not the mistress of her own
fate.

When her family moved to Traverse City, Michigan, she began
teaching in a country school. There she fell in love with the principal,
a young man named Alfred F. Willebrandt, who was planning to
move to Arizona because his health was delicate. Feeling it was her
romantic destiny to look after him, she determined to accompany him
westward. On February 7, 1910, they were married, and shortly
thereafter left for Arizona, where she graduated from Tempe Normal
School (now Arizona State University) in 1911. A year later they
moved to Los Angeles; there she taught in a public school while
attending the University of Southern California law school at night.
She had preferred to study medicine but was forced to settle for law
because medical classes were not offered at night.

After being admitted to the California bar in 1915, Mrs. Willebrandt soon demonstrated her imagination and political ingenuity by
persuading the Los Angeles City Council to appoint her to a position
she herself had conceived—public defender for women in trouble.
Three years and two thousand cases later, she had become so prominent in Los Angeles through her defense of abandoned mothers,
accused prostitutes, and other distressed women that influential people began paying attention to her. In 1917 she became chairman of
the Legal Advisory Board for the Los Angeles Military Draft Board.
Her private law practice had grown so lucrative by 1918 that she gave
up her post as public defender, but by this time she had so convinc-

ingly proven the need for such a service that the Los Angeles City Council established it permanently.

The rapid rise of young Mrs. Willebrandt had not been without personal cost. At the beginning of 1916 she had separated from her husband, who continued to teach school as she developed her career in law and politics. She was elected president of the Women Lawyers' Club, then president of the Women's Professional Club. She became active in the Republican Party, supporting Herbert Hoover for the Presidential nomination in 1920. By this time she had become well acquainted with fellow attorney Doherty, and he was so dazzled by her ability that when the assistant attorney general vacancy occurred after Harding's inauguration, he eagerly recommended her for it.

Though she was applying for the job of chief prohibition enforcer in the Department of Justice, Mrs. Willebrandt's attitude toward liquor was surprisingly tolerant. She had always kept a supply in her house and drank moderately even though her mother was opposed to it. Her mother's brother had been a member of an Oklahoma posse which was wiped out by a gang of drunken hoodlums. Mrs. Willebrandt's parents, both from Protestant backgrounds, had neither professed nor passed on to her any denominational religious affiliation, but they had instilled in her a letter-of-the-law moral code that prompted her to give up all alcoholic beverages when prohibition began. She felt no reluctance or hesitation, therefore, at the prospect of prosecuting people for violations of the Volstead Act.

Through the summer, Doherty and Senator Johnson continued their correspondence on the subject of Mrs. Willebrandt's possible appointment, but as the weeks passed the outlook seemed gloomy. On July 16, in a telegram to a San Francisco friend, Johnson wrote, "At request of Frank Doherty, [I] recommended Willebrandt some weeks ago. Do not know what will be done."

Five days later, on the twenty-first, Senator Johnson said in a letter to Doherty, "Just as a sideline on the application of Mrs. Willebrandt, I want to advise you that the Republican Study Club, Florence C. Porter, president, has endorsed her. Outside of the fact that Mrs. Willebrandt was for Hoover, that recently she has been in consultation with certain ladies who are very strongly against us, and that the Republican Study Club has endorsed her, I have heard nothing to her detriment."

Johnson, a maverick Republican, sometimes reactionary but sometimes extremely progressive, had almost as many enemies in his own party as he had among the Democrats. Perhaps this fact was working to his disadvantage in his efforts to help Mrs. Willebrandt. It was possible also that, since he didn't actually know her, and since he was unenthusiastic about some of the things he knew about her, he was not exerting his maximum effort in her behalf. Doherty, becoming apprehensive, continued to press her case from Los Angeles, and on August 4 he was rewarded by another letter from Johnson which was somewhat more reassuring: "Your recommendation of Mrs. Willebrandt," the letter said, "was sufficient for me to do everything I can with Attorney General Daugherty, and to continue that attitude. . . ."

Thereafter, Doherty and Mrs. Willebrandt could do no more than wait. Finally, on August 13, good news arrived in the form of a telegram from the Attorney General, asking Mrs. Willebrandt to come to Washington for an interview. She knew the interview was only a formality. When she boarded the train in Los Angeles, she was beginning a new life which would soon make her one of the nation's most famous women.

Capt. Robert E. Flora, Chief Prohibition Agent for the Cincinnati District, was alarmed and somewhat chagrined on the evening of Oct. 23, 1921, when prohibition agents from several other cities called to tell him they were in town and invited him to accompany them on a raid they intended to make that night. When Flora went to the Sinton Hotel to meet them, he found five men awaiting him and soon learned that their target was George Remus. They were about to leave for the Death Valley Farm out near Cheviot, the place Remus used as a bottling plant, storage depot, and transfer point. Flora would have been happy to prevent his fellow agents from sweeping down on this establishment. He knew Remus well and enjoyed a profitable friendship with him, as did many of the men in the Cincinnati office.[6] But these were not ordinary agents who had suddenly arrived in town to go after Remus. They included Bert C. Morgan, Federal Prohibition Director for the state of Indiana; W. O. Holman, Chief of the Indiana Field Forces; and G. L. Simons, General Prohibition Agent, of Chicago. And it soon became apparent that they were not simply here on their own initiative. Someone in Washington was making a serious attempt to put Remus out of business.

The Remus operation had become so enormous that everyone connected with prohibition enforcement was aware of it. Besides the Squibb Company in Indiana, he owned several other large distilleries including the Rugby Distillery in Louisville, the Old Lexington Co. near Lexington; the Pogue Distilling Co. in Maysville, Kentucky; and, in Cincinnati, the Edgewater and the Clifton Springs companies. He seemed to encounter no restrictions in procuring permits to withdraw liquor "for medicinal purposes" from any of these institutions, or from a variety of other sources. Within the last year he had moved an estimated three-quarters of a million gallons of whisky. He was now reputed to be a millionaire a few times over and his generosity was so widespread that it would be difficult for Captain Flora or any of the other Cincinnati area officials to mount a raid against him even if they so desired.

It was perhaps for this reason that none of them had been consulted when prohibition officials in Washington (not yet identified but presumed to include even the brand new Assistant Attorney General in charge of liquor law enforcement, Mrs. Mabel Walker Willebrandt) decided to move against Remus. General Agent Simons of Chicago had visited Cincinnati in June to launch the investigation, but his instructions had obviously come from a higher authority.

Simons and Morgan now informed Captain Flora that the Death Valley Farm had been under surveillance, and that they themselves had been out there this very evening to acquaint themselves with the physical setup. They had seen five or six automobiles parked near the main group of buildings, and were convinced that the depot was operating at this very moment. Did Captain Flora wish to accompany them on the mission? He was not in a position to reject the invitation.

It was after midnight when the six men, carrying a search warrant and a variety of firearms, arrived at Death Valley Farm. The place was quiet, with only a few lights burning, but there were still some automobiles in the yard near the farmhouse.[7]

Instead of knocking, the agents, led by Morgan, tried the door. Finding it open, they slipped silently into the farmhouse, then turned on the lights and announced themselves. They found six armed men in the house, some asleep, others dozing. None of them reached for a gun. As Captain Flora read out the search warrant which justified the entry, Morgan's men rounded up the occupants and placed them under arrest, then began a careful search of the building.

Outside, Agent Holman, who was standing guard near the front door, walked around to the side just in time to see a man slip out the back door and run for the hill behind the house. "Stop!" cried Holman, and the man did so, throwing something onto the ground to his left. When Holman reached the man and looked down into the grass, he found a 38-caliber revolver. Picking it up, he marched the man back to the house, where he was placed under arrest with the other six occupants.

The search of the farmhouse yielded more revolvers and ammunition, several casks of wine in the basement, and some bottled goods on the second floor. Equally important as evidence was a stack of books and papers including bank deposit slips bearing the name "George Remus." In a building near the house, the agents found the Remus bottling works, with twelve barrels of whisky waiting to be bottled, plus several cases of whisky, two thousand gallons of wine, five hundred bottles of gin, and twelve bottles of champagne already bottled.

Within three hours, most of this evidence and the seven arrested men were in front of U.S. Commissioner Thomas Gregory at a night session in his Federal Building office. All seven pleaded not guilty to violating the national prohibition act. Morgan announced they would not be the only men arrested in the case.

Five days later, Remus and six more of his men were also indicted on charges of conspiring to violate the Volstead Act. This was a nuisance to Remus, but he did not regard it as a catastrophe. Through an intermediary he was able to contact his Washington protector, Jesse Smith, and shortly thereafter the two men met again in New York.

Smith was not uneasy about the situation. He assured Remus he was in absolutely no danger. The Department of Justice would put up a vigorous battle to convict him, but it would be just a blind. Remus would never see the penitentiary. It was possible, of course, that if he were tried by a jury he might be convicted, but the case would then go to a court of appeals and there it would be reversed.[8]

This was a promise Remus could easily accept because in his judgment as a lawyer, an appeals court would rule in his favor on the merits of the case alone. As far as he could see, the government men had found no evidence that he was doing anything illegal. He had permits to cover the liquor they had discovered, and there was nothing among the records in the farmhouse to prove he was selling it illegally.

When Remus returned to Cincinnati, it was with a confident outlook and a consuming eagerness to get back to business. There was much work to do. He had to reassure his fellow defendants (for whom he had provided bail) and the rest of his employees that they had no reason to worry. He had to get Death Valley Farm back in operation and his trucks back on the road. Besides this, there were several more distilleries he wanted to buy. He was already negotiating for some of them. He didn't have time to worry about his upcoming trial. His lawyers, expensive but intelligent, could handle that. And with the Justice Department cooperating, there could be no doubt about the outcome. As long as he had Harry Daugherty, the Attorney General of the United States working for him, his continued safety and prosperity were assured.

Because the Manhattan office of the Federal Prohibition Bureau was responsible for enforcement in all of southern New York state, the office's most productive agents, Izzy Einstein and Moe Smith, were often sent to raid out-of-city saloons or speakeasies (an old Irish word for illegal bars) which local agents had lacked the enterprise to close. Even for these out-of-town assignments Izzy and Moe had to adopt disguises. They were becoming famous and recognizable throughout the New York area. They had now developed a repertoire of several dozen roles, gaining access to bars as common laborers, football players (properly smeared with mud) coal men, fruit vendors, longshoremen, college students, streetcar conductors, shipyard workers, truck drivers, cloak-and-suiters, and musicians. Izzy even presented himself one day as a judge at a Fulton Street speakeasy called the Assembly, which was frequented by bona fide judges, attorneys, and public officials, all of whom had to find other speakeasies after "Judge" Einstein ruled the place out of order.

Izzy liked disguises. He believed that the primary skill of a dry agent was to be able to look and act as if he weren't one. It seemed to him that most policemen were unsuitable for prohibition work because, in or out of uniform, they acted like cops. Wherever a prohibition agent might go, he should appear to belong there. "Dress clothes for Broadway," as Izzy put it, "and overalls for the waterfront."[9] But his disguises consisted of more than changes of costume. He was an adaptable man and a skillful actor. He could be a fast-talking salesman, a happy jokester, or a timid farmer bewildered by the city. Since he spoke three foreign languages—German, Polish, and Hungarian—almost as fluently as he spoke English, he could also pass as a helpless immigrant. He studied his prospective victims carefully, decided what kind of person they would trust, and presented himself as that kind of person.

When the commandant of the U.S. Military Academy at West Point had complained that bootleggers were selling liquor to his cadets, for instance, Izzy and Moe had gone there disguised as cigar salesmen. In choosing his disguise for that occasion, Izzy had been tempted to promote himself from civilian to general since he felt that, as a five-foot-tall 225-pounder, he was "built more like a general than a private soldier." But he had then decided against such a rapid promotion. "Not feeling up to assuming too high a rank on the spur of the moment," he later explained, "I compromised by being a cigar salesman and took along a colored man carrying two large bags of samples."

Using the cigars as bait, he had dried up the West Point area so completely that the commandant drove him to the station when he was leaving. Izzy had not been certain, though, whether the commandant, who seemed less than friendly, had taken him to the train because he was grateful or because he was eager to get Izzy out of town. Some of the bootleggers Izzy raided may have been supplying officers as well as cadets.

The cigar-selling device had worked so well at West Point that he decided to try it again, on October 25, 1921, when he and Moe visited the hilly, forested area of Wallomsac, a small town near Troy, about 160 miles north of New York City.[10] However, they soon found a major difference between West Point and Wallomsac. The West Point cadets, officers and gentlemen by act of Congress, had given them no trouble. Wallomsac, a lumber town, was full of big, thirsty lumberjacks who, by their very presence, had frightened away other prohibition agents.

Izzy and Moe drove confidently into town, stopped their open car in front of a cluster of men lounging idly on the main street, and proceeded to offer them cigars at four cents apiece. Since the same brand was on sale locally for ten cents, the two cigar salesmen quickly became popular. When they asked their customers where they could buy a drink, a chorus of voices recommended the same place, a landmark called the Chicken-Coop Inn.

Izzy and Moe found this cozy café crowded with about twenty lumberjacks. After peddling more of their bargain cigars to these men, they turned to the proprietor, a gentleman named Eugene Sargood, and offered him the rest of their stock at a price he couldn't resist.

Sargood was so pleased with his purchase that Izzy and Moe didn't have to ask him for drinks. He offered them eight different brands of whisky, wine, and home brew. Izzy, accepting them all, announced that Sargood and his bartender were now under arrest, and the Chicken-Coop Inn was henceforth closed.

When the twenty or more lumberjacks realized what was happening, an ominous silence fell over the room, followed by a shuffle of heavy boots and a chorus of enraged voices. Izzy and Moe, watching the men close in on them, backed away to the nearest wall. Drawing their 38-caliber government pistols, they pointed at the men and ordered them to stop.

For a dangerous few moments, the irate lumberjacks appeared ready to attack despite the guns. Then, grumbling sourly and mouthing obscenities, they slowly becked away, and when Izzy ordered them to leave the premises, they grudgingly complied.

Fortunately for Izzy and Moe, they had parked their car just outside. Loading the proprietor and his bartender into it before a hostile crowd could gather, they drove off, glancing anxiously backward to make sure they weren't followed. Next day their two prisoners were in the Rensselaer County Jail at Troy, while Izzy and Moe were back in Manhattan, thinking of new roles to play in their search for new victims.

As if the cigar salesman disguise hadn't exposed them to enough danger, the two agents were soon trying out an even more perilous deception. For almost a week they kept dropping in every day or so to buy salami, bread, and cheese at a busy delicatessen in the center of Harlem, 456 Lenox Avenue, near 133rd Street.[11] The proprietor, a man named Louis Immerman, and his clerks had begun to accept the two fat, friendly partners as long-time Harlem residents, new to this immediate neighborhood. Izzy and Moe were now speaking in Negro dialects and their skins were convincingly black—at least those portions not covered by clothing. They were trying their most unlikely disguise to date and it was apparently effective, perhaps because they had darkened themselves just enough to look nonwhite.

Izzy was certain the store had some secret system of selling contraband but he couldn't figure out how it worked. A steady stream of customers, mostly men, came and went, but they asked only for groceries, which they carried away in the usual paper sacks. Some groceries seemed more popular with these customers than others, but the significance of this was not made clear until March 2, when one of the clerks apparently decided Izzy and Moe were trustworthy.

You've got to know the passwords, he confided to them. If you want a pint of gin, you ask for "a small can of tomatoes." A pint of whisky is "a small can of beans." A quart is a large can.

After ascertaining that the price of a pint, whether whisky or gin, was two dollars, Izzy Einstein eagerly asked for small cans of both beans and tomatoes. He was surprised to discover, when the clerk handed him his sack, that he had in fact bought beans and tomatoes. However, as promised, the sack also contained whisky and gin. With the contraband in hand, he announced to the clerk and to proprietor Immerman that they had been duped by government agents and that the establishment would soon be padlocked.

Though Immerman received the news calmly, one of his clerks, a man named Daniel Frey, was unable to contain himself. When Moe Smith walked behind the counter to begin searching the premises, Frey barred his way and struck out at him. Frey soon learned he had chosen the wrong agent to attack. Moe was fat, but he had once been a boxer and he was still agile. With two quick hooks he induced Frey to abandon further resistance.

In the back room Izzy and Moe found four hundred pints and quarts of gin, eighty gallons of "moonshine" whisky, and, in a pickle barrel, one hundred pocket-size bottles of gin. The password for these, of course, was "pickles." Since the proprietor and his men were now resigned to their fate, it appeared that the raid would proceed routinely, but before a government truck arrived from the Knickerbocker Warehouse to carry away the evidence, there was a new development. Hundreds of actual Harlem residents gathered outside the delicatessen, pushing and shoving in an effort to get their hands on the two simulated blacks inside. Once again, Izzy and Moe were in deep trouble, but before the infuriated crowd could enter the store and drag out these phony "brothers," the sound of sirens announced the arrival of the police from the West 135th Street Station.

Though Izzy and Moe were saved from the wrath of the people they had so presumptuously impersonated, these citizens of Harlem had delivered a strong message to them. Until now, Harlem had been virtually untouched by prohibition, and it would be a long time before any dry agents decided to try another raid above 110th Street.

Chapter 5

It was only fourteen months since the Republican election sweep of 1920 which had left Big Bill Thompson in political control of the whole state of Illinois, but already he was plagued with problems. The Chicago *Tribune* had instituted a taxpayer's suit against him for defrauding the city of $2,800,000 in overpayment of fees to friends he had appointed as building inspectors. The inference was that he had pocketed a large share of this money through kickback arrangements. At the same time, Governor Len Small, who was wholly owned and operated by Mayor Thompson, had been charged with realizing a $2 million profit for himself and friends when he was state treasurer, by putting several million dollars worth of state funds into banks owned by these friends without collecting any of the interest the state should have received on its deposits.

"Len Small and I will see you all in hell!" Thompson bellowed when the governor's trouble became public. "Whether this is a government of the people, for the people and by the people, or whether this is a government of money, of newspapers and of crooked political bosses against the people, is to be proved. We will go on!"

What worried Thompson more than this fuss about a bit of simple graft was the growing fuss about the epidemic of crime throughout the city now that great armies of organized hoodlums had moved into the bootlegging business. The Chicago police had so far proven themselves almost totally unable to cope with this situation, perhaps because, as Police Chief Charles C. Fitzmorris was frank to admit, "Sixty percent of my police are in the bootleg business."

Fitzmorris was not yet ready to admit this publicly, but he already knew it was true and so did Thompson, who had no strong prejudice against accepting bootleg profits himself. One of his biggest contributors and most helpful supporters was the South Side panderer-hoodlum-bootlegger Johnny Torrio who, having inherited the small empire of his slain uncle, Big Jim Colosimo, was now building an organization unique in the history of crime. As soon as his complacent uncle was out of the way, Torrio had begun a giant expansion of his illicit liquor business, both retail and wholesale. To preempt key territories he opened saloons and cabarets throughout the south and southwest sections of Chicago and in many of the suburbs. To supply these establishments, he put fleets of trucks on the roads, transporting liquor from Detroit, which was the port of entry for Canadian whisky, and from the Ohio-Kentucky region, where men like George Remus had huge stocks of good bourbon for sale. Because this kind of whisky was too good for the average customer, Torrio had also opened cutting plants, where the bourbon could be diluted at ratios of three and four to one, then rebottled for delivery to the saloons. For beer customers, Torrio had established clandestine breweries in several locations and had made a deal with at least one former brewer to reactivate facilities which had stood idle since prohibition began.

To maintain an operation of this size, Torrio had to have police protection. He had already developed a very reliable payoff network when he was managing his uncle's brothels and gambling casinos. He had only to expand this network by recruiting more policemen and more police officials. There was no shortage of cops willing to go on his payroll. A more serious concern was the day-to-day supervision of his growing underworld empire and the protection of his territory from other entrepreneurs who were imitating his methods. Most prominent among them was a well-armed florist and Democratic politician named Dion O'Banion, whose gang controlled much of the North Side. Aware of the constant threat posed by O'Banion and other North Side hoodlums, Torrio had raised an army of a hundred men or more, under the direction of his closest associate and chief enforcer, Al Capone. With increasing frequency, these men were using their guns as instruments of persuasion and negotiation, and as a result, the people of Chicago were becoming alarmed.

Mayor Thompson was getting complaints about all this not only from the churches and the civic betterment organizations but, amazingly, from State's Attorney Robert Emmett Crowe, whom the mayor had helped to elect.[1] When Thompson named his own private secretary, Fitzmorris, to be Chief of Police, Crowe, not having been consulted, resented the slur so deeply he began a virtual vendetta with the new chief. Fitzmorris, after inspiring a flurry of police activity during his first months in charge of the department, had gradually subsided into lassitude like so many Chicago police chiefs before him, and the hoodlums were carrying on their businesses with a minimum of interference. This offered the politically ambitious State's Attorney an exploitable situation. At every opportunity Crowe criticized the police chief for laxity and blamed him for Chicago's obvious increase in crime. After a May 1921 gang murder which, like most other gang murders, resulted in no arrest, Crowe had demanded that a special detail of forty policemen be transferred to his command. That was all he needed, he said, to wipe out crime and vice in Chicago.

Overriding the protests of Fitzmorris, Thompson gave Crowe his forty men, whom he promptly placed under the leadership of a man named Ben Newmark. Within a few months, Newmark and his men had accepted so many bribes that people were referring to them as Ali Baba and the forty thieves. Crime and vice continued to flourish and Crowe continued to blame the chief of police for it.

So much of this criticism rubbed off onto Thompson that in January 1922 he decided to do something about it. On the nineteenth he summoned as many of Chicago's civic and religious leaders as he could squeeze into his office.[2] When he addressed them it was not off the top of his head as usual but from a prepared text.

"Gentlemen," Thompson said, "I have called you into conference not only because you represent the moral and religious sentiment of the community, but also because I feel that your cooperation is absolutely essential to the successful execution of a plan which I have worked out whereby every hell-hole in this city where vice exists and moonshine is sold will be permanently closed."

Did the mayor actually intend to go after the bootleggers and hoodlums? His audience listened eagerly for the details of his plan.

"I have decided," he said, "to appoint a special law enforcement commissioner to be paid out of the mayor's contingent fund, to investigate all complaints of nonenforcement of the law and to aid me in weeding out any incompetent or dishonest public employee, and to furnish legal evidence which will make it possible to close up all places where vice, gambling, or illegal liquor selling is found to exist."

Was this, then, the extent of his plan? Did he think the appointment of one more man to his office staff would banish crime and vice from Chicago? State's Attorney Crowe had at least asked for forty men. Who was this remarkable man Mayor Thompson intended to hire? He didn't say.

"In my campaign of 1914," he reminded his audience, "I pledged the people of Chicago that if elected, I would drive criminals out of Chicago, and that the people would receive honest service for every dollar appropriated for municipal purposes. The fact is that during the last six years Chicago has been made the healthiest large city in the world. The fact is that crime is less in proportion to our population than at any time in Chicago's history. But so long as crime is still prevalent, there will be work to do to reduce that crime to a minimum, and if possible to eliminate it entirely."

When the assembled community leaders filed out of the mayor's office, they realized they had just heard one of Big Bill Thompson's better performances. He had begun by declaring war on crime and ended by declaring he had already won that war. His statement ought to have been reassuring to everybody. Even to people like Johnny Torrio and Dion O'Banion.

George Remus sat at a table with his staff of six lawyers in the U.S. District Court room in Cincinnati and gazed confidently around the large chamber—at Judge John W. Peck on the bench, at the jury of respectable businessmen just a few feet from him, at the four government prosecuting attorneys on the opposite side, and at his thirteen codefendant employees who filled the enclosure behind him. Beyond them he could see his smartly dressed young wife encouraging him with a smile. Imogene had been a great help to him. She took a more than routine wifely interest in his business affairs, though right now she was spending most of her time supervising the reconstruction of the mansion on the ten-acre estate they had purchased in Price Hill. Among other things, she was installing a huge indoor swimming pool. Before she was finished, they would have the finest house in the city.

Despite the fact that Remus and his thirteen employees were on trial for conspiring to violate the Volstead Act, he had no reason to suppose the trial would last very long. The case might even be dismissed on this opening day if Judge Peck were to accept the first motion by the defense.[3]

One of Remus' attorneys, James Kilgarriff, arose to argue the motion. The books, papers, whisky, rifles, and other articles taken by federal agents from Death Valley Farm on October 23 of the previous year should be returned to the defendants, Kilgarriff insisted, because the search warrant which authorized the raid was illegal. The warrant was so indefinite it failed even to name the persons, the place, or the acts these persons were supposedly committing at this place.

If Judge Peck were to accept this reasoning, the government case would collapse immediately. The judge, however, rejected it without pause. He overruled Kilgarriff's motion on the ground that the presence of this evidence at the farm was proof that the search warrant had been justified, and that it had been definite enough. The trial therefore proceeded, but Remus still looked unconcerned. The government agents hadn't caught any of his men selling liquor at the farm.

Before the first day of the trial ended, however, the prosecution presented a sworn statement by a witness named Howard Hughes that he had purchased a case of whisky at the farm. This kind of evidence could be damaging.

On the second day of testimony, May 9, another unpleasant development awaited Remus. Mrs. Mary Hubbard, the wife of one of his night watchmen, appeared as a government witness. "We lived in the house on the hill," she said, referring to one of the smaller structures on the farm. "A great many of the men here were at the farm often." Then, stepping from the stand, she walked over to the defendants, identifying one after another as frequenters of the place.

When she came to the principal defendant, she looked at him and said, "George Remus came to the farm every day, or every other day."

She had often seen trucks come, she said, carrying "boxes and barrels" similar to whisky containers.

"Did you recognize any labels or marks on these boxes or barrels?" one of the prosecuting attorneys asked.

"Yes," she said. "Fleischman and Squibb." And to this she then added the names of other brands from distilleries owned by Remus: "Dearborn, Brady Special, Rugby, Westfield, Clifton Springs, and Highland Rye."

The next day, the government presented a parade of witnesses who admitted they had purchased whisky on the farm at prices ranging from seventy-eight to ninety-one dollars per case, and Mrs. Hubbard returned to the stand to identify some of these men as visitors to the farm. The outlook no longer seemed so promising for Remus, nor did it improve as the trial continued.

Robert Squibb, one of two brothers from whom Remus had bought the Squibb Distillery, said he had retained offices near the plant after he had sold it, and he had noticed that "a great deal of bottling" was done there between June and October, 1921. He also said armed convoys of trucks appeared "as often as three or four times a week" to move large quantities of whisky out of the distillery.

As the evidence mounted, there could be little doubt in the minds of the jurors that George Remus and his men were dealing in liquor on a vast scale. The questions which Remus' lawyers kept raising about the legality of some of the evidence could not obscure the fact that the evidence was convincing; nor was it easy to persuade a respectable, middle-class and middlewestern jury that Remus should be freed because his operations were at least technically legal. His intent, obviously, had been to subvert the prohibition law.

On May 16, 1922, the jury took only two hours of deliberation before finding all fourteen of the defendants guilty. Remus, as the chief offender, received the stiffest sentence, the maximum under the law—$10,000 and costs plus two years in the federal penitentiary at Atlanta. The other sentences ranged down to $1,000 and fifteen months.

Remus accepted the verdict calmly, turning to smile at his codefendants and reassure them that they would, nevertheless, go free. "I did not conspire against the United States government," he said from his jail quarters that evening. "I have been engaged in many business transactions during the last few years, but in none of them have I been conscious of violating the laws of the United States. We will, of course, file our appeal, and I hope for better results if we can obtain a new trial."

By 11:30 that night, Mrs. Remus had raised bond money for her husband and all of his convicted associates. She arrived in the District Court Clerk's office dressed in bright red and sat down to sign her name, "Imogene Remus," beside her husband's signature on each of the papers. A few minutes later she was in her husband's arms and they were driving away together, apparently as happy as honeymooners.

A few days later, Remus was at the Washington Hotel in Washington, D.C., meeting with his protector, Jesse Smith. Remus was more than slightly impatient now with Smith and his pal, Harry Daugherty, whom Smith called "The General." What kind of Attorney General was Daugherty if he couldn't even control the activities of the Justice Department? The Department was a huge organization, of course, and the boss could hardly keep his eye on everything his subordinates were doing. So it wasn't quite fair to blame the General whenever you got into trouble with his men. The advantage of having the General's protection was that he could get you out of trouble after you got yourself into it.

In fact, however, the General hadn't yet made any apparent move to help Remus. This was what Remus couldn't understand. Counting on Justice Department intervention, he had adopted a trial strategy which resulted not only in his own conviction but in the conviction of some of his men who might otherwise have gone free.

"If I had taken the witness stand," he said to Smith, "I could have thrown out at least eight or nine of the boys that now stand convicted." By admitting his own guilt, he insisted, he could have absolved them of responsibility. He had not done so because he had understood there would be no convictions. But now, he and his men all stood convicted. Just exactly what was Smith prepared to do about that?

The Court of Appeals would undoubtedly reverse the decision, Smith said. Attorney Zoline, who had first introduced Remus to Smith and who was present again at this meeting, agreed with Smith, who went on to say that even if it were not reversed in the Court of Appeals, either a commutation would be entered or there would be some kind of reversal in the Supreme Court. Still, he was confident it would not go that far. He was certain the decision would be reversed in the Court of Appeals.

In any case, Smith declared, "The General" had assured him that ultimately neither Remus nor his men would be sent away to the penitentiary.

Remus could hardly ask for an assurance more definite, or from a higher authority. The two men now had only one more item of business to conclude. Smith had several thousand dollars coming to him as part of their continuing arrangement. Remus took a stack of bills from his pocket and counted them out. By the time he got back to Cincinnati, his trial and conviction seemed like nothing more than a routine business problem which would soon be solved—and just as soon forgotten in the glow of expanding operations and profits.

The summer of 1922 had been a difficult period for President Harding. His wife, Florence, a formidable, watchful, and assertive woman who called him "Wurr'n" and whom he called "the Duchess," now knew almost all there was to know about his intermittent affair with Ohio schoolgirl Nan Britten, who had borne a child by Harding in 1919. In addition to "the Duchess'" constant reminders of his past sins and suspicious safeguards against future ones, Harding had also to cope, as Washington's midsummer heat intensified, with an epidemic of political and economic problems.

On June 25, the nation-wide coal strike, already in progress since April, broke into serious violence when strikers at Herrin, Illinois, killed twenty-one strikebreakers. With the strike continuing into August, the prospects of a winter coal shortage were increasing, especially since a strike of 400,000 railroad shop workers had been in progress since the beginning of July. Congress, at the same time, was complicating the President's problems by passing a high tariff bill and a soldiers' bonus bill he opposed, while rejecting a tax reduction he had approved. And the prohibitionists, led by Wayne Wheeler, were pressing for a "supplemental Volstead Act" to stem the alarming flow of liquor "for medicinal purposes." The drys were even beginning to demand that a poison be added to all industrial alcohol so that bootleggers would have to stop using it in the manufacture of their booze. This was not the kind of "normalcy" Harding had wanted to get back to when he coined his famous slogan during the presidential campaign of 1920. His idea of normalcy was a continuous calm which would enable the country to manage itself while he played golf with businessmen in the afternoon and drank with the boys during evening poker sessions.

Before Harding became President, his wife, surprisingly, had shared this vision of the happy life, at least to the extent that she partook of it. When Harding, as a Senator, was invited to the poker soirées of Theodore Roosevelt's son-in-law, Nicholas Longworth, "the Duchess" would accompany him, not to take part in the game, but to sit in the background and tend bar. According to Alice Roosevelt Longworth, who often witnessed the scene, the poker players would say, as they finished their drinks, "Duchess, you are laying down on the job," whereupon Mrs. Harding would get up and refill their glasses.[4] Since she herself drank only sparingly and never played poker, her attendance at these sessions puzzled her acquaintances. Mrs. Longworth speculated that she "could not bear to miss anything," but it was more likely that, knowing "Wurr'n's" weakness for women, she simply preferred not to let him out alone at night. As long as she knew he was only drinking and playing poker she was tolerant. Even after he became President she remained tolerant for more than a year. Mrs. Longworth has described sessions in the White House library which caused rumors to spread all over Washington:

> No rumor could have exceeded the reality; the study was filled with cronies [including Attorney General Harry Daugherty and his pal, Jesse Smith, who was also his contact with bootleggers like George Remus] . . .; the air heavy with tobacco smoke, trays with bottles containing every imaginable brand of whiskey stood about, cards and poker chips ready at hand—a general atmosphere of waistcoat unbuttoning, feet on the desk, and the spittoon alongside.

Another description of these parties came from Charles Forbes, a Harding crony later convicted of bribery but in 1922 the director of the Veterans' Bureau:

> We played at a rectangular table in the north end of the room. On this particular occasion the President sat at one end and Will Hays, who was then Postmaster General, at the other. The others were Albert Lasker, at that time chairman of the Shipping Board; Harry Daugherty, Ned McLean, Mrs. McLean, and Mrs. Harding. Mrs. Harding did not play— she often sat with us at poker games but never played. I remember that it was very hot and that Albert Lasker took his coat off, displaying red suspenders two inches wide. I won $397 and Will Hays won. The losers all paid up promptly.

Warren Harding enjoyed these parties perhaps more than any of the prerogatives the presidency had brought him. As the pressure from

Wayne Wheeler and other drys increased, however, the parties diminished in size and frequency. Wheeler, after asking the President to stop serving liquor in the White House, had followed up his original plea with a more recent and more exacting one. Wheeler asked Harding now if he didn't feel the time had come when, because of the example it would set, he could afford to give up even his "occasional" drink.

"Your example as President of the United States," Wheeler had pointed out, "would mean more than that of any other individual."[5]

The harassed President had never believed in prohibition, but as a native of Ohio, the birthplace of the Anti-Saloon League, he had never felt courageous enough to oppose it publicly. On the contrary, he had an excellent record of helping the cause whenever Wheeler called upon him. Had he not, therefore, done enough for prohibition without going so far as to give up drinking? He thought so but he didn't dare say so to Wheeler. "I am considering that," he said when Wheeler asked him to abstain completely. "One of these days I probably will stop it."

While the day of his renunciation had not yet arrived in the summer of 1922, the days of revelry in the White House had faded, as journalist Mark Sullivan learned when he visited the President on one of the hottest nights of the year. Harding and Sullivan were friends of long standing, but Harding was obviously out of sorts that night when the two men met in one of the downstairs rooms. He didn't even offer his guest a drink. He had asked Sullivan to come, he said, because he wanted to hear the journalist's advice on how to handle the continuing coal strike. Harding's exasperation was not directed entirely at the miners. "Those Goddam operators are so stiff-necked," he said, "you can't do anything with them."

Sullivan, unfortunately, had no easy solution to offer. United Mine Workers' president John L. Lewis was too tough and too strong to compromise, but the stubborn mine owners were not yet convinced of this, so the strike was destined to continue until September before the miners prevailed. After Harding and Sullivan discussed the problem at some length, their conversation began to run down, since neither man could offer any bright suggestions for ending the deadlock.

Finally, Harding said with a sigh, "Oh well, let's go upstairs and have a drink."[6]

Sullivan, following the President up the broad staircase, was surprised to find himself ushered not into the Chief Executive's private living room but into his bedroom. Mrs. Harding soon appeared and, at her husband's suggestion, produced highballs for the two men without involving any White House servant in the process. As they sat down to enjoy their drinks, the atmosphere was so furtive that Harding felt compelled to apologize.

"We both think that we ought not to drink in the White House," he said, "but we feel that our own bedrooms are our house and we can do what we like here."

Rhode Island, one of the two states which still refused to ratify the Eighteenth Amendment to the Constitution, had so blatantly disregarded the Volstead Act during the nearly three years of prohibition that officials in Washington feared other states might soon decide to emulate this smallest but most stubborn of the forty-eight. One of the only three original colonies which granted religious freedom to Roman Catholics in the seventeenth century, Rhode Island had become, through the years, so attractive to Catholic immigrants that almost three fourths of its 604,000 population were now Catholic. As a group, they were no more friendly to prohibition than Catholics elsewhere, and because they represented such a massive sector of the state's population, they were able to show their feelings tangibly by keeping their saloons wide open. There were prohibition agents in the state, but few were brave enough to antagonize such a large majority. Aware of this, national prohibition officials decided to send twenty-six of their best agents from other states into Rhode Island.

Izzy Einstein and Moe Smith from New York, who were among the twenty-six, arrived in Providence on September 5, 1922, and after checking in at the Biltmore Hotel under assumed names, began scouting the city for illicit saloons.[7] They soon realized they wouldn't have to look very hard, and with their usual dispatch they began a series of arrests. In some places they got drinks for the asking. In others, it took only simple subterfuge to make the liquor flow. At one saloon, Moe Smith told the bartender he'd give him a useful tip in exchange for a drink.

"Tell me the tip," the bartender said, "and we'll see if it's worth a drink."

"The tip," Moe said, "is that there are federal agents on the job in this neighborhood."

Moe soon had a glass in front of him, after which the grateful bartender learned that the tip was embarrassingly accurate.

Not all of the places Izzy and Moe visited were such easy marks. In Central Falls, a suburb of Providence, there was a saloon whose proprietor, James C. Taylor, had a reputation for being able to spot federal men. When Izzy, Moe, and a third agent named Peter Reager cased Taylor's establishment, they noticed that the street in front of it was torn up and a crew of laborers was installing a new sewer. Returning to Providence, the three agents bought picks, shovels, and bandannas, then drove back to Central Falls in work clothes and joined the laborers. After shoveling "about a dollar's worth" of dirt, they casually strolled into Taylor's saloon, tools in hand, and asked for whisky.

Taylor welcomed them cordially and was serving them from an earthenware pitcher when Izzy, announcing his identity, darted around the bar to make sure none of the evidence disappeared.

Turning quickly, Taylor threw the entire contents of the pitcher into Izzy's face and, as the drenched agent let loose a string of swear words, dashed for the door.

The three agents rushed out in pursuit and, after commandeering a car, finally caught Taylor several blocks away. Izzy, breathless and smelling like a distillery, asked, "Why did you run?"

"You told me you were Izzy Einstein," Taylor said, "and that was enough."

Taylor was one of forty-six bootleggers arrested by the Einstein team during their three days in Rhode Island, but he proved to be a much less docile victim than the others. Next morning, September 8, several reporters were at the federal commissioner's office in the Providence Woolworth Building when Einstein, Smith, and Reager arrived to testify against the men they had booked. A deputy sheriff asked Izzy and Moe to identify themselves and they did so, whereupon he announced he was arresting them "in the name of the law of the state of Rhode Island."

When the sheriff asked Reager to identify himself, the latter refused, even though Izzy advised him to do so. He also refused to acknowledge his arrest and began to fight when police tried to handcuff him. It took some time for Izzy and Moe to calm him, after which the three were taken to the Providence County Court House, where they learned the nature of the charges against them.

Taylor, having hired a law firm, had sworn out a warrant accusing the three agents of rushing bartenders, intimidating them with revolvers, using extreme, vile, filthy, and obscene language against them, and even assaulting them. "One Izzy Einstein" and "one Moe Smith," Taylor's suit charged, were "guilty of the most flagrant and intentional violations of the Constitution."

Saloonkeeper Taylor might have had an interesting case in law had he been allowed to pursue it. Neither Izzy Einstein nor many of his colleagues were very sensitive to the constitutional rights of their victims. Since the Supreme Court had given full approval to the Volstead Act, they didn't feel any necessity of worrying about the Constitution. Izzy was not deeply concerned about it now. As soon as he and the two others were released, they departed Providence for New York, leaving federal attorneys behind to argue with Rhode Island about the constitutional rights of saloonkeepers. The federal attorneys eventually did manage to quash the charges against the three agents, but by that time the saloons around Providence were open again and the federal Prohibition Bureau's twenty-six-man flying squad could claim no more than a standoff in its tilt against Rhode Island.

Taking advantage of a fresh autumn breeze, Bill McCoy sailed out of Nassau harbor on his first voyage in more than a year as captain of his schooner *Tomoka,* née *Arethusa.* Since his last voyage he had been, in succession, a corporation president, a fleet owner, a potential millionaire, and now a potential bankrupt. After returning to Nassau on the *Tomoka* in August 1921, having lost his schooner *Marshall* to the U.S. government and narrowly escaped arrest, he had decided there might be more prudence and profit in being a shipping executive than a captain. With this in mind he had formed a corporation, the British Transportation and Trading Company, and had bought two more schooners, the *J.B. Young* and the *M.M. Gardner.* For a while, his small but busy fleet of three vessels seemed destined to make him one of the wealthiest men in Nassau. Then, in the spring of 1922, the *Gardner* was seized on Rum Row and towed into New York harbor. In July, the *Young* was run down by a liner outside New York harbor and damaged so badly she had to go into a Canadian port for repairs. Convinced that both of these misfortunes were due to the inadequacies of his captains, and also feeling the tight financial pinch the loss of the two ships imposed upon him, McCoy had decided to go back to sea himself on the *Tomoka-Arethusa*.[8]

Though this beautiful schooner could carry five thousand cases of liquor, McCoy was sailing north with only one thousand cases since he could no longer afford to buy any more. Because of the rum-running concept he had originated, he would not have needed to travel very far north to sell his merchandise. By October of 1922, there were Rum Rows, or floating liquor markets, all the way up the Atlantic coast and across the Gulf of Mexico. Fleets of rumrunners stood off Galveston, New Orleans, Mobile, Tampa, Savannah, Norfolk, New York, and Boston. He had decided to go to New York because the market was bigger there.

After eight easy days of sailing through pleasant autumn weather, McCoy saw the skyscrapers of lower Manhattan arise to his left and the *Tomoka*, with sails trimmed, took her place among the ships standing at anchor off the Fire Island lightship, twenty miles from shore. Unlike most of the rumrunners, McCoy did not anchor his craft. He preferred to glide back and forth at two or three knots under foresail and jumbo, partly because he liked the motion of a ship underway and partly because he thought it best to be already on the move if a prohibition patrol boat or a pirate craft (of which several were operating against rumrunners) should approach him. Actually, the danger was not great while he was on the Row. The pirates were more interested in ships alone at sea. Coast Guard cutters sometimes would glide down the Row, but since the liquor ships were all twenty miles from shore, they had no authority to interfere.

McCoy found one pleasant surprise awaiting him as he sailed slowly along the line. His schooner *J.B. Young*, which had been in port for repairs after suffering a glancing blow by a liner, was back on the Row under command of her mate, who had taken over when the captain deserted. Her sails were ragged and her bearded crew unhappy, but she had liquor to unload, and despite some difficulties with her buyers, she was making money for McCoy again. Best of all, she now had a captain he felt he could trust.

Business was not so good for the *Tomoka*, however, because

McCoy had been away so long that most of the buyers were dealing with other ships. Many of the buyers didn't even know him. Slightly discouraged, he hoisted his canvas and sailed down the Jersey coast to a smaller row of ships off Highland, where he encountered a schooner called the *Jeanette*, manned by old friends of his. Since this craft was selling "cheap rye from Cuba," and McCoy had a reputation for selling only the best, the captain, a man named Bob Cameron, said to him, "Stick around, Bill. If they don't like our stuff, I'll send them over to you. I'll tell the gang you've got the real McCoy goods."

Though Cameron didn't know it, he had just coined a phrase which would soon become popular on Rum Row and would eventually pass into the language. "The real McCoy" came to denote a genuine as opposed to a shoddy product.

Within a few hours, McCoy had made his first sale, to one of the sea skiffs in the shore-to-Row trade, and within two days he had sold his entire cargo. A week later he was back in Nassau with $50,000 in his pocket, buying two thousand cases of the best rye. After one short voyage, he had averted possible bankruptcy. He now had two ships operating again, and at last he had found a reliable skipper for the second one. With himself in command of the *Tomoka*, he could again see great wealth ahead of him.

News of the Remus party had been circulating for weeks and all Cincinnati was talking about it. George and Imogene were unveiling their mansion on Price Hill with a New Year's Eve celebration for a hundred couples. It was rumored that Remus had spent three quarters of a million dollars on the place; it was a known fact that he had spent more than $100,000 on the indoor swimming pool alone, because the pool had already been the subject of a lawsuit in Common Pleas Court. Mrs. Remus, who had supervised its construction, accused the contractor of overcharging her. He insisted she was responsible for the extra costs because she had continually changed the plans. When the contractor won the suit, Remus, who was in the courtroom, had shown his magnanimity by asking the contractor's lawyer, a man named Eli Frankenstein, to work for him. Walking over to Frankenstein after the verdict was read, Remus held out his hand, smiled, and said, "Anyone who can beat me and my coterie of lawyers deserves to be Remus' lawyer."[9] (He had the unfortunate habit of referring to himself in the third person.) Frankenstein had thus become Remus' representative in civil litigations, which added substantially to the young lawyer's income because Remus was incorrigibly litigious. It appeared, however, that he could afford it.

Remus' net worth was now estimated at more than $6 million. He owned or controlled at least nine distilleries and employed three thousand people. During his more than two years in business he had sold an estimated two million gallons of bonded liquor at about twenty-five dollars per gallon, which brought his volume of business to about $50 million. His frequent litigation was, therefore, a habit which seemed well within his means. So was his preoccupation with the thirty-one-room gray stone showplace he was about to show to a select group of business associates, politicians, public officials, and influential Cincinnatians.

As the invited couples arrived at the ten-acre hillside estate (which had originally been the home of one of the city's wealthiest brewing families), they drove up the road through wooded grounds, beautifully landscaped though now covered by winter's gray and white. Servants took their coats and ushered them into the vast living room furnished with carved antiques and featuring a piano decorated with gold leaf. On the walls were expensive early American paintings.[10]

The main festivities did not take place in the living room, but in the marble-columned, classically proportioned Roman bath which housed the huge swimming pool. The whole vast, water-centered room was decked with flowers and exotic plants. Beautiful girls in white tights waited on the fifty or more tables placed along the sides of the pool. The champagne, the bourbon, and the gin were all of first quality. Since it was one of the host's proud boasts that he had never sold anything but fine liquor, he made certain that for guests in his home he had nothing but the finest.

At one end of the pool an orchestra played for dancing, and as the evening progressed, a group of professional swimmers and divers from Chicago suddenly appeared to perform a water ballet, the climax of which was unexpected. Imogene Remus herself danced out onto the diving board, her opulent figure daringly revealed in a one-piece bathing suit, and dived into the water while her husband and all their guests applauded. Remus loved his wife so much that he was pleased even by her lack of inhibition.

George and Imogene Remus had truly become the Baron and Baroness of Booze. The entire Midwest was their fief and Cincinnati was their capital. It was a fitting place for them to reign, since it was not only a distilling center but also a brewing center. So many citizens of Cincinnati were of German descent that public school classes were taught in both German and English. There was very little sympathy for prohibition in this city, and none at all, of course, at this New Year's Eve party in the Remus mansion. The liquor flowed so freely and the merriment reached such a peak that George Remus could feel only one possible regret: because he never drank any alcoholic beverage himself, he couldn't match the convivial mood of his guests. As inconspicuously as possible, he retired to his paneled library which was filled with hundreds, perhaps more than a thousand, newly purchased books, including one he was currently reading about Abraham Lincoln. With a dish of ice cream by his side and the door firmly closed against the noise of the festivities, he settled down for a few hours of reading.

When he emerged, dawn was approaching but the liquor was still flowing and no one had departed, perhaps because of a pervasive rumor that Remus intended to climax the affair with a stupendous surprise. The rumor proved to be true. As soon as the clamor around the pool abated and Remus could be heard, he announced that the time had come to hand out party favors.

First, in front of each couple, a waitress placed a small box which looked as if it might contain jewelry. These boxes, instead of being for the wives, were intended for the husbands but they did, indeed, prove to contain jewelry—diamond tie pins, diamond cuff links, and so forth. Remus had spent a total of $25,000 on these baubles for his male guests.

If any of the wives were jealous, their pique did not last long. For each woman guest, Remus announced, a brand new 1923 automobile was waiting outside the front door.

George and Imogene Remus could watch with childlike pleasure as the first dawn of the new year arose over the parade of 100 new cars moving down their long drive, attesting to their success, their wealth, their generosity, and their popularity. In addition to all this, they had their magnificent house, and they had each other. For anyone observing them as they bade their last guests goodbye, it would have been difficult to imagine a happier couple.

Only one cloud now hung over the Remus horizon. The Volstead Act conspiracy conviction against him and his thirteen aides was currently under review by the Supreme Court.

Chapter 6

As the year 1923 began, the Chicago *Tribune* was still pressing its taxpayer suit against Mayor Bill Thompson for overpaying the city's building inspectors by almost $3 million. A "Pageant of Progress" Thompson had organized through his Chicago Boosters' Club ("Throw Away Your Hammer! Get a Horn! Be a Booster for Chicago!") had not recruited enough boosters to make it a success. Governor Len Small, whom Thompson and his political mentor-partner Fred Lundin put in office, had been subjected to trial for creaming off the interest on bank deposits of state funds, and though he had been acquitted, he was thoroughly discredited. The Democrats were also making an issue of the fact that Small had been pardoning and paroling hoodlums at the rate of three hundred a year. And they were convening a grand jury to determine whether the jury in Small's trial had been fixed. The publicity from all this had been so unfavorable that most of the Thompson-Lundin candidates in the November 1922 election had been defeated. And now, in January 1923, Lundin himself was in a jam. State's Attorney Robert Emmett Crowe, elected with the help of the Thompson-Lundin machine, was about to show his gratitude by indicting Lundin for interfering with Thompson's school board and engineering a million-dollar theft through false contracts, shakedowns, and bribery.

With a mayoral election coming up in April, none of this bode well for Hizzoner Big Bill. Neither did the outcome of the war on bootlegging and vice which he had sonorously declared a year earlier. To augment this war, he had appointed as his "Crime Commissioner" a Protestant minister, the Rev. John H. Williamson, whose zeal for prohibition had earned him the title of "The Fighting Parson." The battle to rid Chicago of bootleggers was one which Williamson soon found himself fighting almost alone. Thompson's police chief, Charles Fitzmorris, refused to cooperate with him, and because Williamson had become a member of the notoriously wet Thompson administration, he eventually earned the ridicule even of his prohibitionist friends. It was obvious that he wielded less influence with the mayor than men like Johnny Torrio, who had now organized almost all of the city's most powerful gangsters into an uneasy but so far effective bootlegging alliance. When the Reverend Williamson finally realized all this, he surrendered his commission, and as far as Thompson was concerned, the war against bootleggers was at an end.[1] But, unfortunately, most Chicagoans were now aware that the bootleggers had won, and a lot of people deplored that fact. Even those who bought booze supplied by these gangsters were against an outright surrender to them. Or at least they said they were, which meant that many of them were now turning against Thompson for giving them what they wanted.

Big Bill had gradually come to realize that if he was to win reelection, for which he had already announced his candidacy, he would need a very weak Democratic opponent. Perhaps that could be arranged. He could be quite accommodating to the Democrats under proper circumstances. But when he began putting out feelers he got bad news in return. The Democrats, aware of his vulnerability, were determined to topple him. They were getting ready to nominate an honest judge named William E. Dever, who was an effective speaker and an imposing figure of a man, even though he did harbor some naive ideas about enforcing prohibition. He seemed to think it could be done. Or so he said, anyway. He'd find out differently if he were elected, but meanwhile, a lot of people liked the way he talked. He'd be difficult to beat.

One day during a conversation with his Corporation Counsel, Sam Ettelson, Thompson asked for an honest evaluation of his election prospects. Ettelson was unsparingly frank. "You won't come within fifty thousand of beating any Democrat," he said.

Thompson could not gainsay this appraisal. And as the month of January progressed, bringing each day more details of the case Crowe had assembled against Lundin, the mayor concluded this just wasn't going to be his year. On the twenty-fifth, he called a press conference and announced that, contrary to previous announcements, he would not seek reelection in April.

"I wish to make plain my continued interest in public affairs," he said, "and my willingness to lead or follow in any contests the people may make manifest their desires."

Like most of Thompson's statements, it didn't quite parse, but its meaning was clear. Big Bill wanted everyone to know he would be back as soon as the heat was off.

The New York state Assembly chamber was crowded when Governor Alfred E. Smith, looking uncharacteristically somber, entered with two aides and took his chair at the front. The ovation that greeted him came mostly from the wets on the floor and in the galleries, though the drys, many of them wearing white badges to advertise their sentiments, stood and clapped politely. The drys, having been coached by their leaders to arrive early in the day, occupied the majority of the good seats. Many of the wets, arriving on late trains from New York City, had been forced to scramble for folding chairs after pushing their way into the chamber. One small group of wets had unfurled a banner that read:

> "The Anti-Saloon League comes
> A preachin that drinking is sinful.
> I'll wager the rascals a crown
> They always preach best with a skinfull."

This literary effort had been confiscated by the sergeant-at-arms and removed from sight before Governor Smith's 2 P.M. appearance.[2]

Smith, who had scheduled the day's hearing for 1 P.M., could be forgiven by any reasonable person for his tardiness today. He was in such an uncomfortable political dilemma that a dedicated dry might even have forgiven him for downing a couple of highballs at lunch. Three weeks earlier, on May 9, the legislature had done something Smith had publicly favored but privately dreaded. Both houses had voted to repeal the prohibition enforcement measure—the Mullan-Gage Act—which was New York state's counterpart of, and indeed an almost exact replica of, the federal Volstead Law.

This legislative action acutely embarrassed Smith because it forced him either to uphold or veto the repeal. If he upheld it, he would openly proclaim himself the champion of the wets, thereby infuriating the drys in his own party and jeopardizing his chances of one day winning the Democratic presidential nomination. If he vetoed the repeal, thus upholding the prohibition enforcement law, he might lose the respect and support of his wet constituency in New York state and severely damage his prestige among the wets throughout the country. Several dry Republicans in the legislature who had voted enthusiastically for the Mullan-Gage bill when it was enacted in 1921 under Governor Nathan Miller had voted for its repeal this year. Since their vote switch was not accompanied by renunciation of their dry sentiments, the general belief was that they now supported repeal simply for the pleasure of watching Al Smith squirm when he was forced to act upon it. If so, these Republicans must have enjoyed themselves for the past three weeks while Smith, cajoled and threatened from both sides, tried to decide which alternative would do him the least political damage.

The minute he learned of the repeal vote in the Legislature, Smith had reportedly said to an aide, "They have me down and out." He had returned to Albany only a few months earlier after defeating his 1920 conqueror, Governor Miller, by a record-breaking 400,000 plurality in the 1922 election, but the Republicans were wasting no time in making him pay for his unprecedented victory. He had a month in which either to sign or veto the repeal, and as the passing days of May brought increasing thousands of letters, telegrams, and petitions from both sides, it seemed he might take that long to make up his mind. The drys, who had expected the worst, became heartened by his indecision, while the wets began to wonder if he intended to betray them. Franklin D. Roosevelt, who was thought to be at least moist, though his wife was publicly and staunchly dry, said to him in a letter, "I am mighty sorry for the extremely difficult position in which you have been placed over this darned old liquor question." Roosevelt warned him that if he signed the repeal he might never be nominated for the presidency. Smith already knew that, and as his daughter recalled, Roosevelt was not one of the people to whom he looked for advice. Charles Murphy and Tom Foley of Tammany Hall, on the other hand, were two people whose counsel he often sought, and even they had become worried about his intentions, especially when, on May 26, he indicated during a Brooklyn speech that he would not sign the repeal.

Since Murphy and Foley had both been saloonkeepers, there was no doubt in their minds as to Smith's proper course of action. When Foley read about the governor's Brooklyn speech the next morning in his Sunday paper, he dispatched one of his men to find out Smith's real intentions. The man returned from the governor's suite at the Biltmore with what sounded like bad news. Smith had been studying the question in its legal aspects and had concluded that repeal would do more harm than good. Murphy and Foley, alarmed at this report, decided to invite the governor out to Murphy's Long Island home for a little chat. Though Smith had already left for Albany by this time, he returned as soon as he received the invitation and the three men talked for most of the night. As they emerged from the library after several hours of argument, Smith looked grim and the other two looked worried. They still didn't know what he intended to do about the Mullan-Gage Act.

The public was now in an uproar. William Anderson, always an enemy of Smith, was mailing out pamphlets warning Anti-Saloon League followers what the governor would do if they did not apply pressure on him. Wayne Wheeler had arrived from Washington to direct a rather more dignified campaign. The Ku Klux Klan was busy in the rural counties, educating the farmers about the fiendish alliance between Al Smith, the Catholic Church, and Demon Rum. Even President Harding entered the debate by sending a letter to a Newburgh prohibitionist which warned Governor Smith not to sign the repeal.[3]

"The executives of the nation and equally the executives of the States are sworn to enforce the Constitution," Harding wrote. "It is difficult to believe that public approval will ever be given to any other than a policy of fully and literally discharging this duty.... The States are equipped with police organization and judicial establishments adequate to deal with such problems. The Federal Government is not thus equipped. I venture that, if by reason of the refusal or failure of any State to discharge its proper duty in such connection, the Federal Government is at length compelled to enter upon the territory and jurisdiction of the State and to set up those police and judicial authorities which would be required, the most difficult and trying situations would inevitably arise. . . ."

What Harding and the drys feared most was the federal government's enforcement costs if the individual states were to deny their responsibilities. Even dry Congressmen were reluctant to spend federal funds on enforcement. The yearly appropriations averaged less than $10 million. Without help from state and local authorities, it might cost fifty times that to hold even a light lid over the rapidly expanding illicit liquor industry. Every effort had to be made, therefore, to prevent New York state and its wet governor from establishing a precedent of noninvolvement.

Buffeted by the demands from wets and drys, Al Smith had decided to stage a public forum where he could listen as each side presented its case, after which he would render an apparently impartial decision. The crowded and highly charged hearing in the Assembly chamber on May 31 was the outcome of this strategy. As soon as Smith was seated and the applause ceased he began the proceedings by reading out the title of the bill and asking representatives of both factions how they wanted to divide the time. The wets said they would need two hours; the drys asked for three. Smith decided each would have two, with an extra hour for rebuttal.

The first speaker for the drys was a Republican from Brooklyn, Mrs. Ida Sammis-Woodruff, who had voted for Smith against Miller. Her intention today was to put him on the spot. "We have watched your distinguished career and have gloried in the courage you have shown in standing for what you believed right," she said to him, "so that when you said to us, in effect, . . . 'I will uphold the laws of my country,' we knew you meant just that."

She then introduced one of Smith's bitterest enemies, the bombastic William Anderson, who could easily have used the entire two hours himself. Surprisingly, Anderson spoke for less than a minute, relinquishing his time to Col. William Hayward, U.S. Attorney for the Southern District of New York. Hayward began in a voice too soft to be heard in the galleries, and when the spectators shouted for him to speak louder, he was unmoved by their pleas. Finally, turning on them with some exasperation, he said, "I am speaking to the governor. He can hear me."

Colonel Hayward spoke at great length and offered some persuasive arguments. "We hear it said, Governor Smith, that the repeal of the Mullan-Gage Law . . . will not produce an orgy of bootlegging ten times as bad as the present serious one and will not turn the underworld loose in a riot of alcoholic anarchy because the police can, and will, assist the federal authorities. If this were true . . . all of this present legislation would be a waste of time, but it is not true.

"The machinery for federal enforcement in this state consists of about one dozen judges, a half dozen United States commissioners, and about 200 federal prohibition agents The machinery of the state, which it is proposed to neutralize . . . consists of 266 judges, besides the magistrates, 350 state constabulary, 62 sheriffs with all their deputies, and 12,000 police in the city of New York alone. In 1920 there were 218 convictions in the counties of this state under the liquor law then in force. In 1921 there were three times as many, or 681, the Mullan-Gage Law then being operative, while last year there were eight times as many as in 1920, or 1,646."

After speaking for almost an hour, Colonel Hayward concluded with a challenge. "If there ever comes a time," he declared, "when there must be what there is not now, a discord between *The Star Spangled Banner* and *The Sidewalks of New York,* there must be no doubt about which tune the Chief Executive of this state will sing."

To present the position of the Anti-Saloon League, Wayne Wheeler arose. He had interrupted preparations for a European vacation to take part in this debate, not only because he realized its importance but also because he knew that if the League actually wanted to influence Al Smith, instead of merely embarrassing him, someone other than William Anderson would have to argue the case. After Anderson's many attacks against Smith and his religion, it was not reasonable to suppose that his plea, however forceful, would persuade the governor. It might have been better for the dry cause if Anderson hadn't even come to this hearing, but here he was, surrounded by a delegation of Protestant clergymen, whose presence, he believed, would have a salutary effect upon the governor. He could hardly have thought his own presence would be helpful, but he was not the kind of man who could be kept away from such an important event.

Wheeler addressed the governor calmly, in reasonable tones, but with aggressive certainty.

"Repeal of the Mullan-Gage Law," he said, "would be a violation of an oath to support the Constitution, a breach of duty by the state, a fruitless effort to nullify the Constitution and a betrayal of sister states which have joined New York in ratification of the Eighteenth Amendment. . . .

"The repeal of this law would be productive of lawlessness. . . . Myriads of police officers, sheriffs and constables . . . would be compelled to look on scenes of lawlessness . . . and would be impotent to raise a hand to suppress it. . . .

"It is suggested that state and local police will continue in law enforcement if the state code were repealed. How can they operate effectively when the one effective tool, the state code, . . . is taken from them? . . .

"By adopting this repealer, New York will be in the position of seeking to retain the protection of a national government of laws without contributing to that protection. To repeal a law necessary to enforce the Constitution and substitute nothing for it is plain and palpable nullification. . . ."

Against such dry arguments, the wets were at a disadvantage. They could hardly deny or deplore the likelihood that the Mullan-Gage repeal would promote disregard for the prohibition law when disregard for this law was what they sought. But could they expect the governor to decide in their favor if his action would leave him open to the charge of violating his constitutional oath and promoting lawlessness? The wets arose, one by one, to try to cover him by justifying their position, but they did not destroy the central legal arguments of the drys.

Playwright Augustus Thomas increased the Governor's dilemma by associating Mullan-Gage repeal with law resistance rather than law enforcement. "We are told," he said, "that the majority makes our laws and it is our duty to obey them. It is—unless the laws are an invasion of our inherent rights. Then it becomes our duty to resist them."

American Federation of Labor President Samuel Gompers, in a letter read by state A.F.L. President James P. Holland, said the members of his union were getting thirsty. "The men of labor have no concern for the liquor, beer or wine interests as such; they are interested in a fair and square deal on an equality with every other citizen, not that they may have cellars full of booze, but that they may have a glass of wholesome beer with their meals."

State Senator Theodore Robinson vaguely defended himself and his colleagues for the Legislature's vote to repeal. "I voted as an American for the repeal of the Mullan-Gage law because I believe it has done more than any other law to break down law and order. The other side say that we voted for secession. We did no such thing. We voted according to our conscience."

None of the wet speakers was very impressive. The hearing ended with the drys jubilant, the wets glum, and the governor grim.

Back at the executive mansion, discussion of the possible options continued between Smith and his aides for the rest of the day and into the next day. The governor's twenty-one-year-old daughter, Emily, as excited as everyone else by the public furor, asked for permission to listen to the inner circle debate. "I promise you I will not speak,"[4] she said. Her doting father welcomed her into the room, where she listened silently as the members of his staff pressed upon him one reason after another why he should sign the repeal. In the end he agreed with them, perhaps because he had basically agreed with them in the beginning. His conscience told him that prohibition was wrong, that it was an unwarranted abridgment of human freedom, and that the Volstead Act was a bad law. But it was a bad law over which he had no control. The Mullan-Gage Act, an almost exact copy of the Volstead Act, was a bad law over which he now had ultimate control. Disapproving of it as he did, could he justify perpetuating it? If the drys had won the debate at the public hearing, it was mostly because the wets hadn't used their best arguments. Yes, he would sign the repeal, and with his signature he would include his own arguments in defense of his action.

At six o'clock in the afternoon of June 1, Governor Smith called a press conference in his office at the capitol and, as a score of newsmen watched, put his signature on the repeal. His aides then handed out a 1,500-word memorandum explaining his action.

"I have read thousands of letters and I have listened to the fullest discussion," his statement declared, "and no one has pointed out to me any provision of the Constitution or of the Statutes or any decision of the United States Supreme Court which imposes upon our state any constitutional duty to maintain a state enforcement act. . . .

"The Supreme Court of the United States [has] said: 'The Constitution, laws and treaties of the United States are as much the part of the law of every State as its own local laws and Constitution.' That means that after repeal there will still rest upon the peace officers of this state the sacred responsibility of maintaining the Volstead Act with as much force and as much vigor as they would enforce any State law or local ordinance. . . . The only difference after repeal is that today the police officer may take the offender for prosecution to the State Court, to the federal court, or both. After the repeal of the Mullan-Gage Law, the prosecution must be where it belongs—in the federal court.

"In law and in fact there is no more lawlessness in repealing the Mullan-Gage Law than there is in the failure of the State to pass statutes making it a State crime to violate any other federal penal statute.

"Let it be understood at once and for all that this repeal does not in the slightest degree lessen the obligation of peace officers of the State to enforce in its strictest letter the Volstead Act, and warning to that effect is herein contained as coming from the Chief Executive of the State of New York. . . ."

As the newsmen, a notoriously wet group, pressed forward to congratulate the governor on his signing, some of them observed that his smile had regained the spontaneity missing for the past three weeks. He had finally made his difficult decision. He was out in the open now as the de facto leader of the wets, and even if he didn't like this realization, he was ready to live with it. But he would also have to pay the price for his decision, as a host of prohibitionists let him know in letters and public statements during the next two days.

William Anderson, pronouncing Smith responsible for the "unbridled lawlessness" which was certain to follow the repeal, declared angrily, "It would have been far better for the governor if he had signed the bill as soon as it reached him, without going through the pretense of a 'hearing.' As an open wet governor, Smith could have been respected even by the drys for frankness and courage. But as a wet who for a month was, or pretended to be, almost persuaded to stand for law and his oath, he has lost tremendously in respect on both sides. . . ."

Wayne Wheeler, back in Washington, where he hoped to see President Harding before the latter's departure on a trip to Alaska, issued

a statement which virtually declared war against New York's governor. "The action of Governor Smith will stir the nation as did the shot
on Fort Sumter," Wheeler declared. "Tammany dictated the signature along with the liquor interests. But the governor's action will
array the country and enforcement will become stronger than ever.
New York will stay in the union in spite of Governor Smith."
   The Anti-Saloon League and its followers had never trusted Al
Smith. They could at least take some satisfaction now in their proof
that they had been right about him. They would not soon forgive or
forget what he had done.

   Since Wayne Wheeler was soon leaving for Europe, and President
Harding for Alaska, this would no doubt be their last conversation for
some time. Wheeler was planning to sail with his wife on a grand tour
which would include attendance at the International Conference on
Alcoholism in Copenhagen. Harding was about to begin a highly
publicized journey westward which he had originally envisioned as an
excursion, but which he now saw as a "Voyage of Understanding."
He had scheduled numerous speeches along the way in the hope of
rallying support for the World Court, which he thought the United
States should join, and for his own administration, which people were
beginning to criticize for general insipidity. Harding felt tired and
harassed. He was also worried about rumors and indications of scandal among his appointees, but this was not yet known even to Washington insiders like Wheeler.
   The only scandal that interested Wheeler was the continued refusal
of so many people to stop selling and drinking liquor. Despite his
constant vigilance, the wet threat simply would not subside. A few
months earlier, the wets in Congress had tried to add a liquor amendment to the ship subsidy bill. Due partly to his efforts they had failed.
Then they had tried to establish a commission "to decide scientifi-
cally" what constituted intoxicating liquor. As if anyone needed a
commission to answer that question. Wheeler had never drunk intoxicating liquor, but he knew very well what it was. It was anything that
contained alcohol. Secure in that knowledge, he had helped round up
the necessary votes to quash the commission.
   Finally the wets had reversed their strategy and criticized the
Prohibition Bureau, directed by Wheeler protegé Roy Haynes, for

laxity in enforcing the law. To Wheeler this was a ludicrous charge. He firmly believed that Roy Haynes was one of the most honest and dedicated public servants in Washington. He did not believe the rumors that the entire bureau under Haynes was corrupt. And he did not know that Haynes was currying favor with Harding's cronies by procuring liquor for them and sending Internal Revenue Service men to deliver it. But Wheeler did know, and was deeply disturbed by the fact that the liquor laws were being disobeyed on a massive scale all over the country, especially in the big cities. He had written a letter to Harding on this subject and had received a promising reply.

"We are going to tighten up in every way possible," the President stated "not because of the urgency of prohibition enforcement in itself, but because of the desirability of putting to an end the process of nullification and contempt for law which are undermining the law-abiding conscience of the Republic. Of course, this does not apply in seven-eighths of the communities of the entire United States. The shocking disregard of law is limited to a few great cities. I do not think the courts are greatly remiss. Our trouble lies in the lax conscience of a very considerable proportion of our citizens."[5]

It was curious that the President, who was so reluctant to suppress his own thirst, should speak out about the "lax conscience" of other people. Perhaps finally, after two years in the White House, Harding was ready to make a personal renunciation of liquor. It might be worth testing him on it. But that was only one of the subjects on Wheeler's mind when he walked into the Oval Room.

The primary issue of the day was New York state's repeal of the Mullan-Gage Act. To fill the enforcement vacuum this created, Wheeler wanted the federal government to send into New York every agent not vitally needed in other states. It was essential to make New Yorkers realize that despite their governor's unwarranted action, they would still have to obey the prohibition laws. In addition, President Harding should make another statement criticizing Al Smith for his irresponsibility.

Harding did not disagree on this point. He was planning a speech about liquor law enforcement which he would deliver en route to the West Coast. Without mentioning Smith by name, he would condemn the repeal of the Mullan-Gage law and the rationale behind the repeal.

With such matters settled to his satisfaction, Wayne Wheeler looked the President in the eye and reopened the subject Harding most dreaded. As the President had to be aware, there were rumors about drinking among federal employees all over Washington. There were even rumors about drinking among some of Harding's closest friends in a house they kept for social purposes on K Street. And there was gossip about bootleggers coming right into the capitol building to sell their wares. Wheeler favored a law which would force the dismissal of any federal employee convicted of a liquor violation. But it would be difficult to insist upon such a law when it was common knowledge that the President himself indulged in alcoholic beverages.

Harding's continued indulgence, Wheeler told him, was a source of deepening embarrassment to the dry cause. He had personally tried on many occasions to defend the President from attacks by fellow dry leaders, but it was becoming almost impossible. The time had arrived when Wheeler could no longer undertake to defend him. Unless he was ready to swear off alcohol completely and make a public announcement to that effect, Wheeler would have to remain silent when he was attacked among prohibitionists. The President had, after all, written to Wheeler denouncing the disregard of liquor laws among people in the big cities. He had called for an "awakened American conscience." As President, he himself should help awaken it by taking a high moral stand, by pledging never to drink again.

Harding was bewildered by this outright demand. Though its presumption may have angered him, its implicit threat frightened him. Conscious of his declining popularity throughout the country, he felt he could not afford to lose the support of the prohibitionists. Yet he so much enjoyed his highballs that he was reluctant to renounce them. His drinking had been a lifelong habit, he pleaded, and therefore it might be harmful to his health if he were suddenly to stop it.

This kind of reasoning did not impress Wayne Wheeler. He had never believed in the medicinal properties of alcohol. On the contrary, if the President was worried about his health, he had all the more reason to abstain. Wheeler was not only a persuasive man. He was tough, he was persistent, and he had the law on his side. Worn down by his arguments, President Harding finally capitulated. If Wheeler considered it absolutely necessary, he would indeed promise to stop drinking. And he would make a public announcement of it, but in his own time.

Despite the vigor of his arguments and the certainty of his moral position, Wheeler was almost as surprised as he was pleased when

Harding finally made this commitment. Though he might have wanted to go further and force the President to name a date for his public pledge, he decided not to press his luck. For the time being he was happy enough with what he had. He was so happy, in fact, that when he returned to his office, he fairly chortled about his victory to one of his aides. He got a special kick out of it, he said, because actually he had been bluffing. If Harding had refused to take the pledge, he would have continued to support him anyway. The prohibitionists needed the President, after all, as much as the President needed them.

During the hot summer days following William Anderson's July 20 indictment for theft and forgery, he brooded heavily about the factors involved in the charges against him, and the more he brooded the more certain he became that the whole matter was a plot to "get" him. He had already explained to the press that he had never actually split commissions with Anti-Saloon League fundraiser C. Bertsall Phillips. He had simply accepted commission-sharing with Phillips as an informal means of recompense for money he had previously loaned to the League. And it was not true that he had falsified the League's financial records. He had simply, as a favor to Phillips, ordered that some of the man's income be listed as expenses.

Anderson could see now, however, that Phillips was both an ingrate and a crook. The man was disgruntled because in April 1922, when he demanded more money, Anderson had refused to give it to him and had accepted his resignation from the League's fundraising staff. Since then, Phillips, according to information Anderson received, had been running around New York, trying to sell his story to Tammany Hall and the liquor interests, and at the same time he had been trying, though unsuccessfully, to blackmail the League with it. Finally he had taken his story to the District Attorney's office and after a grand jury investigation, it was now out in the open.

But why had the District Attorney's office pursued such a flimsy matter? To Anderson, that was the key question. He had no doubt that Tammany Hall controlled all of New York City's law enforcement machinery, and Ferdinand Pecora, the prosecutor assigned to the case, was, in Anderson's opinion, "the main squeeze for Tammany in the District Attorney's office."[6] Yet it was Anderson's understanding from confidential sources that Tammany had refused to touch the story when Phillips first tried to sell it to the Democratic Party organization.

Why then had the Tammany leaders charged their minds and decided to prosecute Anderson? After giving the question considerable thought, he had painstakingly determined their most likely motivations. First of all, Tammany Hall and the Catholic Church worked hand-in-hand, with each other and with the liquor interests. Three years earlier, when Anderson pointed this out publicly, hadn't Archbishop Hayes called him "a brewer of bigotry and a sower of strife?" Yes, indeed he had, and Anderson hadn't forgotten it. Now, he noticed, "a great publicity buildup" was in progress about the chances of Hayes becoming a cardinal. But apparently, Anderson decided, it was "contingent on my being put out of the way."

There was also a more important reason why Tammany and the Church would naturally want him to be put out of the way. They had decided they would try to get Governor Al Smith into the White House in 1924. In order to do so, they would have to have Anderson locked up for most of that year because he had compiled the facts about Al Smith's "liquor record," and had incorporated these facts into a pamphlet which he regarded as "the most deadly document ever produced against a wet politician." He had, after all, "beaten Smith once, in 1920, by arousing the [Protestant] Church forces against him." No doubt Smith, Tammany, and the Catholic hierarchy feared he could do it again.

His next move, Anderson decided, should be to force Al Smith to look at the facts and answer them. But of course there was no way to do this in person. Smith would be too smart ever to confront him face to face. The governor had already ignored a letter Anderson sent him requesting a special session of the Legislature to investigate the operations of the Anti-Saloon League. The governor must have realized that such an investigation would defeat his purposes because it would uncover no wrongdoing within the League. But Anderson had no intention of letting him off the hook so easily. On August 22 he sat down and wrote Al Smith another letter, pointing out some things he had heard from confidential sources and once more demanding a full investigation.[7]

First he stated flatly in the letter that C. Bertsall Phillips and the Rev. Robert G. Davey, once a legislative agent for the League, had "negotiated with the Hon. James J. Walker, Tammany leader of the State Senate, with a view to the sale of 'information' against me to Tammany for a large sum of money."

As the letter progressed, he enlarged upon his theme. "I also happen to know," he wrote, "that Senator Walker went so far as to take this matter up with Mr. Charles F. Murphy, the Tammany boss, and that Mr. Murphy feared it was loaded and decided to hold onto his, or Tammany's money. An investigation would probably not only open Grand Jury minutes, which have been so freely accorded to others and denied only to me, but may turn up some other things. It might disclose for example just why, in the face of Mr. Murphy's contrary judgement, you wanted the District Attorney to revive the effort to 'get' me after he had been called off last spring.

"Mr. Murphy is reported to have told you . . . that you are 'through' politically because of the dry repeal. An investigation may throw some light on the question of your refusal to accept his decision and your own determination to continue as a candidate for President of the United States. . . ."

Governor Smith never did answer this letter, proof enough for Anderson that he simply couldn't, or didn't dare, answer it.

Assistant Attorney General Mabel Walker Willebrandt undertook in the summer of 1923 to smash a bootlegging ring in Savannah, Georgia, which was almost as big as the George Remus syndicate in Cincinnati. Mrs. Willebrandt's special agents in Savannah had discovered an operation there so vast and well-organized that it included, in her description, "a fleet of ships that brought liquor to the coast and a flotilla of small craft that conveyed it to shore, . . . storage caves especially constructed, a small army of Negro laborers to load the stuff, and [railroad] refrigerator cars," in which the liquor shipments were "disguised as fruit." The enterprise was controlled by four members of wealthy Savannah families, led by a man named Willie Haar, the son of a prominent German-born grocer. These men "practically owned the town," Mrs. Willebrandt contended, "through mortgages and business deals."[8]

They were so powerful and elusive that Mrs. Willebrandt's agents had failed in every attempt to build a bootlegging case against them. Finally she decided to try a new approach. In the spring of 1923, she had learned from the Internal Revenue Service that Haar had earned a traceable income of at least a million dollars the previous year though he had filed returns for much less than that. She immediately began to investigate the tax returns, bank accounts, and real estate holdings of other suspects and discovered that many of them had also earned vast sums on which they had either falsified or neglected to file returns.

With this evidence in hand, Mrs. Willebrandt secured indictments against Haar and several others for tax evasion. She then sent another team of agents to Savannah to connect the bootlegging operation with the group's secret income. The new agents, led by a handsome young man named Franklin Dodge, Jr., were more successful than their predecessors.

Finally, in August, their case was prepared. A special federal court term was convened and the grand jury was called into session, presumably to handle the income tax indictments. But what the jurors heard instead was the complex story of the enormous bootleg ring. Agents described the fleet of ships carrying liquor to Savannah not only from Nassau, Bimini, and Canada, but from as far away as Scotland and France. While the forerunner of this fleet, Captain Bill McCoy, was no longer carrying cargo to the Savannah group, having found a preferable market farther north, there was no shortage of other rum-running sea captains engaged in emulating him. When their ships anchored beyond the three-mile limit, fleets of motor boats were on hand to speed their cargoes into the swampy inlets near Savannah, where the hidden storehouse caves had been built. From these caves, the liquor was distributed to wholesalers and retailers throughout the south by freight trains, trucks, and coastal craft.

New indictments under the Volstead Act were quickly handed down, and on August 15, federal men swarmed all over Savannah, making arrests. By nightfall they had rounded up eighty-four men, including Haar and his chief partners, plus a vice president of one of the city's largest banks. Mrs. Willebrandt could now claim she had smashed two gigantic bootlegging syndicates, but she wasn't sure she could make the claim stand up in court. The leader of the first syndicate, George Remus, was still walking free despite his conviction; his liquor operations in the Cincinnati area were still flourishing and expanding. After two years as the nation's chief prohibition prosecutor, Mrs. Willebrandt knew what she was facing when she took a big case to court. In a recent speech to a group of Pennsylvania Republican women, she had described how evidence disappeared and witnesses were suborned or intimidated in trials against wealthy violators. She now had Willie Haar and his confederates in her net, but it would not be easy to get them into prison.

Nils T. Granlund, publicist, promoter and manager of radio station WHN, was in his office on the top floor of the Loew's State Theater Building in Times Square when Larry Fay entered, "six-foot-three, lantern jawed, beefy-handed . . . flashy and splashy." After an abrupt introduction, Fay sat down and said, "I got the whole second floor of this building and I got taxicabs."[9]

This was not news to Granlund. By the latter part of 1923, everyone in New York knew about Larry Fay's taxicabs. Numbering now in the hundreds, Fay taxis were famous for flashing lights, musical horns, nickel trim, black swastika emblems, and tough, aggressive drivers. In charge of these drivers was a hoodlum named Owney Madden who had come out of Sing Sing early in the year. Madden was completely broke and had agreed to work for Fay while scouting a few enterprises for himself. Thanks to Madden's methods of persuasion, virtually all cab drivers in Manhattan now agreed, however reluctantly, that only Larry Fay's cabs could pick up fares at Penn Station or Grand Central, and at several of the larger hotels.

In 1922, even without Madden, Fay had earned an estimated half million dollars from his taxis and his bootlegging operations. This year he had done even better, but true to his original intentions, he was now closing out his bootlegging activities and was also negotiating with an even larger company for the sale of his taxis. He had decided that the cab business, like the bootlegging business, didn't have quite enough class for him.

"I'm going to open a nightclub," he announced to Granlund, "and I want you to be the master of ceremonies."

"You got the wrong boy," Granlund said. "I'm not an M.C. and I'm not an actor."

Fay, having seen Granlund perform as an M.C. on a charity program with George Jessel the previous night, refused to listen. "I'm gonna build a spot for high class people," he said, "and you're gonna be the M.C."

Granlund, equally determined, said, "No, thank you. I'm not your guy." At this second refusal, Granlund could see "the clouded look of disappointment" on Fay's face. Well aware of the pugnacious reputation Fay had cultivated for himself, Granlund decided to offer an alternative. He was acquainted with a forty-year-old Texan, ex-vaudevillian, ex-movie actress and ex-beauty named Mary Louise Cecilia Guinan, currently engaged as a hostess at a speakeasy called the Beaux Arts on Fortieth Street. Having been a partner of Texas Guinan in a restaurant called Gypsy Land, Granlund now described her talents in effusive terms. Fay was not noticeably impressed, but he did agree to go with Granlund that night and meet her.

When Fay saw the Beaux Arts, a gaudy, expensively decorated club on the second floor of a building across the street from the public library, he showed signs of being impressed. "What a swell joint this is," he exclaimed. To him, the measure of taste was cost.

Since Miss Guinan was busy when they arrived, Fay had an opportubity to see her in action and observe her skill in handling people before Granlund invited her over to their table. With a brassy voice and an easy laugh, she directed an endless stream of sassy remarks toward one customer after another. She seemed to have the knack of making everyone think he was the most important person in the room. Though she was no longer pretty, her vivacity and the flair with which she dressed made her attractive.

In introducing her to Fay, Granlund said, "This guy wants to open a cabaret, a swank nightclub. And he wants you in the top spot."

Since Fay had made no such commitment, Granlund watched him carefully, ready to modify the offer if necessary. However, the ex-cab driver, slightly in awe of the plush surroundings and this smartly dressed, smiling woman, followed right along.

"I like the way you work," he said to Miss Guinan, "and I like you. What I got in mind is we'll open a joint and call it the El Fey Club. You come in and I'll give you fifty per cent of the profit up to a thousand a week. That's your ceiling."

It was now Texas Guinan's turn to be slightly in awe. A thousand a week was several times her current salary. She held out her hand in agreement and it was a deal.

Fay wanted his club to be more than a speakeasy with a smart hostess. There were other places like that. He envisioned something absolutely new—a speakeasy so luxurious, intimate, and spectacular that no one would refer to it as a speakeasy. His club would feature a nightly show with so much talent and so many beautiful girls that New York's most fashionable people would compete for admission. A few days later, he and Granlund found an empty second floor in a building at 107 W. Forty-fourth Street, and New York's first "nightclub" began to take shape.

With winter approaching, Bill McCoy, returning from Rum Row, sailed the *Tomoka* not to Nassau but to Bermuda, which was closer. By reloading there, he hoped to get in another trip to the Row before the bitter winds of December overtook the Atlantic. On November 13, with 4,200 cases of Scotch aboard, he and his eight-man crew set sail for New York once more.

McCoy's profits for the year 1923 had surpassed his wildest dreams. After a single voyage in January he had banked $127,000. That same month, his schooner *Gardner* had been released from quarantine to return to the Row with five thousand cases of cargo per trip. In the spring he had sold the *J.B. Young* because he didn't need it. The *Tomoka* and *Gardner* were each clearing about $100,000 per voyage. He was now so popular on the Row, and his merchandise was so highly regarded as "the real McCoy," that he had become the nation's most famous rumrunner. A succession of beautiful women shared his captain's quarters[10] and even the pirate gangs showed their respect by leaving his vessels alone. It was natural that he should take some pride and pleasure in his notoriety, but at thoughtful moments he realized he was in a precarious position.

At the end of summer, the U.S. government had virtually declared war against Rum Row and McCoy knew it. In June the Coast Guard had added to the rum patrol several cutters and eight thirty-knot speed boats with one-pound guns. They were intercepting so many motor launches carrying liquor to shore that bootleggers were being forced to buy new, thirty-five-knot launches. And though the cutters lacked authority to move against ships outside the three-mile limit, they were now harassing the vessels on the Row with frequent inspections.

At the same time, government enforcement officials were taking diplomatic action against the annoying restrictions of the three-mile limit. Secretary of State Charles Evans Hughes had proposed to Great Britain and other countries that the coastal limit be extended by international agreement to twelve miles. This would force the rum ships farther out to sea and give Coast Guard vessels more leeway in pursuing liquor launches to shore. Though none of the twelve-mile treaties had yet been approved, several countries, including Great Britain, had been virtually persuaded by American pressure to accept them.

McCoy was aware that as founder of Rum Row and the best known person frequenting it, he was likely to become the prime target of this new government thrust. The fact that he was already a fugitive from justice as a result of his indictment following the *Henry L. Marshall* seizure two years earlier could provide a reason for arresting him on sight. Before he sailed from Bermuda November 13 he heard rumors that U.S. authorities were determined to get him. But he had two important advantages—the speed of the *Tomoka* and the fact that the vessel was under British registry. As long as he stayed far enough out to sea, the American Coast Guard had no right to touch him.[11]

Despite continual head winds, the sleek *Tomoka* reached Rum Row off Seabright, New Jersey, on November 17. Because of foul weather, no customers appeared until the twentieth. However, during that one night, McCoy sold his entire cargo with the exception of 150–200 cases of Bacardi rum which he had reluctantly taken as a favor for a friend. In the New York area, the great demand was not for rum but for whisky, and especially for the kind of whisky McCoy offered. He usually sold out faster than anyone else.

He would have sailed south on the morning of the twenty-first were it not for a strange compulsion to get rid of the rum. Expecting to sell it at any moment, he wasted three days before finally contacting a friend who agreed to take it on consignment. Late in the afternoon of the twenty-fourth, a reasonably calm but murky day, he was waiting for his friend to come and relieve him of the rum when the Coast Guard cutter *Seneca* loomed up out of the mist, moving directly toward the *Tomoka*. As the *Seneca* approached, McCoy, who was on deck, heard a voice shout: "*Tomoka,* ahoy! I'm sending an officer to examine your papers."

McCoy saw no cause for alarm. But instead of one person, a whole whaleboat full of men approached the *Tomoka,* led by an officer who announced himself as Lieutenant Commander Louis Perkins.

Perkins climbed over the side and when the others moved to do likewise, McCoy said, "Two on board is enough."

Perkins shouted, "All aboard," and his entire party scrambled onto the deck, each man armed with a Colt automatic.

McCoy turned to Perkins and said, "You're going for a ride, then." To his captain, John Downey, who was at the helm, he shouted, "Full speed to sea, captain!"

Convinced he had been boarded illegally, McCoy decided to teach these Coast Guardsmen a lesson. The auxiliary engines in the *Tomoka* were so powerful that he figured the cutter *Seneca* could never catch him in a race, and the *Seneca* was not likely to use her guns when some of her own men were on the *Tomoka*.

As the *Tomoka* swung out toward open water, Lieutenant Commander Perkins demanded that McCoy turn her around.

"Who are you to give orders on my ship?" McCoy asked heatedly.

As the *Seneca* fell farther and farther astern, the two men argued and the two crews, heavily armed, made ominous moves. Across the cabin hatch they faced each other, but neither Perkins nor McCoy gave orders to fire.

Finally tempers cooled and Perkins began presenting some persuasive reasons why McCoy should surrender. "Be sensible," he advised. "If the government has nothing on you now, it will have if you try to kidnap us. And we won't be kidnapped without a fight. Heave her to, McCoy. I'm advising you for your own good."

McCoy, becoming more reasonable as his anger subsided, began to realize the officer was right. He ordered the jib lowered and the *Tomoka,* turning into the wind, waited for the *Seneca* to overtake her. Perkins and his men rowed back to the cutter while McCoy and his men awaited further developments. Meantime, they dumped into the sea every document and every gun they could find on board, including a machine gun which they were later accused of having fired in the heat of the chase. McCoy ordered Downey to clear the cabin of everything but money, of which McCoy had $60,000 in his pocket and $30,000 in his cabin safe. "Destroy every bit of paper you have with you except your Bibles," he told the men.

After some delay, the *Seneca* hailed them again. Perkins had orders from Washington, he said, either to bring in the *Tomoka* or destroy it. "You will follow me into harbor," he demanded. "If you do not, I shall fire one shot across your bow and then proceed to sink you by gunfire. Understand?"

Though McCoy had no way of knowing it, the U.S. government on this day was instituting a new and legally questionable policy of search and seizure beyond the three-mile limit. The *Tomoka* was an ideal vessel on which to test this policy because she was one ship under British registry that the British would be embarrassed to defend. She was American-built, American-owned, and undoubtedly being used to break an American law. Prohibition officials called her "the flagship of the rum-running fleet." Since the British were in the process of accepting the twelve-mile limit (ratification of the twelve-mile treaty was now pending), they were unlikely to protest very strenuously the seizure of such a vessel under such circumstances.

While unaware of these conditions, McCoy nevertheless preferred to avoid a showdown because the *Tomoka*'s registry would not protect him personally against the earlier charge in connection with the seizure of the *Marshall*. After accepting the demand of the *Seneca*'s captain, he turned to his crew and said, "Boys, I think he's bluffing. It's jail or open sea. It's up to you." When the crew voted for the open sea, McCoy added simply, "We'll wait our chance."

With engine running slowly, foresail and jumbo drawing, the *Tomoka* followed the *Seneca* toward port. The wind, McCoy noted, was now brisk from the northwest and they were sailing into it. As the *Tomoka* tacked to compensate for this, the *Seneca* kept drawing farther in front. The *Seneca* was about three-quarters of a mile away when McCoy saw an ocean liner to starboard on a course that would send it across the *Tomoka*'s wake.

"When that steamer gets into line," he said to his captain, "let her (the Tomoka) go off and clap on sail." He was convinced the *Seneca*'s captain would not fire while the liner was within range.

The *Seneca* was about a mile in front of the *Tomoka* when the liner crossed behind the two vessels. Captain Downey spun the wheel. The schooner hung motionless for a long moment, then caught the breeze and drove directly toward the liner. By the time the *Seneca* turned to pursue, the schooner had picked up speed and seemed destined easily to outrace the cutter. The liner, however, had now passed on and there was nothing to prevent the *Seneca* from using her six-pound guns.

McCoy and his men saw a flash from the cutter's bow, then an orange streak arching toward them in the late afternoon light. The first shell raised a fountain of water in front of the *Tomoka*'s bow. There could be no doubt that she was still within range of the *Seneca*'s artillery. The second shell hit the water just behind the speeding schooner. Cursing the cutter, McCoy's crew let out the lashes to gain more speed. Another shell landed beyond the bow, then a fourth passed just overhead, missing the helmsman by about ten feet.

There could be no doubt now that the *Seneca* had them pinpointed. The fifth shell would not miss. McCoy looked around at the faces of his men, then with a sigh of resignation, ordered them to let the jib run down. Bill McCoy watched with tears in his eyes as the Coast Guard cutter came abeam. He and his beloved schooner were caught at last.

Chapter 7

Their private railway car was awaiting them and so were several hundred well-wishers when George Remus and his twelve aides arrived at the Cincinnati depot. They were a prosperous-looking group; they might easily have been taken for a party of businessmen traveling to a convention. Remus himself was attired in a pearl-gray suit and spats. His shirt was of the softest silk. A huge diamond sparkled from the center of his tie pin. With his wife on his arm he walked through the crowd, shaking hands with his friends and thanking them for coming. Then he and his twelve aides, accompanied by Mrs. Remus, boarded their special car for the 450-mile journey straight south to Atlanta.[1] Finally, on January 24, 1924, a year and eight months after their conviction for conspiracy to violate the Volstead Act, Remus and his men, having exhausted all appeals, were on their way to the federal penitentiary to serve their sentences.

With President Harding now dead and his administration under increasing investigation as a result of Teapot Dome and other scandals, Remus had long since abandoned any hope of intercession in his favor from Washington. Jesse Smith, his "protector," had killed himself with a revolver the previous May. Harry Daugherty, Smith's "protector and partner," was still Attorney General, but he was suffering bitter denunciations from all directions for his failure to prosecute any of the Teapot Dome participants. It was apparent now that despite Smith's repeated assurances to Remus, Daugherty had never done anything in his behalf and did not intend to do anything. Remus, nevertheless, showed no signs of bitterness on this, his last day of freedom. He was so cheerful as he and Imogene settled into the plush seats of their private car that one might think they were going to a racetrack for the day, to enjoy his favorite sport.

Despite the two-year sentence looming ahead of him, plus a subsequent sentence of six months to one year for "maintaining a nuisance" at the Death Valley Farm, Remus still had good reason to be cheerful. The worth of the liquor empire he controlled had swollen to approximately $40 million, and with his wife managing his enterprises, they should continue to prosper. He had so much faith in her as a businesswoman that he had given her power of attorney over all his assets. His entire empire was functioning smoothly, including his most recent acquisition, the Jack Daniels Distillery in St. Louis, which seemed destined to become the most profitable of his properties.

Remus had purchased the Jack Daniels Company as the major partner in a six-man combine the previous June 26. With the aid of the distillery's deputy gauger (whose job it was to record withdrawals but who was receiving three dollars per case for neglecting to do so), he had developed a system of pipes through which whisky flowed directly from the vats inside the plant to trucks outside.[2] In the six months since the purchase of the Jack Daniels Company for $125,000, the Remus syndicate had been able by this method to siphon off more than 30,000 gallons, or about $750,000 worth of exceptionally high quality bourbon. The potential for continued siphoning seemed almost limitless.

On the overnight journey to Atlanta, Remus had several last-minute business items to discuss with Imogene, but he also had time to joke and laugh with the twelve employees who would soon be his fellow inmates. (One of the original thirteen convicted with Remus, having begun his sentence immediately without appeal, was awaiting the others in Atlanta but would not be there much longer since he was now eligible for parole.) Needless to say, the private car was well stocked with liquor. By the time Remus and his twelve had finished their last supper of freedom, most of the diners were happy enough to make light of their fate. Remus himself never drank, though a casual observer might not believe it after seeing him join in the merriment. Perhaps he was not enjoying himself as much as it seemed. The prospect of serving two consecutive prison terms could hardly be pleasant. But he apparently felt a strong compulsion to buoy up the spirits of his men.

He was still outwardly cheerful when the train reached Atlanta on the morning of the Twenty-fifth. After sleeping in an upper berth so that one of his men who was heavier though less nimble than himself could have the lower, he had arisen early and spent an hour or so with one of the books he had brought with him, Dante's *Divine Comedy*. Appropriately enough, it was "The Inferno" that he was currently reading.

When his wife awoke, the two of them found a quiet place in the car and had a long, intimate talk, at the end of which he handed over to her all of his personal jewelry, including his diamond tie pin. Then, after breakfast, he excused himself and retired to dress. When he emerged from the washroom to pack his bags, he noticed that one of the porters in the car was approximately his size and, in an impulsive gesture, gave the man one of his expensive silk shirts.

By this time the train was pulling into the Atlanta station and several reporters were on hand to interview the "Bootleg King of the Middle West." Remus answered their questions graciously.

"I'm up to 225 pounds," he said when someone asked him about his weight, "but I expect to reduce that in prison." In answer to another question, he said he would especially miss his personal valet. Indeed, he already missed him. "I shall have to apologize," he said, "for being forced to appear unshaven before the warden."

The day his trial began on a charge of forgery, William Anderson still found it difficult to believe that Tammany Hall, Governor Al Smith, and the Catholic Church, for whom he blamed his plight, had actually been so brazen as to pursue this matter to its conclusion. It seemed to him no one except the District Attorney had made a complaint against him. Even C. Bertsall Phillips, who would presumably be his chief accuser, had not gone that far. And the directors of the New York Anti-Saloon League were quite satisfied with his action respecting the transaction at issue. This whole proceeding would be very damaging to the League and they were unanimously opposed to it. Yet here he sat on the morning of January 21, 1924, arms folded over his ample frame, watching the courtroom of Justice Arthur S. Tompkins fill up around him.[3]

As the jury selection began, Anderson's attorney, former Governor Charles S. Whitman, declared pointedly that the defendant was "one of the most prominent champions of prohibition." In a city as wet as New York, it was imperative to find out whether any prospective juror would be prejudiced against him on that account. Whitman soon proved his wisdom in raising the issue as one after another of the forty-five talesmen expressed open hostility toward prohibition and its leaders. Even the man eventually chosen as jury foreman, a clothing manufacturer named David Alexander, admitted he disliked prohibition, but when he swore under oath that this would not sway his judgment, Whitman accepted him.

Anderson was disheartened to hear so many of these talesmen speak out against his cause. It dramatized all too well his lack of support from his own people. He felt that the Protestant leadership in New York, by failing to support him, was supinely submitting to "an outrage upon an accredited representative of the churches." On the other hand, he was fortunate to have a lawyer like Whitman defending him. It was true, of course, that Whitman was a heavy drinker, and since all the reporters knew it, this could be embarrassing. But despite his predilection for alcohol, Whitman as governor had always supported prohibition, which fact seemed more important to Anderson than the man's personal habits, especially since, drunk or sober, he was an excellent lawyer.

Anderson sensed that he was going to need the best possible lawyer because the bench, he felt, was loaded against him. He had to acknowledge that the "Tammany Catholic judges" in New York had all been ethical enough to disqualify themselves, and Judge Tompkins, besides being a Republican, was New York State Grand Master of the Masons. But Anderson believed that Tompkins had "always played with Tammany to a certain extent, especially catering to Al Smith." Anderson was also convinced Tompkins hated him personally "because I had blasted his gubernatorial ambitions by exposing the fact that he had given 'certificates of reasonable doubt' (in order to keep them out of jail) to bootleggers who had pleaded guilty" in his court.

On the second day of the trial, C. Bertsall Phillips took the stand to tell how Anderson had forced him to split all fund-raising commissions above $10,000 annually. Whitman in cross examination had already caused Phillips to admit that he had taken his story to an official of the Fleischmann Yeast Company (which Whitman called the Fleischmann Brewery) and that he had asked this official for $5,000. Phillips insisted he wanted the money only as a loan with which to sue Anderson for the return of the fees withheld from him.

The next day, William Potter, Anderson's one-time office bookkeeper, identified the two checks, one for $2,500 and one for $1,375, which represented transfers Anderson had ordered from Phillips' account to his own. Unfortunately, Potter quoted Anderson as saying the $2,500 check was for repayment of a loan to Phillips. This testimony disagreed with what Anderson himself intended to say, but he was confident that as soon as the jurors heard his explanation of the whole affair, they would believe him and exonerate him.

On his first day of testimony, January 24, Anderson acknowledged under direct questioning by his attorney that he had split fees with Phillips but insisted that Phillips himself had suggested the arrangement. He, Anderson, had agreed to it as a method of compensating himself for a debt of $24,700 which the League owed to him. When prosecutor Ferdinand Pecora asked him how the League had accrued such a debt to him, he said it was the result of a "confidential publicity campaign" for the League which he had financed with his own money several years earlier. He had received this money, he said under questioning, from a stranger who walked into his Baltimore office in 1912, when he was the Maryland state superintendent of the League. Though the two men had never before met, the stranger asked Anderson to go into business with him for a guaranteed $10,000 yearly, plus a share of the profits, which he estimated would be $25,000 a year. Since Anderson was then receiving $4,000 a year from the League, this was a sum worthy of consideration, yet he rejected it.

The man then said, as Anderson recalled, "I think you're a darned fool to work your life away for $4,000 a year when you could make a lot more money, but I like that kind of a fool and I think you are doing work that benefits me, and therefore I am going to make a little money for you, and to show you that I am no grafter and there is nothing crooked about it I'm not going to ask you to put up any money. I will invest a little money on your account."

As a result of this investment and several reinvestments, Anderson insisted, the man earned for him and presented to him a total of $25,000 within one year. When Pecora asked for this stranger's name, Anderson at first refused to divulge it on the ground of confidentiality. After Judge Tompkins ruled that he must identify the generous stranger, Anderson reluctantly said he was a man named John T. King, but he knew nothing about him except that one of his offices was someplace in lower Manhattan. He was about forty-five years old, and he wore a black mustache. It was this money from King, Anderson declared, that he had spent on the "confidential publicity campaign" for the League. Pecora did not question him about the term "confidential publicity," which appeared to contradict itself.

While Pecora apparently disbelieved Anderson's account, he had not managed to shake it at the end of the first day's cross-examination. When the defendant returned to the courtroom the following morning, his obviously improved mood bespoke a new confidence. As he took the witness stand he smiled pleasantly at six white-collared Methodist deaconesses in the front row of spectators. And he said "Good morning" when Judge Tompkins arrived. His mood seemed quickly to darken, however, when Pecora resumed his questioning.

After a series of exchanges during which Anderson had to admit he knew almost nothing about his great benefactor, John T. King, and even less about a person named Henry Mann, who, he said, conducted the "confidential publicity campaign," Pecora turned to the $24,700 debt the League had owed Anderson for conducting such a campaign. The League had acknowledged this debt, Anderson declared, at a March 26, 1918 board meeting.

Pecora didn't question this. He was aware that the League board had indeed acknowledged the debt, but he had some questions about the circumstances surrounding this action. Anderson had sworn the previous day that he had financed the publicity campaign with the $25,000 from John T. King. But at that 1918 meeting, hadn't he told the League board that he had raised the money by mortgaging his house and securing a loan on his insurance?

Anderson hesitated so long before answering this question that Judge Tompkins looked down and asked if he was unable to answer it.

"Isn't it a fact, Anderson," Pecora insisted, "that you told the board that the way you raised the $24,700 was by mortgaging your house and insurance policies?"

Anderson hedged. "I told the board that in order to do these things, I may have said so, but not specifically."

Pecora, after giving the jury enough time to appreciate the ambiguity of the answer, said, "Is it a fact that you mortgaged real estate to get the money?"

"Indirectly it is."

"When, at any time before January, 1915, did you mortgage your real estate?"

"In the latter part of 1914," Anderson answered, "and solely because I had spent the money I had set aside for the house."

"But you had already spent the money for publicity?"

"Yes."

"Then the money did not come from any mortgages?"

"No, it did not."

Pecora then introduced into evidence an affadavit addressed to the League board and signed by Anderson in which he swore that the publicity money had come from mortgages and insurance policies. The contradiction did not improve Anderson's credibility. Neither did his failure to produce, or even describe adequately, John T. King and Henry Mann, the two people who, if they existed, might have been able to corroborate his story. His case was further damaged by the fact that he could not explain why Phillips, a fundraiser for the League, should have been expected to pay, out of his own earned commissions, a debt the League owed to its superintendent. All of these circumstances seemed to impugn Anderson's motives in ordering the League's books to be altered. Despite the complaisance of the organization's local board of directors in supporting his "confidential publicity campaign" story, it was difficult to believe that when Anderson ordered $4,400 worth of Phillips' earnings to be listed as expenses, he had any other purpose than to cover up Phillips' kickback payments.

When the case went to the jurors on January 29, it took them only an hour and forty minutes to find Anderson guilty of third degree forgery. He was a lonely man as he stood in the dock, listening to the verdict. His friends had helped him no more than his enemies. Perhaps the greatest cross he had to bear was not the prospect of prison but the fact that all the national leaders of the

Anti-Saloon League had forsaken him. None had spoken out in his behalf, and the day he was judged guilty, only one, Bishop James Cannon, Jr., had even been considerate enough to send him a telegram. Bishop Cannon's wire said:

> Verdict not surprising; indeed it was practically a foregone conclusion that a pure-blooded American, representing Protestant moral forces, who has fearlessly, successfully fought beasts at Ephesus, be convicted on any charge, regardless of evidence, in a court with a wet, foreign-born, Tammany District Attorney, absurdly pretending to protect from fraud the Anti-Saloon League constituency, the organization which he really hates and wishes to destroy; and with a jury in a city where confessedly Satan's seat is, and where the attitude of the press as a whole encourages such a verdict by its sneering, ridiculing, nullifying attitude of the foreign-populated city called New York. . . .⁴

Anderson could find only minor consolation in such a telegram. If Bishop Cannon had really wanted to be helpful, why hadn't he come to Anderson's defense before or during the trial? And even now, why had he sent a message so ethnically inflammatory it couldn't be released to the New York public?

On February 8, when Anderson appeared for sentencing, Judge Tompkins condemned him to a term of one to two years in Sing Sing Prison, and he began his sentence two months later. If there was any truth to his assertion that Al Smith, Tammany Hall, and the Catholic Church had been out to "get" him and put him "out of the way," he would have to admit they had succeeded impressively. He would never bother them again.

/WASHINGTON, PA., Apr. 1, 1924.—Almost everyone in a village named Eighty-four beside the Baltimore & Ohio Railroad tracks eight miles east of Washington went on a spree today when a big "furniture" van was wrecked by an east-bound passenger train and 50 five-gallon cans of choice moonshine whisky were tossed into a ditch.

Residents of the town, who went to the scene of the accident suspecting that the furniture with which the truck was loaded was not its only merchandise, bored holes into the vehicle and struck a false bottom which held the liquor containers.

A crowd of thirsty villagers appeared and soon large quantities of the contraband were siphoned into every kind of vessel. When the chief of county detectives arrived on the scene he discovered a hilarious throng of people, each with a bottle or bucket in hand, doing an Indian dance around the wreck.[5] /

The lunch-hour rush was at its height when Izzy Einstein and Moe Smith entered the Silk Exchange Restaurant in the seventeen-story Silk Exchange Building at 432 Fourth Avenue. Izzy, with a bolt of cloth under his arm, was ostensibly a silk salesman while Moe would have people believe he was an "out-of-town buyer." He seemed not quite at ease in such an expensive restaurant and his clothing was slightly less than stylish. In case the management should fail to conclude that he was a visitor to the city, Izzy asked Moe, in the presence of their waiter, what Broadway shows he would like to see while he was in New York.[6]

As their lunch progressed, they talked at some length about silk while the waiter was hovering nearby. Then, as businessmen do, they drifted to other subjects and Izzy began describing the Broadway hits Moe was most likely to enjoy. W. C. Fields was appearing in "Poppy," Irene Bordoni in "Little Miss Bluebeard," Walter Hampden in "Cyrano de Bergerac." None of them seemed to stir Moe's interest. What he really wanted while he was in New York, he said, was to find something decent to drink, a pint of good whisky, if he could get hold of one.

Izzy called the waiter to his side of the table and in a confidential tone repeated Moe's request. Wasn't there some way the waiter could help out? "He's a customer of mine," Izzy explained, "and I've got to make good with him."

The waiter left the room and returned with a well-concealed bottle which he slipped inconspicuously to Moe. Both men were profusely grateful. They would not forget this favor. After overtipping the waiter, they stood up and departed without taking any action against the establishment. It was not Izzy's strategy to raid the place today. The Silk Exchange was a prominent restaurant the kind that probably had a first-class wine supply in addition to a large stock of whisky, gin, and every other kind of liquor. No doubt this stock would be well hidden. In a seventeen-story building it could be almost anyplace. If he were to move against it today, his total take might be one waiter and one bottle of whisky. To get the owner and a big haul, he might have to return several times, until he had gained the full confidence of at least one of the waiters. The project could take a while, but it had its compensations. He and Moe would be eating well for the next few days.

Their first lunch at the Silk Exchange was so good they returned the very next day, April 11, 1924. They were welcomed even more cordially than the day before and were getting quite chummy with their waiter when suddenly they were victimized by the fame they had achieved. One of the customers, walking past Izzy, stopped short as recognition overcame him.

"There," he cried, "is the man of a thousand disguises."

The disguise Izzy was using at the moment, the bolt of cloth which advertised him as a silk salesman, now looked fairly ridiculous in his hands. Other diners, realizing that Izzy and Moe were in their midst, began making jokes about their exploits. The waiters immediately registered alarm. Izzy could see that if he intended to act at all, he would have to act quickly, whether he was ready or not. Jumping to his feet, he declared without hesitation, but also without evidence, that the establishment was hereby charged with violating the Volstead Act.

All Izzy had to do now was to find the evidence, but the uproar over his identification and the attendant confusion had given the waiters enough time to hide a small roomful of liquor. After a thorough search of the entire restaurant, Izzy was convinced they had done just that. A restaurant this size, if it was serving liquor, would have to keep a large supply immediately at hand, yet he had to admit, with considerable embarrassment, that he couldn't produce so much as a glassful. How could they have moved so many bottles so quickly and so quietly?

It was not until he went out into the foyer of the building that a constructive idea hit him. To move a small roomful of anything quickly, one would have to have a vehicle the size of a small room. Here they had several. The building's elevators. Five or six waiters, trained for such an emergency, could fill an elevator full of liquor cases in two or three minutes. Where, then, would they be most likely to take it? Since the basement was the obvious place, Izzy got into one of the elevators and headed straight for the roof. He was too experienced to look in obvious places.

His trip to the roof was richly rewarded. There, nestled against the elevator housing, he found case upon case of the finest wines, champagnes, and whiskies available. However, before congratulating himself for his cleverness, he decided he had better look also in the obvious place. And he was soon glad he did. In the basement he found the restaurant's main supply. When the government trucks arrived, he and Moe had $25,000 worth of evidence to carry away.

As the 1924 Democratic National Convention approached, it became apparent that this year, Governor Alfred E. Smith of New York was a candidate who would have to be taken seriously. Despite his attempts to woo dry votes by declaring himself opposed to saloons and strong liquors, the wets were certain he was wet. Since most of the big city Democrats were also wet, Smith went to the convention in New York's Madison Square Garden with 241 delegate votes in his pocket. Unfortunately for him, the drys were equally convinced he was wet, and under the concealed leadership of Wayne Wheeler they were determined to stop him. Wheeler, who held tight control over one third of the 1,098 delegates, mostly from Southern and Western states, swung them behind William Gibbs McAdoo, who had been President Woodrow Wilson's son-in-law as well as Secretary of the Treasury in his cabinet, and who in recent years had gradually aligned himself with the drys.

Wheeler and the Anti-Saloon League organization had captured their approximately 350 delegates by adopting a simple but energetic and very productive political strategy. As he later explained it, "We got busy many months before the convention and worked out in the field to make certain that more than one third of the delegates were against any wet candidate. Our work was done effectively but in many states it attracted little attention. It was carried on in almost every state in the Union. When we were sure of a comfortable margin above the one third required we eased up somewhat in our efforts as there was no particular need for more dry delegates."[7]

With unshakable control over enough votes to prevent any wet candidate from winning the two-thirds majority required at that time for the nomination, Wheeler could have sat quietly in his room at the Herald Square Hotel, keeping secret contact with floor representatives like William Jennings Bryan, but never having to go near the hot, crowded Garden except for the pleasure of watching his smooth organization at work. Though he had placed his delegates behind McAdoo, he was not committed to the former Treasury Secretary. He didn't actually care who won the nomination, as long as it was not Smith or Senator Oscar Underwood of Alabama, an avowed wet even though he came from a dry state. Wheeler was not displeased at the prospect of a deadlocked convention which would force the Democrats to settle on some relatively obscure compromise candidate. He planned to support in November the incumbent Calvin Coolidge, who had moved into the White House after the mysterious death of President Harding on his way back from Alaska in August 1923. Coolidge might not be brilliant but he was safe. He was untouched by the Teapot Dome investigations now exposing the corruption of the Harding administration. He had spoken out forthrightly in favor of prohibition, low taxes, and high employment. And, beyond that, he had kept his mouth shut.

Also staying at the Herald Square Hotel, in a room near Wheeler's, was his chief rival for Anti-Saloon League power, Methodist Bishop James Cannon, Jr., of Virginia. When these two men held their daily meetings, they looked, ironically, like long-lost brothers. Not only were they outwardly cordial, as if they were truly glad of the chance to get together; they also resembled each other strikingly. They dressed alike, in dark suits and high collars. Both were slender, with receding hairlines and gaunt, ascetic faces; both wore thin-rimmed glasses and stubbly mustaches. Cannon, who was five years older, had worn a beard for twenty-five years because, as he explained it, his daily schedule was so crowded he didn't have time to shave. He seemed as busy as ever now, yet he was managing to keep his face bare except for his upper lip.

Since Wheeler and Cannon were agreed on the primary Anti-Saloon League purpose at the convention—the defeat of Al Smith's candidacy—their meetings were fairly congenial except in one respect. Cannon, a Democrat, could not conceal his resentment against interference in his party's convention by Wheeler, a Republican. Even though Wheeler's interference was in a good cause, Cannon felt that "a man who it was known would be aggressive in his support of President Coolidge for reelection should not try to be influential in the nomination of the Democratic candidate."

Cannon also resented the fact that Wheeler, through Bryan, wielded more influence than he did over the Southern delegations. The bishop tried to counter Wheeler's power by first suggesting, then insisting, that he, as a Democrat, act as the League's official contact with Southern leaders. After initial reluctance, Wheeler affably agreed. If Bishop Cannon was determined to be the League's official spokesman, he should by all means go ahead and assume the position, as long as everyone at the convention realized that Wheeler, through Bryan, was the actual spokesman for the entire dry cause.

Bishop Cannon's standing as a Democrat had been slightly compromised a month earlier, at least among Northern loyalists, by some remarks he made in Springfield, Massachusetts, at the General Conference of the Methodist Episcopal Church. Addressing himself to the question of whom he would support in November if his own party were to nominate a wet like Al Smith, he had said: ". . . while I am a Democrat, I am not a lawbreaker, and should the Republican Party nominate a man who stands squarely for the genuine better enforcement of the Eighteenth Amendment than we have had up to this time, I think I know my people in the South well enough to say that in that event the issue with them would not be Democracy versus Republicanism; it would be law versus lawlessness."

This statement had prompted a May 18 New York *Times* editorial entitled "What Sort of Democrat Is Bishop Cannon?" The *Times* seemed to suggest that Cannon was not only potentially disloyal to his party but also opposed to Governor Smith on religious grounds, and this was a touchy subject because for many years Cannon had been openly attacking the Catholic Church. In the Baltimore and Richmond *Christian Advocate,* a periodical Cannon owned and edited, he had declared, as early as December 17, 1908, that the Catholic Church was the "Mother of ignorance, superstition, intolerance, and sin." In the *Advocate* of January 30, 1913, he had expressed warm praise for a Missouri anti-Catholic paper called the *Menace,* which, he wrote, "should receive the support and approval of every Christian minister, every voter and citizen, and every lover of the American principles of free education, purity, freedom of worship, freedom of speech and press, all the rights a free people reserve to themselves. Remember, papal bans and curses are against all these."

This open anti-Catholicism, often expressed by Bishop Cannon and other Southern Democrats, was a constant threat to the working unity of a party which harbored most of the country's Catholics and, at the same time, most of the country's Ku Klux Klansmen. Wayne Wheeler, who had never been known to express anti-Catholic sentiments, could nevertheless take some satisfaction from such a potentially explosive Democratic cleavage. It was another factor boding well for Coolidge in the fall. Wheeler was naturally pleased, therefore, at the handicap Catholicism imposed on Al Smith. But the New York governor had so much political ability and personal appeal that he was dangerous as a possible unifier of all the wet forces. Wheeler still had enough respect for Smith to fear his nomination despite the religious problem it would cause the Democrats.

One circumstance that acutely concerned Wheeler as the convention began on June 24 was the fact that it was being held in New York City where Smith held power. Wheeler called him "the ace of trumps from the wet standpoint." It seemed to Wheeler the whole city was campaigning to win the nomination for their bluff, cigar-smoking, whisky-drinking hero, "from the newsboys in the streets to the bands in the convention hall with their interminable 'Sidewalks of New York.' " He called Smith's workers "the livest bunch of wires on the wet side." Some of the more prominent campaigners even invited Wheeler to dinner in the hope of impressing their candidate's virtues upon him. Wheeler ate their food but remained unimpressed. He had read about an indiscreet remark by Smith when Senator Walter Edge of New Jersey declared himself for 3 percent beer. Smith was reported to have said, "I'll be glad to go down and help him if that will get us a place where we can put a foot on the rail and blow off the froth." A few days before the convention opened, Wheeler, in a speech at New York's West Side Y.M.C.A, attacked the governor for this slip of the tongue. "The man who makes such a statement has not caught step with the American people," Wheeler told his audience.

Wheeler firmly believed that the people of America had happily embraced prohibition, but he wasn't so sure about the people of New York. Especially those Tammany Democrats, all Smith supporters, who would be packing the galleries at the convention. In an effort to keep them sober, Wheeler arranged a meeting at his hotel with prohibition agent Izzy Einstein, to whom he had already sent several admiring letters. The meeting was highly publicized, with news photographs, and some of the papers suggested Wheeler and Einstein were planning to raid the convention. Wheeler was too smart a politician to contemplate such a move. He wanted only to ask Einstein's help in keeping liquor out of Madison Square Garden.

Izzy was happy to oblige. Between sessions, he hung around the lobby of the Waldorf Astoria, dressed up as a southern colonel with a goatee, listening for tips or rumors about midtown bootleggers and speakeasies. During each session he was at the Garden, wearing a delegate's badge. While he didn't apprehend any bootleggers there, he and his associates did find, after each session, "a truckload of bottles." He later explained, however, "they weren't legal evidence because they were all empty."

As the convention progressed, Al Smith, in his headquarters on the top floor of the Manhattan Club across the street from Madison Square Garden, became increasingly concerned about Wheeler's activities and the dangers they presented. Smith was also worried about the strength of the Ku Klux Klan among the drys. He felt that "the Klan and the antisaloon forces in the convention were practically identical." Though this was not precisely accurate, it was true that the Anti-Saloon League and the Klan were prepared to make common cause against any wet candidate.

The Klan issue was so serious it threatened to break the convention apart almost before it began. The Platform Committee, dominated by the big Eastern states, approved a plank which would condemn the organization's bigotry. Bryan, as the apparent leader of the drys, opposed the plank. McAdoo, hoping for dry support, remained silent about it. Smith, being a Catholic, had always viewed the Klan with contempt and had often said so. He had little to lose by saying so. No Klan delegate was likely to vote for him. But his statements helped make the Klan issue a wet-dry issue and thereby made it easier for people like Wayne Wheeler to keep the Klan bloc united against any wet candidate.

Young Franklin D. Roosevelt from Hyde Park, the Democratic vice presidential candidate in 1920, but subsequently a victim of polio, placed the New York governor's name before the delegates in what many people considered the best speech during the entire convention. "Ask your Republican friends whom they would least like to see nominated," he challenged. And in conclusion, he presented his man to the assemblage with two lines from Wordsworth containing a phrase which would always thereafter be associated with Al Smith:

> This is the Happy Warrior: this is he
> That every man in arms should wish to be.

The New Yorkers who packed the galleries began a stampede so raucous and prolonged, so obviously flavored with alcohol, that it frightened some of the delegates and offended others. Undoubtedly it hurt Smith more than it helped him. McAdoo's demonstration was tame and sober by comparison, and when the first ballot was counted, it was McAdoo rather than Smith who led the parade of twenty candidates. McAdoo was well ahead with 431½ of the 732 votes needed for nomination. Smith showed only his hard core of 241.

As the second, third, fourth, and fifth ballots followed, the favorite son candidates were expected to drop out, but the possibility of a deadlock kept most of them in the race. The frontrunners gained, though not dramatically. By the tenth ballot, people were openly doubtful that either Smith or McAdoo could make it, yet both were still gaining slowly. By the fifteenth ballot, which was completed just before midnight June 30, McAdoo still had only 479 votes to Smith's 305½.

There was no doubt now that a paralyzing deadlock had developed. It might possibly be broken if several of the minor candidates were to release their delegates, starting a surge in one direction or another, but each of the minor candidates was now clinging to his base of support in the hope of emerging as a compromise choice. It was apparent that nothing could be resolved unless either Smith or McAdoo were to concede, yet neither was willing; even if one of them did bow out, it was not likely that the other could win. The drys unquestionably had enough votes to block Smith, and the wets, who were equally stubborn, had enough votes to block McAdoo.

Day after day, ballot after ballot, the deadlock continued. At the conclusion of the thirty-eighth ballot, William Jennings Bryan, who had been visiting each delegation to plead for McAdoo, created sudden excitement in the Garden by rising to ask the chairman for "unanimous consent to explain my vote."

Bryan was old now and unpopular in some quarters, but he was still a major figure in the party and a persuasive orator. When the chairman disregarded vociferous objections from several quarters and alloted him a half hour to speak, there was as much apprehension among the drys as there was anger among the wets.

After the traditional prelude in praise of the Democratic Party, Bryan frightened the McAdoo organization by stating that the party had other candidates in abundance. "We could call the roll of states," he declared, "and find in every state a Democrat worthy to be President of the United States." As he continued talking, it began to look as if he actually intended to name a candidate from every state.

Since Bryan was now living in Florida, and had come as a delegate from there, he began his list there. "We have a man in Florida," he announced. "He is the president of our state university. His name is Dr. A. A. Murphree."

There was laughter in the hall. Several voices shouted, "We want Smith!" This produced more laughter, applause, and cheers.

"He is a Democratic scholar," Bryan said of Murphree, "and he is a scholarly Democrat."

Someone shouted, "Never heard of him!" Others began to hiss and boo. What was Bryan's strategy? Did he intend to present a list of nonentities in the hope that the delegates would turn to him in preference to them? Did he see in the present deadlock a possibility that the party might nominate him once more, for the fourth time? Despite continued heckling, Bryan went on to name seven men as acceptable presidential candidates, most of them Senators, but including his own brother, Nebraska Governor Charles W. Bryan. Finally, with the McAdoo people becoming more nervous every minute, Bryan also named their man. By this time, however, he had already done his damage, having suggested seven others who might be equally good. He did not mention Al Smith or Oscar Underwood, the two men Wayne Wheeler was most determined to keep out of the White House.

Whatever else Bryan's speech may have accomplished, it failed utterly to recommend him to the delegates as a possible compromise candidate. One elderly delegate was heard to say, "He still has his cross of gold but his crown of thorns is on crooked." Franklin Roosevelt, sitting in the New York delegation with a smile on his face, said when the speech ended, "Mr. Bryan has killed poor McAdoo, and he hasn't done himself any good."

As the delegates returned to their balloting, Al Smith decided that if he was to have any chance of victory, he would have to talk to the man who was blocking his path. This man was not the public leader of the opposition, Mr. Bryan. Though Smith had paraded for Bryan in 1896 and 1900, and had campaigned for him in 1908, he neither admired nor respected him in 1924. "Bryan was a man who was never for anything new except to help himself," Smith later said of him.[8] "In not one of his three campaigns for the presidency did he ever speak in favor of woman suffrage or about prohibition. It always seemed to me that Bryan invented issues to get a nomination, but after getting it he never said anything about them." Well aware that Bryan's convention moves were directed by Wayne Wheeler, Smith invited Wheeler up to his Manhattan Club headquarters for a chat.[9]

Their conversation was pleasant. Wheeler was as engaging, personally, as Smith, and Smith found him friendly. But both men knew they hadn't met to exchange the time of day. Within a few minutes they were talking about prohibition. Smith, who advocated legalization of beer containing less than 2.75 percent alcohol on the ground that it was not intoxicating, asked Wheeler why the Volstead Act defined any beverage with more than one half of one percent alcohol as an intoxicant, and why the Eighteenth Amendment offered no definition of an intoxicant.

Wheeler answered frankly that he didn't think the drys could have got the amendment through Congress and out to the states if it had defined such an alcoholic limit. This began an argument between the two men about the intoxicant definition in the Volstead Act. Wheeler said the one half of one percent limit had been taken from the New York state excise law. Smith pointed out that this law had stated the limit only for taxation purposes. What he was trying to suggest was that he would not be at such great odds with the Anti-Saloon League if the League would tolerate light wines and beer. Wheeler was not receptive to this possibility. When Smith pursued the question of why such a low alcohol limit had been written into the Volstead Act, Wheeler simply smiled and said, "Well, we were in the saddle and we drove through."

Smith then tried another approach. If he were to become President of the United States, he suggested, it would not be the same as being governor of New York. His methods of enforcing the prohibition law would be quite different. He did not specify in what ways they would be different, and Wheeler did not pursue the matter. He felt their views were so radically divergent they might as well keep the conversation "noncommittal." Wheeler could not resist one parting stroke, however, when Smith made casual reference to the possibility that he might some day be President.

"Governor," he said, "you will never enter the White House."

This ended the meeting and in effect it ended Al Smith's only chance of breaking his deadlock with William Gibbs McAdoo. Though the balloting continued for almost two weeks, neither Smith nor McAdoo could gain an advantage. After forty-two ballots, McAdoo had 503.4 of the 732 necessary votes; Smith had 318.6, with nine lesser candidates holding onto their blocs.

As the deadlock deepened, Bishop Cannon left Wheeler to tend the convention while he hurried off to a church conference in Chattanooga. As soon as the conference ended, he rushed back to New

York, where the convention was then approaching the 105th ballot. When Cannon discussed this hopeless situation with Wheeler, he found the latter quite pleased that the Democratic Party had been thrown into such confusion. Cannon, as exasperated at Wheeler as he was disturbed at the plight of his party, made a surprising suggestion when the two spoke of possible compromise candidates. Despite his attitudes about the Catholic Church and his bitter opposition to Al Smith, the bishop proposed that the dry bloc swing its support to Senator Thomas Walsh of Montana, another Catholic but an unequivocally dry one from a dry, rural state.[10] Walsh, the convention's permanent chairman, had impressed everyone by his patience and authority in handling the hard-drinking, frustrated, sweaty delegates who crowded the Garden every day during the New York heat of June and July.

Wheeler must have been startled at this idea, but Cannon was sincere and persuasive. If the drys were to support Walsh it would prove to the world that they had opposed Smith not because he was Catholic but because he was wet.

After the 105th ballot, the deadlock was so rigid that Smith and McAdoo both finally acknowledged their inability to break it. Simultaneously, by prior agreement, they announced their withdrawals during the convention's twenty-first session.

Again Bishop Cannon proposed to Wheeler that they turn to Senator Walsh. Though Wheeler was not enthusiastic at the prospect, he did not oppose it. But when Senator Walsh was approached, he refused to make the race.

John W. Davis, a West Virginia lawyer and former Congressman, offered himself as the least controversial compromise choice. Bryan sent a hurried message to Wheeler asking whether the Anti-Saloon League would oppose Davis. Wheeler was acquainted with Davis and felt he "had a fairly good law enforcement record," though he suspected him of being a secret wet. He had "never taken a stand for or against prohibition," Wheeler noted.[11] He also had the virtue of being almost completely unknown to the American electorate, and Wheeler liked him for that. With a man as obscure as John W. Davis leading the Democratic ticket, Republican President Calvin Coolidge looked like a certainty to win in November.

Wheeler's delight at the outcome of the convention soon proved to be too obvious. Ruled by an insatiable ego and hunger for fame, he wrote a press release which made it clear that he had been "the man behind the scenes" preventing the Democrats from choosing a wet candidate. When he showed this statement to Cannon, the bishop lost his ecclesiastical composure and the two men engaged in a bitter argument.

This was their first unrestrained dispute since the previous January when Cannon, before the Anti-Saloon League national convention, had refused to support Wheeler for the General Superientendency unless the latter would relinquish his Washington office and move to the organization's headquarters in Westerville, Ohio. Wheeler had been too intelligent to make such a sacrifice. The reason he was so much more influential than any other League officer, despite his apparently modest title of general counsel and legislative superintendent, was due in part to his presence in Washington, the seat of national power and publicity, while most of the other officers were in Westerville or, like Bishop Cannon, in some other section of the country. Wheeler, due to constant publicity, had become the nation's most famous dry hero. His constituency included, besides the general public, the White House and the dry members of Congress, most of whom feared him, respected him, or depended on his political and financial help. Bishop Cannon could challenge him, and sometimes even exercise restraint upon him, because he too had a large constituency, the members of his church and the southern Democratic politicians. Cannon had been able, the previous January, to prevent Wheeler from becoming the nominal as well as the actual leader of the League. He insisted now that Wheeler suppress his self-serving statement.

Wheeler seemed unable to comprehend that there was anything wrong with the statement. It was true, wasn't it?

Though it may have been true, it was hardly appropriate. Unless he withheld it from the press, Cannon warned, he himself would issue a statement repudiating it.

Finally, Wheeler agreed to abandon his petty victory claim, which gave Cannon a chance to claim a petty victory of his own. He had stood up to Wheeler and made him back down, a feat few men had accomplished in recent years. But this latest contretemps between the two men would change nothing. Wayne Wheeler still controlled the Anti-Saloon League and it was he, the League's Mr. Republican, rather than Bishop Cannon, the League's Mr. Democrat, who had worked his will upon the Democratic Party.

Chapter 8

Dion O'Banion, a man familiar in many environments, was mixing with politicians tonight. He was, in fact, something of a politician himself. In Chicago's forty-second and forty-third wards on the near north side, O'Banion was the one person with the unfailing ability to deliver the vote. In every election, the returns from those two wards tallied with his hopes and predictions. He had a group of persuasive associates with names like Hymie Weiss, Bugs Moran, Louie Alterie, and Schemer Drucci who made certain there were no surprising results. These men policed the polls so aggressively that people who might oppose O'Banion's political views did not feel encouraged to vote. If they voted anyway, they might be forgiven, but they could never be sure their votes were counted.

A man with O'Banion's political influence could expect to be courted by both political parties and he was. A devout Irish Catholic and former choir boy who had grown up in the North Side slums, he considered himself a Democrat, but in recent years, with Chicago Republicans like Big Bill Thompson showing themselves so sympathetic to O'Banion's primary business interests, he could sometimes be persuaded to make certain that the forty-second and forty-third wards did not go Democratic. There were rumors that he had been so persuaded this year, 1924, which explained the affair he was now attending, a gala political banquet at the Webster Hotel on Lincoln Park West.¹ The Democrats were sponsoring the banquet, in O'Banion's honor, not because they were unaware of his rumored defection to the Republicans but because they hoped that by thanking him publicly for his past favors, they might ensure his future favors, especially in this coming election. The guests included the Democratic candidate for the U.S. Senate, Colonel Albert A. Sprague, who was also Chicago's Public Works Commissioner; County Clerk Robert M. Sweitzer, twice an unsuccessful candidate for mayor against Thompson; the Chicago Police Department's Chief of Detectives, Michael Hughes; several other police officials; a full roster of Democratic officeholders, candidates, and contributors; at least four labor leaders, two of whom were also hoodlums; and a half dozen of O'Banion's top lieutenants.

There was so much whisky, wine, and beer on hand that the party continued until dawn. When the speeches began, one prominent Democrat after another stood up to praise the diminutive, baby-faced, gimpy-legged O'Banion. The climax of the evening came when they presented him with a platinum watch encrusted with diamonds and rubies.

One prominent Democrat who did not attend, Mayor William Dever, was furious when he read about the party the next day. In his view, Dion O'Banion was not the kind of man to whom the Democratic Party should look for support, nor was he the kind of man with whom Chicago policemen should associate. Dever immediately called Chief of Detectives Hughes into his office and asked him to resign.

O'Banion, meanwhile, having accepted the Democratic watch and eaten the Democratic food, delivered the forty-second and forty-third wards solidly to the Republicans on election day. Besides earning some Republican cash, he was registering a protest against Dever who, since replacing Thompson as mayor, had done everything in his power to damage the bootlegging business in Chicago. This was the business which was now O'Banion's principal source of income.

O'Banion was also a florist, owning half interest in one of the city's finest flower shops, on North State Street, directly opposite Holy Name Cathedral, where he had sung in the choir as a boy. At one time or another he had tried safe-cracking, burglary, armed robbery, and hijacking, but he didn't find any of them substantial enough, though he still occasionally resorted to hijacking if the prize was particularly attractive. Murder was another of his skills, and for that purpose he carried three guns in special pockets of his well-tailored suits. The police once estimated he had killed twenty-five men, but murder was only an occasional expedient, not a business in itself. It was bootlegging that had made him wealthy and prominent. And he pursued this enterprise so aggressively that he had antagonized some of his associates.

Like the rest of Chicago's gangsters, O'Banion had agreed to a compact devised by Johnny Torrio three years earlier which divided the city into well defined territories for liquor distribution, and which regulated business procedures among the gangs. The purpose of Torrio's intelligent arrangement was to gain a certain respectability for the bootlegging business by imposing order and preventing violence. Except for a few minor lapses into gunfire, the compact had worked quite well under Torrio's watchful guidance. Recently, however, the delicate competitive balance had been disturbed by the retirement of complacent Mayor Thompson and his replacement by determined Mayor Dever, whose raids were beginning to hurt some of the boys.

O'Banion had reacted by giving rein to the suicidal tendencies characteristic of so many gangsters. He had begun invading the territory of a gang operating adjacent to him, and had even hijacked some of their liquor. He seemed to think he could treat his colleagues the same way he was planning to treat Chicago's Democratic Party. His narrow Irish pride made it difficult for him to accept the leadership of Sicilians like Torrio. Never having outgrown the slum-bred prejudices between the Irish and Italians, he was openly scornful of Torrio despite their alliance. On the previous May 19, he had manifested this scorn by swindling Torrio and setting him up for an arrest in connection with an underhanded business transaction.

Thanks to their earlier working agreement, O'Banion had acquired 25 percent of a large illicit brewery controlled by Torrio and his chief lieutenant, Al Capone. Discovering through a police informant in early May that Mayor Dever and federal authorities planned to raid the brewery on May 19 and confiscate its machinery, O'Banion plotted to protect his investment by immediately selling Torrio his 25 percent interest for half a million dollars in cash. The deal had already been consummated and O'Banion had the money when, on the nineteenth, he indulged himself in an impish desire to see Torrio's face at the moment the swindle became apparent. Aware that the police intended that night to raid the brewery, he invited Torrio and his staff to meet him there for the ownership transfer arrangements. When the police and federal men arrived, they found much more than they had expected. Besides confiscating or destroying the brewery equipment and all the available beer, they were able to arrest both O'Banion and Torrio, plus several of their men. Perhaps O'Banion had hoped that if he too were a victim of the raid, he would avert Torrio's suspicion. But Torrio, who had even more police informants than O'Banion, soon learned that he had been doublecrossed and cheated out of half a million dollars. He was not overly upset about the bootlegging charge against him. Annoying as it was, it could be handled in court. What disturbed him deeply was O'Banion's betrayal; he decided that at the right moment, that too might have to be handled, though in a different way.

On November 10, less than a week after the 1924 election in which O'Banion had doublecrossed the Democrats by delivering his two wards to the Republicans, he was in his flower shop engaging in one of his favorite pastimes, the creation of elaborate floral arrangements. He sincerely loved flowers and treated them with a tenderness he did not always show toward people. He and his associates in the shop had been exceedingly busy during the two previous days because a powerful gangster had died a natural death and was scheduled to be buried the next day. Most of the city's important gang leaders had ordered lavish bouquets. O'Banion was working near the rear of the shop when three expensively dressed men entered. He knew at least one of them, whom a witness described as a "tall, well-built, well-shaven man in a brown overcoat and a brown fedora hat." Perhaps this man and the other two had come to pick up a floral offering for the next day's funeral. O'Banion, who was not in the habit of shaking hands with strangers, came forward with hand extended.

In apparently the friendliest of gestures, the man took O'Banion's hand firmly in his, but then, instead of releasing it, he gripped it tightly while his two companions produced pistols and began firing bullets into O'Banion's body. Two slugs went through his chest, two more through his throat, a fifth broke his right cheek, and after he fell to the floor, a sixth entered his brain from so close a range that his head was powder-burned.

At his funeral, one of the most elaborate in Chicago's history, Johnny Torrio and Al Capone were among the most prominent mourners. The $50,000 worth of flowers included a huge basket of roses with the simple message: "From Al." Chicago's Democratic Party did not send flowers, yet no one suggested that O'Banion had been killed by disgruntled Democrats.

Capone offered one possible explanation for the maverick Irishman's death. "Deany was all right and he was getting along to begin with better than he had any right to expect," Capone said. "But like everyone else, his head got away from his hat. Johnny Torrio had taught O'Banion all he knew and then O'Banion grabbed some of the best guys we had and decided to be the boss of the booze racket in Chicago. What a chance! O'Banion had a swell route to make it tough for us and he did. His job had been to smooth the coppers and we gave him a lot of authority with the booze and beer buyers. When he broke away, for a while it wasn't so good. He knew the ropes and got running us ragged. It was his funeral."

O'Banion's apparent successor as chief of the North Side gang, a Polish hoodlum named Hymie Weiss (originally Wajiechowski) had his own ideas about why O'Banion had died, who had killed him, and who had ordered his death. Weiss swore vengeance publicly against Torrio and Capone. The three years of underworld peace under Torrio's guidance were now shattered and Chicago could expect a vicious, bloody gang war in the months and years ahead.

Johnny Torrio, a prudent man, had left Chicago with his wife, Ann, for a two-month vacation shortly after the murder of Dion O'Banion. They toured the Southern states, then sailed for Cuba and the Bahamas, returning through Florida on the way home. Torrio sought thereby to avoid not only the cold of Chicago's winter but the heat of the gang war he had launched by approving the murder of the North Side leader. Torrio's holiday, as it developed, was hardly restful. His secret itinerary did not completely conceal him from the North Side gunmen on his trail, and though they failed to catch him, they came close enough to make him uncomfortable. When he did return to Chicago in mid-January, he found no opportunity to relax. His chief lieutenant and almost partner Al Capone had narrowly missed death on January 12 (his chauffeur had been wounded) when Hymie Weiss, George Bugs Moran and Vincent Schemer Drucci, the most important of the North Siders, had invaded the South Side in person to riddle his car with bullets at State and Fifty-fifth Streets. And the man who replaced Capone's wounded chauffeur had already disappeared in an obvious kidnapping. The O'Banion survivors were showing no respect whatsoever. They had lessons to learn. Until they were properly educated, Torrio wouldn't feel safe in Chicago.

On January 23, Torrio and eleven others had to appear in federal court to answer bootlegging charges as a result of O'Banion's betrayal in the big brewery raid the previous May. After due consideration of his options, Torrio decided that instead of fighting the charge, he would surprise everyone, including Judge Adam Cliffe, by pleading guilty. A prison cell might be a healthy place to spend the next few months while Capone and the boys eliminated the dangers lurking on the Chicago streets.

Judge Cliffe obligingly gave Torrio five days in which to arrange his affairs before sentencing, and this almost proved to be more than the gang genius needed. On the following day he went shopping with his wife in the Loop. It was late afternoon when they returned in a chauffeur-driven car to their South Side apartment building at 7011 Clyde Avenue, about six blocks west of Lake Michigan below Jackson Park.

The chauffeur, opening the rear door of the Lincoln sedan, handed Mrs. Torrio down onto the sidewalk, then helped Torrio gather up the larger parcels to be carried inside. When Torrio stepped onto the sidewalk, his wife was already at the door of the building. He now saw that a Cadillac limousine had pulled up across the street and that two men were running toward him with drawn automatics.

He had no time to reach the building. The first man fired two shots, one hitting Torrio in the chest and knocking him down, the other breaking his jaw. The second man hit him with two more bullets, in the groin and the right arm, as he lay writhing on the concrete. The two men still in the car were firing at his chauffeur, whom they managed to hit in the right leg below the knee. One of the men standing above Torrio bent over as if to administer the final bullet to his head, but before he fired another shot the driver of the Cadillac honked its horn. He and his companion turned and ran back to their car without finishing the job.

Suffering not only from the bullet holes but from mustard that had been rubbed onto the bullets, Torrio crawled toward his wife as she ran to help him. Shortly after he was carried into the Jackson Park

Hospital, Capone himself, burly, porcine, and loud, arrived to protect him from further harm. Capone broke into tears when he saw his mentor's perforated body and shattered jaw, but his emotion did not cloud his judgment. Despite Torrio's critical condition and intense pain, Capone insisted he be moved immediately to an inner room where he could be guarded by four armed gang members in addition to the two policemen stationed at the door.

Though the police showed some curiosity about the identity of the men who had shot Torrio, he suggested, despite his pain, that they not concern themselves unduly with such trivia. Aside from asking a few routine questions and making a few routine arrests, the police took his suggestion. Several days later, when his pain had abated, Torrio mumbled through his broken jaw to a reporter who asked the same question, "Sure, I know all four men, but I'll never tell their names."

The police were certain that one of the men was Bugs Moran, now second in command of the O'Banion gang, and their certainty was increased when a seventeen-year-old boy who had witnessed the shooting positively identified him. This evidence, however, did not impress the judge before whom they took Moran. He was quickly released and the police declined to pester him any more about the matter.

Torrio gradually recovered from his wounds but he did not forget the incident. As a gang executive, he had occasionally decreed that other men be shot, yet he himself had never before experienced it, and he found now that he was not partial to it. As he lay in bed he gave increasing thought to the prospect that he might soon be offered another portion of the same. He was now worth several million dollars, including a million which he and his wife had taken with them to Italy for safekeeping on a recent trip. One day, when the faithful and watchful Capone was sitting by his bedside, Torrio made an important announcement about his plans after he finished serving the jail term awaiting him.

"It's all yours, Al," he said ruefully. "Me, I'm quittin'. It's me for Europe."

The Torrio method of maintaining peace among Chicago's gangs had failed. Al Capone was free now to try his own methods.

By 1925, Izzy Einstein had arrested so many people and confiscated so much liquor that he was an embarrassment to his colleagues (none of whom even approached his productivity) and even to some of his superiors in the New York office of the Prohibition Bureau. He and his sometimes partner, Moe Smith, had been a source of amusement during the early days of prohibition when there was an element of sport in each battle of wits between agent and bootlegger. But bootlegging was now a very large, serious, highly organized enterprise, with millions of customers who were almost as concerned about its continuance as the bootleggers themselves. Many Prohibition Bureau officials were equally concerned because the illicit liquor trade provided them with larger percentages of their annual incomes than did their government salaries. The business was so huge and extensive that an agent like Izzy Einstein could not threaten it, but he could be a nuisance to some very important and influential New York entrepreneurs. It was perhaps for this reason that he and Moe were frequently sent to expose Volstead law violators in other cities.

Izzy and Moe had spent considerable time in Chicago but were able to raid only a dozen insignificant speakeasies because the very sophisticated liquor interests in that city had assigned private detectives to keep Izzy under surveillance every moment he was in town. When Izzy went to Los Angeles, the film companies kept him busy meeting stars and acting as a technical adviser for saloon scenes in movies. After a hopeless sojourn in Detroit, he concluded "it would have taken pretty nearly the entire prohibition force in the United States" to keep that place dry, especially since the Motor City had become one of the major distribution points for the millions of gallons of liquor coming in from Canada. In Mobile, Alabama, he had managed to arrest eighty-five people and seize $100,000 worth of booze, but he couldn't pretend that any Alabamans went thirsty as a result. In New Orleans, one of the newspapers, the *Item*, helped bootleggers guard against him by publishing his picture soon after his arrival.

Between these assigned trips, full of minor triumphs but major frustrations, Izzy kept returning to New York, where he ignored the unwelcome signs and continued his work as if he believed that he and Moe Smith alone could induce the populace to abandon booze and embrace prohibition. He did not, of course, believe any such thing. He had never preached temperance, and though he didn't drink, he showed little indication that he actually disapproved of drinking. His zeal for his work arose primarily from the pleasure he found in it. Catching bootleggers was the most exciting thing he had ever done.

He could conceivably be happy chasing them for the rest of his life, but he had no desire to eliminate them. Once they were removed, he would have no one to chase.

The more elusive his quarry, the more persistent was Izzy's pursuit. In mid-February 1925, he became convinced that a firm called the Pure Olive Oil Company at 181 Chrystie Street, in lower Manhattan, was too busy and too prosperous for an olive oil wholesaler.[2] He didn't believe there was enough demand for the product to justify the number of trucks and cars he saw there. Since the firm was not a retail outlet, he couldn't go in and snoop around as a prospective customer, nor could he get a search warrant without some evidence that there was liquor on the premises.

Unwilling to abandon his suspicions, Izzy took Moe to a cheap hotel nearby called the Mills, and together they rented an upstairs rear room where they could study the comings and goings of barrels and cans. For seven days they took turns watching the place through opera glasses, but not once did they see anything incriminating. At the end of the week, on the nineteenth, they had become so discouraged they gave up the room. But Izzy was determined to have one more close look at the Pure Olive Oil Company before leaving it in peace.

After waiting until a truck pulled up to the door and began unloading five-gallon cans, he and Moe sauntered casually along the street, looking closely at the merchandise being carried into the warehouse. The cans were all labeled "Virgin Olive Oil" and Izzy could see no reason to suppose they contained anything else. Then, as he glanced down at one container which had apparently been bumped onto the sidewalk, he noticed a trickle of liquid leaking from it.

Bending toward it as inconspicuously as possible, he sniffed and said, *sotto voce*, "That's not olive oil, Moe."

His partner, also sniffing but maintaining his pace to avoid drawing attention, said, "It smells like rye to me."

The two men walked away at a rapid pace and hurried to get the necessary search warrant. When they returned, they found $50,000 worth of rye whisky, all labeled "Virgin Olive Oil." Once again they earned headlines, but once again they increased the antagonism against them among their fellow New Yorkers, especially bootleggers and prohibition agents. It was no longer sufficient to send this pair out of town occasionally. Something else would have to be done with Izzy and Moe.

George Remus, having spent more than a year in prison, was growing impatient for release. It had appeared likely that he would be free long before now. In the two and a half years during which he became a multimillionaire illicit liquor dealer, he had purchased the favors of so many public officials that his early release through political influence seemed almost assured. But, alas for him, he had apparently purchased the wrong officials.

The one he most needed on his side, Assistant Attorney General Mabel Walker Willebrandt, had so far resisted all of his bids for freedom. She had argued in person before the Supreme Court against the reversal of his conviction, and she had refused to help him in 1923 when he went to Washington to see her, and in May 1924 she had rejected a request that he be excused from his cell long enough to procure some canceled checks for a U.S. Senate committee which was questioning him. "We do not feel justified," she wrote, "in allowing a man who, during the past two and a half years we have been prosecuting him, has brought pressure to bear on every public official he could approach in an effort to secure favors, to be absent from prison walls for a trip around the country in the informal manner requested." Mrs. Willebrandt wanted it clearly understood that she could not be influenced by Remus' well-known generosity.

Remus had also failed in his expectation of help from the Senate committee before which he had testified in 1924. He had agreed to leave his prison quarters to go to Washington and tell the story of his activities to the committee (which was investigating Attorney General Daugherty) on the understanding that the Senators with whom he cooperated would "get me out of here as soon as possible."

The "here" (to which Remus referred in an August 28, 1924 statement to the press) was the federal penitentiary in Atlanta, where he had spent most of his term so far. His first ten months in Atlanta had been so comfortable it was almost surprising that he should ever want to leave. The warden, a man named A. E. Sartain, ran the institution as if it were a luxury hotel, at least for those prisoners who could afford the luxury. Warden Sartain's special accommodations were expensive—Remus had paid several thousand dollars for his privileges—but they were worth it. Remus' prison "job" was in the library, where he had a secretary helping him. (He was still very busy, of course, with his outside enterprises.) He dined in the quarters of the Catholic chaplain, Father Thomas P. Hayden. It was rumored that a maid came each day to clean his cell and change the flowers, but this seems doubtful inasmuch as his wife was a frequent visitor. Though Imogene Remus had been indicted herself in May 1924, together with her husband and several partners, after federal agents discovered their pipeline method of withdrawing whisky from the Jack Daniels plant in St. Louis, she seemed more concerned about her husband's problems than her own. She had taken a large suite in the Atlanta Biltmore Hotel to be near him and each time she visited him she came laden with special foods as well as flowers.

All of these comforts had faded, however, when Warden Sartain came under investigation for accepting bribes from Remus and other affluent prisoners. Since the warden had been convicted of the charge in December, and was now in the process of becoming an inmate in his own prison, life within Atlanta's high stone walls had lost much of its gaiety, and Remus was more than ever anxious to leave. Even his wife's visits were now closely restricted. When he wanted to contact her, he was often reduced to writing her letters instead of being able to call her in for consultations.

By this time he had learned a few things about the size and breadth of the investigation which had put him in prison. The person who had directed it from behind the scenes in Washington was tall, handsome Franklin Dodge, Jr., who had recently begun to gain fame as the "ace investigator" for the Justice Department in large prohibition cases. Though Dodge was a close associate of Mrs. Willebrandt, Remus heard, perhaps from fellow prisoner Willie Haar (whom Dodge had also helped send to Atlanta) that the "ace investigator" was somewhat approachable. Any ill will Remus might feel against Dodge for the latter's part in arresting him would be a pointless indulgence if this proved to be true. One could forgive Dodge almost anything if he showed himself willing to intercede with Mrs. Willebrandt. Thanks to the inconvenience of being in prison, Remus could not himself approach Dodge, but a third party might be able to do so. What better third party could there be than his wife, Imogene?

Remus began discussing the possibilities with her seriously during her visits. Toward the middle of March, having heard through the remarkably well-informed prison grapevine that Dodge was planning a trip west from Washington, he began probing his sources in an effort to discover the man's precise travel schedule. On the sixteenth, he wrote to Imogene, who happened then to be back home in Cincinnati,

"I have not found out as yet whether Mr. Dodge has been or will be in Cincinnati in the near future."[3]

He did not stop trying to find out. When he wrote to Imogene again, two days later, he had learned that Dodge was expected in Cincinnati on the twenty-fifth.

At her husband's behest, Mrs. Remus did eventually meet with Dodge, but the outcome was apparently not very promising for Remus. Her report of the meeting was such that he soon felt it necessary to boost her spirits, especially since, in addition to their other troubles, she was now feeling poorly. "When you are well," Remus wrote to her on April 18, "it is best to come here and then you and I can discuss this matter calmly and dispassionately. As soon as I hear from Dodge I will phone you so as to ease your mind. In the meantime be brave and courageous and this turbulent storm will blow over, as all others have done."

Mrs. Remus was soon feeling better, but it seemed to her husband in his prison cell that she was not pursuing the possibilities with Franklin Dodge as vigorously as she might. On May 1, he wrote to her, "Why did you not look up Dodge? This is an important matter it seems to me. He knows about things that someone else does not. I do hope you have results. . . ."

Imogene Remus now had a definite assignment, but the results were yet to be seen.

The new, conscientious U.S. Attorney for the Southern District of New York, Emory R. Buckner, made an announcement on March 5, 1925, which caused nightclub owner Larry Fay some concern. Buckner, who had previously admitted he opposed prohibition and liked to take a drink himself on occasion, nevertheless wanted everyone to know that he intended to fulfill his obligation as U.S. Attorney by padlocking any club or café that sold booze. (One of the Volstead Act provisions allowed the government, after securing an injunction, to padlock for a year any property where liquor was sold illegally.) Buckner declared today he already had evidence against fourteen such places because he had spent $1,500 of his own money before taking office to send four young associates on a tour of Manhattan's most popular establishments. Larry Fay's El Fey on West Forty-fourth Street, the city's premiere nightclub, was at the top of Buckner's list.

Like the others, it would be padlocked, he said, as soon as he could obtain an injunction against it.

Was Buckner serious? Other U.S. Attorneys and prohibition officials had spoken just as bravely about closing New York's speakeasies and nightclubs, but despite all the talk, there were several thousand places in the city where one could drink or at least buy liquor. Even the corner candy stores were selling it without interference. If any little shopowner could operate safely, what made Buckner think he could touch a man like Fay, who now had as many connections in the political world as he had in the underworld?

Among Fay's associates and protectors was James J. "Jimmy" Hines, a former blacksmith who was one of the most powerful men in Tammany Hall. A person in Fay's businesses would naturally belong to a Tammany district club, make regular contributions to Hines and other Tammany leaders, and secure their cooperation before deciding to open a speakeasy or cabaret. Tammany leaders could offer their favorites a wide selection of sympathetic New York judges and public officials, and since the death in January of saloon-keeper Tom Foley (who had been Al Smith's first political mentor), Hines had become the underworld's firmest friend in Tammany. Among the bootleggers and gangsters with whom he maintained intimate connections were the Bronx beer baron, Arthur Flegenheimer (better known as Dutch Schultz); William Vincent "Big Bill" Dwyer, now the most powerful man in the rum-running industry; Owney Madden, once Larry Fay's strongman but now a wealthy brewer, launderer, coal mine operator, and nightclub owner; Irving Wexler (better known as Waxey Gordon), millionaire bootlegger, property owner, and angel for Broadway shows; Arnold Rothstein, bootlegger, gambler, narcotics dealer, and financier; and Charles "Lucky" Luciano, liquor, narcotics, and prostitution wholesaler and head of the Unione Siciliane.

Like Jimmy Hines, most of these men were also friends of Larry Fay. Some of them he did not welcome in his Club El Fey for fear he might scare away his regular patrons. The affinity between hoodlums and café society celebrities had not yet been established. But he had been careful to maintain his old relationships, and therefore had at his disposal the power and influence of the New York underworld as well as Tammany Hall. It was not surprising, therefore, that while U.S. Attorney Buckner's announcement bothered Fay slightly, the threat of padlocking didn't alarm him. Club El Fey continued to operate as if Buckner had never issued his edict.

Club El Fey was an unimposing place from the outside. There was simply a canvas awning next to a barbershop, a window sporting Fay's good luck swastika emblem, and a door opening onto a narrow interior stairway. On the second-floor landing was the locked entrance with peephole, where arriving customers were required to show admission cards unless they were known to the management. Buckner did not explain how his men had come into possession of such cards. Those fortunate enough to be admitted found themselves in a room lavishly decorated but so small that no more than eighty persons could be crowded into it. The club's hostess and mistress of ceremonies, Texas Guinan, was now famous for her "Hello, sucker," greeting to newcomers and many arriving customers hoped she would single them out for the special greeting. Often she did. No one could doubt the accuracy of the greeting. Cover charge at the El Fey was three dollars per person. Whisky, watered down to one hundred shots per quart, cost $1.50 per drink, and so did ginger ale. Champagne, which was actually carbonated cider with alcohol added, sold for twenty-five dollars a bottle.

To make sure his customers wouldn't complain about these prices, Fay had chosen most of them from the Social Register, the Directory of Directors, and other compilations of New York's wealthiest citizens. He now had an extensive mailing list of such people to whom he periodically sent chatty "insiders' " letters, written and signed by Miss Guinan.

From about 11 P.M., when the action began, until 5 A.M., Club El Fey was so crowded that on an average night Fay could go to the cashier and relieve the till of a thousand dollars or more, simply for the next day's spending money. Much of this was spent on one of his chorus girls, Irene Delmar, with whom he had fallen in love.

The show at El Fey featured nothing more than Texas Guinan and the girls, but that was enough. Big, blonde Texas would begin it with three loud cheers for prohibition. "Where the hell would I be without it?" she would ask some man at a front table. Then, after teasing her chosen victim with good-natured banter, or goading him into buying more drinks, she would belt out a song or two before introducing the girls.

There were six girls, all beautiful and all good dancers, hired by Nils

Granlund, whom Fay had induced to supervise the show, and who was now in the business of producing shows for nightclubs. Some of these girls were also in the Ziegfeld Follies, hurrying to El Fey after their closing numbers at the theater. One of the headliners was a completely unheralded fifteen-year-old named Ruby Keeler, who had walked in wearing a cheap dress and rundown shoes to ask for an audition. Granlund, recognizing talent, had made her the leader of the chorus immediately.

A girl had to be a fairly good dancer to work at El Fey because the floor space, small at best, diminished to aisle size as the night progressed and additional rows of tables were moved to ringside for arriving customers. Sometimes it could not be said that there was room to dance, but since there was always room for the girls to shimmy, no one complained.

Club El Fey had become such an honored institution among sophisticated New Yorkers that it was difficult to conceive of the U.S. Attorney actually padlocking it, but on April 6 Emory Buckner proved he was serious. Larry Fay and his counsel, Raymond Wise, were summoned to court that day, and unfortunately for them, it was a federal court, where Fay's Tammany friend, Jimmy Hines, had no influence. Unlike many of the state and local judges, the federal judge they faced, A. E. Hand, owed nothing to Hines or Tammany Hall for his job. Club El Fey, he ruled, would be subject to padlock April thirtieth. Did Fay consent? He had no choice if he wanted to avoid a jail sentence for bootlegging. It was an unhappy moment for him but not a tragic one. After all, New York was full of buildings with empty rooms that would make ideal nightclubs. El Fey was too small anyway. Now he could look for a decent sized place, where he could pack in twice as many customers.

Chapter 9

Despite her growing fame as the Justice Department's chief prohibition prosecutor, and despite the tenacity with which she handled the job, Mabel Walker Willebrandt seemed prone to vicissitudes. They continued to increase. She had been completely uninvolved in the Teapot Dome scandal, for instance, yet she had suffered a rough interrogation when she tried to defend her superior, Attorney General Daugherty, before the Senate committee investigating that matter in June of 1924. "My hands were never tied," she told the Senators, "and Mr. Daugherty, when I was hard pressed, stood behind me."

"What do you mean by being hard pressed?" Senator Wesley L. Jones of Washington asked her. "Who brought the pressure?"

She did not endear herself to her inquisitors when she answered, "Senators, Representatives, and lawyers who wanted delays and postponements in [prohibition] cases."

Senator Burton K. Wheeler of Montana then mentioned that George Remus had testified he had paid more than a quarter of a million dollars in graft to Daugherty's friend, Jesse Smith, who was now dead. Wheeler asked her if she knew "the relationship existing" between Daugherty and Smith.

THE LONG THIRST 165

"I looked upon Mr. Smith in a way as a servant," she said; "what I might describe as a glorified servant."

"Don't you think it rather unusual," Wheeler pursued, "that a valet, or even a 'glorified servant,' should have been received and entertained at the White House?"

"Perhaps that was the glorified part," she answered pertly.

Wheeler then tried to trick her into damaging admissions about prohibition enforcement. "Everyone knows," he declared, "that Department of Justice agents pass whisky saloons every day and make no attempt to stop the violations."

"The Treasury Department handles prohibition enforcement," she pointed out, maintaining that her job was strictly to prosecute, and glossing over the fact that she was also in charge of a corps of special agents

Wheeler was not that easily diverted. "The Congress gave the [Justice] Department two million dollars last year to investigate prohibition violations," he reminded her.

"And it gave the Treasury units thirteen million dollars," she reminded him.

No one could deny that Mrs. Willebrandt had stood up well under the unfriendly grilling, yet the very fact that she belonged to Daugherty's staff had been damaging to her. Later in 1924, she had hoped to win a federal judgeship. Once again she had turned for support to California's Senator Hiram Johnson, who had helped her to become an Assistant Attorney General. She had repaid his consideration by supporting his campaign for reelection in 1922 and by calling him "the outstanding figure of the West." And he had grown to admire her abilities though he was indifferent to prohibition. Once again he recommended her, this time for a northern California opening on the federal bench. But she now had too many enemies in Washington. President Coolidge chose not to appoint her.

At about the same time, in a Los Angeles court, she had been forcibly reminded of an unfortunate chapter in her past life. On November 28, 1924, her husband, Frank Willebrandt, who was now teaching horticulture and agriculture in a Lomita, California boys' school, won an interlocutory divorce decree from her with the charge that "on or about the first day of January, 1916, the defendant (Mrs. Willebrandt), disregarding the solemnity of her marriage vow, willfully and without cause deserted and abandoned the plaintiff, and ever since has, and still continues to, so willfully and without cause desert and abandon said plaintiff, and to live separate and apart from him, without sufficient cause or any reason, and against his will and without his consent." The only satisfaction Mrs. Willebrandt could derive from her divorce notification was that her former husband had at least been discreet. He had obtained the decree so quietly that no newspaper noted the proceedings.

Whatever regrets Mrs. Willebrandt may have felt about the failure of her marriage were soon subordinated to more immediate problems in her career. Always troubled by the difficulty of finding qualified prosecutors to work under her, and keenly aware that even good men could be corrupted by the huge sums bootleggers were willing to pay for protection, she carefully supervised the prosecutors in her division and quickly dismissed anyone who lost her confidence. This policy of immediate action against suspected subordinates had led her into a departmental controversy which became public at the beginning of 1925 when she expressed distrust in a man named Walter Van Riper, an assistant U.S. Attorney in Newark. On December 15, she had sent a publicized telegram to his superior specifying that Van Riper should be prevented from handling further liquor prosecutions in New Jersey.

Van Riper did not accept this rebuke quietly. With his superior, New Jersey's U.S. Attorney Walter Winne, he went immediately to Washington for a showdown, not only with Mrs. Willebrandt, but with her superior, Attorney General Harlan F. Stone, who had replaced Harry Daugherty.[1]

When Van Riper demanded to know why Mrs. Willebrandt had so openly and publicly humiliated him, she said it was because he "did not have public confidence" as a liquor law prosecutor.

Upon what evidence, he asked, did she predicate this conclusion? She had received numerous complaints against him, she said, "from leading people in the state, members of the bar," and others.

Van Riper insisted she name these people but she refused to identify them even when Attorney General Stone said, "You must prove your case against this man or I'll have to back water."

After this unpleasant confrontation, Mrs. Willebrandt was able to convince Stone privately that she had sufficient reason to dismiss Van Riper. A few days later she did so, but the voluminous publicity made her position appear equivocal. By the end of January 1925, Washingtonians were floating a rumor, entirely false, that she herself would soon be forced to resign.

To Mrs. Willebrandt it seemed evident that the continuing campaign against her was inspired entirely by the bootleggers and their allies, the wets.[2] She was offended by the opposition of the wets because she was not a rabid dry herself. She often opposed the absolutist position of Wayne Wheeler and the Anti-Saloon League. She regarded prohibition prosecution simply as part of her job, and by no means the best part. Her campaign to modernize the federal prison system, which was also under her jurisdiction was a greater source of satisfaction to her. She was now launching, near Alderson, West Virginia, an experiment in reform—the first rehabilitation center for women, with a school, a library, and attractive cottage quarters, but without walls. As for prohibition prosecution, it was an unpleasant task, but a task she felt she must do well because nullification of the liquor law could lead to the nullification of all law and order. In a recent Los Angeles speech she had said, "One may work in an orderly, lawful way for the repeal of the Eighteenth Amendment and yet be a good citizen so long as one respects the law as it stands. However, he who tries to repeal this law on the ground that it cannot be enforced, while he contributes to its violation, is not a good citizen."

She didn't delude herself about the constantly growing number of people who no longer respected the liquor law as it stood. Such people exasperated her, perhaps because they made her job more difficult, and she never hesitated to scold them publicly. In soaking-wet Boston, when she was speaking to the Chamber of Commerce, she managed to involve almost the entire city in her castigation. After defining "the upper crust which feels itself above and superior to the law," and "the dregs who strike beneath the foundations of American liberties," she went on to couple the two factions. "These two classes exist everywhere," she said, "especially in Boston, where the oldest families, on which the nation looks as representative of the finest in American life, violate the law." Having thus excoriated Boston, she extended her disapproval to all of New England, which, she said, ignored the law "because of the large foreign population."

She was noticeably more candid in condemning the mostly wet, Catholic, and Jewish "foreign population" of New England than she was in discussing the dry, Protestant Ku Klux Klan elsewhere. When a Los Angeles reporter asked her, "What is your idea of the Ku Klux Klan?" she was uncomfortably evasive.

"I have no objections to people dressing up in sheets if they enjoy that sort of thing," she said. "But I do think it is an undeserved reproach to our government to have a group of its people organize to enforce laws."[3]

The reporter persisted. "But what do you think of the platform of the Ku Klux Klan?"

Though it was virtually impossible for a well informed person, especially an Assistant Attorney General, to be unaware of the bigoted, racist aims of the Ku Klux Klan, Mrs. Willebrandt said, "I don't know anything about it."

She was altogether less caustic in Los Angeles than in Boston, either because Los Angeles was her home town or because she considered it more law-abiding than other cities. Los Angeles did have a comparatively dry reputation because it had passed a bone-dry local option law before prohibition, and because it actually harbored relatively few speakeasies. The shortage of speakeasies did not, however, indicate a shortage of booze. Due to the city's lack of centralization and the widespread habit of entertaining at home, bootlegging was a door-to-door business there. Mrs. Willebrandt knew, of course, that thousands of respectable Angelenos were dealing with neighborhood liquor peddlers, and she spoke with some annoyance to this presumably better element.

"The man within the law who patronizes an outlaw business," she said, "is no better than the one whose active disobedience to law renders him most liable to punishment."

For San Francisco she could entertain no approval or hope whatsoever. The sheriff there, Tom Finn, was an avowed wet. The district attorney, Matthew Brady, was also vice president of the California chapter of the Association Against the Prohibition Amendment. When one of his bootlegger friends was arrested across the bay, outside his jurisdiction, Brady and several friends, feeling convivial, drove to Oakland to serenade him in his Alameda County jail cell. With Irishmen like Finn and Brady upholding the law in San Francisco, and thousands of the city's Italians making wine, beer, or gin at home, nobody went thirsty there.

Only the federal government, Mrs. Willebrandt's agents in particular, made any attempt to enforce the Volstead Act in San Francisco. By 1924, the three federal judges had already fallen five thousand cases behind, even though most offenders pleaded guilty and paid their $100 fines. Mrs. Willebrandt's San Francisco prosecutors were so overwhelmed by the load that she helped get the fine for first offenders raised to $600, hoping this measure would deter people from drinking. Unfortunately, it deterred them only from pleading guilty. So many defendants began demanding jury trials (in the knowledge that San Francisco juries were almost invariably sympathetic to drinkers) that the court calendars became hopelessly jammed and the new schedule of fines had to be quietly modified.

By the spring of 1925, Mrs. Willebrandt had suffered so many setbacks in her difficult job that her friends wondered why she stayed with it. Yet her associates and subordinates at the Justice Department would hardly suspect from her manner that her tribulations touched her. The core of her personality was self-discipline. Dressed invariably in a blue or grey suit so severely tailored as to obscure her trim, athletic figure, she was the first to arrive at her office and the last to leave. She took an ice-cold bath every morning before breakfast, and often she walked to work from her studio apartment opposite Meridian Hill Park, about two miles due north of the White House. She maintained close liaison with the staff of one hundred people in her office because she was determined to be fully informed about every case or question that might arise in her division. Possibly because of this insistence on knowing everything that was happening, she was quick and confident when she made decisions, and she had a reputation among her subordinates for efficiency as well as indefatigable energy. One of her secretaries, speaking to a reporter about her work habits, said, "I don't see how she does it. When we were traveling, she would have a square of toast and some orange juice for breakfast. We would work all morning and about three o'clock in the afternoon she'd remember we hadn't had lunch."

Despite Mrs. Willebrandt's personal industry and efficiency plus the dedication of her staff, she could accomplish little in the war against booze unless the whole federal enforcement system worked properly. By 1925, this system had fallen into such a pitiful muddle (thanks partly to the ineptitude of Wayne Wheeler's nominee, Roy Haynes, as Prohibition Commissioner) that President Coolidge, at the prompting of Treasury Secretary Andrew Mellon, decided to try a new approach to the problem—a military approach.

Shunting Haynes aside without stripping him of his title, the President appointed, on April 1, a retired brigadier general named Lincoln Andrews as assistant secretary of the treasury in charge of prohibition, Coast Guard, and Customs. Andrews was a World War hero who made much of his ability to get things done. He was fond of uttering statements like, "It is true psychologically that every group of men working together comes to have a soul of its own." He also said when he was appointed "generalissimo of prohibition," as he called himself, that he intended to divorce liquor-law enforcement from politics. He would do this, he declared, by dividing the country into twenty-two enforcement districts which would ignore state boundaries, and by appointing retired army officers to take charge of these districts. As one of his appointees put it, "there is very little difference between the warfare against the bootlegging fraternity and military operations in the field in hostile territory against a scheming, skulking enemy whose method of warfare is that of the guerrilla."

When Mrs. Willebrandt learned about Andrews' plans, she realized that another tribulation was facing her. To divorce prohibition from politics would be as easy as divorcing Congress from politics. And as for militarizing the enforcement system, she considered that plan disastrously naive. She believed that lack of expertise at field level was already one of the main contributing factors in the ineptitude and corruption of the system. To put the entire organization under the control of former army officers, none of whom had any training in law enforcement, was likely to increase the corruption by intensifying the ineptitude.

Her immediate fears about Andrews were confirmed soon after he took office.[4] One of his first appointees, as administrator for the very critical New Jersey district, was a man named Frank Hale. Mrs. Willebrandt was appalled when she heard the news of Hale's selection because she knew him all too well. He had worked for the Prohibition Bureau before but had been suspended by the Internal Revenue Commissioner after Mrs. Willebrandt stated "on four different occasions" that she "would not direct any United States attorney to conduct a prosecution on evidence he gathered, because of his unreliability." When she looked into the Hale appointment, she discovered how it had happened. A "close personal friend" of General Andrews had written him in Hale's behalf because, "Hale is a good sojer. Nuff said."

When she learned of this disheartening development, Mrs. Willebrandt's composure suffered a severe test. It was a time when she might easily have abandoned the struggle but for the fact that a great personal joy suddenly came into her life. One of her former legal clients, a woman now living in Michigan, wrote to her about a two-year-old girl available for adoption.[5] The woman in Michigan was now taking care of the child but would soon have to relinquish her because she was marrying a clergyman who apparently didn't want children. Did Mrs. Willebrandt know anyone who might take the little girl?

Indeed she did. "I had been wanting to adopt a child for some time," she later explained. "My natural preference would have been for a boy, because in reality I am living the life of a man. But because I have to go about the country on cases and on speaking trips, it would be harder to stamp my training on a boy. I can more easily take a girl with me wherever I go."

Whatever her original preference, she forgot it as soon as she saw the blue-eyed, blonde girl named Dorothy to whom she was introduced in Michigan. A motherly instinct arose in her which seemed to soften the masculine impression created by her job, her cool, efficient manner, and the starkly tailored suits she wore. In May of 1925, she returned to Washington with Dorothy and moved the child into the studio apartment near Meridian Hill Park.

It was a bewildering adjustment for Dorothy. She slept in her own small bed under a slanted ceiling in her new mother's bedroom, and because Mrs. Willebrandt liked to eat raw cabbage as she sat up reading at night, the child was startled at first by the chewing sounds from this strange woman in the big bed nearby.

The adjustment was much easier for Mrs. Willebrandt because she loved the child and was eager to get to the business of molding her in her own well-disciplined image. "I'd like to train Dorothy," she told a reporter, "so that in her subconscious mind she will feel self-restraint and un-self-consciousness, not arrogantly in the way of conceit, but quietly and efficiently."

With this in mind, she soon had Dorothy emulating her own habit of taking an ice-cold bath every morning. "She can now duck all the way under," Mrs. Willebrandt revealed one day, describing the child's progress. "It was a big thing for her to overcome the physical shock of the cold water and of course she had to get used to it by degrees, but her mental reactions to the idea of overcoming a natural dislike to a cold plunge were very interesting."

By the end of summer, Mrs. Willebrandt was so absorbed in her new daughter that even the frustrations of her job and the peculiarities of General Lincoln Andrews seemed tolerable to her. Instead of working late into the evening as she had always done, she began leaving her office promptly at 5:30 to hurry home for a romp with Dorothy.

OMAHA, NEBR., Sept. 20, 1925.—Leaders of the W.C.T.U. are aroused over plans of the "40 and 8," an auxiliary of the American Legion, to plaster Omaha with French posters advertising liquors and displaying semi-nude figures during the Legion convention here next month.

A. C. McCampbell, Prohibition Director for three states, has been asked to interfere.

Samples of the posters have arrived. They show girls and labeled bottles with invitations to drink.

Mrs. Earl F. Bragg, reform leader, said she expects Mr. McCampbell to rule the posters are a violation of the Volstead Act in advertising intoxicating liquor, even though the place of sale is across the ocean.

Officers of the "40 and 8" assert the posters are intended to create a "Parisian atmosphere" for Omaha.[6]

George Remus, serving the last days of his prison term in Atlanta, had to cope with some vicious rumors during the late summer of 1925. Through the grapevine, he began hearing that his wife, Imogene, when she wasn't visiting him, was spending a lot of time with Franklin Dodge, Jr., the Justice Department investigator who had been one of the people most responsible for Remus' imprisonment. Remus could discount the rumors because he was well aware that Imogene was seeing Dodge. Indeed, he had instructed her to do so. While Dodge had failed to secure Remus' early release from Atlanta, he might yet help eliminate the subsequent term still facing Remus at Dayton, Ohio, for "maintaining a nuisance" on his Death Valley Farm.

Remus had too much confidence in Imogene's love and fidelity to believe the things his fellow prisoners were hinting about her. But he was disturbed that such things were being said. If this kind of gossip had reached the inside of the Atlanta Penitentiary, it must be circulating widely on the outside. Knowing its origin, he decided to write out a statement expressing his complete confidence in Imogene. On August 31, just two days before his time was up, he wrote the statement, expressing his love for his wife and praising her for her devotion.

Unfortunately for him, however, Imogene Remus, on this same day, was filing suit for divorce against him in Cincinnati. When Remus was informed of this, the following day, he refused to believe it. And even on the day after that, as he emerged from his cell at the end of his term, he scoffed at the report. When newsmen asked him about the statement he had issued the previous day in tribute to her, he said, "Let it ride."

He did not have time to elaborate, because Ohio authorities had arrived in Atlanta in anticipation of his release. They quickly rearrested him and hurried him away on a train to Dayton.

Larry Fay's new Club Del Fey at 247 West Fifty-fourth Street, with Texas Guinan presiding as hostess, had become, by early autumn of 1925, even more profitable than his Club El Fey, which had been padlocked in April. While Fay enjoyed the profits, he measured the true success of the Del Fey in an even greater currency—its social acceptability. The Del Fey was attracting not only rich and famous Americans, but also visiting European aristocrats. One summer evening Fay had the pleasure of welcoming Lord and Lady Louis Mountbatten, members of the British royal family. To Larry Fay, the opportunity to meet such people, to chat with them on an equal basis, was the very touchstone of success. He still wanted more than anything else to be taken for a gentleman. He had sailed to Europe and made the grand tour in quest of culture. At the same time, he had toured the cabarets of London and Paris in quest of ideas with which to increase the sophistication of his nightclub. And before returning, he had acquired for himself a twelve-trunk wardrobe from one of the best tailors on Bond Street. He wanted everyone to say he was the best dressed man on Broadway, and most of his friends did say so. Other people might tend to think he looked a bit too slick with his indigo blue shirts, loud neckties, and polished fingernails, but no one said so to his face. His reputation as a gentleman was still somewhat retarded by the widespread—though not quite justified—belief that he used the same business methods as his underworld friends.

In early October, Fay mailed to his select list the latest of the "insiders' " letters signed by Texas Guinan. It mentioned some of the notable people who had recently visited the Del Fey and promised that on the Seventh, screen stars Ben Lyon, Bobby Agnew, and Viola

Dana would be Texas' guests at the club. Included in the envelope sent to everyone on the list was an invitation card with an enticing reminder that "It's New Year's Eve every night at Del Fey."

Unfortunately for Fay, his nemesis, U.S. Attorney Emory Buckner, who had padlocked El Fey, got hold of one of these cards, and shortly thereafter some of his men used it to drop in and check out the premises. They didn't stage a raid. After being admitted to the big, crowded room and receiving their "Hello, suckers," greeting from Miss Guinan, they simply sat down and enjoyed themselves, mostly on champagne, since their waiter strongly hinted it would be beneath his dignity to serve them if they ordered anything cheaper. With the government paying the tab, they drank several bottles while they studied the place. None of them had ever seen the like of it. The entire room was a study in silk. The ceiling was draped with it and the walls were damasked with it. Before the men left, it occurred to them that they should have some evidence to present to their boss the next morning. This proved to be no problem. By now, their waiter was so convinced of their good will that he sold them a pint of whisky to go, for ten dollars.

A few days later, on the twelfth, Fay was surprised and annoyed by an incident which had certain ominous aspects. Former feather-weight boxing champion Abe Attell was arrested by prohibition agents who caught him carrying a case of champagne into Club Del Fey. His arrest was much publicized because Attell was well known. Damon Runyon had called him one of the five greatest fighters of all time. More recently, he had been accused of fronting for underworld financier Arnold Rothstein as the instigator of the Chicago "Black" Sox World Series betting scandal of 1919–20. Though neither Attell nor Rothstein was proven guilty, few people doubted that they were involved. If Attell was now working for Larry Fay, it was logical to guess that Rothstein might be associated with Fay in the financing of the Del Fey. This kind of publicity Fay did not need. It was a prelude to more bad news.

Fay's worst fears were realized on the twentieth when Buckner made another of his announcements. This time the U.S. Attorney promised to close thirty notorious clubs by means of padlocking injunctions before Thanksgiving, with Del Fey at the top of the list. To prove his serious intent, he issued grand jury subpoenas to every waiter in the Del Fey.[7]

This was an unnecessary step. Larry Fay hadn't forgotten the loss of his Club El Fey. He needed no more convincing. He wouldn't contest the loss of his second club. It would be pointless. But neither would he test Buckner's persistence by opening another one. He had been thinking of Florida lately. A great population and real estate boom was in progress down there. Maybe he and Texas Guinan should go south, at least until Emory Buckner was replaced by a more amenable U.S. Attorney. When he proposed this plan to his famous hostess, he found her ready and eager. Winter was coming on, and she too had been thinking of Florida. In such a hot, booming atmosphere, they would surely find a lot of thirsty suckers.

When Izzy Einstein reported for work at prohibition headquarters on Friday the thirteenth of November, 1925, he quickly decided it was not a lucky day. On the bulletin board was a notice addressed to all of the 180 general agents attached to the New York office, which was now located uptown at 1107 Broadway.[8] Signed by John A. Foster, the current administrator for New York City, Long Island, and Connecticut, the notice read:

> In accordance with instructions from the department, you are hereby notified that your services as General Prohibition Agent will terminate on Sunday, Nov. 15, unless you are otherwise notified of your retention in the service. You will, therefore, report on Saturday morning at 9 A.M. in Room 800, bringing with you your badge and pocket commission, transportation request and any other property which may have been issued to you.

Did this mean the entire staff was to be fired? A wave of consternation hit the agents milling around the notice. Then word came from Foster's office that the future was more promising than it appeared. All 180 agents were being asked for their resignations to facilitate a change in official titles. Henceforth, New York prohibition officers would be designated simply as agents rather than general agents. Most of them would be retained, and at increases in salary from $1,680 to $1,800 per year.

A wave of relief now replaced the consternation. Izzy Einstein, however, did not share the relief. He thought it likely that if any agents were to be dismissed, he and Moe Smith would be among them.

He was well aware of his lack of popularity among his colleagues. By instigating or taking part in 20 percent of all the arrests in the Lower New York District since the office was opened, he had made everyone else in the bureau look bad with the possible exception of Moe, who could claim a comparable record only because he was Izzy's partner.

The two of them had raided three thousand speakeasies and arrested 4,900 people. They had confiscated five million bottles of bootleg liquor and smashed hundreds of stills. There were times when Izzy thought to himself: maybe I've exceeded my quota by too much; maybe I've trodden on toes that were meant to be protected. But the work was so much fun he couldn't resist it. He enjoyed stalking bootleggers as much as a hunter enjoys stalking deer, and unlike the hunter, he had a twelve-month license with no limit to his bag. He had used this license so relentlessly that he now had legions of enemies. In April he had outraged many of his fellow Jews by seizing several thousand dollars worth of sacramental wine from a shop in Brooklyn. Actually, he had been offensive to a majority of Jews for a long time simply by virtue of being a prohibition agent. Prohibition was no more popular with Jews than it was with Catholics. In May he had garnered the ill will of many New Yorkers when the U.S. Supreme Court upheld his invasion of a private home to seize liquor. In July he had offended the public's sense of fair play by getting himself elected to a private club for actors on Forty-eighth Street, then using his membership to raid the place.

Izzy was now so cordially disliked throughout New York that Administrator Foster had offered him a transfer to the Chicago office, but he had declined because he loved his home town even if his home town no longer loved him. He still lived at 117 Ridge Street and he wanted to continue living there for the rest of his life despite a well-publicized row with his landlord, who had tried to raise the monthly rent from fourteen to sixteen dollars. Izzy had prevailed against his landlord as he had prevailed against so many bootleggers, but he feared now that the combined weight of his enemies might be too heavy for him and he didn't hesitate to say so. When a reporter asked him where he stood in the office shakeup, he said he thought he was one of those who would be fired.

A friendly colleague standing nearby tried to reassure him. "Izzy, they'll never fire you," he said. "You and Moe have made the old organization look like it was running at top speed in slack seasons when it had come to a dead stop."

Izzy was not comforted. When he and Moe reported at the office the next morning with their badges, credentials, and guns, they were still fearful they would be stripped of these tools of their trade, and they had reason. Of the 180 agents who stood waiting for word about their futures, 145 were notified that their release had been only a technicality and that they would now continue their work at higher salaries. The other thirty-five were told that their release would not be followed by reinstatement. Izzy Einstein and Moe Smith were among the latter.

The two men, after turning in their paraphernalia, walked glumly out of the headquarters building. When reporters asked them to comment, both replied that they had nothing to say. They also had, in truth, almost nothing to show for the five and a half years they had spent as the most dedicated workers in the entire Prohibition Bureau. Despite their tireless efforts, New York had infinitely more bootleggers and speakeasies now than when they had begun. And they were leaving government service without either praise or profit. Unlike many of their colleagues, they had no bribe money set aside for the days of their retirement. They had worked for fun and fame and unquestionably they had gained both. They had exchanged pleasantries with Governor Smith. Wayne Wheeler had asked for Izzy's advice and help in trying to keep the 1924 Democratic convention dry. Douglas Fairbanks and Mary Pickford had gone out of their way to meet him when they were in New York. In Hollywood, other movie stars had asked for his autograph. In every household from coast to coast Izzy and Moe were living proof that prohibition agents could be honest and incorruptible. But to be famous for honesty might seem an empty accomplishment when it was rewarded by dismissal.

As for the future, the prospect seemed bleak. Izzy had received offers from time to time. He wouldn't have to return to the Post Office. He might go into insurance, and perhaps, due to his notoriety, he might make more money than he had ever made, but life would never again offer him the zest and luster he had enjoyed as a prohibition agent.

Captain Bill McCoy had looked forward with some eagerness to November 9, 1925. This was the day he had expected to be released from Middlesex County Jail in New Brunswick, New Jersey, after serving eight months of a nine-month sentence for rum-running. But instead of being free, he found himself, on the ninth, answering a contempt charge in the U.S. District Court at Trenton. To be sure, it was no serious matter. It was actually a subterfuge to hold him as a material witness in a criminal action against the warden of the Middlesex County Jail for the treatment McCoy and others had received there.

McCoy was not the complainant. Far from it. He couldn't have wanted better treatment. The jail housed so many liquor law violators that the warden, a man named Charles E. Blue, felt justified in offering certain affluent inmates including McCoy the opportunity to take outside lodgings at a comfortable apartment hotel nearby. Warden Blue had, however, warned these "inmates" about their behavior. "This is a God-fearing jail," he had said. "At nine o'clock in the evening I lock up. If you hyenas aren't in by then, you'll have to stay out all night."

While McCoy and some of his friends were sitting at ringside during the Mickey Walker–Dave Shade welterweight championship fight in New York on the night of September 21, he was recognized by some citizens who considered Madison Square Garden a peculiar place for a jail inmate to be. As a result, Warden Blue had come under investigation and was now accused of running a hotel when he was supposed to be running a jail. At the November 9 hearing, a government agent named Henry E. Leslie said he had personally seen Blue and McCoy returning to the jail in the warden's chauffeur-driven limousine after pleasure trips on the town.[9] He also testified McCoy had admitted his attendance at the Walker-Shade fight in September. This hearing ended with Warden Blue being bound over for trial and McCoy's release being postponed. Rather than returning him to his suite in New Brunswick, however, the authorities invited McCoy to stop awhile at the Mercer County Jail in Trenton, where he could experience life in a cell as other prisoners lived it, and where he would be on hand if needed as a witness in Blue's trial. As it happened, he was scarcely needed. When the warden came to trial in December, he admitted that, among other unusual procedures, he had sometimes allowed McCoy to "escape" from the tiresome routine of life in a cell.

On Christmas Eve, when the ex-warden was himself becoming accustomed to the tiresome routine of life in a cell, Bill McCoy finally finished his term and walked out of Mercer County Jail a free man.[10] His car, driven by his brother Ben, was at the curb waiting for him.

Ben, who had been his silent partner from the start, and had handled his affairs while he was in jail, knew all there was to know about the present status of the rum-running business. He knew what a highly organized enterprise it had become, and he knew the powerful New York hoodlums who controlled it—men like Big Bill Dwyer, Mannie Kessler, and Frankie Yale (whom Chicago police had accused of killing Jim Colosimo as a favor to Colosimo's nephew, Johnny Torrio). If Bill McCoy wanted to reestablish himself in the business, he would have to deal with these men. Even during the fifteen months between his arrest and his trial, when his schooner, the *Gardner,* was still operating on Rum Row, the organized gangsters had pressed him to affiliate with them and had threatened him when he refused. They now had such a firm hold on the liquor importing trade that, though McCoy had founded Rum Row, he would almost have to ask their permission if he wanted to take his old place there again.

It was not Bill McCoy's style to ask anyone for permission to do anything. Rum-running, in his opinion, should be a free, adventurous, dangerous, but profitable sport. There should be some fun in it. Now that it was a cold, ruthless, efficient business, he decided he no longer needed it. Instead of driving north from Trenton to New York, he and his brother, "happy as a couple of kids," drove south to Florida, which they still considered home. He would settle down there and take it easy. Despite some high legal fees, and the losses he had suffered in the forced sales of his impounded schooners, the *Tomoka* and the *Marshall,* he had almost achieved his dream of making a fortune as a rumrunner. For more than a year he had cleared $100,000 a month. Though he publicly belittled his nest egg, perhaps to forestall scrutiny by the Internal Revenue department, he would never have to work again.

Chapter 10

The climax of the liquor conspiracy case involving the Jack Daniels Distillery was at hand in the Indianapolis Federal Court. Mrs. Imogene Remus and twenty-four other defendants sat in the docks as George Remus, accompanied by a federal agent, walked forward to take the stand. Remus looked calm as he passed his wife. He seated himself comfortably on the witness stand and crossed his legs before glancing in her direction.[1]

By this time, December 16, 1925, Remus had lost his illusions about his wife's love and fidelity. She was still pursuing with dedicated energy the divorce action she had instituted in Cincinnati on August 31, though it was now bogged down in bitter property litigation. The $275,000 in cash Remus insisted he had left with her when he entered the Atlanta Penitentiary almost two years earlier had long since been spent. Several of his distilleries and thousands of gallons worth of liquor certificates, over which he had given her power of attorney, were either sold or in the process of sale. For one of the distilleries, the Fleischman Company of Cincinnati, she had apparently received $80,000, a fraction of its value, and had offered him $100 as his share.

In some of the property and certificate transactions, Franklin Dodge, Jr., was listed with her as a participant. She had also given Dodge several expensive gifts, including automobiles. The $40 million Remus bootleg liquor empire was in disarray, and whatever money Mrs. Remus had realized from it was not to be found. Remus believed she was hiding millions of dollars from him despite the protests of her lawyers that she was virtually without funds.

Remus also believed she was at the root of other problems. While free on bail, he still faced his one-year sentence in Dayton, Ohio, for "maintaining a nuisance" at his Death Valley Farm. He believed now that Franklin Dodge, instead of trying to get this sentence canceled on the grounds that it should have been concurrent with the Atlanta sentence, had conspired at the urging of Imogene to make certain it was sustained. Thus Remus would be imprisoned as long as possible so that the two of them would have time to complete the liquidation of his fortune.

Remus had also begun to believe something even more serious. He had been told by a St. Louis *Post-Dispatch* reporter named John T. Rogers that his wife and Dodge were ready to kill him. During the early stages of the trial here in Indianapolis, the St. Louis journalist, who was preparing an extensive series of articles about Remus and his operations, had come to Remus' room in the Claypool Hotel just after visiting Franklin Dodge's room in the same hotel. Dodge, no longer a federal agent, was attending the trial as a friend and supporter of Mrs. Remus, but they were registered in separate rooms.

"You'd better be careful," Rogers advised Remus. "Dodge has two pistols ready for you. I've seen them."

Remus had sprung to his feet and dashed toward the door with the obvious intention of rushing down the hall to Dodge's room. Rogers had grabbed him and struggled with him until he finally calmed. Remus' courage was beyond question. During his early bootlegging days, he had several times taken part personally in pitched battles between his truck drivers and gangs of would-be liquor hijackers.

Rogers, on another occasion, had heard from an underworld source that Dodge and Mrs. Remus were offering a gang of gunmen $15,000 to murder Remus. When Rogers took this tip to the chief government prosecutor in the Jack Daniels case, the prosecutor asked him to go to Remus' room and keep an eye on him until a guard could be assigned there. Rogers had arrived to find Remus raging frantically against his wife and Dodge, while one of his chief lieutenants, a man named George Conners, tried to quiet him. Rogers' story about the $15,000 plot to kill him was not helpful. It took an hour and a half for the two men to subdue Remus.

That evening, when Remus, Rogers, and Conners went downstairs to dinner, they saw Dodge. Remus dashed toward his wife's friend, causing an uproar in the Claypool's huge, crowded lobby. Before the two men could confront each other, Rogers and Conners were able once more to restrain Remus.

Now on the witness stand, Remus could be calm because he was expecting finally to have revenge of a sort against Imogene and her paramour. He had offered himself as a government witness in the Jack Daniels prosecution, and was about to testify against her.

One of the government prosecutors, Albert Ward, had approached the stand to question Remus when the attorney for Mrs. Remus, Joseph C. Breitenstein, arose from his chair at the counsels' table.

"We object to Mr. Remus' testimony," he said, "on the ground that he was the husband of Imogene Remus at the time of the alleged offense in 1922 and is still her husband, and that he is incompetent as a witness."

Remus, an attorney himself, could hardly have failed to anticipate this objection. However, since Imogene had filed suit for divorce and he had filed a countersuit, he no longer acknowledged her as his wife, and he could see no reason why the law should still consider them united. There was a momentary silence in the courtroom while everyone looked to Judge Robert Baltzell for a ruling. Before the judge had time to decide the matter, prosecutor Ward spoke.

"We feel," he said, "that there is too much question about this point to permit such an objection going in the records and for that reason the government moves to *nolle pross* the case as to Mrs. Imogene Remus."

George Remus suddenly saw himself betrayed. The prosecutors for whom he had so willingly agreed to testify were letting Imogene go without a struggle. They were setting her free. They didn't even intend to put up an argument for his right to testify against her. By agreeing to testify he had made their case for them, and in exchange, they were now destroying his opportunity to achieve the vengeance which should rightfully be his.

He listened helplessly while Judge Baltzell ruled that defendant Imogene Remus was hereby discharged. If Remus himself deserved to go to prison, why shouldn't she? She had not only participated in his illicit business; she was now appropriating for herself all the profits from it. Despite his anger at her dismissal, however, he was aware that he had gained for himself one considerable advantage in agreeing to testify. He had saved himself from prosecution in the case.

Bearing this in mind, he answered cooperatively all the questions put to him about the Jack Daniels operation. But when he stepped from the stand, he was still enraged against his wife. As soon as the inevitable crowd of reporters gathered around him outside the court-room, he launched, in his formal, stilted style, into a bitter tirade against her.

"It has appeared in the newspapers," he said, "that I sought a reconciliation with Mrs. Imogene Remus.

"The woman's statement in this regard is false. I did not attempt at any time, directly or indirectly, a reconciliation.

"When the article appeared, Mrs. Remus was a defendant in the Jack Daniels case now being prosecuted here, and I was to be the chief witness for the government in the case. It appears to me that her statement was designed to influence me in her behalf so as to weaken the government's case. If this was her intention, it failed utterly, notwithstanding the fact that she was eliminated by the technicality that a man cannot testify against his wife.

"If Mrs. Remus has any hopes of reconciliation with me let her put such hopes aside. She has become repulsive to me. . . ."

No one could deny Remus' anguish as he spoke of his lost love. Yet the passion with which he harangued his audience of newsmen, his apparent compulsion to expose publicly his marital woes, made it seem that he took some perverse pleasure in his humiliation. It was as if the five years of fame he had earned by becoming the nation's most prominent bootlegger had developed in him such a taste for notoriety that he would gladly accept attention for failure if he could no longer claim it for success.

Newsmen hurried with gleeful anticipation to the Washington office of Wayne Wheeler. They had just received copies of a letter from the Association Against the Prohibition Amendment, addressed to Attorney General John Sargent, and they wanted to see Wheeler's face when he read it.

The A.A.P.A. was an organization of wealthy, conservative businessmen who had always opposed prohibition and were now sharply increasing their activities against it. With George Washington's birthday approaching, one of the group's members who had a remarkable knowledge of the first President's private papers thought of a devilish way to honor him. The plans as they developed included this letter to the Attorney General from the A.A.P.A.'s chairman, Captain William H. Stayton. The letter said, in part:

> The Association Against the Prohibition Amendment will hold a Face-the-Facts conference and banquet at the Mayflower Hotel on Washington's birthday to emphasize several vital facts:
> 1. That George Washington, the father of his country, was the leader of the revolution against an unpopular law that won American independence.
> 2. That he believed in individual liberty, as well as national liberty, and that in the exercise of that individual liberty he made and temperately and moderately consumed wholesome beverages of greater alcoholic content than permitted by the present national prohibition law.
> 3. That he left a recipe for the home manufacture of an excellent beer, a facsimile copy of which recipe is in our possession. . . .
> We wish to have that recipe read at the Face-the-Facts banquet, which will be attended by more than 500 distinguished American citizens, but under the present Volstead Act we are somewhat in doubt as to whether Washington's recipe is in violation of the law. . . .
> Our further information indicates that there are something like 10,-000,000 American citizens exercising the right to make beverages of greater than one-half-of-one per cent of alcohol in their homes, and it is conceivable that some might wish to use the recipe written in his own hand by the father of his own country, but we should not wish to be the unwitting instrument through which these citizens might be led into violation of the law and subsequent prosecution by the Federal Government for following the example of the immortal Washington.
> Will you, therefore, kindly give us your opinion, whether we may read Washington's recipe for making beer at our Face-the-Facts conference . . . without violating the Volstead Act. . . .[2]

It was a letter which didn't call for an answer. Captain Stayton could hardly expect the Attorney General of the United States to rule that the written words of George Washington must not be read in public. Nor would he be able to rule the reading permissible since the dissemination of alcoholic beverage recipes was indeed forbidden by the Volstead Act. The letter was addressed to the Attorney General because he was the logical recipient, but it was intended simply for the amusement of the public. The discovery that the words of America's first and most honored President were now illegal should be funny enough to make most people laugh, and cause at least a ripple of embarrassment among the prohibitionists, although they weren't likely to answer it either. What prohibitionist would want to go on record against George Washington?

To the amazement of many people, Wayne Wheeler, the prohibition leader who seemed least likely to rise to the bait, was the one who proved unable to resist it. What the public didn't realize was that Wheeler was now a diminishing man. His extraordinary power in national politics, which had seemed to reach its zenith with the dry Republican sweep in the 1924 elections, had been gradually fading since then, and Wheeler's health was fading with it. Always slender, he was now so bony and wrinkled that he looked ten or fifteen years older than his age, which was fifty-seven. His face was gaunt and his eyes were tired. His clothing hung loose on him. He badly needed a rest but was unwilling to take one for fear his influence would continue to erode while he was off the job.

He had seen disturbing changes begin a year earlier when President Coolidge, occupying the White House no longer as Harding's inheritor but with his own mandate, began proving himself as stubborn as he was silent. It was then that the President had shown his dissatisfaction with prohibition enforcement by revamping the entire system and appointing General Lincoln Andrews as prohibition "czar." Since Wheeler's surrogate, Roy Haynes, had been allowed to retain his title as Prohibition Bureau director despite his loss of authority, Wheeler had been able to put a good face on this setback by praising Andrews and paying well-publicized visits to Coolidge. But, as he soon learned, his influence with both men was limited. When he proposed in May 1925 that the President use the Navy to stop rumrunners, Coolidge had flatly rejected the idea. Here was a President with such an impeccably dry record he didn't need Wayne Wheeler to vouch for him among the prohibitionists. When Wheeler began to criticize Andrews' impractical enforcement methods, and in September visited the White House to suggest another revamping of the system, the President had simply ignored him.

At the same time, Wheeler's always precarious relationships with top echelon colleagues in the Anti-Saloon League were becoming ever more difficult. Men like Bishop James Cannon, Jr., remained envious of the frequent publicity Wheeler received and disapproving of his assumption that he could speak almost officially for the League. Men like Ernest Cherrington (manager of the League's vast publishing enterprises) were dissatisfied with his pragmatic, political approach to enforcement. They wanted the League to concentrate its major efforts in the fields of moral persuasion and education. After six years of prohibition during which alcohol consumption had increased annually, they were inclined to accept the evidence that legal force alone would not stop people from brewing, distilling, and drinking. But Wheeler still saw the prohibition movement as a war against an evil which had to be fought relentlessly. Wheeler believed the increase in the liquor traffic was due chiefly to the complacence of many prohibitionists who thought the war was won when the Eighteenth Amendment was enacted. These people had given Demon Rum a chance to rise again because they failed to pursue the battle until it was decisively won.

"Some got cold feet, others developed yellow streaks," he said in early 1926, "and the wets were emboldened to demand not only a repeal of the law, but in many places direct nullification of the amendment to the Constitution. That kind of fight has been going on most of the time for the last six years, but it is a long lane that has no turning. It took us seven years to outlaw the liquor traffic from the adoption of our campaign in Columbus, Ohio, in 1913, to the effective date of the Eighteenth Amendment in 1920. Now those who weakened since 1920 are coming back, determined to see the fight through to the end.

"I don't know whether it is going to take seven years more to do it, as it did then, but it will be done even if it takes seventy times seven years."

In this statement, Wheeler seemed to be acknowledging, through his belligerence, a failure he would have denied in earlier years. He had declared in the summer of 1923 that the United States was then already "seventy-to-seventy-five percent" dry. And at the end of 1924 he had said, "We are making progress. . . . In volume, the consumption of alcohol for beverage purposes has been reduced 90 percent. Before the National Prohibition Act, about $2.5 billion was spent for drink. Even with the high prices demanded by bootleggers, the sum now spent is, as an estimate, not more than $500 million. This is a saving of $2 billion a year."

His estimate was astonishingly optimistic. Others put the annual volume of liquor traffic at about $5 billion. Though this estimate was also inexact, it was closer to reality than Wheeler's statement, and he knew it. Each year the difficulties of enforcement became more evident. This was perhaps another reason why Wheeler's health, his patience, and his sense of humor were all beginning to fail him as 1926 began.

When Wheeler read Captain Stayton's letter about George Washington's beer recipe, he saw nothing funny in it. Always quick with a press release, he satisfied the reporters as fast as the office mimeograph machine could reproduce his words. Pouring out his anger untempered by judgment, he gave the cynical newsmen a statement that delighted them:

> It is unlawful to advertise orally or by print anywhere, or by any means or method, liquor or the manufacture of it or "how it may be obtained," according to section 17 and 18 of the national prohibition act. The fact that such a recipe is attributed, rightly or wrongly, to George Washington does not affect the question. . . .
>
> Washington fought the lawless liquor traffic hard and openly. If he ever did consider beer as a possible substitute for spirits it was long before science and experience taught us that beer creates alcoholic appetites. Neither could he foresee the proven criminality and political corruption of the brewers, whose modern rebellion against all law made the whisky rebellion of his Administration a petty skirmish.

After releasing this bitter, humorless thrust, Wheeler seemed to have second thoughts about his violent reaction to such a whimsical incident. As if he realized he had been lured into foolishness, as if he sensed that his frustration and physical exhaustion had drawn him into an unbecoming posture, he held his tongue while the members of the Association Against the Prohibition Amendment had their fun on February 22, publicizing Washington's beer recipe. During a radio broadcast the next day, Wheeler tried to take the curse off the whole incident by making a casual reference to it.

It was "poor citizenship," he said, "to parade the occasional shortcomings of great men instead of their recognized virtues." He had no intention, however, of proceeding against the A.A.P.A. for publication of the recipe. "I think it's too small a thing to go after," he concluded. "If they can get any enjoyment out of violating the law in that way, let them go to it."

Unfortunately for Wheeler, this statement sounded as humorless as the first, and subjected him to almost as much ridicule. Until now he had been respected by all even though he was disliked by some. But never before had he permitted the public to laugh at him. His enemies could begin to wonder whether he was still as formidable as he had once been.

George Remus was in the depths of frustration as he drove the sixty miles along the Ohio River from Cincinnati to Maysville, Kentucky. He had begun to despair of recovering any of the assets his wife had snatched from his grasp while he was in the Atlanta Penitentiary. On April 2 he had sued her, together with Franklin Dodge and two other men, for the return of about a million dollars worth of property, but he was likely to be handicapped in pursuing that legal action because it was apparent now that he could no longer avoid the one-year jail sentence awaiting him in Dayton, Ohio. On April 9, the Cincinnati Court of Appeals had ruled that he must serve this sentence, and he knew it would have to be soon because he had virtually exhausted the possible legal maneuvers to postpone it. The prospect of his wife and Franklin Dodge taking further advantage of him while he languished in jail for another year was intolerable to him. He was determined that, before going to jail, he would at least recover some of the property taken from him.

It was with this intention that he drove to Maysville, May 3, 1926.[3] He still owned the Pogue Distillery there, and three thousand barrels of whisky (almost 95,000 gallons) were stored in its warehouse. He still owned a fleet of trucks with which he intended to move this whisky to a more secluded place. But in doing so, he would have to ignore a slight technicality. His wife had sold the liquor, plus the withdrawal certificates for it to a Cleveland sportsman named Matt Hinkel. Though Remus was suing to recover it on the ground that its sale was illegal, Hinkel was still technically in possession of it. Remus planned to relieve him of it on the ancient assumption that "possession is eleven points in the law."

Moving with his customary boldness and dispatch, he led his trucks directly to the Pogue plant on the morning of May 3 and, after showing his usual generosity to the warehouse custodians, instructed his men to begin loading. Almost immediately an unforseen problem arose. Hinkel, anticipating such an attempt by Remus, had stationed a guard of his own outside the warehouse. The guard did his duty so promptly that before any of the Remus trucks could drive away, federal marshals arrived on the scene with a restraining order.

This was one more in a continuing series of reversals for George Remus since his release from Atlanta—a series that was not yet at an end. On May 14, the Court of Appeals ruled that he would have to begin his jail term immediately, and a few days thereafter he was taken to the Miami County Jail in Troy, near Dayton, to serve his sentence for "maintaining a nuisance" on his Death Valley Farm four years earlier.

Imogene Remus could now be sure of her husband's whereabouts for at least another year. When that year was up she had further plans for him. She and Franklin Dodge had paid a visit in March to an immigration officer in Atlanta named C. A. Coykendall. On July 7, 1926, when Remus was safely confined in the Troy jail, Coykendall announced that the U.S. government was instituting an action to deport him to Germany, where he was born, and from whence he had been brought by his family when he was four years old.[4] Though Remus had always said his father was a naturalized American citizen, Coykendall said government investigators could find no record to prove it. If Remus' father had, in fact, lived and died an alien, then Remus too was an alien and, in the view of both Coykendall and Mrs. Remus, an undesirable one.

When Mrs. Pauline Morton Sabin of New York City and South-hampton, Long Island, declared publicly on September 12, 1926, that she favored a state referendum on modification of prohibition, the news caused a stir. Pauline Sabin was known not only as the wife of a wealthy New York banker (Charles H. Sabin) but as an important figure in the Republican Party, which was on record in staunch support of prohibition and against any appeal to the public that might weaken it. Pauline Sabin was New York's woman member of the Republican National Committee, a group in almost unanimous agreement about the uplifting value of prohibition.

When the Eighteenth Amendment first took effect in 1920, Mrs. Sabin had favored it as much as did most Republicans. Born in

Chicago, the granddaughter of a Republican governor of Nebraska, she had accepted the guidance of that party since birth and still adhered to it even though her husband was a Democrat. Her father, Paul Morton, had been Secretary of the Navy in President Theodore Roosevelt's cabinet, and during her teenage years in Washington she had been a contemporary and friend of the President's daughter, Alice, now Mrs. Nicholas Longworth, wife of the Speaker of the House of Representatives. Mrs. Sabin, after marrying in 1916 and moving to New York, had become a member of the Suffolk (Long Island) County Republican Committee in 1919 and of the party's State Executive Committee in 1920. A year later she was president of the Women's National Republican Club and in 1924 she was a delegate to the G.O.P. National Convention, after which she was appointed to the National Committee.

No one suspected she might doubt the wisdom of prohibition because she had never spoken publicly about the matter. However, her private convictions about it had been gradually changing. When prohibition began she was the mother of two small sons and she felt that "for their benefit," she should approve of it. "I was carried away, I fear, by the word pictures of enthusiasts who depicted what the world would be like with no liquor in it." She soon decided, though, that "these pictures were mirages," and that the question of whether her boys were ever to drink liquor should not be the government's responsibility but her own.

In May 1924 a dry group called the New York Women's Committee for Law Enforcement had solicited her views about prohibition but perhaps because she did not want to embarrass her party, she had replied guardedly to the query. She favored "enforcing the law of the land," she said. "More than that, I am in favor of and advocate law observance." While it was hardly an outright endorsement of prohibition, it satisfied the enforcement women.

But now, in 1926, Governor Al Smith and the Democrats had made a lively issue of the referendum and the state legislature had passed a bill placing it on the November ballot. The wording of the referendum was to be quite circumspect. It didn't mention repeal. It simply asked Congress to consider a slight modification for which Smith had been fighting since prohibition began. The question on the ballot was to be:

Should the Congress of the United States modify the federal act to enforce the Eighteenth Amendment so that the same shall not prohibit the manufacture, sale, transportation, importation or exportation of beverages which are not in fact intoxicating as determined in accordance with the laws of the respective states?

The whole measure was just another attempt by Governor Smith to bring about a change in the legal definition of an intoxicant and allow the sale at least of light wines and 2.75 percent beer. He had failed in earlier efforts and he would no doubt fail now, but whatever the fate of his referendum, Mrs. Sabin felt she must speak out for it even though her party opposed it. What she said annoyed her fellow Republicans as much as it delighted the Democrats. After expressing her unqualified approval of putting the measure on the ballot, she described it as if it were simply a harmless and impartial opinion poll.

"The intent of the referendum," she declared, "is to 'memorialize the Congress' to the effect that either the citizens of New York are satisfied or dissatisfied with the present conditions brought about by prohibition."

Then she addressed herself more bitingly to its opponents, most of whom were her fellow Republicans: "It has been brought to my attention through the press that certain organizations favoring the present prohibition law are urging their members not to vote on the referendum. This seems to me a most amazing viewpoint. Surely no organization should object to having its members go on record as to their stand on a question that is of vital importance."

There could be no doubt after this that Mrs. Sabin's sympathies were now with New York's Democrats rather than the Republicans, at least on the liquor question. Did she therefore intend to resign her post on the G.O.P. National Committee? She showed no sign of such a move, but if she continued to talk this way, she would have trouble holding her high place among the Republicans.

In November the people of New York state indicated they were in closer agreement with her than with her party. The referendum passed by a vote of 1,763,070 to 598,484.

Since his well-advised retirement in 1923, Chicago's ex-mayor, William Hale Thompson, had been waiting patiently for political changes to develop. He wanted to give respectable Chicagoans time to forget the scandals of his 1915–23 regime, and he wanted to give his successor, Mayor William Dever, enough time to alienate the city's drinkers as well as its bootleggers and gangsters. Meanwhile, Big Bill had other projects to keep him busy. There was, for instance, the South Seas expedition he had planned in search of a phenomenon which had so far eluded every other explorer—a fish which could climb trees.

Thompson had announced this expedition in February 1924, when he formed a corporation called the South Seas Research Company, the purpose of which was to finance the quest for the climbing fish. "There are millions of persons interested in fish," he declared at that time. "I have strong reasons to believe that in the South Sea Islands there are fish that come out of the water, can live on land, will jump three feet to catch a grasshopper and actually climb trees, and I figure that pictures of fish climbing trees ought to be profitable. At least I am willing to bet $25,000 that these pictures can be obtained, and while only part of the money has been taken, I hope before my wife has a conservator appointed for me that takers for all of that amount can be found."[5]

In the almost three years since this announcement, he had been unable to locate the climbing fish, but neither had his wife made any effort to appoint a conservator for him, so it might be said that he had broken even on the endeavor.

After abandoning his piscatorial adventure, Thompson had gradually prepared for his return to Chicago politics. Step by step he had renewed or repaired his friendships with fellow Republicans while Democratic Mayor Dever got into deeper and deeper trouble.

Mayor Dever's difficulties arose from an almost insurmountable handicap—his incurable honesty. Whether he liked prohibition or not, he believed he should enforce it because it was the law. He didn't actually enforce it, because he couldn't, but his efforts to do so had antagonized not only the bootleggers and gangsters but their legions of customers as well. By December 1926, Dever's harassment of the liquor trade and his attempts to disrupt the orderly flow of money from the grateful underworld to the greedy police had made him so unpopular he looked as if he would be quite beatable in the April 1927 election.

Thompson decided under these circumstances that the time had come to reintroduce himself to the Chicago voters. He had patched up much of the animosity against him in the Republican party, and while he had irrevocably split with his old mentor, Fred Lundin, he had managed to reinstitute civility with State's Attorney Bob Crowe. In 1922, after their falling out, Crowe had said, "I quit Thompson because he indicated he did not wish me to live up to my oath of office. The immediate cause of my breach with Mayor Thompson was my efforts to close hell-holes of prostitution and vice." In those days, Crowe had been ambitious and naive. More experienced and more tractable now, he was ready to back any effort to get the bluenoses out of city hall.

Thompson needed more than the support of his own party colleagues, however, to secure victory in Chicago of the middle 1920s. It would be difficult to win any public office there without the money and the muscle of the gang world. And by the end of 1926, Chicago's gang world belonged almost exclusively to Al Capone. What Johnny Torrio had nearly but not quite accomplished by shrewd management and territorial agreements between the gangs, Capone had apparently accomplished by unmerciful and irresistible violence. On October 11 he had brought his war with the North Side inheritors of Dion O'Banion to a bloody conclusion by arranging the ambush killing of Hymie Weiss and an associate directly in front of the O'Banion flower shop. After the death of Weiss but before his funeral, Capone had held a press conference to say a few kind words about the deceased and to offer a few words of advice to his survivors.

"Hymie was a good kid," he said. "He could have got out long ago and taken his and been alive today. When we were in business together in the old days, I got to know him well and used to go often to his room for a friendly visit. Torrio and me made Weiss and O'Banion. When they broke away and went into business for themselves, that was all right with us. We let 'em go and forgot about 'em. But they began to get nasty. We sent 'em word to stay in their own back yard. But they had the swell head and thought they were bigger than we were. Then O'Banion got killed. Right after Torrio was shot—and Torrio knew who shot him—I had a talk with Weiss. 'What do you want to do, get yourself killed before you're thirty?' I said to him. 'You'd better get some sense while a few of us are left alive.' He could still have got along with me. Forty times I've tried to arrange things so we'd have peace and life would be worth living. Who wants to be tagged around night and day by guards? I don't, for one. There was, and there is, plenty of business for us all and competition needn't be a matter of murder anyway. But Weiss couldn't be told anything. I suppose you couldn't have told him a week ago that he'd be dead today. There are some reasonable fellows in his outfit, and if they want peace I'm for it now as I've always been. I'm sorry Hymie was killed but I didn't have anything to do with it."

Capone could afford to be magnanimous. He had an army of at least a thousand gunmen working for him. He controlled all of Chicago's South and West Sides plus most of the suburbs. In many of the suburbs he controlled the politics as tightly as he did the liquor, prostitution, and gambling. His gross income was approaching $100 million per year. And he had so thoroughly frightened all the other gang leaders that when he agreed to meet with them at the Sherman Hotel October 21, it was with the understanding that he would dictate the new territorial boundaries and the price each of them would have to pay for peace. None of them had rejected his terms.

Capone was now so powerful, and had become such a popular figure in Chicago, that Thompson considered his tacit approval more important than the open endorsement of any respectable Chicagoan, however prominent. But it would be a delicate matter to seek this tacit approval. Even in Chicago a politician did not ask a hoodlum to support him publicly. And a man who aspired to be mayor would be foolish to meet socially with hoodlums, although many aldermen, judges, and other public figures did so. The safest way to enlist Capone, Thompson decided, was simply by letting him know where you stood. And you could do that without even sending a messenger to him.

On the night of December 10, the members of Thompson's "America First Foundation" (dedicated to the elimination of all British influence—which Thompson considered deleterious—from American life and customs) crowded into the Grand Ballroom of the Hotel Sherman expecting to hear more than just the usual speech about keeping British propaganda out of the Chicago public schools. Thompson, suffering from a severe cold, had hoisted his bulk out of a sickbed to come here and everyone knew what he intended to say. Tonight he would announce his intention to challenge Mayor Dever in the spring.

The proceedings began when representatives of all fifty Chicago wards came forward, one after another, with "bales of pledge cards" signed by people who were eager to vote for him. When these cards had been dumped into a huge round pile, the master of ceremonies, a former prohibition agent named Major Hamlet Ridgeway, gazed upon them rapturously and cried out, "Bill Thompson, look at that ring of cards! There aren't 125,000 pledge cards there. There aren't 250,000. There are 430,000!"

In a prearranged gesture, Ridgeway then reached out, snatched from Thompson's head the hat which he hadn't got around to removing when he entered the ballroom, and sailed it out into the crowd. "On behalf of the voters of Chicago," he shouted, "I throw your hat into the ring!"

Thompson, not feeling well enough to deliver a speech, merely accepted "with grateful thanks," then asked an associate to read a statement which would be his campaign platform. It contained most of the familiar promises which had become dear to him through the years—he would boost Chicago, he would preserve the five-cent transit fare, he would burn all the pro-British text books in the city schools and fire the pro-British superintendent. None of this was surprising. But there was one promise in Bill Thompson's platform which suggested startling implications.

"If I catch a policeman crossing the threshold of a man's home or place of business," he pledged, "I will fire that policeman right off the force."

Did this mean he intended openly to defy the Volstead Act and the federal government? Al Capone could hardly be displeased when he read such a message. Just in case he didn't happen to read it, Thompson reiterated it in different words a few days later at another meeting.

"The Dever administration has made one of the greatest records in Chicago's history," he said, "for closing up business. When I'm elected we will not only reopen places these people have closed, but we'll open ten thousand new ones."

Speakeasies and breweries were the only businesses Mayor Dever had attempted to close. This Thompson promise was so blatant that Capone could not fail to get it. Almost immediately his money began flowing into the Thompson campaign fund. And his men stood ready to help in all possible ways, which included some rather forceful ones.

Chapter 11

As 1927 began, Wayne Wheeler and other dry leaders had to contend with an issue which was causing public alarm. The immediate concern arose from a dispatch out of New York City on New Year's Day which claimed that even before the previous night's revelry had begun, the holiday death toll from poisoned liquor, according to a body count at the Bellevue Morgue, had reached forty-one. The Department of Health announced on New Year's Eve that at least 750 people had died from poisoned liquor in New York City in 1926 "with thirteen cases still under investigation by the Medical Examiner." During the previous year, 1925, 687 people had died in New York City from poisoned liquor. In 1920, the first year of prohibition, the toll had been 98, but it had been rising rapidly each year since then.

If these statistics reflected only the situation in New York City, Wheeler might have been able to point out that New York was the nation's drinking capital, and put the blame on Al Smith's law enforcement policies. But unfortunately the death rate from poisoned liquor was appallingly high throughout the country. In 1925 the national toll was 4,154, as compared to 1,064 in 1920. And the increasing number of deaths created a public relations problem for

Wheeler and the drys because they weren't exactly accidental. They resulted partly from a federal law whose enforcement Wheeler had insisted upon since the first days of prohibition.

The law was the Tax Free Industrial and Denatured Alcohol Act of 1906. It was passed by Congress at the behest of industrialists who argued that alcohol used in manufacturing processes should not be taxed at the same rate as alcohol used for beverages. They insisted that the production of many useful products was being inhibited by the high revenue tax on alcohol needed to manufacture them. Congress, accepting this argument, removed all tax on alcohol for industrial or artistic use, and for heating, lighting, or generating power. But to make sure none of this alcohol found its way into the mouths of thirsty workers, Congress also stipulated, with the approval of the industrialists, that it had to be denatured and rendered unusable as a beverage. In most instances the denaturant used was methanol, commonly called wood alcohol because it was distilled from wood. As a result of Treasury Department regulations enforced at the insistence of prohibitionists, most industrial alcohol now contained about 4 percent wood alcohol, which was more than enough to make it unpalatable. Almost all chemists agreed that 4 percent was enough to kill a human being even if consumed in moderate quantities.

Dr. Douglas Symmers, director of laboratories at Bellevue and Allied Hospitals in New York, added fuel to the New Year's weekend controversy by stating that three drinks containing four percent wood alcohol would be enough to cause blindness.

Dr. Nicholas Murray Butler, president of Columbia University and an avowed foe of prohibition, went even further. He described the continued use of denaturants in alcohol as "legalized murder."

He was quickly contradicted by a manufacturing chemist in New York named William S. Gray, who called Dr. Butler's statement "the worst rot ever uttered." Mr. Gray said, "The thing that kills the unfortunate who, in his craving, will drink anything, is the alcohol itself in its raw state. Alcohol in the raw state is not fit for use and ought to be aged to get the fusel oil out of it; it is hard and raw and disastrous in its effect on the lining of the stomach. . . .

"The wet propagandists have got to have something to hang their hats on, and if a poor wretch who will drink anything to satisfy his craving is found dying with a smell of liquor on him, they shout: 'Wood alcohol!' The fact is it is raw alcohol."

Mr. Gray's remarks did not alter the fact that thousands of people were dying every year from alcohol which was lethal because the U.S. government purposely made it so. The argument that these victims should not have been drinking any alcohol, that they deserved punishment because they were breaking the law, might be persuasive to dedicated prohibitionists, but the general public was becoming incensed about the mortality rate. There was a strong inclination to blame the law and its supporters for causing all these needless casualties. Film star–humorist Will Rogers, who was also the mayor of Beverly Hills, California, remarked that "Governments used to murder by the bullet only. Now it's by the quart."

The New York chapter of the Anti-Saloon League quickly issued a statement to counter the adverse publicity caused by the rash of holiday deaths. Associate Superintendent S. E. Nicholson said: "The advocates of prohibition are the only ones entitled to mourn over the increasing alcoholic death rate. They are the only ones who have made an effort to relieve the situation. They who resist every effort to ban the liquor traffic are shedding only mock tears of sympathy. Put the blame of murder where it belongs, upon those who sell the poison and upon those who tolerate and encourage it by their determination to bring back the liquor traffic. . . . The remedy for the existing order is to return to the prohibition of 1920, when the death rate of alcoholism fell to ninety-eight in the city of New York."

In Washington, Wayne Wheeler's reaction to the poisoned liquor furor was immediate, practical, and political. Though his health was precarious and his weight was down to 130 pounds, he continued to spend his energy as if his supply were unlimited. Since prohibition began he had consistently advocated the use of poisons to make alcohol undrinkable. In 1922 he told a convention of chemists in New York, "The chemist who can devise a formula which will make industrial alcohol entirely unfit for beverage use, and not destroy its legitimate use, will be a benefactor of mankind."[1] He sensed now that if the wets were able to make enough fuss about these holiday deaths, they might persuade Treasury Secretary Andrew Mellon that he should modify the denaturant requirements, which were determined by his department. There had already been published rumors that the government was planning to abandon wood alcohol and other poisons as denaturants. While Wheeler had never believed these stories, the current controversy could conceivably make them come true. To ward off such a possibility, he paid a visit to Mellon on the afternoon of New Year's Eve.

The two men had never been close. Mellon, as a one-time investor in brewery stock, was not in Wheeler's estimation a very reliable prohibitionist. Both men were well aware that Wheeler had used this argument six years before in an attempt to prevent President-elect Harding from appointing the Pittsburgh financier to the Cabinet. Since then they had enjoyed a polite relationship chiefly because Mellon, as the strongest man in the Harding and Coolidge Cabinets, and as one of the wealthiest men in the country, was too powerful for Wheeler to challenge. The only way Wheeler was able to influence him effectively was by keeping him aware of what the drys wanted, and of the political pressures they were prepared to exert if they didn't get what they wanted. Today Wheeler simply wished to make sure that in Mellon's mind the pressure of the drys would overcome the pressure of the wets. Did the Treasury Department, as rumors indicated, have any intention of changing the denaturant requirements?

Mellon assured Wheeler there was no foundation for such a story. The department's chemists were trying, it was true, to develop a non-poisonous formula that would make industrial alcohol completely unpalatable, and if they were to succeed, then changes might be considered. But at the present time Mellon had no intention of softening the department's policy. Poisonous denaturants would continue to be required in all industrial alcohol. The two men talked for an hour and Wheeler left Mellon's office well satisfied with what he had been told.

To the reporters waiting outside he gave a short outline of what Mellon had promised. And he reiterated his own stand on the subject.[2] He definitely approved of the continued use of wood alcohol or other poisons, he told the press, unless an equally effective nonpoisonous substitute could be found. He predicted that modern chemistry would soon develop such a substitute, but in the meantime the government's policy should remain unchanged.

"A surrender to the bootleggers and drinkers of illicit beverages," he said, "would be unthinkable. When a government proceeds on the theory that its laws will be broken, it must fall."

Then, almost as an afterthought, he said something he would soon regret. "People who drink bootleg beverages after the government has warned them of the danger," he declared, "are in the same category as the man who walks into a drugstore, buys a bottle of carbolic acid with a label on it marked 'Poison,' and drinks the contents."

During the next few days, a storm of protest arose against Wheeler in Congress, among the wets, and even among some of the drys throughout the country. He had slandered the dead victims of alcohol poisoning, they charged, by accusing them of committing suicide when all they had done was to take a few drinks of what they had presumed to be unharmful liquor. Wheeler's critics had a strong argument against him. There was no indication that the victims realized they were taking poison. Even though it might be illegal to drink alcohol, most people felt that death was an excessive penalty for a simple violation of the prohibition law. In the public mind, blame for the thousands of alcohol poison deaths rested first upon unscrupulous bootleggers; if there were no prohibition, there would be no bootleggers. More and more people, therefore, considered the drys, and their chief spokesman, Wayne Wheeler, at least partially responsible for the rapidly rising death toll.

During the first week of 1927, Wheeler watched this public reaction with growing concern. Finally he felt compelled to make another statement clarifying his stand. Wood alcohol, he reminded the public, had been the common denaturant since 1906. It was government policy, dictated by law, to add such denaturants to industrial alcohol. Neither the Anti-Saloon League nor any other dry organization, he insisted, was responsible for the denaturants used.

It was a lame reply to his critics. Too many people remembered that only a few days earlier he had gone personally to Andrew Mellon to make sure the use of wood alcohol was continued.

When Larry Fay returned to New York from Florida after the real estate boom there had turned to bust, he was without his partner Texas Guinan, who had gone into the nightclub business on her own. However, his ambitions were more grandiose than ever. Since these ambitions would require financing, and since Fay's name was still less than impressive in the banking world, he went to see an underworld friend named Frankie Marlow, who had been a rum-running partner of Brooklyn's notorious Frankie Yale, and was now the most prosperous beer merchant in mid-Manhattan. Would Marlow like to become Fay's associate in the most opulent nightclub New York had ever seen?

The idea might be appealing, Marlow conceded, but if he was to become Fay's partner in a nightclub, he might like Fay's help in some of his enterprises. Marlow had not retired from the rum-running business when he expanded his beer operations. Though he might own fewer ships on Rum Row than Bill Dwyer or Waxey Gordon, he still had several, and therefore he shared a common problem with all rum-runners—communication with his fleet. Open messages and signals would be intercepted by prohibition authorities. Some sort of code was needed. A radio code, perhaps. Fay's friend, Nils T. Granlund, was still managing radio station WHN. If Fay or some of his boys were to persuade Granlund to play certain songs over WHN at certain times, it might be useful to certain ships on the Row.[3]

Marlow himself knew Granlund, of course, having hired him to produce the show at a club he partly owned, the Silver Slipper on West Forty-eighth Street. But one day Marlow had threatened to kill Granlund for reprimanding the hoodlum's favorite chorus girl, and since then he had not been one of Granlund's favorite people.

Fay, a cordial fellow beneath his tough veneer, got along well with nearly everyone and had always been friendly with Granlund. When some of Fay's boys began hanging around the radio station, requesting that certain of their favorite numbers be played on the music programs, Granlund was happy to oblige. And when Fay himself was ready to pursue his nightclub plans, he went to see Granlund, who had produced the shows for both Club El Fey and Club Del Fey.

"I'm gonna build the biggest cabaret in the world," he told Granlund. "I'm gonna beat Ziegfeld." He had already rented a very large place on Fiftieth Street and planned to expand it to a capacity of a thousand people. "You do the shows," he said, "and I'll cut you in on it."

A year or two earlier, when Fay's name still held magic in the nightclub world, Granlund might have reacted with enthusiasm, but he had learned much about that world while Fay was in Florida, and it seemed to him no one could successfully operate a place which sold bootleg liquor to so many people at one time. It would be impossible to screen them. Some of them would surely be prohibition agents. In that kind of club, you could be raided every night. All of this seemed obvious to Granlund but Fay disagreed. He maintained that New York City was now so wide open there were perhaps twenty thousand speakeasies, blind pigs, and nightclubs doing business without interference. Protection would be easy to buy, especially with his connections. Granlund was not interested in Fay's assurances. "It'll lay an egg," he warned. "I don't want any part of it."

This conversation may have scaled down the scope of Fay's plans, but it did not deter him. A few months later, he and Marlow, with additional financing from Arnold Rothstein, opened a restaurant-cabaret called Les Ambassadeurs. Though it did not seat a thousand people, it was indeed large, and it was what Fay might call "swanky." He had selected the name. It symbolized the elegance with which he liked to be associated. But it was a name that found little favor with his partner, Marlow, who did not aspire to elegance. He identified more readily with nightclub names like "Silver Slipper," which conjured up suggestive images.

The public apparently agreed with Marlow.

Following his usual pattern, Fay sent out engraved invitations to all the celebrities and socialites who used to compete for admission to his El Fey and Del Fey. But without Texas Guinan to greet and insult these people, and without the intimacy which had helped make Fay's other nightclubs so successful, Les Ambassadeurs did poorly from the start. A nightclub is exciting only when it's full, and it was not easy to fill Les Ambassadeurs. Within two months, there were more bills than there were customers, and since Fay had little money left, it was Marlow who had to pay them. The silk-covered chairs which were a trademark of Larry Fay's establishments didn't look very impressive to Marlow when there were no customers occupying them. Nothing about the place looked good to him anymore. As he sat down one day with his checkbook and a pile of bills, Marlow's discontent finally peaked, not against the nightclub itself or even against Fay. It was against the club's elegant name, Les Ambassadeurs. With pen in hand Marlow looked up at Fay and said, "What this joint needs is a partner who can spell it."

Shortly thereafter, Les Ambassadeurs had no partners at all. It had suffered the ultimate ignominy. It wasn't even raided; it was simply closed for lack of business.

Larry Fay had now come full circle. He was as broke as he had been during his cab driving days before prohibition. Worst of all, he seemed to have lost his touch. At a time when hundreds of thousands of people were making big money on booze, he had dropped his whole fortune. Perhaps it was because he still disliked bootlegging. He really ought to start looking around for some other racket, he told himself.

As the April 5, 1927, election approached, Mayor William Dever was the most bewildered man in Chicago. "Dever and Decency" was his slogan, and he seemed to have a majority of decent people on his side. The presidents of both the University of Chicago and Northwestern University were backing him, so was the "Grand Old Man of Football," Amos Alonzo Stagg, and so were most of the city's civic and religious organizations. He had been an honest mayor, and aside from the failure of his efforts to curb the liquor trade, his record was good. Yet he sensed that his campaign was not going well. He was frustrated because he had no idea how to handle a challenger like Big Bill Thompson. In total exasperation, Dever finally admitted to one of his audiences, "I try to get my opponent to talk on issues; I ask him questions. His only answer is, 'America First.' How can I campaign against a brain like that? What kind of a mind has he? I don't know what this King George stuff is all about."

It did seem at times that Thompson was running against the King of England rather than Mayor Dever. On several occasions he had promised, "If King George ever shows his face in Chicago, I'll punch him in the snoot." During his primary campaign he had said, "I want to make the King of England keep his snoot out of America. That's what I want. I don't want the League of Nations. I don't want the World Court. America first, and last, and always. That's the issue of this campaign. . . . What was good enough for George Washington is good enough for Bill Thompson. . . . If you want to keep that old American flag from bowing down before King George of England, I'm your man."

Day after day he returned to this theme, and in Chicago, the capital city of the isolationist Middle West, it proved as popular as it was meaningless. But it was not Thompson's only issue. There was the school issue, which was, of course, related to the British issue. Speaking of Dever, Thompson had asked, "Didn't he refuse to let our school children contribute their pennies to preserve noble *Old Ironsides* [the famous War-of-1812 frigate under restoration as a national monument]? You know why? Because *Old Ironsides* kicked hell out of every British ship she met and the King of England wouldn't like to have us preserve that ship." Thompson promised repeatedly that when he became mayor, he would immediately fire Dever's school superintendent for abetting such pro-British outrages.

Thompson also challenged Dever on the issue of which man could do more to build Chicago. Big Bill's answer to this question was couched in a song which his supporters sang at almost every rally. It was called "Big Bill the Builder," and it went like this:

Scanning history's pages, we find names we know so well,
Heroes of the ages—of their deeds we love to tell.
But right beside them soon there'll be a name
As someone we all acclaim.

Who is the one, Chicago's greatest son?
It's Big Bill the Builder!
Who fought night and day to build the waterway,
To stem the flood he stood in mud and fought for all he's worth.
He'll fight so we can always be the grandest land on earth.
Big Bill the Builder, we're building with you!

All of these issues were difficult for Dever, as indeed they would be for anyone, to answer. But the issue most damaging to the incumbent mayor was a genuine one—Thompson's open stand against prohibition. In his platform he had declared: "I will do all in my power to assist in repealing the Volstead Act [and] repealing the search and seizure laws in the state of Illinois." In addition to his promise that he would fire any policeman who invaded homes or places of business to find liquor, he had also promised to "see that the police be ordered to protect the people of this community by occupying their time in the apprehension of safe-blowers, holdup men, payroll robbers and sneak thieves, instead of letting these criminals run at will to prey upon the people while the police department occupies most of its time in apprehending decent citizens for minor infractions of the so-called dry laws."

In speech after speech he had enlarged on this promise. "Elect me," he said, "and I'll turn the police from sneaking under the mattresses of your homes, looking for a little evidence of a minor infraction of the Volstead Act, to driving the crooks out."

At one rally he had said, "I'm wetter than the middle of the Atlantic Ocean." At another, he renewed his attack on Dever's police force. "Those policemen who aren't poking into private homes," he said, "are at breweries making sure that city officials get their five-dollar rake-off on each barrel of beer turned out. If I'm put in the mayor's chair I'll immediately use all my power to help repeal the Volstead Act."

Dever had protested that he too favored repeal of the Volstead Act, but he had tried so hard to enforce it that people didn't seem to believe him. Late in the campaign, Chicago's gangsters were supporting Thompson so unanimously and so openly (Al Capone had Thompson's photograph on his office wall beside pictures of Washington and Lincoln) that Dever decided this issue might be useful to him. But he soon learned that Thompson was quite undisturbed by the charge that Chicago's hoodlums were his friends. "Well, my hoodlum friends," he said to an audience of wealthy Republican women, "just take one little hoodlum with you to the polls on election day. And remember what George Washington said. He said, 'Keep out of foreign wars and make the King of England keep his nose out of our affairs.' "

Thompson's actual hoodlum friends had been useful to him in several ways. First, they had contributed large sums of money. The president of the Chicago Crime Commission, Frank J. Loesch, estimated after the election that Capone had filtered $260,000 to the Thompson treasury, and though some people guessed it was less than that, no one thought it was less than $100,000. The man who managed the finances, and also most of the brothels, for the North Side (formerly O'Banion) gang, a relatively obscure hoodlum named Jack Zuta, openly bragged that he had given Thompson $50,000. "I'm for Big Bill, hook, line and sinker," he said, "and Bill's for me, hook, line and sinker." Like Capone, he was a card-carrying member of the William Hale Thompson Republican Club. So were the men for whom he worked in the North Side gang—Bugs Moran and Schemer Drucci, who had inherited the leadership after Capone killed Hymie Weiss. Moran and Drucci might still harbor some disagreements with Capone despite the truce they had sought with him the previous October, but they matched his enthusiasm for the candidacy of Bill Thompson.

As the election approached, Drucci had worked hard, using all the methods Dion O'Banion had taught him, to guarantee a strong Thompson plurality, especially in the North Side's Forty-second and Forty-third wards. He had ordered all of his speakeasy people to make sure their relatives and regular customers got to the polls. He had dispatched goon squads to discourage shopowners from displaying Dever posters and to make life as uncomfortable as possible for all Dever supporters or campaign workers in his area. And he had assigned teams of "poll watchers" whose job it would be to make sure that each precinct turned in the desired vote count. But even during this last week before the balloting, Drucci didn't spend all of his time on politics. He had to help supervise the gang's rum-running, speakeasy, and cabaret enterprises, and in one of the cabarets, a place called the Rendezvous at North Clark Street and Diversey, he had a problem.

Across the street from the Rendezvous was another cabaret called the Green Mill in which some of the Capone men had more than a passing interest. The fact that Capone people were invading the North Side despite the territorial agreement of the previous October was irksome enough in itself. What made it worse was that they had a young comedian at the Green Mill, a New York kid named Joe E. Lewis, who was so good he kept the place packed while the Rendezvous lost money. Drucci didn't blame Lewis for this problem. In fact he enjoyed Lewis so much he spent many of his evenings at the Green Mill rather than in his own joint across the street. He had also cultivated Lewis' acquaintanceship. Drucci's intention was to wait until Lewis' one-year contract with the Rendezvous expired, then hire him away.

On the night of April 3, Drucci and his bodyguards went to the Rendezvous to catch Lewis' act, and between shows, Lewis came around to Drucci's table.

"Stay off the street," he cautioned Drucci.[4]

When Drucci showed some annoyance at the suggestion that he might be unsafe in his own territory, Lewis repeated his warning: "Stay off the street, Schemer."

Lewis didn't say why. It was not because he had heard Capone men plotting to kill Drucci, although one of the Capone men who hung around the Rendezvous, a handsome young Italian named Vincent Gebardi, who called himself Machine Gun Jack McGurn, was capable of killing almost anybody. Lewis offered his words of advice to Drucci simply because he had a premonition that some kind of disaster was about to overcome the powerful North Sider.

Drucci, however, did not see himself as the kind of man who suffered disasters. He was accustomed to administering them. The next morning, the day before election, he and two of his men dropped into the office of a pro-Dever alderman, Dorsey R. Crowe, who didn't seem to comprehend the perils of working against Bill Thompson. Fortunately for Crowe, he was not in his office, but what Drucci and his associates did to his furniture and his filing cabinets was enough to show him what might have happened to him if he had been there.

Mayor Dever and his police chief, Morgan A. Collins, were so incensed by this incident and scores of others like it throughout Chicago that they decided to make an immediate move against all the city's hoodlums in the hope of at least slowing up the intimidating tactics of the gangs until after the polls closed the next day. If Dever were to retain any chance of victory, he would have to prevent the gangs from taking control of the polling places. Chief Collins, accordingly, ordered a roundup of every known hoodlum who could be found on the streets that day. Whether by design or coincidence, one of the department's most active and eager anti-gang cops, a patrolman named Dan Healy, was a member of the five-man team which drove north to the Drucci residence, the Bellaire Hotel at 420 Diversey Parkway.

Drucci, expensively dressed as usual, wearing gray spats beneath the cuffs of his well-cut suit, stepped out of the Bellaire in mid-afternoon with Harry Finkelstein (a part-owner of the Rendezvous) and another companion. The three men had walked only a few feet when Healy and his fellow officers accosted them and frisked them. Finding a .45 automatic pistol on Drucci, they had an excellent excuse to arrest him.

At the Detective Bureau where they took him, Drucci called Healy an ugly name because he didn't like the way the patrolman was grasping his arm. Healy immediately let go of Drucci's arm and took a swing at him. Healy then pulled his gun on the gangster and said, "Call me that again and I'll let you have it!"

Despite this threatening gesture, Healy was one of the men assigned to escort Drucci to criminal court, where Drucci's attorney was already waiting with a habeas corpus writ. In the car on the way downtown, Drucci continued to bait the young policeman. "I'll get you," he promised. "I'll wait on your doorstep for you. Go on, you kid copper, I'll fix you for this. You take your gun off and I'll kick hell out of you."

It is possible that Drucci didn't know his man; it is certain he didn't know him well enough. Though Healy had been on the force only a few years, he had already killed one hoodlum and had survived a nasty personal encounter with one of the city's most dangerous criminals, a West Side gang leader named Joe Saltis. Healy was now so furious at Drucci that when the disarmed gangster made what he interpreted as a threatening move, the young cop pulled out his gun and fired four shots at close range. Drucci did not die immediately but he was dead by the time Healy and his fellow officers got him to the Bridewell Hospital on the far West Side. Some people were so suspicious as to suggest that the cops might have found a closer hospital, or at least might have driven faster. A few days later, a coroner's jury decided that Drucci's death was justifiable homicide.

Undoubtedly, his death had one salutary effect on the election. With machine-gun and shotgun-carrying policemen on patrol at all the polling places, there was almost no disorder. But Mayor Dever's belated move to suppress the gangs was a weak answer to their activities and to Thompson's antiprohibition campaign promises. Big Bill was returned to City Hall by a plurality of 83,072 votes.

At his Sherman Hotel headquarters on election night, Thompson sat in shirtsleeves under an engraving of George Washington. As his drinking, singing, cheering supporters swarmed around him, he rolled a cigar in his mouth, smiled jubilantly, and taunted his defeated enemies. In the street below, an even larger crowd chanted his name.

Not until victory was absolutely assured did he make a statement. When he spoke, he told the people where he stood. "I stand today where I have always stood," he declared, "and I will stand there until I die, upholding the principles laid down by George Washington. . . .

"I have permanently organized the America First Association, which has in Chicago 700,000 members. This association will fight on to send to Washington one-hundred-percent Americans, will Americanize again our Chicago schools and revise the histories our children are forced to study, carrying pro-British propaganda. . . .

"In regard to our local situation, I will surround myself with a cabinet competent to forge Chicago forward again as I did when I was mayor before."

He said nothing about the hoodlum and prohibition issue, but he had already decided who his police chief would be—former Chief of Detectives Michael Hughes, the man Mayor Dever had fired for attending a testimonial to Dion O'Banion.

Immediately after Thompson's statement, which was also broadcast on the radio, he and his retinue hurried to an old schooner docked at Lincoln Park's Belmont Harbor. This somewhat decrepit ship, once a lumber carrier, had been converted into a headquarters for the Fish Fan Club of Chicago, another Thompson organization.[5] He had founded the club "to urge and encourage the propagation of fish in American waters." By chance, it had become, in addition, an excellent place for him and his friends to eat or drink together. Tonight about 1,500 of them were doing both in celebration of his victory. But the vessel had not been built to float such a heavy load and the creaking of its hull sounded like cries of protest. When its chief engineer tried to stop some late arrivals from coming aboard, they turned out to be plainclothes policemen. Annoyed at him for barring their way, they arrested him and carted him off to the station, thus depriving the ship of the one man who knew how to operate its pumps.

It was a few minutes after this that Thompson and his party arrived from the Sherman, adding their weight to the ship's burden. The liquor flowed so freely and everyone was having such a good time that no one seemed to notice the slow descent of the deck toward the water line.

Eventually, as the mayor-elect arose to make a speech, the president of the club glanced overboard and realized what was happening.

"For God's sake, Your Honor, get off this ship," he whispered. "She's sinking!"

Thompson, quite naturally, was not expecting such a startling bit of information. He was not in a mood to comprehend it.

The club president, trying to push him toward the gangplank, said, "We've had enough trouble electing you. We can't afford to lose you now!"

When Thompson finally grasped the situation, he took a more general and generous view of it. Instead of running to save himself, he cried, "What about all these people?" and immediately began sounding the abandon ship alarm.

Did his followers succumb to panic and stampede toward the gangplank? They did not. They were having so much fun they continued dancing and drinking as the old schooner settled majestically to the bottom. Fortunately, it was standing in only six feet of water. Everyone was dunked but no one drowned. And when the mayor waded ashore, he could actually prove his campaign claim that he was as wet as the Atlantic Ocean.

Wayne Wheeler's influence, after slowly declining for more than two years, had suffered a severe blow when President Coolidge and

Treasury Secretary Andrew Mellon had dismissed his docile protegé, Roy Haynes, as Prohibition Commissioner. During the spring months, Wheeler had made such a public issue of his campaign to save Haynes that the latter's removal at the end of May had been interpreted as a public rebuff to the Anti-Saloon League leader. At the same time, many people were still calling him a poisoner for having advocated the continued use of wood alcohol as a denaturant in industrial alcohol. And in Congress, attacks against him, which had become more virulent every day, were no longer answered with such prompt enthusiasm by his dry supporters.

After Congress adjourned in the spring, Wheeler had been exhausted and had to spend several days in bed. On the evening of April 23, when he debated the prohibition question against attorney Clarence Darrow at Carnegie Hall in New York, he was so weak that the Anti-Saloon League's national superintendent, C. Scott McBride, had to read his opening statement for him. Despite the hoots and catcalls of the unfriendly New York audience, Wheeler had then stood up and debated Darrow so effectively that newsmen declared the encounter a standoff. Wheeler had looked pale and gaunt, however, and rumors of his illness continued to proliferate.

These rumors had finally become so widespread that he felt obliged to answer them. "According to the wets, I am dangerously ill and about to quit the prohibition work," he said. "This is unmitigated bunk. I have been for thirty-three years in this fight and will never quit as long as God gives me breath to fight the lawless contraband. My health is better than the wets wish it was and it is getting better every week."

In fact, he was suffering from both kidney trouble and heart disease, the latter possibly caused by overwork. He seemed to think an eighteen-hour workday was routine. The task of countering the recently intensified campaigns of wealthy wet groups like the Association Against the Prohibition Amendment, the struggle to neutralize opposition to his methods within the Anti-Saloon League, and the unsuccessful effort to keep Haynes from losing his job had drained so much of Wheeler's energy that he had been forced at the end of May to retire to his rustic cottage in western Michigan, about fifty miles northwest of Grand Rapids.

Even here he spent much of his time in his upstairs study, reading newspapers, magazines, and the usual large volume of mail. But despite the temptation to throw himself back into the battle, he did manage to curtail his activities. He answered his mail and issued an occasional statement, but he also took time to walk in the woods and along the country roads with his wife, Ella, whose parents, Mr. and Mrs. Robert Candy of Columbus, were also staying with them. Mr. Candy, a prosperous merchant now eighty-two years old and retired, had been suffering from a severe heart condition.

In late June, Wheeler issued one statement which caused him additional trouble. Almost obsessed with the fear that New York Governor Al Smith might become the Democratic Presidential nominee in 1928, he was ever on the alert for opportunities to oppose this possibility. After his last visit with President Coolidge on May 14, he had tried to mask his disappointment at Coolidge's coolness toward Roy Haynes by talking to the reporters outside the White House about more general political matters. When Al Smith's name was brought up he had to acknowledge that there was a noticeable trend among the big city northern Democrats toward the governor, but he flatly predicted that Smith would not get the nomination. "He has a reputation that is wringing, sousing wet," Wheeler had told the press on that occasion. "He is too wet to hang out on a line to dry. If by chance he should win the nomination, he will lose all the border states and a number of Southern ones." Now in June the Al Smith momentum still seemed to be growing, and Wheeler couldn't resist sending out a statement from his summer cottage.

About the question of Anti-Saloon League participation in the 1928 election, he said, "There will be at least one of the national dominant parties which will have a satisfactory candidate for the maintenance and enforcement of the Eighteenth Amendment. There is a possibility that both will be satisfactory. Then the League keeps hands off. If Governor Smith is nominated, and the drys in the South would rather vote for an independent dry candidate for President than for a dry Republican, this would give them a chance to register their protest."

Three weeks later, on July 20, Wheeler was attacked by an old in-house rival. Bishop James Cannon, Jr., in his official capacity as chairman of the League's Legislative Committee, issued a joint statement with Dr. Arthur J. Barton, chairman of the League's Executive Committee, to the effect that Wheeler's remarks were his own and that he had no authority to speak for the League about partisan politics. "We do not think it appropriate or helpful," they said, "for any League official to declare that one party, [in this case the Republican Party, as the context clearly implies], will nominate a candidate satisfactory to the Anti-Saloon League of America, while the Democrats may nominate a wet candidate, and furthermore, to imply that many dry Southern Democrats would be too narrow to vote for the satisfactory dry Republican. . . ."

Bishop Cannon's previous clashes with Wheeler had always been in private. Wheeler was astonished to learn that the Methodist bishop would go so far as to rebuke him in public. The best reply he could muster was that Cannon had misconstrued his original words. He would not engage in a public dispute with Cannon. He didn't have the strength for it. First of all, he had to get back his health. As the days of August progressed, he devoted himself firmly to that endeavor.

In the late afternoon of August 13, Wheeler was resting in his upstairs study while his wife prepared the evening meal in the rather primitive country kitchen downstairs. Suddenly he heard a prolonged, agonized scream. Rushing down the stairs, he found her in the living room, engulfed in flames like a human torch. He pulled the rug off the floor, wrapped it around her, and finally extinguished the fire. He could see immediately what had caused it. The gasoline stove in the kitchen had exploded.

Seeking help to get her to a hospital, he looked around for his father-in-law and found him slumped on the floor just a few feet away. The old man, seeing his daughter in flames, had suffered another heart attack and immediately fell dead. Wheeler, unable to get his suffering wife into the family car, called the nearest doctor. As quickly as possible she was taken to the small town of Shelby, which had a hospital, but very little could be done for her. Her entire body was burned, including even the inside of her mouth. The flames had been so thick she had inhaled some of them. Shortly after midnight that night, she died.

Wheeler accepted this tragedy with a composure that astonished his friends. He personally arranged the funerals in Columbus for both his wife and her father, and he did everything possible to comfort his mother-in-law, who was prostrated by shock. A week later he calmly entrained for Winona, Minnesota, where the Executive Committee of the Anti-Saloon League was holding a joint meeting with the World League Against Alcoholism. He had been scheduled to speak. His colleagues unanimously advised him not to do so. He said he saw no reason why he shouldn't speak. When he met with his associates he discussed League business as if he had nothing else on his mind, and indeed, as far as his conscious mind was concerned, this may have been true. The horror of the last ten days had sent him into such severe shock that he seemed scarcely aware of what had happened to him.

On August 22, despite the protests of his friends, he spoke in Winona's Billy Sunday Auditorium and received a standing ovation. His skin was sallow, his eyes sunken. His voice was so weak that only those in the front rows could hear him. Realizing that he lacked the strength to deliver his entire address, he gave a short summary of it and asked his listeners to read the rest from copies which had been printed in advance.

The following morning he returned to Michigan and to the cottage which had been the scene of tragedy. A week later, on September 1, his health had deteriorated to such an extent that he was removed to a sanitarium in Battle Creek. There on September 5, after recovering sufficiently to be able to sit up in a chair, he reached out for a book but, without touching it, lurched forward, dead.

In the week that followed, some of Wheeler's enemies praised him as generously as his friends. He had done more than any other man in the struggle to make America dry. Though he sometimes lacked humor and tolerance, he was always a courteous gentleman and always a courageous fighter. He was at all times faithful to himself and his beliefs.

Bishop Cannon was in Switzerland at the time of Wheeler's death, but later he said of him, "Undoubtedly Dr. Wheeler was one of the ablest, if not the ablest, political leader ever associated with the prohibition cause. He was a firm believer in his own policies, and while he was obliged to admit in discussions in the Executive Committee that he had frequently transcended the bounds of sound, Anti-Saloon League policies, yet he not only always claimed justification for the course which he had followed at any given time, but he honestly believed that he was justified in following the policy which he did." It was a startling appraisal but no doubt a sincere one. The bishop could not be accused of undue forgiveness or of mincing words about the dead.

When Cannon returned from Switzerland, he immediately began devoting his attention to the next year's Democratic Presidential campaign. Once again the beaming face of Al Smith was rising above the political horizon. He had now compiled such an impressive record as New York's governor that Senator Carter Glass of Cannon's home state, Virginia, said of him, "Al Smith has perhaps made the most effective and useful governor of New York since the regime of Samuel J. Tilden. He is highly accomplished in the science of government and experienced in its practical administration. He is undoubtedly one of the most notable men of the age."

Whatever the eminent Carter Glass might think, Bishop Cannon was determined that, for the good of the country, Smith had to be kept out of the White House. He might be more difficult to beat in 1928 than he had been in 1924, but he could be beaten and he would be beaten. Cannon was convinced of that, especially since he would be in a position to work more effectively against New York's wet governor. With Wayne Wheeler dead, Cannon was almost certain to become the dominant figure in the Anti-Saloon League.

It was still dark when George Remus got out of bed in his lonely mansion on Price Hill the morning of October 6, 1927.[6] The house was now empty except for his sister, Annie Ryerson, and her husband, Gabe, who had been looking after it for a few months. Remus was not living there himself. He kept a suite at the Sinton but had decided to stay overnight in the huge house on the hill where he had spent some of the happiest days of his life. Unfortunately, his sleep had not been restful. His estranged wife, Imogene, was scheduled to go to court for her divorce today and he was not ready for that. They hadn't yet arrived at a property settlement despite several attempts to do so during the five months since his return to Cincinnati after his release from jail. Meanwhile, the property to be settled between them had continued to dwindle so rapidly that Remus was now in financial difficulties even though he still lived comfortably. His legal fees alone were almost sufficient to break him. In addition, he was paying several bodyguards because he took seriously the possibility that his wife and her lover, Franklin Dodge, the former Justice Department investigator who had helped send Remus to prison, were now determined to have him killed.

Meetings between Remus and his wife during these last few months had been like military conferences, with armed guards as well as staffs of negotiators on both sides. Though Mrs. Remus insisted she was not in possession of any of the assets which had disappeared, he was convinced she had sequestered at least two million dollars. He had even instigated her arrest in May on a charge of selling some of his liquor withdrawal certificates, but she had won her release on the grounds of insufficient evidence.

Though she said she had no money, she was living at least as lavishly as Remus himself, at the Alms Hotel on the east side of town. Remus, after eating dinner the previous night with some friends in his suite at the Sinton, had been driven to the Alms by one of his bodyguards, George Klug, and had sat in the car near the main entrance on Locust Avenue for fifteen minutes, hoping to catch Imogene arriving or leaving. With the divorce action imminent, he had wanted to see her one more time, but finally he had given up and Klug had driven him to the Price Hill estate.

His sister, Annie, was also up by the time he dressed and went downstairs from the master bedroom, but he had very little to say to her. He had never talked to her about his business affairs or his troubles. Absently he walked through the elegant old mansion which was now stripped of almost all the furniture and art works he had bought for it. His wife had taken even the chandeliers, the built-in window benches, and the clocks from the walls.

At 7 A.M., Remus picked up the telephone, called Klug, and told him to bring the car. Then he went out the back door and through the carefully landscaped grounds to the garage, where he spent a few minutes before returning to the house. When Klug arrived and Remus prepared to leave, his sister saw him to the door and, knowing he was due in court this morning to answer his wife's divorce suit, said to him, "This is going to be your big day today."

He said, "Yes, Annie, I guess so," and got into the front seat of his large blue-green limousine. It was still too early to go to court, but that was not his destination. He told Klug to drive him to the Alms Hotel.

Remus and Klug were sitting in the limousine, parked near the Locust Avenue entrance to the Alms at 8 A.M. when Imogene Remus, wearing a black silk dress and a small black hat, and accompanied by her twenty-year-old daughter, Ruth, emerged from the hotel to get into a waiting taxicab. As the taxi sped away toward downtown Cincinnati, Remus said to Klug, "Catch that cab."

Mrs. Remus and her daughter settled down in their taxi, comfortably unaware that they were being followed. Ruth began reading aloud a letter she had received, and her mother listened as attentively as possible for one whose mind was preoccupied with a bitterly contested divorce action. They were on their way to the office of her attorney, Judge Edward T. Dixon, for a final briefing before their appearance in Domestic Relations Court at 9 A.M. As they turned south into the congested rush-hour traffic of Victory Boulevard, Mrs. Remus looked out the window and saw her husband's huge limousine move up beside them.

"My God! There's Remus in that car!" she exclaimed. Leaning forward, she said to her driver, "Pull over and stop."

"No, don't stop!" her daughter cried. "Go faster!"

Remus was making hand signals to indicate they should stop.

The cab driver, following the instruction of the daughter rather than the mother, put his foot on the gas and drove toward Eden Park as fast as the traffic would allow, with the Remus car in pursuit.

As the cars neared the bridge at the north end of the park, George Klug tried to pull ahead of the cab and cut it off, but failed. Mrs. Remus screamed with fear as the two cars, taking advantage of the diminished traffic in the park, began a race down Eden Park Drive.

About one hundred feet north of the reservoir in the center of the vast park, now bright with autumn foliage, Remus' powerful limousine gradually moved ahead of the taxi and began crowding it to the curb. To avoid a collision, the cab driver pulled to a stop. When Ruth began opening the cab door on the right side as if to get out, her mother pushed her back into the seat and opened the door on the left side.

Her husband, directing a stream of epithets against her, reached the door just as Imogene opened it. Grabbing her by the wrist and shouting "I'll fix you! I'll fix you!" he pulled her down from the running board. As he drew her close to him, she noticed that he held in his left hand a small, pearl-handled revolver which he had once given her for protection.

"Oh, Daddy, you know I love you!" she cried. "You know I love you! Daddy, don't do it! Don't do it!"

Pressing the revolver against her belly, Remus pointed it upward and fired one bullet. His screaming wife fell to the pavement.

His stepdaughter, Ruth, having emerged from the car, ran up to him, grabbed him by the coat lapels, and cried, "Do you realize what you're doing?"

Looking at Ruth but speaking almost to himself, he said of his wife, "She can't get away with that."

Imogene Remus, regaining her feet, climbed back into the taxi, then out the other side. Remus started around the cab toward her but was impeded by his stepdaughter, who clung tenaciously to him in the hope of protecting her mother. As Imogene ran up the road, screaming to curious motorists that she had been shot, her daughter released her hold on Remus and ran after her.

Ruth had reached her mother and was trying to comfort her when one of the passing cars stopped and the driver opened the back door. The two women stumbled into the car and as the man raced away toward Bethesda Hospital, Imogene Remus, now bleeding so freely that her black dress was soaked, sank to a kneeling position against the seat.

"I'm dying!" she cried. "I know I'm dying!"

"No you aren't, Mother," Ruth insisted.

Mrs. Remus was too distraught to accept any words of comfort. "Isn't George terrible for doing this!" she cried out, and as the pain increased, so did her cries. She was soon screaming so loudly that two policemen on foot stopped the car, then, grasping the situation, joined the party on the way to the hospital.

George Remus, satisfied that he had accomplished what he had set out to do, looked around for his limousine and found that it was gone. His bodyguard-chauffeur, George Klug, had decided, when he heard gunfire, that this was not a place where he wished to be. Remus, ignoring the crowd which had begun to gather, and still caught up in the excitement of his action, walked westward, unmolested, toward Gilbert Avenue, where he encountered an acquaintance who drove him to the Pennsylvania depot. Here he got into a taxicab and asked the driver to take him to the First District Police Station.

At Bethesda Hospital, Imogene Remus was rushed into the emergency surgery room, where it was found that the bullet her husband fired had passed through her liver, stomach, spleen, and one lobe of her lungs. At 10:45 A.M. she died.

George Remus was already lodged in a cell, pacing nervously and hammering his left fist into the palm of his right hand when Detective Chief Emmett Kirgan visited him to convey this news.

"You've accomplished what you set out to do," Kirgan announced.

"Is she dead?" Remus asked.

"Yes, she's dead. What do you have to say about it?"

Remus was apparently expecting some such question. "She who dances down the primrose path," he intoned, "must die on the primrose path. I'm happy. This is the first peace of mind I've had in two years."

A few minutes later, when other officers, not knowing Remus had been informed of the death, came to bring him the same news, he seemed to have softened slightly.

"Your wife just died," one of the policemen said.

"Very well, gentlemen, I thank you," he said.

"What do you wish to say?"

"What more is there to say?" he asked rhetorically. Then, after a reflective pause, he added, "It's the penalty one pays for being contrary to the debt one owes society."

In mid-October, 1927, comedian Joe E. Lewis announced he was leaving the Green Mill nightclub on Chicago's North Side to star at the Rendezvous across the street. A day later he emerged from his residence, the Commonwealth Hotel, to find Machine Gun Jack McGurn waiting to talk to him.[7] Lewis knew McGurn and had seen him often at the Rendezvous. He had even dated some of McGurn's girlfriends, though never while McGurn was still interested in them. Joe Lewis loved girls but not that much. McGurn was reputed to have killed twenty-two men, the first four or five in revenge for the murder of his father, who had been an alcohol cooker. In preparation for this revenge (against North Side gang members who were punishing his father for selling his alcohol to someone else), McGurn had engaged in target practice until he became an expert marksman. Lewis, surprised yet hardly apprehensive at seeing McGurn, smiled and said hello.

After they had walked a half-block or so along Diversey, the flashy killer with the slicked-down hair got around to the business on his mind. Why had Lewis decided to leave the Green Mill?

"My contract's up," Lewis said. "I'm not renewing."

"We're renewing," McGurn said softly. "You know I've got a piece of the joint."

Lewis undoubtedly had known this but could see no reason to be impressed or frightened by it. If you were a nightclub comedian you had to work for hoodlums, since they owned most of the clubs, but that didn't mean they owned the performers. "I'm sorry," he said. "I start at the Rendezvous on November second." It too was at least partly owned by hoodlums, members of the North Side gang, but its manager, a veteran bootlegger named John Fogarty, had offered Lewis a thousand a week plus a percentage, which was a big jump from the six-fifty he had been getting at the Green Mill.

In a low, gentle voice, as if he were merely offering felicitations, McGurn said to Lewis, "You'll never live to open."

Lewis did not immediately absorb the gravity of the remark. "I'll reserve a table for you," he said, and walked away. It was inconceivable that McGurn would actually kill a comedian. Gangsters killed each other. They did not kill outsiders. But when you worked for gangsters, did they consider you an outsider? That was a frightening thought, especially in Chicago, where the gangs had been operating with almost no restriction since Big Bill Thompson's return to City Hall.

Having appointed as police chief the one-time chief of detectives, Michael Hughes, whom former Mayor Dever had fired for associating with gangsters, Thompson, after his inauguration, had gone about cementing his relations with Jack McGurn's boss, Al Capone. He had named one of Capone's errand boys, a first ward politician named Danny Serritella, as the Official City Sealer. Serritella's official duty was to make Chicago's merchants adhere to honest weights and measures. His unofficial duty was to act as Capone's representative and messenger in the mayor's cabinet. Perhaps to shorten the distance Serritella would have to carry his messages, and also to dramatize the friendly bond between himself and the mayor, Capone had moved his headquarters from suburban Cicero to the Metropole Hotel, 2300 South Michigan Avenue, where he had always kept a suite for himself. He now took over two whole floors.

With the city in capable hands, Mayor Thompson had spent much of the spring, summer, and fall in travels, ostensibly to promote three of his favorite causes—America First, flood control, and inland waterways—but actually to build a groundswell for himself as a 1928 presidential candidate. In April, a week after his inauguration, he had traveled to New Orleans, in June to Washington D.C., in July to St.

Louis, in August to Toledo and Springfield, in September to California, and in October to Wisconsin, then South Dakota. To prevent anyone from misconstruing the purpose of all these junkets, he had made his hopes quite clear on October 19, during one of his infrequent trips to Chicago. Warning his fellow Republicans about the likeliest Democratic strategy in 1928, he declared at the Sherman Hotel, "There is one thing that disturbs me about the situation more than anything else. If Al Smith, a wet, is nominated for President by the Democrats . . . we'll have a fight on our hands if we nominate a dry for President."

He then went on to spike a base libel which he said the Democrats had been leveling at him: "The statement of the Democrats regarding Thompson as being dry is about on a par with their statement that they follow the ideals of the Great Commoner, Thomas Jefferson [sic], and because they stand with Jefferson they stand for the League of Nations, which is absolutely contrary to his teachings. . . . Apparently the Democrats would sell the flag for a glass of beer. Bill Thompson will not. I'd like to have the beer, but I love the flag more."

Having thus put the record straight, and shown the Republican Party how it could best retaliate if the Democrats were to nominate a wet, Hizzoner the Mayor of Chicago hurried off again to Toledo, then on to Washington, from whence he intended to journey to his native Boston, and finally New York.

Thompson's presidential ambitions did create one problem for Al Capone. Because the mayor realized he could never win the Republican nomination (which President Coolidge had announced he would not seek) unless he could point with pride to his record as a crime fighter, he ordered Police Chief Hughes to launch a well-publicized drive against the gangs. In the hope of making this drive look genuine, Hughes and his men had to close some breweries and speakeasies, arrest some hoodlums, and pledge once more to drive the crooks out of Chicago. All of this was a nuisance, but anyone who thought it was hurting the bootleggers should have been at the Rendezvous nightclub on Diversey Parkway for the Joe E. Lewis opening the night of November 2.

All the tables were filled, all the standing room was occupied, and plainclothes policemen, aware of McGurn's threat, were sifting watchfully through the crowd. Lewis himself entered the club with manager Fogarty and a bodyguard, just before the first show was scheduled to begin. The policemen, who were led by a captain named

Joseph Goldberg, were not here to enforce the Volstead Act by closing the place. Goldberg, a friend and admirer of Lewis, had told him it would be futile to resist the Capone gang, especially in view of continuing phone threats which had followed McGurn's quiet warning. Since Lewis insisted on opening at the Rendezvous despite the danger, Goldberg and his men were here to enjoy Joe Lewis' act and protect him.

After the show began with twelve—count 'em—twelve "unadorned daughters of Eve" displaying their talents, Lewis appeared in a white suit. Holding a drink as usual, he took everybody's mind off murder with his songs and funny lines. An hour later he had made an idle boast of Machine Gun Jack McGurn's threat that he would never live to open at the Rendezvous.

During the week ahead, that threat looked less likely each night as the Rendezvous filled up with people eager to listen to Lewis in his new surroundings. The danger to his person seemed gradually to diminish; so did the vigilance of the police guarding him, and so did his own personal concern.

At 10:30 in the morning of November 9, when Lewis was asleep in his room at the Commonwealth, he was aroused by a knock at the door. When he opened it, still drowsy, three men, all strangers to him, shouldered their way inside. One of them drew a .45 automatic and said, "Just one favor, Joe. Don't yell."

The second man, holding a .38, moved around behind Lewis and hit him on the head with the butt, hard enough to open a hole in his skull. As Lewis fell, not yet quite unconscious, he saw the third man produce a hunting knife. Both gunmen then went to work on him with the butts of their weapons. The knife man began by plunging his blade as far as it would go into the comedian's left jaw. With quiet, indifferent savagery he stabbed and slashed in all directions until it was reasonable to suppose his victim could not possibly survive. Then the three men departed, closing the door behind them.

After perhaps half an hour, Lewis slowly regained consciousness to find he was still alive. But when he realized that blood was spurting from an open hole in his head, that his face and much of his body had been ripped to shreds, and that he had been pounded so unmercifully he couldn't organize his thoughts, he began to wish he would die, and the sooner the better. It was some time before the idea occurred to him that he might survive.

He tried to stand up but failed. He tried to reach the telephone but managed only to knock it off the bedside table. Finally he dragged himself through pools of his own blood to the door, and after five minutes or more, though his bloody hand kept slipping on the knob, he managed to open it.

A chambermaid eventually found him in the hall. At Columbia Memorial Hospital, doctors decided, after six hours of surgery, that they would be able to save his life despite the fact that his head was broken open, his body was slashed from head to toes, he had twelve gashes in his throat, his tongue was cut, his brain was clouded, and he was unable to use his right arm. Perhaps after a few years of tedious therapy he might regain most of his faculties, but it would be a long time before Joe E. Lewis could perform before another nightclub audience.

He had become so famous in Chicago by now that the attack against him created a sensation in the newspapers. It brought no immediate reaction, however, from Mayor Thompson, who was barnstorming in the Eastern states. While Lewis lay speechless and partly paralyzed in the hospital, Thompson and his entourage were in New York, where reporters tried to embarrass him by asking him why such things kept happening in Chicago.

Thompson did not stand still for their abuse. Chicago, he informed them, was free of crime. What about all the murders? "That's a lot of newspaper talk," he said.

Two stories dominated the nation's newspapers on November 14, 1927. Charles A. Lindbergh arrived triumphantly in Washington that day after his return from his epoch-making flight across the Atlantic. And George Remus went on trial in Cincinnati for the murder of his wife. The Criminal Court-room of Judge Chester R. Shook was crowded to overflow when he tapped his gavel to begin the proceedings at 11 A.M.[8] About forty newspapermen from all over the country were squeezed uncomfortably into the press section, even though it had been enlarged for the occasion. As the first motions were read, Judge Shook demonstrated his cooperation with the press by allowing photographers to take pictures.

Cincinnati, the Midwest, and indeed the entire nation were fascinated by the trial of this criminal lawyer who had become a millionaire bootlegger, then an unrepentant wife-killer. Remus, dapper as ever (he kept twenty suits in his private quarters on the top floor of the Hamilton County Jail), had entered the courtroom early, escorted by a bailiff and carrying an armful of law books and notes. Shortly after his arrest he had announced that "Remus the lawyer" would argue the case of "Remus the defendant." And he was still prepared to do so, though he had subsequently hired one of Cincinnati's most distinguished lawyers, former District Attorney Charles Elston, to assist him.

Elston, who arrived in court after his client and went into immediate conference with him, had already exercised a profound influence over both "Remus the lawyer" and "Remus the defendant." On the day after his arrest, Remus had ridiculed the suggestion of newsmen that he might plead innocence by virtue of temporary insanity. "Anyone who thinks I am insane," he said with a smile, "needs a mental examination himself." Later, when Elston suggested the same defense, Remus cried out, "What! Remus insane?" Elston then asked, "What do you want to plead?" "Why, justification," Remus insisted. "Unfortunately," Elston reminded him, "there is no such defense."

Remus, though not persuaded, finally agreed to a compromise. His defense would be that even though he was temporarily insane when he killed his wife, he was also justified by the unwritten law that a man has the right to protect his home. Instead of standing trial himself, he would put the dead Imogene and her lover, Franklin Dodge, on trial. And he would offer such proofs of his own "insanity" that the prosecution would be forced to declare him sane. If the jury was then persuaded more by the defense than the prosecution, this declaration might be useful later. To augment this strategy, Remus, with the aid of Elston and his staff, had secured an astonishing variety of defense witnesses.

A few minutes after Judge Shook opened the trial, Remus stood, faced the bench, and said, "Before you call the jury I have a motion to present, Your Honor." He then read a request that the court serve processes upon his wife's daughter, Ruth Remus, his wife's sister, Mrs. Grace Campbell, her brother, Harry F. Brown, and her lover, Franklin L. Dodge, Jr., ordering them to bring to court "all receipts, accounts, bills, telegrams, and letters" passing between Dodge and Mrs. Remus, certificates for whisky in government warehouses, and a variety of other records bearing on his contention that his wife wished to destroy him so she could marry Dodge.

County Prosecutor Charles Taft, a son of William Howard Taft, former President of the United States and now Chief Justice of the Supreme Court, quickly grasped Remus' intention and arose to object on the ground that these documents weren't needed.

"The Court feels it is unnecessary," Judge Shook agreed, "but the request will be granted."

Remus had already won a significant victory. The Court, by summoning these documents, was virtually acknowledging that the conduct of Imogene Remus was material to her murder. Even before the trial moved into the jury-selection phase, young Charles Taft was beginning to see the pitfalls Remus and Elston had prepared for him.

It was not until a week later, Monday, November 21, that the ten-men-and-two-women, mostly middle-aged jury had finally been chosen and arguments could begin. Assistant prosecutor Walter Sibbald opened with an outline of the state's case. "We're here to try the charge of murder and no other charge," he said, in anticipation of the defense strategy. "The state doesn't think that the evidence should go back further than twenty-four hours" (previous to the killing of Mrs. Remus).

After this plea to prevent the defense from exploring the victim's behavior during the two years before her death, Sibbald went on to an even more crucial aspect of the state's case. Remus, he said, had ordered dinner for four persons in his hotel suite the night before the slaying. These people were, in addition to himself, his chief assistant, George Conners; his bodyguard-chauffeur, George Klug; and another employee, a woman named Blanche Watson. The state expected to prove, he announced, that these four had taken part in a conspiracy to kill Mrs. Remus, and that the killing was therefore premeditated. The state intended to call George Klug as a witness to testify, on the basis of certain statements he made after the killing, that he and Remus had driven to Mrs. Remus' hotel that same night before her death, and had "laid in wait at the entrance for this woman to appear, so they might at that time murder her." The prosecutor's expectation that Klug might say such things, thus implicating himself as well as condemning Remus, was a sensational development.

Because Remus had caught a severe head cold, he left his opening statement to Elston, who began by saying, "We do not deny the killing, but we do deny that it was with deliberate and premeditated malice which the law says must exist for murder. The defense is insanity. . . . It was an insanity brought about by a series and set of circumstances and acts which turned an otherwise normal man into an insane man." He then proceeded to outline what he termed "a definite conspiracy between Dodge and Mrs. Remus" to deprive Remus of his wife, his property, his freedom, his residence in the United States, and ultimately even his life.

"In spite of all this," Elston concluded, "Remus for a long time hoped that the affectionate relations between himself and his wife might be restored. But Mrs. Remus made the statement to several that she intended to marry Dodge when she got her divorce. She had taken all the Remus silver and eliminated the letter 'R' and had it engraved with the letter 'D.' She had taken an automobile and had 'F.D.' placed thereon, 'F.D.' being for Franklin Dodge. She used the defendant's money to hire assassins to take the defendant's life.

"These things the defendant turned over in his mind a thousand times a day. She bought seven automobiles when he was in Atlanta, and they were used by herself and Dodge. He turned these things over in his mind day and night. The more he thought about them, the more they preyed on his mind and tortured him. . . . We do not deny that Remus was at the Sinton on the night before the killing, but we do deny that there was any conspiracy. Further we believe the state will not be able to produce one syllable of testimony to prove that there was any murder conspiracy."

When prosecutor Taft called George Klug as a state witness the next day, he was embarrassed to learn that Elston was right. The sullen, reluctant Mr. Klug seemed to have forgotten almost everything he had known about the killing. Taft's embarrassment was compounded when the waiter who had served the dinner to four people in Remus' Sinton Hotel suite the night before the killing said on the stand that he could identify none of them except Remus.

The defendant sat calmly through a difficult day on the twenty-fifth, when Ruth Remus dramatically described her mother's death. But he was heartened the following day when Judge Shook told Taft in court, "A good deal of your theory of the case has been dissipated by the evidence." And for two weeks of court sessions thereafter, Remus could watch with growing satisfaction the jurors' reaction to a long parade of defense witnesses who described the iniquities of his wife and her lover and the violent "brainstorms" into which Remus erupted whenever their names were mentioned. A succession of lawyers, reporters, businessmen, and even one former prosecutor testified to these fits of rage at various times and places since the day Imogene Remus instituted her divorce action. St. Louis *Post-Dispatch* reporter John Rogers, who was a recent Pulitzer Prize winner, offered additional testimony that Dodge and Mrs. Remus had instituted the deportation proceedings now pending against Remus and had planned to have him murdered. George Conners, claiming Remus was now virtually without funds, described his wife's liquidation of the Remus fortune. A petty criminal named "Hamilton Harry" Truesdale swore that Mrs. Remus had hired him for $10,000 to kill her husband. And renowned criminal lawyer Clarence Darrow, once a colleague of Remus in Chicago, came to Cincinnati with several other prominent Chicagoans to testify as a character witness for him.

After all this praise of Remus, and the damaging descriptions of Mrs. Remus, prosecutor Taft, perceiving that the victim and her lover were now the defendants in the trial, decided to provide some testimonials to her wifely virtues. More important, the voluminous defense allegations about Remus' fits of insane rage forced Taft to show the jury on December 15 the report of three state-appointed alienists who had interviewed Remus at length after his arrest. All three of these experts declared firmly and positively that George Remus was sane when they examined him and had been sane the day he shot his wife.

When the time arrived for final summations, Elston described soberly all the evils Imogene Remus and her lover had perpetrated upon her husband, while Remus launched a more general attack. Early in his meandering oration to the jury, he delivered a testimonial for the kind of liquor he sold, a denunciation of the Volstead Act, and an excoriation of the kind of public servants it had spawned—especially Franklin Dodge.

"But for the Volsteadian law this defendant would not have been here," he declared. Then, in an obvious reference to Dodge, he added, "and but for this deuce of society that Volsteadism made." He referred to Dodge also as "the ace of the prohibition department and a deuce with women." He called him a "human parasite" and a "moral leper."

Turning for a few moments to one of the two central themes of his defense, he read for the jury's benefit a dictionary definition of "transitory insanity." He praised Judge Shook, thanked Sheriff William

Anderson (who had provided spacious quarters for him on the top floor of the jail, even allowing him to keep a liquor supply for his endless stream of guests), and paid tribute to the members of the press (many of whom had been visiting him regularly to drink his liquor between court sessions).

After attacking the "hypocrisy" of the prosecutors, he touched, perhaps unintentionally, upon one of the central attitudes behind his aggressive ambitions. Reminding the jurors, all from modest origins, that Taft had asked them if they would want a man like Remus as a neighbor, he proudly declared, "This defendant started in life at five dollars a month, and he may have contaminated his neighbors, but ladies and men of the jury, we could not all be born with a golden spoon in our mouths like Charles P. Taft the Second."

In these few words, George Remus illustrated the enigmatic quality of the American dream as he and millions of others conceived it, combining that sharp hatred of the wealthy with an obsessive desire to join them. He had known all the disadvantages of a poor immigrant background. He had also observed that many of America's wealthiest men were once impoverished outsiders. More important, he could hardly conclude from watching some of their methods that fastidious scruples eased the route to the top. Many of the nation's most colossal millionaires had amassed their fortunes by evading or disregarding the law. He could argue that when he embraced bootlegging he had done no more, and that the law he disregarded was a bad law.

If Remus had fallen short of his dream, it had been by only a narrow margin. His failure had not arisen from ineptitude in business; he had actually amassed the kind of fortune he coveted. Had he, then, chosen the wrong business? He could point to many other men, some of them highly respected, who had made and kept millions of dollars in the illicit liquor trade during the first seven years of prohibition. Might it be said that he had brought on his own destruction by flamboyantly attracting attention and thus getting caught? He could see no reason why his wife should have been unable to handle his affairs, with his continuing guidance, while he was imprisoned. Was his essential mistake, then, merely his choice of Imogene as a wife? He not only thought so; he was unshakeably certain of it. To demonstrate how she had ruined him, how much money she had stolen from him, he rolled back his coat sleeves and dramatically displayed what he called "penny cuff buttons" on his shirt.

Finally, after a rambling peroration which took almost two hours, Remus walked over to the jurors and addressed them dramatically: "The defendant does not desire any sympathy or compassion," he declared. "If you, who have a higher power than the President of the United States in this case, feel that the defendant should go to the electric chair, do not flinch. The defendant will not flinch.

"The defendant stands before you in defense of his honor and the sanctity of his home. The defendant is on trial for that. If that is a crime, punish him. As you ponder your duty bear in mind that that which is most sacred is your home and family. I thank you. Merry Christmas to you."

Thus ended, six days before Christmas, 1927, the final plea in the murder trial of George Remus. Judge Shook, apparently alarmed by the prospect of acquittal, gave extraordinary instructions to the jury. A verdict of acquittal, he ruled summarily, was not open to them. If they wished to pronounce Remus innocent, they could do so only "on the sole ground of insanity."

At 2:35 on the afternoon of December 20, the jury left the courtroom. At 2:54 they reached a decision and returned to court. After nineteen minutes of deliberation they had voted that Remus was innocent "on the sole ground of insanity." When the verdict was announced, the jubilation which ensued was described as "the wildest scene ever known in the Hamilton County Court House."

One of the jurors said, "If we could have acquitted him clean, we surely would have done so. We decided that the man had been persecuted long enough."

For Remus, however, the celebration had its limits. The verdict did not free him. He would now have to undergo a "lunacy hearing" in Probate Court, and he might yet face a lifetime behind bars in an asylum for the criminally insane.

When he appeared before Probate Judge William Lueders in Cincinnati, it seemed possible that he would be freed immediately. Three state-appointed alienists had certified at his trial that he was sane. Could the state repudiate or ignore its own expert witnesses? Remus summoned all three to appear, albeit reluctantly, as defense witnesses at his hearing and repeat their earlier certification. Unfortunately for him, however, two of the doctors had now changed their views. Dr. David I. Wolfstein had decided that Remus was "ruthless, reckless, selfish, eccentric; the kind of man who takes the law into his own hands." Though he did not go so far as to contradict flatly his original analysis and declare Remus insane, he did pronounce him dangerous. "He could be vile," said Dr. Wolfstein. "He has shown he can be dangerous." Dr. Charles Kiely, also falling just short of self-contradiction, agreed that Remus was "a very dangerous man." Dr. E. A. Baber simply confirmed his earlier statement. He was not prepared, he said, to call Remus "dangerous." But his testimony wasn't needed. Judge Lueders, deciding that two out of three experts should be enough, had ruled that Remus was "a dangerous person to be at large," and also, in his own opinion, insane.

Even as Remus entered the Lima prison-hospital, his attorneys were filing writs on his behalf, and though he was denied a second sanity hearing, a Court of Appeals did grant him a habeas corpus writ on February 1, 1928. Unlike Judge Lueders, this three-judge panel was persuaded by Remus' contention that the state should not be allowed to have it both ways. If he was insane, the state should not have certified him sane during his trial. If he was sane, as three state alienists had said, then he did not belong in an asylum.

To help the appeals judges decide he was sane, Remus produced six alienists who so testified. The panel of judges was convinced. The Court of Appeals declared him sane on February 21 and ordered his release. The state appealed the case to the Ohio Supreme Court, but to no avail. On the morning of June 20, 1928, the Ohio high court affirmed the Court of Appeals decision ordering Remus' release.

The former "Bootleg King" was jubilant. "It's wonderful! It's wonderful!" he cried. "I'm going back to Cincinnati and make my home there."

A few hours later, smiling broadly at the few reporters on hand, he walked out of Lima State Hospital and into the automobile of one of his attorneys. George Remus was free at last, and on his way back to the world he had helped create, the world of booze and bribery, high living and high finance. But, alas for Remus, he no longer fitted into the world he helped create. He had lost his place there. His fortune was gone. His associates had scattered. His flamboyance had faded and even his fame had begun to dwindle. No longer newsworthy, he faced an obscure, lonely, drifting life which would finally end on January 20, 1952, in a "modest" Covington, Kentucky house he was then sharing with a recently acquired third wife.

Chapter 12

In January, Mrs. Pauline Sabin had announced she would not seek to become a delegate to the Republican Party's 1928 national convention. It was perhaps as much a tribute to her personal charm as it was to the great wealth and social position she represented that she had been elected to the delegate slate even though she hadn't sought it.

Mrs. Sabin had sufficient reason not to seek the honor. As time passed, she found that she had less and less in common with her fellow Republicans on what she considered the foremost issue of the day, prohibition. And now she had written an article for *Outlook Magazine* which was due to appear in June, just before the convention.[1]

When the article was published June 8, Mrs. Sabin became, as she had expected, an immediate embarrassment to those Republicans supporting the presidential hopes of Herbert Hoover, the Secretary of Commerce. Hoover was striving mightily to play down the prohibition issue.

"I was one of the women who favored prohibition when I heard it discussed in the abstract," her article began, "but I am now convinced it has proved a failure. It is true we no longer see the corner saloon:

but in many cases has it not merely moved to the back of a store, or up or down one flight [of stairs] under the name of a speakeasy?

"It is true that in our universities groups can no longer go together to a ratskeller and drink their beer genially and in the open. Is it not true that they are making their own gin and drinking it furtively in their own rooms? Indeed, the authorities of certain colleges have instituted the practice of searching the students' rooms without their consent and during their absence."

Mrs. Sabin then turned her scorn toward a group which was seldom publicly attacked—the dry women of America who fostered and fought for prohibition. Even the most outspoken wet champions seldom attacked such women because it was ungentlemanly and because it was generally accepted that a woman, a wife and mother, had good reason to detest liquor. It threatened her home.

Unlike most champions of the wet cause, Mrs. Sabin had no need to be gentlemanly, and she refused to accept the notion that it was inherently sensible for women to embrace prohibition. To those who favored it because they thought it would protect their children from drink, she pointed out that their children were now growing up "with a total lack of respect for the Constitution and the law." She was especially critical of women who would vote for a dry candidate "without taking enough interest to question his stand on other matters of vital importance." These women, she wrote, have "one-plank minds, and even go so far as to support men they know will personally break the prohibition law but who will be sure to vote to sustain it."

She attacked such organizations as the Women's Christian Temperance Union and the Law Enforcement League because they claimed to speak for the women of America. "It may be that they speak for a good many but their number is steadily diminishing." There were millions of American women who had changed their minds, she argued, and now considered prohibition a menace as well as a failure. For them she had an important suggestion.

"As soon as the women opposed to prohibition organize and become articulate," she insisted, "they will be able to do more toward bringing about a change in the conditions which exist today than any organization composed solely of men."

This concluding suggestion in Mrs. Sabin's article was profoundly disturbing to many intelligent drys. As it happened, her husband was treasurer of the nation's most prominent antiprohibition organization "composed solely of men"—the Association Against the Prohibition Amendment. The A.A.P.A. was now rapidly expanding in size and scope, but its results were limited by the fact that most of its members were so busy handling their own enterprises they didn't have time to assume active roles in the antiprohibition movement. Their wives, on the other hand, had time to spare. With servants and governesses to take care of their homes and children, such women could exercise considerable force if they were ever organized. Educated, sophisticated, and articulate, they would provide a sharp contrast to the energetic but simplistic ladies of the W.C.T.U.

If Mrs. Sabin's plea for women to organize against prohibition was more than rhetoric, the drys might find her difficult to handle in the years ahead. She was well acquainted with the kind of women on whom she was calling. She was one of them. If she had changed her mind about prohibition, many others were probably doing so too. She was also politically knowledgeable. At forty-one years of age, she was mature and still as attractive as she was persuasive. During one of her visits to Washington on National Committee business, a Senator said of her, "Thank God, a pretty woman in politics at last."

The opening day of the Democratic Convention in Houston was approaching. Party leaders realized they would face a hard fight in the fall because the Republicans, earlier in June, had nominated a formidable candidate—Herbert Clark Hoover of California. Hoover had first gained fame and high praise as administrator of American relief for war-torn Belgium in 1919. As Secretary of Commerce since 1921, he considered himself largely responsible for America's booming prosperity. For seven years his office had released a flow of press releases to remind the public of his role in expanding the economy and keeping it free of controls. His laissez-faire economic views made him a hero to business men and his unfaltering support of the liquor laws made him highly acceptable to the prohibitionists. He would be difficult for any Democrat to beat.

It seemed apparent to most Democrats that the job of beating Hoover would probably go to Al Smith. However, many of them, especially Southerners, were not reconciled to this likelihood. Bishop Cannon, who would be coming to the convention as the chief spokesman for the Anti-Saloon League and thirty other dry organizations, had been preaching to the nation for nine months in an effort to slow the tide of Smith's growing popularity. But since the "Happy Warrior's" election in 1926 to a fourth term in Albany, his progress toward the nomination had been relentless. William Gibbs McAdoo, who had stymied Smith in 1924, was not in the race. Two of the key men behind McAdoo, Wayne Wheeler and William Jennings Bryan, were now dead. Throughout the country, even in the rural Western states, the Smith machine was functioning smoothly and Smith-for-President clubs were blossoming, fully financed. In April, Smith had won the Wisconsin and Michigan primaries. In May, after he ran away with the California primary, two of his challengers—Senator Thomas Walsh of Montana and Governor Albert E. Ritchie of Maryland—decided to retire from the race, leaving only Senator James A. Reed of Missouri in serious contention.

Inasmuch as Reed was even more notoriously wet than Smith, Bishop Cannon had slight hope of enjoying the convention outcome, but he was not ready to accept it complacently, nor was he willing to fold up his campaign against Smith merely because it appeared unlikely to succeed. He had said in April and again in October of 1927 that "the position of Governor Smith . . . would make the paramount issue of the campaign to be nullification versus law enforcement."

On December 7, 1927, while discussing Smith in a speech at the Anti-Saloon League's convention in Washington, he quoted from an article in the November 30 *Nation* by Oswald Garrison Villard:

> Do you believe in electing to the Presidency a man who drinks too much for his own good, and is politically a rampant wet? Does Al drink, and does he drink too much? I am reliably informed that he drinks every day, and the number of his cocktails and his highballs is variously estimated at from four to eight. It is positively denied that he is ever intoxicated, much gossip to the contrary notwithstanding.

After quoting Villard, Bishop Cannon asked, "Would not any nation which should elect such a 'cocktail President' to uphold the Constitution and to execute the laws pertaining to prohibition be properly the object of the amazement, the ridicule, indeed the contempt, of the other nations of the world?"[2]

(The bishop did not question the accuracy of Villard's charge that Smith drank from four to eight cocktails a day. It is doubtful that

Smith drank that much habitually, but no doubt he did so on occasion. A long-time friend and Smith supporter, William F. Kenny, maintained a private barroom in the penthouse of an office building he owned at Fourth Avenue and Twenty-third Street in Manhattan. It was known as the "Tiger Room," partly because the tiger was the Tammany Hall symbol. Many Tammany leaders went there to drink Kenny's excellent booze while they talked politics, and so did Smith when he was in New York City.)

Up to this point, Cannon's opposition to Smith had been conducted on the very legitimate basis of the New York governor's prohibition record. On May 14, 1928, at a Kansas City meeting of the General Conference of the Methodist Episcopal Church, the bishop began shifting the emphasis in his attacks against Smith. He first regaled his fellow Protestant clergymen by quoting an article in the Vatican newspaper, *Osservatore Romano,* which said:

> The attempt to enforce prohibition in America has become so useless, not to say dangerous, that it would be better to abolish it, especially since unbridled passion is always more rampant as soon as there is an attempt to enforce complete abstinence.

After criticizing Vatican officials for attacking the American prohibition law, and pointing out that he personally knew Catholic priests and laymen who genuinely advocated prohibition, Cannon launched a polemic which added a pungent anti-Catholic flavor to his anti-Smith campaign:

> It is not surprising . . . that this position of high dignitaries of the Roman Catholic Church will be reflected in the attitude of many loyal sons of Romanism who are members of legislatures, members of Congress. It is a fact that the attacks upon the prohibition law come principally from men who are Roman Catholics or who represent Roman Catholic centers like Boston, Baltimore, New Orleans, and New York. . . . Certainly Governor Alfred E. Smith, who is prominently spoken of for President, is likely to be tremendously influenced by the views of the Pope and the Romish cardinals on the subject of prohibition, for when he gave an official reception to Cardinal Hayes and visiting cardinals he knelt and, as Governor of New York, kissed the rings of the cardinals, thus emphasizing the idea of the subordination of the state to the Romish Church.[3]

By the time the convention opened in hot, steamy Houston on June 26, Al Smith realized that Bishop Cannon and his followers offered the only threat to his nomination. But if the bishop was spoiling for a disruptive battle, or expecting the Smith forces to reveal some vulnerability he could use against them, he was due to be disappointed. One of the first things Cannon noticed when he entered the huge new Sam Houston Convention Hall was that his Virginia delegation had been seated right across the aisle from the New York delegation. As Cannon put it, "There was no finer looking, better dressed, more polite, less demonstrative delegation in the convention than the delegation sent by Tammany Hall." It was, he decided, "a remarkable contrast to the delegation to the New York convention in 1924," because it had "no red-nosed, red-faced men with large stomachs indicative of their liquor habits. On the contrary it was composed of the highest type of citizenship which the New York City Democracy could secure. It was led by such persons as George Gordon Battle, Henry Morgenthau, Mrs. Charles Dana Gibson, Franklin D. Roosevelt, and others of like quality. Every effort was made to impress the southern Democrats that Tammany Hall was composed of a high type of men and women."

Though the nominal head of the delegation was young Roosevelt, Bishop Cannon knew very well who actually controlled all these proper New Yorkers. It was the Irish Catholic Tammany boss George Olvany.[4] Indeed, the whole convention, as far as he could see, was going to be an Irish Catholic show. Frank Hague, for instance, was running the New Jersey delegation, and George Brennan the Illinois contingent. Bishop Cannon viewed this Catholic ascendancy with alarm, but what could he do about it? He had been unable to repeat Wayne Wheeler's 1924 accomplishment of assuring that more than one third of the delegates were committed to the dry cause. He couldn't hope, therefore, to stymie Smith by stopping him short of the required two thirds unless he could swing some of Smith's Western delegates back into the dry column where they belonged. His only hope of managing that was by starting a battle with the Smith forces over the prohibition plank in the platform.

The situation looked promising when the Smith-dominated platform committee met and one of its subcommittees introduced the draft of what Cannon considered a shamefully wet prohibition plank. Here was his chance. If he could turn the convention into a wet-dry contest, he might yet be able to lure away enough of Smith's marginal delegates to defeat him. As quickly as they could gain the floor, Cannon and the Southern leaders arose to threaten that if such a wet plank were adopted, the dry minority would take the issue to the convention floor.

Cannon could not know that the Smith forces had their instructions. They had placed their slightly damp sentiments on record and that was all they were expected to do. Graciously they bowed to Bishop Cannon's threats, and furiously he accepted his trivial victory. His prohibition enforcement plank, almost identical to the 1924 model, went into the platform, but when the platform was adopted on the twenty-eighth, and the balloting began, Cannon realized that his party had forsaken him.

Governor Smith, surrounded by friends at the executive mansion in Albany (his wife and family, except for married daughter Emily Warner, had gone to Houston) listened to the balloting on the radio. It was the first coast-to-coast radio broadcast of a convention ever attempted. Many of the Smith supporters couldn't get over the fact that Houston was coming through as clearly as if it were right here in the parlor. The room was crowded to capacity and thousands stood outside, awaiting the good news. Smith leaned forward toward the radio, cigar in hand, as the balloting began.

"Mr. Chairman, Alabama casts one vote for Smith, eight votes for [Senator Walter F.] George, and six votes for [Cordell] Hull."

Al Smith had expected very little support from Alabama. But Arizona came through for him with all six of its votes, then Arkansas with seventeen of its eighteen, followed by clean sweeps from California, Colorado, Connecticut, and Delaware. The Smith bandwagon seemed to be on its way. When the first ballot was completed, however, his total of 724 2/3 votes fell ten short of the necessary two thirds and the tension among the radio listeners in the executive mansion was increasing.

Former Senator Atlee Pomerene of Ohio then petitioned the chair for recognition. His delegation had passed during the vote count. "Mr. Chairman," he said, "I ask that Ohio's entire forty-five votes be recorded in favor of Al Smith."

In Albany, as in Houston, the celebration erupted. Smith's daughter, Emily, jumped up and threw her arms around his neck. The crowd outside, hearing the cheers, brushed past the one state trooper guarding the door and began overrunning the executive mansion from top to bottom, pushing and shoving to get near their hero, snooping in one room after another, and waving hip flasks.

When the crowd was finally cleared out at about dawn, Smith talked by phone to his wife in Houston, and to New York Senator Robert Wagner, whose opinions he deeply respected. Then he sat down to a breakfast of bacon and eggs and, after a short rest, composed an acceptance telegram which would be read to the convention before it adjourned.

Against the advice of many of his close friends, he devoted almost half of this telegram to a restatement of his policy on the prohibition problem. "I was unwilling," he said later, "that the convention adjourn without knowing my views and what I proposed to say in the campaign and to do about this much discussed and debated question."

In the telegram, he said that whoever became President, it would be his duty "to point the way which in his opinion leads to a sane, sensible solution" of a situation "entirely unsatisfactory to the great mass of our people." While stating once more that he was against bringing back the saloon, he suggested that "Democratic principles of local self-government and states' rights" be applied to end the lawlessness prohibition had fostered.

What Smith seemed to be proposing was that the national prohibition law be replaced by local option laws which would, of course, nullify prohibition in many of the country's urban-dominated states. Bishop Cannon, when the telegram was read to the delegates in Houston, quickly called a meeting of Southern dry leaders at the convention. Within a few hours after the Democrats had adjourned, Cannon made the ominous announcement that Southern dry Democrats would convene at Asheville, North Carolina, July 11 "to organize at once for the election of dry Democratic Senatorial, Congressional, and state nominees for public office and for the defeat of the wet Tammany candidate for President."

If Smith wanted to win in November, he was going to have to beat a very angry bishop as well as a very popular Secretary of Commerce. But could the bishop, on the dry issue alone, convince Southerners they should break a sixty-year tradition, dating back to the Civil War, of voting only for Democrats?

The whispering campaign against Al Smith because of his religion began immediately after his nomination. Not only in the South but throughout the country, the rumor spread—and some labeled it as verified truth—that if a Catholic were elected President, the Pope would soon arrive from Rome and move into the White House. During the course of the campaign, Smith's managers collected and burned "whole trunkloads" of scurrilous anti-Catholic pamphlets about him, most of which also accused him of being a drunk. The Ku Klux Klan sent speakers all over the South and into selected Northern areas to point out the danger of putting a Papist into the White House. Smith was accused of driving drunk in Manhattan, though he never drove, and his wife, Katie, was accused of tippling in nightclubs though she never drank.

On July 19 at Asheville, North Carolina, Bishop Cannon adjourned his Southern Dry Democratic convention and opened anti-Smith headquarters in Richmond, Virginia, with branches in fourteen states. The Baltimore *Sun,* reporting on his convention, said that four fifths of the delegates questioned were willing to admit that they felt Smith's religion was a more important reason to oppose him than his wet record. During the convention, however, Bishop Cannon made no reference to Smith's religion, and as the campaign began, he seemed personally to be avoiding the subject. It may be that his primary bias against Smith was on the basis of the liquor question, or perhaps liquor and Catholicism were hopelessly linked in his mind. After all, wine was drunk during Mass and many Catholic immigrants had come from countries where some kind of alcoholic beverage was a staple of life. Cannon's willingness, in 1924, to support for the presidency Senator Thomas Walsh, a Catholic dry, indicated he was capable of a degree of flexibility on the religious issue, whereas he was capable of none on the prohibition issue.

Surprisingly, it was Assistant Attorney General Mabel Walker Willebrandt rather than Cannon who first provoked Al Smith into speaking out against the bigotry which was stalking him. Mrs. Willebrandt had been the first high official in the Coolidge administration to announce her support for Herbert Hoover, and at the Republican convention, as chairman of the Credentials Committee, she was criticized by Senator George Norris of Nebraska because, he said, she was "careful to seat all the Hoover delegates from the solid South." On the night of June 28, while Al Smith was winning his first-ballot nomination in Houston, a hundred of her prohibition agents had swooped down on a score of New York nightclubs, arresting such celebrities as Texas Guinan and singer Helen Morgan in a drive to dramatize the wetness of Smith's home town. Mrs. Willebrandt said later she had personally helped plan the raids.

After conferring with Secretary Hoover in Washington on August 31, she began a speaking tour in his support which would eventually take her from coast to coast. In her first major address, at Springfield, Ohio, before 2,500 ministers and their wives at the state conference of the Methodist Episcopal Church, she perhaps thoughtlessly gave Smith a wedge to use against her by calling for a concerted, clergy-led, Protestant drive to defeat him.[5]

She first attacked "the members of the intelligentsia who organized the Association Against the Prohibition Amendment," and accused the group of helping Tammany Hall win the nomination for Smith by using their "New York money" to buy up and convert to the wet cause previously dry newspapers in rural and Southern communities. Then she concentrated her attack on the New York governor himself. "He was the one governor in all the American states," she declared, "who, notwithstanding his oath to support the Constitution of the United States, pulled down one of the forty-six pillars the people had erected for its support. New York had ratified that amendment. That ratification was a pledge to concurrent effort. But the audacious governor was unconvinced by such reasoning. Tammany wanted the least possible prohibition. Tammany had reared him; gave him his power. Tammany's desires were his convictions."

After warming up to her subject, she continued. "There are two thousand pastors here. You have in your churches more than 600,000 members of the Methodist Church in Ohio alone. That is enough to swing the election. The 600,000 have friends in other states. Write to them. Every day and every ounce of your energy are needed to rouse the friends of prohibition to register and vote."

When she finished speaking, the clergymen, on a standing vote, unanimously endorsed Hoover.

Smith, meantime, had embarked on an extensive campaign trip through the Western states in an eleven-car special train. On September 20, as the train neared Oklahoma City on the way from Omaha, Smith and his party could see a succession of flaming Ku Klux Klan crosses in the fields they were passing. When the train pulled into the Oklahoma City station, a large crowd was there, but it seemed to Smith a sullen, frightening crowd. He decided to strike back at the bigots, and do it right here where there seemed to be so many of them. When his advisers unanimously argued against it, he listened to them and announced he would go ahead anyway. "I felt deep in my heart," he said later, "that I would be a coward and probably unfit to be President if I were to permit it to go further unchallenged."

His courage did not make him comfortable, however. Before leaving his hotel that evening for the Oklahoma City Coliseum where he was to speak, Smith said to his speechwriter, Charlie Michelson, "I'm scared, Charlie. I'm wondering how it will go. I don't know those people out there. I don't speak their language."⁶

Including standees, there were perhaps 15,000 jammed into the 10,000-capacity Coliseum, and they gave Al Smith a tremendous ovation when he was introduced as "the next President of the United States." Somewhat heartened by the applause, he wasted little time getting to his point. His second paragraph began: "In this campaign an effort has been made to distract the attention of the electorate . . . and fasten it on malicious and un-American propaganda. . . . I shall speak openly on the things about which people have been whispering to you. . . . I specifically refer to the question of my religion. . . . I can think of no greater disservice to this country than to have the voters of it divide upon religious lines. It is contrary to the spirit not only of the Declaration of Independence, but of the Constitution itself."

After pointing out that as governor of New York, he had appointed to state offices more Protestants than Catholics, he got around to the matter of Mabel Walker Willebrandt's speech twelve days earlier to the Ohio Methodist ministers. It was her final exhortation to the pastors that he found offensive, her plea that they recruit their 600,000 church members to vote for Hoover.

"Mrs. Willebrandt holds a place of prominence in the Republican administration in Washington," he reminded his audience. "By silence after such a speech, the only inference one can draw is that the administration approves such political tactics. . . . What would the effect be upon these same people if a prominent official of the government of the State of New York under me suggested to a gathering of the pastors of my church that they do for me what Mrs. Willebrandt suggests be done for Hoover?"

By this time his listeners were enthusiastically with Smith. When he paused they would encourage him with shouts like, "Pour it on 'em, All!" When he finished, they cheered. But the majority of these people were Democrats who had been given tickets because the party organization considered them loyal. Was the speech actually a success? Smith was eager to get back to his hotel and phone New York for the reaction of advisers there who would have heard it on the radio.

When he entered his suite, he immediately put in a call to Mrs. Belle Moskowitz, who was managing his New York headquarters.

"Where are you?" she asked when she heard his voice.

"Back at the hotel," he said.

"Thank God for that," she sighed.

The religion and prohibition issues, strangely entwined in the public mind, had now become so inflammatory that all of his advisers were worried. In fact, nobody could figure out how the Oklahoma City speech was received. Supporters were quick to applaud it, but reaction was minimal from the people to whom Smith had actually been addressing his remarks.

Mabel Walker Willebrandt was one exception. She was genuinely shocked at Smith's interpretation of her Ohio speech. It simply hadn't occurred to her that she was putting the election on a religious basis.[7] She did not consider herself anti-Catholic. It was a Catholic, Major Frank Doherty of Los Angeles, who had done more than anyone else to make her an assistant attorney general. In the days following Smith's speech, many Democrats and some Republicans continued to chastize her for bigotry. Finally, on the verge of tears, she called Doherty one afternoon and said, "Surely you and Sarah [his wife] do not believe these things of me." As Doherty reassured her in his "warm Irish voice," she collapsed into a weeping spell.

The speech had been ill-conceived, no doubt, because it did call for a political division along religious lines, but as she pointed out, it contained no anti-Catholic remarks. Her rationalization was to some degree suspect. She had not exhorted the churches to "go into politics," she said. She had simply pointed out "the fact that prohibition for which Protestant churches had consistently fought for fifty years did not belong in politics and had never been there, but had been dragged into the political arena by Governor Smith's telegram repudiating his party platform respecting the Eighteenth Amendment."

Mrs. Willebrandt was too well acquainted with the operations of the Anti-Saloon League and other dry groups to pretend that prohibition "did not belong in politics and had never been there." As she well knew, prohibition had been the nation's primary domestic political issue for nearly a decade, and Al Smith had as much right to oppose it as the dry groups had to support it. He had not been unreasonable in criticizing her for trying to make the campaign against him a religious issue, yet when he did so, he exposed her to more censure than she perhaps deserved. Aside from her 1924 refusal to condemn the Ku Klux Klan, Mrs. Willebrandt had never been on record in support of bigotry. (And it may be noted parenthetically that before she died in 1963, she became a Roman Catholic.)

Bishop Cannon, who had interrupted his campaigning for a short trip to Europe, returned to Richmond on September 12. Though his health was delicate and his wife was gravely ill (she suffered so severely from high blood pressure she was in danger of dying at any time), he immediately turned his attention to fundraising for his Anti-Smith Democrats. Much as he had always detested New York, he wasted no time before going there, leaving Richmond after only one day at home with his wife. New York was where the money was, and if he wanted to raise significant funds for his cause, he could hardly ignore the place.

Cannon arrived on the fourteenth, for what would prove to be a very profitable visit.[8] After meeting a friend named C. Bascom Slemp, he went to the office of Joseph Frelinghuysen, a one-time New Jersey Senator, who quickly contributed $10,000 to his cause and promised another $10,000 if it was needed.

The bishop and Mr. Slemp then went to the office of Edwin C. Jameson, a lawyer and insurance executive who had the highest possible Republican political connections. Slemp introduced Cannon to Jameson, then retired while Cannon, perhaps needlessly, explained the purpose of his organization and described a very satisfactory meeting he and an associate had had with Secretary Hoover, whom they now supported. Hoover, he said, had made a "clear-cut declaration that he stood for the vigorous, effective enforcement of the Prohibition Law." After these preliminary remarks, Cannon got down to the purpose of his meeting with Jameson. In addition to the money already collected or expected, he said, he would need another $50,000 for the Virginia campaign alone. Could Jameson provide that much for him?

Jameson said he would be glad to help "a movement based upon moral principles as over against purely political party allegiance." He had a number of friends in Virginia who no doubt felt the same way. Without hesitation he promised the $50,000.

Cannon, determined that there would be no burdensome conditions attached to the promise, made it clear that he would accept the money only if he could spend it as he saw fit, "without giving any itemized report of how the money had been used." Unless Jameson was confident he would use it wisely and efficiently, Cannon would refuse to take it.

In answer to this, Jameson simply asked him when and how he would like the payments to be made. Bishop Cannon said he would want $10,000 a week for five weeks, and that he himself would come to New York and collect it each week.

By this time, Cannon had another, personal reason to visit New York each week. Early in the summer, when he had come to the city for a speech about the dangers of Al Smith, he had seen in the lobby of the McAlpin Hotel, at Broadway and Thirty-third Street, a tall, blonde, good-looking woman who might have been in her forties but didn't "look a day over thirty." Though she was with another woman, something about her made him think she might be friendly. He walked up to her and introduced himself as Stephen Trent, a writer. The two women were so engaging he offered to take them to their destination in his car. The woman who had first attracted his attention introduced herself as Mrs. Helen McCallum. Her friend was Mrs. Joan Chapman. They went to Mrs. Chapman's apartment, and before leaving his winsome new acquaintances that evening, the bishop gave Mrs. McCallum twenty dollars to help her out of a financial difficulty.[9]

Thereafter, Bishop Cannon often visited Mrs. McCallum when he came to New York, and at least on one occasion helped her solve another financial problem with a gift of a hundred dollars. Whether he saw her during his September 14 visit to New York has never been established. For most of that day he was busy with his fundraising efforts. That night he went up to Harlem with "some friends," but he never disclosed the identity of these friends.

Harlem at that time, besides being a black ghetto, was a popular entertainment center for downtown whites. The Cotton Club on Lenox Avenue (in which Larry Fay had once been a partner with Arnold Rothstein and others), the Paradise and Connie's Inn on

Seventh Avenue, were among the most expensive and spectacular nightclubs in the city, featuring such attractions as Duke Ellington, Louis Armstrong, and Cab Calloway, plus floor shows with beautiful chorus girls. Lenox Avenue swarmed with people every night until dawn as the crowds pushed their way in and out of the hundreds of cabarets and speakeasies. In just one block, between Lenox and Seventh Avenue on 133rd Street, there were "several dozen restaurants, cabarets, and nightclubs." Booze flowed so openly and freely at all of these places that it looked as if the authorities had forgotten to tell the people of Harlem about prohibition.

Bishop Cannon observed the blacks there in "shops and stores and theaters and dance halls." He didn't say which dance halls he had seen, nor did he mention seeing anyone drink liquor at these places, which would indicate he didn't stay long at any of them. He did stay long enough, however, to discover that these blacks were overwhelmingly for Al Smith. Perhaps Smith's sympathy for liquor was one of the reasons, but the bishop found another. He learned that "while the Negroes are historically and politically naturally allied to the Republican Party (since Abraham Lincoln, a Republican, had freed the slaves), yet they had been thoroughly organized under the Tammany system, had been given offices in the city government, and were counted upon to cast an almost solid vote for Governor Smith."[10]

In contrast, when Cannon stopped at Washington the next day on the way home to Virginia, and observed black government employees, he found that "most of them worked in groups apart from the white employees, and that the attitude of the United States government was far more in accord with the Southern ideas than were the methods of the Tammany politicians. This information concerning the attitude of Tammany, of which organization Governor Alfred Emanuel Smith was a Sachem, toward the Negroes was of great value in combatting the propaganda which was issued against Secretary Hoover, that he had compelled white and colored clerks to work side by side in his department."

Armed with this further damaging information about Smith, the bishop launched a campaign that was to last for the remaining seven weeks before election day, a campaign during which he spoke almost every night and two or three times a day, at dozens of cities and towns throughout Virginia. He also spoke in Delaware, Maryland, Washington D.C., West Virginia, Kentucky, both Carolinas, Georgia, Tennessee, Arkansas, Texas, Mississippi, Alabama, and Oklahoma. It was a prodigious effort, but he was afterward modest about it.

"My own speaking was, of course, quite a minor matter," he said, "compared with the numerous meetings held in all the Southern states and the addresses made by ministers and laymen in their local communities."

Important as these speeches were in spreading the word against Al Smith, Bishop Cannon felt that his organization's literature was even more effective. "Literally millions of pages," he said, "were printed and circulated in every section of the South. Copies of most of the publications were sent to all the religious press (Protestant only, of course) North and South, and to the leading secular newspapers of every section."

Governor Smith, on September 29, came upon a city in middle America which was sympathetic to his views about both religion and prohibition. When he got to Milwaukee, the nation's beer brewing capital, the German and Polish Catholic populations turned out to greet him with enthusiasm despite a downpour of rain. At the City Auditorium where he spoke that night, 16,000 people filled the air with confetti and hats when he came down the aisle grinning his famous grin and waving his famous brown derby. The moment he arose to speak, one of the two bands played "Sidewalks of New York" and the 16,000 Milwaukeeans sang it. After a short delay while the rectangular-framed radio microphones were adjusted, Al Smith stepped forward and announced this would be the last major speech of his western campaign trip. He recapitulated the other speeches on the trip, and when he again mentioned Mabel Walker Willebrandt in connection with his Oklahoma City remarks against bigotry, the crowd booed her name. "I shall let the Republican campaign managers worry about her," he said. "From comments in the public press all over the country, they have abundant reason to do so. We all have something to be grateful for. I haven't got Mabel on my hands." The crowd cheered.

Approaching the theme of this evening's address, he said, "If there is any one subject above all others concerning which the welfare of the country requires plain speech and constructive leadership, it is the subject of the Eighteenth Amendment and the Volstead Act."

At the very mention of the Volstead Act, the Milwaukeeans jumped to their feet to urge him on with shaking fists and raucous cries. In this city, with its many large breweries, prohibition was more than a drinking problem; it was an employment problem. Smith attacked it forthrightly.

Quoting various sources, including prohibition officials, to prove that the liquor laws had produced more thirst and more crime but no prohibition, he declared that "a great army of the American people oppose these laws. Nobody can say that that is a healthy condition in our democracy. Nobody can say that people like ours are comfortable when so many of our thinking citizens resist the attempt on the part of the government to regulate their conduct by law. The natural result of it is the breeding throughout the length and breadth of the country of a disrespect for all law."

He then listed his recommendations: that the Volstead Act be amended to contain a sensible definition of what constituted an alcoholic beverage; that the Eighteenth Amendment be modified "to allow each state to determine for itself what it wants to do about the question of local habits"; and that a national referendum be held on the whole prohibition question.

"The cure for the ills of democracy," he concluded, "is more democracy. Hand this back to the people. Let them decide it."

For the first time since the Eighteenth Amendment was adopted, the question of modification or repeal was now an open, declared issue in a Presidential race. Secretary Hoover, as he gradually increased the pace of his campaign, found it a much less troublesome issue than did Smith. Hoover was uncomfortable discussing the subject but most people failed to notice this because he was a much more formal, stiff-collared man than Smith, and he seemed somewhat uncomfortable discussing any subject. Several years later he wrote: "The prohibition issue was forced into the campaign by Governor Smith. My innumerable contacts in life had confirmed that alcohol was one of the curses of the human race."[11] But his views about prohibition were not governed solely by that simple observation. "At the time the Eighteenth Amendment was adopted, . . . I had expressed to my friends the reverse of enthusiasm for that method of advancing temperance, saying that I did not believe that the Constitution was the place for sumptuary legislation. I resolved in the campaign not to commit myself to prohibition as a fixture of American life but first to see if the law could be enforced."

Hoover said the above in 1951. If he had said it during the 1928 campaign, he would have heard some loud cries of anger and anguish, not only from people like Bishop James Cannon but from millions of other prohibitionists who believed him to be solidly dependable on the issue. What he said in 1928, during his acceptance speech, was the following:

> I do not favor the repeal of the Eighteenth Amendment. I stand for the efficient enforcement of the laws enacted thereunder. . . .
> Our country has deliberately undertaken a great social and economic experiment, noble in motive and far-reaching in purpose. It must be worked out constructively.
> Common sense compels us to realize that grave abuses have occurred—abuses which must be remedied. An organized searching investigation of fact and causes can alone determine the wise method of correcting them. . . .
> . . Change in the Constitution can and must be brought about only by the straightforward methods provided in the Constitution itself. There are those who do not believe in the purposes of several provisions of the Constitution. No one denies their right to seek to amend it. They are not subject to criticism for asserting that right. But the Republican Party does deny the right of anyone to seek to destroy the purposes of the Constitution by indirection.

After saying this, Hoover said as little as possible about the subject. Prohibition was Smith's problem, not his, and Smith was welcome to it. The only difficulty the issue presented to the Republican candidate was the phrase, "experiment, noble in motive," which the Democrats distorted to "noble experiment." Hoover had to explain repeatedly to the drys that he didn't actually think of prohibition as an experiment, that it was as permanent a fixture to him as it was to them. They had to accept his explanation because they couldn't support his opponent; even if they were distrustful of him, they had to face the fact that he was the likely winner. Thanks to Bishop Cannon and his associates, the Democratic candidate was in danger of losing even the solid South, while Hoover's popularity continued to rise throughout the country despite one small difficulty in the South—that recurring accusation that he had been too nice to Negroes.

Governor Theodore Bilbo of Mississippi, a notorious racist, was spreading the rumor that during a visit to his state in 1927, Secretary Hoover had paid a call on a colored woman in Mound Bayou, and later had danced with her. The image of Herbert Hoover dancing with anyone amused everyone except Hoover himself. He directed his personal assistant on October 19 to issue a press release which called Bilbo's remark "the most indecent and unworthy statement in the whole of a bitter campaign."[12]

Fortunately for Hoover, he was seldom faced with such embarrassing crises. Most of the time he was able simply to go from speech to speech, pointing with pride to the prosperity which was evident everywhere in 1928, and for which the Republicans took full credit.

As Smith swung into the cities, especially from Chicago eastward where the Irish Catholics were concentrated, he drew one record-breaking crowd after another. It was no surprise that the cities were behind him. The question was, how had he done out West and how would he do in the South? Frances Perkins, at that time Chairman of the New York State Industrial Board, who had accompanied him on his western swing, admitted ruefully, "He did not sound like a man who knew pigs and chickens."

It was still early in the evening of November 6, election day, when Al Smith began to realize all his efforts had been in vain. As he watched the returns with gubernatorial candidate Franklin D. Roosevelt at the Sixty-ninth Regiment Armory in Manhattan, Smith received a New York *World* report from the South that Virginia (Bishop Cannon's home state), North Carolina, and Florida were definitely going Republican. Worse than that, as the evening progressed, it became evident that Hoover was winning even in New York state. (In the governor's race, Roosevelt was slightly behind his opponent, Albert Ottinger, but before morning, he was destined to pull ahead by a narrow 25,000 margin.)

When Smith's defeat began to dawn on him, his smile faded and so did his ruddy complexion. By midnight it was obvious to him that he had been smashed. He had even lost seven of the supposedly solid Democratic Southern states. It looked as if he would win less than 100 electoral votes. (In the final tally, Hoover won the Presidency with 22 million popular votes to 15½ million; 444 electoral votes to 87.)

Al Smith was reported to have said before going home, "Well, the time hasn't yet come when a man can say his [Rosary] beads in the White House."

Chapter 13

Still somewhat down on his luck but not sufficiently impoverished to lose his reputation as Broadway's most stylish dresser, Larry Fay was managing an elegant boite called the Rendezvous for his bootlegger friend Frankie Marlow when a more promising opportunity came his way in November 1928. Through his connections with Tammany leader James J. Hines, he learned that ninety-four milk wholesalers in the New York area had organized an association for the purpose of maintaining profitable prices and protecting themselves against each other as well as the big competitors. Hines was aware of this development because he had recently secured the appointment of one of his men, Bernard Plunkett, as secretary of the city Board of Health, the agency which regulated milk dealers. Hines now had such a strong influence over the board and its policies that he decided the independent milk dealers might be quite eager to cultivate his good will, which they could best do by accepting another of his confederates as the czar of their new association.

Fay would be ideal for the job. He was bright; he could be tough, but he didn't use the extreme methods of other Hines associates like

Dutch Schultz, Owney Madden, Louis (Lepke) Buchalter, or Lucky Luciano. One of Hines's more gentle associates, Arnold Rothstein, had the ability to handle the job with ease, but even if Hines had considered him, he could now forget it. On November 5, Rothstein was found full of bullets at the Park Central Hotel. His death, incidentally, provided a substantial monetary gain for Fay, who owed Rothstein $11,500, which he would not have to repay.

. The prospect of becoming identified with a more socially acceptable beverage than booze appealed mightily to Fay because of his long-time dislike of the illicit liquor trade. While it had brought him his first taste of money and fame, it had also brought him public identity as a hoodlum and he was eager to rise above this image. "I'm a businessman," he once protested. "Just a regular businessman like any broker or merchant."

The day he presented himself to the members of the New York Chain Milk Association as their prospective leader, they showed themselves remarkably eager to accept him. He was a well-known personality, of course, and he had a reputation for being able to get things done.[1]

"I'll get action in two weeks," Fay promised, and they, being aware of his political and underworld connections, didn't hesitate to believe him. These were not simple, naive men. They knew what their group needed—influence and muscle. And they were willing to pay for it, though they may not have been willing to pay as much as they were destined to pay.

Fay had a few stipulations to make before he agreed to join the group. First he would have to be president and chairman of the board. He would also decide territorial disputes, prevent cutthroat practices between members, protect them from territorial invasions by the large dairies, and set fixed prices to which all members would have to adhere. He was confident that within a short time he could get the price of New York milk up from the present $4 to $4.40 per forty-quart can, and he was also confident he could make the grocers accept the higher price. If they didn't, he would make it difficult for them to get any milk at all. As for the quality of the milk, if the Board of Health inspectors showed signs of becoming unreasonable, it was understood that there were certain people to whom Fay could speak, and who might be expected to make the inspectors more responsive.

To provide all these services, Fay would hire a staff of men who would, in his words, "adjust difficulties" in the milk industry. No one had to guess where he would get these "staff" members. Friends like Owney Madden and Frankie Marlow had plenty of formidable men Fay could employ.

To pay for the services, each wholesaler would contribute five cents for every forty-quart can of milk shipped into New York. And for the purpose of handling these fees, Fay was also willing to become the association's treasurer. Out of these funds he would compensate his "staff" and take care of all operating expenses. Anything left over would be considered his salary.

A few days later, Larry Fay was once again sitting in a lavish office at 1775 Broadway near Columbus Circle. He had already found nine "difficulty adjusters" and he was hiring a staff of pretty girls to handle the fees from the ninety-four milk wholesalers. Within a short time, these fees were totaling $900 per day, but his members weren't complaining because the price of milk had already gone up a few cents. Some grocers grumbled, but not after a visit or two from Fay's "adjusters." Since his payroll and expenses totaled about $2,000 a week, his "salary" amounted to somewhat more than $4,000 a week, which would come to more than $200,000 per year. Larry Fay had apparently succeeded at last in getting out of the bootleg liquor trade. Now perhaps people would stop calling him a hoodlum. What could be more respectable than the milk business?

The defeat of Al Smith had been a great victory for Bishop James Cannon, Jr., and he did not hesitate to share his pleasure with the world at large. The day after the election, he issued a statement rejoicing in the fact that, despite Tammanyism, the nation was still strong, progressive, and patriotic:

> The unprecedented defeat of Governor Smith, the wet, Tammany candidate for the Presidency, is an indignant, overwhelming repudiation of the proposal by [sic] the people of our country to place the national government in the hands of the wet sidewalks of our cities, aided and abetted by a selfish, so-called liberal element of high society life.

The "high society" people he was castigating were probably members of the increasingly active Association Against the Prohibition

Amendment. His reference to putting the government "in the hands of the wet sidewalks of our cities," might have been difficult to visualize, but his meaning was clear because Cannon had used the "sidewalk" reference before, during one of his anti-Smith campaign speeches. At Cambridge, Maryland, he had said:

> Governor Smith wants the Italians, the Sicilians, the Poles and the Russian Jews. That kind has given us a stomach-ache. We have been unable to assimilate such people in our national life, so we shut the door to them. But Smith says, "give me that kind of people." He wants the kind of dirty people that you find today on the sidewalks of New York.[2]

Now that America had repudiated Governor Smith and his kind of people, Bishop Cannon could get down to the work of guiding the nation along the path of "genuine, idealistic, truly progressive Americanism" which he perceived so clearly. Because he had been exceedingly helpful to President-elect Hoover during the campaign, he would henceforth be able to enjoy the kind of access to the White House that the late Wayne Wheeler had enjoyed during the Harding and early Coolidge days. Bishop Cannon had become, unquestionably, the most powerful of the prohibition leaders, the strongest figure in both the Anti-Saloon League and the Methodist Church. The future looked bright for him. Yet he did have one personal worry.

Just before the election, the New York *World*, a notoriously wet newspaper, had informed him that it was in possession of affidavits describing his transactions with a stock brokerage firm, Kable and Company, which had gone bankrupt and was now under investigation. Kable and Company was the kind of firm referred to in Wall Street as a "bucket shop." It sold stock to speculators on precariously narrow margins, and sometimes it produced better results for favored customers than for its average clients. Its reputation had always been poor, and it finally failed because, in anticipation of a market drop, it had withheld purchase of several million dollars worth of stock ordered by its clients. If the market had dropped, the company would then have been able to fill its clients' orders at lower prices, thus realizing significant secret profits for itself. When the market rose sharply instead of dropping, the company had insufficient funds to pay the profits its clients thought they had earned.

Bishop Cannon had not been among the losers when the enterprise went bankrupt. In late 1927 and early 1928, he had been one of its more favored customers. During that eight-month period, Kable and Company had purchased for him stocks worth $477,000 and had sold them for $486,000. To realize this $9,000 profit in eight months, Bishop Cannon had invested only $2,500.[3]

When the reporter for the *World* informed Cannon of the affidavits describing his transactions, he also asked the bishop for a statement of explanation. Cannon had indignantly refused to reply. It was his own business, he said, and the *World* had no right to inquire about it. This whole attempt to probe his personal affairs was, in his opinion, "a contemptible Tammany trick."

His firmness in the face of this threat had apparently impressed the editors of the *World*. The paper hadn't yet published a word about the matter. Yet, with Kable and Company under investigation, all the facts might eventually come out. And while Cannon could assure himself he had done no wrong, he was aware of the public opprobrium which attached to "bucket shop" operators. He was even more keenly aware of the Methodist Church's sanctions against profiteering in commercial enterprises, plus its ban against gambling. His enemies would no doubt welcome the opportunity to argue that stock speculation was a form of gambling.

This annoying market affair necessitated Bishop Cannon's presence in New York City perhaps more than he might have wished during the days and weeks following the election. His wife was gravely ill in Washington, and it was unfortunate he couldn't spend more time with her. On the other hand, it was fortunate that in New York, he could be with Mrs. Helen McCallum, to whom he had become quite attached after meeting her in the McAlpin Hotel lobby.

Bishop Cannon was in his wife's hospital room in Washington the night of November 25 when she suffered a paralytic stroke. He had to go to New York early the next morning because he was scheduled to make a speech on the twenty-sixth to the New York Methodist Preachers' Association about the happy outcome of the recent election. While he was in Manhattan that day, he found time to have lunch with Mrs. McCallum, and he apparently found it difficult to tear himself away from her because he also spent that night in New York despite the serious condition of his wife in Washington. He did make several long distance calls to his sons, who were at their mother's bedside. When they told him that her condition was worsening, he decided to leave for Washington as early as possible the following day.

The bishop was with his wife when she died that night. They had been married forty years and three months, and had raised a family of nine children. Born Lura Virginia Bennett, she was the daughter of the president of Randolph-Macon College in Ashland, Virginia, the Methodist Episcopal school from which Cannon had graduated in 1884. A few days after her funeral, his grief was such that he hurried back to New York in quest of consolation from Helen McCallum.[4]

The de facto mayor of Chicago, Al Capone, was spending most of his time in his Miami mansion in February 1929. Meantime, his organization, which now included several judges and other public officials plus an army of policemen, gunmen, and rumrunners, managed the affairs of Chicago with a minimum of law but a certain amount of order. Aside from recurring troubles with the malcontents of the North Side gang, now led by Bugs Moran, who didn't seem to know when he was beaten, Capone had just about everything going his way.

At the same time, the official mayor of the city, William Hale Thompson, had fallen into political and personal difficulties which threatened to engulf him. Big Bill's problems had begun in the spring election campaign of 1928. Though he himself had not been up for reelection except as a Republican ward committeeman, State's Attorney Robert Emmett Crowe, who had become his close political ally, was facing a difficult opponent in the Republican primary, Judge John A. Swanson, the chosen candidate of U.S. Senator Charles S. Deneen.

Several days before the election, a few of the boys, perhaps Capone men, had shown too much enthusiasm in their support of the Thompson-Crowe machine. They had planted bombs against the Chicago homes of both Swanson and Deneen, and while no one had been hurt, the Chicago public had drawn the unfortunate inference that the explosions were a meaningful part of the Thompson-Crowe campaign.

At about the same time, a young black lawyer named Octavius Granady, who was running for Republican committeeman of the Twentieth Ward, was shot to death by four men who caught him in the street after a long chase. Granady's opponent was the incumbent committeeman and ward boss, now also the City Collector in the Thompson administration, Morris Eller.

These incidents prompted the Chicago Crime Commission to withdraw its support from Crowe and to point out that Eller's son, Emanuel, a Superior Court judge, had waived indictments against sixteen hoodlums for carrying concealed weapons during the first three months of 1928, and had waived robbery indictments in twelve other cases.

When the voting public reacted to these events by giving Swanson an almost two-to-one victory over Crowe, and by rejecting Mayor Thompson as Republican committeeman in his own ward, Big Bill reacted to the defeat by having a nervous breakdown. He increased his already high consumption of liquor. He indulged in temper tantrums and at times seemed to lose completely his always tenuous grasp of reason and logic. Though he did attend the Republican national convention in Kansas City, his once-high hopes of winning the presidential nomination had been shattered so completely that he controlled only sixteen of Illinois' sixty-one delegates. One of these Thompson delegates was Morris Eller.

After the convention, Thompson's physical and psychological condition was so distressing to his friends that they secretly arranged for him to spend a few weeks in seclusion at the estate of a friend in northern Wisconsin. When he returned to Chicago in September of 1928, he was a subdued, bewildered man. He couldn't figure out where his supporters had gone and he didn't know how to bring them back. He spent hour after hour dithering in his unofficial office on the sixteenth floor of the Sherman Hotel, making disjointed statements in reaction to the events around him but showing none of his old enthusiasm for shaping events.

In contrast, Capone had lost none of his initiative. He was enlarging his liquor business, issuing orders to judges and police officials, intimidating aldermen, and branching out into the labor rackets. He had also decided the time was ripe to eliminate his long-time problems with the North Side gang, whose members were still hijacking his liquor shipments. From his Miami home (where Chicago's City Sealer, Dan Serritella, was staying as a house guest) he ordered Machine Gun Jack McGurn to go to work on the project. McGurn devised a plan which necessitated the importation to Chicago of five gunmen whom none of the North Siders would recognize. The men he chose were led by a bank robber and murderer named Fred "Killer" Burke, a former member of the Egan Rats gang in St. Louis. Burke was an expensive but dedicated and dependable practitioner of his trade.

On the cold, snowy morning of February 14, a black Cadillac touring car, the kind police often used, with two uniformed men in the front seat plus three wearing plain clothes in the back, turned off Webster Avenue onto North Clark Street near Lincoln Park and stopped in front of a one-story garage or warehouse building marked "S-M-C Cartage Co." Its address was 2122 North Clark and it was well known in the area as one of the Moran gang's liquor transfer depots. As it happened, Moran and an associate were approaching the building when they saw the Cadillac stop and the two uniformed men get out. Having no desire to be caught in a police raid, however routine and insignificant it might be, Moran and his friend quickly reversed their steps toward the Parkway Hotel, from whence they had come.

The two uniformed men and two of the plainclothesmen, armed with machine guns and shotguns, quickly entered the building, surprising a pair of Moran's hoodlums in the front office and five more men beyond the wooden partition in the garage section toward the rear. One of the men there was a mechanic working on a truck. Another was a young optometrist who was a friend of Moran and liked to hang around gangsters. The rest were veteran members of the gang. They had been sitting near a coal stove in the chilly building, drinking hot coffee and eating crackers while waiting for the chief himself to arrive. Moran had told them all to be on hand this morning because he had received a phone call from someone promising to deliver a load of hijacked liquor.

The two uniformed invaders apparently announced that this was a raid and ordered all seven to line up facing the whitewashed brick wall of the building. All seven complied. Police raids were an annoyance but professional gangsters did not resist them. Even if arrested, they would be out of jail by midafternoon. As the seven stood against the wall, their noses almost touching the bricks, two of the men behind them systematically frisked them, relieving them of their guns. This, too, was an exasperating inconvenience but no more than that. The guns could be replaced and Chicago's courts were full of judges who, like Emanuel Eller, almost automatically dismissed hoodlums charged with carrying concealed weapons.

There is no reason to suppose any of the seven men against the wall anticipated what was about to happen to them. They showed no sign of resistance. When the machine guns of the two uniformed men began to bark, it was too late to resist. In less than two minutes a hundred bullets poured forth, a dozen or so per victim. Only eight were found later to have missed flesh and hit the wall. At least three of the men did not die immediately, but two of them did so when shotguns were fired at their faces from a few inches away. The third lived just long enough to observe the gangster code by refusing to help police identify his killers.

People who lived near the building heard what sounded like a pneumatic drill. Then they heard what sounded like a car engine backfiring. A few moments later two men in plain clothes emerged from the garage with their hands up, followed by the two uniformed men holding guns to their ribs. All four got into the Cadillac, where the fifth man was waiting, and drove away. A woman named Mrs. Max Landesman, in a rooming house next door, glanced out her window at the scene. Just another police raid, she decided, and gave it no more thought.

When the bloody result of the St. Valentine's Day massacre was discovered and the newspaper reporters arrived with the police about an hour later, Chicago was able to claim it had produced the worst gang killing in history. But a lot of Chicagoans, surprisingly, did not relish that claim. They had been complacent about the gangs long enough. They were getting tired of the slaughter and the disgrace, just as they were getting tired of the politics of Big Bill Thompson.

What could Chicagoans do about this monstrous situation? They had allowed it to develop by electing officials like Thompson. The mayor himself was one of the few people in town who didn't cry out against this latest horror. He did make it clear, though, that it wasn't his fault. The new state's attorney, John Swanson, was to blame for it. Hadn't he promised the previous April, when he defeated Thompson's ally, Bob Crowe, that he would drive out the crooks and wipe out crime?

GENEVA, ILL., Apr. 30, 1929.—The Kane County Grand Jury today decided not to indict Roy Smith, deputy sheriff, who shot and killed Mrs. Lillian De King during a dry raid on the De King home at Aurora on the night of March 20. Joe De King, Mrs. De King's husband, was told he could consider himself fortunate that he was

not indicted for having resisted the officers who entered his home.
The Grand Jury wished to indict De King according to George
D. Carbary, State's Attorney, on the theory that De King should
not have objected to his home being invaded. Enough votes were
available for his indictment, Mr. Carbary said, but the prosecutor,
entering the Grand Jury room just in time, told the jurors he felt
De King had been punished enough through the loss of his wife, the
mother of his only son.

The Grand Jury did not consider action against Gerald De King,
12 years old, who shot Deputy Sheriff Smith after the latter had
knocked down his father and shot down his mother.[5]

The day after Herbert Hoover's inauguration, Pauline Sabin resigned from the Republican National Committee. Her immediate
reason was disappointment at the new President's refusal to come out
against prohibition. When the Women's National Republican Club
gave her a farewell testimonial April 3, however, she said her main
reason for resigning was that "I want to devote my untrammeled
efforts toward working for a change in the prohibition law. . . .
Prohibition . . . has led to more violations of and contempt for law,
both by private individuals and public officials, and to more hypocrisy
than anything else in our national life. . . . To tell citizens what they
must or must not do in their strictly personal conduct as long as public
safety is not affected is a function which government should not
attempt."

Surprisingly, many of these Republican women cheered her. In the
next few days, after her remarks were published, she was inundated
with letters from other women who said they agreed with her. These
letters also included about $5,000 in contributions toward the wet
cause. Immediately Mrs. Sabin began recruiting women of like mind
for an anti-prohibition organization which she hoped would become
national in scope.

On May 28, 1929, at Chicago's Drake Hotel, fifty prominent
women from seventeen states gathered for a luncheon the purpose of
which was to found such a group.[6] Mrs. Sabin had chosen Chicago
rather than New York as the site of this first meeting because she
wanted to give the organization a national rather than an Eastern
regional identity. At the moment, however, the movement she was
trying to found was dominated by very wealthy women from Eastern

states. There was Mrs. Pierre du Pont of Delaware, Mrs. William Lowell Putnam and Mrs. Lothrop Ames of Massachusetts, Mrs. Samuel Harden Church of Pennsylvania, Mrs. R. Stuyvesant Pierrepont of New Jersey, and eleven prominent New Yorkers including Mrs. Caspar Whitney, Mrs. Edward S. Harkness, Mrs. Cornelius N. Bliss, Mrs. Archibald Roosevelt, Mrs. William K. Draper, and, of course, Mrs. Sabin herself.

The husbands of many of these women were active in the Association Against the Prohibition Amendment, not solely in every case because they deplored the social evils and human restrictions caused by the dry laws. Pierre du Pont, for instance, deplored the money it was costing him and other members of the du Pont family in taxes. He had sent a letter to a list of America's biggest taxpayers arguing that they would save great sums if legal liquor were restored and properly taxed. "The British liquor policy applied in the United States," he estimated hopefully, "would permit the total abolition of the income tax, both personal and corporate."

As the Drake Hotel waiters cleared the luncheon dishes, Mrs. Sabin, slender and graceful, her reddish hair showing strands of gray, stood and began the official proceedings. Since all of the women knew why they were there and none had to be convinced that their course was right, they quickly got down to business. The name of their group, they decided, would be the Women's Organization for National Prohibition Reform. Its self-evident purpose would be "to unite the women of the country in a fight against the Eighteenth Amendment." Their first convention would be held in the fall, at which time they hoped delegates from every state would take part in electing permanent officers. Until then, Mrs. Sabin as chairman would head a slate of temporary officers to get the group started, and a national advisory council would immediately launch a membership drive to enroll women by the hundreds of thousands or even millions if possible. With their husbands eagerly providing as much money as they would need, these women envisioned no limits to their potential effectiveness.

After the luncheon meeting, Chairman Sabin was all enthusiasm and determination as she met the press. "The women of the country," she said, "are beginning to realize the deplorable effects of the operation of the law upon their country and their children. This organization is a result of a demand from women all over the country that an

aggressive effort be made for the protection of the American home.
. . . When the truth in regard to existing conditions is more fully
known among all women, they will unite in requiring such a change
as will replace the present corruption and hypocrisy with sobriety and
honesty."

The prohibitionists quickly took notice of this new, well-financed
threat. But they gave no indication that they were as yet frightened
by it. Clarence True Wilson, Secretary of the Board of Temperance
of the Methodist Episcopal Church North, who had once advocated
that purchasers of bootleg booze be given five-year prison sentences,
said of Mrs. Sabin's fledgling organization, "The little group of wine-
drinking society women who are uncomfortable under prohibition
will have as much influence in assaulting the Constitution of their
country as they would have blowing soap bubbles at Gibralter."[7]

Dr. Mary Armor, president of the Georgia state Women's Christian Temperance Union, offered an even more fascinating image. "As
to Mrs. Sabin and her cocktail-drinking women," Dr. Armor said,
"we will outlive them, out-fight them, out-love them, out-talk them,
out-pray them, and out-vote them."[8]

President Hoover announced on May 28 an undertaking he hoped
would satisfy an important promise. During the 1928 campaign, he
had said he would appoint a commission to investigate the whole
prohibition situation and make recommendations for needed changes.
He now named the members of that group (to be called the National
Commission on Law Observance and Enforcement) and described the
scope of its inquiry. But he was less than pleased to do so. By this time
he realized that the project was more difficult and politically dangerous than it had seemed.

When he began putting the commission together shortly after his
inauguration, Hoover had asked Charles Evans Hughes, one of the
nation's most distinguished men, to take charge of it.[9] Hughes had
been governor of New York, justice of the U.S. Supreme Court,
Secretary of State, and once Republican nominee for the presidency.
He was now a judge on the World Court in the Netherlands. In a
March 25 letter, Hoover had declared to Hughes that the work of the
commission would be "the outstanding necessity of the next four
years," and that he knew of only two men big enough to direct it,
Hughes himself and Justice Harlan Stone, who was now on the Su-

preme Court and unavailable. Would Hughes accept the post? No, thank you, Hughes answered, and his determination was so firm the President had to look elsewhere.

Next he tried corporation lawyer Owen J. Roberts, but he too refused it. Everyone seemed to see the pitfalls the commission would encounter. Hoover settled for his fourth choice, one-time Attorney General George W. Wickersham, to head the commission. Then came the problem of selecting ten other members. Both the wets and the drys applied pressure to have their representatives appointed. Bishop Cannon, who was in Egypt, sent a cablegram suggesting, quite reasonably, that the group include at least one prohibitionist, one "honest, outstanding opponent of the prohibition law," and one woman.

The commission members as announced on May 28 included at least four drys, but it also included at least two wets and one woman, Mrs. Ada L. Comstock, president of Radcliffe College. The apparent drys were Wickersham himself, plus federal judges William I. Grubb, Paul J. McCormick and William S. Kenyon. The apparent wets were one-time Secretary of War Newton D. Baker and New Orleans attorney Monte M. Lemann. The other commission members were Kenneth Mackintosh, former chief justice of the Washington state supreme court; Roscoe Pound, dean of the Harvard Law School; Henry A. Anderson, a Virginia attorney, and Frank J. Loesch, director of the Chicago Crime Commission. The group as a whole was considered to be safely prohibitionist in sentiment.

The personal inclinations of the commission members were important to Hoover because if they were to recommend liquor law changes intolerable to the drys who had helped elect him, he would be caught in the middle. This consideration may have gone through his mind even before his inauguration. In his inaugural address he subtly changed his promise about the commission. Its duty, he said, would be to make "a searching investigation of the whole structure of our federal system of jurisprudence, to include the method of enforcement of the Eighteenth Amendment and the causes of abuse under it."

This change in Hoover's commitment had not gone unnoticed. Wet Congressmen and some journalists saw it as a method of diminishing the prohibition aspect of the planned investigation by saddling the commission with the bewildering task of examining the entire judicial system.

The wets were not reassured by Hoover's statement accompanying the appointment of commission members. The group would be limited, he revealed, to a consideration of the methods of enforcing the laws against liquor. It would not be asked to decide whether there should be such laws. The Eighteenth Amendment had already decided that question.

The dedicated drys showed no displeasure at the composition of President Hoover's commission or the limitations he placed upon it. The dedicated wets grumbled that under such limitations nothing would come of the inquiry. The rest of the country gave Hoover credit for instituting some kind of action in what everyone agreed was a difficult situation. Meanwhile, the nation's hundreds of thousands of speakeasies continued to do business as usual. But Hoover showed no sign of complacency on the prohibition issue now that he had launched his commission. He continued to intensify his efforts to fulfill his other promise—more rigid enforcement of all liquor laws, including the new Jones Law which threatened bootleggers with five years imprisonment and $10,000 fines. Hoover seemed sincerely dedicated to enforcement.

To a convention of Associated Press editors he said, "If a law is wrong, its rigid enforcement is the surest guaranty of its repeal. If it is right, its enforcement is the quickest method of compelling respect for it." Under his close supervision, federal liquor law arrests had already begun to rise.

After recurring rumors of proceedural conflict between herself and Attorney General William D. Mitchell, her new boss since President Hoover's inauguration, Mrs. Mabel Walker Willebrandt, the Assistant Attorney General in charge of all federal liquor law prosecution, resigned her post May 28, 1929. She did not resign, however, for the rumored reason. She was getting along quite nicely with Mitchell, who had already adopted several of her suggestions about organizational changes in the department. Nor was she resigning because she felt she had fallen short in her job or that prohibition was a hopeless cause.

In a newspaper interview during a January visit to her home city of Los Angeles, she had declared that prohibition was making "reasonable progress toward success."[10] Drinking had become less fashionable, less "smart," less the "expected thing to do" within the last two years or so. The decrease in alcoholic consumption was perhaps not great, but she felt it was sufficient to promise a further decrease. Prohibition would win out, she told the reporter, first because it was a matter of law, and second because it made sense. Those who did not observe it because it was the law should do so on the basis of ordinary intelligence.

"The election of Hoover was not precisely a referendum on the wet and dry issue," she said, "but Hoover's success and Smith's decisive defeat plainly showed that the country as a whole wants strict enforcement and may be depended upon to support the incoming administration in the measures it undertakes to dam the alcoholic flood."

If she believed that, despite the gains of prohibition, strict enforcement was still necessary to "dam the alcoholic flood," why then should she quit her job just when the President she had worked so hard to elect seemed to need her so badly? The reason was simple. She was giving up her job because she felt that eight years of complete devotion to prohibition was enough. The long days and evenings she was forced to spend in her office and the weeks she spent traveling every year kept her away from her adopted daughter, Dorothy, who was now six years old, and from their home at 3018 Dumbarton Avenue in "uptown" Washington. Situated on a corner lot with broad lawns, evergreen trees, and barberry hedges, this large, white, shingled house into which they had moved the previous year was commensurate with her government position but difficult to maintain on her government salary.

The limitations of her income had been a problem to Mrs. Willebrandt ever since she had come to Washington in 1921. She was keenly aware that an attorney as prominent as she had now become could expect great financial advantages in leaving government service for private practice.

President Hoover didn't want to see her go. He had felt some pressure from politicians she had offended by refusing to save their bootlegging friends from prosecution. And he had no doubt been told by some of his advisers that she was a political liability because of the supposedly anti-Catholic speech she had made against Al Smith during the 1928 Presidential campaign. But Hoover recognized that she had done valuable work in his behalf and he had rejected her offer to resign when he took office. He now accepted her resignation "with deep regret" and with high praise. "In view of the very great opportunity which has come to you for re-entry into private practice of the law, and in view of the seven [sic] years of sacrifice you have already made to public service, I do not feel that I am justified in again asking you to reconsider. . . . The position you have held has been one of the most difficult in the government, and one which could not have been conducted with such distinguished success by one of less legal ability and moral courage."

The opportunity the President mentioned was an offer by a firm called the Aviation Corporation, representing the aircraft industry, to become its Washington counsel and to undertake for it "a comprehensive study of national and state laws affecting the industry." This offer did not represent Mrs. Willebrandt's only lucrative prospect in private practice. The grape and wine industry of California, her home state, was understandably depressed because of prohibition, and very anxious to secure government assistance in solving some of its problems. Since the closing of the wineries nine years earlier, the industry had been able to develop a national market for about 80,000 railroad carloads of grapes to be used mostly in home wine-making, but this left yearly surpluses of several hundred thousand tons. California grape growers were desperately seeking a new way to sell this product. The industry's chief spokesman, Thomas C. C. Gregory of San Francisco, was a friend of President Hoover and also a friend of Mrs. Willebrandt.

Shortly after his March 4 inauguration, Hoover had called a special session of Congress to pass legislation he hoped would relieve some growing indications of economic hardship among farmers. One of the measures passed during this session was the Agricultural Marketing Act, which created the Federal Farm Board, a body empowered to issue government loans for farm cooperative groups.

The President approved this legislation June 15 and on July 15 the Farm Board opened for business with another California friend of Mr. Hoover, C. C. Teague, as one of its members. Two weeks later, July 29, a California organization called the Grape Control Board Ltd. was founded under the direction of Thomas C. C. Gregory, for the purpose of seeking a government subsidy. This group, which represented 20,000 grape growers and 85 percent of California's yearly product, then launched a corporation called Fruit Industries Inc., for the purpose of selling more grapes.

Mrs. Willebrandt, shortly thereafter, was engaged on a confidential basis to represent Fruit Industries Inc. With President Hoover's two other friends, Gregory and Teague, she completed a trio which proved remarkably effective in convincing the Farm Board of the needs of the California grape growers. Their industry soon received the first of several multimillion-dollar loans from the federal government.

Fruit Industries Inc. then announced the introduction of a new product onto the market, a liquid grape concentrate called Vine-Glo, which was available in sherry, port, tokay, muscatel, reisling, moselle, sauterne, burgundy, and champagne flavors. Vine-Glo contained no alcohol, but if the buyer added water and sugar to it, and allowed it to stand for sixty days, he would have wine with an alcoholic potency of about 12 percent. Vine-Glo was soon selling in all but one of the forty-eight states, priced between ten dollars and thirty dollars per keg, without interference from federal prohibition authorities. Mrs. Willebrandt had made an auspicious entrance into private law practice.

WASHINGTON D.C., May 14, 1930. The administration bill transferring prohibition enforcement from the Treasury to the Department of Justice was passed by the Senate today without a rollcall after an amendment by Senator Millard Tydings (Maryland Democrat) to eliminate wood alcohol as an adulterant of industrial alcohol was defeated by a vote of 54 to 19.

Senator Tydings offered a number of other minor amendments but centered his fight on his proposal to substitute nauseous drugs approved by the American Medical Society for wood alcohol as an adulterant. Senator Felix Hebert (Rhode Island Republican) in charge of the bill, approved the intent of the amendment but said it had no part in the transfer bill. He assured Senator Tydings that the Judiciary Committee would promptly report a separate bill if one was offered.

Senator Tydings proposed that pyridine, malachite green, or giethylpthalate be used as a substitute for wood alcohol.

The debate became intense after Senator Morris Sheppard (Texas Democrat) denied that wood alcohol was used in quantities sufficient to kill.

Senator Tydings declared that the arrogance of the drys was

increasing the wet sentiment in the country. "The very fact is," he said, "that the government, driven by fanatics who have no regard for human life in the furtherance of this law, advocates the death penalty for doing no greater thing than drinking a pint of liquor."[11]

Chapter 14

When Mrs. Helen McCallum sailed from New York for Europe with Bishop James Cannon, Jr., in late June of 1930, it was her second such trip with him and she was traveling as his secretary. She had also accompanied him to the Holy Land in February of the previous year. Their lives since then had been so complicated the bishop scarcely had time to carry on his prohibition work.

Shortly after their return from that earlier trip, in June 1929, several wet newspapers had begun attacking the bishop by publishing the full story of his stock market transactions with Kable and Company. Recognizing this whole matter as a "purely political" maneuver "to destroy or weaken the effect of my opposition to wet Tammany candidate Smith" (who was looming as a Presidential threat again in 1932), Cannon had strode defiantly and aggressively through the whole storm of investigation and accusation which followed. Even when one of the Kable partners testified during bankruptcy hearings that except in one transaction the bishop had been exclusively a speculator, Cannon had refused to admit he had gambled in the market or done anything else inconsistent with the moral teachings of his church.

To prove that this impertinent invasion of his private affairs could not distract his attention from his most cherished public crusade, he had led the struggle that autumn to amend the Volstead Act, making the purchase of liquor as much a crime as its sale, and thus exposing all drinkers to the danger of jail sentences. "The purpose of the Eighteenth Amendment," he had pointed out, "is to prohibit the traffic in intoxicating liquor, the use of which causes men to lose control of their physical, intellectual and moral power. . . . The time has come to put the buyer and seller on exactly the same footing before the law."

While the 1928 election had made the current Congress the driest in history, its members were not prepared to take such a drastic step, especially under Cannon's leadership. Belligerent as he had been in proclaiming his righteousness, he could not stem the criticism leveled against him by some of his own dry Methodist colleagues as well as the wet press. Even President Hoover, who apparently hadn't been disturbed by Cannon's racism and religious bigotry, who had invited him to lunch at the White House several times during the first months of his administration, now began to shy away from direct contact with him.

The bishop, in spite of this, did not shy away from Hoover, who was, no doubt, the first Republican he had ever endorsed. When the President submitted the preliminary Wickersham report to Congress in January 1930, Cannon bitterly attacked the document's critics. Nicholas Murray Butler, the outspokenly wet president of Columbia University, had called it "pathetic evidence that Washington, like the Emperor Nero, fiddled while Rome is burning." Ignoring the literary deficiency of the great educator's remark, Cannon had accused him of "egotistical arrogance." But Butler was an old, tired target. The bishop found a newer, more attractive one when Mrs. Pauline Sabin also belittled the first Wickersham report, stating she could find "nothing of value" in it.

Mrs. Sabin's seven-month-old Women's Organization for National Prohibition Reform, now about 60,000 strong and still in the midst of its initial membership drive, had begun with some success to publicize itself by provoking the drys into controversy. The drys, increasingly concerned about the group's potential, couldn't resist giving it serious and angry attention. Bishop Cannon was especially obliging in this respect. Describing Mrs. Sabin as "the leader of a group of society women opposed to prohibition," he declared that she "utterly fails to recognize that there is morally no distinction between those whom she contemptuously brands as 'prohibition's criminal offspring, the bootlegger, smuggler and the racketeer,' and those who she declares 'in their resentment of the law's invasion of their personal liberties will continue in their every-day lives, deliberately and completely to disregard the law's very existence.' "[1]

With that stinging rebuke, he felt he could dismiss Mrs. Sabin from his mind. He had other women making more urgent demands upon his attention. In the spring of 1930, a personal problem had arisen between Bishop Cannon and Helen McCallum because, even though he was paying the rent on her apartment at 210 E. Sixty-eighth Street in Manhattan, he was now a widower, famous, popular, and well traveled, which meant he had frequent opportunities to meet other women. On April 12, when he was absent from Mrs. McCallum touring Africa and Europe as part of his ecclesiastical duties, New York newspapers received a United Press dispatch from Huntsville, Alabama to the effect that Bishop Cannon had married Mrs. Mary McCoy of Athens, Alabama.[2] Mrs. McCoy's sister-in-law said she had "indirect word of the wedding," and a niece said, "The whole family knows that my aunt and Bishop Cannon are married."

As it happened, Mrs. McCoy was also traveling abroad, and a similar report of their marriage had surfaced a few weeks earlier, only to be denied by the bishop in a dispatch from Berlin. When Mrs. McCallum, in New York, read this second dispatch, she did not wait for a second denial from her traveling sweetheart. In the presence of three New York *Evening Journal* reporters, she signed an affidavit that very day, describing how she had met the bishop and tracing the progress of their two-year relationship. Two days later, on April 14, she was still so angry that she substantiated her account by taking one of the reporters to her bank and producing for him, from a safety deposit box, a sheaf of letters the bishop had written to her.

Fortunately for the bishop, he was able to return from Europe within a week, and on April 21, after assuring Mrs. McCallum he had not married Mrs. McCoy, he wrote for her another affidavit which she signed, repudiating the first one. The bishop's love life became serene once more, but his religious, fiscal and political woes continued to proliferate.

Because many of his fellow Methodists remained skeptical of his innocence, Cannon was even subjected to a secret hearing before his denomination's Committee on Episcopacy at Dallas in May 1930. After testifying for three hours, he had convinced these colleagues that there were no grounds for instituting ecclesiastical proceedings against him.

No sooner had he cleared this hurdle than another loomed. In the spring, Rep. George H. Tinkham, an aggressively wet Republican from Massachusetts, had charged that New York insurance executive Edwin C. Jameson handed over to Cannon $65,300 in cash during the 1928 Presidential campaign, that this was actually Republican money filtered through Jameson to Cannon so it could not be traced, and that Cannon had reported receiving only $17,000 of it. Due to Tinkham's pressure, this matter soon came under investigation by the Senate Lobby Committee, which convened in late May primarily to question the current president of the Association Against the Prohibition Amendment, Henry H. Curran. Four of the committee's five members were staunchly dry, and the group was as reluctant to question Cannon as it was eager to question Curran. Realizing the strong political position in which this placed him, Cannon displayed open defiance from the moment he entered the hearing room on June 3. Walking with the aid of a crutch because he had recently turned his ankle, and looking tired because he had just arrived in Washington from his ecclesiastical inquisition in Dallas, he nevertheless showed no lack of energy as he proceeded to flail the assembled Senators.

He began by asserting that the whole affair was a Roman Catholic attempt to discredit him because of his crusade for prohibition. When acting chairman Senator Thomas Walsh of Montana (a Catholic dry whom the bishop had once discussed supporting for the Presidency) took gentle exception to his remark, Cannon only partially softened it. "I do not charge you, Senator, with persecution," he said, allowing the accusation to stand against other Catholics. When the questioning began, he refused flatly to explain his activities or his financial arrangements as head of the anti-Smith campaign in the South. As for the details of how he had spent the unaccounted $48,300 he had received from Jameson (over and above the $17,000 he had reported), he told the senators that was entirely his business. "You'll never see that account," he said.

On the second day of the hearing he was equally implacable, rejecting with open scorn all questions about his 1928 political activities and expenditures. That night he made a lengthy statement to the press which contained an unverifiable accounting for the $48,300 in vague round numbers and without receipts or itemization. Incomplete and unsatisfactory as this information was, he made it perfectly clear that no one need expect any further disclosures about the matter, and that in divulging this much to the public, he would still refuse to divulge it to the Senate Lobby Committee.

"In my statement to the committee," he reminded the reporters, "I said I would make a further statement to the press concerning the Jameson contribution and expenditures. . . .

"I refused, however, to admit the right of the committee to single me out and require a report from me concerning my activities. . . . I insisted then and insist now that this singling out of myself and of the Virginia Anti-Smith Democrats because we fought the wet Tammany candidate is a deliberate, intolerable infringement upon the rights of American citizens."

When he appeared before the committee the next day, he was more confident than ever of his dominion over it. All the members except Blaine of Wisconsin were from dry states and some of them had received contributions from the Anti-Saloon League. Instead of answering questions at this session, Bishop Cannon simply read a short statement against his persecutors, ending with a challenge which could not be defined as anything but outright contempt of Congress.

"I must respectfully state," he said, "that having answered all questions addressed to me by the committee on which I volunteered to appear as a witness, I shall now withdraw as a voluntary witness. If the committee desires to subpoena me, that is its right."

Thereupon he picked up his crutch and as the crowded galleries erupted into a mixed chorus of cheers and catcalls, turned his back upon his inquisitors, walking deliberately toward the door.

Senator Walsh, a man who disliked raising his voice, had to do so in order to be heard. "You take your own course," he said, "but we have not excused you. Senator Blaine wishes to question you."

Bishop Cannon glanced back without slowing his pace and the crowd quieted in anticipation of his parting remark. "I will be at my office," he said, "if the committee wishes to subpoena me."

In the days that followed, it became evident that the bishop was a better judge of Senators than was the press. Newspapers and magazines throughout the country predicted he would be cited for contempt. But the committee didn't even ask him to return. Instead, it initiated a very vigorous probe of the Association Against the Prohibition Amendment.

Having confounded his ecclesiastical and political critics, Bishop Cannon could once again turn his attention to his sweetheart, Mrs. McCallum. It seemed likely he would one day marry her, but even when they sailed back to Europe together two weeks later, the bishop's friends did not expect the ceremony to take place for some time. The prospective bride's health had been delicate and he was planning to leave her in England while he took a side trip to South America.

A few days after they reached London, while they were staying at the home of Sir Henry Lunn, editor of the *Review of the Churches* and an old friend of the bishop, Mrs. McCallum surprisingly decided she was quite well enough to be married and to accompany the bishop on his South American trip. Because the decision was so sudden, Sir Henry had to use his influence with the Archbishop of Canterbury in securing a special license for the couple to marry immediately. The ceremony was performed July 15 at Christ Church on Westminster Bridge Road, a towering edifice built in 1876 partly with American funds as a memorial, ironically, to Abraham Lincoln, a man who was no hero to Bishop Cannon. Sir Henry and another friend of the bridegroom were the only witnesses. Thereafter, the happy couple boarded the steamship *Arianza* en route to Madeira and Rio de Janiero.

An unfortunate development arose to mar their honeymoon. While they were in Brazil, the bishop received word of serious troubles to come. Four ministers in his church had filed with the College of Bishops formal charges relating to his "character and conduct." The charges included immorality (specifically adultery in his relations with Mrs. McCallum), bucket shop gambling, flour hoarding (when he was president of Blackstone [Virginia] College for Girls during the World War), and gross moral turpitude.

The day after he learned of these charges, Bishop Cannon and his bride cut short their honeymoon to return to New York. When their ship docked, so many reporters and photographers crowded around them that the flashbulbs reduced Mrs. Cannon to hysteria. The bishop did not lose his composure. He made it clear that in his opinion the action taken against him was invalid because it had not followed the rules laid down by the Methodist Discipline.

As the campaign for the New York governorship approached, the stock market crash of the previous October had already been followed by astonishing increases in business failures and unemployment. Still, the most prominent 1930 political issue in the state was prohibition. The Democratic leadership was openly wet as usual except for one important man, Governor Franklin D. Roosevelt, who was to be the party's candidate for reelection. Everyone was aware that Eleanor Roosevelt was a convinced dry but no one seemed to know exactly where her husband stood on the issue. For the entire previous decade he had staunchly supported Al Smith in one election after another, twice delivering presidential nominating speeches for the "Happy Warrior" at national conventions, without once announcing his own attitudes about liquor. Always artful at dodging questions, Roosevelt even kept Smith guessing about the matter, a circumstance the former governor did not appreciate.

The two men, never close personal friends despite their long-time political solidarity, had become almost distant since Roosevelt's ascendancy to the governorship. Smith, understandably bitter as a result of the bigotry in 1928 which helped keep him out of the White House, may have resented the fact that his protegé had outpolled him in New York, winning the governorship while Smith failed even to carry his own state against Hoover. It was in the dry, Protestant northern areas that Smith did poorly. When Roosevelt carried many of those areas, Smith may have felt it was because Roosevelt was a Protestant, whereas it may actually have been because Roosevelt had never acknowledged himself a wet. Smith, having declared himself so openly for repeal, may also have resented, even in 1928, Roosevelt's refusal to do so.

Despite Smith's apparent reservations about Roosevelt, he had volunteered all possible help to the governor who succeeded him, and if he was still resentful of Roosevelt in 1930 it might be because the latter, wishing to prove himself his own man, had insisted on getting along without Smith's help. Publicly they were still friends and Al Smith was gracious enough during the Democratic state convention to insist on delivering the renomination speech for Roosevelt.

"No man," Smith declared, "has accomplished more in the office he occupied than Franklin D. Roosevelt. He has a clear brain and a big heart. For his humanity, the love and devotion he has shown the poor, the sick and the afflicted, Almighty God has showered down on his head the choicest graces and His choicest blessings."

To oppose Roosevelt, the Republicans nominated United States Attorney Charles Tuttle, an able prosecutor with a reputation as a shrewd politician. Aware of the governor's reluctance to occupy wet ground, and aware also that this was where a growing number of urban Republicans plus most of the Democrats were now to be found, Tuttle decided it would be wise to move in and preempt. But unfortunately for him, he was up against an even shrewder politician. Roosevelt, getting wind of Tuttle's intentions, quickly set about beating him to it.

From his Hyde Park estate on the Hudson he sent an open letter September 9 to his friend Senator Robert Wagner, who was campaigning for him in New York City. In the letter, Roosevelt wrote:

(. . . It is my belief that in the state of New York an overwhelming public opinion is opposed to the Eighteenth Amendment. The crux of the matter is that the Eighteenth Amendment has not furthered the cause of a greater temperance in our population, but on the other hand (quoting from language used in a resolution adopted by the American Legion) it has "fostered excessive drinking of strong intoxicants" and has "led to corruption and hypocrisy," has brought about "disregard for law and order" and has "flooded the country with untaxed and illicit liquor." I personally share this opinion.)

Roosevelt then went on to suggest that a new amendment be promulgated to supercede the Eighteenth, allowing each state to decide on the legality of liquor within its borders. When this letter became public, making Roosevelt's views unequivocally clear, Tuttle saw his best chance of victory slipping away. Roosevelt in a few words had deprived him of his only hope of winning Democratic votes and at the same time had made a strong bid to take from him a sizable bloc of urban Republican votes. Mindful of wet groups like the Association Against the Prohibition Amendment and Mrs. Pauline Sabin's companion force, Tuttle decided he had better dive into the wet stream even though his opponent had got there before him. Lamely he followed the governor in calling for the repeal of the Eighteenth Amendment. Even as he did so he must have wondered with sinking heart how the upstate dry Republicans would react to his announcement.

Tuttle was not left in suspense long. The upstate Republicans, at a rump convention, nominated a third candidate on a "Law Enforce-ment" ticket. The result was devastating. Though Tuttle tried to capitalize on some new Democratic Party scandals which were just becoming public, there was no suggestion that they involved Roose-velt, who acted upon them deftly by asking the Appellate Division of the state Supreme Court to investigate. On November 4, Roosevelt won reelection by a plurality of 725,000 votes over Tuttle, a larger margin than Al Smith had ever been able to compile.

On the following day, Roosevelt's campaign manager, James A. Farley, said in a victory statement, "I do not see how Mr. Roosevelt can escape becoming the next presidential nominee of his party, even if no one should raise a finger to bring it about."

When Farley told Roosevelt about this statement, the governor did not rebuke him. "Whatever you said, Jim, is all right with me."[3]

Under President Hoover's guidance, federal agents during the 1929–30 fiscal year had arrested 68,173 persons for liquor law viola-tions and had confiscated 8,633 vehicles plus 64 rum-running boats. The personnel of the Bureau of Prohibition had been improved by new requirements that all agents pass civil service examinations. And Mabel Walker Willebrandt's replacement, G. Aaron Youngquist, an-nounced that 206 more liquor law cases had been brought to the bar of justice than in the previous year. Anyone reading these figures might get the impression that Hoover was making progress in his campaign for enforcement. When he sent a message of felicitation to the Women's Christian Temperance Union convention in Houston, the women stood and cheered him for ten minutes. But despite the statistics and the W.C.T.U., the nation's liquor traffic continued una-bated and wet sentiment was increasing. In addition Hoover had lost the support of numerous drys because his economic policies had not yet ended the depression which followed the market crash of 1929.

There was so much clamor now about the economic situation, the unemployment, the breadlines, the hunger in the streets that Hoover had already gone even farther than he thought proper toward reliev-ing the suffering and anxiety. At year's end he had signed a bill which he hoped would stimulate business by appropriating $116 million for the construction industry. The same day he had signed another pro-viding $45 million in drought relief for farmers, and two days later he had approved a supplementary appropriation of $150 million for the Federal Farm Board, which agency had already loaned $250 million to large farm cooperatives throughout the country. (These loans now included almost $20 million to Mabel Walker Willebrandt's California grape growing clients.) But Hoover's measures had not so far prodded the lethargic economy. The hard times continued and millions of Americans were now suffering real privations. The Democrats in Congress were taking advantage of this situation by demanding a federal relief bill which would provide direct payments to the needy. Hoover was not inclined to listen to such a blatant cry for federal funds. Relief was the responsibility of state and local agencies. It would be improper for the federal government to give handouts to the poor. He even had some reservations about offering federal money to help businesses, although he had been able, in some instances, to stifle such reservations.

In his second Annual Message to Congress, December 2, he had declared: "Economic depression cannot be cured by legislative action or executive pronouncement. Economic wounds must be healed by the action of the cells of the economic body—the producers and consumers themselves. Recovery can be expedited and its effects mitigated by cooperative action. That cooperation requires that every individual should sustain faith and courage; that each should maintain his self-reliance; that each and every one should search for methods of improving his business or service. . . . The best contribution of government lies in encouragement of this voluntary cooperation in the community."

Hoover had said this because it made sense to him. Basically he agreed with Calvin Coolidge and most of his fellow Republicans that the best government was the least government. Except, of course, in matters like prohibition, which deserved maximum governmental regulation. If Hoover felt any inconsistency in supporting governmental interference with people's drinking habits while refusing to augment their eating habits, he never expressed it, even when his enemies accused him of trying to keep people from eating as well as drinking. It was distressing to him to see how many people thought the federal government had a duty to help feed the hungry. Hoover was confident prosperity would soon return and such people would understand he had chosen the wise course by allowing the economy to remedy itself. Until then he would continue to pursue sound economic policies, and as for those drys who seemed to be defecting because they disagreed with his economics, they could be expected to support him once more when the depression was over.

On January 18, 1931, George Wickersham, Chairman of the National Commission on Law Observance and Enforcement, delivered to President Hoover the final report of the Commission, henceforth known as the Wickersham report. As Hoover had expected from earlier progress reports, it was not the kind of document he envisioned when the group was formed. Many of the commissioners, thought to be dry when he appointed them in May, 1929, had apparently become wetter month by month as they dove deeper into the prohibition probe.

It is not possible to determine exactly how much the President knew about the report before it was submitted to him in its final form although it is known he had received the first findings a whole year earlier, in January, 1930. Neither is it possible to determine whether he was responsible for any changes in the report before its release to Congress on the 19th, but it is evident that if he did make any changes, he didn't make as many as he would have liked.

In an apparent effort to prepare the public for the report and to shape general reaction to it, Hoover sent a message about it to Congress before sending the document itself. His message was as reassuring as possible to his dry supporters:

> . . . The commission considers that the conditions of enforcement of the prohibition laws in the country as a whole are unsatisfactory, but it reports that the Federal participation in enforcement has shown continued improvement . . . and it outlines further possible improvement. It calls attention to the urgency of obedience to law by our citizens, and to the imperative necessity for greater assumption and performance by State and local governments of their share of responsibilities. . . .
>
> It recommends that further and more effective efforts be made to enforce the laws. . . .
>
> The commission, by a large majority, does not favor the repeal of the Eighteenth Amendment as a method of cure for the inherent abuses of the liquor traffic. I am in accord with this view. . . .
>
> I do, however, see serious objections to, and therefore must not be understood as recommending, the commission's proposed revision of the Eighteenth Amendment which is suggested by them for possible consideration at some future time if the continued effort at enforcement should not

prove successful. My own duty and that of all executive officials is clear
—to enforce the law with all the means at our disposal. . . .

Only in the latter part of the message did the President indicate any
dissatisfaction with the report. When the report itself reached Congress and the public, reaction was somewhat similar, though on a
lesser scale, to the public bemusement forty-three years later when
Richard M. Nixon released a message describing six of his office tape
recordings, then released transcripts of the tapes which didn't fit the
description. The Wickersham report, many decided, didn't quite say
what President Hoover said it said.

The report's general "conclusions and recommendations" seemed
to fit his message fairly well. The commission as a whole did declare
itself "opposed to the repeal of the Eighteenth Amendment," "opposed to the restoration in any manner of the legalized saloon," and
to the "manufacture and sale of light wine and beer." But when one
read the reports of the individual members and their individual
recommendations, it was difficult to determine how the commission
had arrived at its general recommendations. Two of the eleven members were in favor of immediate, outright repeal. Five suggested a
revision of the amendment which would be tantamount to repeal
because it would restore legal liquor under control of a government
monopoly corporation. Two others, convinced that the amendment
was not working, believed it should be given one more chance but only
after extensive revision. Of the eleven members, no more than two
were willing to say the Eighteenth Amendment should be left in force
as it stood.

President Hoover was startled by the next day's reactions. Several
newspapers suggested that if the commission's conclusions were at
odds with those of its members, some "outside pressure" must have
influenced the general report, and that "outside pressure" could have
come only from President Hoover. Senator Millard Tydings of Maryland proposed a Senate inquiry "to determine how the commission
reached its conclusions and if it received suggestions from outside."
Two Congressmen proposed legislation to repeal the Eighteenth
Amendment and one of them, Fiorello LaGuardia of New York, also
proposed an inquiry "to give the public the whole story of prohibition."

Senator William E. Borah of Idaho, one of the most influential drys in Congress and leader of the debate in support of the harshly punitive Jones Law, made no effort to conceal his disgust at the published results of the nineteen-month investigation. "The torpedoing of the report of the commission," he said, "by the individual views of the members of the commission leaves the report without any force or effect in the ultimate solution of the problem." Most of the drys, however, including Senator Wesley L. Jones of Washington, who introduced the Jones Law, were pleased with President Hoover's reaction to the report even if they were disturbed by the report itself. "The President's message I liked very much," Jones said. "I like the clear-cut, definite stand he takes."

Chairman Wickersham felt constrained to deny that the President had anything to do with the inexplicable differences between the individual and general reports. "At no time has the President in any manner attempted to influence the recommendations of this commission," he said.

The drys may have believed him. The wets did not. They snickered delightedly at the whole fiasco and in both houses of the New York legislature resolutions were introduced calling for repeal. These resolutions were supported, perhaps even instigated, by Governor Franklin D. Roosevelt, an increasingly serious possibility for the Democratic Presidential nomination in 1932. When asked about the resolutions, Roosevelt said, "They are all right with me. Any constitutional proposal that carries out the party platform is all right with me."

The evident effect of the Wickersham report was to damage the dry cause by showing that even a dry group of moderate conservatives, after a careful study of prohibition, had to admit it wasn't working. The effect of President Hoover's reaction to the report was to pin him inescapably to the dry cause. The White House, in an effort to deemphasize this result, released quotations from "a close friend" of the President insisting he had not "closed his mind" on revision of the Eighteenth Amendment. But by this time the damage had been done and it bode ill for Hoover's future because the wets were now definitely on the offensive. Their gain of seventy House and four Senate seats in the 1930 election had given them momentum at a time when the drys were faltering, partly because their most dynamic leader, Bishop James Cannon, Jr., was embroiled in so much peripheral controversy.

Even more important, the wets were now able to flood the country with propaganda. Hundreds and thousands of businessmen and industrialists, at one time hopeful that prohibition would make their employees more sober and efficient, were now disillusioned with its results and were contributing financially to the repeal drive. They were also sending their wives out to join Pauline Sabin's rapidly expanding group, the Women's Organization for National Prohibition Reform. With 300,000 insistent women on its rolls, the WONPR could no longer be ignored, as President Hoover soon learned.

In the spring of 1931, Mayor Bill Thompson was not the same man he had been when he returned victoriously to City Hall four years earlier, and Chicago was not the same city. Here as elsewhere, the gaunt reality of the depression had subdued the boozy, festive atmosphere of the '20s, and people were more worried about bread than beer. Relief rolls increased. Property values fell, diminishing the city's income from taxes, bringing it perilously close to bankruptcy, and confronting civil servants, policemen, firemen, and school teachers with the possibility of working for no pay.

When Thompson had decided, in December 1930, that he would run again, he must have known he would face these problems for which he was not responsible, plus several others of his own making. He had been so indolent that his machine had virtually ceased to function and so stubborn that he had lost many of the friends he needed in his own party. Only thirty-three of the fifty Republican ward committeemen were willing to support him. His nervous breakdown had plunged him into a lethargic funk which was intensified by his diminishing popularity.

His tolerant liaisons with the bootlegging gangs, the Capone syndicate in particular, brought Thompson new embarrassment with each new outburst of violence. Since the St. Valentine's Day massacre of February 1929, the people of Chicago had finally begun to grow weary of gang warfare. Even their hero-worship of Al Capone was fading, perhaps because they thought he had gone too far in that Valentine celebration, or perhaps because he too was now having his troubles. Capone's knack of staying above or beyond the law, a knack many people seemed to envy and admire, was beginning to fail him. During a visit to Philadelphia in May 1929, he had been picked up on a concealed-weapons charge, and instead of getting the two-or-three month sentence he expected and might have welcomed (since Bugs Moran and other North Side survivors of St. Valentine's Day were on his trail), he was hit with a one-year sentence of which he had to serve ten months. On his return to Chicago, he found the police, goaded by public opinion, somewhat less cooperative than they had been. They quickly introduced harassment tactics against him which were not necessarily legal but were annoyingly effective. Whenever he or his men appeared on the streets, they were in danger of arrest for vagrancy, and even if they beat the rap, they might be picked up on a similar charge the next day.

The depression had also hurt the liquor business and diminished gang income, while a squad of federal agents dubbed "The Untouchables" had at least increased the cost of beer production by raiding and smashing several Capone breweries. But the most serious difficulty Capone faced was the intensified snoopiness of the Internal Revenue Service. Capone's organization had grossed an estimated $400 million since he assumed control of it in 1925, yet he had never filed an income tax return. The I.R.S. had first manifested its curiosity about this phenomenon in 1927, and the election of President Hoover had produced a new impetus to persuade Capone that he should have corrected his oversight.

Hoover was so exasperated by the impunity with which Chicago's supreme ganglord defied the law that he assumed a personal role in the matter. Because of his belief in physical fitness, he began inviting members of his Cabinet to the White House every morning for exercise sessions during which they tossed heavy medicine balls back and forth to each other. Hoover would begin these sessions by throwing the ball to Treasury Secretary Andrew Mellon and, with it, the invariable question, "Have you got that fellow Capone yet?" He would then end the exercise with a final reminder to Mellon, "Remember, now, I want that man Capone in jail." Mellon had forcefully relayed this instruction to the Prohibition Bureau and the I.R.S., both of which were under his supervision.

By 1930, the I.R.S. had already put Capone's brother, Ralph, in prison for tax evasion, and was prosecuting several of his men. Federal agents were investigating Capone himself so intensely that he was prepared to take drastic steps in his efforts to thwart them. He said to one of them, after a tough session of interrogation, "How's your wife? You be sure to take care of yourself."

In early June 1930, this same federal agent, Frank J. Wilson, received information that led him to think a Chicago *Tribune* crime reporter named Alfred "Jake" Lingle might have some very direct personal knowledge about Capone's finances. Wilson made an appointment to interview Lingle in Tribune Tower on the morning of June 10.⁴ At noon on the ninth, Lingle became the victim of Chicago's eleventh gang-style murder within a ten-day span. He was killed by a gunman who was either accompanying him or came up behind him as he walked through a crowded pedestrian tunnel under Michigan Avenue at Randolph Street.

In the first days after Lingle's death, the *Tribune* and all the other Chicago newspapers pronounced his killing a retaliation by gangsters against an honest reporter who had tried to expose them. But as the investigation continued, a new picture of Lingle emerged. Probers discovered he was exceedingly well connected for one whose newspaper job seemed so routine. He was simply an information gatherer for the *Tribune*. He didn't even write his own stories; he had never earned a byline. Yet he had developed first-name friendships with most of Chicago's important public officials. He was such a close friend and confidant of Mayor Thompson's current police commissioner, William P. Russell, that some insiders called him Chicago's unofficial police chief. At the same time, he was such a close friend of Al Capone he had several times been a guest at the gangster's Miami mansion, and he wore a diamond-studded belt buckle Capone had given him. Lingle had also managed, though his *Tribune* salary was $65 a week, to compile an income of at least $60,000 a year. In addition to the home on the West Side where he lived with his wife and two children, he kept a summer cottage at Long Beach, Indiana, and a suite in the world's largest hotel, the Stevens, on south Michigan Avenue. His Lincoln limousine was driven by a chauffeur. He vacationed in such places as Florida and Cuba. His stock portfolio was extensive, and when he went to a racetrack (which happened to be his destination the day he died), he often bet a thousand dollars on a single race.

Investigators quickly concluded from what they learned about Lingle that Al Capone, to whom he had become very useful in police, gambling, and political matters, was the principal source of his income, and that he, therefore, must have been quite well informed about certain sources of Capone's income. Perhaps this was why I.R.S. agent Wilson had arranged to interview Lingle June 10, 1930. Whether Capone, on learning of this scheduled interview, had arranged to preclude it is a matter of conjecture. But a short time later, within the hearing of an undercover government agent who had infiltrated his gang, Capone indicated he knew all the details of the murder, including the identity of the man who had fired the gun at Lingle's head.[5]

If Capone did kill Lingle, why should he have wanted to eliminate someone who had been so useful to him? No one but Capone could know for certain. It was possible, however, that Capone feared Lingle might betray him to the federal tax agents because, not being a gangster, he could hardly be counted upon to observe the gangster's rule of silence.

While the death of Lingle may have been opportune for Capone, it had not shaken the I.R.S. men from his trail. On March 13, 1931, at the height of Mayor Thompson's reelection campaign, a federal grand jury, after digesting all the information collected by the government agents, indicted Capone for income tax evasion.

By this time, the mayor's campaign had begun to droop and he couldn't understand why. Aware of his disadvantages, he still had confidence in his campaign methods. He had been certain that as soon as the Thompson bandwagon got into the streets of Chicago, the crowd would once more climb aboard, but he was finding now that people no longer laughed and cheered at his loud, rough-and-tumble antics. He continued, nevertheless, to pursue his old methods because he knew no others. He insulted not only his Democratic opponent, Cook County Board President Anton Cermak, but also all of Cermak's fellow Bohemian-Americans by asking his audiences, "Do you want a Bohunk for mayor?" And he accused Cermak of being a tool of England's King George V because one of Cermak's supporters was a founder of the World Bank. He also called Cermak "the biggest crook that ever ran for mayor," a title which Chicagoans, accustomed as they were to some very sizable crooks, considered laughably hyperbolic. Others had accused Cermak of feeding at the public trough during his long, upward career through Democratic ranks, but no one had been able to prove the charges.

While campaigning against Cermak, Thompson also lashed out against his old nemesis, and now Cermak supporter, the Chicago *Tribune*. In a pamphlet entitled "THE TRIBUNE SHADOW— Chicago's Greatest Curse," the mayor included a statement by the City Sealer in his administration, Daniel Serritella, who was also the president of Chicago's Newsboys' Union and an almost publicly avowed Capone factotum. The Serritella testament, dated February 14, 1931, purported to show that Capone was not a friend of Thompson but an ally of the *Tribune* and its publisher, Col. Robert R. McCormick. Serritella stated in the pamphlet:

A little over two years ago, Max Annenberg, director of circulation of the Chicago *Tribune*, called me on the telephone and said he wanted to meet me at the Drake Hotel and have a talk with me. I asked him what he wanted to talk about and he told me the *Tribune* was having some trouble with their chauffeurs and drivers. . . . They were going to call a strike . . . for the following Saturday and he wanted to get someone to talk to the executive committee of the chauffeurs and drivers union to see if the strike could not be called off. . . .

I told him that as president of the newsboys' union there was nothing I could do. Then Max Annenberg said he would call up Capone and see if he could do anything in the matter, which he did and made an appointment with Capone to meet him in the *Tribune*'s office. I attended this meeting, at which Capone agreed to use his influence to stop the strike, which prevented the same. Max Annenberg then brought in Robert McCormick, editor and publisher of the Chicago *Tribune*, and introduced McCormick to Capone. McCormick thanked Capone for calling off the strike for the *Tribune* and said, "You know you are famous like Babe Ruth. We can't help printing things about you, but I will see that the *Tribune* gives you a square deal."

McCormick, when he was told of this statement, offered a quite different version of his only meeting with Capone. "I arrived late at a publishers' meeting," he said. "Capone walked in with some of his hoodlums. I threw him out and after that I traveled around in an armored car with one or two bodyguards. Capone didn't settle anything."

A week before the election, Thompson had reason to regret drawing Serritella so openly into his campaign. On April 1, State's Attorney John Swanson sent a squad of his men to raid Serritella's City Hall office. They came away with stacks of records indicating that the City Sealer had a cozy arrangement with many of Chicago's merchants, allowing them to short-weight Chicago's housewives. Here was a charge which, even if untrue, could hardly be refuted before election day.

"Your Democratic-Republican State's Attorney stepped on the gas this morning," Thompson said after the raid. "Well, watch the city administration go into high. They have invited it and they are going to get a fight, and I hope our people will be benefited when the end tells the truth."

He advised Serritella, who was also a state senator, to introduce a senate bill calling for an investigation of Swanson. More positive measures than this were needed to placate Chicago's housewives, most of whom were prepared to believe the worst about a city official with undeniable Capone connections. Though Thompson climaxed his campaign with a frantic tour of the city, shaking thousands of hands and talking to every crowd he could gather, he awoke on election day without confidence. Cermak was formidable, not because his speeches were more reasonable than those of Mayor Dever four years earlier, but because, unlike Dever, he was a clever politician with a united Democratic Party behind him. And on the critical issue of prohibition, he had made it clear he was as wet as Thompson.

At 7:15 election night, partial returns indicated Thompson was already 150,000 votes behind his challenger. In his headquarters on the fifth floor of City Hall, the mayor refused to concede defeat. "We are not ready yet," he said, then disappeared into the office of the Assistant Corporation Counsel, where he was separated by guards from all but his closest advisers and a few newsmen. He sat slumped in the room's biggest chair, the only one big enough to hold his prodigious bulk, with his soft, fat hands on a desk in front of him and his eyes cast down. His usual thick cigar was in his mouth and sometimes, when he removed it, tobacco juice drooled down his chin. Though he made a few attempts at wisecracks, there was no real jollity in him tonight. He was an exhausted, beaten man. At about ten oclock, when he was almost 200,000 votes behind, he made a weary concession speech on the radio.

"The people of Chicago have spoken," he said. "I cheerfully abide by their decision. I congratulate you [Mr. Cermak] on your victory."

In a low, solemn voice, he announced the only plans he had for his future. "I will redouble my efforts for the completion of the waterways [from Chicago to the Atlantic and the Gulf of Mexico], to bring to Chicago a greater prosperity and work for the unemployed. To this end I have chartered the Mississippi river steamship *Cape Girardeau* and will leave on a tour of the Illinois, Mississippi, Ohio, and Tennessee Rivers Thursday.

"I invite those Chicagoans who are interested to join with me on this trip. I shall continue to uphold the teachings of George Washington and fight foreign entanglements."

The excursion down the inland waterways to New Orleans had been advertised before the election as a "triumphal victory tour," and hundreds of people had reserved space on the *Cape Girardeau*. But two days after the election, when the *Cape Girardeau* steamed south from Peru, Illinois, Thompson was accompanied by only fifty of his followers rather than the "hundreds of leading business and professional men and public officials" who had been expected to make the trip. Instead of an entire train, one car had been sufficient to carry the excursionists from Chicago to Peru. As the few passengers straggled aboard, several of them asked, "Where's the gang?" There was no answer because there was no longer a Thompson "gang." Big Bill Thompson's power in Chicago politics was gone for all time, and so were most of his friends.

One old friend still remembered him, however. Minutes before the Rock Island train pulled out of Chicago for Peru, two men loaded a cargo of heavy brown parcels aboard the special car. A knowledgeable spectator on the platform called it "Capone's bouquet of bourbon for the wake."

When Pauline Sabin and her associates in the Women's Organization for National Prohibition Reform scheduled their second annual convention at Washington's Mayflower Hotel on April 14, 1931, they expected about five hundred delegates to appear. Actually, eight hundred women arrived from thirty-three states that morning. But Mrs. Sabin had hoped for an overflow and was ready for it.[6] She had reserved the Mayflower's largest auditorium, the Conference Hall, and had stationed a corps of young page girls inside and outside, waiting to be helpful. To avoid confusion in the corridors, she had arranged for each of the state leaders to gather her delegates at designated places and march them to the hall under state banners. One result of her meticulous planning was that even the first session began on time.

To make all the delegates feel they were participating, without turning the plenary sessions into endless, unmanageable debates, Mrs. Sabin had made certain every delegate was placed on at least one committee where she could talk as much as she wished. "Please don't hesitate to have full discussions," she told the committee chairmen. "That's what you're here for." By encouraging unlimited talk in the committees she hoped to prevent it in the full sessions, and she succeeded.

She herself opened the convention with some wry comments on the recently released Wickersham Commission recommendations.

"The separate statements of all but one of its eleven members," she said, "compose a document which should be adopted as the handbook of the antiprohibitionists. Though by some feat of Japanese sword-swallowing, the commission managed in its summing up as a unit to eat its own words, nevertheless for the findings which it spread upon the record and for the plain demand of ten of its eleven members for repeal or revision, we owe it a debt of gratitude."

Mrs. August Belmont followed with another short speech in which she said, "I have a passionate resentment of the amount of time and attention that this subject is taking from the American people. There is only one way, however, to move it out of the center of the picture. . . . I believe this organization has a very real mission to perform in doing that."

Within an hour the committees were at work giving the delegates their chance to talk while Mrs. Sabin and the other leaders got into a more private discussion of methods to gain maximum attention for the group, especially during its convention. Several days earlier, as it happened, President Hoover had welcomed to the White House a few prominent dry women. It was suggested that he might therefore feel obliged to meet some women representing the opposition. Mrs. Sabin was skeptical. She had not considered asking for a reception at the White House, she said later, "because our purpose is the repeal of the Eighteenth Amendment and Mr. Hoover has said several times he is opposed to repeal." However, some of the women from Massachusetts believed they could get an invitation from the President, and they were women whose judgments on the subject could hardly be ignored. One of them, Mrs. Robert Lovett, had been Massachusetts chairman of the Women's Committee for Hoover in 1928. Another, Mrs. Christian Herter, was currently staying at the White House with her husband, as a guest of President Hoover. It was decided finally that Mrs. Lovett would call the White House and find out if a WONPR delegation would be welcomed there.

The convention was already in session the next morning, with more than five hundred of the delegates present, when Mrs. Lovett came to Mrs. Sabin and told her the President would indeed be willing to receive a delegation from the WONPR. How large a delegation? The President hadn't specified. In that case, Mrs. Sabin would decide how many women should go to the White House. Without hesitation she decided they should all go. But first they should pass a resolution to present to him, asking him to change his mind and join the growing campaign for repeal of the Eighteenth Amendment.

A few minutes later, with the resolution quickly agreed upon, this plenary session was adjourned while 534 delegates rushed out of Conference Hall and through the Mayflower lobby to taxicabs or to their own automobiles, many chauffeur driven, en route to the White House.

Even when he realized what an avalanche was descending upon him, President Hoover retained his good humor. Mrs. Sabin entered the Oval Office first with Mrs. Courtlandt Nicoll, the organization's secretary, who handed him the freshly passed resolution, then recited a few remarks she had prepared to accompany it.

"At the second annual convention of the Women's Organization for National Prohibition Reform, comprising a membership of over 300,-000 from every state," she nervously intoned, "it was voted the copy of the resolution passed by the convention this morning be presented to you and to the Congress. I therefore have the honor to present you with this resolution."

President Hoover was never an effusive man, but he was polite. "I am very glad to have it," he said.

He then stood patiently by his desk, shaking hands with every one of the organization's officers and delegates as they filed past him. He was acquainted with quite a few of them, and some he had regarded as friends. That was one of the more disturbing aspects of this strange intrusion upon his busy day. These women, to whom liquor probably meant nothing just a few years earlier, were now imbued with an evangelistic passion for its legal restoration. And it wasn't necessarily because they liked to drink. Perhaps some of them enjoyed cocktails, as the prohibitionists seemed to think, but many of them probably didn't drink at all. They were working for repeal because they believed in it and had become dedicated to it.

After all the women had shaken the President's hand, they hurried back to the Mayflower Hotel, where they immediately passed another resolution urging all rank-and-file WONPR members to vote only for candidates "who have openly declared themselves in favor of the repeal of the Eighteenth Amendment."

That seemed to exclude quite pointedly their gracious host of an hour earlier.

Undercover prohibition agents George Markham and Michael Reardon walked into the New York store of Vino Sano Distributors at 277 Fifth Avenue on August 3, 1931, and looked at the merchandise displayed on the counter.[7] Vino Sano was the trade name of a grape brick manufactured by the firm and sold in competition with the grape concentrate, Vine-Glo, which was made and marketed by the large, government-subsidized California cooperative, Fruit Industries Inc. Legal counsel for Fruit Industries, Inc. was Mrs. Mabel Walker Willebrandt. Her firm, which sold Vine-Glo at ten to thirty dollars per keg, was less than enthusiastic about the competition from Vino Sano, priced at two dollars per brick.

This trade rivalry was no concern of agents Markham and Reardon, who had been sent to the Vino Sano store simply to learn what they could about the product and, if possible, make a purchase. They had no trouble gaining entry. The store was operating openly on the assumption that the sale of the grape brick was legal because it contained no alcohol. It's advertising instructions even included an amusing note of caution about its use:

> Dissolve one brick in one gallon of plain water. Treat this exactly as you would freshly pressed fruit juices for home use.
>
> Sugar may be added according to taste, usually one pound for the dry types [of grapes], two pounds for the sweet types. The beverage should be consumed within five days, otherwise, and in summer temperature, it might ferment and become wine.

Markham picked up one of the empty Vino Sano cartons on the counter and was examining it casually when a clerk said, "What can I do for you?"

"Is it true," the agent asked ingenuously, "that a man can make good wine from this preparation?"

"Absolutely," the clerk said, handing him a circular and showing him a list of available flavors.

Markham, pointing to muscatel, said, "This is the kind I want to make. I'm not interested in grape juice. What I want is good wine with a kick in it."

"Here's what you want then," the clerk said, offering him a muscatel grape brick, together with a package of anti-acid, a cork, and a rubber hose. "It's all that's necessary," he assured the agent, "to make muscatel as good as you ever tasted."

Markham and his partner paid their money, took their goods, and left the store. They had been instructed only to gather evidence, not to stage a raid. Two days later, other federal agents descended upon the establishment, confiscated 3,000 grape bricks, and arrested the manager and two of his clerks.

Prohibition Administrator Andrew McCampbell announced that the raid had resulted from a complaint by Fred A. Victor, current New York State Superintendent of the Anti-Saloon League, whose office was nearby, but attorney David Siegel, who represented Vino Sano Distributors, was skeptical of this information. He suspected that the real instigator of the raid was Vino Sano's competitor, Fruit Industries Inc.

If Vino Sano's top executives at the main office in San Francisco agreed with Siegel, their reaction was imaginative. Instead of complaining to Fruit Industries about these alleged tactics, the Vino Sano general manager, a man named Karl Offer, sent a telegram to the firm's attorney, Mrs. Willebrandt, asking her to take over the defense of the three arrested men.

It was an astute move. Mrs. Willebrandt obviously knew how to get things accomplished. Thanks partly to her persuasiveness, the Federal Farm Board, since its inception in 1929, had loaned a total of $19,-187,622 to the California Grape Control Board, of which Fruit Industries Inc. was an off-shoot. Of this approximately $20 million, Fruit Industries itself had received $2,555,330. Former Senator James Reed of Missouri, an avowed wet and long-time critic of Mrs. Willebrandt, had charged that these loans were made "after secret negotiations" between her and the Farm Board. ("It seems absolutely impossible for the federal government to keep out of the bootlegging business," Reed wrote in an article for *Cosmopolitan Magazine*. "However, it remained for the administration of Herbert Hoover to finance the business as a nationwide project with the taxpayers' money.")

Mrs. Willebrandt's company, Fruit Industries, was now selling its government-subsidized product in forty-seven of the forty-eight states without interference. One of its four New York plants had been raided the previous April and "three hundred gallons of alleged wine" had been seized, but nothing had come of the incident. It might provide a good argument for the Vino Sano people to use, however, in trying to persuade her to represent them. Since both companies were in the same business, she would be helping to avert future raids against Fruit Industries if she could successfully defend Vino Sano's right to sell its product.

The telegram from Vino Sano's manager reached Mrs. Willebrandt at her Washington office in the Investment Building. She was obviously doing very well in private practice. She also maintained a Los Angeles office in the Union Bank Building there. She had added four more attorneys to her firm and many more clients in addition to the aviation industry and the major portion of the California grape industry. She was doing so well that she now rode in a chauffeur-driven automobile, and when she gave parties in her home on Dumbarton Avenue near Rock Creek Park, the guests often included Supreme Court justices and other government dignitaries.

Mrs. Willebrandt was somewhat embarrassed to receive the wire from Vino Sano, asking her to represent them. It was the next day before she answered their request. She sent a short return telegram to the company's manager in San Francisco.

"I'm very sorry," the telegram said, "but I do not take prohibition cases."[8]

Chapter 15

Would there be no end to the succession of crosses Bishop James
Cannon, Jr., was asked to bear? When he returned on the *Mauretania*
September 17 from one of his frequent trips to Europe (this time as
a delegate to the International Congress Against Alcoholism at Geneva), he was besieged by reporters about a U.S. Senate investigation
that indicated he had deposited in his own checking account at least
$8,000 which had been contributed to the Anti-Smith Democrats in
1928. Was it true that he had done such a thing?

"Every check that I received," he told the reporters, "was used in
the political campaign, and I never took one penny for my own
personal use. I shall make a written statement as soon as I get to
Washington."

But was it true that he had put campaign funds in his own checking
account? What about certain moneys contributed by former New
Jersey Senator Joseph Frelinghuysen and former Republican National Committee chairman Claudius Huston?

All the money sent to him for the political campaign, the bishop
insisted, had been used for that purpose exclusively. "As I have writ-

ten in a letter," he said, "I do not have any recollection of correspondence on this matter."

He then turned his defiant attention to the Senate Campaign Funds Committee, which was expected to seek his testimony about the charge, hurling a special challenge to its chairman, Senator Gerald Nye of North Dakota.

"If Senator Nye or anyone else thinks I am going to neglect my church work to attend a meeting that is illegal," he said, thus denying the committee's jurisdiction in the matter, "they are mistaken. If Senator Nye wants to see me, I'll see him, but if there is to be any investigation of my private affairs, my business as an executor, or my relations with my own family, let it be in legal order and by the grand jury."[1]

He seemed to be implying that anyone who doubted his ability to defy the U.S. Senate with impunity should bear in mind the ease with which he had handled the Senate Lobby Committee the previous year. The reporters turned to another subject. Did he believe the current estimates that there were now more wets than drys in the United States? He most certainly did not believe any such thing, and if the reporters believed it they should take a look at the 1930 election, which had left Congress staunchly dry. (Actually the wets had gained four Senate and seventy House seats in 1930.)

What about the 1932 election, they asked. The bishop would obviously not support Al Smith for the Presidency, but would he support New York state's other possible candidate, Governor Franklin D. Roosevelt, who was a Protestant?

Bishop Cannon was quite aware that Roosevelt was a Protestant, and from a good American family,[2] but he was also aware of the letter Roosevelt had sent to Senator Robert Wagner the previous September denouncing prohibition. No, indeed, he didn't like New York's current governor any more than its former one. He would work, he said, for the nomination of William Gibbs McAdoo, the man who had blocked Al Smith's nomination in 1924.

When the bishop issued his challenge to Senator Nye and the Campaign Funds Committee, he calculated well. The committee continued investigating his use of 1928 campaign contributions, calling the treasurer of his organization, Ada L. Burroughs, to testify, but did not call Cannon even after Miss Burroughs refused to answer questions on the ground that the committee lacked jurisdiction. Once again Bishop Cannon had proven himself more formidable than a committee of U.S. Senators.

However, he did not frighten Assistant U.S. Attorney John J. Wilson, then an eager young prosecutor in the District of Columbia office. (Wilson later gained public notice when, as a private attorney representing H. R. Haldeman and John Ehrlichman during the 1973 Senate Watergate hearings, he called Senator Daniel Inouye of Hawaii "that little Jap".) Since Bishop Cannon had insisted that only a grand jury could legally investigate him, Wilson took the case to a District of Columbia grand jury, and on October 16 that body indicted both the bishop and Miss Burroughs on ten charges of violating and conspiring to violate the Federal Corrupt Practices Act. The government accused them of irregularities in failure to account for much of the $65,300 Cannon had received through Edwin C. Jameson.

The day the indictments were announced, Bishop Cannon was in Atlanta attending a convocation of his denomination's College of Bishops. He was ready for the reporters when they reached him.

"This is merely a plot to discredit me," he said, "a persecution by a Roman Catholic District Attorney (he was apparently under the mistaken impression that Wilson was a Catholic) acting under orders of his priest. I am not surprised at anything the Roman Catholic District Attorney in Washington does."[3]

Later, after he had examined the indictments, Cannon ordered his attorneys to file a demurrer on the ground that the Corrupt Practices Act could not possibly relate to a presidential campaign because the purpose of a presidential election was to choose electors. These electors, he argued, were purely state officers, not governed by federal statutes.

While his lawyers went to court to argue the legal aspects of the case, Bishop Cannon himself continued to set before the public what he considered the real story behind the charges against him. In a letter to the Richmond *Times-Dispatch* he wrote: "By a check up, twice made by reliable persons, it appears that twelve of the twenty-three of this particular grand jury are Roman Catholic. . . .

"In my Episcopal labors for thirteen years I have been brought in close touch with Roman Catholic methods and work in Mexico, Cuba, South America, and the Belgian Congo, and while I have some Roman Catholic friends for whom I have a very high regard personally, yet when the Roman hierarchy determines to punish or destroy the influence of a man who has helped to defeat their pet candidate, Alfred Emanuel Smith, the three years of continued attack added to my former experience in other lands, have taught me that I must be exceedingly watchful and vigilant at every turn, or the Romish hierarchy will, by one instrumentality or another, accomplish its purpose."

MADISON, WISC., Jan. 31, 1932.—Jennie Justo, 23, today calmly faced the fate she knew "must some day overtake me."

"I knew it was coming from the time I started selling liquor to support my mother and family," the attractive young woman said Saturday in reference to the six months' sentence to the Milwaukee house of correction and $500 fine imposed by Judge R.C. Baltzell in federal court.

Her black eyes flashed as she told how the basement of her home had become a rendezvous for University of Wisconsin students for five years as she sought to "support my mother and educate my brothers and sister."

"I wish people wouldn't think I'm as bad as I've been painted," Jennie said wistfully. "I'm not a criminal, though I know that I've broken the prohibition law.

"I'm not the queen of the bootleggers. Why do they continue calling me that? There are lots of girls here bootlegging—beautiful girls," she declared.

"The college boys like them, but there's no money in bootlegging in Madison any more. There's too many places to buy liquor. Why, there must be 3,000 in Madison and the surrounding small towns. And besides, people don't have the money to spend."

Her mother, her three brothers and her younger sister seemed to concern the raven-haired Jennie more than the six months in jail which awaited her.

"I wish that I could serve them here so mother and the baby brother could visit me. What are we going to do? Mother can't work and the little money we had went to pay for this house."

Jennie traced her life back nine years to the days when she was a happy school girl. Then her father was murdered in one of the unsolved crimes of Madison's "bush" (Italian district). She went to work in a drug store to support her mother and her younger brothers and sister "so they might have an education I missed."

Her deep, throaty voice choked slightly as she told how the drug store was closed after three years and she was unable to get another job. "I had lots of Italian boy friends and they got me delivering alcohol, whisky and gin. What else could I do? The family needed my support and I was too young to get a job. Then spiked beer ruined that. People too began to want to spend less for liquor. I had to open up a place here."

She told how she sent an allowance every month to her brother Joe "Pep" Justo while he received the high school education "I missed." It was she who urged and encouraged him to "train hard and live a clean life" that aided him in attaining his present reputation as a boxer.

Federal prohibition agents from Chicago staged the raid which resulted in Jennie's plea of guilty Saturday. "They phoned from Chicago and said they were Pep's friends coming to Madison for a good time," she declared without a touch of rancor in her voice. "I met them at the station and took them to my home. They said they were Pep's friends and I didn't want to charge them for drinks, but they insisted. That's the evidence presented against me."

All this was told Judge Baltzell Saturday morning when Jennie appeared to enter her plea. Lyman T. Powell, assistant district attorney, said Dean Scott H. Goodnight (of the University of Wisconsin) had made frequent complaints based on her reputation for selling to students.[4]

On June 6, the wet army gained a new recruit who represented a colossal loss to the drys. John D. Rockefeller, Jr., announced that day that he favored repeal of the Eighteenth Amendment.

Heretofore Rockefeller had been the nation's most prominent prohibition supporter; over the years he and his family had been the largest contributors to the Anti-Saloon League. But now, in an open letter to Columbia University president Nicholas Murray Butler, he said the evils of prohibition more than outweighed its benefits, and these evils "unless promptly checked are likely to lead to conditions unspeakably worse than those which prevailed before."[5]

He had revised his views "slowly and reluctantly," he said, but was now convinced that prohibition had increased drinking, that it had substituted the speakeasy for the saloon "not only unit for unit but probably two-fold if not three-fold," that it had stimulated the spirit of law-breaking and increased crime "to an unprecedented degree."

He contended that "many of our best citizens, piqued at what they regarded as an infringement of their private rights, have openly and unabashedly disregarded the Eighteenth Amendment," and as an inevitable result, "respect for all law has been greatly lessened."

Rockefeller's purpose in announcing such a public stand just a few days before the 1932 national conventions was self-evident. He hoped, he said, that prohibition would now be taken out of partisan politics. He urged both parties to adopt repeal planks.

The Rockefeller statement delighted the Democrats because it intensified the already enormous difficulties of the Republicans and President Hoover, whom the public was blaming for the depression. When the GOP delegates convened in Chicago June 14, many of them would have been happy to replace President Hoover as their nominee, but since he was the incumbent, this was out of the question. He controlled the party machinery so firmly that winning renomination was the one problem he didn't face. His deepest concern was what to promise in the platform about the depression and prohibition.

About the depression he had definite views. Prosperity, he believed, was just around the corner. The possibility of a business upturn was clearly discernible. The present unfortunate situation called for drastic reduction of federal expenditures, maintenance of the gold standard, and, to reduce the alarming number of mortgage foreclosures, the creation of home loan discount banks. At Hoover's prompting, these measures were incorporated in the platform.

About prohibition, his views were no longer as definite as they had been. Aware of the Rockefeller statement and the growing wet strength even in his own party, but also of his strong commitment to the drys, Hoover wanted a platform plank wide enough for both wets and drys to stand on without crowding each other. He got what he asked for, though it's doubtful that he got what he wanted. On the subject of prohibition, the Republican platform said:

. . . We do not favor a submission limited to the issue of retention or repeal. . . . The progress that has been thus far made must be preserved while the evils must be eliminated.

We therefore believe that the people should have an opportunity to pass upon a proposed amendment the provisions of which, retaining in the federal government power to preserve the gains already made in dealing with the evils inherent in the liquor traffic, shall allow states to deal with the problem as their citizens may determine, but subject always to the power of the Federal Government to protect those states where prohibition may exist and safeguard our citizens everywhere from the return of the saloon and attendant abuses.

Even though the President was in control of the convention, it took an all-night battle in the Resolutions Committee before he managed to get this wording approved. Instead of pacifying both the wets and the drys as he had hoped, it left both sides dissatisfied and deepened the gloom which already enveloped the GOP delegates as a result of Hoover's inability to cope with the depression.

When the Democrats met in Chicago June 27, their usual raucous belligerence was intensified; it looked as if this time they would find it hard to lose. Republican troubles over the depression, and to a lesser degree prohibition, endowed the Democratic nomination with a value it hadn't had since 1916, and encouraged a host of hopefuls to fight for it.

New York's Governor Franklin D. Roosevelt had begun his quest for the nomination after his 1930 reelection, after sounding out Al Smith's intentions. When Smith told Roosevelt's political manager, Jim Farley, that he didn't intend to run again for the presidency, Farley began talking to party officials around the country and building a springboard for Roosevelt, whose governorship of the nation's largest state had favorably impressed most people. Roosevelt's only major problem appeared to be the question of how he would handle an emerging New York City scandal which involved Tammany Hall and the playful Mayor James J. "Jimmy" Walker. Roosevelt's need of Tammany support balanced against his need to maintain his own untarnished image made this a delicate issue for him. He tried to straddle it by simply agreeing with Republicans who were demanding a legislative probe of New York City corruption. He seemed to be treating the boys as gently as they could expect, but they didn't think so. Tammany leaders demonstrated how they felt about Roosevelt's failure to protect them by letting Al Smith know he still looked like an attractive candidate to them, especially now that the depression was becoming a bigger issue than either prohibition or religion.

It was the kind of encouragement for which Smith had been waiting. His public friendship with Roosevelt was such a sham he could scarcely maintain it. To Clark Howell, publisher of the Atlanta *Constitution,* he said one day in a fist-banging outburst, "Do you know, by God, that he [Roosevelt] has never consulted me about a damn thing since he has been governor?"[6]

In April 1932, when Massachusetts held its presidential primary, Smith not only entered it; to everyone's surprise he won it, inflicting upon Roosevelt his first setback in what had looked like an irresistible drive toward the nomination. A month later, when Speaker of the House of Representatives John Nance Garner beat Roosevelt in the California primary, the coming convention took on dramatic prospects.

The nation's economic depression was now so deep that an unprecedented eleven million (almost one fourth of the normal work force at that time) were unemployed. Every city had breadlines and soup kitchens for the hungry. Around the outskirts of many towns, especially near the dumps, people evicted from their homes by mortgage foreclosures or inability to pay rent were building shacks out of old packing crates and cardboard boxes. Their political feelings were indicated by the fact that communities of such shacks were called "Hoovervilles." Thousands of businesses had failed since the end of 1929 and even the speakeasies were feeling the economic pinch. Though many of them continued to prosper, more of them were being closed now by lack of solvent customers than by prohibition agents.

Chicago was in dismal condition when the Democrats arrived. The city was unbearably hot and humid. Worse than that, the streets of the Loop were full of idle men, cadging dimes, nickels, or even pennies. The streets were also full of waste paper, trash, and potholes because municipal services under the new mayor, Anton Cermak, weren't much better than they had been under "Big Bill" Thompson. Thompson was now living, comfortably retired, in a luxurious lake shore apartment, with at least $2 million, mostly cash, stashed away in safe deposit boxes. One of the few improvements noticeable in Chicago since Thompson's defeat had been the removal to a federal penitentiary of his long-time supporter, Al Capone, convicted the previous October of income tax evasion. Most of Capone's speakeasies and cabarets were still open, however, so the Democratic delegates would not be deprived of booze during their deliberations.

A surprise arrival at the Democratic Convention was Bishop Cannon. Inasmuch as he had supported Hoover in 1928, most people hadn't expected him to show up, but the bishop still regarded himself a Democrat. Despite all his personal troubles, he had come to Chicago to try to save his party.

He was destined to have a hard time of it. Shortly after his arrival in Chicago, a Virgin Island delegate named Judge Lucius J. M. Malmin walked up to him in a crowded hotel lobby and shoved a bottle of Virgin Islands bay rum into his hand. A photographer, who had been forewarned, snapped pictures.

Cannon, taken aback, didn't react for a moment, but when he realized the trick that had been played on him, he cried: "Framed! I'll smash it!"

The Virgin Island delegate grabbed the bottle from Cannon's hand just in time to save it. As spectators laughed, the bishop walked away with his dignity and his righteous indignation intact.

On June 25, Cannon was to address the prohibition subcommittee of the party's Resolutions Committee. The large hearing room and the galleries were crowded as he made his way forward. At the same time, Senator Carter Glass of Cannon's home state, Virginia, was leaving the room because, as he explained to newsmen, he didn't want to listen to "such a man." A long-time opponent of the bishop, the crusty old senator had heard all his arguments.

The spectators were in an uproar even before Cannon began to speak. The highly vocal wets, who filled the rear of the room and one half of the balcony, tried to shout him down. They were hissed by drys, mostly women, who occupied the other half of the gallery. When the chairman, former Senator Gilbert M. Hitchcock of Nebraska, finally restored order, Cannon began by reading a telegram from friend and colleague Dr. Arthur James Barton, who warned that the state of Virginia would vote Republican if the Democrats declared for repeal.

As Cannon finished reading the telegram, the wets in the room began booing and refused to stop for five minutes. An Illinois Congressman, Michael Igoe, who was a subcommittee member, stood up and, referring to the bucket-shop stock market charges against the bishop, shouted at him, "Your broker wants you!"

Cannon shouted back testily, "I thought I was addressing gentlemen."

When the noise subsided, he continued his exhortation. "The people whom I represent," he said, "did not hesitate to put moral principle above party loyalty in 1928 as was shown by the electoral votes of Virginia, North Carolina, Kentucky, Tennessee, Florida, Texas, Oklahoma, and, we believe, Alabama, if fairly counted in 1928."

No one could accuse the bishop of lacking courage. He was brazenly reminding his fellow Democrats of what he and his anti-Smith forces had done to the party four years earlier.

"Those same people," he now promised, "will register their conscientious convictions without hesitation if confronted with a similar issue in 1932. And this is a naked fact which the Democratic Party must face. The people of the South will not stand for a wet platform." Raising his hand and pointing his finger at the wet section of the gallery, he punctuated his remarks with defiance. "It is a fact that you don't like, apparently," he shouted.

"We don't like traitors, either," a man next to Igoe shouted back. Once more pandemonium reigned, and Bishop Cannon was forced to give up his attempt to educate these people.

More than a dozen other people, both wets and drys, spoke before the subcommittee. Among them was Pauline Sabin, who accused her own Republican Party of failure to meet the liquor issue squarely. "In behalf of our membership of one million, ten thousand, nine hundred and forty women," she said, "I ask you to adopt a resolution pledging the Democratic members of both Houses of Congress to propose to state conventions a resolution to repeal the Eighteenth Amendment. Were this a question of drink, I would not lift my finger to change this law. When history is written, it will be shown that our organization was fighting for good government and not for drink."

Throughout the hearing, the room was crowded and reactions were sharp, but while the public excitement continued to boil in the Resolutions Committee, the real prohibition contest was taking place behind the scenes between the Smith and Roosevelt factions. After his 1930 declaration in favor of repeal, Governor Roosevelt had tried to placate the drys in the party by saying as little as possible about the issue. Smith, perceiving this strategy, had tried to lure him into the open. In March 1931, Smith had fought to put the party on record for repeal through a National Committee resolution, but Roosevelt had joined forces with the Southerners to block the resolution. In December, Smith had said to Clark Howell, "Why the hell don't he speak out? He's been more outspoken on the question than even I've been, and now ain't the time for trimming."[7]

Smith knew exactly why Roosevelt had been avoiding the issue, and in the Resolutions Committee proceedings Smith hoped to use Roosevelt's reluctance against him. Roosevelt had firm control of the committee, but if it produced anything less than a repeal plank, and if the minority were to challenge this plank on the floor, he would be unable to control a majority of delegates. Smith was eager to go to the floor with a minority report and provoke such a test. He was confident he could win it because prohibition was one issue on which he knew most of the delegates were with him. His one best chance for the nomination was to make prohibition the major issue.

Unfortunately for Smith, Roosevelt also knew this, and as soon as he realized Smith would actually go to the floor with a minority report, he wasted no time preempting his political mentor's position. If the party must have a repeal plank, Roosevelt, not Smith, would be its author. Suddenly, the Roosevelt members of the Resolutions Committee were in favor of a repeal plank, and it became the majority position before Smith had a chance to register it as his minority position. Once again Roosevelt had proven his political skill.

As the balloting approached, however, Roosevelt foresaw difficulties because of the two-thirds rule at Democratic conventions. He held a majority of the 1,154 delegate votes but not two thirds, and decided to launch a drive to suspend the two-thirds rule. This drive caused such an adverse reaction (especially from Southern leaders for whom the two-thirds rule provided virtual veto power) that he was forced to abandon it, and he lost some prestige for having fostered it. Once again Al Smith and the seven other candidates in the race began to think they might yet defeat him.

At the end of the first ballot their hopes were sustained by the fact that Roosevelt had only 666¼ of the 740 votes he needed. At the end of the second ballot, in which Roosevelt gained only eleven, their hopes were raised, and at the end of the third, on which he picked up only 4¾ votes, bringing him to 682, he was in deep trouble. Smith's headquarters issued a gleeful announcement: "We have Roosevelt licked."

It was almost but not quite true. The three ballots had taken the entire night of June 30–July 1, and as the weary delegates finally adjourned at nine o'clock in the morning of the first (leaving Chicago Stadium littered with sixty tons of debris, including 5,000 liquor and pop bottles), Roosevelt's backers were desperate but not defeated. One of them, Joseph P. Kennedy of Boston, had made a significant phone call the previous day to publisher William Randolph Hearst, who was sojourning at his San Simeon castle estate in California. Hearst at that time was such a powerful political figure that he actually controlled the California delegation even though William Gibbs McAdoo was its nominal leader. Hearst also had strong influence with John Nance Garner, who controlled the Texas delegation, and for whom the California delegation had voted in the first three ballots. On the telephone Kennedy pointed out to Hearst that unless California and Texas were to vote for Roosevelt, he would lose the nomination, in which case not Garner but Al Smith or Newton D. Baker would win it.[8] Though Baker was a wet, having been one of the two Wickersham Commission members to advocate outright repeal of the Eighteenth Amendment, the isolationist Hearst disliked and distrusted him because he also advocated American membership in the League of Nations. As for Smith, Hearst detested him because several years earlier, when Smith was a candidate for governor of New York, he had refused to accept the politically ambitious publisher as a running-mate in the Senate race.

Kennedy played upon these prejudices now with an effectiveness that did not become evident until the evening of July 1 when the convention was preparing for the fourth ballot. The Mississippi delegation and parts of several others had been planning all afternoon to leave Roosevelt's fold. The Smith forces had begun a serious push for their man. But then came news that McAdoo of California was asking permission to address the delegates.

For the first time since the convention began, Chicago Stadium was absolutely quiet as the tall, slender, ascetic-looking McAdoo began to speak.

"Mr. Chairman, ladies and gentlemen, I thank you for the privilege accorded me to say just a word in explaining the vote of the state of California," he said. "California came here to nominate a President of the United States. She did not come here to deadlock this convention, or to engage in another desolating contest like that of 1924."

It was McAdoo, of course, who had thwarted Al Smith in 1924 by battling him to a 104-ballot stalemate. He was now about to strike a final, decisive blow against Smith's political career.

"We believe," he continued, "that when any man comes into this convention with the popular will behind him to the extent of almost seven hundred votes . . .”

With these words he had inadvertently made the rest of his speech redundant. The Roosevelt forces delightedly leaped to their feet while the New York, New Jersey, and New England delegates, most of whom were loyal Smith men, sat in glum silence watching the short but loud demonstration that now took place. By the time McAdoo resumed his speech, few people seemed to be listening. But everyone heard his last sentence.

“And so, my friends, California casts forty-four votes for Franklin Delano Roosevelt.”

After the bedlam subsided, the delegations supporting other candidates hastened to follow California's example in an effort to make the nomination unanimous. But this effort failed to overcome the bitterness of one man's eight-year frustration. When the final ballot was counted, Al Smith, having refused to release his delegates, still held 190½ of the 201¾ votes with which he had begun the convention.

For almost a month Bishop James Cannon had controlled his feelings about the shocking defection from the dry ranks of John D. Rockefeller, Jr. Automobile maker Henry Ford spoke out more often for the dry cause but Rockefeller, perhaps because he said so little, carried more weight with the public when he did speak. Furthermore, he carried more weight with the wealthy, many of whom considered Ford an upstart. Rockefeller's abandonment of the crusade would no doubt swell the already alarming wet tide.

Bishop Cannon, on the Fourth of July, decided he could remain silent no longer. Speaking at an Independence Day celebration for Methodists in the Ocean Grove, New Jersey, Municipal Auditorium, the bishop did his best to explain to the 3,000 faithful prohibitionists in his audience why one of their number had deserted them. Mr. Rockefeller, he said, had developed “an inferiority complex” about the liquor question.[9]

He took special exception to one contention in Rockefeller's public statement “that many of our best citizens, piqued at what they regarded as an infringement of their private rights, have openly and unabashedly disregarded the Eighteenth Amendment.” The bishop asked his audience, "How can a man be one of our best citizens and flaunt the Constitution?"

However, the bishop was not without compassion for Rockefeller. "Mr. Rockefeller lacked adequate knowledge of the subject he was discussing," Cannon said, mentioning Henry Ford, Jane Addams of Chicago's Hull House, and Evangeline Booth of the Salvation Army as examples of citizens who were better equipped to speak about prohibition. Cannon then went on to suggest that the environment in which Rockefeller lived might have been partially responsible for his sudden heresy.

"Mr. Rockefeller," the bishop reminded his listeners, "is surrounded by lawlessness and the rotten and unspeakably filthy government New York City has had under Tammany for the past several years."

With this patronizing castigation of John D., Jr., Bishop Cannon had now come full circle in his pronouncements about the Rockefellers and their vast wealth. In 1905, at a time when John D., Sr., received more publicity for his questionable business methods than for his philanthropies, Cannon, not yet a bishop, called him the "representative of the greatest evil in public life."[10] If the Methodist church were to accept gifts from such a robber baron, he said, it would thereby "padlock the lips of the pulpits." But the kind of "maturity" which modifies such strong idealistic views came quickly to the young clergyman. A year later, when a Rockefeller philanthropy offered $10,000 to his alma mater, Randolph Macon College, Cannon was one of those who gave public thanks for the gift. And through the years from that time on, he had often expressed his gratitude as the Rockefellers poured at least $350,000 into the Anti-Saloon League before 1920, plus an estimated $75,000 per year thereafter. It was understandable if he was distressed by their apostasy. They would be sorely missed.

Izzy Einstein had lived in quiet obscurity as an insurance salesman during the seven years since his sudden and unwarranted dismissal from the federal Prohibition Bureau in November 1925. But now he had written a book about his rum-sleuthing experiences entitled *Prohibition Agent No. 1.* October 26, 1932, was publication day, and Izzy was welcoming the gentlemen of the press in the Manhattan office of his publisher, Frederick A. Stokes.[11] Some of these newsmen had known him in the old days when he was the funniest as well as the most feared of government men; they had always treated him familiarly, at times cavalierly.

Today, they appeared to be on their best behavior. When the publisher passed out cigars, no member of the fourth estate accepted one until after Izzy himself had gathered a fistful. Then the reporters waited patiently while Izzy sat back in one of the publisher's upholstered armchairs and chose the cigar he planned to smoke first. Once he had it lit, he looked up at the pads and pencils in front of him and began the press conference.

"Ask me something," he challenged.

"Did you write the book yourself?" one of the reporters ventured.

"Sure. Ain't my name on it?" Izzy rejoined. "Somebody helped me. I got a couple of sons—lawyers, only they ain't admitted yet to the bar. But they're smart. I dictated and they wrote it down."

Exhaling a cloud of cigar smoke, he challenged the newsmen again. "Ask me something else."

"Are you proud of your first book, Mr. Einstein?"

"I'll be more prouder," he said, "when I see the sales, how they go."

Some of the reporters had received advance copies of the book and one of them at least had actually read it. He noticed, he said, that Izzy's descriptions of his adventures on the trail of demon rum did not mention his partner, Moe Smith. Could Izzy please explain that oversight?

Izzy's answer indicated that the partners were no longer the closest of friends. "Maybe Moe will write a book," he said, "so why should I write about him?"

He quickly veered away from the subject of Moe Smith and began describing the reaction of a Brooklyn restaurant manager he once had occasion to arrest. "He fainted," Izzy recalled. "He got real sick, in fact. He never stood trial. He died, in fact."

Izzy was warming up to his subject now and didn't need to be prodded. He described the funnel he had invented which allowed him to pour evidence apparently into his vest pocket but actually into a hidden flask in the lining. He told about the futility of his raids in Detroit, where no one had ever been able to slow the flood of liquor from across the border, and he recalled with a smile the time he got "the bum's rush" from a Detroit speakeasy operator for ordering buttermilk. He described the disguises he had invented and the cleverness with which he used them to trap bootleggers. He became so absorbed in his stories that he seemed to be reliving them.

Finally one of the reporters drew him back to the present by asking him about the current status of prohibition. How many speakeasies did Izzy think there were in New York? His book stated there were 100,000, and that a half-million New Yorkers were involved in supplying and selling liquor. Where did he get those figures?

Izzy was slow to answer and reluctant to give sources, but he had methods of estimating. What were his methods? He wouldn't say. "It's mostly theory," he admitted.

Since the matter of theories had now arisen, another reporter asked him about his theory of prohibition. "What are your convictions, Mr. Einstein? Do you believe in the moral principle of prohibition?"

The usually voluble Izzy Einstein fell silent. A frown came over his face and he fiddled nervously with his cigar, tearing loose the wrapper. Obviously bewildered, he stared at the reporter and said, "I don't get you."

No one pursued the question. It was apparent that he really didn't understand why anyone would ask such a thing. Principles and theories were not matters of concern to Izzy. All he knew about prohibition was that for five years he had been agent No. 1, that he had raided 3,000 speakeasies and arrested about 5,000 people, and it had been more fun than anything else he had ever done in his life.

As the presidential campaign got under way, it quickly became evident that the paramount issue of 1932 was bread rather than wine. The economic depression was now so deep and all-pervasive that the dry rank-and-file had become apathetic to the battle against the bottle. Worse than that, when President Hoover delivered his August 11 speech accepting renomination, the dry leaders realized they had even lost their place on the presidential ballot.

The murky and confusing prohibition clause Hoover had sponsored in the Republican platform should have warned the drys of what was to come. With men like John D. Rockefeller, Jr., deserting them, Hoover, who had always entertained personal reservations about prohibition, could hardly be expected to remain steadfast. When he came to the prohibition segment of his acceptance speech, he began by asserting to everyone's bemusement that his views on the subject were "clear and need not be misunderstood." Then he inched forward, but not very far, in an effort to stop people from misunderstanding him. He didn't want the country, he said, "on the one hand to return to the old saloon with its political and social corruption, or on the other hand to endure the bootlegger and the speakeasy with their abuses and crime." What he favored was a change in the Eighteenth Amendment allowing each state to determine its own liquor policy so long as it didn't interfere with neighboring states.

He had now promulgated as a personal policy what he had already written into the GOP platform, and he had stated it in such a way that he seemed to suggest elimination of federal enforcement. Despite his boast of clarity, he had remained especially vague on this point, and he hadn't in any way explained how the dry states under his plan would prevent the import of liquor without posting armies of guards at all their borders. He hadn't moved wetward far enough to win many wets, but he had gone far enough to lose a lot of drys.

Bishop Cannon, who had hurried off to Geneva after abandoning his efforts to save the Democratic Party, now felt constrained to launch a cablegram denouncing his 1928 Republican champion for giving in "to the speakeasies, bootleggers, and nullifiers of the Constitution."

On the opposite side of the issue, Pauline Sabin received the President's acceptance speech with cool disdain. "President Hoover's change in attitude in regard to the failure of national prohibition is very gratifying," she said. "While this organization [the Women's Organization for National Prohibition Reform] is unalterably opposed to the return of the old saloon, we believe that the way to prevent it is to return the power to the several states to enact laws responsive to the sentiment of the people."

By coming out almost but not quite for repeal, Hoover appeared to have lost everybody. Even the Women's Christian Temperance Union refused to endorse him this year, suggesting instead that its members vote as they please while applying dry pressure to both candidates.

Thanks to Hoover's equivocation, Governor Roosevelt, having declared for repeal, was able to take for granted his edge in the issue, and concentrate on the more acute problems of the depression. In speech after speech he promised to relieve the plight of America's

"Forgotten Man," a phrase which encompassed farmers, workers, the unemployed—everyone who had a complaint to air. When the question of prohibition came up, Roosevelt handled it with aplomb. In St. Louis, one of the nation's leading brewery centers, his list of economic promises was interrupted by a shout from the audience: "What about repeal? Will you bring back beer?"

Pausing only for effect, Roosevelt inserted his answer into his speech as smoothly as if it were part of the written text. "And in the meantime," he declared, "I propose to increase the federal revenue by several hundred million dollars a year by placing a tax on beer." It was perhaps the first time in history that an American audience cheered the announcement of an intended new tax.

Roosevelt also gained political strength in his home state of New York and in New England by making a patient effort at reconciliation with Al Smith. It was not easy. Smith's first public pronouncement of the campaign, in a September 30 *New Outlook* magazine article, ridiculed Roosevelt's repeated references to the "Forgotten Man." Though Smith said in the article that he endorsed his party's ticket, he didn't mention Roosevelt by name.

Four days later, at the New York Democratic state convention in the Albany Armory, Smith reluctantly ascended the platform to shake Roosevelt's hand.

"Hello, Frank, I'm glad to see you," he said.

Roosevelt greeted his one-time sponsor with a beaming smile. "Hello Al. I'm glad to see you, too, and that's from the heart."[12]

The two men then joined forces, ironically, to help Herbert Lehman win the gubernatorial nomination despite stubborn opposition from Tammany Hall. Smith told Tammany boss John F. Curry that if the boys didn't get behind Lehman, he (Smith) would run for mayor of New York City in 1933 and use all his power against the Tammany machine.

"On what ticket would you run?" Curry asked.

"On a Chinese laundry ticket," Smith replied defiantly.

As Curry knew, Al Smith could become mayor of New York City if he ran on a parking ticket. Lehman got his nomination and New York state looked safe for Roosevelt. Smith was sufficiently mollified to make a few campaign speeches for him. In Manhattan on October 19, he pleased Roosevelt and soothed his old Tammany friends at the same time by saying, "The loyalty, the devotion of the great Democratic organization of this city will be exerted to the last degree in favor of the election of Roosevelt."

Five days later, Smith repeated this endorsement before a crowd of 17,000 people (plus an overflow of many more thousands) in Newark. He also told this Newark throng that he had written the Democratic repeal plank and that "thirsters for wine and beer must look to the Democrats." In addition, he recalled his own travail of four years earlier by reminding his audience of the religious issue which was used against him. Referring to Mrs. Mabel Walker Willebrandt by name, he said, "let it be written into the political history of this country that what she did she did at the behest of the Republican National Committee. All the bigotry and intolerance that arose throughout the country because of her remarks can be directly charged to that political committee."

Once again, he was using Mrs. Willebrandt, perhaps unfairly, as a symbol of all the bigotry in 1928. Mrs. Willebrandt, now practicing law privately and quite prosperously in Washington, responded with good nature: "I am greatly flattered that a gentleman of such high position as Mr. Smith should remember me so long."

Smith also spoke at a testimonial dinner on October 26 for Pauline Sabin, who had become a valued friend since her conversion to the wet cause, and who was now actively campaigning for Roosevelt. Many of the women in the WONPR had been life-long Republicans, and Mrs. Sabin had exercised considerable diplomatic skill in bringing the group securely into line behind a Democrat. One of the most formidable women in the WONPR, Mrs. August Belmont, had tried to splinter the organization and lead its Republicans back to Hoover after he offered his qualified endorsement of repeal, but Mrs. Sabin had kept the organization intact by the sheer force of her personality and her devotion to hard work. Under her guidance her million members throughout the country had developed active political organizations in every state and every election district. Furthermore, they were women who had access to Congressmen, governors, mayors, and state legislators. Mrs. Sabin kept in direct touch with each of these local units. One of her associates, Mrs. Grace Root (daughter-in-law of former U.S. Senator and Republican statesman Elihu Root) described her affectionately as a "taskmaster" who knew how to get maximum performance out of the members.

"She always required her women to know their facts and to win their point," Mrs. Root recalled. "Once they had signed up it was without mercy she put them at their job."[13]

The WONPR may have been a voluntary organization but according to Mrs. Root, "There was nothing elective about the work which Mrs. Sabin laid before her women to accomplish as repealists. In dealing with governors, Congressmen, district attorneys, business and newspaper men, social service workers and detectives, she required that "The Sabine Women" beat them at their own game."

In two years, Mrs. Sabin had built the WONPR into the nation's most effective citizens' group against prohibition. Al Smith confidently told her, at the Commodore Hotel dinner in her honor, that she was about to receive her reward.

"The fight to repeal the prohibition laws," he said, "has virtually been won."

Even Bishop Cannon would have difficulty in challenging that assessment. When he returned from Europe late in the campaign, he again accused President Hoover of abandoning the cause, but there was none of the bishop's old fire in this latest salvo. He also sent letters to Roosevelt and to Hoover asking them how they could make good their promises to prevent the return of the saloon if prohibition were repealed. He apparently received no reply to either letter.

The once powerful Methodist bishop was now a figure of fun even among many of his fellow drys. And his personal troubles were not yet at an end. On the last day of October, Justice Department prosecutor John J. Wilson reinstituted the indictment against him for allegedly putting 1928 campaign funds in his own pocket. While Cannon eventually beat this charge, it was a final blow to his public influence and his claim to moral leadership.

On November 4 in Birmingham, Alabama, he told a conference of his church colleagues that despite his serious reservations about Hoover, he would vote for him anyway "as the only way to defeat Roosevelt." It was the last significant political statement of his career, and he ended it with a remark which proved him consistent to the end. The "final lineup" behind Roosevelt included, he said, "the able, shrewd, intolerant Smith, with treacherous, grafting Tammany." When Bishop Cannon got his teeth into an enemy, he held on but the strength was now gone from his bite. His crusade was on its way to defeat. There is no record in his home precinct at Blackstone, Virginia, that he even bothered to vote on election day.

President Hoover, as the last days of the campaign dragged on, felt just as disillusioned as Bishop Cannon, and much more exhausted. On his final swing across the country toward his Palo Alto, California residence where he intended to vote, he came near to collapse.[14] During a St. Paul, Minnesota speech, a man was assigned to sit behind him on the platform, ready to push a chair under him if he began to fall.

Hoover knew by this time that he and prohibition were about to share the same fate. On November 8, he received only 15,759,930 votes to his opponent's 22,815,535. Governor Roosevelt had carried all but six states to win a larger electoral victory than any Democrat before him, and his party had increased its Congressional majorities to 59–37 in the Senate and 312–123 in the House of Representatives. Prohibition was now doomed.

During late December 1932, few people were more depressed than Larry Fay. Always a man of changing fortune, he was now totally broke and had no means of livelihood except a small, uncertain income he earned as front-man and nominal owner of a speakeasy called the Casa Blanca which had just opened at 33 West Fifty-sixth Street. He lived in a small apartment at the Carnegie Plaza, also on Fifty-sixth Street two blocks west.

Fay would begin his day by walking down Broadway to his favorite restaurant, Dinty Moore's on Forty-sixth Street, where he still had credit and where he would sit talking for hours to the proprietor about the elegant new nightclubs he planned to open. Moore would listen patiently but could hardly take Fay seriously. No one was opening elegant new nightclubs in 1932.

After lunch, but before the Casa Blanca's opening hour, Fay would make the Broadway rounds, occasionally borrowing a few dollars from friends—if he could find any and if they had money to lend. The depression had become so widespread that even his most prominent friends felt the pinch. Prominent surviving friends, that is. Many had gone their full route. Arnold Rothstein was now four years dead. Beer distributor and nightclub partner Frankie Marlow had been found dying from three bullet wounds near Flushing Cemetery in 1929.

Charlie "Chink" Sherman, who was Fay's financial backer in several enterprises, had been found dead in a Catskill quick-lime pit in 1931, a few months after engaging in a bloody brawl with Dutch Schultz at a speakeasy called the Club Abbey on Fifty-fourth Street. (Fay himself had been at the Abbey that night but missed the brawl by leaving prudently a few minutes before it began.) Owney Madden, who had worked for Fay after coming out of Sing Sing as an impecunious young thug in 1923, was now a millionaire entrepreneur in liquor and laundries, but he was also, at the moment, inconveniently back in Sing Sing because of parole violations. Almost everyone seemed to be in some kind of difficulty. For Fay the last three years had been all bad.

In October 1929, his sweet arrangement as czar of New York's wholesale milk dealers had collapsed when he was indicted on charges of conspiracy in restraint of trade. The indictment accused him of intimidating grocers, fixing milk prices, and making cozy agreements with large milk companies. He beat this rap like every other one he had faced since 1911, but it took fifteen months and a lot of money in legal fees. In January 1930, Fay was arrested (but subsequently cleared) on a disorderly conduct charge after hitting a process server in the face. A month later he tried to organize the city's taxi drivers as he had organized the milk dealers but the cabbies lost interest when they learned they would be paying him at least $72,000 a year. In February 1931 he was foiled in an attempt to revive the milk dealers' association. In June 1931 he married a twenty-year-old showgirl named Evelyn Crowell, but the marriage didn't last much longer than the honeymoon. In May 1932 the federal government charged him with evading income tax on receipts at the Club Rendezvous in 1929. This charge was still pending.

Receipts at the newly opened Casa Blanca were so low that a few days after Christmas, Fay, as manager, decided he had to cut corners. He was going to dispense with the services of the doorman, a six-foot, two-inch 200-pounder named Edward Maloney who was receiving $100 a week and drinking away a sizable part of it. Fay hadn't yet notified Maloney of his dismissal when he had a change of heart. There was so much unemployment he didn't want to fire anyone. Even though Maloney was drinking too heavily to continue as doorman, there were other things he could do at the club if he would accept less money. Instead of firing him, Fay hired a new doorman for only forty dollars a week and notified Maloney he would have to take a pay-cut.

At the same time, Fay posted a notice in the kitchen: "All salaries of employes will be reduced 30 percent." He didn't expect many complaints. Times were so hard that millions of workers throughout the country were accepting pay-cuts gracefully in the realization that a smaller wage was better than none at all.

At eight o'clock in the evening of New Year's Day, Fay was standing alone in the draped and carpeted foyer of the Casa Blanca, hoping to greet more customers than the few who had already arrived. He was wearing a black, double-breasted business suit, well cut and expensive but not new. There was a commotion outside the front door and Maloney, the demoted doorman, came staggering into the foyer followed by his successor, who was trying vainly to restrain him.[15]

Maloney was so intoxicated that he stumbled and almost fell just inside the door. After regaining his balance, he looked around and saw Fay. Drawing himself erect as if to proclaim sobriety, Maloney began to belabor his boss. He pointed out that he had money coming to him for the previous week's work and demanded it on the spot.

Fay did not take exception. Though he was sometimes belligerent, he could also be conciliatory if the occasion demanded. He told the new doorman to go upstairs and get the money from one of his associates in the office. Then, speaking softly, he tried to soothe and quiet Maloney before the man's shouting disturbed the customers inside the club. But Maloney was too drunk and angry to listen. Fay had treated him badly and he had come prepared for revenge.

Pulling a pistol from the right pocket of his heavy overcoat, he stepped close to Fay and began firing bullets into his chest. When Fay raised his hands to protect himself, he caught one slug in the left forearm but three went into his torso, one of them piercing his heart. As he fell, the upper part of his body sprawled across a sofa while his legs dangled to the floor. Maloney ran out the front door and disappeared. (It was two days before he surrendered to a traffic policeman.)

When detectives arrived at the Club Casa Blanca, Fay was already dead. There were white powder stains surrounding the bloody holes in his otherwise impeccable black suit. In his pockets they found only thirty cents—three dimes. Elsewhere in the establishment, to the embarrassment of his associates, they also found three hundred bottles of what they described as "alcoholic beverages." Despite all his efforts to go "respectable," Larry Fay had never quite managed to escape the illicit liquor business.

In the assembly hall of the Utah state House of Representatives at Salt Lake City, the federal government's fourteen-year effort to banish liquor from the land came to a sudden end on the fifth of December, 1933. That afternoon at 3:32 (Mountain time), the last delegate to Utah's ratification convention—S. R. Thurman of Salt Lake City—cast a resounding "Yes" vote for the Twenty-first Amendment to the U.S. Constitution. The new amendment stated that "The eighteenth article of amendment to the Constitution of the United States is hereby repealed."

A great cheer arose from the floor and galleries as Thurman cast his vote. Everyone in the chamber realized that this made Utah the thirty-sixth state to ratify, and that the new amendment now had the three-fourths-of-all-states majority required for adoption. The convention's president, Ray L. Olson of Ogden, gaveled for silence and announced the official result. This was immediately transmitted to the White House in Washington, both by special wire and by the radio facilities of the Columbia Broadcasting Company.

The proclamation President Roosevelt had written for the occasion was admonitory rather than jubilant. "I enjoin all citizens," he said, "to cooperate with the government in its endeavor to restore greater respect for law and order by confining such purchases of alcoholic beverages as they may make solely to those dealers or agents which have been duly licensed." Finally, the time had come for a serious drive against bootleggers. The government could collect its newly levied taxes on liquor only if it were purchased through "duly licensed" dealers.

Roosevelt also promised to prevent a recurrence of the "social evils" of the pre-prohibition era and asked that no state "authorize the return of the saloon either in its old form or in some modern guise." This last plea was nothing more than a political gesture. Roosevelt knew as well as everyone else that the saloon would now come back, but as a politician he was expected to deplore this fact. Even the most ardent wets had long since accepted the necessity to deplore the evils of the old saloon. The President, after paying homage to this well-established political custom, then put an end to it with the kind of simple but practical action for which he was becoming famous. Henceforth, he said, Americans must eschew the word "saloon," substituting for it the word "tavern." During these first months of his presidency, Roosevelt was such a popular figure that no one seemed to notice he was actually proclaiming the return of the saloon, if not "in its old form," then "in some modern guise."

The new Democrat-dominated Congress, apparently unable to move against the depression until the new President arrived to prod it, had nevertheless moved against prohibition without any prompting two weeks before his March 4 inauguration. On February 16 the Senate had voted 63–23 to submit the Twenty-first Amendment for ratification by state conventions. Four days later, the House of Representatives had done likewise by another overwhelming vote of 289 to 121. When Roosevelt entered the Oval Office, there was only one significant repeal gesture left for him to make. On March 13 he proposed that Congress immediately modify the Volstead Act to allow the sale of light wines and 3.2 percent beer. As a result, Congress passed the Cullen Bill and on April 7 much of the nation enjoyed a small beer binge in preparation for the big hard-liquor binge expected to take place the minute the Eighteenth Amendment was repealed.

Everyone assumed the country was ready for a celebration. A dismal blight had been lifted from the land. Despite the social and personal miseries caused by excessive drinking, liquor had proved as impossible as sin to eliminate, and the attempt at its prohibition had produced a fiasco as tragic as it was expensive.

(The day this fiasco ended, the Justice Department tried to add up the cost of prohibition and discovered that the federal government alone had spent $129 million in the attempt to enforce it. Ninety-two federal agents and 178 civilians had been killed in acts of violence against each other. More than a half-million people had been convicted in federal courts for offenses against the liquor laws. In addition, millions of others had repeatedly broken these laws, thereby encouraging in themselves and the people around them a diminution of respect for all law. And billions of man-hours had been wasted in the continuous fourteen-year debate between the wets and the drys— a debate in which each side poured forth upon the other a constant deluge of misinformation, delusion, and deceit./

It was not surprising that President Roosevelt should welcome repeal with sober warnings. Much more surprising was the fact that the nation itself welcomed repeal with fairly sober celebrations.

Chicago, of course, was an exception. Its more than seven thousand illegal drinking establishments began filling up long before the moment of Utah's ratification. Only the big wholesalers and hotels, watched closely by federal revenue men, observed the deadline. St. Louis remained technically dry even after the deadline because the state of Missouri hadn't yet got around to canceling its enforcement law. The city's bars became crowded anyway as people left their offices after 5 P.M., but those who hoped to enjoy their first legal drinks on the way home that night had to settle once more for bootlegged drinks.

Missouri was one of twenty-eight states that still had constitutional or statutory prohibition, although most of them were in the process of annulling it. Nevada was not among them. Nevadans were so well prepared for repeal that within ten minutes of Utah's ratification, liquor stores throughout the state were selling well-known brands across the counters. Some of the state's speakeasies, long since as wide open as its brothels and gambling casinos, didn't even stop serving long enough to observe the moment when they were declared legal. It was simply business as usual.

There was no celebration in Los Angeles or Hollywood. While numerous nightclubs were open, most of the movie stars stayed at home, perhaps to avoid the crowds which were anticipated but did not materialize.

In Detroit, Henry Ford offended the drys and startled everyone else by serving bottled beer at a public luncheon in honor of his new 1934 V-8 model. In most Eastern cities, where the time was already 5:32 P.M. when Utah ratified, it was too late for all but a few wholesalers to supply the newly licensed retailers. Philadelphia, as a result, was even more quiet than usual the night prohibition ended. Boston, where prohibition had never been honored very seriously, treated this night like any other one.

In New York, Pauline Sabin said hopefully, "I am confident that whatever celebrations usher in the return of legal liquor, they will be short-lived, and that once the custom of drinking is no longer shrouded in secrecy we shall settle down to temperance and moderation."

Meanwhile, the city's entire police force of 19,000 men was mobilized to handle the throngs expected in the streets. Surprisingly, only the Times Square area filled with people, and even there the crowd was well behaved. Arrests did not exceed the daily average for the previous five years. Perhaps this was because many would-be celebrants had trouble finding drinks. The police, after fourteen years of tolerating speakeasies, had suddenly begun raiding all those which hadn't procured licenses. Since licenses had been issued to only three thousand establishments in the metropolitan area, repeal brought an immediate drop of several thousand in the number of drinking places. And few of the three thousand licensed places had been able to procure liquor between the time it became legal and the time the warehouses closed. The city's two largest warehouses had closed even before Utah ratified. From those which stayed open later, only fifty-four truckloads of bonded whisky had been released.

Consequently, liquor was so scarce that some New Yorkers longed for the return of prohibition so they could buy a drink. Only those fortunate enough to find tables at the large hotels or ex-speakeasies such as the Stork Club, the Embassy, and Twenty-One, which had been transformed into supper clubs, could be assured of as much liquor as they wished. In order to be served, customers had to be seated at tables, because New York had passed a law (soon to be revoked) forbidding the sale of drinks at a bar.

Late in the afternoon of December 5, an enterprising newsman, finding almost nothing to report about repeal on the streets of New York, decided to interview former Governor Al Smith.

Having been the first significant national political figure to declare himself wet, and having fought against prohibition since the moment it began, Smith could be said to have sacrificed his career to the wet cause. As a result he now suffered great bitterness—a bitterness compounded by the fact that his protegé, Franklin D. Roosevelt, was reaping the benefits of the spade-work Smith had done, and at the same time was imposing on the country a socioeconomic program which Smith considered unsound.

Today, however, there was no apparent bitterness in Al Smith. When the reporter and his photographer entered the paneled office he now occupied as president of the Empire State Building Corporation, the former governor came forward to greet them with his famous beaming smile. He had just received the news of Utah's ratification and he was delighted.[16]

In honor of the occasion, the reporter asked, would Smith be willing to pose for a picture with a drink in his hand?

Smith declined with a laugh. "I never drink," he said, "in the daytime."

Notes and References

CHAPTER 1

1. New York *Times,* Jan. 17, 1920
2. Los Angeles *Times,* Jan. 17, 1920
3. Steuart, 148 *et seq.* New York *Times,* Apr. 2, 1926.
4. *Ibid.,* 113 *et seq.*
5. Anderson, Oral History
6. Odegard, 96
7. New York *Times,* Jan. 17, 1920
8. Einstein, 1 *et seq.*
9. Van de Water, 6
10. Emily Smith Warner Oral History. Mrs. Warner said: "At public functions there wouldn't be anything served, but for private dinner parties we had cocktails and wine."
11. New York *Times,* Jan. 2, 1933
12. Granlund, 118
13. New York *Times,* Mar. 5, 6, 9, 1920
14. *Ibid.,* Mar. 5, 1920
15. Anderson, Oral History

CHAPTER 2

1. *Ibid.,* Dec. 16, 17, 1927. Cincinnati *Enquirer,* Dec. 16, 1927.
2. Kobler, *Capone,* 71 *et seq.*
3. Steuart, 162
4. New York *Times,* Apr. 3, 1926
5. Steuart, 163
6. Van de Water, 9–11
7. Einstein, 14; New York *Times,* Aug. 15, 1920.
8. *Saturday Evening Post,* Sept. 10, 1949
9. Based on a story in the New York *Times,* Nov. 2, 1920.

CHAPTER 3

1. Graham, 100 *et seq.*
2. Chicago *Herald & Examiner,* Nov. 11, 1920; New York *Times,* Nov. 11, 1920.
3. New York *Times,* Jan. 2, 1933
4. Based on a story in the New York *Times,* Jan. 21, 1921.
5. Willoughby, 23
6. Van de Waters, 16 *et seq.;* New York *Times,* Nov. 29, 1923.
7. Trial proceedings as reported in New York *Times,* Jan. 22, 23, 24, 25, 1924.
8. Excerpted from New York *Times,* May 12, 1921.
9. Remus testimony before the United States Senate Special Committee on Investigation of the Attorney General, May 16, 1924.

CHAPTER 4

1. Cannon, 304 *et seq.*
2. Steuart, 170 *et seq.*
3. *Ibid.,* 175 *et seq.*
4. Columbus, Ohio, *Dispatch,* July 12, 1921
5. Telegram, Johnson to Doherty, in the papers of Sen. Hiram Johnson, Bancroft Library, Berkeley.
6. Cincinnati *Commercial Tribune,* trial proceedings, May 9–17, 1922.
7. Cincinnati *Enquirer,* Oct. 24, 1921
8. Remus testimony at Senate hearing, May 16, 1924.
9. New York *Times,* Mar. 26, 1922
10. *Ibid.,* Oct. 26, 1921
11. *Ibid.,* Mar. 3, 1922

CHAPTER 5

1. Wendt and Kogan, *Big Bill of Chicago,* 192 *et seq.*
2. Chicago *Herald & Examiner,* Jan. 20, 1922
3. This account of the Remus bootlegging trial is based upon the Cincinnati *Commercial Tribune,* May 9–17, 1922; New York *Times,* May 17, 1922, and the Remus testimony at the Senate hearing, May 16, 1924.
4. From Alice Roosevelt Longworth's memoirs, *Crowded Hours.*

5. From a special article written by Wheeler in the New York *Times,* Apr. 2, 1926.

6. An incident related by Sullivan to Samuel Hopkins Adams, and quoted in Adams' book, *The Incredible Era.*

7. Einstein, 108–19; New York *Times,* Sept. 9, 1922.

8. Van de Water, 132 *et seq.*

9. Related to the author by Frankenstein.

10. The best description of the Remus New Year's party is in the Cincinnati *Enquirer,* Jan. 21, 1952. Other references appear in the *Enquirer,* Dec. 6 and 16, 1927, and Oct. 1, 1934.

CHAPTER 6

1. Wendt and Kogan, *Big Bill of Chicago,* 202 *et seq.*

2. New York *Times,* June 1, 1923

3. New York *Times,* May 17, 1923

4. Emily Smith Warner, Oral History

5. New York *Times,* Apr. 2, 1926

6. Anderson, Oral History

7. New York *Times,* Aug. 24, 1923

8. Mrs. Willebrandt in a special New York *Times* article, July 6, 1924.

9. Granlund, 117 *et seq.*

10. Willoughby, 42

11. Van de Water, 243 *et seq.*

CHAPTER 7

1. New York *Times,* Jan. 26, 1924

2. New York *Times,* Dec. 17, 1925; Kobler, 245 *et seq.*

3. This account of the Anderson trial is based on descriptions of the trial in the New York *Times,* Jan. 22, 23, 24, 25, 26, 30, and Feb. 9, 1924; also the Anderson Oral History.

4. *Bishop Cannon's Own Story,* 327

5. Based on a story in the New York *Times,* Apr. 2, 1924.

6. Einstein, 42; New York *Times,* Apr. 12, 1924.

7. Steuart, 216 *et seq.*

8. Smith, 211 *et seq.*

9. This account of the Smith-Wheeler meeting is derived from Smith's own description of it, *Up to Now,* 286 *et seq.,* and Justin Steuart's description of it (*Dry Boss,* 217) as Wheeler had related it to him.

10. Cannon, 333 *et seq.*
11. New York *Times,* Apr. 3, 1926

CHAPTER 8

1. Wendt and Kogan, *Big Bill of Chicago,* 240 *et seq.*
2. Einstein, 120; New York *Times,* Feb. 20, 1925.
3. Cincinnati *Enquirer,* Dec. 6, 1927

CHAPTER 9

1. New York *Times,* Jan. 1, 1925
2. Mrs. Willebrandt's feelings in these matters were expressed in her book, *Inside of Prohibition.*
3. A dispatch from the Los Angles *Times* News Service, Sept. 11, 1924.
4. Willebrandt, 119
5. This account of Mrs. Willebrandt's adoption of her daughter comes basically from the daughter herself, now Mrs. Dorothy Van Dyke, who was interviewed at her home in Alameda, California, June 9, 1974. Supplementary information was found in *Better Homes and Gardens,* March, 1928; and the St. Louis *Post-Dispatch,* Jan. 17, 1926.
6. New York *Times,* Sept. 21, 1925
7. New York *Times,* Oct. 21, 1925
8. Einstein, 257 *et seq.;* New York *Times,* Nov. 14, 15, 1925.
9. New York *Times,* Nov. 10, 11, and Dec. 2, 1925
10. Van de Water, 241, 260, 282, *et seq.*

CHAPTER 10

1. This account of the Jack Daniels trial was compiled from the Cincinnati *Enquirer,* Dec. 17, 1925, and from information reported in the New York *Times,* Oct. 23, Nov. 22, Dec. 1, 2, 3, and 18, 1927.
2. New York *Times,* Feb. 20, 1926
3. *Ibid.,* May 24, 1926
4. *Ibid.,* July 9, Aug. 22, 1926
5. *Ibid.,* Feb. 21, 1924

CHAPTER 11

1. New York *Times,* Sept. 12, 1922
2. Steuart, 279
3. Granlund, 100 *et seq.*
4. Cohn, 14 *et seq.*
5. Stuart, 318 *et seq.*
6. Much of this scene was constructed from testimony at the trial of George Remus in November and December, 1927.
7. Cohn, 3 *et seq.*
8. This account of the Remus trial was compiled from the records of the Hamilton County, Ohio, Criminal Court and from the daily reports of the Cincinnati *Star-Times* and *Enquirer* during November and December, 1927.

CHAPTER 12

1. *Outlook* Magazine (later called *New Outlook*), June 8, 1928
2. Cannon, 389
3. *Ibid.,* 407 *et seq.*
4. *Ibid.,* 415
5. Willebrandt, 304 *et seq.*
6. Josephson, 383
7. Willebrandt, 10 *et seq.*
8. Cannon, 439 *et seq.*
9. Dabney, 229 *et seq.;* Philadelphia *Record,* July 23, 1930.
10. Cannon, 441
11. Hoover Memoirs, 1920–1933, 200 *et seq.*
12. New York *Times,* Oct. 20, 1928

CHAPTER 13

1. Thompson and Raymond, 289 *et seq.* New York *Times,* Oct. 2, 9, 1929.
2. Dabney, 188
3. *Ibid.,* 195 et seq.
4. Philadelphia *Record,* July 22, 1930
5. Exerpted from the New York *Times,* May 1, 1929.

6. Root, 9 *et seq.*; New York *Times,* May 29, 1929 and May 8, 1932.
7. New York *American,* May 30, 1929
8. New York *Tribune,* June 18, 1930
9. Sinclair, 164
10. Los Angeles *Times,* Jan. 13, 1929.
11. Excerpted from the New York Times, May 15, 1930.

CHAPTER 14

1. New York *Times,* Jan. 25, 1930
2. Dabney, 245 *et seq.*
3. Burns, 123
4. Kobler, *Capone,* 289, 295 *et seq.*
5. *Ibid.,* 309
6. Root, 42 *et seq.*
7. New York *Times,* Aug. 7, 9, 1931
8. Pasley, 215

CHAPTER 15

1. New York *Times,* Sept. 18, 1931
2. Cannon, 415
3. New York *Times,* Oct. 17, 1931
4. Interview in the Madison, Wisconsin, *State Journal,* Jan. 31, 1932.
5. New York *Times,* June 7, 1932
6. Josephson, 435
7. Sinclair, 403
8. Oulahan, 114 *et seq.*
9. New York *Times,* July 5, 1932
10. Dabney, 311
11. New York *Times,* Oct. 27, 1932
12. Josephson, 442
13. Root, 133 *et seq.*
14. Allen, *Since Yesterday,* 74
15. This account of Larry Fay's death is based largely on stories in the New York *Times,* Jan. 1, 3, and 4, 1933.
16. New York *Times,* Dec. 6, 1933

Bibliography

BOOKS

Adams, Samuel Hopkins. *The Incredible Era.* Boston: Houghton Mifflin, 1939.

Allen, Frederick Lewis. *Only Yesterday.* New York: Harper, 1931.

———— *Since Yesterday.* New York: Harper, 1939.

Allsop, Kenneth. *The Bootleggers.* London: Hutchinson, 1961.

Anderson, Sherwood. *Memoirs.* New York: Harcourt, Brace, 1942.

Anti-Saloon League. *Catechism.* Westerville, Ohio: 1910.

Asbury, Herbert. *The Great Illusion.* Garden City: Doubleday: 1950.

Barbican, James (pseudonym). *The Confessions of a Rum-runner.* Edinburgh: Blackwood, 1927.

Barnes, Harry Elmer. *Prohibition Versus Civilization.* New York: Viking, 1932.

Barrett, Marvin. *The Jazz Age.* (Based on NBC Project 20.) New York: Putnam, 1959.

Boettiger, John. *Jake Lingle.* New York: Dutton, 1931.

Boole, Ella. *Give Prohibition Its Chance.* New York & Chicago: Revell, 1929.

Bright, John. *Hizzoner, Big Bill Thompson.* New York: Cape and Smith, 1930.

Britton, Nan. *The President's Daughter.* New York: Elizabeth Ann Guild Inc., 1927.

Bruere, Martha. *Does Prohibition Work?* New York: Harper, 1927.

Burns, James MacGregor. *The Lion and the Fox.* New York: Harcourt, Brace & World, 1956.

Cannon, Bishop James, Jr. *Bishop Cannon's Own Story.* R. Watson, editor. Durham: Duke University Press, 1955.

Carse, Robert. *Rum Row.* New York: Rinehart, 1959.

Cherrington, Ernest H. *History of the Anti-Saloon League.* Westerville, Ohio: Anti-Saloon League, 1913.

Cohn, Art. *The Joker Is Wild.* New York: Random House, 1955.

Colvin, D. Leigh. *Prohibition in the United States.* New York: George H. Doran Co., 1926.

Dabney, Virginius. *Dry Messiah: The Life of Bishop Cannon.* New York: Knopf, 1949.

Daniels, Jonathan. *The Time Between the Wars.* Garden City: Doubleday, 1966.

Darrow, Clarence and Victor S. Yarros. *The Prohibition Mania.* New York: Boni & Liveright, 1927.

Dedmon, Emmett. *Fabulous Chicago.* New York: Random House, 1933.

Dobyns, Fletcher. *The Amazing Story of Repeal.* Chicago & New York: Willett, Clark, 1940.

———— *The Underworld of American Politics.* New York: Published by the author, 1932.

Dohn, Norman H. *The History of the Anti-Saloon League.* Columbus, Ohio: Doctoral thesis at Ohio State University, 1959.

Douglass, Earl L. *Prohibition and Common Sense.* New York: Alcohol Information Committee, 1931.

Einstein, Izzy. *Prohibition Agent No. 1.* New York: Frederick A. Stokes, 1932.

Finney, Ben. *Feet First.* New York: Crown, 1971.

Fowler, Gene. *Beau James.* New York: Viking, 1949.

Franklin, Fabian. *What Prohibition Has Done to America.* New York: Harcourt, Brace, 1922.

Graham, Frank. *Al Smith.* New York: Putnam, 1945.

Granlund, Nils T. *Blondes, Brunettes and Bullets.* (Sid Feder joint author.) New York: McKay, 1957.

Hancock, Harold. *The History of Westerville, Ohio.* Westerville: Published by the author, 1973.

Haynes, Roy A. *Prohibition Inside Out.* Garden City: Doubleday, 1923.

Hoffman, Frederick J. *The '20s.* New York: Macmillan Free Press, 1949.

Hoover, Herbert C. *Memoirs: 1920–1933.* New York: Macmillan, 1952.

Hoover, Ike. *Forty-Two Years in the White House.* Boston: Houghton Mifflin, 1934.

Josephson, Matthew and Hannah. *Al Smith: Hero of the Cities.* Boston: Houghton Mifflin, 1969.

Kobler, John. *Ardent Spirits.* New York: Putnam, 1973.
––––––– *Capone.* New York: Putnam, 1971.

Lee, Henry. *How Dry We Were.* Englewood Cliffs, N.J.: Prentice Hall, 1963.

Livingstone, Belle. *Belle Out of Order.* New York: Holt, 1959.

Lomax, Alan. *Mister Jelly Roll.* New York: Duell, Sloan & Pearce, 1950.

Long, J. C. *The Great Commoner.* New York: Appleton, 1928.

Longstreet, Stephen. *Chicago.* New York: McKay, 1973.

Lynch, Dennis Tilden. *Criminals and Politicians.* New York: Macmillan, 1932.

Lyons, Eugene. *Our Unknown Ex-President—A Portrait of Herbert Hoover.* Garden City: Doubleday, 1945.

Means, Gaston B. *The Strange Death of President Harding.* New York: Guild, 1930.

Merriam, Charles E. *Chicago: A More intimate View of Urban Politics.* New York: Macmillan, 1929.

Merz, Charles. *The Dry Decade.* New York: Doubleday Doran, 1931.

Mezzrow, Milton, and Bernard Wolfe. *Really the Blues.* New York, Random House, 1946.

Moray, Alastair. *The Diary of a Rum-runner.* London: Allen, 1929.

Morris, Lloyd. *Incredible New York.* New York: Random House, 1951.

Odegard, Peter. *Pressure Politics.* New York: Columbia University Press, 1928.

Ostrander, Gilman M. *The Prohibition Movement in California, 1848–1933.* Berkeley: Doctoral Thesis. California University Publications: History, V.57. 1957.

Oulahan, Richard. *The Man Who . . .* New York: Dial, 1971.

Pasley, Fred. *Muscling In.* New York: Washburn, 1931.

Pickering, Clarence R. *The Early Days of Prohibition.* New York: Vantage Press, 1964.

Pollard, Joseph P. *The Road to Repeal.* New York: Brentano's, 1932.

Preston, Robert L. *The Remus Trial.* Leesburg, Va.: Privately printed, 1928.

Reed, James. *The Rape of Temperance.* New York: Cosmopolitan Books, 1931.

Reeves, Ira L. *Ol' Rum River.* Chicago: Rockwell, 1931.

Root, Grace Cogswell. *Women and Repeal.* New York: Harper, 1934.

Rourke, Constance Mayfield. *Trumpets of Jubilee.* New York: Harcourt, Brace, 1927.

Russell, Francis. *The Shadow of Blooming Grove—Warren G. Harding in His Times.* New York: McGraw-Hill, 1968.

Sann, Paul. *The Lawless Decade.* New York: Crown, 1967.

Shaw, Elton R. *Prohibition, Going and Coming.* Berwyn, Ill.: Shaw, 1924. (Foreword by Wayne B. Wheeler.)

Sinclair, Andrew. *Prohibition, the Era of Excess.* Boston: Little Brown, 1962.

Smith, Alfred E. *Campaign Addresses, 1928.* Washington D.C.: Democratic National Committee, 1929.

———— *Up to Now.* (An Autobiography.) New York: Viking, 1929.

Steuart, Justin. *Wayne Wheeler, Dry Boss.* Chicago and New York: Revell, 1928.

Stuart, William H. *The 20 Incredible Years.* Chicago and New York: Donohue, 1935.

Sullivan, Edward Dean. *Chicago Surrenders.* New York: Vanguard, 1930.

Sullivan, Mark. *Our Times, Vol. VI—The Twenties.* New York: Scribner's, 1935.

Thompson, Craig, and Allen Raymond. *Gang Rule in New York.* New York: Dial, 1940.

Thrasher, Frederic M. *The Gang.* University of Chicago Press, 1927.

Tumulty, Joseph P. *Woodrow Wilson as I Know Him.* Garden City: Doubleday, 1924.

Unger, Samuel. *A History of the Women's Christian Temperance Union.* Columbus: Doctoral thesis, Ohio State University, 1933.

United States Senate. Proceedings of the Select Committee on Investigation of the Justice Department. Washington D.C. Library of Congress, 11 parts. 1924.

Van de Water, Frederic F. *The Real McCoy*. Garden City: Doubleday, Doran, 1931.

Walker, Stanley. *The Night Club Era*. New York: Frederick A. Stokes, 1933.

Warburton, Clark. *The Economic Results of Prohibition*. New York: Doctoral thesis, Columbia University, 1932.

Warner, Emily Smith. *The Happy Warrior*. Garden City: Doubleday, 1956.

Wendt, Lloyd and Herman Kogan. *Big Bill of Chicago*. Indianapolis: Bobbs Merrill, 1953.

_____ *Lords of the Levee*. Indianapolis: Bobbs Merrill, 1943.

Whipple, Sidney B. *Noble Experiment*. London: Methuen, 1934.

Willebrandt, Mabel Walker. *Inside of Prohibition*. Indianapolis: Bobbs Merrill, 1929.

Willoughby, Malcolm F. *Rum War at Sea*. Washington D.C.: Treasury Dept. U.S. Coast Guard, 1964.

MANUSCRIPTS

New York Public Library. Correspondence of M. Louise Gross.

Bancroft Library, Berkeley, California. Correspondence and Papers of Sen. Hiram Johnson.

TAPE RECORDINGS

Columbia University Oral History Project. Recorded interviews of William H. Anderson, Ella Boole, and Emily Smith Warner.

MAGAZINES

Baltimore and Richmond *Christian Advocate*
Better Homes and Gardens
Outlook and *New Outlook*
The Saturday Evening Post
Time

NEWSPAPERS

Baltimore *Sun*
Chicago *Herald Examiner*
Chicago *Tribune*
Cincinnati *Commercial Tribune*
Cincinnati *Enquirer*
Cincinnati *Post*
Columbus, Ohio, *Dispatch*
Los Angeles *Times*
Madison Wisconsin *State Journal*
New York *American*
New York *Times*
New York *Tribune*
Philadelphia *Record*
Richmond Va. *Times-Dispatch*
St. Louis *Post-Dispatch*
Washington *Post*
Washington *Star*
Westerville, Ohio, *Public Opinion*

Index

Index